The ENGLISH TEACHER'S COMPANION

FOURTH EDITION

The
ENGLISH TEACHER'S
COMPANION
FOURTH EDITION

A *Completely New* Guide to Classroom, Curriculum, and the Profession

HEINEMANN
Portsmouth, NH

Heinemann
145 Maplewood Ave., Suite 300
Portsmouth, NH 03801
www.heinemann.com

Offices and agents throughout the world

The author and publisher wish to thank those who have generously given permission to reprint borrowed material:

Excerpts from *Common Core State Standards* © Copyright 2010. National Governors Association Center for Best Practices and Council of Chief State School Officers. All rights reserved.

Figure 2.2: "America's Leaky Education Pipeline" graphic, copyright © 2007 by the National Council on Education and the Economy (NCEE), Washington, DC. Used with permission.

Figure 2.7: "The Engagement Factor" originally appeared in *Teacher Magazine Professional Development Sourcebook* (October 12, 2010). Reprinted with permission from Editorial Projects in Education.

Figure 2.8: "The Four Cs of Academic Success" from *School Smarts* by Jim Burke. Copyright © 2004 by Jim Burke. Published by Heinemann, Portsmouth, NH. All rights reserved.

Excerpts from "A Lesson for Teachers" by Mike Rose in the *Los Angeles Times* (June 4, 2010). Reprinted by permission of the author.

continues on page xvi

Library of Congress Cataloging-in-Publication Data
Burke, Jim.
    The English teacher's companion : a completely new guide to classroom,
curriculum, and the profession / Jim Burke. — Fourth edition.
        pages   cm
    Includes bibliographical references and index.
    ISBN-13: 978-0-325-02840-8
    ISBN-10: 0-325-02840-0
1. English philology—Study and teaching—Handbooks, manuals, etc. I. Title.
    PE65.B87 2008
    428.0071'2—dc23   2012033297

Acquisitions Editors: Lisa Luedeke *and* Tobey Antao
Production Editor: Patricia Adams
Cover and Interior Design: Lisa A. Fowler
Cover Photographer: Marc Fiorito
Typesetter: Kim Arney
Manufacturing: Steve Bernier

Printed in the United States of America on acid-free paper
9 10 11   VP   24   23   22
PO 34192

My deepest thanks to

you, my fellow English teacher,
for we are all in this work together

Carol Jago, for your guidance
and the gift of your friendship
these many years

my family for all your love,
your lessons, and our life together

CONTENTS

CHAPTER 5 Teaching Reading *136*

CHAPTER 6 Speaking and Listening *203*

CHAPTER 7 Language Study: Vocabulary, Grammar, and Style *256*

CHAPTER 8 Assessing and Grading Student Learning and Work *293*

This book was born of an invitation from Lois Bridges to write about what I do in the classroom. That invitation began a conversation between us that has continued for 15 years and shaped me (and this book) profoundly, as has our friendship. Lisa Luedeke, editor of the third and the first half of this fourth edition, challenged me in new ways as a writer and thinker and her influence culminates in *What's the Big Idea?* and this edition of *Companion*. As with all great editors, though, her influence and our relationship extends well beyond these pages. It is difficult to lose an editor at any time but especially in the middle of a project; this loss, however, was much easier to bear for two reasons: my great happiness for Lisa as she came out with her first novel and my relationship with this book's third and most recent editor, Tobey Antao. She picked up where Lisa left off and brought her own fierce intelligence and energy to the project. To all three women I am indebted and grateful as this is a book I could not have hoped to write on my own.

Throughout the process of writing one edition or another, I have been blessed with many guides—people who have been essential teachers through their example, our conversations, and their own books. I entered the profession at a time when I was fortunate enough to know and learn from some of the great forces in our field: Arthur Applebee, Nancie Atwell, Sheridan Blau, Fran Claggett, Ralph Fletcher, Don Graves, James Gray, Judith Langer, James Moffett, Miles Myers, Tom Newkirk, Carol Booth Olson, Linda Rief, Bill Robinson, Regie Routman, Robert Scholes, and Bill Strong.

This book and my own teaching are further shaped by a new generation of thinkers whose books have taught me, whose friendships have sustained me, and whose example challenges me daily to be worthy of counting them as my friends and colleagues: Janet Allen, Deborah Appleman, Kylene Beers, Smokey Daniels, Kelly Gallagher, Stephanie Harvey, Carol Jago, Penny Kittle, Donalyn Miller, Bob Probst, Laura Robb, Alan Sitomer, Michael Smith, Vicki Spandel, Alfred Tatum, and Jeff Wilhelm. Of these people, I am especially grateful to Jeff Wilhelm for the chance to work with him these last 15 years; to Kylene Beers for giving me the opportunity to write for *Voices* during those great years under her editorship and to join the conversation she led through the National Adolescent Literacy Coalition; and to Carol Jago and Laura Robb for their deep, sustained mentoring and friendship these many years.

I also wish to acknowledge and express my genuine gratitude to those with whom I worked or still do work on the AP English Course and Exam Review Commission; the Adolescent Literacy Standards Committee of the National Board for Professional Teaching Standards; my fellow authors and our editors at Holt McDougal Harcourt; those with whom I work on the Common Core Standards project through the PARCC Consortium; the U.S. Holocaust Memorial Museum, in particular Pete Fredlake; and the many presidents and fellow board members with whom I served on the California Association of Teachers of English and the National Council of Teachers of English over the years.

I have always been grateful for the communities of which I have been a part through my years in the profession; and where I could not find one, I worked to create the community I needed to keep me strong and help me enjoy my work. Thus, I give thanks to the thousands who joined CATENet, the first online community I created and maintained for years. My deepest gratitude when it comes to such communities, however, is reserved for the English Companion

Ning, a community I started in 2009 after returning home from that year's NCTE convention. That was when I realized newer teachers could not get to such conventions and were not joining the conversations that had so influenced me as a young teacher. The "EC Ning"—that place "where English teachers go to help each other"—has given me a deeper appreciation for the benefits of such communities and their ability, at their best, to improve our practice and give us "the courage to teach." In particular, I must thank Karen LaBonte, Meredith Stewart, Gary Anderson, Teresa Bruner, Jennifer Ansbach, Jeff See, Mike Umphrey, and Mark Childs who, as I began working on this edition of the book, suggested it would be cool if we turned it over to the English Companion Ning community and wrote it together and made it available online to all. In a way, it would seem we did this: the EC Ning community has shaped this book in many, many ways and, in the process of its composition, we all worked to create an online community to which we contribute and through which we help the larger community of English teachers around the world.

No author ever felt more supported throughout the process of writing a book than I did by the many people at Heinemann, which really does live its credo of being "dedicated to teachers." In particular, I must thank Lesa Scott, Anita Gildea, Vicki Boyd, Roberta Lew, Lisa Fowler, Sarah Fournier, Eric Chalek, Patty Adams, Kate Montgomery, Michelle Flynn, and Cheryl Savage for their help in all aspects of my work on this book and with the company.

As I write these words, I am mindful of those whose words and example have contributed to this book in so many ways, going all the way back to my days as a special education teacher, when I learned that all students deserve our best so that they might discover and fully develop theirs. As a Peace Corps volunteer in Tunisia, I learned how to work across cultures and languages, as well as to persevere through my own feelings of incompetence as I struggled to learn Arabic. At Castro Valley High School, where I began so many years ago, I was mentored so well by Doug Rogers, Steve Poling, Anne Parris, and Clare LePell. Finally, I must thank those colleagues at Burlingame High School where I still teach (and will until I retire), the colleagues who have taught me so much over the years. I am particularly grateful to Elaine Caret, Diane McClain, Sandy Briggs, Rebecca Shirley, and Morgan Hallabrin for the hours of conversations during which they have shared so much of their wisdom about teaching with me.

It is the students, however, at all these schools, especially Burlingame High, to whom I owe my largest debt, my deepest and most sincere gratitude in terms of the content of these pages (with special thanks to former student Marc Fiorito for the wonderful photographs on the cover). This book is one, in many ways, we have written together through our exploration of language, literature, and life. They are, in the end, my most important teachers, showing me every day what is possible and how I might go about achieving it so long as they feel they have a place at the table and I am still listening to what they are telling me.

The first edition of *The English Teacher's Companion* was published nearly 15 years ago. For models I looked at all the great books of that time, especially those by Nancie Atwell and Regie Routman, and those from the years before to guide me; but the books that helped me understand what I was trying to become were books such as *What to Expect When You're Expecting*—books that guided my wife and me through the beginning years of parenting when we needed someone who knew the territory ahead to help us find our way. And those three kids, the ones we needed the books to help us raise? They are now in college, high school, and middle school. I wonder whether there is a new book out there titled *What to Expect When You Have No Idea What to Expect* for parents of young adults. Boy, could we use that!

Why then do I write an entirely new edition of this book? Because to offer you anything less would suggest I had not grown, had not changed, had not learned or evolved in response to all the movements, policies, and challenges we have faced as teachers and Americans these last 15 years. How could I come to you as your fellow traveler, your colleague, your companion and not bring the best of all I have learned from writing all those other books, teaching all those new classes—both the lowest and the highest levels—at a school that has itself, as have all our schools, gone through so many changes? I cannot give you a slightly new version of the same book for I am not the same teacher I was when I first wrote it. How could I be after watching my classes change so much, seeing my school declared a "failing school" under No Child Left Behind (despite the fact that we attain some of the highest scores in the county year after year)?

To say I am not the same teacher is not to say I am not as good; nor do I dismiss anything I said in this book's previous editions. Rather, I am a *different* teacher, a better teacher, one made more conscious of my practice through the writing of this and my other books. When I wrote this book the first time, I had no cause to believe it would be embraced by so many, that I would have the opportunity to amend it across multiple editions. Doing so made me the writer I have since become, that no writer can be when he or she writes a first book. I am grateful for the opportunity to write this whole book anew, having learned so much from so many in my class, my department, and schools around the country.

But it is so much shorter, you will say: Where did all those pages go? By way of an answer, I shall borrow from Blaise Pascal, who apologized to his friend for writing such a long letter, saying "I did not have time to write a shorter one." Or, I might steal from Mark Twain, who responded to his editor's telegraph that said "NEED 2-PAGE SHORT STORY TWO DAYS" by sending this in return: "NO CAN DO 2 PAGES TWO DAYS. CAN DO 30 PAGES 2 DAYS. NEED 30 DAYS TO DO 2 PAGES." In other words, I have spent three times longer writing this book (more than three years) than I did writing the first edition (one year). In fact, I have spent more time on this book than any I have ever written.

You wonder: *What have you added, or was it all subtraction?* I have read more widely and deeply and seriously within the professional literature than ever before, drawing from the latest and best research by authors, such as Judith Langer and Arthur Applebee, to offer substantial validation of any methods suggested. In addition, throughout the chapters I have integrated ideas about how to work with struggling students as well as those with special needs of one sort or another. I have also tried to show what technology looks like when situated in the curriculum instead of separating it in its own chapter. Each chapter begins by framing the subject within the context of its history and the arguments for its importance, then identifies the related Common Core State Standards (CCSS) for that section, sometimes going on to consider other standards that seem relevant or even more rigorous in that particular domain.

One other strand warrants mention: We have been so focused on the needs of struggling students, those underachievers whom we care about, that we have often found it difficult to give equal consideration to those at the other end of the spectrum in our classes. Throughout the book, sometimes in overt ways—a subsection in the reading chapter titled "Teaching Advanced Reading"—and through more covert ways such as the examples provided, I have tried to address the dilemma of meeting the needs of all at whatever level they enter our classes in August. (When I wrote the first edition, we still began school *after* Labor Day.)

So please don't think of this book as *less*; instead, think of its fewer pages as *more*—more said in fewer words, more time for you to think since it asks you to spend less time reading it. Lois Bridges, this book's first editor, the one who invited me to write it in the first place, always told me, "If you are learning as you write it then that means your readers will, too." By this standard, the book seems a success, for I learned so much while writing it that I cannot help but feel I became a better teacher during that time.

Which is as it should be, for you and I both have much to learn if we are to meet the challenges we face in our classrooms these days. When I wrote the first edition of *Companion* and decided to include standards in the curriculum chapters, many opposed this; I said simply that it was the reality we faced in the classroom, so they should be included. As I write now, so many years later, nearly all the states have adopted the CCSS. So I have anchored this book in those standards. I am, after all, still teaching every day at Burlingame High School, and these standards are *my* standards too; thus, they guide my own daily practice as I assume they do yours.

Certainly the standards and this era challenge me, as they no doubt do you, to be the teacher I have spent my life trying to be. To be that teacher, though, I desperately need the many companions I have picked up along the way. When I wrote the first edition, Kelsey Parker, a wonderful girl, was a freshman in my class. As I was finishing that book, she wrote in one of her papers that "without companions, the world is a sea of stories with no one to listen." How fitting that I should go online tonight, Kelsey long since having become a professional counselor, and find this quote on her blog after I entered the search term "companion quotations":

> Without books the development of civilization would have been impossible. They are the engines of change, windows on the world, "Lighthouses," as the poet said, "erected in the sea of time." They are companions, teachers, magicians, bankers of the treasures of the mind. . . . Books are humanity in print.

What a summation of all I hope this edition of the book will be to you! If you are a new or student teacher, I hope it will be the "lighthouse" you need to guide you through the sometimes rough waters of the early days we all experience. If you are nearer to the middle of the path Danté described—as I am—I hope it might light your way as the stars did his en route to the other side of his own trials or be your Virgil to help you through the tests we must all pass every day. Most of all, though, I hope this book will be for you, as you see the images of my students at work and read of what we do in my class, "humanity in print" as Kelsey's quotation says. For we are all very much striving to maintain our humanity in the midst of so many political, professional, technological, and cultural changes that would strip our classes and curriculum of the very humanity that places our discipline in the Humanities.

I have taught English for nearly 25 years and I love it. If we were to list our relationship with English or our work as teachers on Facebook, which did not exist when I wrote the first edition, we would no doubt have to say, "It's complicated." And it is. And sometimes it's just plain *messy*. But that's what I love about it. I tell my students that their job is to find a problem or a question that interests them so much, that is *so* important and fascinating to them, that they will want to spend the rest of their lives trying to solve or answer it—even though they will not be able to do so.

The point, I tell them and you, is to be in the game, to be at the table, to be part of the conversation, to contribute what is yours to give to help all those who come along behind you—to not just be part of the story but to be one who helps write that story. Here, in these pages, you will find all I have learned along the way these many years. I offer it to you so you might take into your own mind my ideas, and those of the others represented here, and someday give that wisdom—seasoned with your own—back to the profession that we might then learn from you as you, too, become a companion and a teacher to colleagues and students.

—Jim Burke
San Francisco

Credits, *continued from p. iv*

The
ENGLISH TEACHER'S
COMPANION

FOURTH EDITION

CHAPTER ONE

What We Teach

(Re)Defining English as a Discipline

> Students need to be prepared to make a living, to make a life, and . . .
> to make a difference.
> —Carol Jago (2009)

Teaching English in Our Brave New World

Students spend more time studying English than any other discipline. Ours is the only subject students are required to take every year. Nearly 1300 hours of English classes over seven years; up to 4000 or 5000 hours, in the case of some students, if one includes the time spent on homework. As Elbow (1990) says, "from the corporation president to the homeless person huddling in the bus station" (112), they have all passed through our classes, thus making each English teacher's classroom a sort of cultural Ellis Island.

To what end, all this English?

Is it all about learning to read Shakespeare so that students might understand Miranda when she speaks in *The Tempest* of the "brave new world"? So that they might catch Huxley's allusion to Shakespeare when later they read his *Brave New World*? So that they will be ready, through their study of literacies and literature, for the brave new world of the future for which we are expected to prepare them? What does "English" even *mean* as a discipline in the era of "Twitterature" and www.sixwordstories.net, "vooks," and e-books that allow writers to embed audio, video, and images? What *is* "English" in a world where we must know how to convey the same idea in 3000, 300, 30, 3, 1, or no words, using an image instead? What *is* "English" when ideas must be able to be effectively communicated on an $8\frac{1}{2} \times 11$ sheet of paper but also via e-books, webpages, blogs, wikis, tweets, 10-foot screens, or smartphones that fit in our pockets? And writing and reading, those most fundamental literacies? What will *they* look like in a world where one can speak into a device that transcribes speech into editable text or have that same device read *you* the *New York Times* or a novel? O brave new world, indeed, that has such people, such problems and possibilities in't!

PAUSE & REFLECT What questions, comments, or concerns does this opening raise for you?

Each discipline develops in students not just bodies of knowledge—facts, theories, and concepts to memorize—but ways of seeing, thinking, and communicating, all of which rely

1

on the fundamental literacies they learn in our English classes. As Nystrand notes, in a report titled "English: Not Just for English (Class) Anymore," students face increasingly similar interdisciplinary demands that require these core literacies (1998). Each discipline has its own customs and conventions into which the teachers in those areas must initiate their students, as one would an apprentice.

Literacy in the Workplace: Putting Our Discipline to Work

It is not, of course, the English teacher's primary job to prepare students for the workplace, though this is surely an important obligation we share with teachers of other disciplines. Literacy, as Deborah Brandt says in *Literacy in American Lives* (2001), is a *resource*, an "economic, political, intellectual, spiritual [resource], which, like wealth or education, or trade skill or social connections, is pursued for the opportunities and protections that it potentially grants its seekers" (5). To this I would add, the nation to which they belong, for as Brandt says "Literacy is a valued commodity in the U.S. economy, a key resource in gaining profit and edge" (21). Such an emphasis on literacy as a resource stresses the fact that it is a resource that people trade, thus focusing on the competitive nature of literacy and its relation to individual and social success. Brandt notes that "literacy looms as one of the great engines of profit and competitive advantage" and is cultivated by what she calls "sponsors," those "agents, local or distant, concrete or abstract, who enable, support, teach, and model, as well as recruit, regulate, or withhold, literacy—and gain advantage by it in some way" (18).

> **"** IT IS NOT, OF COURSE, THE ENGLISH TEACHER'S PRIMARY JOB TO PREPARE STUDENTS FOR THE WORKPLACE, THOUGH THIS IS SURELY AN IMPORTANT OBLIGATION WE SHARE WITH TEACHERS OF OTHER DISCIPLINES. **"**

Echoing others' comments (Alliance for Excellent Education 2007; Hayes 2008; Tapscott 2008; Darling-Hammond 2010; Godin 2010) about the changing nature of work in the global economy, Brandt (2001) drives home the extent to which:

> the nature of work in the United States puts a premium on the ability to traffic in symbols generally and verbal symbols particularly, as print and print-based technologies have penetrated into virtually all aspects of money making. In an information economy, reading and writing serve as input, output, and conduit for producing profit and winning economic advantage. Systematic information has replaced direct experience as the basis for knowledge making and decision making, turning texts into the principle tools and literacy into the principle craft of the information economy. (25)

The problem is that high school and even a large percentage of college graduates are showing up for work without the skills and knowledge needed to compete in this economy (Wagner 2008; Darling-Hammond 2010). At the same time, a growing number of adults in other countries are showing up *with* these qualifications as part of what Zakaria (2008) calls "the rising of the rest" of the world in an increasingly global marketplace of labor and ideas. As the National Center on Education and the Economy (NCEE) says in its critical 2007 report, "Tough Choices or Tough Times," "this is a world in which a very high level of preparation in reading, writing, speaking, mathematics, science, literature, history, and the arts will be indispensible . . . in which comfort with ideas and abstractions is the passport to a good job, in which creativity and innovation are the keys to a good life" (xviii).

A report by the Conference Board on "basic knowledge and applied skills" for the twenty-first century workforce, titled *Are They Really Ready to Work?*, reinforces the critical tone and grave concern expressed in the NCEE report. It concluded that the future U.S. workforce is "woefully ill-prepared for the demands of today's (and tomorrow's) workplace" (Casner-Lotto and Benner 2006, 9) particularly in four areas, each of which involves literacy in one form or another:

- Professionalism/work ethic
- Oral and written communications
- Teamwork/collaboration
- Critical thinking/problem solving

PAUSE & REFLECT Visit the Bureau of Labor and Statistics to see the latest trends for future employment: www.bls.gov. What do you notice when you look at these trends? What are the implications for what you should be teaching?

The Conference Board's report goes on to point out, that in the decade ahead, approximately 85 percent of newly created U.S. jobs will require education beyond high school (12). While the employers surveyed identified reading comprehension as an area of concern (38.4 percent), many more (80.9 and 69.6 percent, respectively) are very concerned about graduates' written communication and critical thinking/problem-solving skills. That these two areas emerge as the greatest concerns is significant, particularly in light of the extraordinary emphasis on reading skills in the last decade (College Board 2011; Applebee and Langer 2009; Gallagher 2009). Moreover, while so much of the discussion in the media focuses on basic literacies, it is more sophisticated skills—communicating, thinking critically and creatively—that most concern businesses (Pink 2006; Friedman 2007; Wagner 2008; Friedman and Mandelbaum 2011).

Echoing the Conference Board report, the NCEE report says, "the universal complaint of employers and colleges is that our students cannot write well . . . [and] our schools are hostile to ideas, [as evidenced by] tests that ask students to come up with the one right answer . . . [and thus] penalize the creative student rather than rewarding him" (32). Ravitch (2010), responding to such a "measure and punish" curriculum, called for "a strong, coherent, explicit curriculum that is grounded in the liberal arts and sciences with plenty of opportunities for children to engage in activities and projects . . . that ensure [they] gain the knowledge they need to understand scientific ideas, political debates, and the world they live in" (13). Indeed, it is this repeated emphasis on and call for attention to the importance of "the crucial new factor, the one that alone can justify higher wages in this country . . . creativity and innovation" (29) that unites so many (Pink 2006; National Adolescent Literacy Coalition 2007; Sternberg, Jarvin, and Grigorenko 2009; Robinson 2011). In a paper titled

"THE PROBLEM IS THAT HIGH SCHOOL AND EVEN A LARGE PERCENTAGE OF COLLEGE GRADUATES ARE SHOWING UP FOR WORK WITHOUT THE SKILLS AND KNOWLEDGE NEEDED TO COMPETE IN THIS ECONOMY (WAGNER 2008; DARLING-HAMMOND 2010).**"**

"I<small>F WE ARE TO</small>
<small>REMAIN GLOBALLY</small>
<small>COMPETITIVE IN</small>
<small>WHAT HE CALLS</small>
<small>THE 'C</small><small>ONCEPTUAL</small>
A<small>GE,'</small> <small>GREATER</small>
<small>CREATIVITY WILL</small>
<small>BE REQUIRED THAN</small>
<small>IN THE PREVIOUS,</small>
<small>MORE ANALYTICAL</small>
'I<small>NFORMATION</small> A<small>GE'</small>
<small>IN WHICH PEOPLE</small>
<small>WERE DESCRIBED</small>
<small>AS 'KNOWLEDGE</small>
<small>WORKERS' (49).</small>**"**

"Creativity in the Classroom, Innovation in the Workplace," Ken Robinson reports that, "it is not that there aren't enough graduates to go around, it's that too many of them can't communicate, work in teams, or think creatively" (2009a, 1).

Pink (2006), who shares Robinson's concerns about creativity, declares that students need "a whole new mind," arguing that all work dependent on the left-brain capacities—logic, sequence, literalness, and analysis—is increasingly sent abroad or, more frequently, done by computers, whereas the right-brain work—synthesis, emotional expression, creating context, and thinking about the big picture—is what should be our focus. If we are to remain globally competitive in what he calls the "Conceptual Age," greater creativity will be required than in the previous, more analytical "Information Age" in which people were described as "knowledge workers" (49).

Tony Wagner, in his book *The Global Achievement Gap* (2008), illustrates the difference between these two ages through his conversation with the CEO of a chemical engineering company. When Wagner asks the CEO which skills he looks for when hiring "young people," the CEO responds immediately: "First and foremost, I look for someone who asks good questions. . . . For employees to solve problems or to learn new things, they have to know what questions to ask. . . . The ability to ask the right questions is the single most important skill" (2). When Wagner asks him which other skills matter most, the CEO says, "I want people who can engage in good discussion" and can communicate effectively in writing (4).

Wagner, along with others, including the NCEE and Conference Board, found people in the workplace reiterating the CEO's priorities: "the preparation that mattered most for their companies' jobs was less about technical skills and knowledge than about learning how to think, and *their* concern was that time spent on test preparation [in K–12 schools] and memorizing more content knowledge comes at the expense of teaching students to use their minds well" (6). For those who would argue that such cognitive demands are not needed by those who work with their hands and not their minds, Rose (2004) found the "cognitive demands" of the workplace much more complex and challenging, concluding that we "tend to underestimate the significance of common workplace literacy" (207).

Representing Wagner's and others' ideas, Darling-Hammond (2010) identifies the following skills as those needed to close the global achievement gap and ensure America's continued success:

1. Design, evaluate, and manage one's own work so that it continually improves
2. Frame, investigate, and solve problems using a wide range of tools and resources
3. Collaborate strategically with others
4. Communicate effectively in many forms
5. Find, analyze, and use information for many purposes
6. Develop new products and ideas (2)

PAUSE & REFLECT Visit the website for the Partnership for 21st Century Skills. What are your thoughts about the ideas offered here? How do they correspond with what you are teaching in your classes?

Not all agree with or support this emphasis on new literacies that assume an entirely digital world and economy. Two authors—Matthew Crawford and Mike Rose—question the direction and value of all this change toward Pink's Conceptual Age. While conventional wisdom holds that everyone in the future will need a college degree, Crawford (2009) attacks this "dichotomy of mental versus manual [work]," adamantly resisting the assumption that "all blue-collar work is as mindless as assembly line work, and second, that white-collar work is still recognizably mental in character" (31). Rose (2005) seconds Crawford, talking about how the "current distinction between an 'old work order' and a 'new work order' [rhetorically] renders twentieth-century industrial workers as cognitively substandard" (209). In his study of literacy in the workplace, Rose reveals a complex "occupational landscape" rich in "cognitive processes" that require workers to use a range of symbol systems, modes of expression, written and oral communication, cognitive collaboration, notetaking and visual representation in the course of the ongoing learning that most experience over time due to the rapidly evolving workplace (Rose 2005).

The intelligence and dignity inherent in labor and the trades are obvious and personal to me: I saw these qualities every day in parents of my childhood friends, my uncles, and my own father, who worked in the printing industry for 38 years in nearly every capacity as he rose to management. As was Mike Rose, I was the first in my family to graduate from college (Burke 2004), an experience that helped me to understand how much intelligence my uncles possessed about people, materials, business, and making or fixing things. Yet even as I understand the truth in Rose's findings and appreciate Crawford's certainty that his work as a mechanic cannot have denied him because it "cannot be delivered through a wire" (33), I also see these same twenty-first century literacies, the survival skills described by Wagner, the Partnership for 21st Century Skills, and the NCEE, increasingly at play in the small shops where people do the work Rose and Crawford honor with their words.

> *I ALSO SEE THESE SAME TWENTY-FIRST CENTURY LITERACIES, THE SURVIVAL SKILLS DESCRIBED BY WAGNER, THE PARTNERSHIP FOR 21ST CENTURY SKILLS, AND THE NCEE, INCREASINGLY AT PLAY IN THE SMALL SHOPS . . .*

Joe's Ice Cream, three doors down from my house in San Francisco and serving its award-winning ice cream since my wife's mother went there as a child, maintains a lively website and encourages people to post reviews on Yelp! American Cyclery, the oldest cycling shop in San Francisco, a cool old place with wooden floors and vintage bikes hanging on the walls, blogs and tweets about upcoming events, repair tips, and recommended rides. My mechanic has replaced his newsletter with a Facebook page he regularly updates with useful information; and my plumber, not to be outdone, regularly posts information and videos on his website and YouTube portal, which he uses to promote not his plumbing skills but his circus abilities as an acrobat, contortionist, and stunt cycle rider.

My point? Everyone, even the artisanal baker who markets his bread online and ships from France through FedEx while the bread is still warm, requires the survival skills Wagner

"It seems like we are roaming far afield from English as we have previously taught it. Yet what am I talking about? Communication by various means for a variety of purposes with real audiences."

describes. When my father, who dropped out of high school at fifteen, got hired by the printing plant, he had neither experience nor skills but possessed a willingness to learn; by the time he retired 39 years later, people applying for entry-level positions needed degrees in graphic arts and advanced-level computer skills. Oh, and why was my father still there to run that division? Because he realized that if he didn't acquire these new literacies he would end up on the scrap heap like all his other coworkers who dismissed computers as a passing phase and, as a consequence, lost their jobs.

It seems like we are roaming far afield from English as we have previously taught it. Yet what am I talking about? Communication by various means for a variety of purposes with real audiences. Collaborating with others to solve problems and create solutions. Learning new literacies to tell the story of a business such as Joe's Ice Cream or American Cyclery. Drawing on the different personae outlined later (see page 17) to serve the company your students will create or work for in the future. (See Figure 1.1.) In a perfect world, students would graduate and live the rich, literate lives of Sam Calagione, owner of Dogfish Head Brewery who describes how he and his wife end their day—typical of the new world of work, it doesn't quite end the way it used to thanks to the digital and global lives many of us now lead:

> By the time I'm done reading to [the kids], it's 8:30. . . . Once in a while, I come down and watch *Entourage* or *Flight of the Conchords* with Mariah while she's typing away at her computer, posting updates on Facebook and Dogfish.com. But usually, . . . I read until 10:30 or 11. Sometimes, it's culinary or wine magazines. I have a little notebook next to my bed, and if something I'm reading inspires me, I'll jot down some notes. For the last half-hour, I'll read some fiction just to take my mind off of work. . . . I obsessively notch the pages, even when I'm reading fiction. If it's notched up and folded back, it means it's an actual idea that applies to Dogfish. If it's notched down, it's more about the feeling—part of what's written reflects our off-centered philosophy. Every word that I read, I filter through this Dogfish prism. Every thought that I have in some way pertains to Dogfish. It's kind of sick in a way—that Dogfish is that prevalent in my thought patterns. But after 5:30, I stop focusing on the nuts and bolts of the business and let my mind wander to the more fun and creative parts. (Calagione 2009)

PAUSE & REFLECT What are your thoughts about the relationship between what you teach in your classroom and its connection to the world of work?

Academic Literacy: Learning to Be a Student—Forever

Caglione and others mentioned in the previous section provide a telling example of Toffler's argument that "the illiterate of the 21st century will not be those who cannot read and write, but those who cannot *learn*, unlearn, and relearn" (1999). What are Calagione and his wife doing? They are *learning*. Taking notes. Asking questions. Engaging in both critical and creative

Workplace Literacies and Expectations

Note The following list of traits derives from actual performance evaluations from different fields.

SOCIAL SKILLS AND WORK ETHIC	Fall	Spring	Δ
• Demonstrates appropriate and measured self-confidence			
• Uses feedback on performance to improve and identify areas for further improvement			
• Works well under pressure			
• Shows ability to work with and lead others in variety of situations			
• Seeks opportunities to gain and improve skills related to current and future work			
• Maintains a positive attitude toward those with and for whom they work			
• Demonstrates a strong work ethic and perseveres through problems encountered on job			
• Accepts responsibility for his or her own work; offers help to others when able			
• Shares knowledge, ideas, and strategies with others			
• Makes ethical decisions when working with others and on personal projects			
• Requests feedback from others in order to improve or learn new solutions			
• Seeks to understand and support clients and colleagues			
• Receives respect from clients and colleagues with whom he or she works			
• Understands and follows protocols, practices, and policies			
• Raises questions and makes suggestions about how to improve performance			
• Identifies ways to do additional work that improves the process, product, or performance			
• Seeks ways to better serve those with whom he or she works			
• Takes initiative instead of waiting for others to serve clients, solve, complete, or address issues			
WRITTEN AND ORAL COMMUNICATION			
• Writes logically organized and detailed documents that are free of mechanical errors			
• Gathers appropriate details through interviews and discussions			
• Listens respectfully but actively, showing understanding through questions and comments			
• Shows understanding of and respect for others' perspectives and validates their positions			
• Evaluates audience and crafts written or verbal communication accordingly			
• Communicates in language that is appropriate and correct for the audience, occasion, and purpose			
PROJECT, TIME, AND RESOURCE MANAGEMENT			
• Prioritizes tasks and uses time appropriately			
• Meets deadlines and arrives at scheduled meetings and appointments promptly			
• Anticipates the next steps in a project without prompting from colleagues or supervisors			
• Follows instructions and protocols reliably and accurately			
• Keeps all materials, resources, and information in safe, organized, accessible place and format			
• Evaluates and double-checks all work before sending or submitting			
• Requires minimal supervision and asks for help when necessary			
• Works with an appropriate sense of urgency and finishes all assigned tasks on time			
• Shows adaptability and agility as demands and conditions change			
KNOWLEDGE AND ANALYSIS			
• Demonstrates appropriate knowledge of subject			
• Evaluates and interprets data from various sources			
• Chooses and applies appropriate tools and strategies to solve problems			
• Draws logical conclusions based on facts and analysis			
• Demonstrates the ability to research and document complex ideas and processes			
• Understands and is able to use a variety of applications to complete tasks			
• Uses standard software applications to improve project quality and productivity			
• Knows and applies knowledge of methods, practices, and solutions that lead to success			
• Knows and applies knowledge of professional and corporate standards			
• Uses downtime to improve knowledge of practices, procedures, applications, and field			
TOTAL SCORE			

Reflection What does this evaluation tell you about your own strengths and weaknesses as they relate to any future job or career you might consider? What surprises or concerns you the most? Which strengths show the greatest promise in helping you succeed in the future? What experiences or education should you consider to address your weaknesses and further improve your strengths?

FIGURE 1.1 Workplace literacies and expectations. I ask students to fill this out at the beginning of the year to help them identify those areas of need and to help them think about the larger set of skills this class will teach them and this world expects them to possess. They give themselves a score of 0 to 10 in each row.

thinking. Writing *and* discussing. Reading a range of types of texts, including fiction, but doing so with a purpose—in this case, improving their business. Calagione and his wife are, in other words, not merely businesspeople but lifelong students who illustrate the notion of academic literacy we will discuss next as part of the Big Picture of teaching English.

Just as we do not exist solely to prepare students for the workplace, nor do English classes serve the other disciplines and universities as if our classroom were some academic pit stop, where we do a NASCAR-quick fix-up, before sending students back into the halls to their other classes. Yet, as with preparing them for the demands of the workplace, so must we play our part in developing the academic literacies students need to succeed in school now and college or other postsecondary education later. And they do need that preparation. According to "Ready or Not: Creating a High School Diploma That Counts," a report by the American Diploma Project (ADP), at least 28 percent of entering college students nationwide require remedial English or math courses; in California, the ADP reports that the number was 55 percent in 2007 (ADP 2004).

Of course not all high school graduates enroll in college; others go straight into the workplace where they find themselves, as we have already discussed, needing more advanced literacies than previous generations ever did. According to the ADP report mentioned previously, the cost of remediating such students in the workplace ran as high as $40 million a year for a single state. What about entering middle and high school students, though? Here, too, we find many in need of those "academic literacies" we once assumed they already had. As Cziko (1998) writes, "Although I have been teaching English for over twenty years in both middle and high school classrooms, I hadn't thought explicitly about teaching reading" (1).

Figure 1.3 represents all that I have come to consider essential to academic success. These "academic essentials" (Burke 2007a; 2010) represent the skills, abilities, and qualities students need—and that I had to learn the hard way when I finally went to college—if they are to succeed in high school and, eventually, college and the workplace.

Five Generations of Literacy in the Burke Family

My great grandparents came from Russia to farm in Oklahoma then later moved West during the Dust Bowl to settle in Fresno, California.

My grandparents settled in Sacramento after moving from Kansas. He worked as a self-employed painter and wallpaper hanger.

My father (*middle*) left high school early, as did his brothers pictured here, to begin working in the printing trade where by retirement age he advanced as his literacy skills improved to become one of the supervisors.

I graduated from high school in 1979 in the bottom 10 percent of my class and took a job in a printing factory. Upon enrolling in community college, I was placed in the remedial English class, then graduated in 1983 with BA in developmental psychology.

Our three children (from L to R): Nora, Whitman, and Evan. At this time, Evan and Whitman are in college and Nora is thriving in middle school.

FIGURE 1.2 Five generations of literacy in the Burke family

THE ACADEMIC ESSENTIALS

What students must know and be able to do to succeed in middle/high school, the workplace, and college.

4. CAPACITIES | **3. COMPETENCIES** | **1. COMMITMENT** | **2. CONTENT**

	READ • Literary • Informative • Persuasive • Visual/graphic • Multimedia	**WRITE** • Arguments • Informational • Narrative • Explanatory	**SPEAK & LISTEN** • Interview • Discuss • Speak/present • Perform	**REPRESENT** • Image • Graphic • Infographic • Numbers • Multimedia	**OBSERVE** • People • Processes • Performances	**TAKE NOTES** • Lecture/discussion • Research • Reading literature • Reading Info/argumernt	**TAKE TESTS** • Multiple choice • Essay • Short answer
GENERATE • Questions • Hypotheses • Claims • Connections • Alternatives • Categories							
EVALUATE • Importance • Effectiveness • Validity • Accuracy • Quality							
ANALYZE • Cause/effect • Problem solve • Implications • Logic • Results							
ORGANIZE • Spatial • Cause/effect • Chronological • Importance • Problem solve • Classification • Compare/contrast							
SYNTHESIZE • Info/data • Events • Ideas • Sources • Perspectives							
ASSESS • Product • Process • Next steps • Strategies • Alternatives							
REFLECT • Process • Progress							

FIGURE 1.3 The Academic Essentials Matrix represents those key skills needed to succeed in all academic courses and in today's workplace. It is formatted as a matrix to suggest that when we read, for example, we also generate, evaluate, analyze, and so on. The outside frame contains the Four Cs of academic success as described in detail in *School Smarts* (Burke 2004).

© 2013 by Jim Burke from *The English Teacher's Companion*, Fourth Edition. Portsmouth, NH: Heinemann.

Many have examined the demands of college-level work (Intersegmental Committee et al. 2002; Conley 2005a, 2003; Cox 2009), arguing that the following are essential for college readiness:

- *Habits of mind:* those skills necessary for learning college-level content, including critical thinking skills such as analysis, interpretation, problem solving, and reasoning.
- *Key content knowledge:* the essential knowledge of each discipline that prepares students for advanced study, the "big ideas" of each content area.
- *Academic behaviors:* those general skills, such as reading comprehension, time management, and note-taking, which students need to engage in college-level work. Also includes metacognition, or self-awareness of how one is thinking and learning, is crucial if students are to work independently in and after college. (Alliance for Excellent Education 2007, 3)

"THUS, ONE PART OF OUR JOB AS ENGLISH TEACHERS IS TO WELCOME *ALL* STUDENTS INTO THE 'HOUSE' OF ENGLISH . . . "

I had none of these literacies when I entered college. Nor do I fault my high school teachers. It was a different time: No one expected everyone to go to college then. Schools today often use something like the form shown in Figure 1.4 to help students. Prior to the late 1990s, few thought about the cognitive demands of academic work in these ways. Schoenbach, Greenleaf, Cziko, and Hurwitz (1999) began that process of demystifying these demands and showing teachers how to address them strategically within the content areas without displacing what teachers considered their "real" subject. Echoing other teachers' sentiments no doubt, Christine Cziko said, when first approached about incorporating academic literacy into her English class, "but I'm an English teacher not a reading teacher!" (Cziko 1998).

Academic literacy is about more than reading or even academic work, however; there are cultural, social, and even emotional elements, as well (Tatum 2005, 35). As I wrote in *School Smarts: The Four Cs of Academic Success*:

> Learning is natural; schooling is not. Schools are countries to which we send our children, expecting these places and the people who work there to help draw out and shape our children into the successful adults we want them to become. As with travel to other countries, however, people only truly benefit from the time spent there to the extent that they can and do participate. If someone doesn't know the language, the customs, the culture— well, that person will feel like the outsider they are. As Gerald Graff, author of *Clueless in Academe* (2003) puts it, "schooling takes students who are perfectly street-smart and exposes them to the life of the mind in ways that make them feel dumb." (Burke 2004, 2)

Thus, one part of our job as English teachers is to welcome *all* students into the "house" of English, give them a tour, and be patient while they fumble around and orient themselves in the process of reinforcing or developing their "academic identity" (Lampert 2001). If we do not accept this role, if we do not see our students as "apprentices" to a discipline we have spent our lives trying to master, they will be unable to gain from us all we hope to share when we turn to the rich tradition of words and ideas that is what *we* consider English (see Figure 1.5). It is toward that home, the real core of our discipline, that we now turn.

Name: _____ Date: _____

Major: _____ School: _____

DOMAINS (Score yourself 0–3. 0 = don't know it/can't do it; 3 = major strength)	Fall	Spring	Δ
WRITING			
• Write to think, using notebooks, blogs, and online discussions to generate and refine ideas.			
• Use appropriate and correct grammar, usage, and mechanical conventions.			
• Show a sound understanding and mastery of the style and conventions of academic writing.			
• Construct a coherent, defensible argument that you support with evidence from reliable sources.			
• Find, evaluate, choose, integrate, cite, and correctly format sources.			
• Support and illustrate your ideas and assertions using evidence and examples.			
• Generate and refine your own topic and ideas when writing.			
• Follow the writing process to generate ideas, draft, revise, proofread, and publish your work.			
• Write 5-10 page papers that defend an argument with insight and analysis—not summary.			
• Apply a range of rhetorical strategies appropriate to your audience, occasion, and purpose.			
• Write with great clarity, cohesion, and coherence about compelling ideas and complex texts.			
• Demonstrate a commitment to writing well and ethically.			
READING			
• Read critically as evidenced by comments, writing, annotations, and notes.			
• Use textual evidence to support and illustrate your inferences and interpretations.			
• Identify, analyze, and critique an author's argument.			
• Recognize and understand words with multiple meanings (i.e., different connotations).			
• Read and understand a range of types of texts for different purposes.			
• Identify, analyze, and critique author's rhetorical and stylistic choices.			
• Analyze literary, expository, and informational pieces in light of literary and rhetorical style and effect.			
• Select and read books that challenge your own assumptions, knowledge, and abilities.			
• Show obvious interest in and commitment to reading a range of challenging texts.			
SPEAKING AND LISTENING			
• Give effective speeches or presentations on an idea or text using appropriate means and media.			
• Participate in and contribute substance to both group and full-class discussions.			
• Use language appropriate to the audience, occasion, and purpose when speaking			
• Provide evidence, examples, and commentary when contributing to discussions or presenting.			
• Listen and respond to others' ideas and opinions with respect.			
• Demonstrate knowledge of social conventions in discussions (acknowledge, respond to others).			
• Show a commitment to participating in and ensuring the success of any discussion.			
THINKING			
• Exhibit curiosity (80%).			
• Experiment with new ideas (79%).			
• See other points of view (77%).			
• Challenge their own beliefs (77%).			
• Engage in intellectual discussions (74%).			
• Ask provocative questions (73%).			
• Generate hypotheses (72%).			
• Exhibit respect for other viewpoints (71%).			
• Ask questions for clarification (85%).			
MANAGING YOURSELF			
• Self-Awareness: Know your needs and strengths; know what you need to succeed and improve.			
• Self-Management: Control stress, impulsivity, attention, and energy to achieve desired outcomes.			
• Social Awareness: Respond and show respect to other perspectives, cultures, and values.			
• Relationship Skills: Communicate and interact with a range of people; ask for and provide help.			
• Responsible Decision Making: Solve problems by making responsible, ethical choices.			
• Work Ethic: Come on time, prepared, all work completed as assigned and when it's due.			
• Personal Ethos (Character): Demonstrate that you are trustworthy, ethical, and committed.			
TOTAL SCORE			

Note: The items listed under "Thinking" come from a UC/CSU report titled *Academic Literacy;* the percentage refers to the number of professors who reported they were very concerned about students' performance in each area.

FIGURE 1.4 College Prep: Are You Ready? I ask students to complete this form in the fall and again at the end of the year to help identify what they need to learn and, at year's end, what they have learned but still need to improve on if they are to succeed in college.

FIGURE 1.5 Meeting with senior Michelle in the last week of the year during our exit interviews to discuss her readiness for college according to the College Prep assessment

PAUSE & REFLECT How do the issues raised here about academic literacy relate to your own experience as a student? How would you describe yourself as a student—and what are the implications of that as they relate to the needs of your students?

Revising Our Discipline: What English Is—and Is Not

So what *is* English—and why does our discipline merit more of students' time and attention than any other subject? For starters, it attempts to do what we have already discussed: develop those literacies students need to succeed not only in school but in college and at the workplace. The National Council of Teachers of English (NCTE) offers the following description of 21st Century Literacies they believe English teachers should accomplish:

> Literacy has always been a collection of cultural and communicative practices shared among members of particular groups. As society and technology change, so does literacy. Because technology has increased the intensity and complexity of literate environments, the twenty-first century demands that a literate person possess a wide range of abilities and competencies, many literacies. These literacies—from reading online newspapers to participating in virtual classrooms—are multiple, dynamic, and malleable. As in the past, they are inextricably linked with particular histories, life possibilities and social trajectories of individuals and groups. Twenty-first century readers and writers need to:
>
> - Develop proficiency with the tools of technology
> - Build relationships with others to pose and solve problems collaboratively and cross-culturally
> - Design and share information for global communities to meet a variety of purposes
> - Manage, analyze and synthesize multiple streams of simultaneous information
> - Create, critique, analyze, and evaluate multi-media texts
> - Attend to the ethical responsibilities required by these complex environments (NCTE 2008)

PAUSE & REFLECT How does this statement relate to your values and principles about teaching English? What is missing? What would you change? Which of these elements is most important in your opinion?

But English is so much more than these literacies, none of which appeared in Applebee's landmark 1993 study "Literature in the Secondary School: Studies of Curriculum and Instruction in the United States." Applebee noted that English studies, up until that time, fell into three different "traditions." The first of these, which he argued stemmed from the world of Matthew Arnold, "emphasized the importance of a common cultural heritage to both the growth of the individual and the preservation of national values and traditions" (3). Anticipating much of the work of Bloom (1995), Hirsch (1988, 2007, 2009), and Ravitch (2001, 2010), this tradition stresses the "development of the intellect through engagement in great ideas" (Applebee 1993, 3) and is sometimes referred to as the "cultural heritage model," which argues that all students "need exposure to the greatest works, and that attempts to make the curriculum more 'relevant' and 'accessible' to students will also make the curriculum less worthwhile" (3).

The second tradition, which emphasizes the development of essential language skills, is more "utilitarian and even vocational in emphasis," calling for greater focus on "'functional' skills, on 'minimum essentials,' on 'minimum competencies,' and on the 'basics,'" thus giving greater importance to practical reading at the exclusion of the "great works" (3). Moreover, in this more functional literacy model, "contemporary nonfiction is likely to receive more attention in the curriculum than 'great books,' and the value of literary studies is more likely to be discussed in terms of practical reading skills that result than in terms of cultural values or intellectual discipline" (Applebee 1993, 3).

> **"**IN THIS TRADITION, WHICH HAS ITS ROOTS IN THE WORK OF JOHN DEWEY, 'BOOKS ARE LIKELY TO BE CHOSEN FOR STUDY ON THE BASIS OF THEIR INTEREST AND APPEAL TO THE STUDENTS RATHER THAN THEIR PLACE IN THE COMMON CULTURE' . . . **"**

The third, and final, tradition focuses on the child not the subject, placing greater emphasis on "appreciation" and "engagement" than essential skills or cultural heritage. In this tradition, which has its roots in the work of John Dewey, "books are likely to be chosen for study on the basis of their interest and appeal to the students rather than their place in the common culture" (4) and work will tend to focus more on process and projects. All three of these traditions are still very present today, though where academic literacy and, more recently "new literacies" (Lankshear and Knobel 2006; Coiro, Knobel, Lankshear, and Leu 2008), would fit is difficult to say given that Applebee's 1993 survey of English studies includes no reference to computers let alone the Internet.

PAUSE & REFLECT Which of these three "traditions" best describes your beliefs about your role as an English teacher? Discuss where your position comes from and how it shapes your thinking about what and how you teach.

Prior to Applebee's 1993 study, the 1987 English Coalition Conference gathered some sixty of the profession's leaders to answer one question: What is English? After *three weeks* of discussing the question—and, of course, others that arose along the way—Peter Elbow (1990), charged with documenting the conference, wrote: "English is . . . the grab-bag, garbage-pail, everything-but-the-kitchen-sink discipline. Or, recasting this with the dignity that English professors love, English is peculiarly rich, complex, and many-faceted. More so, I think, than any other discipline" (110).

Carol Jago, former president of NCTE, advocates a literary education for the intellectual and cultural benefits it affords students: "Writing about literature disciplines the mind. It challenges students to look closely into what they read, and express clearly and powerfully what they find there. . . . It requires deep reading and analytical thinking—skills that will serve students well whatever their futures may hold" (2009, 1). Arguing that literature can change lives, Jago continues: "The young people trusted to our care need to know how to make a life. And real life all too often poses moral dilemmas like the one Atticus Finch confronted . . . Walking a mile in Atticus's shoes, vicariously experiencing both his fear and his courage, can help to prepare students for the hard choices they will make in their own lives" (2). Others (Nussbaum 1995, 2010; Lickona, Schaps, and Lewis 2003; Wilcox 2004; Sion 2004) echo and extend Jago's call for such character education as the English language arts are able to provide.

Still others (Denby 1996; Prose 1999; Bloom 2000; Atwell 2001a; Bauerlein 2008) share this faith in "the religion of literature" (Scholes 1998, 76), arguing that literature, the study of great works, is capable of cultivating not only one's cognitive faculties but also one's moral sensibilities. Edmundson (2004), who favors a more philosophical approach to literature as a means of achieving "The Great Confrontation," such as Atticus experiences, asserts that we read to answer this question: "What does this book tell us about how we should live our lives?" As Jago (2009) reminds us, students' lives take place in the real world, and

> to thrive in the real world, students need to be able to do more than Twitter. They need to be able to develop extended arguments that demonstrate a careful analysis of complex ideas. They need to be able to criticize a brave new world in which reading is reduced to skimming and scanning websites, in which templates replace writing, in which the arts are extracurricular and in which culture is reserved for the few rather than the many. (5)

What Jago and Edmundson, all English teachers in one way or another, celebrate is the English teacher as described by Pat Conroy (2007):

> I have read like a man on fire my whole life because the genius of English teachers touched me with the dazzling beauty of language. . . . I've been in ten thousand cities and have introduced myself to a hundred thousand strangers in my exuberant reading career, all because I listened to my fabulous English teachers and soaked up every single thing those magnificent men and women had to give. I cherish and praise them and thank them for finding me when I was a boy and presenting me with the precious gift of the English language.

Reading Conroy's words, as well as those authors mentioned earlier, one cannot help notice the extent to which fiction is not only emphasized but nonfiction is simply dismissed, ignored; it does not even appear on any of the reading lists Stotsky, Goering, and Jolliffe (2010b) assembled when studying what students in middle and high school were required to read (see their Figure 1.6, p. 15).

Noting this absence of nonfiction, *Washington Post* columnist Jay Mathews (2010) wrote: "It wasn't until I was in my fifties that I realized how restricted my high school reading lists had been, and how little they had changed for my three children. I am not dismissing the delights of Twain, Crane, Buck, and Wilder. But I think I would also have enjoyed John Hersey, Barbara Tuchman and Bruce Catton if they had been assigned."

After celebrating the new generations of nonfiction prose writers, such as Gladwell, McCullough, Kearns Goodwin, Mathews laments that they are not being assigned and that fiction remains nearly the exclusive focus of the secondary language arts curriculum; this is despite the overwhelming emphasis in college and the workplace on reading challenging nonfiction once students graduate. What nonfiction is included in the language arts classes often seems, so far, to be related to preparing students for such writing as they will encounter on state or other standardized exams. One exception is the Advanced Placement Language and Composition course and its emphasis on rhetoric and composition, usually in the junior year (see Figure 1.6).

The other exception to this fiction-centric curriculum is, of course, the Common Core State Standards (CCSS) that emphasizes the close reading of informational texts, which they explain as follows in the CCSS document itself:

> To become college and career ready, students must grapple with works of exceptional craft and thought whose range extends across genres, cultures, and centuries. Such works offer profound insights into the human condition and serve as models for students' own thinking and writing. Along with high-quality contemporary works, these

Most Commonly Taught Titles in Grades 9–11

9th Grade	10th Grade	11th Grade
1. *Romeo and Juliet*	1. *Julius Caesar*	1. *The Crucible*
2. *The Odyssey*	2. *Antigone*	2. *The Great Gatsby*
3. *To Kill a Mockingbird*	3. *To Kill a Mockingbird*	3. *The Scarlet Letter*
4. *Animal Farm*	4. *Of Mice and Men*	4. *Of Mice and Men*
5. *Night*	5. *A Separate Peace*	5. *To Kill a Mockingbird*
6. *Great Expectations*	6. *Night*	6. *Huckleberry Finn*
7. *The Miracle Worker*	7. *Animal Farm*	7. *A Raisin in the Sun*
8. *The Outsiders*	8. *Fahrenheit 451*	8. *The Glass Menagerie*
9. *Lord of the Flies*	9. *Lord of the Flies*	9. *The Red Badge of Courage*
10. *The Giver*	10. *Anthem*	10. *Our Town*
11. *A Separate Peace*	11. *Oedipus Rex*	11. *Macbeth*
12. *Anthem*	12. *A Raisin in the Sun*	12. *Hamlet*
13. *Huckleberry Finn*	13. *Huckleberry Finn*	13. *Their Eyes Were Watching God*
14. *Of Mice and Men*	14. *The Outsiders*	14. *Night*
15. *Wish You Well*	15. *The Crucible*	15. *Fahrenheit 451*

FIGURE 1.6 The most commonly taught titles in grades 9–11 according to Stotsky, Goering, and Jolliffe (2010b). With regard to other genres and texts used, they found that: no book-length nonfiction was assigned or mentioned (out of 350 classes investigated) and between 61 and 70 percent of respondents used textbooks, with most teachers teaching fewer than half of the selections contained in them.

texts should be chosen from among seminal U.S. documents, the classics of American literature, and the timeless dramas of Shakespeare. Through wide and deep reading of literature and literary nonfiction of steadily increasing sophistication, students gain a reservoir of literary and cultural knowledge, references, and images; the ability to evaluate intricate arguments; and the capacity to surmount the challenges posed by complex texts. (National Governors Association 2010, 35)

While I accept the power, even the truth, of what so many argue here, while I experience the power of literature every time we discuss it in my classes—and we do, as you will see throughout the book—there is also another view, one we need to make room for in our own professional minds. In *The Rise and Fall of English: Reconstructing English as a Discipline*, Robert Scholes (1998), challenges the conviction long held by many that "literature offer[s] quasi-sacred texts that [can] be expounded by a licensed teacher/preacher to reveal the entrance into the kingdom of light" (15). He continues in this vein, observing "that two world wars and the Holocaust have . . . demonstrated that high culture is not necessarily a guarantee of the 'sympathy, tolerance, and understanding'" (19) many expected it to be.

> " . . . FICTION REMAINS NEARLY THE EXCLUSIVE FOCUS OF THE SECONDARY LANGUAGE ARTS CURRICULUM; THIS IS DESPITE THE OVERWHELMING EMPHASIS IN COLLEGE AND THE WORKPLACE ON READING CHALLENGING NONFICTION ONCE STUDENTS GRADUATE. "

What does Scholes (1998) argue in his "reconstruction" of English as a discipline? Rhetoric and craft, and "a canon of concepts, precepts, and practices rather than a canon of texts" (120). "The pendulum is swinging back to rhetoric," he argues. "Not only is our world dominated by political and advertising rhetoric, but literary texts themselves now appear to us more and more as instances of interested rather than disinterested language" (20). What he is suggesting is "that we stop thinking of ourselves as if we had a subject matter and start thinking of ourselves as having a discipline [that] we can offer our students as part of the cultural equipment that they are going to need when they leave us" (68).

For Scholes, this means dismissing our blind faith in the "religion of literature" (76) and developing instead our own and students' knowledge of craft as "producers and consumers of text," thereby reinforcing the apprenticeship model mentioned earlier. This notion of craft, however, conflicts with our romantic view of English as art, for "art is high, craft is low. Art is unique; it can't be taught. Craft is common; it can be learned" (Scholes 2001, xiii). He would have us turn students into "textual animals."

As Scholes explains, "our English word comes from the Latin verb *texere*, which meant specifically "to weave" and, by extension, "to join or fit together anything; to plait, braid, interweave, interlace; to construct, make, fabricate, build. From *texere* also comes *textum*, 'that which is woven, a web'" (73). This way of thinking about text, as something we are either composing or trying to comprehend, is what I call "textual intelligence":

Textual intelligence (TI) is all about how texts are made, and how different grammatical structures create meaning for or affect the reader. Writers use their TI when they do everything from choose the format (poem vs. prose vs. play) or the purpose (to entertain vs. to inform) or the structure (narrative vs. expository), the medium (word or image, page or screen). They make TI decisions as they choose the point of view, the tense of the story (past tense, present tense), the use of foreshadowing or flashbacks, the organizational structure (linear or episodic). All these choices come from, in part, the writer's understanding of how texts and language work. Therefore, the more a student understands these structures, the more options he or she has when . . . writ[ing]. (Burke 2001, 164)

Perhaps what I am doing now in these pages is what English teaches us to do best within the democratic tradition: consider a subject from multiple sides, allow for differing, even conflicting interpretations and arguments, so long as they are carefully reasoned and well supported. While Jago and Scholes, along with many others, represent different views, there is a center to their thinking—a place akin to the common center of a Venn diagram—where we can reach some agreement that makes sense to us all.

One person who has considered these questions in great depth is Judith Langer. Having spent her entire career researching and reflecting on our discipline, she concluded in a speech to the International Reading Association that English teachers have a unique role among the disciplines: to develop in our students "a literate mind," which she defines as involving "the kinds of thinking needed not only to do well in school, but outside as well. It's the kind of mind children need to get on in life and adults need to keep up with life. It involves the ability to use language and thought to gain knowledge, share it and reason with it. We do this when we read, write and use the symbols and signs that permeate our society" (2004b).

To Langer's ideas, I would add that English also aspires to ensure that students learn certain types of knowledge:

- **Procedural:** How to *do* something: communicate, comprehend, compose.
- **Cultural:** Who *is* . . . when *was* . . . what *were*? What *do* we value?
- **Historical:** What was it *like* during . . .? What did people *believe* then?
- **Structural:** How does *x* work? How is *y* constructed?
- **Rhetorical:** What *is* language? How to *use* it to achieve a given effect?
- **Existential:** *Who* are we? *Whose* are we? *Why* are we here?
- **Ethical:** *Should* we? What are our obligations to . . . ? What if . . . ?
- **Psychological:** *Why* do we act that way? What do we need, want—and *why*?

PAUSE & REFLECT What are your thoughts so far about English as I have discussed it? Do you agree? Disagree? Why?

Adopting the Eight Personae of the English Language Arts

Yet we need to do more than teach skills and knowledge: We need to cultivate within our students a range of personae, each of which is necessary if they are, as Jago says, "to make a living, make a life, and make a difference" (2009, 1). Note that each of the following personae has two sides: one devoted to comprehending, interpreting, and analyzing the text or content created by others; the other dedicated to communicating one's own ideas and content through whichever means or media that person deems most appropriate to the task and occasion. In other words, each role involves both comprehension and composition. Here is a brief description of the eight personae English teachers attempt to develop in students—and ourselves:

- **Storyteller:** Whether a salesperson or politician, parent or teacher, everyone must be able to use a range of means and media to tell the story of an experience, an event, a situation, or a problem and its proposed solutions; moreover, we must be equally able to understand and analyze the stories, in whatever form and format they are produced, others tell us. Such stories would include those composed on paper as well as computers (i.e., digital storytelling). As Turner (1996) says, "Narrative imagining—story—is the fundamental instrument of thought." See the works by Daniel Pink, Peter Guber, or Christopher Volger.

- **Philosopher:** Whether in literary or expository, visual or written texts, students encounter increasingly complex ideas they must be able to understand and grapple with by posing questions and considering a subject from multiple angles; in addition, they must be able to convey their own perspective on and response to these ideas through words, images, numbers—or some mix of them all—when writing about or discussing the ideas they study through a range of texts. See the works by Martha Nussbaum, Mark Edmundson, or Hubert Dreyfus and Sean Dorrance Kelly.

- **Historian:** All texts and ideas are situated in a larger historical context; thus we must know how to gather, assess, and apply background knowledge relevant to the text or task at hand to comprehend its ideas and arguments; we must also know how to reason like the historian when assembling and communicating our ideas about trends, events, or texts. As we move into a more global, connected world where we not only read the texts but confront the history of other countries, we must become more historically adept readers and communicators. See the works by E. D. Hirsch, Thomas Friedman, and Charles Hill.

- **Anthropologist:** We must all develop the ability to understand not only our own but also others' cultures as we encounter them within the classroom, the world, texts, and online communities; this means also developing the ability to observe, examine, and communicate insights about these cultures—such skills are fundamental to our personal and economic success. People have spoken often of President Obama and the extent to which the influence of his anthropologist mother contributes to his ability to understand and communicate with people from various backgrounds in different situations. See the works by Malcolm Gladwell, Louise Rosenblatt, and Brian Boyd.

- **Reporter:** Everyone today must be able to search for, locate, evaluate, and analyze a remarkable amount of data from different sources; in this context, we must develop and continually refine our ability to investigate, research, and navigate through the ever-increasing sea of information available. Once we have done all this investigating, it is time to convey the results; thus we must be able not only to understand but also sift through and effectively communicate insights from these investigations of people, places, ideas, processes, or texts in the most appropriate form and format. This may involve traditional genres of written discourse but also may include mixed media, audio, or video depending on the context and purpose. See the works by Laura Hillenbrand, Michael Lewis, and Michael Pollan.

- **Critic:** Whether it is a literary or informational text, a written, multimedia, or visual text, a commercial or personal text, we all need the skills critics use to evaluate and analyze the work itself within the larger tradition to which it belongs. Indeed, such critical skills are fundamental to success in both professional and personal realms as we are increasingly expected to navigate the commercial, political, and financial waters ourselves. Whereas the critical mind once had to focus on what it thought about books and film, now it must also train itself to examine retirement plans, medical options, and competing products and services. Naturally, as with all critics, we must also be able to formulate and express our opinions about the subjects we critique, offering insights about the given literary or other text we have considered. See the works by Deborah Appleman, James Wood, and Helen Vendler.

- **Designer:** Design is such a crucial aspect of any text—on paper, online, or in the physical world. We need to know how to "read" for it, noticing the features used to instill the text with meaning; people even speak of "designing experiences," which means that the very tablecloths and arrangement of the room are designed with some intention in mind. The critical designer's eye will notice and understand it; so, too, must we consider design when we compose documents, create online content, produce videos, or otherwise communicate with people. It is important to take into consideration not only the means and media but also the available features and functions of every element. Communication, whether received or created, is too crucial to leave to chance; we are all designers now—or must learn to be. See the works by Daniel Pink, Robin Williams, and Garr Reynolds.

- **Traveler:** All the other personae are very purpose-driven—that is, related to success in one domain or another. While success is a fundamental objective of all education, we fail if students do not leave our classes having learned to enjoy the journey and wanting to continue it in the future. If they do not want to read, do not take any pleasure in viewing, observing, thinking, or communicating, we have not been successful. Thus, the final persona represents a person who *wants* to know more about the world and takes pleasure in exploring it, who sees reading as being about the destination of the journey. Travelers want to know, visit, see, and understand; we, as their teachers, must constantly be models of such a persona, cultivating this curiosity in our students, playing guide to each as they seek to find in themselves those subjects they want to study, those domains they want to explore and come to understand. See the works by Nancie Atwell, Teri Lesesne, Donalyn Miller, and Kelly Gallagher.

I end this chapter on *what* we teach by recognizing the role the CCSS will play in our work in the future and directing you to the inside covers of the book, where you will find the anchor standards for English language arts. Developed and published in 2010 by the National Governors Association, the Common Core Standards challenge us all in new and not always comfortable ways. As Fine (2010) writes, "What we need is to infuse the work around the common core with an element of visionary thinking. The standards themselves do not confine teaching to the realm of the scripted or undemocratic, but without serious reflection and rethinking, they will. The balance depends on our collective ability to come to terms with the standards and to use them as an opportunity for reflection and growth" (18).

PAUSE & REFLECT **Common Core Connection:** See the inside of the covers for the standards referred to throughout this book. For the latest information related to the Common Core Standards, visit www.corestandards.org.

Whether teaching or writing, I always try to have a "big question" I am trying to answer (Burke 2010). In this chapter, that question has been "What *is* English?" I have offered my perspective, one that continues to evolve as I do even after 25 years in the classroom. As Applebee (1996) says, a good curriculum is always a conversation. I have thought long and hard about the conversation we have had throughout this chapter; now it is your turn to have this same conversation with yourself and your colleagues: What do *you* think English is in this brave new world you, as a teacher, help to create and strive to prepare your students for every day in your class?

PAUSE & REFLECT Visit one of the following standards documents, preferably the one most relevant to your own classes. After reading the document, reflect on and discuss it with yourself and your colleagues as it applies to your classes.

- Common Core Standards
- Advanced Placement Literature or Language and Composition Claims
- Partnership for 21st Century Skills
- State standards for your region

Recommended **Resources**

PRINT

- *Curriculum as Conversation: Transforming Traditions of Teaching and Learning*, Arthur N. Applebee (University of Chicago 1996).
- *Envisioning Literature: Literary Understanding and Literature Instruction, Second edition*, Judith A. Langer (Teachers College Press 2010).
- *The Rise and Fall of English: Reconstructing English as a Discipline*, Robert Scholes (Yale University Press 1998).

ONLINE

- National Council of Teachers of English (www.ncte.org)
- The English Companion Ning (www.englishcompanion.ning.com)

CHAPTER TWO

Who We Teach

*Understanding and Teaching
the Next Generation*

Adolescence is a purgatory between childhood and adulthood.
—Intrator and Kunzman (2009)

The two elderly white women huddled together in the quiet, empty hallway of my school, wondering aloud about the kids depicted on the "World Cultures Map" that covered the wall. They jumped a bit when I stopped and asked whether they needed any help. "Oh no, thank you! We are part of the 60-year-reunion committee. We have a meeting down in the Alumni Room," they explained. Polite smiles. Then one asked, pointing at the map, "Who are all *those* people?" I knew what they were thinking. Sixty years earlier, when they graduated from Burlingame High School, just about every classmate was white. Real estate offices all had maps with "red-lined" areas to indicate those neighborhoods that were off-limits to nonwhites and Jews. If there had been Japanese students, they would have been gone, interned at Tanforan Race Track, which is where Seabiscuit once trained and our students now shop—the racetrack long ago having been converted into a large shopping mall.

Now these two nice women found themselves standing in the same halls of the same school where approximately 50 percent of the students live in apartments, dozens of languages are spoken, and kids come from a wide range of cultural, religious, and social backgrounds. "*They* all go *here*?" the women said in unison, their eyes wide, their voices filled with dismay. "They sure do!" I said. "Do they take classes with all the . . . *regular* kids?" they asked in disbelief. "*Of course* they do. Some of our best students are on that wall," I boasted, pointing to the photograph of a Latino boy in my AP Literature class and proudly saying, "That's Luis Gonzalez! Wonderful boy! Just got accepted into Berkeley, Stanford, *and* Santa Clara, which gave him a full academic scholarship!"

As if this were all too much to process, they wished me a pleasant day, then turned and moved off together, whispering their own private thoughts to each other about the school—and the past—they had come to remember and celebrate. When they attended the school, our country was at war with Japan. Had the two women looked at the walls on their way to the Alumni Room, they would have seen election posters from some of our school's top students whose grandparents or relatives may well have been kept at Tanforan while these two women prepared to graduate. And those election posters? Nearly every one of them featured an ambitious young woman whose options were unimaginable to these two women when they graduated from high school sixty years earlier, when women may have attended college in numbers equivalent to men (Francis 2012) but graduated into a world that expected them to be secretaries, nurses, or teachers.

Meet the **Next** Generation

Although my characterization of these two women is accurate—this was how they spoke, how they reacted, what they said—I mean them no disrespect, but want only to emphasize just how much the world and our student population has changed. Most schools today bring together three distinct generations, not all of which see and live in the world the same way, something that inevitably affects the relationship between teachers, students, and their parents. In my own house, we have three generations rubbing up against each other: Greatest Generation (mother-in-law, b. 1927), Baby Boomer Generation (my wife and I, b. 1961), and Generation Y (now sometimes referred to as the Connected Generation or Generation C, b. 1992, 1994, and 1999).

Today, one in three American teens belongs to a minority racial or ethnic group (Magazine Publishers of America 2004). Within this group, Asian American teens are expected to grow in number by 31 percent in the coming decade; the Asian population overall is growing

> **"**Most schools today bring together three distinct generations, not all of which see and live in the world the same way, something that inevitably affects the relationship between teachers, students and their parents.**"**

faster than any other major race group between 2000 and 2010 (Humes, Jones, and Ramirez 2011, 4). Latinos, however, who now represent one in six U.S. residents, are expected to make up 30 percent of the total population by 2050 (Humes, Jones, and Ramirez 2011) with as many as 33 percent of those students having Hispanic roots (Fry and Passel 2009). As of 2010, 78.3 percent of all Latinos lived in 10 states (with my state, California, claiming 40 percent more than second place Texas), though many of the fastest-growing Latino populations are now in the southeastern region of the United States (Lee et al. 2011, 5). According to the Pew Hispanic Center, Hispanic children account for approximately 25 percent those who are under 18 in the United States, the majority of whom are second- or third-generation Americans, not recent immigrants (Fry and Gonzales 2008).

While Latinos have typically lived more often in urban and rural communities, they now live increasingly in suburbs (Fry 2009; DeParle 2009) where, even though many certainly struggle, every year more enroll in and take a growing number of Advanced Placement exams to help them prepare for and get accepted to college. According to the College Board, Latino students represent 15.9 percent of the public schools' graduating classes and 15.5 percent of the AP exam examinee population, while African American and American Indian students represent 14.5 percent and 8.2 percent, and 1.2 percent and 0.6 percent, respectively (College Board 2010, 2). Still, while AP participation rates continue to climb for Latino students, a 2010 report highlights a second, more troubling trend that is emerging: low graduation percentage rates for Hispanic students (55.5), African American students (53.7), and Native American students (50.7), compared with 80.7 percent for Asian and 76.6 percent for white students (Swanson 2010, 2).

A report from the College Board specifically emphasizes the mounting concern about boys of color (2010), although another report (Robelen 2010) shows strong evidence that "Americans of different backgrounds are earning high school diplomas and college degrees at higher rates" (Adams 2011, 6) and taking more rigorous courses. Regardless of the various gains, a 2011 report emphasizes the persistent gap between achievement of white and Hispanic students (Hemphill, Vanneman, and Rahman 2011) in the eighth grade; most significant is the fact that "while Hispanic students' average scores [on the NAEP exam] have increased across the assessment years, White students had higher scores, on average, on all assessments" (1). This effect—of one group outpacing another while both get more instruction—is what Stanovich (1986) calls "the Matthew Effect," comparing it to the Gospel of Matthew, which says that the "rich get richer and the poor get poorer."

There are as many variations within and across immigrants (see Figure 2.1) as there are students. This chart is not meant to create a set of types into which we can or should sort students; instead, I offer this chart to help us think about students in more useful, insightful, and diverse ways as we try to better understand and meet their needs in our classes. For other information, see Olsen and Jaramillo (1999), Whiting (2003), Roberge (2003), Freeman and Freeman (2007); the figure was adapted from these.

> *I OFFER THIS CHART TO HELP US THINK ABOUT STUDENTS IN MORE USEFUL, INSIGHTFUL, AND DIVERSE WAYS AS WE TRY TO BETTER UNDERSTAND AND MEET THEIR NEEDS IN OUR CLASSES.*

Immigrant Student Typologies

Accelerated	Newly Arrived	Underschooled	Long-Term ESL
• Been in United States 4 years or less	• Been in United States 3 years or less	• Been in United States 2 years or less	• Been in or born in the United States 7 years or more before high school
• Come from all different countries	• Come from all different countries	• Come from all different countries	• Come from all different countries; raised in United States
• Attended good schools in native country	• Some attended good schools; others are unprepared	• Have little or no schooling or it was interrupted	• Come from same local schools as others; also called "Generation 1.5"
• Move rapidly through ESL program	• Move through ESL program steadily	• Move slowly through ESL classes; often repeat classes	• Stay in transitional or support classes; tend to be fluent in oral English
• Earn higher grades than rest of students	• Earn grades similar to other students	• Tend to struggle, fail, and/or barely pass	• Divided: Some do well; others struggle
• Graduate on time	• Need more than 4 years to graduate	• Do not graduate or pass exit exams	• Tend to graduate; some enter community college
• Succeed in mainstream classes (despite limited English)	• Succeed if content classes offered in native language	• Find classes too difficult in any language	• Perceive their performance as higher than grades show it is

FIGURE 2.1 Immigrant Student Typologies. These are, of course, not meant to be definitive categories.

Race and ethnicity are obviously only two of the many lenses through which we view our students. Other important trends, all of which have a substantial impact on our English classes, include:

- As of 2007, 6.7 million (9 percent) students received special education services. Within this population, autism is the fastest-growing disability, with 1 out of every 91 children being born on the autistic spectrum (Yavorcik 2009).

- About 40 percent of all children receiving special education services have specific learning disabilities (i.e., those affecting the processes involved in using language, spoken or written, as related to listening, speaking, reading, writing, spelling, or calculating), according to the *2009 Condition of Education* report (National Center for Education Statistics 2009).

These numbers all become more meaningful and urgent for English teachers as the number of full-inclusion students in mainstream classes grows.

PAUSE & REFLECT Visit the IDEA homepage on the U.S. Department of Education website. After looking around, read those reports and findings relevant to your school and students. What conclusions can you draw that apply to your students?

The most troubling trend perhaps, for it transcends race and gender, is the gap opening up between the rich and the poor in the United States. As recently as 2009, 20 percent of children lived in poverty, a figure that represents an 18 percent increase over the last decade (National Center for Education Statistics 2009). Tavernise (2012) summarizes a series of new reports on poverty and its effects on educational performance and opportunity; she highlights several key developments:

- Family income appears to be more a factor in educational success than race
- The gap in standardized test scores between affluent and low-income students has grown by approximately 40 percent since the 1960s and now doubles the testing gap between white and African American students
- Students from affluent backgrounds are 50 percent more likely to complete college, which is the single most important predictor of success in the workforce
- Affluent children spend 1300 more hours than low-income children before age six in places outside their homes (which, one could argue, inevitably enriches background knowledge and language development)
- Affluent children enter school having spent an average of 400 hours more than poor children engaged in literacy-related activities (A1)

PAUSE & REFLECT Take time to consider the information in Figure 2.2. How does this mesh with your observations and experiences in school and around the community where you teach? Visit www.skillscommission.org to view the slide presentation about the report from which this diagram comes.

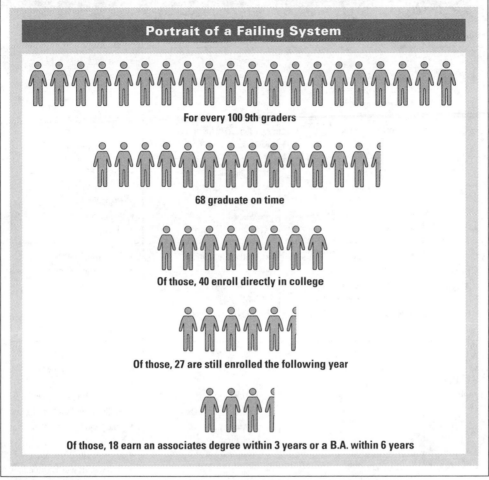

Portrait of a Failing System

For every 100 9th graders

68 graduate on time

Of those, 40 enroll directly in college

Of those, 27 are still enrolled the following year

Of those, 18 earn an associates degree within 3 years or a B.A. within 6 years

FIGURE 2.2 America's Leaky Education Pipeline. You can read the report and learn more about this at the website for the National Council on Education and the Economy (www.skillscommission.org). The data for the NCEE's graphic comes from James Hunt and Thomas Tierney, *American Higher Education: How Does It Measure Up for the 21st Century?* National Center for Public Policy and Higher Education © 2006.

PAUSE **&** REFLECT After reading all this information about the kids we teach and the trends for the future, much of which seems to contradict itself at times, what thoughts and concerns do you have? How would you describe the student population you teach?

So far, this chapter has focused mostly on ethnicity and race, two areas in which schools are undergoing a "vast . . . transformation" (Frankenberg 2008, 5), which will culminate in most states across the nation eventually reporting "a majority of nonwhite students" (see Figure 2.3). A separate change is also well underway, however: the generational change, which has led to the next generation being called the "Millennials" (Taylor and Keeter 2010).

Who We Were, Who We Are, and Who We Teach			
Generation	**Baby Boomers**	**Generation X**	**Generation Y**
	• Teachers • Administrators • Parents of teachers • Parents of students	• Teachers • Administrators • Parents of students	• Teachers • Students
Years/Size	• 1946–1964 (born) • 77 million	• 1965–1978 (born) • 45 million	• 1979–2000 (born) • 80 million
Ethnic Breakdown	• White: 77% • African American: 12% • Hispanic: 9% • Asian: 1 • Other: 1%	• White: 68% • African American: 14% • Hispanic: 14% • Asian: 3% • Other: 1%	• White: 61% • African American: 13% • Hispanic: 19% • Asian: 5% • Other: 2%
History: **Influential Events and Experiences**	• Korean and Vietnam Wars • Television • Nuclear/Sputnik era • Rosa Parks/Civil Rights • Rock-n-Roll • JFK, RFK, MLK killed	• Watergate scandal • Computers • Reagan era • AIDS • Title IX (women's sports) • Divorce/one-parent family	• 9/11 attack and wars • Columbine shootings • Dot.com boom/bust • No Child Left Behind • Internet/cell phones • Busy, overplanned life
Media: What They Watched, Played, and Used to Communicate	• *Leave It to Beaver* • Walter Cronkite • Elvis Pressley • 4 TV stations • Radio/record albums • Letters • Telephone • Face-to-face • *Monopoly*	• *Brady Bunch* • Dan Rather • The Beatles • 4 TV stations; VCR • Radio/albums/CDs • Letters/email • Telephone • Phone-to-phone • *Pacman*	• *Family Guy* • Jon Stewart and *Oprah* • Tupac Shakur • 100s of TV stations; DVR • Radio/CDs/iPods/iPhone • Email and texting • Cell phone • Facebook/texting/videochat • *Angry Birds* (via smartphone)
Attitudes: Life and Work	• Live to work • Value rewards other than $ • Hard-working • Focused on family • Seek flexibility in work • Devoted to company • Committed to equity, justice • Want to make a difference • Collaborative, social	• Work to live • Value material rewards • Optimistic about personal future but not world • Resist/resent supervision • Fragmented as a group • Need/resist feedback • Comfortable with change • Effort, commitment vary	• Live to work (but expect reward and recognition) • Value rewards other than $ • Optimistic • Close to parents • Globally aware • Open-minded about other cultures, sexual preferences • *Very* social, collaborative
Qualities	• Service-oriented • Ambitious • Disciplined • Cooperative • Considerate • Involved/active	• Flexible • Technoliterate • Independent • Unintimidated by authority • Informal • Creative	• Collaborative • Optimistic • Persistent • Ambitious • Able to multitask • Tech savvy

FIGURE 2.3 Who We Were, Who We Are, and Who We Teach.

© 2013 by Jim Burke from *The English Teacher's Companion*, Fourth Edition. Portsmouth, NH: Heinemann.

PAUSE **&** REFLECT   Where would you place yourself on the chart in Figure 2.3? What are the implications for you as a teacher? What would you change or add to this chart that would help you better understand the students you teach?

The Millennials: The Dumbest, the Smartest— or Just the Next Generation?

The Millennials (also called Gen Y, Generation Y, Generation C, the Net Generation) invite equal measures of concern and celebration from scholars and critics, CEOs, and leaders. To some they are idiots; to others, savants. Some worry they mark the beginning of the end; others insist they signal the beginning of a new era of brilliance and will redefine work, culture, and life as we know it. Both *Time* (Fisher 2009) and the *Harvard Business Review* (Erickson 2009), among others, are trying to make sense of the Millennials, to whom businesses are trying as hard to sell products as we are to sell poetry. All of which leads back to the question: What does Gen Y bring to the table—besides a cell phone and the ability to text without looking at the keypad during class?

Should we be worried? Bauerlein (2008), Jackson (2009), and Carr (2010) certainly think we should be. Each paints a picture of our society moving headlong into a new "Dark Age" in which everyone knows everything about their friends' personal lives but little else and nothing of the past, thus leaving them unprepared to meet the demands of the present—or the future. Bauerlein leaves no room for doubt in his assessment of the "intellectual condition of young Americans":

> The 21st-century teen, connected and multitasked, autonomous yet peer-mindful makes no great leap forward in human intelligence, global thinking, or netizenship. Young users have learned a thousand new things, no doubt. They upload and download, surf and chat, post and design, but they haven't learned to analyze a complex text, store facts in their heads, comprehend a foreign policy decision, take lessons from history, or spell correctly. Never having recognized their responsibility to the past, they have opened a fissure in our civic foundation, and it shows in their halting passage into adulthood and citizenship. (201)

If Bauerlein worries about their lack of knowledge, others worry about the lack of attention and critical perspective (Jackson 2009; Gallagher 2009; Lanham 2006; Carr 2010). This concern about whether students pay attention emerges as a dominant concern, along with the ability to sustain that attention long enough and with adequate critical distance to be able to separate the "noise from the message" in a world of information that is more akin to drinking from a fire hydrant than sipping from a stream. A 2012 report about this "hyperconnected" generation presented findings to a range of experts, asking them to offer predictions about the year 2020, several of which are relevant to our work as English teachers:

- Millennials' brains are being rewired to adapt to the new information-processing skills they will need to survive in this environment.
- Memory is changing, beginning to function more like hyperlinks to information triggered by keywords and URLs, which the brain stores and recalls, but not the full memory.

- Some students will be "supertaskers," able to handle several complicated tasks simultaneously and do them well, allowing them to work in ways most others cannot.

- Adolescents who are used to "quick-fix information nuggets" will struggle to engage in deep, critical analysis of issues and challenging information.

- Many young people will make shallow choices, seek instant gratification, and lack the patience needed to learn what does not come quickly or easily to them.

- Young adults and graduates will require such skills as the ability to conduct rapid, efficient searches, browse for and evaluate the quality of information on a topic, and synthesize often large quantities of information. One researcher suggested that "the ability to read one thing and think hard about it for hours will [be useful] but it will be of far less consequence for most people." (Anderson and Rainie 2012, 4)

Another group cannot help but see this generation of students in a more positive light, having embraced the digital culture the NetGeners helped create (Ito et al. 2008; Tapscott 2009; Richardson 2010; Davidson 2011). Where Bauerlein (2008), for example, dismisses the Millienials' ways as superficial, Tapscott calls them an elite learning force that "instinctively turns first to the Net to communicate, to understand, to learn" (9). Davidson (2011) takes a different tack, suggesting that "pundits are convinced that kids today know nothing, [but] it may well be because they know nothing about what kids today know" (57). Returning to the earlier data about poverty, we can easily imagine such digital elites developing skills that many low income students do not even know exist.

Another, more troubling, perspective has also begun to emerge regarding the Millennials: Damon found that only one in five 12- to 22-year-old males and females surveyed (see Figure 2.4) possessed "a clear vision of where they want to go, what they want to accomplish in

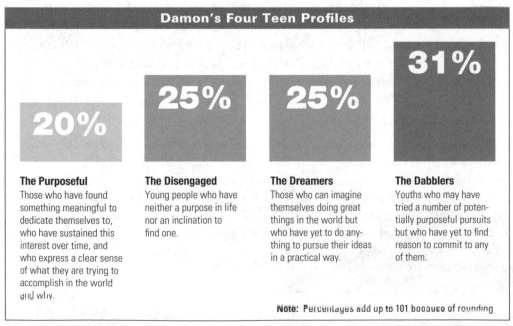

FIGURE 2.4 Damon's Four Teen Profiles. Adapted from his book *The Path to Purpose: Helping Our Children Find Their Calling in Life* (2008).

life, and why" (2008, 8). By contrast, Damon reports that "almost 60 percent may have engaged in some potentially purposeful activities, or they may have developed some vague aspirations; but they do not have any real commitment to such activities or any realistic plans for pursuing their aspirations" (8). (Visit the website of the Stanford Center on Adolescence for more information.) So, regardless of whose perspective we share about the kids in our classes, students face profound and often troubling existential questions that we as English teachers are in a unique position to address in the context of our classes and curriculum.

The irony, of course, is that the very skills critics complain about—multitasking, limited attention, frustration with "old-school" ways—are the very skills the twenty-first century workplace expects. When asked to describe the skills needed in the emerging global, fast-paced, 24/7 workplace of the future, Rob Carter, chief information officer at FedEx said that the best training

> for anyone who wants to succeed in 10 years is the online game *World of Warcraft*. *WoW* offers a peek into the workplace of the future. Each team faces a fast-paced, complicated series of obstacles, and each player must contribute to resolving them or else lose his place on the team. The player who contributes most gets to lead the team—until someone else contributes more. (Fisher 2009)

PAUSE **& REFLECT**   Compare the Workplace Literacies Self-Evaluation in Figure 1.1 with what Carter and others are saying in the preceding.

In an effort to understand how to reach and teach this generation, Tapscott (2009) identifies several "norms" he says we should keep in mind when working with NetGeners. In short, this generation expects to be able *to choose* what they read, watch, do, or create; *to customize or personalize* their work, their tools, their environment; and *to work together* in person or online, in an atmosphere or a way that is entertaining and exciting, in part because the work is fast-paced, using tools, texts, or techniques that are new and engaging (35).

PAUSE **& REFLECT**   What are your thoughts about what this chapter has discussed so far regarding generations, culture, the media, and the implications of all these for teaching and learning?

Engagement: Winning the Hearts and Minds of All Students

The 2009 Gallup Student Poll, which began tracking the "state of mind" of American students in grades 5–12, reported that half of all students are "hopeful" and "engaged," feeling very positive about school and their future; almost two-thirds of respondents described themselves as "thriving" (Lopez 2009). The poll, which focuses on three domains—hope, engagement, and well-being—concluded that around one-third of students are "struggling or suffering" (3). Tapscott's study echoes much of Gallup's findings, declaring that "9 in 10 [Millennials] in the United States describe themselves as "happy," "confident," and "positive" (2009, 32).

Several recurring themes emerge at this point regarding students' relationship with and attitude toward teachers, schools, and the curriculum. One of these is the tension related not only to what we ask students to do but also how and why we ask them to do it. Such tension also includes the texts and tasks, as well as the media and means students use to convey their understanding of what they read. It also involves the culture and expectations of the teacher and those of the students in the class; this notion of culture is not just ethnic or racial, but technological and experiential, economic and political, and gender- and generation-based.

Such differences—owing to political, economic, and social trends—have never been more pronounced (Beers 2009). Within any one class, a teacher in most schools is likely to have illegal immigrants, gay students, conservative and liberal students, native and nonnative speakers, Christians, Jews, and Muslims, haves and have-nots, not to mention students of every ethnicity and race, as well as those of mixed race who are part of what Richard Rodriguez (2002) calls the "browning of America." As a result of this potent mix of cultures, Whitaker (2010) argues that we must all become "culturally responsive teachers" in the broadest, most inclusive meaning of those words. In the absence of such responsive teaching, we run the risk of imposing on students a model that calls to mind the imperialists of the past who ardently believed that those from less developed nations or backgrounds were "if not patently inferior to, then in need of corrective study" by those from the superior culture (Said 1994, 41) who possess the knowledge and power necessary to survive and thrive in the modern world.

Finally, we are likely to have, playing out in classrooms across the country, those generational and cultural tensions that will have an inevitable effect on not only what, but also on why and how we teach. Can we continue to teach only Hamlet, Huck, Holden, and Harry (Potter) when more and more of our students are named Jesus, Hishem, or Xiaohui Han? Nor can the curriculum consist of literature by and about (mostly dead) white men when you have had a Supreme Court justice named Sonia Sotomayor, a Secretary of State named Hillary Rodham Clinton, or a President named Barack Obama. Nor, from a more utilitarian perspective, can we have students read only authors from the United States and England when they are increasingly likely to work with—or even *for*—companies in Japan, Brazil, India, or China. Am I saying we should toss out books such as *Heart of Darkness*? I'll let President Barack Obama respond:

> I tossed [*Heart of Darkness*] into my backpack. "Actually, [Marcus] is right . . . it is a racist book. The way Conrad sees it, Africa's the cesspool of the world, black folks are savages, and any contact with them breeds infection."
>
> Regina blew on her coffee. "So why are you reading it?"
>
> "Because it's assigned." I paused, not sure if I should go on. "And because—"
>
> "Because . . ."
>
> "And because the book teaches me things," I said. "About white people, I mean. See, the book's not really about Africa. Or black people. It's about the man who wrote it. The European. The American. A particular way of looking at the world. If you can keep your distance, it's all there, in what's said and what's left unsaid. So I read the book to help me understand just what it is that makes white people so afraid." (2007, 103)

Obviously students such as President Obama are not our problem; yet these questions he addresses are at the heart of student engagement. After her year-long study of high school students, Pope (2003) concluded that most students feel "caught in a system where achievement depends more on 'doing'—going through the correct motions—than on learning and engaging with the curriculum. Instead of thinking deeply about the content of the courses and delving into projects and assignments, the students focus on managing the work load and honing strategies that will help them to achieve high grades" (4).

More recently, a national study reported that, according to students, "teachers very rarely—or never—speak to them personally about things that matter to them" (White 2010, x). In her investigation of student motivation and engagement, Cushman (2010) found that "every one of these youth could name something they were already good at . . . [which many] were even growing expert at, although sometimes the adults in their lives had not noticed" (3). The question, "What does it take . . . to get *really good* at something?" drove her inquiry, evolving into what she called the "Practice Project," which asked students to study how people got really good at something that mattered to them. In Cushman's project, I hear echoes of others—Tapscott and his "net norms," for example—demanding that students have choice, room to customize, make their learning their own. At the end of the project, Cushman, who has a rare ability to bring students' voices into the conversation about teaching and learning, asked students what conclusions we should draw from the Practice Project; it has many similarities to projects discussed elsewhere in this book such as Life Studies (which asks students to read about the lives of people they might want to emulate) and The Expert Project (which asks students to study one subject for the whole year in progressively more depth). Here are their recommendations for increasing motivation as kids work toward mastery of content in a course:

> ❝ MORE RECENTLY, A NATIONAL STUDY REPORTED THAT, ACCORDING TO STUDENTS, 'TEACHERS VERY RARELY—OR NEVER—SPEAK TO THEM PERSONALLY ABOUT THINGS THAT MATTER TO THEM.' ❞

- Link school to a purpose that has meaning to us.

- Keep the community of learners small enough to know each other.

- Make exploring new fields a big part of our learning.

- Don't try to cover everything.

- Organize learning around themes and projects.

- Model collaboration among adults.

- Connect us with experts in the community.

- Provide opportunities for us to develop initiative and leadership.

- Give us choices about how to learn important subjects.

- Make performances part of learning.

- Do away with class rankings.

- Listen to the perspectives of others, including youth. (2010, 154)

Figures 2.5 and 2.6 show the results of the Center for Evaluation and Education Policy's 2009 High School Survey of Student Engagement (HSSSE) with regard to activities engaged and amount of time spent on each while attending school. Figure 2.7 shows the percentages of students' rating of various types of instructional methods that either excite or engage them.

Lampert (2001) brings some coherence to this large and complex question of engagement as it relates to personal and academic success (see Figure 2.8). As have others (Burke 2004,

HSSSE 2009—Number of Hours Spent on Particular Activities					
	Number of Hours				
Activities	**0**	**1 or fewer**	**2 to 5**	**6 to 10**	**10+**
Doing written homework	7%	32%	39%	15%	7%
Reading/studying for class	11%	39%	37%	10%	3%
Reading for self	16%	38%	29%	10%	6%
Participating in school-sponsored activites	26%	18%	25%	14%	17%
Watching TV/playing video games	6%	25%	38%	18%	12%
Surfing/chatting online	12%	27%	35%	16%	10%
Talking on the phone	8%	34%	30%	14%	14%
Socializing with friends outside of school	4%	11%	33%	27%	26%

FIGURE 2.5 HSSSE results for number of hours spent on particular activities in a typical seven-day week

HSSSE 2009—Importance of Particular Activities					
	How Important				
Activities	**Not at All**	**A Little**	**Somewhat Important**	**Very Important**	**Top Priority**
Doing written homework	7%	14%	33%	36%	10%
Reading/studying for class	9%	18%	33%	31%	9%
Reading for self	17%	27%	32%	19%	5%
Participating in school-sponsored activites	20%	16%	23%	30%	11%
Watching TV/playing video games	22%	36%	27%	10%	5%
Surfing/chatting online	22%	33%	28%	12%	4%
Talking on the phone	16%	30%	30%	17%	7%
Socializing with friends outside of school	4%	10%	26%	42%	18%

FIGURE 2.6 HSSSE results for the importance of particular activities

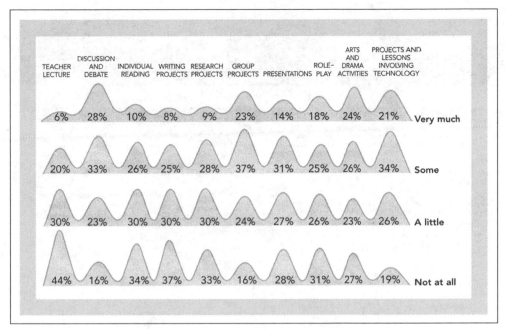

FIGURE 2.7 HSSSE results concerning the engagement factor. Adapted from *Ed Week*.

2005; Delpit 2006; Mahiri 2004), Lampert stresses the role that academic identity plays in school success and engagement:

> Although some students show up at school as "intentional learners"—people who are already interested in doing whatever they need to do to learn academic subjects—they are the exception rather than the rule. Even if they are disposed to study, they probably need to learn how. But more fundamental than knowing how is developing a sense of oneself as a learner that makes it socially acceptable to engage in academic work. The goal of school teaching is not to turn all students into people who see themselves as professional academics, but to enable all of them to include a disposition toward productive study of academic subjects among the personality traits they exhibit while they are in the classroom. If the young people who come to school do not see themselves as learners, they are not going to act like learners even if that would help them to be successful in school. It is the teacher's job to help them change their sense of themselves so that studying is not a self-contradictory activity. One's sense of oneself as a learner is not a wholly private construction. Academic identity is formed from an amalgamation of how we see ourselves and how others see us, and those perceptions are formed and expressed in social interaction. How I act in front of others expresses my sense of who I am. How others then react to me influences the development of my identity. (265)

The Four Cs of Academic Success

COMMITMENT

Commitment describes the extent to which students care about the work and maintain consistency in their attempt to succeed.

Key aspects of **commitment** are:

- *Emotional investment*: Refers to how much students care about their success and the quality of their work on this assignment or performance.
- *Effort*: Some students resist making a serious effort when they do not believe they can succeed. Without such effort, neither success nor improvement is possible.
- *Consistency*: Everyone can be great or make heroic efforts for a day or even a week; real, sustainable success in a class or on large assignments requires consistent hard work and "quality conscience."
- *Faith*: Students must believe that the effort they make will eventually lead to the result or success they seek. *Faith* applies to a method or means by which they hope to achieve success.
- *Permission*: Students must give themselves permission to learn and work hard and others permission to teach and support them if they are to improve and succeed.

CONTENT

Content refers to information or processes students must know to complete a task or succeed on an assignment in class.

Content knowledge includes:

- *Discipline- or subject-specific matter* such as names, concepts, and terms.
- *Cultural reference points* not specifically related to the subject but necessary to understand the material, such as:
  – People
  – Events
  – Trends
  – Ideas
  – Dates
- *Conventions* related to documents, procedures, genres, or experiences.
- *Features, cues, or other signals* that convey meaning during a process or within a text.
- *Language* needed to complete or understand the task.
- *Procedures* used during the course of the task or assignment.

COMPETENCIES

Competencies are those skills students need to be able to complete the assignment or succeed at some task.

Representative, general **competencies** include the ability to:

- *Generate* ideas, solutions, and interpretations that will lead to the successful completion of the task.
- *Manage* resources (time, people, and materials) needed to complete the task; refers also to the ability to govern oneself.
- *Communicate* ideas and information to complete and convey results of the work.
- *Evaluate* and *make decisions* based on information needed to complete the assignment or succeed at the task.
- *Learn* while completing the assignment so students can improve their performance on similar assignments in the future.
- *Use* a range of tools and strategies to solve the problems they encounter.

CAPACITIES

Capacities account for the quantifiable aspects of performance; students can have great skills but lack the capacity to fully employ those skills.

Primary **capacities** related to academic performance include:

- *Speed* with which students can perform one or more tasks needed to complete the assignment or performance.
- *Stamina* required to maintain the requisite level of performance; includes physical and mental stamina.
- *Fluency* needed to handle problems or interpret ideas that vary from students' past experience or learning.
- *Dexterity*, which allows students, when needed, to do more than one task at the same time (a.k.a. multitasking).
- *Memory* so students can draw on useful background information or store information needed for subsequent tasks included in the assignment.
- *Resiliency* needed to persevere despite initial or periodic obstacles to success on the assignment or performance.
- *Confidence* in their ideas, methods, skills, and overall abilities related to this task.

FIGURE 2.8 The Four Cs of Academic Success originally appeared in *School Smarts* (Burke 2004); this remains an important tool for me to use when planning and assessing student learning.

What Gender Is English?

To speak of concern about academic success is to speak, to some extent, about adolescent boys. According to a 2010 College Board report:

> Across the board, young women are outperforming young men with respect to high school graduation rates. White women perform 4 percentage points better than white men, while African American, Hispanic, Native American, and Asian women outperform the men in their ethnic or racial group by 9 percentage points, 9 percentage points, 7 percentage points and 2 percentage points, respectively. (2)

Despite the media attention the "boy crisis" has received in recent years, (Smith and Wilhelm 2002; Tatum 2005; Whitmire 2010), some reports suggest the truth is more complex (Corbett, Hill, St. Rose 2008).

For example, the academic performance of boys is not declining; rather, girls' performance is soaring. The number of boys enrolling in college has steadily increased (Rooney, Hussar, and Planty 2006), but women have enrolled in larger numbers, outpacing the boys. In California, for example, 58 percent of those admitted to state universities in 2009 were female, 42 percent male—a statistic that is consistent with other, more national trends. In fact, college graduation rates for men stopped growing in the late 1970s, some attributing it to the end of the Vietnam War and the draft deferments that previously motivated many to attend and stay in college (Dorning 2011, D9).

Still, there *is* a crisis within the population of young men in our society, one some (Crawford 2009; Rose 2009a; Rosin 2010) might say is caused by a loss of types of work and ways of living that once seemed more compatible to those boys who did not aspire to work in an office. That crisis does not, however, include all adolescent boys. Instead, it tends to involve boys from low-income Hispanic and African American families, but also those with learning disabilities, two-thirds of whom are boys. Despite the cause for concern, there is evidence of progress even among these students. As the *NAEP 2008 Trends in Academic Progress* report states, "the national trend in reading showed improvement from 2004 to 2008 in all three ages [9-, 13-, and 17-year-olds]" (Rampey, Dion, and Donahue 2009, 10). Such progress is, admittedly, more complex than a first glance reveals: Average NAEP reading scores for 13-year-olds and 17-year-olds rose for those at the lowest percentiles but showed no significant change for middle- and high-performing students of the same age.

> **"** FOR EXAMPLE, THE ACADEMIC PERFORMANCE OF BOYS IS NOT DECLINING; RATHER, GIRLS' PERFORMANCE IS SOARING. **"**

How They Feel About School—and English

The real question is: Do students see what happens in school as relevant and able to prepare them for the larger world beyond? Moreover, do they see themselves as *able* to do, and the sort of person who *does,* what a teacher asks? To the extent they do, students commit; otherwise, school seems a distraction, an unwelcome interruption to the satisfying day they had planned for themselves. If the teacher gives the message that he or she will help students and, with persistence and effort students believe they can learn and succeed, they evolve into successful students (Intrator and Kunzman 2009; Burke 2004).

The 2009 High School Survey of Student Engagement (HSSSE) found that 75 percent of students reported being bored because "the content was not interesting" and 39 percent complained material in courses "wasn't relevant" (Yazzie-Mintz 2010, 5)—a feeling that consistently appears in others' research (Smith and Wilhelm 2002, 2006) on adolescent literacy experiences. It's not just that they are bored; rather, the crisis is that many students do not feel supported or challenged when learning new material. One student in the HSSSE summed up this point when she said, "I wish school could be intellectually as well as academically challenging" (Intrator and Kunzman 2009, 1).

This concern, about intellectual—as opposed to only academic—engagement troubled Applebee and Langer (2009) also when they studied middle and high school writing instruction. Smith and Wilhelm (2002), Intrator and Kunzman (2009), and Csikszentmihalyi and Schneider (2008) all found that students need texts and tasks that challenge them; while adults are often quick to argue that many students cannot meet such expectations, Vygotsky (1978) found that it was possible as long as teachers engaged in the "kind of instruction which marches ahead of development and leads it" (1962, 104), through scaffolding of some sort, to that mastery we all seek to cultivate in students. Asking students to complete some sort of survey at the beginning of a semester can be very helpful because it gives you a chance to get useful information about how each one feels about the subject of the class, perceived weaknesses, and interests. Figure 2.9 shows Andres completed survey form.

PAUSE & REFLECT Read the latest HSSSE online and write about or discuss with your colleagues those details or trends that apply to your students.

End Note: Welcome to My Classroom

Nothing I have described in this chapter is foreign to me: It is the world in which I teach, the world I see when I visit other schools and districts around the country. We have had enough numbers for a while in this chapter, so let's have some names.

My most recent freshman College Prep (CP) English class began the year with 35 students and ended with 31, several moving to other classes at the semester shuffle but not leaving school. Thus, I will focus on the remaining 31 who were with me for the second semester. Of these, 19 were boys, and a very squirrelly, social group of boys at that, with the exception of Francisco who sat quietly in the back (or wherever I asked him to sit) and did his work and earned an A–. Of the 31, 17 identified themselves as Latino, their original or ancestral countries ranging from Brazil to Mexico and several in between. Of the remaining 14, 7 were white; the remaining were divided between Asian/Pacific Islander, Middle Eastern, and biracial.

Out of everyone in the class, 8 were enrolled in the ACCESS class, a program I created for struggling readers who lacked the academic essentials (see Burke 2005); 6 other students, none of whom were in the ACCESS class, received special education services for everything from Asperger's syndrome to ADHD. Several others, all boys as it happens, told me they had been diagnosed with ADHD but were not receiving special education support services for it. As one of them, who was utterly failing my class at that time explained patiently, confidentially to me, "Oh I have ADHD, Mr. Burke, but it doesn't affect my school work at all." At another point, he assured me that he "does better on tests when [he] doesn't study," a statement he was hard-pressed to defend given his standing in the course, but such is the logic of students.

Student Survey

Student Survey   *Andres*

Please be honest in your responses as they will help me help you and create a more engaging, useful class.

Past   It is useful for me to get some sense of your past so I can help you in the present.

1. What words would you use to describe your experiences with English up till now:
   _____fun_____, ____enjoyable____, _confident-building_
   Choose one of these words and tell me a bit more so I can understand better.
   Since my teacher last year liked me a lot, my English experience was enjoyable. Since I also enjoy writing stories and other literary works.

2. Have you passed the California Exit Exam in English?   (Yes)   No

3. Did you do the summer reading as assigned? If so, what did you read:
   Novel: _____
   Auto/bio: *Pelé*

Present   Now for a little info about your life in the present moment:

4. What is your attitude toward reading and writing at this point? Explain.
   I cannot read fast. It makes reading such a task that I try to stear clear. Writing on the other hand is incredibly fun for me.

5. Do you have a job? (Yes)   No   If yes, doing what? *train young kids in soccer*

6. What do I need to know about you as a person if I am to be an effective teacher for you?
   visual learner; concept of what we are doing must be clea

7. Who and/or what matters most to you? *Passing this class :*

8. What are your most difficult or demanding classes this year? *Spanish AP*

9. List three areas of greatest interest for you. Put a star by the area that interests you *most*.
   *Soccer*____, *Cinema*____, *Languages; Spanish & culture*

10. Please check all that apply:
    ✓ I have a computer at home
    ✓ I have Internet access at home
    ✓ I have a cell phone
    ✓ I have internet access on my cell phone

11. *In context to Engl ??* What are your areas of greatest strength and need of improvement?

Strengths	Areas to Improve
Language Theme	Reading Structure in writing

12. Check all that apply to you. I know how to create and/or use the following:
    o Blogs
    o Wikis
    ✓ Tweets
    ✓ Facebook
    o Videos
    o Other: _____

Future   And now for the future, which is what this year is all about in many ways.

13. At this time, when I graduate, I expect to (circle all that apply):
    ✓ Attend a two-year college
    o Attend a four-year college
    o Enroll in a special vocational program (e.g., certified mechanic, HVAC, etc.)
    o Find a job or work for a family business
    o Join the armed forces
    o Other (please explain): _____

14. What do you want to leave this class having learned, done, and accomplished? Explain.
    Hopefully by the time I graduate I will have written at least one paper that will show you I'm intelligent, because in person I'm quiet or may even come off as a nusense.

FIGURE 2.9 A filled-in Student Survey form

In addition, of these 31, approximately 13 had been enrolled in an English Language Development (ELD) program at some point prior to coming to high school, 4 of whom remained in the ELD Transitional English class for the duration of the year they were in my class. They were remarkably social across all cultural, gender, ethnic, and other boundaries. I should say that I loved this class entirely, though this is true of any class that comes to mind. They were, however, a joy to work with that year.

How did they do? What did I notice? Final grades for second semester were revealing: of the 31 students, 4 failed, 3 of whom were increasingly absent as the semester rolled along, until they rarely ever came during the last month despite the collective and persistent efforts of teachers, counselors, and administrators. Still, all 3 students showed at different times that they *could do* the work; one in particular did remarkable work on a personal narrative about her friend who died in middle school after being hit by a car. Of these 4 students who failed, 3 were girls; of the 4, all were Latino. This led to what, for me, was a fascinating observation by semester's end: of the 12 girls in the class, all earned either Fs or As and Bs; there were no girls who earned Ds or Cs. They seemed to be all in or all out as far as commitment. Of the 12 girls, 2 (not those who failed) were out several times for extended absences due to mental health issues that were serious enough to warrant hospitalization after attempting or threatening suicide.

What about the boys? Of the 19, only 1 failed but only 2 earned As; some showed tremendous progress, particularly when the unit (e.g., on *The Kite Runner*) was one that engaged them, something I will discuss in much more detail in the next chapter. Of the 19 boys in that class, I can say with confidence that they all read *The Kite Runner*, even the one boy who failed the class. The boys roller-coastered their way through the year, some dropping at times to a D or even an F, but responding to my mentoring, coaching, outreach—in class, in the hallway between classes, by phone, online, through notes—to them and their parents.

It was a very masculine class: they almost all wore dark clothing, usually black jeans and "hoodies," and nearly all participated in sports. I had five wrestlers, four football players, two baseball players, two basketball players, the star of the badminton team, two lacrosse players, and several elite soccer players—one of whom, Eduardo Trujillo, wrote with great enthusiasm about his experiences with the Junior Olympic soccer team the previous summer. On some days, it felt more like a gym than a classroom as boys prior to, sometimes even during, class would spontaneously start wrestling, grabbing each other or their things. The girls laughed or rolled their eyes, or let out exasperated exclamations of "Juaaaaaaannnnn!" or "AnnnDDDDyyyyyyy!" with equal exasperation and amusement. Figure 2.10 shows one of my typical classes, which usually range between 30 and 35.

This particular class, which is very representative of those I have had in recent years, came after the morning break of 15 minutes. On a typical morning, as many as 8 or 10 kids, mostly boys, would be in the room goofing, talking—with me or others. I

FIGURE 2.10 My freshman class at Burlingame High School.

worked hard, as I always have, to connect with them. During the year, several had parents who split up; others lost family members or had family members who endured serious health crises, most notably Krikor whose three-year-old cousin underwent treatment for cancer. Several of the Latina girls had their *quinceañera*, a rite of passage that, for most of them, trumped all other commitments until it was over—see Julia Alvarez, *Once Upon a Quinceanera: Coming of Age in the USA* (2007). And my Tongan students left school for a week at one point, despite major assignments that were due, to attend ceremonies held in another part of the state for the visiting prince and princess who had come from Tonga to speak to Tongan youth about the importance of education, faith, and morality.

They began the year slowly, nearly all of them telling me that they had become used to not being held accountable for their work in past years; more significantly, however, they struggled to do the increasingly complex work I demanded from the beginning (and which you will begin to see examples of starting in the next chapter). In particular, I found that they all, nearly to a student, had difficulty doing anything that required evaluation, analysis, and synthesis—or what some might call critical, divergent thinking, the sort that requires patient, sustained, close analysis. When I counted back in time from ninth grade, I realized that they had all begun elementary school around the time that No Child Left Behind had begun to exert its influence on what and how teachers, especially in the elementary grades, taught.

I began teaching in 1988, before cell phones, Facebook, or even the Internet; but also before the wars in Iraq or Afghanistan, before 9/11 and the Great Recession of 2008—all of which have directly or indirectly affected all my students. Into my classes now come a generation that has been raised in a different world than the one in which I grew up. They often do not look like me, nor do they speak the same language when they go home. In this class of 31 students, they spoke Spanish, Tagalog, Mandarin, Portuguese, Armenian, Japanese, Persian, Arabic, Tongan, Hindi, and, of course, English when they went home. And yet they are, in their own way, the same kids we were in so many ways as a couple glimpses show: the first from a student blog response by a Latina girl with great potential and pain, the second from an in-class prompt response by a Latino boy with great potential and the desire to heal others' pain:

> A stream to me has a kind of ability to erase your pains and painful memories. Combined with a hot day that relaxes your tensed up muscles seems to set my mind free. My routine day is to get up. Out of responsibility I prepare myself for the day I have no meaning for. I usually run out of my so called home and race to the bus hoping it would not intrude into my life any more than it already has. I look into the lives of random people who have endured more pain than they show for about ten minutes. I can feel my muscles dragging themselves not wanting to take the next step for the fear of falling. Before I know it I am at school, where every teacher I encounter looks into the bottom of my heart that seems to barely beat. These teachers that even take the time to realize what they have just encountered tell me straight up that I have so called brains and have a full life waiting for me to begin it. This is something my heart rejects but my brain fully absorbs. I go through

❝On a typical morning, as many as 8 or 10 kids, mostly boys, would be in the room goofing, talking—with me or others. I worked hard, as I always have, to connect with them.❞

my day moping. I have the love of my friends and yet it is not enough to make my pain go away. I have endured so much I'm surprised that I'm still thinking. At the end of my school day, I mope to the train or to go my appointments set up by my social worker to help my life from ending. I see the face of my demon as I take each step toward the train. Before I know it, I have stepped off and forced my legs to go home, never again do I want to call it that but what other title should I give it. It is the first and same foster home I have lived in for more than a year. Through all this pain, my biggest relief is to even think about a hot summer day dipping in a cold stream in Nicaragua.

***

What I want my life to be like when I'm thirty. I want to be out of college with my degree and having a high-end job that I enjoy such as sports or a related field. One thing that I want though, to go with my education, is a beautiful but intelligent fiancé and being able to wait a few more years till I have a child (praying for a boy). Also, one thing I need to know to get to the job I want is to know the human body if I want to get into sports medicine, but I think I may need a bachelors degree too and a degree in psychology for those who come in and are so depressed about their injury, but what I need to depend on to do this job is my hands and my mind because if someone comes in with a pain they don't know I have to use my hands to find the pressure point of the pain and my mind to know what may have triggered it so I can heal them.

You will get to know these students—my kids—as well as those in my Advanced Placement and honors classes, in the coming chapters. I love them all, perhaps at this point because I see in them all the student I was, the student I became, and the student I am now, one who knows he will never be done, never know enough. In addition, because they are the same ages as my own three children. Now that we have learned *who* these kids are, let us turn our attention to how best to teach them.

Recommended **Resources**

WRITTEN

- *"Doing School": How We Are Creating a Generation of Stressed Out, Materialistic, and Miseducated Students*, Denise Clark Pope (Yale University Press 2001).
- *Fires in the Bathroom: Advice for Teachers from High School Students*, Kathleen Cushman (New Press 2003).
- *Tuned in and Fired Up: How Teaching Can Inspire Real Learning in the Classroom*, Sam M. Intrator (Yale University Press 2005).

ONLINE

- Pew Research Center (http://pewresearch.org)
- Digital Youth (http://digitalyouth.ischool.berkeley.edu)
- What Kids Can Do (www.whatkidscando.org)

CHAPTER THREE

How to Teach So Students Will Learn, Use, Remember—and Enjoy

> Every good teacher I've known, regardless of grade level, subject or style, has the equivalent of what musicians call "big ears"; they are curious, open, on the lookout for anything they can use in the service of some larger goal. That is what it means to think like a teacher.
>
> —Mike Rose, "A Lesson for Teachers" (2010a)

PAUSE **& REFLECT** Before you read this chapter on teaching and learning, explain your own ideas about what effective instruction looks like and how you think we learn. On what do you base your pedagogical philosophy about teaching and learning?

Most of what I know about teaching and learning I learned in the garage with my father, on the tennis court with my coaches, or in the bright rooms of a school in Tunisia where, prior to beginning to teach in the Peace Corps, I struggled to learn how to speak Arabic (and teach "woodshop" six hours a day to a group of special needs students despite having no wood). In the garage, my father showed me how to perform a task, explaining as he did so what he was doing but also why and how; then he guided me through my first attempts until I showed myself ready to work independently. Even then, however, he still checked my work, mentoring me with his easily remembered rules such as "measure twice, cut once." If I made a mistake, he simply said, "Let's try that one again, but this time do it *this* way next time," and he would mime the action.

My tennis coaches were not much different: They would tell me what to do, then model it, guide me through it, watch and correct me as I learned it, sometimes bringing out cameras to record my stroke to help me better see what they meant. Later, when I joined the Peace Corps, I came to understand how difficult and humiliating learning can be and how important it is that the teacher find ways to sustain students' faith in themselves, the teacher's methods, and the content itself. Perhaps more than any other time, I learned that real learning necessarily involves failure as we fumble forward through our frustration and, at times, fear on our way to learning and, ultimately, mastering something we truly want to know or do. But such experiences also taught me perhaps the most important lesson of all: *how to learn*. These experiences taught me that *learning by doing* applies to any "game" we want to play, including the "school game" (Perkins 2009, 9).

Instructional Approaches: Is One Better Than Another?

Effective instruction teaches students the essential skills and knowledge they need to answer the questions and solve the problems we all encounter in our personal and professional lives. Such questions provide a purposeful context in which to learn the skills and knowledge students need to answer such questions (Burke 2010; Hillocks 2009b; Applebee 1996). In other words, good teaching engages both the heart *and* the head, instilling in students the abilities and information as well as confidence and, what Escalante called *ganas*, which he defined as: "determination plus hard work plus concentration" or "the urge to succeed, to achieve, to grow" (Mathews 1988, 191). They need to succeed in school and beyond. Good teaching does more, though. In such classrooms, students are initiated into the discipline by knowledgeable teachers much as apprentices were by the masters of different crafts were centuries ago. The question is: Does *one* of these instructional methods offer "that 'silver bullet': the teaching method that always works" (Smagorinsky 2009, 15)?

Smagorinsky (2009) identifies three main instructional paradigms for us to consider. **The environmental or structured process**, associated with George Hillocks (see Hillocks 1999), requires that the teacher identify the big ideas and essential questions the course examines, then design lessons to facilitate that study. Such work, often done in groups, seeks to achieve a specific, identified goal related to the larger ideas the unit explores. This approach emphasizes procedural knowledge (knowing *how*) over declarative knowledge (knowing *that,* for example, Washington is the nation's capitol).

Nancie Atwell (1998) and Kittle (2008) are two teachers who represent the **individualistic or workshop model**, which concentrates on teaching skills and knowledge in the context of individual or small-group learning. This approach emphasizes the *process* of learning to do or to use things—tools, techniques, ideas—in authentic contexts, during which the teacher guides and helps as needed.

Finally, **the presentational or product-oriented model**, which is not associated with any one source, is best understood as direct instruction that delivers information by lecture; this would include means such as PowerPoint and other computer-based delivery systems that students might encounter through programs (e.g., *Read 180*) or the online courses. This method is best suited for providing background knowledge, information, or procedures needed to learn what something is, what it does, and how it works. According to Applebee (1994), this method is not effective as a primary means of instruction because it tends to be passive (i.e., students sitting, listening, watching, taking notes).

These three paradigms offer a context for what follows. They are not so much irreconcilable schools of thought as different modes the effective teacher uses as the subject and situation demand. For it *is* our knowledge—of the subject, the kids we teach, the teaching methods we use—that has the biggest effect on student learning. More than class size, more than socioeconomic status, more than any other variable, the teacher's knowledge most consistently and powerfully determines student success when it comes to learning (Schmoker and Graff 2011; Darling-Hammond 2010; Darling-Hammond and Bransford 2005).

" GOOD TEACHING ENGAGES BOTH THE HEART *AND* THE HEAD, INSTILLING IN STUDENTS THE ABILITIES AND INFORMATION AS WELL AS CONFIDENCE . . . **"**

PAUSE & REFLECT Which of the three paradigms just outlined best describes your own instructional approach? What evidence do you accept as a measure of its (and your) effectiveness?

At the heart of our inquiry is the question of whether there is such a thing as "best practice" in literacy instruction (Graham, MacArthur, and Fitzgerald 2007; Daniels and Bizar 2004). Zemelman, Daniels, and Hyde (2005) describe the term as teaching that is "serious, thoughtful, informed, responsible," noting that the concept derives from the "professions of medicine, law and architecture, where 'good practice' or 'best practice' are everyday phrases used to describe solid, reputable, state-of-the art work in a field" (vi). Applebee (1986) calls such work "principled practice," a term Smagorinsky (2009) defines as challenging "teachers to think about what is appropriate given the unique intersection that their classroom provides for their many and varied students; their beliefs about teaching and learning; the materials available for them to use; and the public, professional, and policy contexts in which they teach" (20).

What I am *not* advocating, what we do *not* need, given all that we must accomplish in our classes, is a range of instructional fads and distractions that undermine the instructional narrative of our classes. Instead, we want what Schmoker describes: "a simple, emphatic insistence on a common curriculum, sound lessons, and authentic literacy" (2011, 23). Describing his ideal teacher, Schmoker offers what might seem a bland exemplar, but this is his point: Being an effective teacher is within the grasp of all. In the following, Schmoker tells us of an experienced teacher who, after transferring to the lowest-achieving high school in Tempe, did nothing more than:

> *actually teach* a sound English curriculum, rich in reading and writing, using ordinary, structurally sound lessons. . . . [He] taught whole-class lessons focused on a clear learning objective in short, instructional "chunks" or segments, punctuated by multiple cycles of guided practice and formative assessment ("checks for understanding"). And he did this every day. He was neither particularly charismatic nor theatrical. He was what any teacher or team can be. The result? The success rate in his classes alone was so high that his *entire school* made the largest writing gains of any high school in the state (from 59 percent to 85 percent passing the high school exit exam). (21)

We see this same clarity of purpose and focus on effective instruction in the Excellence in English (EIE) project which captures best the "patterns" of effective literacy instruction in both middle and high school English classes (Langer 2002, 13). Despite high levels of poverty and often large numbers of English-language learners, these schools—Langer calls them "beat the odds" schools—"scored higher on high-stakes tests than students in demographically comparable schools" while also supporting "high literacy," which

> refers to a deeper knowledge of the ways in which reading, writing, language, and content work together. This kind of literacy . . . belongs at the heart of the teaching and

> **"WHAT I AM *NOT* ADVOCATING, WHAT WE DO *NOT* NEED, GIVEN ALL THAT WE MUST ACCOMPLISH IN OUR CLASSES, IS A RANGE OF INSTRUCTIONAL FADS AND DISTRACTIONS THAT UNDERMINE THE INSTRUCTIONAL NARRATIVE OF OUR CLASSES."**

learning of English across the grades. It is reflected in students' abilities to: engage in thoughtful reading, writing, and discussion in the classroom; use their knowledge and skills in new situations; and perform well on a wide variety of reading and writing tasks, including high-stakes tests. (3)

The EIE project identifies three instructional modes, each reflected in the instructional paradigms we have described earlier, common in all effective classrooms where English teachers teach both skills and content within the context of exploring complex questions, important ideas or, as Langer calls it "building envisionments" (2004a):

Through **separate** instruction (Langer 2002, 13), the teacher creates an opportunity to introduce or emphasize specific skills and knowledge outside of the context of the larger assignment. In Figure 3.1 I am providing separate instruction in a sentence structure I want my students to learn and use in a subsequent paper they will write.

Once students have shown an initial understanding of the lesson I taught through separate instruction, I move on to **simulated** instruction, which requires students to apply what they learned in a specific way related to the larger unit of instruction. For example, Figure 3.2 shows a way to extend the lesson on sentence structures to include *Heart of Darkness*—the book they were reading at that time. After initial examples, students receive less and less support, beginning with cloze sentences here and culminating in generating their own examples from scratch.

"THIS NOTION OF APPRENTICESHIP, OF MOVING FROM NOVICE TO PRACTITIONER, REITERATES THE IMPORTANCE OF SCAFFOLDING OUR INSTRUCTION**"**

After students show an initial mastery of the skill or knowledge, they then get **integrated** instruction which, in this case, requires them to incorporate the sentence structures into their papers. In the photograph in Figure 3.3, Jenny and Gabriella evaluate each others' use of these sentence structures and look for additional places to use them in their papers on *Heart of Darkness*.

Together, these different approaches form an instructional continuum that ranges from apprenticeship to what Lave and Wenger call "full participation" as legitimate members of the "community of practice" (1991, 42). As Judith Langer writes, these three types of instructional activities "all

These Three Images Define and Explain *Separate*, *Simulated*, and *Integrated* Instruction

FIGURE 3.1

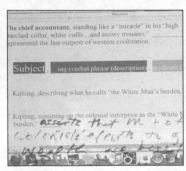

FIGURE 3.2

FIGURE 3.3

can occur when needed within the ongoing instructional program" (2002, 14). This notion of apprenticeship, of moving from novice to practitioner, reiterates the importance of scaffolding our instruction, to teach students what they cannot initially do—or do well, at least—on their own.

As I often say to my students: "You do not come to school to learn what you already know. If you are not struggling on some level, you are not learning; or, as the skiers say, 'if you are not falling down, you are not trying hard enough.'" Perkins is emphatic about this stage of learning: to improve one *must* "work on the hard parts . . . [since] . . . real improvement depends on deconstructing the game, singling out the hard parts for special attention, practicing them on the side, developing strategies to deal with them better" (2009, 10). This "hard part" is what Godin (2007) calls "The Dip," which he defines as the "long slog between starting and mastery" (17). It is the point at which more effort does not, for the moment, lead to improved results (and may even lead to diminishing returns).

Real learning, real success—for individuals, businesses, and teams—comes to those who push through The Dip to achieve greater and more sustainable gains. I often talk about this phenomenon with my students, especially my AP students who are used to just "getting it" and succeeding. When roughly 5 out of 70 incoming AP students earn As on their summer reading essays, however, they quickly realize they are really in a world of new expectations and standards. It is the one that creates in them the sense of disorientation that Vygotsky (1978) refers to in his theory of zones of proximal development; that in, "'good learning' is . . . [what comes] in advance of development" (89).

Just as Stephen King determines a story's plot by putting characters in situations to see how they will react (2010, 161), so must teachers design experiences that push students just beyond their current development, then help them learn the skills and knowledge they need to succeed. Angel Pérez, vice president and dean of admissions at Pitzer College, wrote of the importance of such learning, describing a memorable interview with a prospective student. When asked what he looked forward to in college, the student said, "I look forward to the possibility of failure"; he then went on to explain that his parents and teachers had worked so hard to help him succeed that they never let him take risks or learn how to fail. As Pérez says at the end of his commentary, "Failure is about growth, learning, overcoming, and moving on" (2012, 23).

Pearson and Gallagher (1983) represented this process in their gradual release of responsibility model, which traces the steady progression from an initial period of demonstration through shared demonstration and guided practice to independent practice, with teacher support decreasing and learner control increasing every step of the way.

Of course, actual learning is not such a linear process, as the diagram in Figure 3.4 suggests; rather, it is recursive, more cyclical, for just as we reach the next level, we encounter new, more complex material, which returns us to the status of novice, though this time we have the knowledge of how to learn and the confidence that we can.

> **"REAL LEARNING, REAL SUCCESS—FOR INDIVIDUALS, BUSINESSES, AND TEAMS—COMES TO THOSE WHO PUSH THROUGH THE DIP TO ACHIEVE GREATER AND MORE SUSTAINABLE GAINS."**

PAUSE & REFLECT Reflect on Langer's three approaches in light of the other paradigms discussed and your own teaching. What questions and concerns remain at this point about these ideas in general and as they relate to your own teaching in particular?

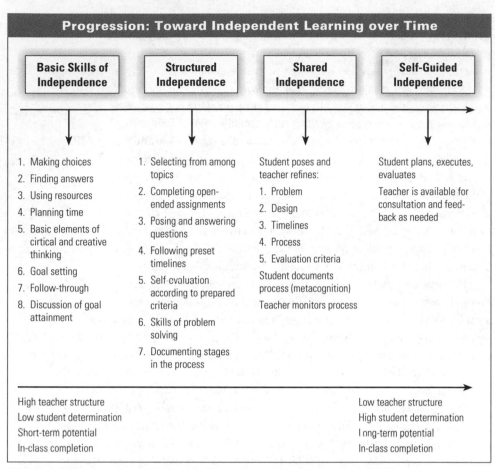

Progression: Toward Independent Learning over Time

Basic Skills of Independence	Structured Independence	Shared Independence	Self-Guided Independence
1. Making choices 2. Finding answers 3. Using resources 4. Planning time 5. Basic elements of cirtical and creative thinking 6. Goal setting 7. Follow-through 8. Discussion of goal attainment	1. Selecting from among topics 2. Completing open-ended assignments 3. Posing and answering questions 4. Following preset timelines 5. Self-evaluation according to prepared criteria 6. Skills of problem solving 7. Documenting stages in the process	Student poses and teacher refines: 1. Problem 2. Design 3. Timelines 4. Process 5. Evaluation criteria Student documents process (metacognition) Teacher monitors process	Student plans, executes, evaluates Teacher is available for consultation and feed-back as needed

High teacher structure	Low teacher structure
Low student determination	High student determination
Short-term potential	Long-term potential
In-class completion	In-class completion

FIGURE 3.4 Progression: toward independent learning over time from Tomlinson (1993)

How **We** Learn

What method you use matters little, as I have mentioned, if you do not know your content or how to use the methods to achieve the intended results (Darling-Hammond 2009, 2); you must also *believe* your students can learn whatever you are teaching (Whitaker 2010; Burke 2004; Shulman 1999). Before we look more closely at how to teach, let's consider how we learn so that we can increase the likelihood that students will do, understand, and remember what we teach them.

PAUSE & REFLECT What does it mean to "learn" something? What was the most difficult thing you ever learned? Describe the process by which you learned it, identifying the specific steps or aspects of that process that might apply to students' learning process.

Applebee notes that "what we learn is in large part a function of how we learn it" (1994, 50), an observation Ellen Langer echoes in her book about "mindful learning" in which she says, "the way information is learned will determine how, why, and when it is used" (1997, 3).

Frank Smith would add that what (and how) we learn depends on "the company we keep," by which he means the other members of the community we already joined or will soon, seeing in them the person we are or want to become (1998, 9). Thus, to the extent that students learn to see themselves as members of "the literacy club," they will choose to learn and do whatever reinforces that identity.

This extends to the larger, more complicated "academic literacy" club, as well. Not all kids see themselves as *students*; nor do they all believe in the value of what we offer or their ability to learn it. In such cases, we must back up, seek first to understand why they feel this way, then take time to develop in them an academic identity that will sustain them through the inevitable struggle to learn what they do not know yet (Burke 2004, 2005). If the teacher inspires in such students a sense of fear or futility, students will, "instead of learning to read and write . . . to behave in thoughtful, respectful, and democratic ways . . . learn that these are areas of life beyond their interests and reach" (Smith 1998, 29). We want students to know "what opportunity *feels* like . . . [to teach in ways that cultivate in our students] a sense of possibility, of hope . . . made concrete, specific, hope embodied in tools, practices, or sequences of things to do—pathways to a goal" (Rose 2009a, 14).

> **"**. . . ATTENTION TO STUDENTS' THINKING AND THEIR PERSONAL EXPERIENCES IS ESSENTIAL IN TODAY'S CULTURALLY AND COGNITIVELY DIVERSE CLASSROOMS.**"**

In its inquiry into how we learn, the National Research Council (NRC) identified three key findings about our learning process. First, "teachers must draw out and work with the preexisting understandings that their students bring with them" (Bransford, Brown, Cocking 2000, 23). This attention to students' thinking and their personal experiences is essential in today's culturally and cognitively diverse classrooms. If their knowledge, experience, culture, and interests have a place in the classroom, students will feel they, too, can find a place within such a class and will engage with the questions the class asks (Tatum 2009; Smith and Wilhelm 2002, 2006; Echevarria, Vogt, and Short 2008). As Marzano and Kendall argue in their model of teaching and learning, "if an individual does not perceive a specific piece of knowledge to be important at a personal level [or cannot improve their understanding or competence in this area] he or she will probably not be highly motivated to learn it" (2007, 107). Another important application of this first finding is students' reluctance to cast off "preexisting misunderstandings"—of what a text means or how to write an essay—until new methods or knowledge have proven to be safe. This explains the enduring faith in and hanging onto the security blanket of the five-paragraph essay, for example, in my AP Literature seniors.

Second, the NRC found that teachers must teach some "subject matter in depth, providing many examples in which the same concept is at work and providing a firm foundation of factual knowledge" (25). But these facts are best taught within the context of a unit of inquiry that has both personal and public importance, a unit that provides a context for learning the skills and knowledge, since at the core of our curriculum—reading, writing, and speaking—"are forms of inquiry, [that] are best learned in the contexts of inquiry" (Hillocks cited by Wilhelm 2007, 10; Applebee 1996; Lave and Wenger 1991). Other leading researchers and practitioners strongly concur with the importance of such background knowledge (Hirsch 2007; Harvey and Goudvis 2007; Marzano 2004) and depth (Egan 2010; Schmoker 2011).

Finally, the NRC suggests that "the teaching of metacognitive skills should be integrated into the curriculum" (Bransford, Brown, and Cocking 2000, 14). Developing metacognitive processes requires guidance and instruction as students are initiated into the process of "thinking about their thinking." As Schoenbach et al. found in their research on "academic literacy" and their "reading apprenticeship" model, "as students started to be comfortable thinking about thinking, [they were able] to guide more targeted discussions of the reading process" (1999, 58) by providing them with questions and prompts to promote such reflective thinking.

Eventually, however, that kind of support must be gradually dismantled so that students themselves can internalize and independently apply the most important lesson of all: how we learn best. Tomlinson (1993) offers a more visual representation of this same process (refer to Figure 3.4), one consistent with the gradual-release method (Pearson and Gallagher 1983), zones of proximal development (Vygotsky 1978), and instructional scaffolding (Lave and Wenger 1991, 48). Tomlinson, however, focuses on what the learner does, not the teacher.

What joins all these ideas about learning is the notion that we learn things best "as wholes" (Perkins 2009) and that, to borrow Perkins' language, one best "learns the game" by playing it. Thus, by having students play the game—of writing a paper, reading a book or discussing it with others—we create the sort of capacity-building event that Vygotsky (1978) argues "creates a zone of proximal development . . . [that] awakens a variety of internal development processes . . . [which] are internalized . . . [and thus] become part of the child's independent developmental achievement" (90). By learning *as they play the game*, students receive the added benefit of not just learning in context but of finding in that context more meaning in what they learn.

The Elements of Effective Instruction:
Ten Principles to Practice

What we want, what we need is a clear set of teaching moves we can use to make teaching consistently effective despite the inherent complexity of the classroom. Every year it seems we are asked to do more, though never, of course, given more time in which to accomplish the goals. One year I kept track of *every minute* taken from my instructional time—whether for interruptions from the counseling office, extended lunch activities, mandatory state testing, or anything else: it added up to, cumulatively, *29 hours*. As our classes grow larger and more diverse, the core of our work—teaching students to read, write, speak, and think—grows more complex. Atul Gawande, writing about a similar though inevitably more accelerated trend in medicine, identifies three kinds of problems related to work: simple, complicated, and complex (2009, 49).

> **As our classes grow larger and more diverse, the core of our work—teaching students to read, write, speak, and think—grows more complex.**

Simple problems, explains Gawunde, have established steps, such as using a recipe to bake a cake, one can follow. Complicated problems, such as sending a rocket to the moon, can be broken into a series of simple problems. Complicated problems, such as building that rocket, require greater expertise; however, since this problem has already been solved, success can be achieved with some reliability. Complex problems, such as teaching a class of 35 adolescents, however, have no inevitable, replicable solution given their inherent—dare I say it?—complexity. As a parent of three children (two boys and a girl), I can attest to the lack of any available recipe that delivers a predictable result. After teaching adolescents for more than 25 years, I know only one thing for sure: they are complex.

As Gawande (2009) notes in his book about the practice of medicine (surgery in particular), "a doctor must be prepared for unpredictable turns . . . [because] medicine contains the entire range of problems—the simple, the complicated, *and* the complex" (51). Teaching is not so different, something I realized while working in an emergency room (as the admissions clerk) at night and doing my student teaching credential during the day. (I often had notes for the next day's lesson plan or student papers in my lap while completing the admission forms or stamping blood work requests!)

Gawande set out to create what he called the "safe surgery checklist," a brief list of actions a doctor could complete before, during, and after any operation, under any conditions, to ensure a safe and successful procedure. This idea, that there should be some list of practices we could turn to when designing and teaching, and then reflecting on the effectiveness of those lessons, mirrors similar projects in education: the Excellence in English project (Langer 2002), the "essential nine" techniques of "classroom instruction that works" (Marzano, Pickering, and Pollock 2004), and the 49 techniques to help you "teach like a champion" (Lemov 2010). Most of us, however, need a little more specific guidance when actually teaching or preparing our lessons. We need a list to consult and use on the run, not 49 techniques. We need a Swiss Army knife—not a tool chest with dozens of drawers.

Perkins (2009), adopting the medical practitioner's hat for a moment and applying it to teaching in a way Gawande would no doubt appreciate, diagnosed teachers as often suffering from two afflictions when approaching complexity in the classroom: "elementitis" and "aboutitis." Instead of getting students *doing* so they can learn, we "focus on elements," leaving little time to have students *do* the thing they came to learn (e.g., construct an argument)—a condition Perkins calls *elementitis* (5). Or, we spend so much time teaching *about* something (e.g., the theater in Shakespeare's time) that we never get to the thing students are supposed to *do* (e.g., read *Hamlet*), an ailment Perkins calls *aboutitis* (5).

A teacher might, for example, spend weeks teaching about mythology (*aboutitis*) or the poetic form of the epic (*elementitis*) to prepare students to read *The Odyssey* instead of just having kids *read* it and learn about myths and literary elements in the context of the story as they encounter them. Perkins' solution to these afflictions is to have students "play the whole game" (8), which is what Schmoker means when he calls for teachers to focus on a "coherent curriculum, sound lessons, and meaningful opportunities to read and write" (2011, 13).

After analyzing many studies on effective literacy and English language arts instruction, I arrived at the following 10 elements of effective instruction which, if implemented consistently, will improve both your teaching and students' performance. These elements appear on my lesson plan template (refer to Figure 3.13 so that I can consult them when planning the next day's lesson. I find, as Gawande did when he demanded of himself that he use his own safe-surgery

> **❝Instead of getting students *doing* so they can learn, we "focus on elements," leaving little time to have students *do* the thing they came to learn.❞**

checklist, that I am more consistently effective and have become, over time, more conscious of what I do that makes a difference.

The Ten Elements of Effective Instruction

1. ***Provide the necessary conditions*** for optimum learning and engagement: a safe and supportive environment in which students can *do* what you want them to so that they learn within a meaningful, authentic context.

2. ***Establish and communicate clear, specific learning objectives*** aligned with established state and national academic and career standards.

3. ***Make explicit connections*** between present and past lessons, students' lives, other texts or subjects, the real world, and the Big Ideas around which lessons are organized.

4. ***Prepare students*** by teaching relevant background knowledge, skills, and academic language and literacies.

5. ***Integrate assessment*** throughout the instructional process, using the data to establish initial understanding, measure progress, provide feedback, refine instruction, and prepare students for future performances; this includes students reflecting on and assessing their own performance and progress.

6. ***Teach students strategies*** for learning, remembering, and doing.

7. ***Demystify literacy practices and performances*** by modeling, providing examples, and giving clear directions as students graduate from dependence on you to responsibility for their own learning.

8. ***Use different instructional methods, modes, and media*** in clear, coherent ways.

9. ***Ask students to generate*** a range of ideas, interpretations, solutions, questions, and connections.

10. ***Provide meaningful opportunities to practice, perfect, and perform*** all lessons in class and at home.

Let me briefly address one immediate concern that any such list of elements raises: control, or the exercise of professional knowledge. As Gawande (2009) observes, "We don't like checklists. They can be painstaking. They're not much fun. . . . It somehow feels beneath us to use a checklist, an embarrassment. It runs counter to deeply held beliefs about how the truly great among us—those we aspire to be—handle situations. . . . The truly great are daring. They improvise. They do not have protocols and checklists" (173). Gawande then suggests that "maybe our idea of heroism needs updating" (173).

So, too, perhaps with teaching: What helps our students learn best is what must guide us. What causes them to learn the skills and knowledge they need to live rich lives is what must guide us. Thus, the elements listed above offer a guide, not a mechanistic, lockstep solution to the problem of how to teach any student at any level. They provide what I find to be a succinct, useful, and effective set of solutions to the problem of how to teach 35 students to read, write, speak, and think. Which order you use, the way you implement these elements—those are your calls to make; I am suggesting, however, that at some level, each of these elements applies to every lesson, every day, regardless of what you are teaching.

Now let's get into the classroom to see what these look like and to better understand not only how to use these techniques but why we should.

Classroom Connection: What a Period Looks Like

The period I describe here is a typical period, not some fireworks show; most days of effective, even great teaching, look about as exciting as a bunch of people in an old workshop hammering and sawing and shaping wood. This is important to understand: the movies too often imply that every minute of every day should resemble a scene (complete with inspiring soundtrack, of course) from a movie, such as Freedom Writers, in which lives are changing before our eyes. The real work of the classroom is quieter than that, often taking place off camera and over a longer period of time. So here's a sample of one period with my College Prep (CP) freshman class; they were reading The Kite Runner in the last month of the school year and under great pressure to finish in the short time we had. We had the opportunity to pilot the book to determine its viability and appropriateness as a freshman text. It was an actual period: All the photos you see were taken in the period I describe.

A few other details are worth mentioning, just to round out the picture: this freshman class, which met right after the morning break, had 31 students: 19 were boys, 5 were in transitional English, 11 were in the ACCESS class or identified as having learning difficulties. It was a 51-minute period with a construction site right outside our window. Oh, and it was spring and they could smell summer only a month away.

As kids enter the classroom, I greet them and give each one a copy of an article from the previous day's New York Times titled "Pakistani Taliban Are Said to Expand Alliances" by Carlotta Gall and Sabrina Tavernise (May 6, 2010). Only days before, a Pakastani Taliban attempted to detonate several car bombs at Times Square. We are at a point in The Kite Runner where the Taliban are overtaking Afghanistan and imposing their laws on the people.

I am trying to provide the necessary conditions (1) by not only welcoming and talking with students before the class begins, but also by providing challenging work during which I circulate around the room helping them to do well. This support prevents disruption, reduces anxiety, increases effort, and generally contributes to the positive, productive classroom atmosphere they need (and desire) if they are to do good work.

Before having students read the approximately 500-word article, I ask them to each generate a purpose question ("PQ") based on the title, doing this first on their own before comparing their PQ with their partner's.

After discussing their different PQs briefly, we generate one we can all use: "Why and how are the Pakastani Taliban expanding their influence outside of Pakistan?" I then direct them to read the article on their own and underline those details that relate to and will help them answer the PQ when they finish (see Figure 3.5).

Before turning them loose, I use the opening paragraph of the article to demonstrate what they should do, thinking out loud about what I am doing as I read and mark it up. Finally, I go through the article to identify and discuss those words they may not know but must if they are to understand the article.

FIGURE 3.5 Ardy and Eduardo mark up the article prior to discussing it and how it relates to *The Kite Runner*.

The students then read and apply my example to the next paragraph to show me that they understand what I want them to do and how I want them to work.

By teaching students strategies, such as generating a PQ, annotating texts, and taking notes as they read, I teach them strategies for learning, remembering, and doing the work (6) while also preparing them for their careers and college.

These efforts to incorporate strategies also provide, along with the checklists and examples on the homework handout you'll see at the end of this lesson, effective opportunities to demystify the literacy practices associated with this lesson as well as the demands of this particular assignment (7).

While they read, I circulate to make sure that all the students, especially the English learners and struggling readers, understand what to do and are able to do it. After finishing the article, we briefly discuss what it says and how it relates to our world and The Kite Runner—a conversation that prepares them for the subsequent discussion and homework about the relationship between the Taliban and the people of Afghanistan. The previous day we had watched short portions of a documentary available on YouTube, Meeting the Taliban, and read a short article titled "Who Are the Taliban of Afghanistan?" from the CNN.com website.

The assignment and my observations as I move around the room and talk with students allow me to integrate assessment and accountability throughout the lesson (5) through writing, homework, and discussion in class. These same features also allow students to assess their own performance and progress.

At this point in The Kite Runner, we learn that Sohrab, the orphaned boy Amir is trying to rescue, has been sold to the Taliban to entertain them. In addition to the in class articles and videos, I tell them about (but say we cannot watch) a powerful Frontline documentary titled The Dancing Boys of Afghanistan, which they can watch at home if they want and their parents approve. It is on the PBS site but has some mature content that makes it inappropriate for the classroom and our class wiki for the book's unit.

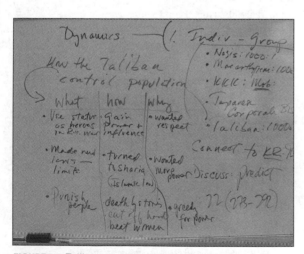

FIGURE 3.6 Taliban notes on the whiteboard from our class discussion of the novel prior to writing an analytical paragraph about the Taliban

After our full-class discussion of events in Times Square and the connection to the Taliban in the book, we transition to groups to discuss the relationship between the Taliban and the people of Afghanistan. After a few minutes, I interrupt to ask them to use a more structured way of discussing the material so that they will be prepared for the paragraph they will begin writing in class in a few minutes. On the board, I draw (and direct them to do the same on their notes), a three-column chart that says "How the Taliban Control the Population" at the top and then What, How, and Why at the top of each column (see Figure 3.6). After giving them a few minutes to complete this, during which time I am working with different groups to check on certain kids, we talk about the chart together as a class. Throughout this discussion, I pose questions intended to help them clarify or extend their thinking and tell them all to add these ideas to their notes, as I add the details to my own diagram on the board.

Like using PQs and annotating text, using graphic organizers is a strategy that will not only help students with this lesson (6) but also demystify the learning process (7) and prepare them for their lives after school.

At nearly every turn, students are both required as well as taught how to generate a range of ideas, interpretations, questions, and connections (9), all of which provide them, throughout the period and for homework that night, opportunities to practice these different skills and perform them within the context of the class assignment this one period (10).

When we finish this short conversation, we use those notes, as we do nearly every day, to write a paragraph about some aspect of the book that relates to the homework and our Big Idea of relationships—between people and themselves, their faith, their family, their new and home country, and so on. (See Figure 3.7) In today's class, students write a paragraph about the nature of the relationship between the Taliban and the people of Afghanistan and how the Taliban control such a large population. Students

FIGURE 3.7 Kollin and Krikor writing about the novel after generating ideas during their discussion

FIGURE 3.8 After group and class discussion, students turn to write

get about 10 minutes to write this paragraph, which is not a personal response, but a focused, organized, developed expository paragraph. This assignment has required them to read the text analytically, take notes (annotating and using structured notes), discuss their ideas, and write an analytical paragraph with evidence to support and illustrate their ideas (see Figures 3.8).

Throughout the lesson, whether we are discussing an article or watching videos, writing or reading, they (and I) are making explicit connections to past and present lessons, as well as to their own lives and experiences (3), not to mention the Big Idea of relationships in the novel. We are also reading for recurring patterns, imagery, themes, and words that convey key ideas in the novel. We have used different methods—writing, reading, discussing, watching, listening—different media (written texts and video footage); and, finally, a mix of instructional modes: full-class discussions, small-group conversations, paired interactions, and individual work (8); separate, simulated, and integrated instruction. (See classroom notes examples in Figures 3.9 and 3.10.)

When they finish the paragraph, they get that night's homework assignment for Chapter 21 (see Figure 3.11); we briefly discuss it to be sure they all understand. They then have the last 10 minutes of class to begin the homework, something I realized I had to do because of the length of the book and how little time remained in the semester.

Using this handout, which looks the same for all the chapters they read except for the three reading questions at the bottom, I establish and communicate clear objectives (2) that I further reinforce through my comments when introducing and explaining what they read,

Classroom Notes

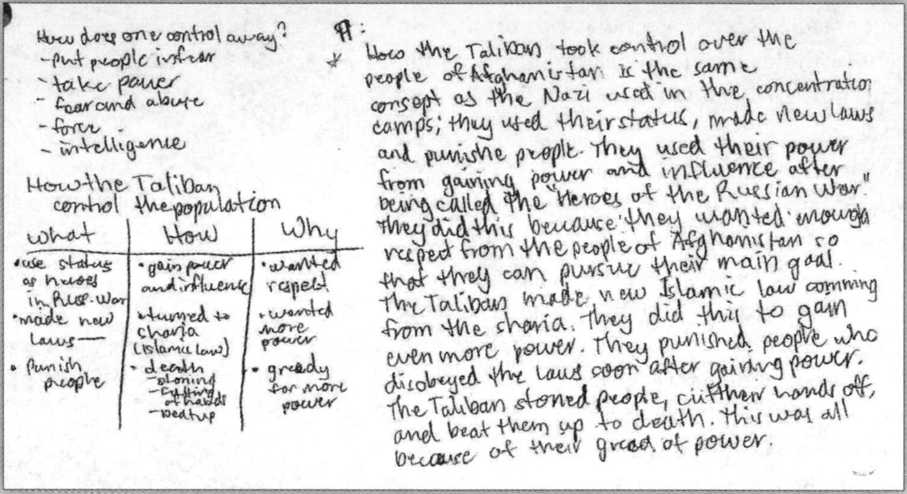

How does one control away?
- put people in fear
- take power
- fear and abuse
- force
- intelligence

How the Taliban control the population

What	How	Why
• use status as heroes in Russ. War • made new Laws — • punish people	• gain power and influence • turned to sharia (Islamic law) • death - stoning - cutting of hands - beat up	• wanted respect • wanted more power • greedy for more power

How the Taliban took control over the people of Afghanistan is the same consept as the Nazi used in the concentration camps; they used their status, made new laws and punish people. They used their power from gaining power and influence after being called the "heroes of the Russian war." They did this because they wanted enough respect from the people of Afghanistan so that they can pursue their main goal. The Taliban made new Islamic law comming from the sharia. They did this to gain even more power. They punished people who disobeyed the laws soon after gaining power. The Taliban stoned people, cut their hands off, and beat them up to death. This was all because of their greed of power.

FIGURE 3.9 Jan's notes on the Taliban and his subsequent paragraph.

Classroom Notes

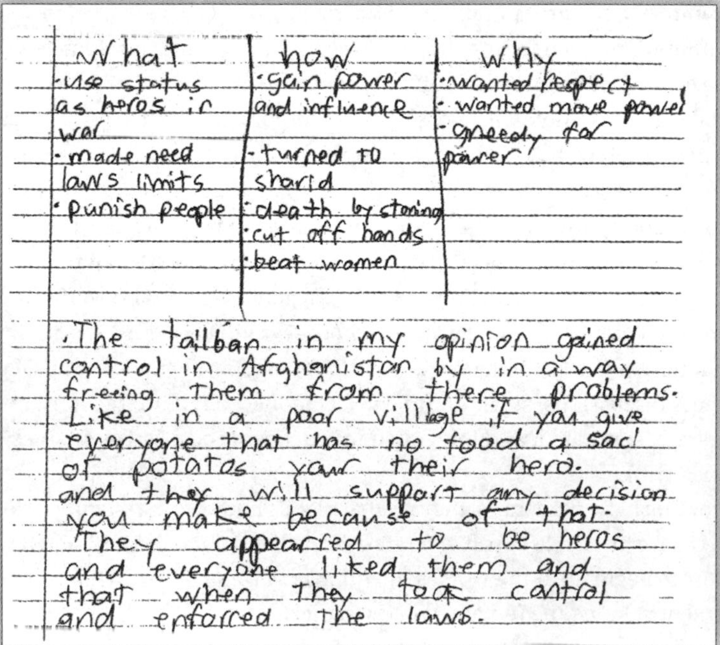

What	how	why
• use status as heros in war • made need laws limits • punish people	• gain power and influence • turned to sharid • death by stoning • cut off hands • beat women	• wanted respect • wanted more power • greedy for power

• The tailban in my opinion gained control in Afghanistan by in a way freeing them from there problems. Like in a poor village if you give everyone that has no food a sac of potatos your their hero. and they will support any decision you make because of that. They appearred to be heros and everyone liked them and that when they took cantrol and enforced the laws.

FIGURES 3.10 These notes, taken by an ELL transitional student, show how they help him gather ideas and details he can then organize into a paragraph.

Name: _____ Date: _____ Period: _____

Burke/English 2CP
Chapter 21 (259-272)

Develop your answers fully. You should be able to check each of the following:

❏ You answer *all parts* of the question as precisely as possible.

❏ You provide examples (from the book or, if appropriate, your own life or the world at large) to illustrate what you say.

❏ You explain the meaning and/or importance of your comments and/or examples as these relate to the question you are answering.

❏ You answer *all* the questions listed.

Here is a sample question and response to show you what I expect:

SAMPLE QUESTION: How does the relationship between Amir and Hassan change based on what Amir learns in this chapter? Also, explain why this knowledge changes the relationship.

| Establishes a focus specific to the question | | Explains what changes, why, and how; illustrates with an example |

> 1. I think the relationship took a very large turn even though Amir does not show it. Now that Amir learned that him and Hassan were related I think it changes their relationship in a way that Amir is hurting even more on the inside but that if Hassan would have known, he would have loved Amir even more. Now that Hassan has passed away Amir is probably going to have to live with all the mistakes he made and how he treated Hassan. This will take a huge effect on Amir unless he does something to make him feel like he redeemed himself.

| Further explains why previous ideas are important in relation to the story | | Expands on the previous idea to explain its importance and meaning |

1. Explain what Amir's dream means and why you think that.
2. Discuss Amir's visit to "Baba's house," focusing on what he does, what he thinks, what the visit means, and what it tells us about Amir.
3. What happens in the stadium and what does it say about the society of Afghanistan at that time? Discuss why you think this, providing examples to support what you say.

FIGURE 3.11 Sample of *The Kite Runner* Reading Response homework assignment. (Note that the only thing that changes from chapter to chapter are the questions.)

Sample of Jesus' Homework for *The Kite Runner*

Chapter 21

1. I think the dream that Amir meant had some connection to Sohrab. Maybe Sohrab was the turtle in his dream and Amir and Hassan were trying to protect it from danger. Although the dream was very random i'm sure it had something to do with Sohrab and Amir's/Hassan's relationship to him. When it say's that Amir and Hassan were both excited to find the turtle I think it might have meant the happiness that Hassan had when his wife gave birth to Sohrab and the happiness for Amir to be able to try and redeem himself by trying to recover Sohrab.

2. I think Amir's visit to Baba's house was very strange. In a way I think he might have related his new life with the past, for example, when he saw all the broken windows and how old the house was it kind of reminded him that he was not young anymore and that the Afghanistan that he had grown up in was gone. I think one of the reason's that Amir went to visit the house was to remind himself that the old Afghanistan that he grew up in was gone because he was sort of confused on what was going on in Afghanistan as well as shocked by the things he saw.

3. When Amir went into the stadium he saw a man and a woman who had commited adultery get stoned to death. I think this communicates to Amir that the Taliban have complete control over Afghanistan and that not only have they brainwashed the people by scaring them but that they do as they wish around the country. In my opinion for a whole stadium to clap when people who have sinned get murdered, there has to be something that has altered the minds of those people somehow.

FIGURE 3.12 Sample of Jesus' homework for *The Kite Runner,* which then serves as the basis for much of our work in class the next day and notes for the paragraph he will write.

watch, write, discuss, and do for homework. I use the same handout not only to help them make connections and to self-evaluate their own performance and progress but also to prepare them by providing examples, checklists, and background knowledge through a variety of means (4).

When they come to class the next day, students continue this cycle, using their homework (see Figure 3.11) from the previous night as the basis for close reading, discussion, response, and writing. Such an instructional cycle might be summed up as a recursive process of reading, writing, speaking, representing, all taking place in the context of a Big Idea or Big Question around which instruction is organized.

FIGURE 3.13 Daniel, who struggles with reading due to learning difficulties, benefits from the time in class spent closely reading or re-reading the text before writing about it.

This is one day in a unit that lasts a little less than a month and culminates with them writing an in-class final essay on the last day of school about one relationship they choose (from the book) using all those notes and draft paragraphs. In the next section, we will look at what goes into planning such a unit, and consider this one lesson in the larger context of the week and month during which it occurred.

Planning for Success: The Week and the Unit

Nice class, you may be thinking, but what are they doing the rest of the week—and for the rest of the unit—you wonder? And how to stitch that all together into an effective instructional sequence that is not just engaging but effective? Good questions.

It's useful to think of each day as a paragraph in a larger essay about whatever the unit is you are teaching. Thus, in the case of *The Kite Runner* unit, the class-as-essay would be not only about relationships but also the skills and knowledge the unit is designed to teach (not just to give them a chance to prove they have). The instructional design model in Figure 3.14 offers one way to think about and to plan for these instructional goals. It also provides a means by which to evaluate my lesson on the other side, to ask whether the activity I thought would lead to more advanced, cognitively demanding work did so or somehow ended up merely asking students to identify key details without engaging in any analysis of those details.

A more articulated, structured means of planning a day's lesson would involve using a tool like the backwards design planning tool in Figure 3.14. Such a tool complements the elements of effective instruction I offer here by providing a structure for planning a day's lesson. Also see the template in Figure 3.15.

This sample lesson, the one I have chosen to discuss in some detail, falls at the end of the last week of the unit, though it is representative of the previous days. Here is a slightly larger glimpse—that lesson set in the context of the rest of the week (see Figure 3.16). It happens during the last week before the day of the final exam.

On the day of the final, they come in with their notes, the paragraphs they have been writing nearly every day, the book, and any sort of outline they may have created. Before we can write (we have a two-hour final), we have to carry the textbooks to the library and wait in line

Note: This is meant to be used to design, assess, and refine your lesson plan to ensure you are asking students to work and think at the highest levels; the rest of the chapter is meant to help you teach to these levels.

		Representative Actions	Descriptions	Examples
Wisdom	**LEVEL 6**	• Challenge • Judge • Refine • Reflect • Revise • Speculate • Teach	• Reflective, analytical thought • Knowledge of craft, process • Internalize principles, practices, processes • Transcendent goal: mastery • Demonstrated independence • Computer cannot do this	• Having read and written about *Lord of the Flies* (*LOTF*), students reflect on processes and decisions in light of their understanding of their own writing and thinking processes as well as established standards in a given area such as writing.
Knowledge	**LEVEL 5**	• Assess • Compose • Create • Design • Imagine • Synthesize • Troubleshoot	• Active, creative, critical thought • Fluent, native understanding • Create new ideas, iterations • Big goal, objective • Monitored independence • Computer cannot do this	• Students read *LOTF* and put William Golding on trial for slander against humanity for his portrayal. Students adopt roles and use ideas from research and the book to support ideas and verdict. Write a paper drawing on readings, trial, research.
Knowledge	**LEVEL 4**	• Apply • Articulate • Construct • Decide • Demonstrate • Generalize • Observe	• Active, critical thought • Critical understanding of content, context, criteria • Apply and/or refine criteria, terms, approach • Possible end—or means • Provisional independence • Computer cannot do this	• Students read *LOTF* and Golding's Nobel speech about human nature; generalize about human nature of boys in book as well as people in general based on speech, text, and their own observations. Consider subject from multiple perspectives.
Knowledge	**LEVEL 3**	• Analyze • Compare • Elaborate • Generate • Infer • Investigate • Predict	• Active, critical thought • Deeper understanding of content and context • Generate the criteria used • Possible end—or means • Dependence to independence • Computer can do some of this	• Students read *LOTF* and generate criteria for leaders and followers; classify characters accordingly and write comparative analysis using evidence from the novel (and other sources) to support inferences and make predictions.
Data/Information	**LEVEL 2**	• Collect • Comprehend • Describe • Evaluate • Paraphrase • Represent • Summarize	• Limited thought • Surface learning • Minimal action using others' criteria • Entry-point, not an end • Guided dependence • Computer can do most of this	• Students read *LOTF* and collect key details to include in a summary of the chapter; they describe characters based on criteria or terms (e.g., antagonist) given by the teacher or textbook. May summarize using a graphic representation.
Data/Information	**LEVEL 1**	• Identify • List • Mimic • Recall • Reference • Repeat • Retrieve	• Minimal/no thought • Rote learning • Passive • Entry point, not an end • Dependent on others, directions, teacher • Computer can do this	• Students read *LOTF* and take quiz on which they match names and details based on surface reading of the book. Students take multiple-choice test or jot short answers on handout; take notes on facts for background information.

FIGURE 3.14 Teaching by Design. Think of the arrow as similar to a thermometer: The more the assignment demands intellectually, the higher it should go. Today should, in some way, be more challenging than the day before.

Lesson Plan Template

Date: _____ Class: _____ Unit: _____

Instructional Checklist	ACT 1:
❏ Provide the necessary conditions.	
❏ Establish and communicate clear, specific learning objectives.	
❏ Make explicit connections.	
❏ Prepare students.	
❏ Integrate assessment throughout; include time for reflection.	
❏ Teach students strategies.	
❏ Demystify literacy practices and performances.	
❏ Use different instructional methods, modes, and media.	
❏ Ask students to generate.	
❏ Provide meaningful opportunities to practice, perfect, and perform all lessons in class and at home.	
Remember and Reflect	ACT 2:
Homework	ACT 3:

FIGURE 3.15 This is the lesson plan template I designed for myself. The checklist to the left is an abbreviated version of the instructional protocols discussed earlier.

Weeklong Instructional Sequence	
Day and Notes	**Main Course (Core Text)**
Monday (Day 1) **News • Events • Notes**	• Ch 21 *Kite Runner* (*KR*) discussion of relationship between Taliban and Afghanistan's people • Teach essential skills, language, knowledge • Generate ideas, questions, connections via discussion • Choose and apply strategies to write comp/contrast ¶ • Assess: understanding of book, ability to write ¶ • Go over homework to prepare for reading Ch. 22 • Last ten minutes to read; time for me to check in, help • HW: Read Ch 22 and respond to assigned questions
Tuesday (Day 2) **News • Events • Notes**	• Ch. 22 *KR* emphasis on changes within relationships • Groups examine causes and effects of changes in relationship between people and their country • Generate examples of causes and effects from book • Model and discuss sentence structures for cause/effect • Write 10-minute ¶ on how/why relationships changing • Introduce homework and reading questions prior to reading • Read last ten minutes, guided by reading questions • HW: Read Ch 23 and respond to assigned questions
Wednesday (Day 3) **News • Events • Notes**	• Ch 23 questions focused on our many different selves (e.g., public/private) and our relationship with each self • Groups discuss homework and generate the different types of selves we might have, then connect to *KR* • Facilitate class discussion, using organizer on the board to structure conversation about different selves • Write 10-minute ¶ about Amir's different selves and his relationship with each one • Introduce homework questions for Ch 24, taking time to explain Maslow's Hierarchy of Human Needs • HW: Read Ch 24, focusing on what motivates characters and how they try to meet their different needs.
Thursday (Day 4) **News • Events • Notes**	• Create a 3-column organizer on the whiteboard to guide group and then class discussion: What does the character need? How does the character try to satisfy that need? Why do they need it? • After groups pool their ideas in response, we discuss these questions as a class, generating examples and commentary on those examples to prepare for writing • Write a 10-minute ¶ on the subject of needs and how their efforts to satisfy these needs affects relationships • Introduce homework: Choose **one** relationship we have studied that runs throughout the book and jot down ideas about the type of relationship and how/why it changes • HW: Read the last chapter of the book; write as already directed about the one relationship they choose
Friday (Day 5) **News • Events • Notes**	• Tie up all conversations about book by revisiting first Big Question of the year: What does it take to be a survivor? • Ask groups to generate the qualities of a survivor, recalling earlier conversations in the year about this and applying those ideas to this book now that they are finished • Lead discussion about the book, this topic • Ask students to give feedback on the book and instructional techniques • Introduce and give handout with steps for the final essay • Field any remaining questions about book, topics, final

FIGURE 3.16 Weeklong instructional sequence for *The Kite Runner* unit.

to turn them in along with all the other kids. Then, we have to wait until I get the key for the computer lab. Then, we have to wait for everyone to get seated at a working computer; get their notes and books out; get the final set of directions; and finally they are free to write! Outside, we hear the faint ruckus of seniors who have finished high school calling to each other; inside, my students buckle down one last time to write what for many is their longest essay on the longest book of the year. Figure 3.17 shows the final assignment sheet as they got it.

By the time they print and submit their papers, each of my students has written, with few exceptions, a 3- to 4-page typed essay on the longest book most have ever read (see Figure 3.18). With time to revise, these papers would be all the more impressive and refined; as they are, however, they show young minds wrestling with real ideas as they convey their ideas about a book they all had read (with the exception of the two who had cut school for the last month) discussed, and enjoyed. Figure 3.19 shows the essay, which marks a great end to a year that began poorly for Kollin.

Wrap Up

Throughout this chapter, I have focused mostly on what Hillocks describes as "personal practical knowledge" of teachers (1999, 2) in which he quotes Connelly and Clandinin as referring to the images, metaphors, and rules we each have about what it means to be a teacher and how we should act. Hillocks goes on to describe what he calls the "personal philosophy" of teachers, which "names the way a teacher thinks about him- or herself in teaching situations, but stated in narrative form" (4). Thus, the question, as I see it, is what metaphor or image informs my teaching and in which way? That is, what is the story I tell myself about my role in the class?

One teacher Hillocks (1999) mentions compares her classroom to a "home" where her role is to "plant seeds" to see whether students "will be interested in an activity" (3). My fondness for gardening, coupled with my respect for research on effective instruction, suggests some variation on this homegrown metaphor: the teacher as gardener. As the elements of effective instruction emphasize, one must provide the necessary conditions if the garden is (or their minds are) to grow. Nor do all plants have the same needs or grow at the same rate. Thus, I must learn what they each need, recognizing that both plants and students have certain common needs such as, in the case of the plants, sun, water, and healthy soil. Fundamental to the enterprise of gardening is the notion that things *can* grow, thrive, and serve some greater good—to feed, to bring joy, to calm the mind riddled with the white noise of the modern world.

PAUSE & REFLECT Which metaphor would you choose to describe the complexity of the classroom and your role in it? What is that metaphor?

Mike Rose, who understands and accepts the complex nature of teaching and learning more than most, offered the following in an address to graduates:

> Get ready to fail. A lesson will flop, or your understanding of a kid's problem will be way off base. . . . [This] happens to all of us . . . It will be painful and disorienting. So learn how to handle failure, for at those moments you will be vulnerable to your own insecurities and those who are cynical about young people . . . It is imperative, then, that . . . you start figuring out who the good teachers are. Get to know them, for when you fail, you'll need them to convert those failures into knowledge rather than doubt or bitterness. (2010a)

Mr. Burke/English 2CP

Overview	We have spent the last three weeks preparing for this final in one way or another. You have the period today to show me (and yourself!) what you can do as a writer, reader, and thinker after a year's worth of study. I expect great things but only because I know you are capable of them (and because I have *seen* you do them!). You have the whole period to write this paper and should use it to ensure it is your best work.
Step One	Find a computer and get out your book and notes. Set up all your goodies. (notes, books, etc.)
Step Two	Open a Microsoft Word document, and save it with this title: **yourname_kr final essay.doc** (e.g., jimburke_kr final essay.doc).
Step Three	Write an essay in which you examine one of the following relationships in the book *The Kite Runner*. • Amir and Hassan (friend to friend) • Amir and Baba (parent and child) • Amir and Assef (victim to aggressor/abuser/enemy) • Amir and himself • Amir/Baba and America/Afghanistan (adopted vs. homeland) • Hassan and Baba • Individual with past and present Begin by sketching out a plan or outline using your notes and the book to guide you. Then write an introduction, the body paragraphs, and a final conclusion. As you write, be sure that you: ❏ Have good FODP throughout the whole paper and in each paragraph ❏ Include specific examples and quotations from the paper ❏ Explain *how* these examples or quotations relate to your main idea and *why* they are important (hint: Keep asking, "So what?") ❏ Show how the relationship changes over time and in response to different events ❏ Use appropriate and effective transitions to clarify and emphasize your ideas ❏ Have an introduction, body paragraphs, and a conclusion ❏ Include a title on the first page
Step Four	Proofread and edit your paper as time allows. Put your name and the page numbers in the header.
Step Five	Print your paper and staple it; in the event that we have a problem with printing, open up School Loop and send it to me as an attachment so I can print it later.
Step Six	Staple all your notes to the back of the paper and turn in your paper and the reflective bibliography assignment, which is also due today.
Step Seven	Return your copy of *The Kite Runner* and any other books you still have.
Step Eight	Have a great summer.
Step Nine	Do your summer reading.
Step Ten	Visit me next year!

FIGURE 3.17 *The Kite Runner* Final Essay handout.

It is appropriate to end this chapter on how to teach by stressing the extent to which, as teachers, we must never forget how to learn—or that we must continue to do so. My first day of teaching, a lesson I spent *days* creating, went up in smoke as soon as I called the class to order. I turned to address my very first class as my master teacher, Bill Robinson, looked on. I said, "Welcome! Today we are going to learn about _____" and turned to write "Appositives" on the board—my mind went as blank as that board. The words, all that learning, *it was all gone* for the day, the silence of the class broken only

FIGURE 3.18 Fietonga uses all his notes and drafts of his previous paragraphs for the assignment to write a winning final essay on the last day of the semester.

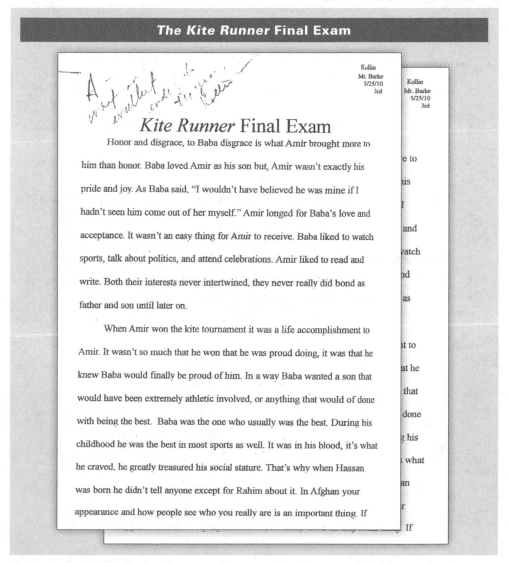

The *Kite Runner* Final Exam

Kollin
Mr. Burke
5/25/10
3rd

Kite Runner Final Exam

Honor and disgrace, to Baba disgrace is what Amir brought more to him than honor. Baba loved Amir as his son but, Amir wasn't exactly his pride and joy. As Baba said, "I wouldn't have believed he was mine if I hadn't seen him come out of her myself." Amir longed for Baba's love and acceptance. It wasn't an easy thing for Amir to receive. Baba liked to watch sports, talk about politics, and attend celebrations. Amir liked to read and write. Both their interests never intertwined, they never really did bond as father and son until later on.

When Amir won the kite tournament it was a life accomplishment to Amir. It wasn't so much that he won that he was proud doing, it was that he knew Baba would finally be proud of him. In a way Baba wanted a son that would have been extremely athletic involved, or anything that would of done with being the best. Baba was the one who usually was the best. During his childhood he was the best in most sports as well. It was in his blood, it's what he craved, he greatly treasured his social stature. That's why when Hassan was born he didn't tell anyone except for Rahim about it. In Afghan your appearance and how people see who you really are is an important thing. If

FIGURE 3.19 Sample *The Kite Runner* essay by Kollin, a student who struggled first semester but really engaged with this book and our study of it.

by Bill Robinson dismissing the students (it was a college composition class), telling them we would meet again the next day.

And the next day I returned, having reviewed, rehearsed, and restored myself that night. I taught that lesson with more passion than any appositive ever received. The lesson went well. Walking down the hall after class, a little bounce in my step, I dared to ask Bill, who was notorious for his exacting standards and blunt judgment, "So what did you think, Bill? I thought it went quite well!" Looking down as we moved through the throng, he said only, "You have a lot to learn, a lot to learn," and kept shaking his head as we walked down the hall. And he was right.

I still do. We always will. Which is why Rose's words are so true, so important. But as teachers, we soon realize our first and most enduring students are and always will be ourselves. So if you want to know, as this chapter has discussed in such detail, how to teach, begin by remembering how to learn—and never stop.

Recommended **Resources**

Print

- *Focus: Elevating the Essentials to Radically Improve Student Learning*, Mike Schmoker (ASCD 2011).
- *Envisioning Literature: Literary Understanding and Literature Instruction*, Judith A. Langer (Second Edition) (Teachers College Press 2011).
- *Holding on to Good Ideas in a Time of Bad Ones: Six Literacy Principles Worth Fighting For*, Thomas Newkirk (Heinemann 2009).
- *Ways of Thinking, Ways of Teaching*, George Hillocks, Jr. (Teachers College Press 1999).

Online

- Read Write Think (www.readwritethink.org)
- English Companion Ning (www.englishcompanion.ning.com)
- The National Council of Teachers of English (NCTE) (www.ncte.org)

CHAPTER FOUR

Teaching Writing

I never know what I think about something until I have written on it.
—William Faulkner

Introduction: All Writing Is Personal

Throughout high school, where I worked little and wrote even less, I wrote poetry. This troubled and confused me. After a few years, the tension became too much: I burned all my poems for fear someone would find and read them. (Don't worry: they were awful!) After barely graduating from high school, community college was next, where I was placed in a remedial writing class based on a test I do not remember taking. Then, teacher Mace Perona made us keep a journal, which changed everything. I filled three composition notebooks in one semester. Poetry returned, slightly improved once I realized I could—and should—*read* poetry. Also, by this time, I was reading *everything*, all the time. But academic writing, the more formal sort, came slowly—an F on a 10-page essay on *Hamlet* with the word "So?" in large red letters covering the front page. Psychology papers returned with notes across the top in jittery, grad student scrawl: "This is a formal academic paper not a short story!" By graduation, however, I had mastered the academic writing genre.

First job after college: Working full time, one-on-one with an autistic boy at a private school, during which time I kept extensive journals about what I did, how I did it, why I did it, and how he responded. Next, two years in the Peace Corps writing Susan in Japan long detailed letters on onion skin paper using the little manual typewriter I lugged to Tunisia. Then my first published article (in the *San Francisco Chronicle*) while still a student teacher (and newly married to Susan!). Several failed novels, the main benefit of which was the discipline to sit and think and write and rewrite for hours and days. But here and there, an article published about teaching in one journal or another. Some success with poetry: regularly published, even a few awards! A master's thesis that earned special honors.

Then, Lois Bridges, who would become my first editor, saying: Write about what you do in your class. So, I wrote what became the first edition of the book you now hold. And since then? Many more books. Articles. Speeches. Blogs. Tweets. Websites. Wikis. Nings! Plus, text messages to Susan, whom I have never stopped writing (or loving) after all these years and our three children.

What's my point with this brief history of my origins as a writer? Writing is a craft people can learn and even master no matter where they begin. But there is another, more subtle point to this story: All writing is personal, an extension of ourselves, a record of the process by which we create ourselves, discover our ideas; it is a performance of ourselves (Newkirk 1997).

PAUSE & REFLECT Write your own writing autobiography, identifying the key moments, people, and assignments.

Writing: Past, Present, and Future

We write, especially as adults, on an increasingly wide array of devices (iPads, computers, cell phones) using a growing number of platforms (social networks, websites, text messages, emails), incorporating more media (words, images, sounds, video, infographics) to be read in more formats (cell phone screens, computer screens, presentation screens, ebooks, and, of course, paper pages) than ever before (see Figure 4.1).

These days writing and, in particular, the teaching of it suffers from something akin to a multiple personality disorder. Although students are writing more than ever in their private lives (Lenhart, Arafeh, Smith, and Macgill 2008; Robb 2010), they do not define writing done online or on phones as "writing" (Lenhart, Arafeh, Smith, and Macgill 2008, ii). Instead, they describe it all generically as "communication." Students are also writing more in both middle and high schools than in the past, although not "of any significant length or complexity" (Applebee and Langer 2009, 21) and in middle school are writing more to improve reading comprehension and prepare for standardized state writing exams (Hillocks 2002; Applebee and Langer 2009, 21). Neither of these prepare students for the demands of postsecondary education or the workplace, which spends more than $3 billion a year—states spending an additional $200 million—in writing instruction and remediation (National Commission on Writing 2003).

Writing Outside of School

% of students who write outside of class by type of writing
(agree or strongly agree to . . .)

	% of All Students	5th	6th	7th	8th	9th		Males	Females	
Writing in a journal (Q1)	30.5%	38.5	28.9	25.6	31.0	25.4	**	16.9	46.3	***
Respond to blogs	24.1%	18.6	21.6	30.7	24.7	22.5	**	22.6	26.5	NS
Write stories	37.3%	45.2	43.0	34.4	27.9	33.8	***	29.2	46.8	***
Write poems	22.4%	19.7	23.0	22.2	23.3	27.1	NS	11.5	33.9	***
Write email to friends	62.1%	45.0	61.2	72.1	69.1	52.1	***	55.3	71.2	***
Text friends	63.2%	43.6	58.1	75.4	71.9	66.2	***	57.5	69.1	***
Write letters	36.2%	39.0	38.6	34.5	35.5	22.5	NS	25.0	49.8	***
Do at least one the above	89.4%	83.6	89.5	93.2	92.0	85.9	***	84.1	96.6	***
Do 3 or more of the above	47.0%	44.6	47.4	46.8	50.7	40.8	NS	29.7	66.9	***

Nine out of ten students engage in some type of writing outside of class.

Two and three asterisks mean that it's highly unlikely that chance had anything to do with the results. Three askteriss are even more unlikely than two.

FIGURE 4.1 "Writing Outside of School" table from Laura Robb's *Teaching Middle School Writers* (Heinemann 2010)

In their national study of writing instruction, Applebee and Langer note that, despite all the attention writing received in the years prior to the focus on testing, "the most striking aspect . . . is how slow changes in performance have been" (2009, 19). Such written communication as blogs, text messages, emails, social network posts, and journals is what many call "expressive writing" (Kinneavy 1971; Hillocks 2002; Newkirk 2009b). Researchers and policy makers distinguish between this kind of personal writing and more academic writing that focuses on informing, explaining, and persuading—each of these modes being vital to success in college and the workplace (College Board 2010a; NCTE 2008; National Governors Association 2010).

Moreover, writing on computers shows consistent benefits in terms of performance and improvement, yet "30% of teachers report that they do not use a computer when teaching writing because it does not match the format of the state assessment, and 4.4% [of teachers] report that school or district policy actually prohibited computer use for the teaching of writing" (Applebee and Langer 2009, 23). Such policies consequently prevent students from learning to use the tools required by higher education and/or the workplace. Summing up the initial findings from their national study of writing, Applebee and Langer (2009) concluded:

> What is clear is that even with some increases over time, many students are not writing a great deal for any of their academic subjects, including English, and most are not writing at any length. Some 40% of twelfth-grade students, for example, report never or hardly ever being asked to write a paper of three pages of more. . . . Writing [itself] seems to have evaporated from public concern, [thus] high school students who aspire to attend college will likely be unprepared to tackle the complex reading and writing tasks they will encounter. (26)

As with reading, we are expected to teach students advanced and new literacies to meet the demands of the changing world of communication, even as we try to remediate the same students whose abilities may be three to four grade levels below (National Adolescent Literacy Coalition 2007). Our work then is to move students from one phase to another (see Figure 4.2) to prepare them for the demands they will face as employees, students, and citizens. No doubt, this work makes great demands on both students and teachers. As Olson and Land (2007) write in their study of the Pathways Project in the Santa Ana Unified School District, where 93 percent of the students are ELLs and face other educational challenges:

> Many teachers of struggling students and English language learners (ELLs) avoid teaching strategic reading and analytical writing to their secondary students because they feel the skills required (analyzing text and forming interpretations, development of a meaningful thesis, control of organization, effective use of evidence and supporting details, sentence variety, and control of the conventions of written English) are too sophisticated for the population they serve. (271)

" OUR WORK THEN IS TO MOVE STUDENTS FROM ONE PHASE TO ANOTHER TO PREPARE THEM FOR THE DEMANDS THEY WILL FACE AS EMPLOYEES, STUDENTS, AND CITIZENS. **"**

PAUSE **&** REFLECT Discuss your thoughts and feelings about teaching writing to the students in your class. Which of the phases in Figure 4.2 represents the student you were and the students you teach?

Identifying Students' Phase of Interest for Writing

Phase One Students
- ❏ Do not think they know much about writing and do not think they are good at writing
- ❏ Think writing is a lot of work
- ❏ Do not revise much, mostly out of confusion about how to approach the task
- ❏ Like feedback that feels specific and manageable
- ❏ Dislike peer conferences because they feel unable to critique others' work

Phase Two Students
- ❏ Think of writing as something that must be "done right" to please the teacher
- ❏ Put work into their writing but no more than they put into other assignments
- ❏ Revise in an effort to incorporate teachers' comments
- ❏ Like feedback when it tells them how to do things "right"
- ❏ Like peer conferences but don't use them as they were intended; work near partners, not with them, and consult teacher a lot

Phase Three Students
- ❏ Think of writing as an art form and consider themselves writers
- ❏ Gladly spend time working on writing projects, both for school and for personal enjoyment
- ❏ Revise a great deal, mostly to "make it sound right"
- ❏ Dislike feedback when it feels like the commentator is trying to tell them how to write; appreciate recognition of their work
- ❏ Dislike peer conferences for the same reasons: they are skeptical of feedback

Phase Four Students
- ❏ Think of writing as a craft; think they are good writers but also have an awareness of their place in the greater writing community
- ❏ Gladly spend time working on writing projects, both for school and for personal enjoyment
- ❏ Revise a great deal to improve content, structure, style, and mechanics
- ❏ Welcome all constructive feedback; get frustrated when only praise is offered with no suggestions for improvement
- ❏ Appreciate peer conferences, but only if they feel constructive

FIGURE 4.2 "Identifying Students' Phase of Interest for Writing" (Lipstein and Renninger 2007).

What They Write: The Common Core State Standards and Beyond

The focus of this chapter is on *how* to teach writing but we must first clarify *what* we should teach when it comes to writing. The Common Core Standards for English Language Arts specify that all students in grades 6 through 12 should learn that "writing is a key means of asserting and defending claims, showing what they know about a subject, and conveying what they have experienced, imagined, thought, and felt. To be college- and career-ready writers, students must take task, purpose, and audience into careful consideration, choosing words, information, structures, and formats deliberately" (National Governors Association 2010, 41).

While these standards imply a clarity, comparable to a chain restaurant menu, of what to teach, they are overwhelming in their scope once you begin to examine the minutiae at each grade level. Anticipating the Common Core Standards and responding to such documents in general, Newkirk (2009b) argues for an "uncluttering" of the curriculum, drawing on the ideas of Kinneavey (1971) and echoing others (Graham and Perin 2007; Jago 2009) who also emphasize a select few modes of discourse: expressive, informational, persuasive, and literary (or what I refer to later as "imaginative" and the NAEP framework calls "writing to convey experience"). Figure 4.3 sums up these four types of writing.

To these models of discourse, we might add yet another perspective, which distinguishes between public and private writing, personal and professional, and vocational versus academic writing. It is this last form, academic writing, that often causes so much trouble for students. Smagorinsky, Daigle, O'Donnell-Allen, and Bynum (2010) examined the notion of such a "secret English" governed by "conventions of academic discourse . . . characterized by a particular social register, a way of perceiving, organizing, and communicating information in particular contexts" (375). These authors go so far as to examine, in their research, the notion of "academic bullshit" (375), describing it as "the ability to produce [a] text that appears to meet a disciplinary standard yet masks the author's insufficient grasp of the appropriate content knowledge" (376).

The authors conclude, however, that such academic BS is rarely an attempt to deceive but rather a sincere effort to gain "genre knowledge" through the use of "academic bullshit . . . which serves as a useful, and perhaps indispensible, [exploratory] tool enabling one's development as

Types of Texts			
Persuasive	**Explanatory**	**Imaginative**	**Expressive**
Description Provides arguments that support claims about topics or texts using evidence and logic.	Explains or conveys ideas and information about concepts, procedures, events, places, or people.	Captures and conveys a real or imagined experience through a story, poem, or other form or medium rich in detail and design.	Uses informal, loosely organized language intended to convey attitudes, feelings, thoughts to an interested audience.
Examples Ads Debates Editorials Essays Letters Literary analysis Proposals Reviews Speeches	Articles Essays Manuals Presentations Reports Resumes Summaries Websites Wikis	Biographical narratives Digital stories Graphic fiction Mixed media Monologues Personal narratives Poems Scripts Fiction	Blogs Emails Journals Personal statements Reader's responses Reflections Reviews Social network posts Text messages

Sources: Adapted from Newkirk 2009b; Jago 2009; Lindemann 2001; Kinneavey 1971. Note that the 2011 NAEP writing framework assesses writing in three areas: to persuade, to explain, and to convey experience (ACT 2007, 28).

FIGURE 4.3 Types of Text. The Common Core Standards challenge us to integrate a wider range of texts, especially nonfiction ones that become progressively more complex over the course of each school year.

© 2013 by Jim Burke from *The English Teacher's Companion*, Fourth Edition. Portsmouth, NH: Heinemann.

" . . . ACADEMIC PROSE IS UNFAMILIAR, EVEN UNNATURAL TO MANY STUDENTS, A LANGUAGE ALL ITS OWN THAT STUDENTS, ESPECIALLY THOSE FROM NONACADEMIC BACKGROUNDS, MUST LEARN AS ONE WOULD A FOREIGN LANGUAGE. **"**

a scholarly writer" (376). Ignoring the authors' use of an otherwise offensive term for a moment, we realize that they go to the heart of the challenge most secondary English teachers now face: Helping all students master "the moves that matter in academic writing" (Graff, Durst, and Birkenstein 2010), which are fundamental to the enterprise of preparing students for college (Shaughnessy 1979, 3; Olson and Land 2007, 271). Of these different forms, it is argument that is at the heart of the academic enterprise and thus merits our greatest attention (Schmoker and Graff 2011; National Governors Association).

Yet such academic prose is unfamiliar, even unnatural to many students, a language all its own that students, especially those from nonacademic backgrounds, must learn as one would a foreign language (Bailey 2007; Zwiers 2008). Shaughnessy, writing of these same students, calls academic writing a "trap" (1979, 7). Such academic writing poses unique challenges to all students but English learners in particular, as this "academic English language" includes content specific vocabulary, specialized grammatical structures, complex functions of language and discourse—all for the purpose "of acquiring new knowledge and skills, interacting about a topic, or imparting information to others" (Bailey 2007, 10). However, as Olson and Land's impressive results show, using such cognitive strategies as sentence starters (see Figure 4.4), students in the Pathways Project showed dramatic gains (averaging 32 percent greater success in improving scores on writing assessments over seven consecutive years) (2007, 289).

Clearly, my emphasis so far has been on academic genres, those necessary for success in secondary and postsecondary institutions. Yet other, more personal forms of writing certainly merit a place in students' writing diet. Writing only academic prose would be the equivalent of eating only protein bars. Atwell teaches only those "genres found in the real world of literature—kinds of writing that a reader can locate in a reasonably good bookstore or library" (2002, 92). She goes on to say that she "avoids . . . school genres" and focuses instead on "poems, memoirs, letters, essays, book reviews, gifts of writing, reports, profiles, and parodies" (92). For Atwell, "poetry is an essential genre to teach in grades K–12" (92).

" WRITING ONLY ACADEMIC PROSE WOULD BE THE EQUIVALENT OF EATING ONLY PROTEIN BARS. **"**

Romano (2009) argues with equal passion for the multigenre paper. Still others (Kittle 2008; Kirby and Kirby 2007) emphasize the importance of memoir. And many (Hicks 2009; Richardson 2010; Robb 2010; College Board/National Writing Project/Phi Delta Kappan 2010) ask with growing urgency where in all these genres such new media as blogs, wikis, tweets, and other emerging forms fit. It is, when you stop to think about it, staggering to realize all that we are asked to accomplish in so little time (my classes are 50 minutes long) with so many students (I typically have 35).

PAUSE **&** REFLECT What type of writing do you do best? What sort of writing do you do on your own, outside of school? What form of writing is most difficult for you? Why is that? Ask your students to write about the same questions.

Sentence Frames: Helping Students Discuss, Read, and Write About Texts

Overview

Students at all levels struggle to find language that expresses their ideas and helps them achieve their rhetorical purpose. Sentence structures offer a useful means of getting students up and running with academic language through either sentence starters or sentence frames. Both approaches are useful for writing about and discussing different types of texts.

Sentence Starters	Sentence Frames
Making Predictions • I predict that . . . • If x happens, then . . . • Because x did y, I expect z.	**Summarizing** • Readers often assume that . . . • While many suggest x, others say z . . . • (Author's name) agrees/disagrees with x, pointing out . . .
Making Connections • X reminds me of . . . • X is similar to y because . . . • X is important to y because . . .	**Responding** • X claims . . . , which I agree/disagree with because . . . • X's point assumes x, which I would argue means . . . • While I agree that _____, you could also say . . .
Making Inferences • X means . . . since x is . . . • Early on the author says . . . which suggests x is . . . • X causes y as a result of . . . which shows . . .	**Agreeing** • Most will agree that . . . • I agree with those who suggest that . . . • X offers an effective explanation of why y happens, which is especially useful because most think that . . .
Summarizing • The main idea is . . . • The author argues that . . . • In _____, (author's name) implies . . .	**Disagreeing** • I would challenge X's point about y, arguing instead . . . • X claims y, but recent discoveries show this is . . . • While X suggests y, this cannot be true since . . .
Evaluating • The author's point is/is not valid because . . . • The author does/does not do a good job of . . . • The most important aspect/event/idea is . . .	**Taking the Third Path: Agreeing and Disagreeing** • While I agree that . . . , I reject the larger argument that . . . since we now know . . . • I share X's belief that . . . , but question . . . due to . . . • Most concede x though few would agree that y is true . . .
Analyzing the Text • The author uses _____ to show/achieve . . . • The author assumes _____, which is/is not true . . . • The use of _____ strengthens/weakens the author's argument by . . .	**Arguing** • Although x is increasing/decreasing, it is not y but z that is the cause . . . • While x is true, I would argue y because of z. • X was, in the past, the most important factor but y has changed, making it the real cause.
Clarifying • What the author is saying is . . . • Given that x happened, the author is trying to show . . . • X is not _____ but is, instead, _____ since . . .	**Explaining Importance** • Based on x, people assumed y, which made sense at the time, but now we realize z, which means . . . • This change questions our previous understanding of x, which means that now we must assume . . . • While this conclusion appears insignificant, it challenges our current understanding of x, which means that . . .
Synthesizing • These elements/details, when considered together, suggest . . . • Initial impressions suggested x, but after learning _____ it is now clear that . . . • It is not a question of x but rather of y because . . .	

For more about the use and effectiveness of sentence starters, see "A Cognitive Strategies Approach to Reading and Writing Instruction for English Learners in Secondary School," by Olson and Land in *Research in the Teaching of English* (Feb 2007); to learn more about sentence frames, consult *They Say/I Say: The Moves that Matter in Academic Writing*, by Graff and Birkenstein (Norton 2006).

FIGURE 4.4 Sentence frames designed to help students adopt the academic voice when writing

The Elements of **Effective Writing**

All these new forms raise a set of increasingly complicated questions: Is "writing" merely words or is it evolving into a more complex form? Is there such a thing as a set of traits that apply to all writing—or does each form demand its own unique set of qualities, come with its own conventions that determine how effective the writing is? When we first begin teaching English, we think we know what writing is, how it works, what it is made from; after all, haven't we been doing it for most of our lives—and, since we are college graduates and English teachers(!), doing it well?

We know that good writing must be clear, concise, correct, consistent, cohesive, compelling, and concrete. Williams (2006) adds that good writing must be ethical and elegant, and use whatever structures are necessary to emphasize one idea or detail over another. While related to concision, simplicity is another attribute of good writing according to Zinsser, who commands that we "simplify, simplify . . . [by getting rid of all the] clutter, [which] is the disease of American writing" (1998, 7).

Johnson (2011), offering a more modern take on Zinsser's admonition, coined the term *microstyle*, which applies to everything from text messages and tweets to domain names and slogans. He explains that "the function of microstyle is to get messages noticed, remembered, and passed along" (8). Thus, effective writing, in this more modern context of the attention economy, is not just brief but witty so as to increase the likelihood that someone will choose to read your words over all the others out there and remember them if they do (see Figure 4.5). Instead of emphasizing mere brevity for these micromessages, those messages that "take at most a few seconds to hear or read" (8), Johnson argues that such messages are "about *expressive economy*, a basic design principle that is not limited to verbal messages" (8).

Many now discuss writing in the context of an "economy of attention" (Lanham 2006; Davenport and Beck 2002; Johnson 2011) in which one attempts to "win the battle for attention" (Lanham 2006, viii). Carr goes further, suggesting that the Internet is actually changing our brain and thus "changes in reading style will [necessarily] bring changes in writing style as authors . . . adapt to readers' new habits and expectations" (2010, 104). In short, Carr predicts that word choice will be determined not only by style but also searchability, as all writing increasingly migrates to the Internet. Several other qualities emerge that Strunk and White and Williams and Zinsser never had to consider: brevity, design, readability, and memorability. It is essential to remember: Real writing these days must consider an audience made up of people across the country and around the world.

❝ It is essential to remember: Real writing these days must consider an audience made up of people across the country and around the world. **❞**

Indeed, the very definition of "writing" is growing so loose, as "new literacies" continue to emerge, that we find people referring to "writing with cameras" (Lankshear and Knobel 2006, 203). Others, such as Bruce, enthusiastically discuss "writing as assemblage," by which he means "a process of assemblage . . . aided by the *convergence* of communication technologies [such as] print, images, databases, instant messaging, conferencing, email, fax, radio, video, interactive programs, and virtual reality" (2007, 6). Kress captures the changes these others celebrate, suggesting that "writing as design," which may or may not use words, is a fundamental aspect of writing in a world of "dominance by the screen" (2007, 6). Such new

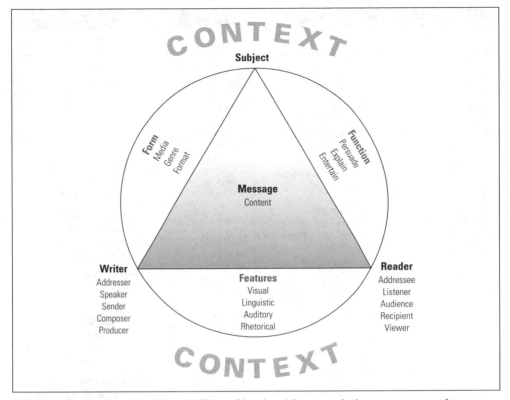

FIGURE 4.5 The New Rhetorical Triangle. The traditional model seems to lack a way to account for many new forms and ways these forms are being used to persuade us.

© 2013 by Jim Burke from *The English Teacher's Companion*, Fourth Edition. Portsmouth, NH: Heinemann.

thinking challenges people, including those revising the AP Language and Composition standards, as they wonder whether a stack of PowerPoint slides is the rhetorical equivalent of the "old school" persuasive essay.

The question is: Do our past notions of the qualities of effective writing still apply regardless of what we are writing—or writing on, or with, or for? Spandel (2009) and Culham (2010) identify the following traits of good writing: ideas, organization, voice, word choice, sentence fluency, conventions, and attention to layout, design, or presentation. Hicks (2009) and Kittle (2008), in their examination of "digital writing" or "new writing," conclude that the qualities of multimodal compositions are more aligned with these traits than anticipated. Hicks observes that the medium often determines the organizing structure, which in turn is driven by the ideas the writer seeks to emphasize; rhetoric furthermore informs the selection of words, organization, and voice in relation to the writer's purpose.

These different models helped me identify what has remained a simple but very effective set of qualities that inform my instruction and thinking about the texts we read and those we write, whether on paper or screens, for pages or slides. Simply called "FODP" in my class, these four elements—Focus, Organization, Development, and Purpose—offer a succinct but useful guide to the territory (see Figure 4.6). They are not meant to capture all the qualities of writing;

Writing FODP

Name: _____ Period: _____ Date: _____

Focus	Organization	Development	Purpose
Subject What you are writing about (e.g., Hamlet, the Depression, modern art)? **Main Idea** What you are trying to say about the subject. This is also known as your "point," as in "What's your *point*?" **Claim** The thesis statement or other statement your essay or paragraph is supposed to prove or defend.	**Cause-Effect** Arranged to show connections between a result and the events that preceded it. Also known as **Problem-Solution**. **Classification** Organized into categories or groups according to various traits. **Comparison-Contrast** Organized to emphasize similarities and differences. **Listing** Arranged in a list with no consideration for other qualities. **Mixed** Organized using a blend of patterns. Might, for example, classify groups while also comparing or contrasting them. **Order of Degree** Organized in order of importance, value, or some other quality. Also known as **Order of Importance**. **Sequential** Arranged in the order that events occur. Also known as **Time** order or **Chronological** order. **Spatial** Arranged according to location or geographical order. Also known as **Geographical order**.	**Examples** Primary text Secondary texts Class discussions Outside world **Details** Sensory Background Factual **Quotations** Direct Indirect Primary text Secondary texts **Explanations** Importance Meaning Purpose Effect **Elaborations** Connections Clarifications Comparisons Contrasts Consequences Concessions	**Cause and Effect** Answers the question, "Why did it happen?" **Classification** Answers the questions, "Which kind is it?" or "What are its parts?" **Compare-Contrast** Answers the questions, "What is it like?" or "How is it different?" **Definition** Answers the question, "What is it?" **Description** Answers the question, "What does it look, sound, smell, taste, or feel like?" **Illustration** Answers the question, "What is an example?" **Narration** Answers the question, "What happened and when?" **Persuasion** Answers the question, "Why should I want to do, think, or value that?" **Problem-Solution** Answers the question, "What is the problem and how can it be solved?" **Process Analysis** Answers the question, "How did it happen?"

FIGURE 4.6 The FODP Model of academic writing is my attempt at a succinct, descriptive model that accounts for the key elements in academic writing. (Originally published in *Tools & Texts for 50 Essential Lessons.*)

still, they give me and my students a way to think and talk about writing—one that demystifies it without simplifying it because these four elements apply to the shortest and simplest page, the longest paper, or a text created for a slide or a smartphone screen.

The Elements of **Effective Writing Instruction**

Now that we know what writing is, the question is *how* to teach it? Nancie Atwell (1998) sums up her evolving notions of writing instruction thus:

> Just as there are times when kids need a mirror, someone to reflect back their writing to them, there are times when they need an adult who will tell them what to do next or how to do it. Bottom line, what they need is a Teacher. Today I'm striving for the fluid, subtle, *exhilarating* balance that allows me to function in my classroom as a listener *and* a teller, an observer *and* actor, a collaborator *and* a critic *and* a cheerleader. (21)

Atwell achieves all this by "handing-over" (19) to the students increasing control of a process in which "an adult intervenes and gradually provides less assistance to the learner" (19). Kittle (2008), applying many of these same ideas in her own high school classroom, concludes that "apprenticeship with a master in the field is still the best model for learning" (8). As Atwell does, Kittle writes with her students, arguing that "you [the teacher] are the most important writer in the classroom . . . a writer just . . . trying to write—like them" (8).

Atwell, too, speaks of overcoming her "anxiety about revealing to the world how hard and slow" writing is for her (1998, 26), but finds this liberated her as both a writer and a teacher, an experience I have had myself and with which I have grown increasingly comfortable. Atwell captures what Kittle describes and I do regularly and, which the instructional findings that follow confirm, makes the difference:

> Most importantly, I take off the top of my head and write out loud in front of them on overhead-projector transparencies. I show them how I plan, change my mind, confront problems, weigh options, make decisions, use conventions to make my writing sound and look the way I want it to and my readers will need it to, and generally compose my life. I'm not writing the great American novel in these demonstrations. I am tackling the tasks that are part of my everyday existence. (25)

Writing Next, a report summing up the research about secondary writing instruction, identifies eleven elements of effective writing instruction, each grounded in research into specific instructional methods that show significant gains in students' writing.

Elements of Effective Writing Instruction

1. **Writing Strategies**, which involves teaching students strategies for planning, revising, and editing their compositions

2. **Summarization**, which involves explicitly and systematically teaching students how to summarize texts

3. **Collaborative Writing**, which uses instructional arrangements in which adolescents work together to plan, draft, revise, and edit their compositions

4. **Specific Product Goals**, which assigns students specific, reachable goals for the writing they are to complete

5. **Word Processing**, which uses computers' word processors as instructional supports for writing assignments

6. **Sentence Combining**, which involves teaching students to construct more complex, sophisticated sentences

7. **Prewriting**, which engages students in activities designed to help them generate or organize ideas for their compositions

8. **Inquiry Activities**, which engages students in analyzing immediate, concrete data to help them develop ideas and content for a particular writing task

9. **Process Writing Approach**, which interweaves a number of writing instructional activities in a workshop environment that stresses extended writing opportunities, writing for authentic audiences, personalized instruction, and cycles of writing

10. **Study of Models**, which provides students with opportunities to read, analyze, and emulate models of good writing

11. **Writing for Content Learning**, which uses writing as a tool for learning content material. (Graham and Perin 2007, 4)

PAUSE & REFLECT After reading through the report's recommendations, identify those you need to work on the most to be a better teacher of writing. Reflect on what you do and do not know, and how you might go about addressing those gaps in your knowledge.

The **Process** of Teaching Writing

When it comes to the writing process model, everyone agrees that there *is* a process; few, however, seem to agree about its stages beyond conceding that it has three parts: before, during, and after. Newkirk (2009a) attempts to remove the clutter from this sphere of the writing curriculum by suggesting five stages: invention, focusing, ordering, revision, and editing (149). Murray, one of the founding fathers of the process model, identifies three stages, which he advises we reapply throughout the process until the piece is done: collect, plan, and develop; then passing "through that same sequence, again and again, emphasizing one stage of the process, or two, or all three—or even part of a stage—doing what is necessary to produce increasingly effective drafts" (2004, 57).

Connors and Glenn list three generic but still useful steps: prewriting, writing, and rewriting (1999, 123). Offering a slightly different version, Flower describes a process that involves planning, generating ideas in words, designing for a reader, revising for effectiveness (1997, 59). My own synthesis of the different models honors these others but offers a variation that accounts for the changing nature (and media) of writing and composing. The model in Figure 4.7

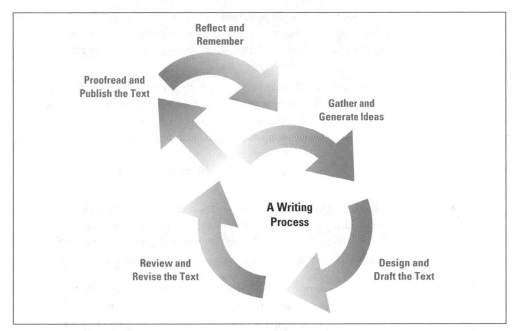

FIGURE 4.7 One view of a writing process we often use in my class. It reminds us all that good writing takes time.

applies to writing not only those traditional forms common to school but also to composing the more modern forms such as slides, tweets, and other digital productions.

Before examining the process, let me briefly describe the stages and provide a rationale for the model in Figure 4.7.

- **Gather and Generate Ideas:** This takes place throughout the composing process, though it is especially important as part of the prewriting stage. As the process unfolds, writers should—as a result of further reading, discussing, or inquiring—continue to seek out and evaluate new ideas or refine those they already had as they learn more. This vital part of the composing process ends only when the paper is complete.

- **Design and Draft the Text:** The word *design* includes planning and organizing, but also those aspects of composition related to newer forms and media—blogs or websites, slideshows and mixed media compositions—that require serious attention to format and function, appearance and substance. Drafting, while common to all writing process models, takes place throughout any composing process since one is always writing to discover what they mean and convey that discovery to the reader. This is what Murray calls a "discovery draft" (2004, 57).

- **Review and Revise the Text:** This stage, which often marks the end of the first phase but not completion of the process, demands that writers check the map to ensure they are still going in the right direction. In this case, the "map" might be the directions on an assignment, the prompt, or just the initial plan the writer had in mind. This stage also asks the writer to begin reading with the reader in mind so as to determine whether it is clear or needs further information or additions (e.g., quotations, images, hyperlinks, infographics, embedded video) to achieve its purpose. It is here that one also reads for clarity and coherence, for style and voice, taking time to revise not only what one wants to say but also how they say it. Again, as with the previous phases of the process, this one continues throughout since, with each change in any one phase of the process, other pieces may need to be refined, replaced, or removed.

- **Proofread and Publish the Text:** As the saying goes, "a piece is never finished, only abandoned." So students (and their teachers) must, at some point, accept that it is finished, that within the constraints of time, topic, and talent, they have done all they can do. All that remains—although it is no small task—is to proofread for errors of any sort, including formatting, citations, and hyperlinks, before submitting it to the teacher, hitting the Post button on the blog, or otherwise sending it out to the audience for which they wrote it.

- **Reflect and Remember:** Once the whole process is complete, students should take time to reflect on the challenges they faced and how they overcame them. Were there questions they asked? Strategies they used? Tricks they tried? These should be identified and stored in some useful way for students to access and use for future assignments.

One could easily describe this process as linear, yet it rarely works that way in practice. The more time we can allow students to work through the back-and-forth, two-steps-forward-three-steps-back process of composition, the more they (and their text) will improve and the more we will have an authentic context within which to teach all the skills and knowledge student writers need if they are to become fluent, effective writers.

Gather and Generate Ideas

Writing is only as good and as interesting as the ideas it examines. As Newkirk says, "for my money, the bias [within the writing process] should always be toward invention, toward generation" (2009a, 149). Nothing makes a greater difference in teaching writing than taking time to generate a rich hoard of ideas and teaching students a range of strategies they can use to come up with such ideas on their own. The time spent preparing students to write particularly benefits ELLs, according to Echvarria, Vogt, and Short (2000, 56). Lindemann (2001) sums up the role of such prewriting (*inventio* in classical rhetoric) and its key benefits in her overview of this phase of the writing process:

> As a rule, the more time spent on a variety of prewriting activities, the more successful the paper will be. In working out the possibilities an assignment suggests, students discover what they honestly want to say and address some of the decisions they must make if the paper is to express a message effectively. Writing the first draft becomes easier because some writing—notes, lists, freewriting—has already taken place. Drafting also becomes more productive because students are less preoccupied with formulating ideas from scratch and freer to discover new messages as the words appear on the page. (110)

This first of several steps in the process is hardly separate; rather, as Flower describes it, "planning, generation, and organization of your ideas form a creative trio" (1997, 127). In other words, good writers "constantly shift back and forth from one mode of thought to another as they work on a problem" (128). The strategies that follow help students generate ideas for either a thesis or supporting ideas within the paper. Such generative thinking, according to Langer

(2002), is necessary for effective literacy instruction in middle and high school (33). As writing comes to blend with and incorporate more media, writers will increasingly have to gather and generate not only ideas and words but also images, diagrams, clips, and design concepts depending on their means, mode, message, and media.

Here, then, are some different ways students can gather and generate ideas, including examples that I show my students using the following strategies. Students use cell phones to look up words in Figure 4.8.

Reading

Students read a range of texts related to the subject with the specific purpose of finding topics or ideas to explore in their papers. Also, they read a variety of models written by other students or professionals (or the teacher) designed to spark ideas for the writing assignment. To prepare for an essay about food (the idea was that we are what we eat), for example, my students read several different food blogs, which I linked to on our class wiki. In addition to the blogs, they read articles, essays, infographics, poems, and photo essays; they also listened to several audio readings from *This I Believe*, *The Kitchen Sisters*, and *This American Life*.

Writing

Students make lists, take notes—from lectures, reading, viewing movies—do freewrites, or use their journals to gather ideas. Flower (1997) distinguishes between brainstorming, which is "a goal-directed search for ideas" (129), and freewriting, suggesting it is most useful when writers "feel blocked or . . . insecure about [their] writing or [their] ability to say anything sensible on the topic" (129). Flower offers three rules to consider when brainstorming: don't censor any possibilities—just write them down; do not try to write "polished prose"; and keep your eye on the question to be answered or problem you are trying to solve.

Brainstorming, Flower reminds us, "is not free association; it is a goal-directed effort to discover ideas relevant to your problem" (129). Online discussions and social networks offer students exciting new ways to use writing to gather and generate ideas, as the example of students using Google Groups to brainstorm ideas for an upcoming paper about *Hamlet* shows (see Figure 4.9a). You might sum up the different types of generative writing here as "writing to think," an idea that many strongly endorse for these early stages of the composing process (Elbow 1990; Zinsser 1998; Murray 2004). Also see Figures 4.9b and 4.9c.

Speaking

Students talk with neighbors to spark new ideas; they also discuss ideas in larger groups, in full-class discussions, or through online discussions. During such conversations, students capture ideas in notebooks, on organizers, butcher paper, transparencies, Smart Boards or other electronic devices designed to record information. Depending on the topic, students can interview each other, experts, members of the

FIGURE 4.8 Girls in my senior class use the dictionary function on their cell phones to look up the etymologies of words as a way to generate ideas for analyzing a poem we read in class that day.

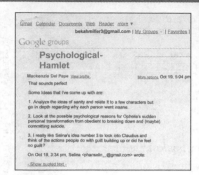

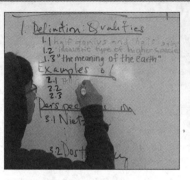

FIGURE 4.9a Mackenzie and her group used the online discussion group they set up to generate possible ideas for an upcoming paper on *Hamlet*.

FIGURE 4.9b Carlos adds to our "whiteboard wiki," which we used to capture and organize our ideas prior to a discussion about different conceptions of the "superman" idea in *Crime and Punishment*.

FIGURE 4.9c Hannah and Eunice capture their visual explanation of tragedy using a cell phone. They then sent the image to their other group members who subsequently incorporated the image into their essays.

community, or their families for additional ideas and alternative perspectives. Boscolo and Gelati (2008) found that "collective discussion," when combined with writing, further aided idea generation and had the added benefit of increasing student motivation for the writing assignment (214). A study by Nystrand (2006) also confirmed the value of purposeful discussion in helping students harvest new ideas and revise old ones (101).

Heuristics

Students use a variety of devices—questions, categories, analogies, lists, topics—to jump-start their brain for ideas or synthesize several into one compelling, specific idea. Olson and Land (2007) single out cognitive strategies—planning and goal setting, tapping prior knowledge, asking questions—as particularly effective when working with diverse student populations, in particular ELLs (277). Specific sets of questions, often referred to as the Reporter's Questions, offer an efficient means of generating ideas: who, what, when, where, why, how (to which some suggest adding, so what).

Visuals

Students work alone or with others to create clusters, mind maps, or other visual representations of their ideas. Some techniques, such as mind maps, anticipate and prepare for the drafting phase by establishing the connections between ideas. Students can also develop ideas by using graphic organizers and software applications such as Glogster or Inspiration. Although it could be placed under other categories, outlining has more in common with visual strategies such as mapping since it shows the relationship between ideas and the categories into which they might be sorted; like mapping, it also serves as a half-step toward drafting.

Finally, graphic organizers and structured note-taking tools offer another powerful strategy for generating and organizing ideas, typically in a more spatial format than the other techniques listed. Figure 4.10 offers a range of tools to consider. These visual tools often work best

The Shapes of Thought: Tools for Writers and Readers

Shape	Variations	Discussion
1. Circle		Circles suggest cycles, spaces, objects, towers, rings, and concentric waves radiating out from a disturbing force. Circles imply boundaries to keep out—and in. Such circles also call to mind the round table, different personae, and the notion of the center.
2. Square		Squares evoke strength, the shape suggesting four walls, space, balance on all sides. Within the walls, within the space, division can occur, most commonly into quadrants or halves, though other spaces are possible.
3. Triangle		The triangle evokes the idea of foundations and hierarchies; it also emphasizes the idea of foundations and thus strength. Triangles by their nature have different sides, not all equal, as with status and perspective. When drawn in three dimensions, triangles become pyramids.
4. Spreadsheet	Spreadsheet Matrix	Spreadsheets suggest logic or order; they also emphasize relationships and associated criteria used to examine such relationships. It can also be reduced to two columns (T-chart) or formatted as a matrix for comparing items against an array of factors or elements.
5. Arc	Beginning End Bridge Fall	The arc, when applied to a story, represents the growth (or evolution) over time of a character, business, or other narrative subject. Such change comes in response to events experienced over time. The arc also serves as a bridge, the process of crossing over from one phase to another.
6. Graph	x y x y	Graphs give us ways to think about events across time and the factors that affect them. This format also suggests levels and relationships between elements. A useful tool when analyzing trends, changes, effects, and relationships between key factors.
7. Branches	A B A C B tournament branches	Branches symbolize the fork-in-the-road moments when we see multiple options and must consider which one to take (or which one others might take in a given situation). Such a "decision tree" emphasizes the extent to which authors, people, or organizations have options and invite readers to examine what affects those decisions.
8. Storyboard		Though not a shape, the storyboard is a tool that reveals the episodic nature of events or stories, and invites us to consider how one episode relates to another—or does not. Also allows user to combine visual thinking and writing. Storyboards are not meant to be works of art; they are spaces in which to visually represent and examine how different elements in a story relate to and affect each other.

FIGURE 4.10 Tools for Writers. The primary shapes in the left column are those that, over time, I have come to use the most often. Their shapes are familiar and natural, thus allowing for easier and more effective use than traditional graphic organizers.

in conjunction with writing and speaking, thus allowing students to elaborate on their thinking as represented on the page. Marzano (2007) found such visual strategies to be very effective, as have others (Burke 2002; Buehl 2009; Hyerle 2009) for generating and giving shape to ideas. The three images in Figure 4.11 show students using visuals to generate ideas.

DESIGN AND DRAFT YOUR DOCUMENT

Regardless of how writing evolves, ideas will always remain at the core of the enterprise; as we have discussed already, though, the nature of writing itself—how it looks, what it is made of, what it is written with, for, on—is changing. This becomes more apparent when we move into the act of actually composing, taking those ideas and accompanying details—examples, quotations, information—and deciding how to arrange them rhetorically, stylistically, or visually. It is this notion of purpose—the idea that we are trying to accomplish something through the act of writing—that shapes the choices we make during this stage of the composing process.

As with the first stage, during which students gather and generate ideas, this next phase requires time, because good, real *writing requires time*. To write is to *think*—at least it should be. The essay should be treated as an invitation to explore, to reflect, to persuade; it is not a form to be filled out, nor is each paragraph a box into which a certain number of items should be stuffed. The real spirit of this phase, then, is to discover what you have to say about the idea(s) you chose from that first step of the process and figure out how you can best say it. Newkirk (2005) expresses best what I am saying here: "Do current approaches to teaching expository writing promote or do they actually foreclose possibilities for open-ended, conversation-like, exploration? Or does the 'thesis-control essay' . . . actually limit the inquiry that writing supposedly should foster?" (33).

Thus students, at this stage, must not only begin gathering additional ideas but also coming up with the way to arrange them that will, to borrow from Newkirk, "open" instead of "foreclose" thinking. It also means deciding whether words alone are adequate to the task or whether you should consider including images, hyperlinks, diagrams, or (eventually) even embedded video into your text. In my class, and many others', it now also means asking whether the "paper" should even be written on paper or should (as with my freshman class' multimedia essay about "what it takes to be a survivor") be written for the screen, using an application like PowerPoint, so that you can incorporate color, images, video, sound—and, of course, words.

As students compose for ever more interactive, mixed media environments, they will have to think, as this stage says, like "designers" as they draft, making crucial decisions throughout the remainder of the process about not only the content of their message but the form and function of the text itself and the features they choose to use, including fonts, colors, and layout. (See Figure 4.12.) Several key elements of this stage emerge as challenges, each with its own difficulties:

- Discovering what it is the writer wants to say about the subject
- Establishing a controlling idea or focus to the paper
- Arranging ideas to achieve a purpose
- Adding ideas, details, quotations, images or graphics to the draft

As we have already discussed, there are many different types of writing appropriate to the English class; here, however, we focus primarily on expository prose in general and the

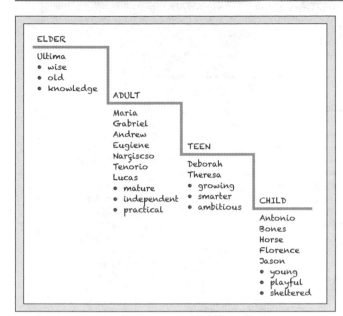

FIGURE 4.11a The stages of life shown here illustrates a more analytical approach to reading the book; students are then ready to write with greater insights about it and its ideas.

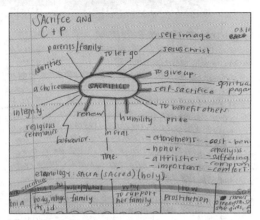

FIGURE 4.11b Sample from a student's notebook showing the use of visual thinking to generate ideas for subsequent writing assignments that also help them read more closely

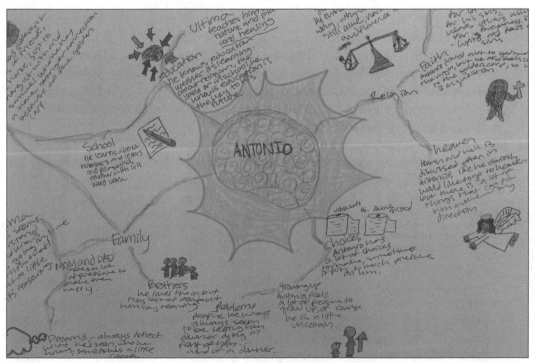

FIGURE 4.11c This visual explanation of the relationships between different characters in Anaya's *Bless Me, Ultima* builds a better understanding even as it prepares them to write more analytically.

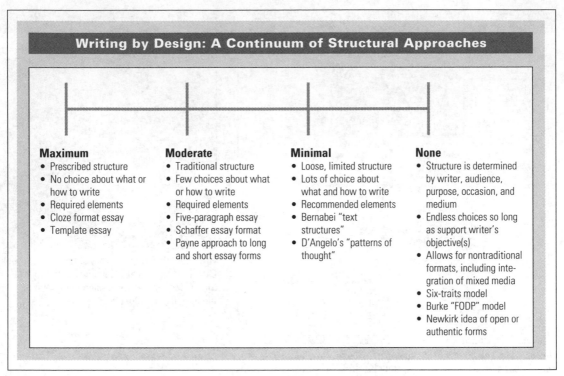

FIGURE 4.12 Writing by Design: A Continuum of Structural Approaches

academic essay in particular as that remains one of the greater challenges all students face. The "schoolified essay" (Bernabei 2005) is too easily reduced to triangles and rectangles (Payne 1969, 41). This traditional model, along with those of Jane Schaffer and the Six-Traits models, form something of a continuum. As Bernabei notes, "within the recommended structures are tons of variation and possibilities, all leading to lots of choices. It's all in the implementation" [of these structures] (personal communication 2010).

Students routinely move back and forth along this continuum as they attempt increasingly difficult assignments and topics. I certainly see this developmental progression play out in my classes, both college prep and AP Literature. Students entering in August show a fierce adherence to the five-paragraph format (see Figure 4.13), which seems to offer the comfort and security of childhood's blanket that many clung to with such tenacity. Of course, when I ask them what they will do in college given that most papers are expected to be at least 10-pages long, they get a confused look, wrinkle their brows, and say, "Hmmm, yeah. . . . I hadn't really thought about that. . . ."

As Corbett and Connors point out, there comes a time when the writer must "[select] material [from all that they have generated and gathered] and put [it] in some order, for without order, the force of even the best material, though chosen with the keenest discretion, will be weakened" (1999, 250). A certain tension, more intensely felt for some than for others, characterizes this stage of writing. This tension boils down to structural control and the extent to which students are allowed to choose and approach a topic in their own way. Ironically, Payne

(1969), who goes on to offer a highly structured model of the inverted triangles with which we are so familiar, proclaims that "a student is no machine when he writes an essay; he is a human being—judging, evaluating, interpreting, expressing not only what he knows but what he *is*. Thus every attempted essay is a kind of voyage toward self-discovery" (14). It is this notion of discovery that Murray (2004, 51) emphasizes, insisting that students be allowed to work like real writers, who want first to find out what they think—something the highly structured model Payne offers prevents since it suggests the writer already knows what they think before they even begin writing.

I use the following techniques in my classes, with kids of all grade and ability levels, to help them through the design and draft phase, which begins with students figuring out what

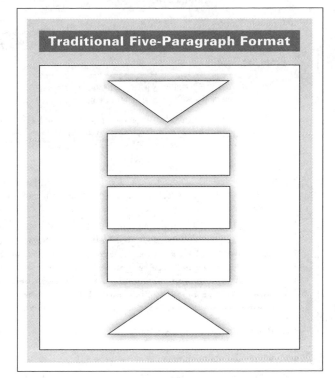

FIGURE 4.13 The traditional five-paragraph format

they want to know and what they think they will learn about their chosen topics after gathering all those ideas about it. One way of doing this, which I use for bigger, more formal papers, is to have students write a proposal for the paper they want to write (see Figure 4.14); a less formal variation would be to ask them to jot down their ideas and goals for the paper on an index card that I can approve or use to help them refine their thinking. This has the benefit of not only helping them improve their ideas, but also teaching them some real-world writing skills as many professions require people to submit proposals.

Once students have some sense of what their topic is and what they want to say about it, we often take time (usually a full period) to craft a *working* thesis using the Thesis Generator (Figure 4.15). This working thesis functions more like what Murray calls a "focal point" (2004, 18) or what I describe as a "focus line" (Burke 2009, 40). The idea is not to lock in a claim but to establish a "focus line" as a map for the territory ahead (see Figure 4.16), the sort of thing Lewis and Clark might have drawn out to represent what they thought they might see on their journey; of course, they had to begin revising as they learned more about the territory through which they passed.

When helping students through this phase, I give each of them a printed copy of the Thesis Generator then display the same handout on the screen. Moving back and forth, from my model and our discussion of it, to their emerging thesis, we spend the period engaged in close discussion about ideas, what a thesis is, what it must accomplish, what makes one better than another—or not a thesis at all. By period's end, students leave ready to start the next

Hamlet Critical Theory Paper Proposal Worksheet

Proposal Details

1. **Critical Theory**: Which theory have you focused on while reading *Hamlet*? What interests you most about this theory as you understand it at this point? Why does that interest you?

   While reading *Hamlet*, our group focused on the Psychological critical theory. What interests me about this topic is that it deals with analyzing the mind and how it works. This interests me because it enables us to better understand human behavior and provides reasoning behind one's actions.

2. **Focus**: What is the *subject* (e.g., madness, power, identity) of your paper? What is it about that subject that interests you? What will you say about this subject? Why does this interest you? How would it help you or your readers better understand *Hamlet*?

   The subject of my paper will be about Hamlet's sanity throughout the play and if he is actually turning mad or just pretending. Also, I will include the idea of cognitive dissonance and how Hamlet is faced with conflicting thoughts. I think these ideas are interesting because even though you may think someone sane, they could be fighting internal battles that the outside person knows nothing about. This will help us understand *Hamlet* in that we will better understand why Hamlet does what he does and what drives him to do so. It also helps us grasp whether Hamlet is fully conscious of what he is doing.

3. **Organization:** How will you organize your paper? What are the chunks and how will they be arranged? Why those chunks and this arrangement?

   I will start the paper off by describing Hamlet in his actions and thoughts that he expresses to the reader in the play. I will then go deeper in analyzing what these actions or thoughts mean in psychology terms. Then I will make the claim, using the analysis I have created of Hamlet, of whether he is sane or not by the end of the play. I feel this arrangement is best because it shows example, analysis, and reasoning behind my claim/thesis.

4. **Development**: What evidence, details, examples, or key quotations will you use to support and illustrate your main idea? What are the sources of your information?

   The evidence I will use to support my main idea is mostly the soliloquies Hamlet has in the plays. These soliloquies are good examples of Hamlet's saneness and shows when Hamlet loses control of himself, but also how he gains back control of his emotions. Also, it's good evidence because he is alone in these scenes and there is no one around to influence his behavior. Seeing how he behaves alone tells a lot about his mental state.

5. **Purpose**: What are you trying to achieve in this paper? How will the contents of the previous answers help you achieve this purpose?

   In this paper I will try to come to a consensus on Hamlet's state of mind throughout the play. I will try to make a justified claim on whether he is sane or insane. By creating a psychological analysis of Hamlet, I will be able to come to this conclusion.

6. **So What?** What is the *So what?* about your paper? What are you trying to say and why should we find it so interesting or important? Why should we care?

   So what? Well, by understanding Hamlet's state of mind, we will then be able to better understand why Hamlet behaves the way he does. We will be able to comprehend the things we were unsure of before and come to a new consensus of Hamlet's character, or find that our original view of Hamlet was accurate. Our view of Hamlet will be sharpened with this psychological analysis.

FIGURE 4.14 Meaghan's *Hamlet* paper proposal. Note how much thinking she has to do to conceive of the paper before ever writing it. All authors have to first submit proposals for the books they want to write.

The Thesis Generator	
For a literary paper, I use the following:	
1. Identify the *subject* of your paper	The development of one's own identity.
2. Turn your subject into a guiding question	How does a young man go about developing his own identity apart from his parents?
3. Answer your question with a statement	Telemachus realizes that he must set out on his own journey to find his identity.
4. Refine this statement into a *working* thesis	In the absence of his father, Telemachus assumes the role, sending himself on a quest that will transform him into the man he needs to be.

1. Identify the *subject* of your paper	
2. Turn your subject into a guiding question	
3. Answer your question with a statement	
4. Refine this statement into a *working* thesis	

For a nonliterary paper, I use the following variation:	
1. Identify the *subject* of your paper	Relationships between teenagers and their parents.
2. Turn your subject into a guiding question	How does the relationship between teenagers and their parents change?
3. Answer your question with a statement	As teens grow more independent, they resent and resist the limitations and expectations their parents impose on them.
4. Refine this statement into a *working* thesis	Conflict between teenagers and their parents is a difficult but necessary stage in kids' development.

FIGURE 4.15 The Thesis Generator for both literary and nonliterary papers

phase: designing or downloading (from their brain) the draft, which often means drafting the first page and listing out the chunks and rationale for their importance and placement, and notes about where they should go for the rest of the paper.

Defining Terms

Argument: the reason(s) one gives to persuade others that a certain action or idea is right

Assertion: a statement of fact or belief made with great confidence or force

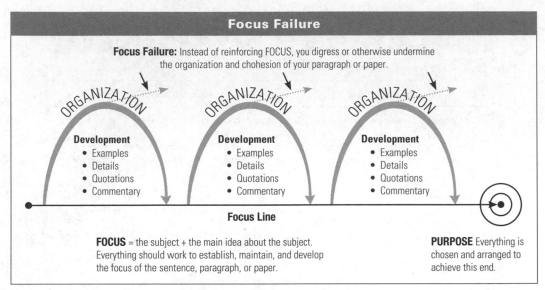

FIGURE 4.16 The Focus Line, a diagram I often draw on the whiteboard or on paper during writing conferences to reinforce the importance of structure. Each arch represents a paragraph or chunk of the essay.

Claim: something one states or asserts is true, but must support

Opinion: a statement or judgment not based on fact or knowledge

Proposition: a statement expressing a judgment or opinion

Thesis: a theory or statement one puts forward as a premise one must prove

---

Lindemann suggests a technique she calls "'chunking' which resembles more closely . . . what writers do as they shape a draft" (2001, 138). Such thinking, which is more visual and schematic, helps generate new ideas, new connections, and new possibilities (see Figure 4.17). At this stage, it is essential that writers' minds remain open to new insights and connections (see Figure 4.18). Moreover, such thinking promotes greater creativity, inviting students to open instead of limit their minds. A number of leading advocates for the importance of creativity (Hyerle 2009; Buehl 2009; Buzan 2010) single out visual, generative approaches for their ability to reveal the new, the unsuspected, the undiscovered angle.

Chunks offer the added benefit of not evolving into paragraphs at this point; they are merely units of thought, each of which consists of however many paragraphs the writer decides they need to fully develop their focus. They also allow the writer to examine the rhetorical relationship between them. Those students wishing to be more tactile and manipulative might consider writing chunks on index cards or even sticky notes so that they can experiment with different arrangements. Those wishing to use more digital formats could try applications, such as *Inspiration* or *Glogster*, or use features such as Notebook View or Outline View in Microsoft Word.

Chunking

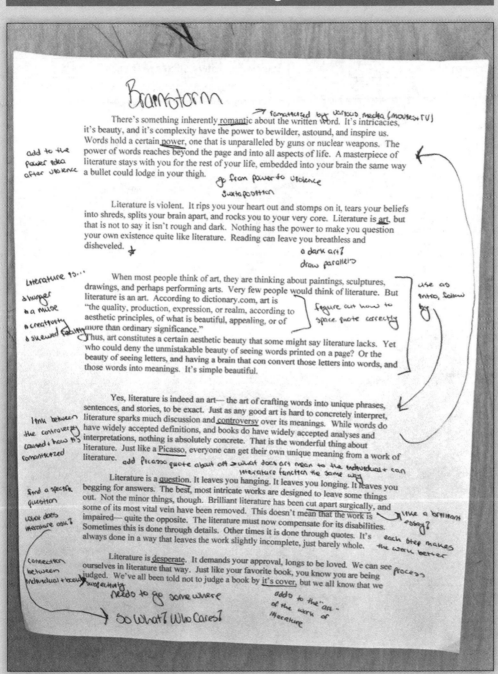

FIGURE 4.17 Here Rachel "chunks" her ideas about literature for a paper in which students had to define just what counts as literature in a world of so many different changing forms and formats.

The following "moves" are designed to help students write more effective analytical sentences and paragraphs. While many of these examples complement each other (e.g., you could organize a paragraph around an analogy in order to define something), they often work fine or even best on their own. The goal here is to help students arrange their ideas and paragraphs as they draft and revise in light of their purpose.

Type and Description	Sample Expository Sentence Frames
Analogy Connects things or ideas based on common elements, such as structure or qualities, to illustrate or emphasize similarities and/or differences.	• Despite their relationship, they were more like enemies than allies . . . • His mind, by this point, resembled a pinball machine as ideas bounced . . . • Like a game of chess, the plot advanced, guided not by x but y.
Cause and Effect Examines and reveals causes, effects—or both. Explaining **why** focuses on causes; focusing on **what** did, will, or could happen involves effects.	• It was x, not y, that explained his decision to do z. • Doing x caused y, which ultimately led to z, an outcome that shows . . . • True, x stemmed from y, but z did not; rather, z was caused by a and b.
Chronological Emphasizes time sequences to show when things happened, the order in which they occurred. Used to describe events, processes, experiences.	• After x happened, y began, which led to z, the final phase of . . . • First, they did x, after which they did y, all of which culminated in z. • They tried x; then they attempted y; finally, they turned to z.
Classification Breaks down or links subjects and processes based on differences (divisions) or similarities (classes).	• X belonged to a class of people who . . . • Among them there were differences which at first were not apparent . . . • X and Y rejected z; however, Y, as a member of the _____ class, accepted . . .
Comparison and Contrast Focuses on the similarities to compare; examines the differences to contrast. It's possible, even wise, to both compare *and* contrast.	• X and Y were both z, while A and B were c . . . • X shared the sentiments of Y but not Z, believing . . . • Though X and Y agreed that . . . . Y alone argued that . . .
Definition Explains what something means, what it is, in order to define; clarifies how it is similar to or different from other ideas, subjects, to define it by classifying or comparing/contrasting.	• By any measure, by any criteria, x was . . . • X was y but not z, a but not b . . . . • According to X, Y was . . . a as well as b . . .
Illustration Shows what we mean, what something looks like in order to *illustrate* our point by using examples to clarify or define.	• One example of x appears early on when Y does z . . . • X proves this when he does y, a gesture that clearly shows z . . . . • In case we doubted that X was y, we need only remember that he . . .
List Provides a string of reasons, examples, ideas, features, or other factors; tries to make a point by repetition, quantity of examples, or force of multiples.	• X was many things. It was y but also z. It was a and b. It was also c and d. • Everyone had a theory about x. Y thought . . . Z argued . . . . A believed . . . . • At this point, he offered a string of reasons for his actions. He said he did it because of x. He then said he did it for y. Then he said it was really z . . .
Narration Uses stories and anecdotes to illustrate ideas or make a point. Narrative power stems from its ability to inspire, or move people.	• One time, X left for y, heading off to discover z, an experience that . . . • He had, in the past, done x but only when he began to suffer from . . . • They were different from others; they would run away and be happy . . .
Pros and Cons Considers the pros and cons (ad/disadvantages) in order to allow/force readers to consider a subject or choice from multiple perspectives.	• Of course x offered advantages, chief among them being y, which . . . • One could not consider x without realizing y, which was unacceptable . . . • True, x was . . . ; however, y offered an alternative, one that promised . . .

FIGURE 4.18 Patterns and Purposes: A summary of the different ways we can organize and frame our ideas

Type and Description	Sample Expository Sentence Frames
Problem and Solution Emphasizes the problem(s) or identifies solution(s) by way of framing the subject, process, or argument.	• X lacks y, which means z will have to happen. • The cause of x is most often y; however, x can be solved by doing z. • Many argue that X undermines Y, causing it to . . . ; however, Z addresses . . .
Process Focuses on the steps or causes that led to the result or current situation; emphasizes the causes and effects; can be mental, physical, or structural.	• Such a problem does not happen all at once, but in stages . . . • While he seems to have suddenly become x, the truth is that it was the culmination of many such small decisions, each of which led to . . . • X slowly begins to reveal y, which leads to z and, eventually, a and even b.
Spatial Emphasizes the location, arrangement, or direction of elements, people, processes; helps readers visualize what it looks like or how x relates to y within a space.	• Upon entering x you see y near z; look to the left of z to find a . . . • X appears between y and z, which results in a further down the page. • In the first quatrain, the poet does x; in the next two, however, he . . .
Agree Refers to another's point and explains why you agree with or support the idea. May involve a *brief* summary of the other's idea to create context for your agreement.	• X argues . . . , a point I agree with since it suggests . . . • In her article, X states that . . . which confirms my assertion that . . . • X could only be y, something Jones verifies in her article, saying . . .
Disagree Refers to another's point and explains why you disagree or oppose it. May involve a *brief* summary of other's idea to create context for your opposition or rejection.	• While X says . . . , this makes little sense in light of . . . • True, x is . . . , but Y forgets . . . , which undermines her argument by . . . • Several argue that x is . . . ; however, I disagree as it is clear that . . .
Agree *and* Disagree Refers to another's point and explains why you both agree *and* disagree. May involve a *brief* summary of the other's idea to create context for your position(s).	• Yes, x is . . . , a point clearly established by Y early on; however, this same point comes into question later, when Z demonstrates . . . . • It is not difficult to see that both are correct: X is, as Jones (2007) says, crazy; X is also, however, as Smith (2002) shows . . . • I agree that X is . . . but reject the notion that X could be . . .
Acknowledge Alternatives Recognizes that academic writing makes a claim of some sort; inevitably, others will accept or reject this claim; anticipates and discusses these "naysayers," using their counterarguments to further clarify and emphasize your own argument.	• Some will argue that x is, in fact, y, a point many (Jones 2007; Smith 2002) bring up when considering z. • Indeed, as many have noted, x is y, even, in some cases, z. • Not everyone agrees, however. Jones (2007) contends . . . Others, including Smith (2002), go so far as to argue . . . .
Alternative Strategies Recognizes that in addition to other strategies that are equally useful but fall between the tidy definitions offered above.	• *Element-by-Element*: Each ¶ focuses on a different element of the subject. • *Text-by-Text*: Each ¶ focuses on a different text in relation to the subject. • *Idea-by-Idea*: Each ¶ focuses on a different idea within the text. • *Character-by-Character*: Each ¶ focuses on character A or B (or C and D). • *Event-by-Event*: Each ¶ focuses on a different event and its relationship to those that came before it (e.g., the relationship between each of Hamlet's soliloquies and how they evolve and build on each other).

FIGURE 4.18 *Continued*

Sample of D'Angelo's Paradigms

Definition Paradigm

- Extended Definition A
  - Introduction (includes logical definition)
  - Expansion of the genus
  - Expansion of the differentia
  - Conclusion (includes clincher sentence)

- Extended Definition B
  - Introduction (includes logical definition)
  - Supporting details
  - Supporting details
  - Conclusion (includes clincher sentence)

- Extended Definition C
  - Introduction (includes thesis)
  - Meaning 1 (partial definition of key term)
  - Meaning 2 (partial definition of key term)
  - Meanings 3, 4, 5, . . .
  - Conclusion (includes clincher sentence)

Classification Paradigm

- Introduction (includes thesis)
- Type 1 (or subclass 1)
- Type 2 (or subclass 1)
- Types 3, 4, 5, . . .
- Conclusion (includes clincher sentence)

In addition to chunking, Lindemann (2001) and others (D'Angelo 1985; Bernabei 2005) suggest more structured but no less generative approaches to designing and drafting the paper. D'Angelo's "paradigms" demystify with and clarify the "moves" or "chunks" of various academic essays. In the sidebar, for example, are two sample paradigms teachers might use or adapt to illustrate the structure of the definition and classification paradigms.

Throughout this design and drafting phase, many writers—I am certainly one of them—need feedback, need to talk about and share their ideas to help them find the way to tell their story or structure their arguments. Whether this means first verbally rehearsing their essays by talking about their ideas or having their drafts read by a trusted (but critical) friend then discussing it with me or their peers (in class or online), this is an important part of what Bernabei calls "fleshing it out" (see Figure 4.19). During my conversation with Marissa (Figure 4.20), for example, we considered other ways she might arrange ideas in her *Hamlet* paper, chunking it out character by character, idea by idea, event by event, change by change—the decision about which approach to take depending on her goal.

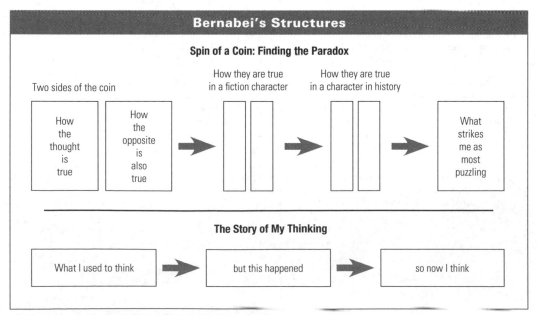

Bernabei's Structures

Spin of a Coin: Finding the Paradox

Two sides of the coin | How they are true in a fiction character | How they are true in a character in history

How the thought is true → How the opposite is also true → → What strikes me as most puzzling

The Story of My Thinking

What I used to think → but this happened → so now I think

FIGURE 4.19 Gretchen Bernabei offers an effective alternative to chunking and other models through her essay "kernels," in her book *Reviving the Essay* (2005).

Having taken this time to develop a schema for their ideas, students are now ready to begin actually *writing*. In this case, since we are focusing on academic or analytical writing, let us consider the introduction and how to help students write one, now that they have a working thesis—or at least a focus. I provide students with the "Introductions" handout, though most textbooks offer some version of the list shown in Figure 4.21a. After discussing introductions as a whole class, we examine several examples, each one taking a different approach or using a different voice. I display these on the whiteboard via my projector so I can annotate them—with a marker, or by using features within Microsoft Word such as color, bold, or highlighting.

FIGURE 4.20 Marissa and I confer at the front of the class while others respond to classmates' papers during a writing workshop.

I then send students home to write a draft of their introduction. I tell them that as a writer I nearly always toss out my initial introduction once I really know what I am trying to say (often replacing it with my conclusion, at which point I finally realize what I am trying to say in the essay).

When students come in the next day with their introductions, I ask them to draft two additional leads for the same paper, choosing two different strategies from the list of possible ways to begin their essays. I usually give students minimal time (10–15 minutes) to create a sense of urgency but also to bypass the brain's initial resistance and force them to just get it done. Students then trade the three introductions they now have—one from the previous night's homework and the two they just wrote—with peers who must then identify the lead they think is most effective (see Figure 4.21b). Respondents need to explain which one they like best and why, passing it then to a second reader who should not know which one the previous respondent liked most.

More often than not, it's the third introduction—the one the student wrote in class, under pressure—that emerges as the favorite. Why? Because students have begun to write their way into their topics and, consequently, their papers, and are thus gaining a footfold on both what they want to say and how they want to say it. Whenever possible (or necessary), I create three sample introductions myself to help students see what I mean and to better understand the demands of writing such essays. I cannot emphasize enough how much I learn from doing—even just part of—my own assignments.

> **"**I CANNOT EMPHASIZE ENOUGH HOW MUCH I LEARN FROM DOING—EVEN JUST PART OF—MY OWN ASSIGNMENTS.**"**

Now that students have a focus and some form of an introduction, they need to generate complete drafts, which means most of them need time for a whole new round of gathering and generating ideas. Depending on the book we are reading or the type of essay we might be writing, I sometimes find that a visual arrangement (see Figure 4.22a about *Siddhartha*) is more useful as students look for ways to capture when, how, and why the character changes over the course of the book, and the

Crafting a Strong Introduction

Effective Introductions:

- Establish the focus by introducing the subject, narrowing it down, and making a statement (claim, thesis statement) about the subject.

- Place the **thesis statement** near or at the end of the introductory paragraph. It is the main point you will try to prove.

- Try one of the following strategies for an effective introduction:

  - Use an intriguing **quotation** or series of quotations.

  - Ask a **question** or pose a series of questions about the subject.

  - Begin by **defining** the subject (though avoid the overly familiar "According to *American Heritage Dictionary*, a crime is a . . . ").

  - Make an unexpected or compelling **comparison**.

  - Open with a **controversial statement** that challenges but does not offend or distract from the point you want to make.

  - Lead with a relevant but engaging **anecdote**.

- Introductions should **draw the reader in** with the promise of new insights or information about a subject that interests them.

- Introductions should **establish your credibility** as a writer through a combination of *what* you say and *how* you say it.

- Introductions should **set up some sense of structure** so that the reader knows **how information will be organized** and can read it effectively.

FIGURE 4.21a Effective introductions

stages into which his journey can be divided for further analysis. Figure 4.22b offers several other approaches to consider.

Sometimes students need the visual of an actual sample paper like the one they are writing. I provide such examples in different ways. When we are just focusing on how to begin, for example, I sometimes project a sample of a successful beginning page from a previous student's essay on the whiteboard. We then discuss what makes it effective as I underline and circle different elements by way of trying to illustrate what they need to do.

Another variation of this approach is to fire up the LCD projector and stand at the laptop facilitating discussion about, for example, *Siddhartha*. When an idea comes into focus, I will say to the whole class, "What I hear you saying is that (and I will begin typing) 'As a result of his experiences with a variety of teachers, Siddhartha comes to realize that he must be his own teacher.' Does that capture what you were just saying?" If it does, kids can write it down as is or in their own words. I will use the color feature of Word to make that sentence red on the screen to indicate it is our focus line, the one we need to unpack and develop. We call this collaborative writing in the class.

FIGURE 4.21b Fiona, Dana, and Margarita swap and read each others' papers as they learn how to write strong introductions.

We then go from there, discussing and drafting together as we hear the language of our ideas emerge; all the while, I am telling them they can write down initial sentences exactly as we compose them or, if they prefer (and are more confident), in their own voices. Once they know what the writing assignment should look and sound like, I turn students lose to write the rest of it on their own. On other occasions, depending on my students' needs, I use the more guided

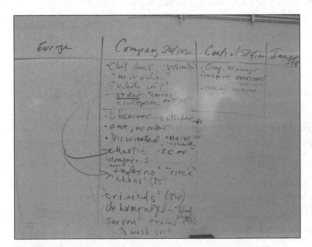

FIGURE 4.22a Notes generated in the form of a spreadsheet or matrix help establish order but also reveals more subtle connections for many writers.

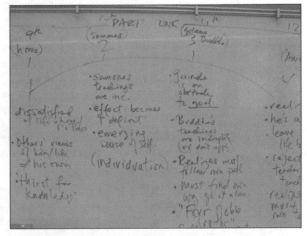

FIGURE 4.22b Visual formats allow us to see how one idea or section in a story relates to another.

FIGURE 4.23a Jesus and Carmen respond to others' writing as part of the process in the early stages of drafting the paper.

FIGURE 4.23b Students eventually end up on-line, responding to each others' papers using Microsoft's Track Changes feature or a similar function in Google Docs.

approach of a cloze sentence as a lead ("Of the many words one might use to describe Huck Finn, none fits better than _____."); I put it on the board and ask students to generate possible ideas to fill in the blank before we choose one and begin to draft the introduction together, as I stand ready at the laptop, facilitating our conversation—and the composing process (Figure 4.23a).

One final strategy, a variation on collaborative writing, is to have students draft their papers using Google Docs. During this process, students write papers and send invitations to classmates, asking them to read and respond to the drafts as they are creating them. Using annotation tools and other features of Google Docs, students suggest ideas and connections to peers. While they are in the computer lab, students sometimes search for links, images, or infographics to incorporate into their papers as they shape ideas into the draft (Figure 4.23b). Some begin to realize that instead of writing a whole paragraph about Maslow's hierarchy of human needs or the journey cycle, they might insert a graphic in much the same way they would an example or commentary. Such images and other embedded media can also be added later, during the revision process, as writers begin to realize they might save space and make their point more effectively with an image, graphic, or embedded media clip. To this end, I encourage them not to stop drafting in order to go find or to create such content, but to put a placeholder in the text (e.g., "Find image related to x and put here"), then return later to clean up any such loose ends when they are ready.

Before we proceed to the next stage, which involves reviewing and revising the draft students have now written, let us briefly revisit two important parts of this phase: responding to students' writing and generating further ideas. The role of responding to student writing (and writers) is crucial at this stage. Our conversation with them about their paper unfolds throughout the process, taking place during both structured and impromptu conferences in class, with each other as well as with me. Often, though not always nor for all students, this conversation extends beyond the classroom, occurring online through opportunities they seek out or I create (see Figures 4.24a and b).

On some occasions, I realize students will be writing, for example, their in-class essays about their independent-reading books, or there will be some other occasion—say, counselors

FIGURE 4.24a Dana and I demonstrate for the class how to respond to each others' papers before I turn the class over to their peer response groups.

FIGURE 4.24b Matthew and Jan apply the strategies Dana and I modeled. Such modeling and the opportunity for structured, targeted response are helpful for all students but especially English learners such as Matthew (*left*).

coming in for the period or mandatory district testing—when I can collect drafts and give them a quick but useful response (*yes, to all 35 papers*) by the end of our 51-minute period! How do I do that? I scan through the papers until I see two or three patterns or issues and then jot those as bullets (e.g., • Elaboration, • Examples!) at the top. If they do not know what the bullets refer to, they can ask me later that period and then address these needs for homework that night.

As Sommers notes, when responding to student writers, "the most articulate and insightful comments will have no influence on students if they don't understand how to use them" (2010). More recently, computer and smartphone applications have become available that allow me to give, in Sommers' words, more "articulate and insightful comments" because I can simply talk to the student as I read, narrating my thinking and responses without having to struggle with whether to take the time to write my illegible comments (which must then be translated in class by me or those who accept the challenge and become expert crytographers).

One example of such a response in our class is a 10-page College Prep senior English paper that we spent a long time working on and receiving feedback on throughout the process. The comments can run to a length we would never write by hand; yet when responding orally, using appropriate software, you are hardly aware of it until you finish. Thus, one has the feeling of effortlessly responding in much greater depth and at greater length. A variation on dictated comments would be to use your cell phone to record and send your notes to students as an attachment for them to listen to while they go through their own papers.

PAUSE & REFLECT Describe your own experience with and attitude toward revision as a writer and a teacher. A student once snapped at me, "If I want praise, I can have my mother read it. Tell me what I'm doing wrong so I can improve!" What would you say to him?

Review and Revise

Revision is not a linear, paint-by-numbers process in which writers move from one phase to the next as Britton suggests in his description of the writing process as "a series of stages described in metaphors of linear growth, conception—incubation—production" (Sommers 2009, 323). Rather, the composing process is recursive, looping back on itself as the writer discovers new ideas and works to improve the content, structure, and style of the draft. Sommers rejects these "linear conceptions of the writing process [which represent it] . . . as a separate stage at the end of the process—a stage that comes after the completion of a first or second draft and one that is temporally distinct from the prewriting and writing stages of the process" (323). She describes it instead as a "sequence of changes in a composition—changes which are initiated by cues and occur continually throughout the writing of a work" (324). Murray (2001) proclaims that "writing *is* rewriting, and the writer's craft is largely a matter of knowing how to discover what you have to say, develop and clarify it, each requiring the craft of revision" (2).

Applebee and Langer (2011) found that only 19 percent of students studied (they examined over 8500 assignments) did any extended writing of a paragraph or more and characterized most work as "writing without composing" (15), which is to say writing—and *rewriting*. The key distinction here is, of course, whether students—and teachers!—see this piece of writing as a mere assignment to be completed or an invitation to engage with and develop an idea more fully (see Figure 4.25). For this is the turning point in any piece of writing, the point at which students, if they do not feel any ownership of the work, will go through the motions or simply quit, accepting what they have as "good enough."

Atwell herself struggled with issues of ownership in her "early years of writing workshop when [she] worked so hard not to usurp students' 'ownership' of their writing, not to advise or instruct or praise writers . . . not to appear to be teaching" (2002, x), and to recognize that "sharing practical knowledge is [her] responsibility as a classroom teacher" through what she calls "mini-lessons" and others, such as Fletcher and Portalupi (1998) call "craft lessons." Fletcher and Portalupi are emphatic about this phase of writing that calls on writers to focus on the *craft* of writing—a phase they contend that "gets the least attention . . ., [a] part of the authoring cycle [during which] students are left on their own to make a thousand decisions" (3). As they say, in summing up their argument for the importance of this crafting phase, "craft is the cauldron in which the writing gets forged" (3). Craft also implies the notion, mentioned earlier, of apprenticeship, of being educated into a way of working that is "quality-driven" (Sennet 2008, 241).

Revision is not just a phase in the writing process but a way of living—a worldview: things can be improved; there are other ways to see or say this; I can do better. As Murray says, "Revision gives us a second chance at life. In fact, it gives us many more chances to revise understand—our childhoods; our relationships with family, friends, enemies, classmates, employers; our ethnic and racial

FIGURE 4.25 Hannah turns to Patrick for advice on her draft that shows her need to manipulate different elements en route to discovering the best organization for the ideas in her paper. Patrick takes the role very seriously, offering her specific suggestions that lead to a better paper.

backgrounds, how our gender shapes us; our world" (2001, 3). This is the point in the composing process at which I must emphasize, as I have in the two previous stages, *the importance of time*, which the Common Core Standards describes as writing "routinely over extended time frames (time for research, reflection, and revision)" (2010, 47). As Applebee and Langer concluded in their national study of middle and high school writing instruction, "writing as a way to study, learn, and go beyond—as a way to construct knowledge or generate new networks of understandings—is rare" (2011, 26).

PAUSE & REFLECT After reading about these different perspectives on revision, which one(s) most validate or challenge your own beliefs or practices—and why?

This process of revision often marks a whole new phase of generating ideas as we begin to write our way into a more genuine understanding of what we do and do not think. Lindemann argues that "at least *one-third* of our teaching should emphasize how writers rework drafts" (2001, 195). Such instruction might include showing examples from previous students' drafts as they moved toward what became a distinguished paper. The teacher might also show examples, such as those found in the series of *Paris Review* books (see Gourevitch 2006), of early and subsequent drafts of a poet's or novelist's work. Perhaps most effective, however, is for you as the teacher to share your own writing with the students, to go public about your process as Gallagher (2011b) and Kittle (2008), among others, urge us to do. I often show students samples of pages with my revisions or my editor's marks all over them as a way of illustrating for them that a piece can always be improved and that learning never ends.

We must provide the necessary conditions, however, not just say that revision is a requirement that students must meet on their own time. In 1981, Applebee reported that 59.3 percent of teachers said revision was an important instructional technique. Twenty years later, Hillocks found no substantial change (2002). By 2008, however, this number dropped to 45 percent according to Hillocks (2008, 316) as a result of increased and sustained emphasis on timed writing (which allows no room for any sort of authentic writing process), a result other major studies of writing also showed (MacArthur 2007; Applebee and Langer 2011).

Before we examine some specific strategies for teaching (and doing) revision, we should be clear what we even mean by the term *revision*. Some confuse *revision* with *editing* and *proofreading*, both of which may occur throughout the revision process. Sommers, for her study of student writers, distinguished between four "operations": deleting, substituting, adding, and reordering words. Inexperienced writers focus only on these surface details which, while important, lead to correct, errorless prose, not good writing. The changes that Sommers studied took place on four levels within a piece of student writing: word, phrase, sentence, and theme, which she defines as "the extended statement of one idea" (2009, 325). In contrast, Sommers noted that experienced writers focused much less on such surface concerns and more on the "form or shape of their argument" (329).

Specifically, Sommers observed that inexperienced student writers tended to "scratch out" and "review every word to make sure everything was worded right" and looked, in general, for ways to "reword," practicing

> **"**WE MUST PROVIDE THE NECESSARY CONDITIONS, HOWEVER, NOT JUST SAY THAT REVISION IS A REQUIREMENT THAT STUDENTS MUST MEET ON THEIR OWN TIME.**"**

what she called a "thesaurus philosophy of writing" (2009, 325). These writers, in other words, see revision as a clean-up activity during which students add or replace words with "better words" or remove words to "avoid repetition" (326). These findings corroborate those in the different studies MacArthur surveyed (2007, 143). In those cases when the writing flowed out of students with (what they perceived to be) ease and grace, Sommers notes "they say they cannot see any reason to revise" (326), a tendency that is particularly common to Generation Y students who have been raised to feel that whatever they say or do is good, even great—because they did it, because "that's what I think."

On the other hand, experienced writers, who referred to revision as "rewriting," stress their ongoing efforts during this stage to find "a pattern . . . or a design for their argument" (Sommers 2009, 329). Such seasoned writers establish more specific objectives when revising according to Sommers (2009) and MacArthur (2007): the effect they want to have on and the needs of the reader. Thus, experienced writers engage in a more nuanced conversation that takes them outside of themselves and forces them to examine the content, style, and rhetoric of their writing in light of their medium, message, audience, purpose, and occasion. Experienced writers, says Sommers, view this phase as a vital, ongoing process of "*discovering meaning . . . a repeated process of beginning over again, starting out new—that inexperienced writers failed to have*" (328). During this phase, experienced writers concentrated more on sentence-level changes (as opposed to the word-level) but also made changes on all other levels, using all the revision operations Sommers identified.

Given the benefits of composing on the computer, it is worth noting that only 42.3 percent of middle and high school students compose first drafts on computers, 48.6 percent use it to edit and revise (Applebee and Langer 2011, 23). Unfortunately, even here state testing and an overemphasis on timed writing intrude on writing instruction: Some schools officially forbid teachers to allow students to write on word processors because they are not allowed to use them on high-stakes tests (Russell and Abrams 2004).

PAUSE & REFLECT How do these observations about experienced and inexperienced writers match your experience as a writer or teacher? At what point did you become an "experienced writer" as described by Sommers?

Teaching Revision: Strategies

My life is often in peril during this phase of the writing process when I say things like, "Okay, so the final draft of the paper we have worked so hard on is due Monday!" It might be a Thursday when I say this. And when they come in Monday, bleary eyed and spent, I often say, "Great! Now we have a great *rough draft* and the rest of the week to really make it into something we can all be proud of. So let's get to work!"

At this point, I introduce a specific lesson based on my informal assessments of their papers (conferences, quick-checks, observations while circulating during peer response sessions). After the lesson, they work in class and finish it, whatever specific work I assign, at home that night (see Figure 4.26). When I first put them through this process, I assure them that they will thank me, that these additional, targeted lessons will improve their skills, their papers, and, of course, their grades. Over time, they believe me, but the first time? Well, it can be a little intense. But you know what? That communal lament unifies the class and challenges me to make sure that what we do will, as promised, improve their papers and their writing abilities.

PAUSE **&** REFLECT What are your thoughts about this less-is-more approach to teaching writing? What does your school require? Do you find it effective?

MacArthur (2007) identifies several traits common to solid instruction in revision. First, teachers have the greatest opportunity to teach students how to revise well "when students evaluate and change what they have already written" (142). Students must also be able to read critically but at some distance when evaluating their own work, and therefore must also possess good reading comprehension. It is such criti-

FIGURE 4.26 Jorge poses questions to a classmate in the margins of the paper by way of helping that classmate see where a reader gets lost or simply wants more information.

cal reading skills that make the next approach possible: Teach students to evaluate their writing or that of their peers using specific criteria, then allow them to revise their papers using the results of their evaluation.

Thus, "teaching self-evaluation is a key part of strategy instruction" when it comes to teaching revision. Specific evaluation criteria consistently yield greater and more reliable gains than general criteria such as content and organization. For that reason, MacArthur recommends teaching students evaluation criteria appropriate to a specific genre, using a list of questions one might ask to determine whether their papers include all the elements of an argument. It is also important that students learn to evaluate their papers but only after learning the criteria and having the chance to practice applying them (145).

Flower distinguishes between two types of revision: "global" and "local" (1997). Global revision "affects how the paper works as a whole . . . , and involves changes in the purpose, in the gist, or in the major ideas . . . or the logic of an argument or the writer's stance toward the reader" (233). Local revision is the "familiar process of evaluating individual words, phrases, and sentences . . . [which] affect only a small, local part of the text [but do not] alter the gist or overall structure of the text" (232).

GLOBAL REVISION A great deal of our time and effort at this phase is spent analyzing the structure, development, and organization of the paper as a whole. Students need to get a sense of how writing works, how one thing flows into and affects another within the context of the larger argument of the paper. While it is useful for me to guide such structured analysis, students must continually be moving toward independence and fluency. Independence requires that students learn now to engage in close peer reading and response on their own, with a partner in class, or online via programs such as Google Docs or Microsoft Word's Track Changes feature.

As students move toward the end of all such response, they have only the guidelines and criteria on which all assessment of their work will be based. Rubrics at this stage remain tools students can use to do one final check to be sure they have everything done or included. The checklist at the top of the rubric is important: it provides a set of must-dos that summarize many qualities of effective, successful papers in the past; I include it as a guide to success (see Figure 4.27). This is for a definition paper but the features of the rubrics stay pretty consistent regardless of the type of writing.

A panel of leading composition scholars headed by Braverman and Lunsford, speaking about key findings from their research at a national convention, singled out this technique as one of the more reliable and effective, one of the panelists saying that he did not provide students with checklists for what a paper should have but found that it made a difference if they knew what previously successful papers had *done* (Braverman and Lunsford 2005).

At this point, the paper is written and ready to submit; this is the point when you ask them to consider how they might transform it into something compelling. Given that the paper now consists of words on the page, the writer might ask whether there are images, video, infographics, or links that might add substance in a way that helps students more effectively achieve their purpose. Links? Audio? Video? Yes, all of these and probably more over time as students begin to write *for* and *with* multimedia devices such as iPads. Or they will send you the link to their multimedia essay, or perhaps, having done it your way (via the traditional essay) will ask whether they can recast it as a short film or in some other more interactive format (see Figure 4.28).

Writing Moves

When speaking of "moves" in my class, I sometimes use the following set of prepositions as lever-words to help them understand and address this aspect of their writing.

- **Against**: The writer challenges, contradicts, or offers a counterargument against her own claim or another's she was considering.
- **Away from:** The writer moves away from the established focus to consider seemingly unrelated issues, sources, or comparisons in order to highlight some connection or idea in the paper.
- **Behind:** The writer digresses or pauses to look behind, to consider precedents or his own past experience in light of the current subject of the paper. The idea is that whatever happened in the past can shed light on the present.
- **Beyond:** The writer moves beyond the current subject, perspective, or text to consider others that may provide insight about the text or topic the student is examining.
- **For:** The writer advocates for a position or idea; when they move for something, writers are in the persuasive mode, using their details to argue for something.
- **Into:** The writer moves down into the text or topic to get below the surface; this is an essential move for academic writing because it begins to get the student away from summary.
- **Between:** The writer looks between the ideas he is examining to find those ideas not immediately visible without scrutiny and a sense of what these in-between ideas mean, why they matter. This is a nuanced move that often requires the writer to work with smaller, more subtle ideas.
- **With:** The writer agrees with or goes along with established ideas or those of the writers she is discussing; it is a move one can make for a time in order to set up a tension that leads to a move *against* this position.

LOCAL REVISION   Picking up where the global section left off, one might suggest that the student begin this next level, or last stage of revision, by returning to those notes in the margin that indicate the "smaller problems of correctness to which the student can return later." While local revision certainly demands that writers pay attention to grammar, usage, and mechanics—all of which might be said to be more a part of "editing" than revising—the stress here remains more on logic, clarity, cohesion, and the more subtle but vital elements of style and rhetoric.

Some of these ideas are expressed through the notion of "thinking moves," which Dombeck and Herndon (2004) characterize as a "progression of ideas, introduced and interwoven as the essay progresses . . . [through] a number of turning points, surprises, twists—moments when the essay's established thinking is added to, revised, called into question, problematized, or transcended in some way" (34). These "moves" happen within and between the sentences and paragraphs, creating "rhetorical emphasis . . . by shaping sentences and paragraphs that are designed to frame the turn in a rhetorically powerful way so that it is clear to the reader not only that the writer's thinking is *moving*, but that it is moving in a particular, intended

Definition Paper: Writing and Scoring Guide

Name: _____ Period: _____ Date: _____

Does your paper:

❏ Define the idea or term using a specific strategy (e.g., analogy, extended definition, examples, stipulation)?
❏ Establish the general category to which the idea or word belongs?
❏ Add qualifiers (what it is/is not, does/does not do) to distinguish it from others in the same category?
❏ Consider alternative or opposing definitions/perspectives—and accept/reject them based on your criteria?
❏ Anticipate readers' assumptions or perceptions and somehow answer or respond to them?
❏ Present your definition as an argument you must make, support, and rebut?
❏ Define or otherwise clarify any words?

Exceeds the Standard	Meets the Standard	Approaches the Standard	Misses the Standard
Comprehension: Understands the text in light of the author's purpose, style, rhetorical strategies, genre, and audience.			
Shows novel or compelling insight about the topic; understands author's purpose/ text when using secondary and primary sources.	Shows insight about the topic; understands author's purpose/text when using secondary and primary sources.	Shows limited insight about the topic; limited understanding of author's purpose/text when using secondary and primary sources.	Shows little or no insight about the topic; minimum or flawed understanding of author's purpose/text when using sources.
Thesis: Develops an appropriate topic, research question, interpretation, or assertion.			
Develops a specific, compelling, defensible definition.	Develops an appropriate, compelling, defensible definition.	Offers a plausible definition.	Develops a flawed or indefensible definition; or offers no definition.
Evidence: Integrates evidence from different primary and secondary sources to support the thesis and any assertions.			
Integrates various reliable primary/ secondary sources; uses them to support and challenge thesis or assertions in sophisticated, effective way.	Includes several reliable primary/secondary sources, uses these to support and challenge thesis or assertions in plausible, useful way.	Integrates few if any primary or secondary sources; attempts to use them to support thesis or assertions; chooses unreliable sources that are not used well.	Integrates no reliable primary/secondary sources; if does, uses them ineffectively or not at all.
Development: Elaborates on and articulates the reason, effect, or meaning of evidence, examples, and assertions.			
Develops compelling, logical progression of commentary and analysis about the definition; considers other perspectives; responds to/defends against them.	Develops a plausible progression of commentary and analysis about the definition; attempts to consider other perspectives, responds to/defends against them.	Offers an obvious or flawed progression of commentary and analysis about the definition; minimal or no consideration of other perspectives; little or no response to/defense against them.	Offers no substantive or coherent commentary or analysis about the definition; does not consider other perspectives or respond to or defend against them.
Organization: Organizes ideas and details for in light of audience, occasion, purpose.			
Uses a variety of organizational patterns and strategies, transitional words and phrases, to emphasize/clarify ideas within/between paragraphs.	Uses several organizational patterns and strategies, transitional words and phrases, to emphasize/clarify ideas within/between paragraphs.	Uses few organizational patterns and strategies, transitional words and phrases, to emphasize/clarify ideas within/between paragraphs.	Uses no organizational patterns and strategies, transitional words and phrases, to emphasize/clarify ideas within/between paragraphs.
Style: Uses stylistic elements and rhetorical strategies to achieve intended effects and stated purpose (to define).			
Uses a variety of sophisticated and effective rhetorical strategies; uses precise, powerful words that create a distinctive voice.	Uses a variety of effective rhetorical strategies; uses words that give the writing a voice.	Makes an effort to use some rhetorical strategies; uses words that offer the hints of a voice.	Uses no or inappropriate rhetorical strategies; uses plain or ineffective words that achieve no voice.
Conventions: Observes appropriate conventions of grammar, usage, document format.			
Observes all conventions of standard written English—including tense, agreement, parallelism—and MLA format.	Observes most conventions of standard written English—including tense, agreement, parallelism—and MLA format.	Observes some conventions of standard written English—including tense, agreement, parallelism—and MLA format.	Observes few conventions of standard written English—including tense, agreement, parallelism—and MLA format.
Documentation: Cites and uses sources accurately and ethically, and follows recognized citation guidelines (e.g., MLA).			
Uses source materials ethically and accurately, quoting all sources correctly and in context; cites sources using MLA guidelines.	Uses source materials ethically and accurately, quoting most sources correctly and in context; cites most sources using MLA guidelines.	Uses source materials inconsistently or inaccurately, quoting some correctly or in context; cites sources incorrectly using MLA guidelines.	References no source materials, quoting few or none correctly or in context; cites no sources or does so incorrectly using MLA guidelines.
Requirements: Include or do in your paper all that the assignment stipulates.			
Exceeds assignment requirements, which might include adding images/graphics, including more than requisite number of sources, writing more than required number of pages. Has WOW!	Does what the assignment requires in terms of elements, features, layout, and length.	Does most of or nearly what the assignment requires in terms of elements, features, layout, and length.	Does not complete or do what the assignment requires in terms of elements, features, layout, or length.

_____

FIGURE 4.27 Sample rubric for English classes. It serves as a template for other types of papers.

FIGURE 4.28 Tommy puts the final polish on his paper about food, working on the design and layout of the paper itself in the process of also making any other final edits.

direction" (34) that guides "readers through a careful choreography that displays each new idea as flowing from those that have come before" (34).

This concept of "moves" (Graff, Birkenstein, and Durst 2010) captures what we most often feel as readers when the writer executes some daring stylistic or rhetorical feat: *Nice move!* we want to say, and I sometimes do, right in the margin of the paper. Such moves, however, go unseen if the writing itself lacks the clarity Joseph Williams helps writers achieve through his book *Style: Lessons in Clarity and Grace* (2006): "Once we've formulated our claims, organized supporting reasons, grounded them on sound evidence, and motivated readers to read attentively, we must still express it all clearly, a difficult task for most writers and a daunting one for many" (4).

Let us turn now to this final part of the revision process and look at what we can do to help students learn *and apply* those strategies that will result in prose that is clear and coherent, compelling and cohesive, concise as well as correct. It is often difficult to separate the methods related to the sentence from those specific to the paragraph. So let us begin with the paragraph and work toward the sentence, which, according to Lanham, is the foundation on which all else is built (2006, iv).

A couple approaches deserve fuller treatment before we move on. First, the Paramedic Method was developed by Richard Lanham (2006) in an attempt to rid the world of the bureaucratic or what he calls the "Official Style" by teaching people how to "translate their own or someone else's [Official Style] into plain English" (v). He stresses the importance of following each step of his Paramedic Method of revision to the letter instead of arguing with it. Also, his concern is with the single sentence, for as he says, "Get the basic architecture of the English sentence straight . . . and everything else will follow" (iv). Thus he tells us to find all the "lard" by looking for *all* the prepositions and variations of *is* verbs, replacing whenever possible those weaker words with actions expressed as simple verbs. He also counsels that writers begin building up to their point quickly instead of slowly with a bunch of unnecessary words. Finally, he strongly encourages writers to read their pieces out loud to hear where the points of emphasis are—or should be—and to break the sentences into rhythmic units to better understand and refine the sound and cadence of the writing, both of which are often undermined by a lot of clutter in the sentences.

This method, used effectively, can dramatically reduce what Lanham calls the student's Lard Factor, which he calculates by dividing the difference between the number of words in the original version and the revised version by the number of words in the original version (2006, 4). As Lindemann says, commenting on Lanham's Paramedic Method, "Lard adds up when it accumulates over several sentences. Removing it is sometimes simply a matter of making every word count—and deleting words that don't" (202). Of course, this work demands time! But then again, real learning and excellence always do.

Such work as this provides perfect context for minilessons—targeted instruction delivered at the point of need. Examples of such lessons might include citing sources, using gender neutral or Standard English, incorporating quotations for flow and effect, or resolving some final questions related to tone and style (see Figure 4.29). In my classes, whether College Prep ninth graders or Advanced Placement seniors, I struggle, as we all do, with getting kids to use and properly cite sources when writing academic papers. I address this problem by making it a direct lesson, as outlined in Figure 4.30.

One final technique demands attention—the computer as a tool for revision. We must *teach* students how to use computers to improve efficiency and the quality of writing; grammar and spell-checkers offer help but by no means are the only available tools on the computer. Just using computers to write does not inevitably result in better writing or a greater willingness to revise. Rather, combining instruction in the use of computers

FIGURE 4.29 Working at the overhead (I now use a document camera or my iPad attached to an LCD projector), I provide a minilesson on how to choose, use, and incorporate quotations into the text of their essay.

and revision strategies leads to improved writing and revising (MacArthur 2007, 147). The first thing I do is teach students to use the Search function to find those details that cause trouble; I do this by modeling it on my laptop and projecting it onto the whiteboard so that I can mark up and discuss the sample paper. Such interactive annotation will become increasingly easy and common as emerging technologies for both tablets and computers arrive on the market in the coming years. I am already experimenting with this on an iPad, but it is hit and miss and thus not worth recommending for most at this time.

For example, to check whether students have properly formatted all citations, they can type Command-F and enter just one parenthesis or quotation mark. Each time the program finds, for example, a parenthesis, students check to see if the parenthetical citation is properly formatted; if it is, they hit the Find Next button and work through the paper. Other possible searches that can be useful include: *is* (and its variants), *for example*, and words they know they tend to misspell or otherwise confuse (there/their, its/it's, affect/effect).

As students work through their papers one key stroke at a time, I take the opportunity to confer with them while they work on the computer because this allows me to use the mouse to highlight sections to discuss, and to quickly show them potential problems, patterns, and alternatives; they can then try it themselves while I watch. In addition, students with special needs benefit from this method because it gives me access to more tools to help them see what they might not otherwise notice (see Figure 4.31). By "special needs," I mean anyone from the special education student with language-processing disorders to English learners struggling to find the right word, to advanced writers whom I challenge by showing them how to use more complex syntactic structures or stylistic moves.

Finally, on those occasions (typically major papers) when I comment in detail and call for revisions, they learn and must use Microsoft Word's Track Changes feature (or its equivalent in Google Docs). I demonstrate

"WE MUST *TEACH* STUDENTS HOW TO USE COMPUTERS TO IMPROVE EFFICIENCY AND THE QUALITY OF WRITING; GRAMMAR AND SPELL-CHECKERS OFFER HELP BUT BY NO MEANS ARE THE ONLY AVAILABLE TOOLS ON THE COMPUTER.**"**

Integrating Quotations

1. Embedded Within One Sentence

Introduction/lead to quotation, *the quotation*, discussion/explanation of quotation.

Example   **Stafford argues that we are intimately related to nature, *for when he says "I stood there and thought hard for us all,"*** he makes the man just another one of the animals, no more important than any other living thing in the surrounding forest.

2. Broken Into More Than One Sentence

Introduction/lead to quotation. *The quotation*, discussion/explanation of quotation.

Example   **Stafford argues that we are intimately related to nature. *When he says, for example, "I stood there and thought hard for us all,"*** he makes the man just another one of the animals, no more important than any other living thing in the surrounding forest.

Introduction/lead to quotation, *the quotation*. Discussion/explanation of quotation.

Example   **Stafford argues that we are intimately related to nature *when he says "I stood there and thought hard for us all."*** These words make him just another one of the animals, no more important than any other living thing in the surrounding forest.

INTEGRATING EXAMPLES

1. **Animals and nature in general are certainly big business. *The San Francisco Zoo, for example, profits from the tigers,*** the tragic death and news coverage both advertising how exciting the zoo is and how dangerous the animals really are.

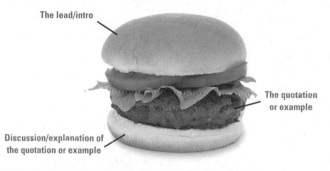

The lead/intro

The quotation
or example

Discussion/explanation of
the quotation or example

FIGURE 4.30 Sample of the sort of page I create for students as part of a minilesson. On the screen, certain phrases and words appear in different colors to bring attention to their function.

how to use this and provide for them a handout with detailed directions. They must use the tracking feature to indicate that they made each change I suggested or requested (see Figure 4.32). They then print a final copy, staple it to the other drafts, specifically the one with all my comments, and resubmit their paper. My usual approach for this is: If they made *all* the changes, the paper's grade goes up a full grade; if they made most changes, it goes up a bit; if they made only a few and those just the surface fixes, the grade stays the same; if they make no changes at all, the grade goes down a full grade. This seems to be incentive enough to get them back to revising their papers.

In case you needed one more reason to justify the time spent revising, I provide this: Nothing works better as a defense against plagiarism. Some report that as many as 87 percent of college-level students admit to plagiarizing work, typically through what is now called "cyber-plagiarism" or "cyber-cheating" (Wiebe 2006, 1). In short, these efforts amount to copying and pasting, sometimes with minimal changes, material from the Internet which the students do not cite, but instead treat as their own original writing. When we have students revise across multiple drafts, have them do the dirty work of writing as I have described it here, they are less likely to be able (or inclined) to plagiarize. And if they do, when all those drafts come due, it is much easier to spot, especially if they claim they have no drafts, that they "did it all on the computer."

FIGURE 4.31 Dom and I steal a little time together during our work in the computer lab to work more closely on his paper. This allows me to better meet his different needs as one who has a variety of learning difficulties.

As I mentioned earlier, many adolescents feel they have already said what they mean, that it's good enough as it is. This attitude stems, no doubt, from our collective prejudice against the idea of a "do-over," which equates to: my writing is bad, I'm a bad writer, a terrible person! As Murray says of revision, "We . . . think that we are only asked to rewrite if we have failed. In fact, that is what usually happens in school and at work. Only when we become experienced and mature writers do we understand that rewriting is an essential part of the process" (2001, 2).

I often tell my students a story to illustrate my own growth and beginnings as a writer. When I wrote my first piece that was published, it was 5000 words long. The editor called and said, "You know, I think you have a very good 500-word piece in here and I would like to work with you on that." He was right, of course. Absolutely. And nothing has so marked my own transformation into a writer than my ability to listen to others' suggestions, which often amount to removing the parts I think are just so witty, so smart.

FIGURE 4.32 Alejandro incorporates changes using Track Changes in computer lab. The margin comments are not my remarks but his changes. I simply look at these to see what he changed when I re-evaluate the paper.

This attitude toward revision, which is so familiar and comfortable for me, is not so for some, even most. However, it is often the most problematic for our most advanced students as I was reminded when one of my best former students, who had gone to UCLA to study English, visited me after graduating from college. He explained that he had never revised a paper in high school, nor in his first year in college. His belief was that if you were, as he felt he was, a good writer, you didn't need to revise. Then sophomore year, his As began to drift down to Bs, and Cs, even into the D range. He had found the boundary of his talent and his approach no longer worked. He was so troubled by this experience that he entered therapy, for he knew he definitely wanted to write, perhaps to teach, so he had to work through this.

What he came to realize was that his reluctance to revise stemmed from his own insecurities, as if revising meant that he was not as good as he had always been told he was, as great as he thought he was. So he panicked. Then he began looking at books about writing and realized that *real* writers revise over and over, seeing it as the real work of the creation, not a sign of failure. And so, having realized that it was not only okay but expected that you would, Byron learned to think as Samuel Beckett wrote: try, and fail, but "no matter. Try again. Fail again. Fail better" (2006, 471).

Proofread and Publish

In the Common Core Standards for language arts, the Production and Distribution of Writing section states:

- Produce clear and coherent writing in which the development, organization, and style are appropriate to task, purpose, and audience. (Grade-specific expectations for writing types are defined in standards 1–3.)

- Develop and strengthen writing as needed by planning, revising, editing, rewriting, or trying a new approach, focusing on addressing what is most significant for a specific purpose and audience.

- Use technology, including the Internet, to produce, publish, and update individual or shared writing products, taking advantage of technology's capacity to link to other information and to display information flexibly and dynamically. (National Governors Association 2010, 46)

Proofreading, apart from editing and revising, occurs throughout the composing process in some form. We see flaws as we work on an earlier part, changing them on the fly. But we also need this final check, as the pilots go through before taking off, to ensure the small details are in order. While students want to believe correctness does not matter, especially in this era of texting (which has eradicated the writer's conscience), the conventions of grammar, punctuation, and spelling, as well as formatting and layout do matter. (See Chapter 7 for a detailed treatment of these aspects of writing.) These errors undermine confidence. They raise questions about one's knowledge, one's commitment, one's ability to write. And sometimes these mistakes cost, which students often want to dispute. But when a business or a university evaluates thousands of applicants, every flaw makes it that much easier to reject an application.

"While students want to believe correctness does not matter, especially in this era of texting (which has eradicated the writer's conscience), the conventions of grammar, punctuation, and spelling, as well as formatting and layout do matter."

What then can we do when it comes to proofreading? I generally take one final day and use the period to put them through the paces on different aspects that they neglected or did not know. These items often link to lessons I taught. So, for example, I might ask students to find every title—of websites, articles, magazines, songs, novels, and more—and circle them. We then review: How do you format the title of a poem? Why do you do it that way? What if the title of that poem was also the title of the book in which it appeared—would you format them both the same way? Why or why not? And so we check each one. And then we do the same thing—yes, *again*—with citations. And works cited entries. And quotations. And so on.

In our English department, we use as our primary reference a style guide our English department developed together through a series of extended discussions and many drafts. We talk about how, when proofreading, one can only really process one thing at a time. Spelling. Then punctuation. Then capitalization. And quotation formatting. And so on.

The computer can help here again: Show them how to use the Search function to find all periods and check that they are in the right place. Or search for one quotation mark; then let it find each instance, which you can then check and, if necessary, repair before moving on to the next. My final suggestion to students, which many find helpful after their initial amusement, is to read their paper aloud, or even better, backward one sentence at a time. This technique, used by many professional copy editors, prevents the brain from running ahead over the paper's too-familiar terrain. Thus, the errors are more noticeable.

Which brings us, finally, to the question of publishing, which is a noble goal for the teacher to have. Yet we are pressed for time and must ask whether the effort to publish something does not, in many cases, displace time that could be better spent working on writing the next piece and thus improving still more. Am I against publishing? Not at all. Some teachers have more than 40 kids (I have 35) in a class, though; so if you are in a class that allows you to have students publish their work, then the following ideas are of greater interest than for those who simply cannot muster the time, resources, or energy to do it. Such teachers would be rare, however; Applebee and Langer found that only 8.2 percent of high school teachers provided students with an audience outside of class, while 11 percent of middle school teachers did so; students at that age are still willing to show parents, for example, their work (2011, 17). I should say, to be clear, that I have had my students do the following in some form at one time or another:

- Post online through various venues, including students' own blogs, wikis, websites, or other web-based platforms. My students have been blogging for several years now and find it very satisfying, though we do not publish their academic papers online as part of their blog.

- Send the work to others who constitute an authentic audience and may respond to the writer. My students, for example, wrote letters, which we spent time perfecting, to members of the Rotary Club. These letters were, in turn, read aloud at the next Rotary Club meeting (Burke 2012).

- Publish in local or school newspapers, literary magazines, or other venues in print and online.

- Create their own literary journal or other publication to which they each contribute a piece of work appropriate to the theme and audience.

- Present their papers as abbreviated presentations to the class, as one might a dissertation—they must "stand and deliver"; after that they respond to questions from a panel of guests or classmates.

- Have their parents or other interested people in their lives read and write responses to the students' papers, stories, or poems.

- Perform their writing if it is literary or otherwise lends itself to performance or public speaking.

What students want, above all, as all writers do, is to know they are heard, that their words were given a genuine reading by an interested reader. Writers do not "publish" everything they

> "What students want, above all, as all writers do, is to know they are heard, that their words were given a genuine reading by an interested reader."

write. It is not a rule that we do so; some stuff is better left in the drawer. That doesn't mean it was not valuable nor that it was a mere exercise or a waste of time. One might sum up the whole notion of publishing with these words: *post* (online, around school), *perform* (by reading, acting out), or *publish* (by some other, more traditional means). Or you can get a book, such as Chris Weber's *Publish with Students: A Comprehensive Guide* (2002), and use his suggestions and the abundant resources provided.

REFLECT AND REMEMBER: STUDYING THE GAME TAPES

When it is all over, but before they turn it in, I always ask students to reflect on a few things, just as coaches of many sports ask (okay, *insist*) that their players review the game tapes to learn from what they did well—or did wrong. Only by becoming more aware—through such deliberate metacognitive study of their processes, the choices they made, the strategies they used—can students become better writers (see Figure 4.33). Any success is just an accident unless students learn what they did to achieve such success (or failure). Sometimes the focus of reflection is very specific; also, it is often as much for my benefit as for theirs. For example, if I used a new technique, I want detailed feedback about how it did or did not help them. If I tried a different assignment, such as the "digital essay," I want to know whether they were engaged and challenged, frustrated or bored so I can revise or reject the assignment in the future.

On most occasions, however, the purpose of such reflection is to improve their own self-awareness of what they did: how, when, and why. So I have them respond to one or more of the following questions, usually the day I collect the papers:

- What did you do well?
- What was difficult—and why?
- What helped you overcome those difficulties? How did this help?
- What did you do differently this time? What was the result?
- What can you tell me about your process on this paper?
- How is this similar to or different from your previous papers?
- In what ways or areas is your writing improving?
- What do you need to keep working on as a writer?

Sometimes I just ask them to tell me about the three Ps: their **performance** (how well they did), their **progress** (how it compares to previous papers), and their **process** (what they did and how they did it to get this final result). It is succinct but useful.

PAUSE & REFLECT How does the process of teaching writing just outlined compare with your own process or experience?

Designing Writing Assignments and Prompts

Lindemann describes writing assignments as "specific invitation[s] to write" and attributes the problems students experience more often to poorly designed assignments than the students themselves (2001, 213). Writing, in other words, can only be as clear as the directions, questions, or prompts students receive; Williams simply says there is no such thing as the "perfect

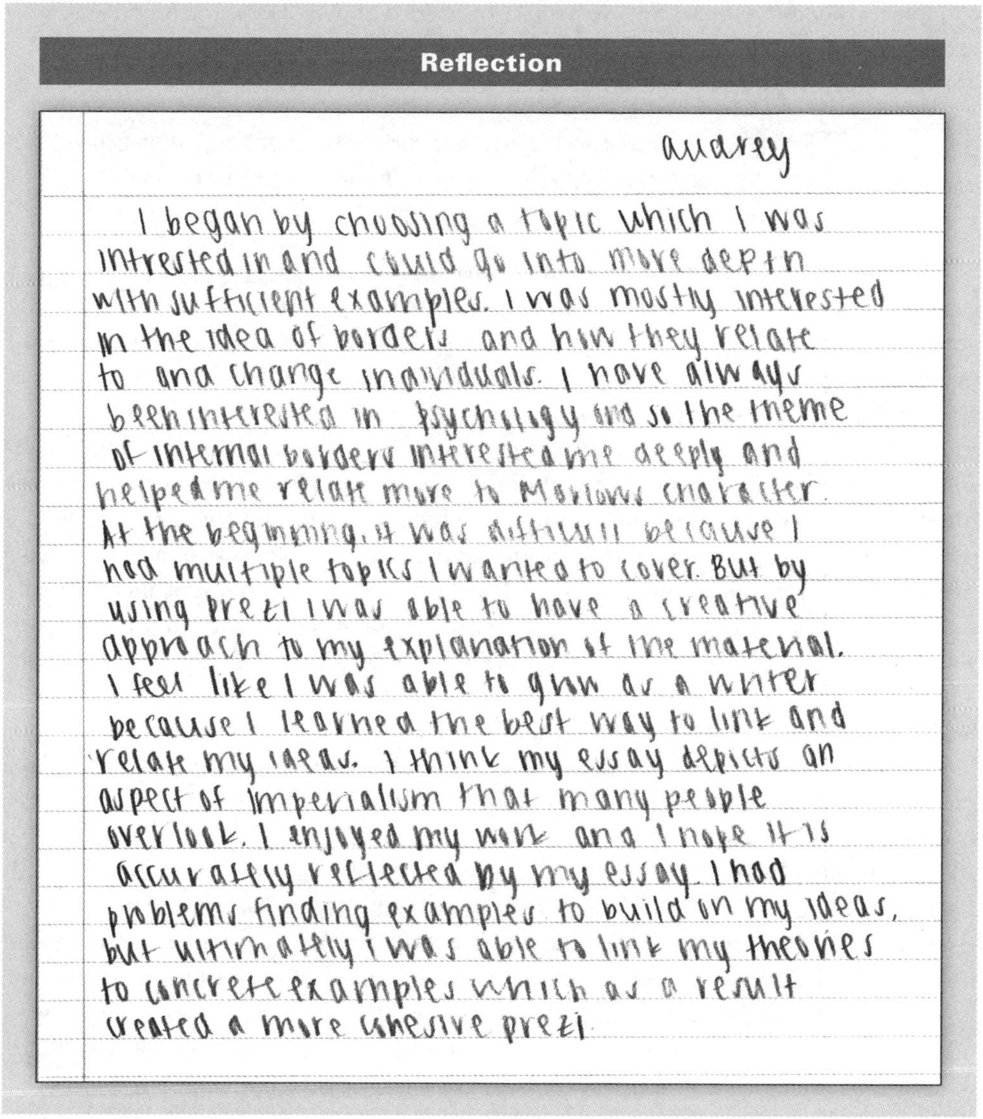

Reflection

> Audrey
>
> I began by choosing a topic which I was intrested in and could go into more depth with sufficient examples. I was mostly interested in the idea of borders and how they relate to and change individuals. I have always been interested in psychology and so the theme of internal borders interested me deeply and helped me relate more to Marlows character. At the beginning, it was difficult because I had multiple topics I wanted to cover. But by using prezi I was able to have a creative approach to my explanation of the material. I feel like I was able to grow as a writer because I learned the best way to link and relate my ideas. I think my essay depicts an aspect of imperialism that many people overlook. I enjoyed my work and I hope it is accuratly reflected by my essay. I had problems finding examples to build on my ideas, but ultimately I was able to link my theories to concrete examples which as a result created a more cohesive prezi.

FIGURE 4.33 Audrey reflects back on the process she followed en route to writing a great paper.

[writing] assignment" (2003, 279). Combine these different perspectives with the various standards we all struggle to teach and you have a perfect storm of complexity that makes it difficult to design effective and engaging writing assignments.

All the more difficult if one aspires to create assignments that both inspire and instruct students in those skills the state and universities look for and measure, while also cultivating the independence of mind real writing (and thinking) requires. As one Texas high school English teacher summed up the dilemma regarding formulaic writing, "We tend to be repetitive of what we want them to write, what we want them to include, and . . . the process that they need to use in order to get everything included. [So] we become repetitive . . . [telling the students] this is what you have to write, this is what has to be included, you have to include this number of quotes" (Hillocks 2002, 92). Yet, Bernabei, Hover, and Candler (2009), also from Texas, offer useful and compelling examples in their book of what robust writing instruction is that prepares kids for state tests while also making them all-around better writers.

PAUSE & REFLECT Download the extensive guidelines and sample assignments, available on the "Writing Assignment Framework and Overview" document from the National Writing Project website. Use to evaluate and improve your own assignments.

Some resist the idea of teacher-designed writing assignments. Atwell "avoids . . . school genres, [focusing instead on] poems, memoirs, letters, essays, book reviews, gifts of writing, reports, profiles, and parodies" (1998, 92). Although Atwell surely prepares students for the demands of the university and adult world, hers is an ideal situation that is not available to most teachers in the public schools these days.

Kittle suggests something of a middle path, one that reflects much of what I have illustrated throughout this chapter: We should develop assignments that teach the skills through the study of craft in all genres, including academic writing and writing on demand. This approach expects much more than the assignment that reads like a checklist to be completed instead of an essay to be created. These assignments develop, as Kittle says, independence that demands the students do the difficult work of generating and shaping those ideas (personal communication 2011). In other words, we must conceive of assignments in terms of the gradual release of responsibility model (see Figure 3.4).

The problem, according to Stotsky (2010b), is that teachers, in an attempt to engage and include, focus almost exclusively on personal writing, thus allowing students to graduate from high school without having learned, for example, to craft an argument—what is "the essence of thought, . . . the soul of an education and is at the heart of inquiry, innovation, and problem solving" (Schmoker and Graff 2011, 31). Such personal, reader-response assignments, according to some (Robb 2010), do not provide an "intellectually progressive curriculum sequence" (Stotsky 2010b, 24) and thus result in the intellectual equivalent of time spent at the gym lifting a bar without any weights on it. Williams, however, distinguishes between "cognitive" and "rhetorical" difficulty, asserting that while "[on the *cognitive* level,] narrative-descriptive writing *is* easier than argumentation. . . . [O]n the *rhetorical* level, narrative-descriptive writing is much more difficult . . . as [the writer] must provide a fact-based representation of reality that builds on a theme or themes and that conveys a message or messages through the interaction of events, characters, setting, dialogue, etc." (2003, 287).

PAUSE & REFLECT List all the writing assignments your students do during the year. Label each of your assignments according to categories listed in Figure 4.3. Do you tend to favor one over another? Where do you get the ideas for your writing assignments? How would you gauge the rhetorical and difficulty of these cognitive assignments over time?

We have talked so far about what makes writing assignments difficult; what we have not addressed is what these effective writing assignments include so that we can be sure to include those features when we create assignments for our classes. Lindemann (2001), who offers the clearest thinking on this subject, identifies several key ideas for teachers to consider when choosing or creating writing assignments. First, each assignment should present "more complex rhetorical problems" than those before it. These rhetorical demands, as we have discussed, should require closer reading and greater intellectual analysis. Such demands should also vary across assignments. We might think of writing assignments as involving the four Ts: topics, tasks, types of writing, and texts to which they must sometimes respond or refer. It is through such variation of tasks that students develop the agility and fluency they need as writers.

Several other considerations arise when creating a writing assignment. We must consider the students' interest in and understanding of the subject, as well as their objective in writing about it. In addition, we should ask who the audience of their writing will be on this occasion, and what stance students should take in relation to both the audience and subject of the composition. Finally, we should ask what form of discourse, which might include the media or permissible variations on the traditional essay, is most the appropriate for this assignment and occasion, and what the criteria for success should be so students have some guidelines when composing (see Figure 4.34).

To these considerations, we must add the standards we are required to teach and the skills the assignment was intended to teach. We must also account for the time we will have taken for this assignment, as well as emerging considerations, such as the forms and features, we might allow in this era of new media. In short, we must identify those "moves" we want our students to master, many of which can be expressed through the verbs we use in writing assignments—*compare, contrast, describe, persuade, describe, examine, discuss, embed, link, animate*, among others.

> **"** IT IS THROUGH SUCH VARIATION OF TASKS THAT STUDENTS DEVELOP THE AGILITY AND FLUENCY THEY NEED AS WRITERS. **"**

Analyzing the Language of Writing Prompts

1. Select a novel, play, or epic . . . then
   a. write an essay in which you
      i. analyze
         1. how the character's experience
            a. with exile is
               i. both alienating and enriching, and
         2. how this experience
            a. illuminates the meaning of the work as a whole.

1. Read the passage carefully. Then
   a. write an essay in which you
      i. define the narrator's attitude toward the characters and
      ii. show how he directs the reader's perceptions
         1. of those characters
            a. through his use
               i. of stylistic devices such as
                  1. imagery,
                  2. diction,
                  3. narrative structure, and
                  4. choice of specific details.

FIGURE 4.34 Analyzing the language of writing prompts reveals just what we or others really expect our students to do.

Writing *assignments* differ from writing *assessments* in that they are designed not only to measure but also to teach. Lindemann concludes her 2001 study of effective writing assignments by offering a "Heuristic for Designing Writing Assignments" in which she recommends we ask the following questions:

- What do I want the students to do?
- How do I want them to do the assignment?
- For whom are students writing?
- When will students do the assignment?
- What will I do with the assignment? (219)

To these questions I would add the following in light of recent changes and challenges in the classroom:

- Which skills and academic language must my students, especially my English learners, acquire if they are to succeed on this assignment?
- Why are they doing this assignment at this time?
- What are my criteria and are they similar to, easier or more demanding than those of previous assignments?
- Whtch other forms or features might I be willing to accept for this assignment if we had access to the appropriate media and digital resources?
- Which standards can I most effectively, unobtrusively, and authentically teach to in this assignment as it is currently conceived? How might the assignment be tweaked to revisit previously taught standards, or to reinforce those on which you are currently focusing?

PAUSE **&** REFLECT Use these questions to evaluate your own assignments, perhaps choosing one you think is effective and another that you think could be improved. What differences do you notice between the two?

I have included here several writing assignments that represent a range of types and purposes. Some are from my College Prep (CP) classes; others are from my AP Literature class (see Figures 4.35–4.37). Assignments such as the "multimedia essay" exemplify those new forms which challenge both students and teachers as they evolve in their early years.

I recognize that my assignments can be long, averaging nearly a full page; however, this structure allows me to clarify and convey to my students (and myself) what I am trying to achieve on each assignment. There is nothing wrong with a good, clear prompt that tells students what to write about and what form to use. Still, when I have to include some or all of the following elements, it challenges me to be clear and provide the support students need if they are to write successfully:

- ***Overview:*** This brief portion, which always appears at the top, provides a general sense of the assignment, the topic, the task, and the rationale for it. In other words, it frames what I expect students to learn and do, why they are doing it, and how they should do it.
- ***Standards:*** It is impossible to include all the standards relevant to any given assignment; however, what is useful for both students and teachers is the identification of key

English 2CP

Overview   This assignment asks you to read the book from a variety of "angles of vision." What does this mean? You will choose a different topic to focus on for a few chapters, taking notes on and thinking about that subject, then writing a one-page paper about that subject using the guidelines below.

Requirements   This assignment asks you to:
- Choose a topic from the list provided below
- Read the assigned chapters with that subject in mind
- Take notes in your Reader's Notebook (about that subject) as you read the chapters
- Use these notes to write four one-page typed papers about that subject that follows the guidelines spelled out below

Guidelines   Each one-page paper should include:
- Your name, the chapters, period, and date
- An original title
- Topic sentence that introduces the angle of vision
- Textual detail(s): Each paper must include a quotation or specific reference to a textual detail
- Any examples or quotations must have a lead and follow-up discussion about the meaning of the quotation/example
- Transitional sentence in which you make a connection between the text, your own experience or ideas, and your angle of vision
- Concluding sentence

Chapters:
1. 1-6
2. 7-12
3. 13-18
4. 19-22

Jim Burke
Chapter 1–6
3/5/08

All the World Is a Classroom

All the world is a classroom if we open our eyes to the lessons around us. Within the walls of a school one learns about language and laws, food and physics, history and health. Yet outside those walls we learn about relationships and values, taking these lessons from not only our parents, but also from our friends and the authors we study, the shows we watch, the people we meet. In *Bless Me, Ultima*, seven-year-old Antonio learns important lessons long before he shows up for his first day of school. From the curandera Ultima, who brings Antonio with her into the hills, he learns the power of plants to heal. She would teach him "to observe where the plant grew and how its leaves looked" (39), for Ultima believed that "even the plants had a spirit" (39). Through such lessons and conversations with Ultima, Antonio learned to respect "the *presence*" in nature. From Jason, Antonio learned about the "magic of letters," a lesson he learned more fully from his teacher, Miss Maestas, who by lunchtime on the first day had taught him to write his name. Unfortunately, he also learned about "*la tristesa de la vida*" (the sadness of life) the same day from classmates who laughed at him and made him feel like an outcast. As with Tony, I have learned lessons from many teachers, some of whom cannot be found in schools. I learned early on, while not much older than Tony, that kids can be cruel. I was often beaten up by kids at my elementary school, an experience that taught me to be tough but also to be kind. Some teachers certainly taught me important lessons, though I often did not realize it at the time. Mr. Kitchener, for example, taught me to love writing and to appreciate the power of words by letting us write on typewriters in his backroom, an experience that made writing seem somehow exciting, special. And my father taught me how to make and fix things, spending long hours in the garage showing me how to cut and hammer, prep and paint as the summer evening passed. Such lessons remind us that every place is a classroom and anyone a teacher if we would simply open our eyes, step in, and allow ourselves to learn.

Transitional sentence in which you make a connection between the text, your own experience/ideas, and your AOV.

Possible Topics
- Family
- Education
- Faith
- Duty
- Growing up
- Relationships
- Stories
- Evil
- Dreams
- Reputation
- War
- Honor
- Conflict
- Teachers
- Choices
- Nature
- Wisdom
- Parents
- Siblings
- Loss
- Culture

FIGURE 4.35 Angles of Vision handout for my CP freshman class reading *Bless Me, Ultima*

Mr. Burke/English 2AP

Overview   This paper draws on new aspects of writing, such as hotlinks embedded in the text, and other such interactive or multimedia features. The point is that writers increasingly must write using not only the traditional words, but images, sounds, video, and links.

Requirements   To satisfy the requirements for this paper, you must:

❏ Write a 3- to 5-page essay (this is actually a little difficult to measure if you use Prezi).

❏ Type the paper on the computer and format it appropriately.

❏ Format it according to the MLA BHS Style Guide.

❏ Incorporate into your paper, where appropriate, <u>hot links</u>, images, video, or graphics. These should be incorporated into the paper, not tacked on or serving any evident purpose other than satisfying the requirements of this assignment.

❏ Submit it to turnitin.com by TBA. I will access each paper through turnitin.com and read it as a digital paper (so the links are live).

❏ Include a Works Cited with all appropriate sources, each properly formatted. If you access documents online and cite them, you must hot link them in your Works Cited, also, so the link goes directly to the source cited.

❏ Turn in all drafts, revisions, and evidence of work—drafts, notes, etc.—with a hard copy of final draft on top on the designated date.

Standards   This assignment is aligned with the following English standards for college:

• Consult and cite a variety of credible, appropriate sources.

• Develop a compelling argument about a narrow subject appropriate to *Heart of Darkness*.

• Provide evidence (e.g., quotes, examples) that supports your argument.

• Include and properly format in-text citations and Works Cited (at the end).

• Use a range of media and means to convey your ideas most effectively.

Topic   The topic for this paper is up to you. You must revise as directed; keep all drafts and show evidence of change throughout the process. Here are some ideas and subjects that came out of our class discussions:

• Work

• Othering

• Power

• Cognitive dissonance

• Complexity/chaos

• Ambition

• Evil

• Human nature

• Morality

• Salvation

• Order/disorder

• "The horror!"

• Other?

Links/Embeds   A quick word about links and content—images, sound, or video—embedded in the text. Links come in at least two forms: required and optional. "Required" links take the reader to information/content that is necessary to understand what they have not yet read; "optional" links offer additional or background information for those unfamiliar with the subject. Be mindful of which type you are including and write your sentence so as to make it clear how the reader should respond. Other embedded content should be incorporated into (i.e., referred to, alluded to, used by) the paper seamlessly.

FIGURE 4.36 *Heart of Darkness* digital essay handout for AP literature class.

AP English Literature

Directions   Follow the guidelines below as you write your paper on this subject. If, when you finish the book and are preparing to write your paper, you have an idea you really want to write about and feel the assignment does not account for it, see me.

Standards   These standards come from *Standards for Success*, a document that includes the standards for college-level performance in the main academic areas:

- D.1. know and use several prewriting strategies, including developing a focus; determining the purpose; planning a sequence of ideas; using structured overviews; and creating outlines.

- D.2. use paragraph structure in writing as manifested by the ability to construct coherent paragraphs and arrange paragraphs in logical order.

- D.4. present ideas to achieve overall coherence and logical flow in writing and use appropriate techniques, such as transitions and repetition to maximize cohesion and elegance to writing.

- D.7. use a style manual, such as the Modern Language Association (MLA), to apply writing conventions and to create documentation formats in a manner consistent with the manual.

- E.2. articulate a position through a thesis statement and advance it using evidence, examples, and counterarguments that are relevant to the audience or issue at hand.

- E.3. use a variety of methods to develop arguments, including compare-contrast reasoning; logical arguments (inductive-deductive); and alternation between general and specific (e.g., connections between public knowledge and personal observation and experience).

- E.4. write to persuade the reader by anticipating and addressing counterarguments, by using rhetorical devices, and by developing an accurate and expressive style of communication that moves beyond mechanics to add flair and elegance to writing.

Requirements   This paper, your last major paper of your senior year, must do or include the following, all of which are spelled out in the newest (seventh) edition of the *MLA Handbook for Writers of Research Papers*:

- ❏ Be at least ten pages, double-spaced, typed, with 12-point serif font and standard margins.

- ❏ Refer to or include quotations from at least five sources—seven if you want to be eligible for an A. In addition to *Crime and Punishment*, these must be substantial sources—scholarly articles, essays, or books. Sources such as *shmoop.com* will not count; essays from the *Stanford Online Encyclopedia of Philosophy*, for example, do count, as would articles from Google *Scholar* or *Knol*.

- ❏ Follow all manuscript formatting guidelines outlined on the attached BHS Style Guide.

- ❏ Provide a list of Works Cited formatted according to MLA guidelines (see attached BHS MLA Style Guide for further details and assistance).

- ❏ Place a title on your first page: centered, *not* bold, italicized or underlined.

- ❏ *Use subheaders* throughout your paper to help organize and generate ideas. These subheaders should be formatted using a **bold font** and establish a clear focus to the material that follows (e.g., **Raskolnikov's Existential Troubles, Is Raskolnikov a "Superman"?** or **The Wisdom of Sophia**).

- ❏ Upload your paper to turnitin.com and submit a hard copy on the assigned date. **Papers not submitted to turnitin.com will receive no credit. If you have no drafts, no evidence of revision as implemented within the class—your paper will receive no credit.**

**Process and
Procedures**   In the coming week we will use much of our time in class as a writing workshop for research, writing instruction, feedback, the conferencing with me in class or the library. You should come to class each day with all your materials related to your paper, including all notes, books, and other resources. I am also available to meet during lunch with those who sign up on the calendar. **Your final draft will be due by Friday, May 6th.**

FIGURE 4.37 *Crime and Punishment* paper assignment for AP literature class.

standards that both parties recognize as important to learn. Again, this step is as much for the teachers as for the students since it forces them to identify their intended instructional outcomes. The samples here draw on different sets of standards; going forward (the CCSS are not yet being fully implemented as I write this), I will anchor all such assignments in either the Common Core State Standards or those AP English Literature standards developed by the College Board.

- *Requirements:* Here, students find itemized the demands of the assignment which include everything from length to deadline, format to features. I format these elements as a checklist to visually reinforce the idea that they should be able to check off each item. This is where I spell out any particular features—for example, the requirement that they embed images or links in their papers or include a certain number of sources, which they must list in the Works Cited; I would also list this under the requirements.

- *Directions:* This is where the actual writing prompt and related directions or guidelines appear. It spells out the writing task in detail, including the genre, for example, that students must use. I take extra caution to consider which verbs I should use here and whether I will need to teach them how, for example, to "*analyze* x and *explain* how it contributes to the meaning of the work as a whole."

- *Process:* This does not necessarily appear on all assignments, only those that require an articulation of the different steps we will follow, some of which might warrant a separate grade. This part of the assignment, if included, helps me envision not only where we are going but also how we will get there and what role I must play along the way.

- *Assessment Criteria:* While these may sometimes say little more than "This paper will be assessed using the 9-Point AP Rubric" (which they all have a copy of for reference) including assessment of the information demands; I determine up front what will be assessed and how. Depending on the assignment, a full rubric, with a checklist of factors common to successful performance on this particular one (see Figure 4.27 for a sample of such a rubric) may appear on the back of the assignment sheet.

- *Resources:* Although not present on all writing assignments, this element appears when the topic requires them to explore a variety of sources. So, for example, on a biographical assignment called the "Life Studies," I include resource links on our class wiki from several key websites, such as the *Time* 100, that feature profiles of people my students might study for the project. Sometimes, though not always, I include as a sample a previous student's paper that I have annotated using those tools available in Adobe Acrobat or Microsoft Word to indicate the strengths and weaknesses of it.

- *Other Content:* On occasion, if space allows and the need exists, I include a sample of what the work could look like. I say "could" because I often do not want to limit their thinking by providing a model they will treat as a template. Whenever possible, I include a range of topics to choose from on the assignment sheet, usually three or four. This increases buy-in and challenges me to think about the topic from different perspectives in relation to not only a text they may have read but also experiences they have had and skills they still need to learn.

This process of developing such a detailed assignment, either by myself or with those colleagues on my department team with whom I collaborate, helps me establish standards *for myself*. If I write a basic prompt like "Recall a time when you met someone who taught you a lesson

Teaching vs. Assigning Writing	
When Writing Is *Assigned*	**When Writing Is *Taught***
• Students are asked to write only on the teacher's topics. • The teacher selects writing topics for papers without consideration of audience and purpose. • Most of a teacher's time is spent correcting papers. • Students are asked to analyze, compare, describe, narrate, review, and summarize, without the strategies to successfully complete these tasks. • Students are not aware of significant improvement in their writing. • Students are required to rewrite—in some cases. But rewriting usually is limited to correcting grammar, usage, etc. • Students are required to write without much forethought. • Students and teachers are bored by what students write.	• Students have opportunities to create topics that matter to them. • Audience and purpose for papers are specifically identified in assignments. • Most of a teacher's time is spent in class teaching writing skills and strategies. • Students are given writing models, assignments, and strategies to guide each of their different writing tasks. • Students reflect on significant growth—or lack of it—in specific writing skills. • Students are encouraged to revise, edit, and improve—and to correct drafts and then resubmit. • Students think about what they write through brainstorming, freewriting, role-playing, discussion, or other prewriting activities. • Students and teachers are excited about what students write and make efforts to display and publish it.

Source: National Writing Project, adapted from *Because Writing Matters: Improving Student Writing in Our Schools* 2006

FIGURE 4.38 In this table, Nagin (2006) examines the difference between merely assigning and actually teaching writing.

you will never forget," I have not had to identify what that prompt gives me the chance to assess or teach. Instead, I prefer to write up an assignment sheet, thinking about the assignment as one might a trip they spent the evening planning and envisioning—while still leaving room for the unexpected discovery, which is always the best part of traveling—but also making a detailed list of what to pack so they will be sure to have a great experience along the way. The difference between these two approaches to writing assignments is often the difference between *assigning* writing and actually *teaching* writing as the comparison in Figure 4.38 shows.

Daily Writing and Beyond

As this chapter nears its end, I want to discuss the place of writing in our curriculum, especially on the daily and weekly level. Writing daily just to write does little more than develop students' stamina unless they write for a purpose that engages them and develops their skills and knowledge. Notebooks of artists reveal pages filled with sketches of hands, noses, faces, and more—all of these evidence of artists learning and refining their craft. Such drawings are never just idle doodling: They are evidence of an artist (or apprentice) working to master an effect, a line, a technique. So it should be in class when we have students write; time is too precious

FIGURE 4.39 Prior to reading *Siddhartha*, students head to the football field with their notebooks to reflect on where they are at this stage in their lives versus where they are going. They sit on the yard line that corresponds to their age and imagine that they get a full 100 yards of life.

to spend it carelessly. Though not necessarily done in notebooks, students *in math* classes were found to spend more time as measured by "pencil on paper" in high-performing high schools than other subject areas—almost twice as much as English! English classes in the study tended to ask for writing of greater length (Langer 2011a). The notebook is such a "think space" as it allows me to have them put "pencil on paper" more often than I would if I had to collect and slap a grade on everything they wrote.

The "notebook" goes by many names, each of which emphasizes a different aspect of its purpose and value. The alternative names include: the daybook (Brannon et al. 2008; Murray 2004); writer's notebook (Kittle 2008; Buckner 2005; Fletcher 1996); *Reader's-Writer's Notebook* (Rief 2007); and, with an emphasis on English-language learners, the Interactive Notebook (Carter, Hernandez, and Richison 2009). Such notebooks offer a place, similar to the artist's sketchpad, to practice, capture, and think; as I will show later, this place is expanding to include more public, digital writing that is similar to notebooks but now goes by the names wiki, blog, tweet, and/or Facebook. What all such spaces have in common is the safety of a place where students can take intellectual risks without fear of failure or low grades (see Figures 4.40a and b).

In my classes, we use the notebook (and blogs, wikis, Facebook, tweets) for analytical or academic writing, the sort that reports (Stotsky 2010a; Arum, Roksa, and Cho 2010; Applebee and Langer 2009) emphasize our students need to develop if they are to be ready for the demands of college and/or the workplace. But we also use them to generate ideas, reflect on

FIGURE 4.40a Jesus, Alex, and Daidyn using notebooks to practice their writing in class. Such writing offers a safe opportunity for students to rehearse the types of academic writing they are attempting to master.

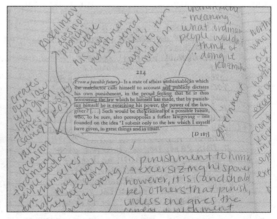

FIGURE 4.40b On occasion, I have students tape a piece of text into their notebooks, giving them more space to work on close reading and annotating.

progress and connections, and just think—about everything. Penny Kittle (2008) offers a vivid description of what a Writer's Notebook is and how she uses it in her class:

> I expect that most of my students are not keeping writing notebooks, so I start with my personal notebook tour so they get to know me, as well as develop a sense for how writing comes to be. . . . The first page of each of my notebooks is a collage. . . . I tell my students why I chose the pictures, quotes, or ideas that help me write. The first notebook assignment is to create a collage for the inside cover of the notebook. . . . Even in the first week of school we begin filling our writing notebooks with quick, free writing . . . and "now you try it" exercises from minilessons. It's all rehearsal—the prewriting work that will lead us as writers. Using the notebook is a daily expectation in class . . . , a storehouse for . . . all the rubble of thought . . . the notebook is where we mine the world for story." (23)

I do my best to write with them as much as I can, which I find sets the tone and gets my own head in the game that is about to begin in class; sometimes I even write on my iPad and project it to show them my own thinking as it unfolds. (See Figure 4.41.) In our notebooks, we do, on any given day, at least one of the following in class or at home:

- Take notes
- Jot observations
- Write draft paragraphs
- Reflect on our performance
- Reflect on progress
- Write sentences based on language and craft study
- Represent ideas in graphic form
- Generate ideas for papers, discussions, projects

Figure 4.42 shows the handout I give students, which you will note has additional examples of what we do in and with the notebook (and blog).

The notebook offers, as I have already discussed, a place for daily writing, a place to practice, think, respond, and reflect (see Figures 4.43–4.46). How you respond to or evaluate the notebook depends on how your students use them. Sometimes I bring students' notebooks home, one box at a time, at the end of each grading period to evaluate them; other times I go over them in class while they are busy working in groups, thus allowing me to confer on the side with them individually as we discuss the notebook. The truth is that I am monitoring students' use of the notebooks almost daily as I circulate around the room.

FIGURE 4.41 I keep a notebook in class for all such in-class writing that I do with them about the books we read. Here you see me writing about own personal reading book after we had time for SSR in class.

Thinking about *how* you read

- I was distracted by . . .
- I started to think about . . .
- I got stuck when . . .
- I was confused/focused today because . . .
- One strategy I used to help me read this better was . . .
- When I got distracted I tried to refocus myself by . . .
- These word(s) or phrases were new/interesting to me . . . I think they mean . . .
- When reading I should . . .
- When I read today I realized that . . .
- I had a hard time understanding . . .
- I'll read better next time if . . .

Thinking about *what* you read

- Why does the character/author . . .
- Why doesn't the character/author . . .
- What surprised me most was . . .
- I predict that . . .
- This author's writing style is . . .
- I noted that the author uses . . .
- The main character wants/is . . .
- If I could, I'd ask the author/character . . .
- The most interesting event/idea in this book is . . .
- I realized . . .
- The main conflict/idea in this book is . . .
- I wonder why . . .
- One theme that keeps coming up is . . .
- I found the following quote interesting . . .
- I _____ this book because . . .

Elaborating on what you think

- I think _____ because . . .
- A good example of _____ is . . .
- This reminded me of _____ because . . .
- This was important because . . .
- One thing that surprised me was _____ because I always thought . . .
- The author is saying that . . .

Sample bookmark

The Book of Ideas

Capture • Conceive • Compose • Connect • Create • Converse • Contemplate

Purpose

To think. To generate. To open up, break down, crack open, work through. To wonder. A place to play, experiment, try on, try out. An idea lab, think tank, a Walden Pond made of paper. Who keeps a record of their ideas in order to discover, refine, extend, or understand their ideas? Philosophers, presidents, scientists, inventors, artists, CEOs, designers, bloggers, professional presenters, researchers, explorers, chefs, directors, and, of course, writers, poets, screenwriters.

Standards

The work in your Idea Book should show you constantly:

- Generating insights and connections between current studies, other subjects, and the world
- Analyzing causes, effects, and implications of details, actions, and events
- Responding to and reflecting on what you read, what we discuss, what you think
- Synthesizing different perspectives and concepts across, within, and beyond the texts we study
- Drawing, listing, diagraming, doodling, writing, brainstorming, playing with ideas
- Reflecting on meaning, importance, process, practice, performance
- Explaining why you think one thing or another; or one thing *and* another
- Capturing ideas from wherever/whomever however you can: copying, jotting, notetaking, etc.
- Thinking: about language, literature, life, learning

Assessment

The Idea Book is the equivalent of one major paper each semester, though it is evaluated each grading period. The criteria are spelled out in spirit here; a more detailed rubric will be provided prior to collecting and evaluating your Idea Book.

Notebook

Each Idea Book should do or include the following:

- Include a table of contents on the first six pages where each entry is identified and dated
- Date and label each entry clearly (e.g., "10/25 Sonnet 29 Response")
- Use a standard composition notebook like the one pictured.
- Show your sense of style: if that means making it personal with images inside and out, that's great; if it means keeping it as it comes, that's fine.
- Each day should have writing whether about what we do in class or what you read and think about outside of class.

Blogging: Blogger • Tumblr • Other?

General guidelines for blogging:

- Post to the class blog (http://seniorwanderers.blogspot.com/)
- Post to the class blog on Tumblr (englishcompanion.tumblr.com)
- Respond to blogs by students in the class
- Choose your *three* best blogs and print, along with comments, then paste these into your Idea Book at the end of each grading period.

FIGURE 4.42 The details of the Idea Book are outlined above. The full handout includes images of a range of notebooks from different professions to show students how major thinkers, designers, scientists, and writers have used notebooks to capture ideas for research, products, and more. The sample bookmark pictured to the left can be used to guide students' writing in their Idea Books as needed.

A Student Notebook Page

Sarah

Needleman

- Needleman portrays the meaning of happiness in the time we surround our lives with.
- Evil originates from desire because mans goal in life is to understand it.

Lombardo

- The importance of how people view time, and the difference in their choices shows the importance true happiness because the choices that play into it.
- If a person wishes to wait and live for the future they must have obtained the knowledge that this is, what they want and their true happiness and desires play into it.

happiness

Siddhartha?

- Siddhartha's arduos journey, in an effort to find himself and therefore true happiness and truth for every part of his life, is an exemplary example of the path to happiness.
- His struggles and desire to reach this point through all of the trials and teachers is an extreme example of the journey we must go through if we truely want to be happy and free.

Sarah

- To know what I truely-w/o doubt- want to be happy is somewhat impossible w/o going on the struggling journey Siddhartha went through. To be truely happy— not just on the surface or on the moment but future you must know who you are.

FIGURE 4.43 We nearly always use the notebook to write about ideas that connect our own lives to the ideas in the book but, as you see here, in substantial ways that can be used as the basis for subsequent writing assignments. Here you see Sarah also connecting the subject to the novel we were reading and two nonfiction articles, one by philosopher Jacob Needleman and the other by psychologist Philip Zimbardo.

Siddhartha Roles Roundtable

You Cant Always Get What You Want

Friday December 11, Indiana became the 19th state; Nitrous oxide was used for the first time in dentistry; Germany and Italy declared war on the United States; and I was deferred from my future. While I would love to say I am ecstatic because I still have a chance-- I am actually frustrated beyond belief. So I was good, but not good enough? If I had just studied a little harder, signed up for a few more of that, done a little more of this... the possibilities of the game "what if" are never ending, and with it is my anger toward myself. Trying not to compare myself to the people who got into Stanford is one of the hardest things I have ever done. Friday December 11th was filled with some extreme downs on this roller coaster of college applications. Thankfully I had some good people around me that were truthful in helping me understand that I cant always get what I want and that life goes on and I must go with it. Earlier in the semester Mr. Burke asked us to think about the nature of true desire. At the time I thought about the idea that for one to truly know what they want they must be in complete and total suffering. Growing up I was convinced that I wanted to go to this school---that it was my truest desire. But, as I sit here today I believe that those desires were clouded by a synthetic wish because of the people around me and their influence on my life. I'm not saying I have hit rock bottom and therefore know my true desires now. But I do believe that because this is out of the way, or half out of the way, I have a clearer view of my wants and needs. While I cant always get what I want I may be able to get what I need out of this... and for that I am thankful.

FIGURE 4.44 "You Cant Always Get What You Want" is a sample personal entry that shows so powerfully why students need a chance to reflect on their lives throughout the process of creating those lives.

Notetaking Tools: Paragraph Prep

Name: ______________________________ **Date:** ______________

Subject:	**Main Idea:**

Who	Loses	What	How	Why it matters/What it means	Pg #
Gregor	loses	not only his role in the family, but his identity and dignity	when Grete calls him "a monster," then refers to him as "it," telling them to "get rid of the idea that it's Gregor."	This shift in language reveals a mental shift in Grete and, eventually, her parents, that allows them to accept the loss of their son, Gregor, who at the same time thinks "on his family with deep emotion and love."	53 and 54
Who	**Gains**	**What**	**How**	**Why it matters/What it means**	**Pg #**
Gregor	gains	a new appreciation for all he did for his family in the years after the "business disaster"	when he learns that his father, having saved the money Gregor gave him to provide for the family, in fact had "accumulated . . . a tidy principal."	This has the effect of making him feel irrelevant now that they have what they need without his salary. It also means that Gregor worked longer and harder than necessary because he "could have paid off more of his father's debt."	27 and 28

Note: Now go back to the top and fill in the Subject and Main Idea sections to establish a focus for your paragraph.

FIGURE 4.45 Paragraph Prep is a handout we use to take structured notes prior to writing in notebooks. The notes are then used as the basis for that paragraph.

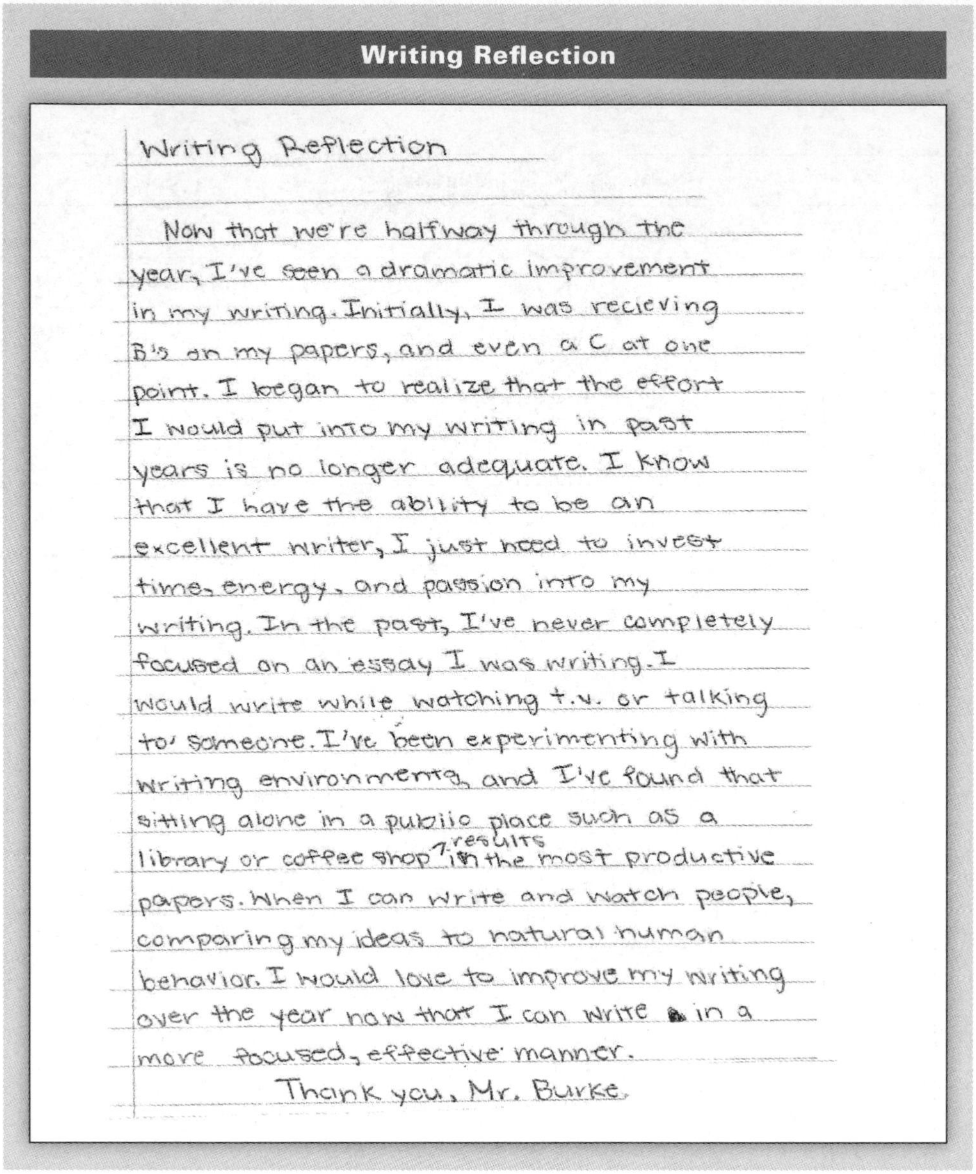

Writing Reflection

Writing Reflection

Now that we're halfway through the year, I've seen a dramatic improvement in my writing. Initially, I was recieving B's on my papers, and even a C at one point. I began to realize that the effort I would put into my writing in past years is no longer adequate. I know that I have the ability to be an excellent writer, I just need to invest time, energy, and passion into my writing. In the past, I've never completely focused on an essay I was writing. I would write while watching t.v. or talking to someone. I've been experimenting with writing environments, and I've found that sitting alone in a public place such as a library or coffee shop results in the most productive papers. When I can write and watch people, comparing my ideas to natural human behavior. I would love to improve my writing over the year now that I can write in a more focused, effective manner.
   Thank you, Mr. Burke.

FIGURE 4.46 Hallie reflects on her growth as a writer. Her sense of progress and confidence is all the more important in light of where she began at the beginning of the year.

Evaluating notebooks, however, poses several challenges. Some kids write more than others; others have smaller handwriting and *seem* to write less than many classmates, but on further scrutiny may actually write more. Boys often resist the use of the notebook, seeing it as busywork; girls often exceed my expectations. Some students write so illegibly you are torn as to how to make sense of and grade it. And some go so far beyond even your most ideal standard as to make you blush with guilt that a student took so much time for your one class when they have so many others. The scoring guide shown in Figure 4.47 allows me a measure of flexibility and efficiency while offering them some accountability for the content and its quality.

Name: _____ Period: _____ Date: _____

Performance	Description
Exceeds the Standard A	**Completion** ❑ Includes all assigned entries and *three* representative blogs from the last grading period. ❑ Shows extra effort in completing these assignments through notes taken in class, additional entries, quality of thought, personal/world/other text connections, or thoroughness. **Compliance** ❑ Follows all guidelines, including dating and clearly labeling all entries. **Content** ❑ **Insight**: Observations, connections, and analysis are precise, compelling (as opposed to summaries or general/personal responses based only on opinion and feelings). ❑ **Reasoning**: Claims and observations are routinely supported by textual evidence, which the writer consistently explains by elaborating on the assertions and connections. ❑ **Understanding**: Entries show insight beyond the obvious or literal meaning/importance. **Consistency** ❑ Maintains quality of content and analysis throughout the notebook and blogs.
Meets the Standard B	**Completion** ❑ Includes assigned entries and *three* representative blogs from the last grading period. ❑ Shows serious effort in completing these assignments through notes taken in class, additional entries, quality of thought, personal/world/other text connections, or thoroughness. **Compliance** ❑ Follows all guidelines, including dating and clearly labeling all entries. **Content** ❑ **Insight**: Observations, connections, and analysis are usually precise and compelling. ❑ **Reasoning**: Claims and observations are generally supported by textual evidence, which the writer usually explains by elaborating on the assertions and connections. ❑ **Understanding**: Entries show substantial insight beyond the obvious meaning/importance. **Consistency** ❑ Maintains quality of content and analysis throughout most of the notebook and blogs.
Approaches the Standard C	**Completion** ❑ Includes most assigned entries and *three* representative blogs from the last grading period. ❑ Shows modest effort in completing these assignments through notes taken in class, quality of thought, personal/world/other text connections, or thoroughness. **Compliance** ❑ Does not follow all guidelines. Does not date and clearly label all entries. **Content** ❑ **Insight**: Observations, connections, and analysis lack precision and analysis. ❑ **Reasoning**: Claims and observations are not always supported by textual evidence; the writer sometimes explains by elaborating on the assertions and connections. ❑ **Understanding**: Entries show limited insight beyond the obvious meaning/importance. **Consistency** ❑ Quality of content and analysis varies throughout the notebook and blogs.
Misses the Standard D F	**Completion** ❑ Missing most assigned entries; missing many or certain important entries. ❑ Most assignments missing or incomplete: few connections to text, self, or world. **Compliance** ❑ Rarely follows all guidelines. Does not date and clearly label entries. **Content** ❑ **Insight**: Shows little or not analysis; may not understand the text or assignment. ❑ **Reasoning**: Claims are rarely supported by textual evidence; no elaboration. ❑ **Understanding**: Entries show little/no insight beyond the obvious meaning/importance. **Consistency** ❑ Quality of content and analysis is extremely inconsistent throughout the notebook and blogs.

FIGURE 4.47 This is the scoring guide I use to evaluate the Reader's Notebooks. It will evolve, however; for we are always tweaking and trying to get it right.

Blogs, wikis, and specific platforms, such as Twitter and Tumblr, represent the next generation of journals; in addition to digital daybooks, people use notebook applications like *Evernote* (I *love* this one: You *must* check it out!) and Microsoft's *OneNote*. Soon enough it seems, both students and teachers will have some durable digital device—call it a tablet, pad, e-book, whatever—on which we will compose, read, capture, even discuss through interactive video applications now common on smart phones. But whether the tablet is stone, as it was so long ago, or a sleek slab of silicon with enough memory to hold all the books ever written, we will be writing, an act itself that Plato worried would lead to the demise of our memory, our minds, our civilization (Plato 1997, 551).

Digital Writing

Such sentiments as Plato expresses, and those wedded to the "scribal society" of the past (Purves 1990), echo concerns about what some call "new writing" (Herrington, Hodgson, and Moran 2009) or, more commonly, "digital writing" (Hicks 2009; Nagin 2010). Others conceive of this writing as "post-typographic forms of text" (Lankshear and Knobel 2006, 23) or "multimodal" documents (Kress and Van Leeuwen 2001; Gee 2007). In a world where people—for reasons both personal and professional—post to Facebook, blog, tweet, podcast, text, and more, digital writing stands to become the dominant means of communicating as we all master "the art of writing little" (Johnson 2011).

> **"**IN A WORLD WHERE PEOPLE—FOR REASONS BOTH PERSONAL AND PROFESSIONAL—POST TO FACEBOOK, BLOG, TWEET, PODCAST, TEXT, AND MORE, DIGITAL WRITING STANDS TO BECOME THE DOMINANT MEANS OF COMMUNICATING . . . **"**

The tools and "apps," once dismissed as little more than extras or frills, have since become the digital equivalent of utilities, such as water, gas, and electricity (Kirkpatrick 2010, 144), for individuals, businesses, and even governments—as well as those who would overthrow those governments. Twitter and Tumblr show substantial gains in the teen population, which finds blogging ineffective since, as one teen put it, "all the people I am trying to reach are on Facebook" (Kopytoff 2011).

Digital writing is not new to teens, of course; it has been part of the air they have inhaled since birth. On Facebook, teens are as likely to communicate using images, links, or songs as they are YouTube clips (or even words!) to craft the modern-day equivalent of coded messages to escape the watchful eyes of all adults. Teens are, in this sense, sophisticated authors who can, and do, use any mode, medium, or means needed to convey their intended message as this article from *Wired* (Thompson 2011) shows:

> If you're in high school these days, a lot of your socializing happens online, but your parents usually insist on being "friended" so they can check what you're posting. This creates a communication dilemma. You want to post candid updates about your life so your friends know what's going on—but not so candid that your folks catch wind of it.
>
> The solution is   to post status updates that have two layers: A bland surface meaning intended for parents, and a deeper, richer significance that can be decoded only by close friends.

It is precisely such sophisticated compositions about the *sturm und drang* of teenage life that inspire some to hail today's youth as smart, savvy, and innovative and others to dismiss them as dumb, superficial, and distracted. Still others, as I have noted throughout this chapter, see such personal and inevitably informal compositions as responsible for the demise of craft, language in general, and conventions in particular. Guzzetti and Gamboa (2005) counter, based on their study of adolescent girls' online writing, that such communication develops confidence, ownership, and a voice, while preparing students for the changing literacy demands of a global society, and addresses the growing digital divide (201).

As Kress (2007) says, trying to capture the changing nature of composition and text, "the *world told* [through writing] is a different world than the *world shown* [through images and other media]" (1). My own inclination to link when writing, as noted in the two bracketed remarks, characterizes the shift in writing, making it almost more appropriate to use the word *composing* instead, as some have suggested we should. Such links though, also represent one of the criticisms of digital writing: It fragments the reading experience, sending the reader out of the primary text and into other texts where the reader then finds other links to follow, eventually losing track of time and not getting back to the primary text they sat down to read in the first place. Thus, as writers of digital texts, we will have to learn not just how to compose but how to *design* texts in ways that direct the reader to whatever end we originally set out to achieve.

" . . . AS WRITERS OF DIGITAL TEXTS, WE WILL HAVE TO LEARN NOT JUST HOW TO COMPOSE BUT HOW TO *DESIGN* TEXTS IN WAYS THAT DIRECT THE READER TO WHATEVER END WE ORIGINALLY SET OUT TO ACHIEVE. **"**

How then do we *teach* digital writing skills? This chapter, after all, is about not just *what* to write but *how* to write. Let me say first that nothing can teach you more about what digital writing is and how to do it than writing such texts. We do not have to *like* Twitter or Facebook, but we have a professional obligation to understand and keep in mind how written communication is evolving in the world for which we are preparing our students. Does a tweet or Facebook update fall into the rhetorical triangle? Most definitely. Can a candidate become president or a company launch a new product line without writing about them on these social media venues? No way.

A recent blog I wrote had embedded within it: hyperlinks to streaming interviews of authors, newspaper articles, *Wikipedia* entries, book reviews, an essay in the *New Yorker*, or a TED Talk video. None of these are essential to click away to; I wrote it as a stand-alone piece. The links merely offer further information for those interested in certain things—Paulo Coelho, Michelle Rhee, the human brain, white boys, and why "Amy Chua is a 'wimp'"—they can read *after* they read my blog.

As I wrote it, I had to make decisions about which links to include, why those links, and whether I wanted those links to be optional or required reading. I also had to make a separate but equally important set of decisions, all of which are somewhat unique to digital writing: How to format it? What to include as links and what to include as embedded images or video in the text's body? Which images (if any) are most appropriate for my purpose and audience? I ended up deciding to use only hyperlinks since images add interest but can also confuse the reader about how to read the text, what to look at, what to read. The resulting text reads quickly (another important element of the digital text in a hurried world reading such texts on screens) and would not fill more than a typical tablet screen.

The list of digital texts most common to the English class would include the following:

- Blogs (which include, for some, Twitter)
- Wikis
- Google+ (which is new as of this writing but shows great potential)
- Multimodal documents (aka mixed or multimedia texts)
- Slide presentations (e.g., Keynote, Prezi, PowerPoint)
- Surveys (e.g., Survey Monkey, Google Forms, Zoomerang)
- Google Docs (various tools and applications within that set)
- Online discussions (through Skype, Facebook, or Google+)
- Scripts (for podcasts, video, or mixed media productions)

Some of these, such as blogs (see Figure 4.48), differ little from the essay or the journal in their general intent or subject; they are, of course, infinitely more public because they are *published* for all the world to see. In short, however, these are texts composed by an individual for the purpose of communicating information, ideas, or opinions to a larger (and more authentic) audience than their teacher. Other forms, such as wikis, online discussions about texts, or a classmate's essay, are more collaborative and restricted to those engaging in that conversation.

As these few examples (and those throughout the book) show, digital writing includes much more than sending an email or writing an essay on a computer. Nor is it limited to personal writing. In her book *Teaching Middle School Writers*, Laura Robb (2010) found strong support, both in teachers' classrooms and research studies, that "analytical exchanges online" not only engaged students but allowed them to discuss literature using blogs, wikis, email, online discussion forums, and even (oh my!) text messages (259).

Providing further evidence of the prevalence and value of digital writing in the curriculum, Lunsford identified several key results in her national Stanford Study of Writing, which examined the writing performance of undergraduate students across disciplines for all four years and their first year after graduation in the workplace or graduate school. Their experience of writing online had led them to expect writing to "make things happen" and to imagine other, often more compelling ways, to communicate information by either using other media or blending them in a multimedia form. Lunsford wonders how we will answer as more students ask, "I know you'd like me to write an essay, but [would it be possible] to make a documentary [instead]?" (Lunsford 2008).

In their study, Lunsford and Lunsford also found that students during the five-year period of the study gradually increased use and integration into their writing of visual (tables, charts, graphs, and illustrations) and multimedia (video, audio, slide shows) elements (Stanford Study of Writing 2008). My own students already routinely ask whether they can incorporate images or other digital content into their papers, even when I have not required or even suggested it. Lunsford observed that students "organize their content and material by association. Like a well-crafted essay, one idea leads to another in an associational framework—more akin to organizing a website" (Karp 2010).

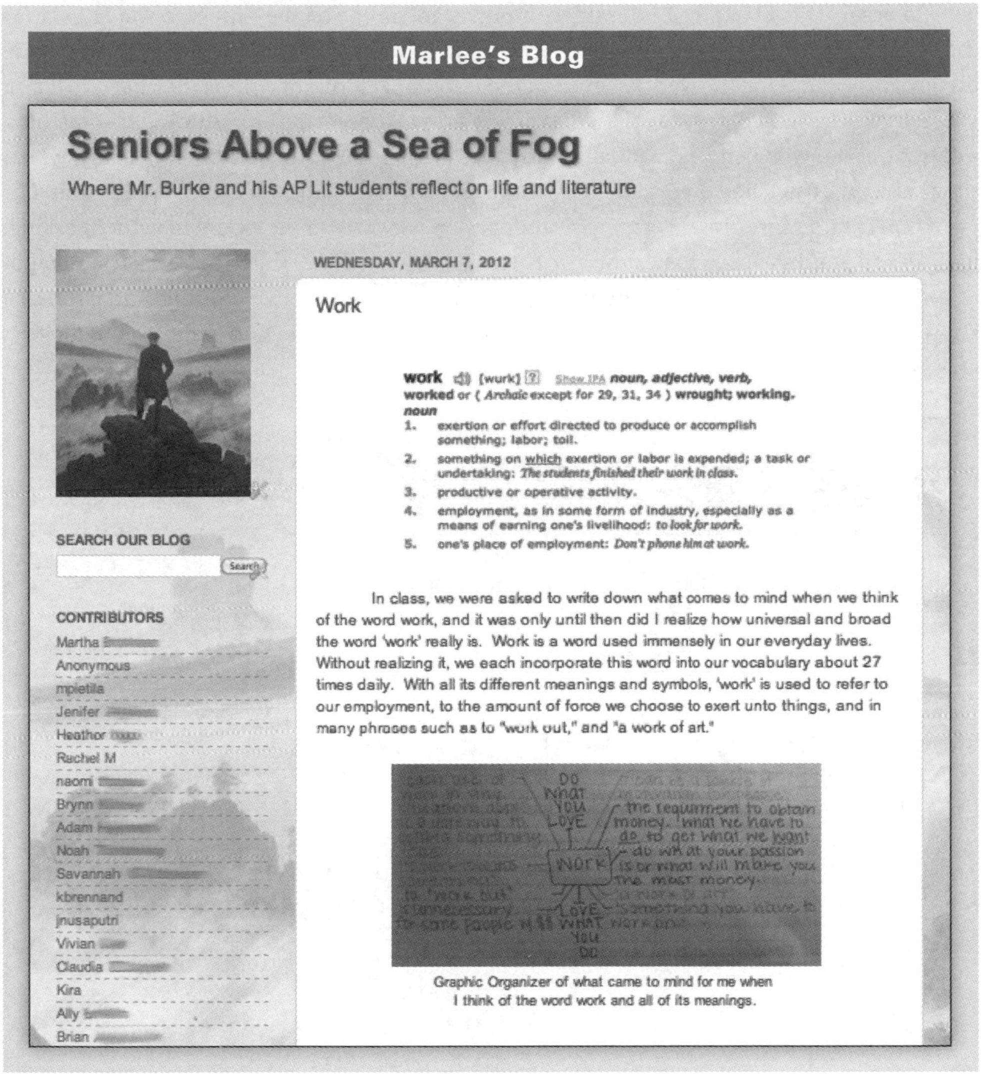

FIGURE 4.48 Marlee's blog in which she shows her thinking across media and, more to the point, deep thinking about ideas such as work.

Where some see such developments as deficits, Lunsford says she sees "a student who can get across a complex idea in 140 characters or less [on Twitter] and . . . [sees] versatility." One of the most compelling findings from Lunsford's study is the awareness students, after years of writing online, show for audience. According to Thompson (2009):

[S]tudents were remarkably adept at what rhetoricians call *kairos*—assessing their audience and adapting their tone and technique to best get their point across. The modern world of online writing, particularly in chat and on discussion threads, is conversational and public, which makes it closer to the Greek tradition of argument than the asynchronous letter and essay writing of 50 years ago.

So are my kids hanging out in the computer lab, online all the time? No way. I look for the opportunities to incorporate digital writing into my courses when we have already made the progress and done the work we must in the traditional forms of writing they need to learn. When they have written several essays and time seems to present the opportunity for something different, then I will come up with another assignment, such as the multimedia essay, which they can compose using presentation software instead of a word-processing application. But even now, I find more kids incorporating, not always when required and often without asking, images and graphs to represent, sum up, or elaborate on some idea they discuss in a paragraph.

Alison, one of my senior students, captures nicely the range of emotions and issues, as shown in Figure 4.49, when it comes to digital writing in her reflection at the end of the first semester.

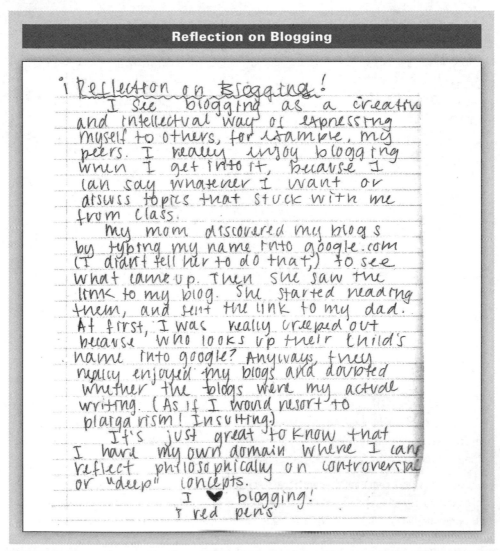

Reflection on Blogging

"Reflection on Blogging!

I see blogging as a creative and intellectual way of expressing myself to others, for example, my peers. I really enjoy blogging when I get into it, because I can say whatever I want or discuss topics that stuck with me from class.

My mom discovered my blogs by typing my name into google.com (I didn't tell her to do that,) to see what came up. Then she saw the link to my blog. She started reading them, and sent the link to my dad. At first, I was really creeped out because who looks up their child's name into google? Anyways, they really enjoyed my blogs and doubted whether the blogs were my actual writing. (As if I would resort to plagarism! Insulting.)

It's just great to know that I have my own domain where I can reflect philosophically on controversial or "deep" concepts.

I ♥ blogging!
8 red pens"

FIGURE 4.49 Alison reflects on blogging, which she had never done but became a big fan of by year's end.

Conclusions **and** Implications

Blogs, of course, did not exist when I left for Tunisia in the 1980s with my portable typewriter, carbon paper, and extra ribbons. By the time we concluded our work there two years later, I had written some 500 pages of letters, mostly single-spaced and duplicated using carbon paper, to Susan, whom I married a few years later. Before all volunteers departed, the Peace Corps brought us to the island of Djerba, rumored to be the site of Homer's Lotus Eaters. It was beautiful in a timeless and ancient way, as all Mediterranean islands are during the summer.

> **"**I . . . LOOK FOR THE OPPORTUNITIES TO INCORPORATE DIGITAL WRITING INTO MY COURSES WHEN WE HAVE ALREADY MADE THE PROGRESS AND DONE THE WORK WE MUST IN THE TRADITIONAL FORMS OF WRITING [STUDENTS] NEED TO LEARN.**"**

To prepare us for our return, Cynthia, the Peace Corps nurse, asked us all to describe our last two years in as much detail as we could in 15 minutes. We scribbled feverishly. Then, Cynthia said, "I know this is crazy, but I want you to further reduce that down to one paragraph that includes the main events." We all insisted it could not be done; then we did it. Finally, after admitting it was absurd, Cynthia asked us to write *one sentence* that captured the last two years. We complied, agreeing it was absurd and laughing at the same time. We inevitably ended up with sentences that said next to nothing: "It was always so hot," or "I built a school." After we read them aloud, Cynthia said, "That's about as much as people are really going to want to hear about all this when you return home." And she was right. When we said these things to friends and family back home, they would often respond with breathless wonder that "It was always hot" or that I "built a school."

I share this story because it now illustrates the change in writing these past 25 years, especially when you compare my experience with today's generation. It seems almost anachronistic to speak of "writing"; better, perhaps, to speak of *composing*—a word that somehow captures more fully the sense of creating something substantial, made from elements one has carefully chosen and arranged with a purpose in mind. Bateman (1990) and Newkirk (1997) apply these notions of composing to the self, suggesting that we present (or even *create*) ourselves through our writing, trying to capture in language and represent to our audience "that idealized sense of who we should be" when we write. This observation complements Smagorinsky's notion that "academic bullshit" (i.e., academic discourse) is an early but necessary part of developing an academic identity (Lampert 2001).

We want students to have what Newkirk calls a "repertoire of performances" available (1997, 5), but we also want them to write in ways that others will read, understand, and use. We want students to know that they can, if they receive an unfair parking ticket (as I did recently), write with enough authority and power to get it dismissed (as I did), thereby putting that writing to work for real ends. For *real writing is read*—by customers, colleagues, officials, community members, and those, such as my wife, we would win over with our words and with whom we would compose our own wedding vows (as we did).

In her 2008 NCTE presidential address, Kathleen Yancey spoke of the "impulse to compose," citing not only those documents through which we composed our country's freedom, but those through which Obama won an election the Founding Fathers could not have imagined as they declared our freedom in 1776. Obama "won . . . for *his* writing—his two books, his eloquent speeches, his graphic posters, his emails with embedded video, and his text messages that announced Joe Biden as vice president; [he] asked you to contribute to the Red Cross, . . . reminded you and your neighbors to vote, . . . and then thanked you for helping make him victorious" (Yancey 2009, 316).

While I would be thrilled, would feel so very proud to have a student grow up and use what I teach them to become the U.S. President, I am just as committed to the writing demands of the junior college student and what Yancey calls the "everyday genres" at home and work: letters, notes, memos, recipes, reviews, and reports (322). Collier (2009) further investigated these forms of everyday writing, going into a range of workplaces to see what most people write in their daily lives to earn a living. She found people in all kinds of jobs filling out requisitions, making lists, writing memos, sending emails, updating Facebook pages and sending tweets for businesses. This writing seems, at a glance, so limited as to not count as writing; yet as one man said, he "spends half of each shift writing (7).

The people Collier studied took writing very seriously, recognizing that mistakes could cost jobs, customers, and even, in extreme cases, lives. Studying those entering vocational schools and community colleges after high school, sometimes as late as their 20s or 30s, Mike Rose noted how central writing was to many of these jobs, and how much learning to write meant to people who studied welding one period and art history the next, both requiring extensive notetaking and writing (2011, 36). These working people represent my own past, my roots. How well I remember as a child, perhaps 10, watching my parents study to get licenses and earn promotions, my father taking writing classes at the community college so that he could write the job evaluations for those who worked in his department.

When I graduated from high school in 1979, my own literacy skills were hardly more advanced than my father's when he left high school at 15 and began working. Thanks to good teachers who showed faith in me and had patience, I endured my placement in remedial writing my first year in college. I survived the six-inch bold red SO WHAT? and the accompanying F on my first (10-page!) paper (on *Hamlet*) when I finally took my first college English course. I overcame the early struggles to learn how to write for all the different academic disciplines, each having its own style, conventions, and language.

> **"With your help, your students will do the same and feel as grateful to you as I do to my own teachers even now, so many years later. They were not just helping me become a writer, they were helping me become who I am today . . ."**

At every turn, I met teachers who took the time to show me how to do what I did not know how to do; in this way, I progressed and improved, one word, one page, one paper at a time. With your help, your students will do the same and feel as grateful to you as I do to my own teachers even now, so many years later. They were not just helping me become a writer, they were helping me become who I am today, just as I did for one of my students named Jennifer Morales who wrote:

Thanks Mr. Burke. Your letter means a lot to me. You have always put in a little extra effort to push me to become greatness. Some people will push me too hard but when you tell me that I've got to keep writing not because it sounds good because it will keep my soul alive and well, I feel more of a reason to keep writing.

Recommended **Resources**

PRINT

- *A Rhetoric for Writing Teachers*, Erika Lindemann (Oxford University Press 2001).
- *Teaching Middle School Writers: What Every English Teacher Needs to Know*, Laura Robb (Heinemann 2010).
- *Write Like This: Teaching Real-World Writing Through Modeling and Mentor Texts*, Kelly Gallagher (Stenhouse 2011).
- *Write Beside Them: Risk, Voice, and Clarity in High School Writing*, Penny Kittle (Heinemann 2008).
- *Critical Passages: Teaching the Transition to College Composition*, Kristin Dombek and Scott Herndon (Teachers College 2004).
- *A Writer Teaches Writing*, Donald M. Murray (Thomson 2004).

ONLINE

- National Writing Project (www.nwp.org/)
- Readwritethink.org
- The Purdue Online Writing Lab (OWL) (http://owl.english.purdue.edu/)
- Institute for Writing and Rhetoric at Dartmouth (www.dartmouth.edu/~writing/)

CHAPTER FIVE

Teaching Reading

Every text . . . is a lazy machine asking the reader to do some of its work.
—Umberto Eco, from *Six Walks in the Fictional Woods* (1994, 13)

Introduction: The Process of Becoming a Reader

I was not born a reader. Before I became a serious athlete in my teen years, I whiled away my days along the American River in Sacramento where I hunted snakes and lizards, built forts with friends, and floated downstream on hot summer afternoons. I was too busy *being* Huck Finn to *read* about him. Later, when I put away these childish things, I picked up the tennis racket and began reading for very specific purposes that had nothing to do with school: I devoured anything related to my favorite players, improved techniques, product reviews, or major tournaments, reading these articles the way I would later read *The Carpenter's Manifesto*: to learn how to do or improve something. Yet I also enjoyed this reading, for it fed some new, more ambitious self I did not then realize I was in the process of creating. Reading for school or any other reason during those years—well, that was a different story.

During my junior year of high school, despite being very ill, I went down to school to take the SAT; friends picked me up early that morning. Moments after the test began I left, seeking shelter under a tree outside Mr. Baxter's class where I was busy failing English. I woke hours later, very confused as to where I was. Stumbling my way back to the cafeteria, I found everyone gone, the campus empty, and myself too weak to do anything. So I shuffled over to my locker and took out *Bless the Beasts and the Children* by Glendon Swarthout, returned to my shade—and read. Hours later, when I looked up from the book, it was late afternoon in the sleepy suburbs of Sacramento; but I had been elsewhere, doing other things, with kids my own age whom I only just met but now felt I knew better than most of my "real" friends who that day had left me behind. By the time I walked the couple miles home that day, I was changed in ways it would take me years to understand. (Burke 1999, 2)

When, two years later, I began attending the local community college, I faced a new challenge: how to read textbooks for introductory classes such as economics and psychology. I saw people highlighting words as they read; so I got a blue highlighter. Apparently they highlighted the important ideas. I highlighted whole chapters at first. I quickly realized, however, that it was not particularly helpful to have whole chapters highlighted in blue.

Soon, in addition to all my required reading for classes, I began gorging on the canon of early adulthood: Kerouac, Rand, Hesse, *Zen and the Art of Motorcycle Maintenance*, and others. After that first year of college, I read constantly, as if my life depended on it: at home, on the job, and, at one point, even in the car until, on my way to college one day, I rear-ended a woman's car.

I spent my summer that year parking cars in the Y Lot at the California State Fair, a vast expanse of dirt that offered no shelter. There I stood, in heat that often exceeded 100°, my flag hanging uselessly in one hand and a book held up in the other. Wasn't it obvious where to park? Out there in that lot, working 12 to 14 hour days, I read. And I read. And read. *Lord of the Flies*. Kesey. Steinbeck. Hemingway. All things Kerouac, whose author bio I consulted for suggestions that told me what to read next.

I was making tremendous progress, filling up my word hoard every day. Until one book made me feel completely stupid. Only years later would I really understand that *Finnegans Wake* was just not a book I was ready to read at that stage, never mind that I was trying to read it while standing in Y Lot where cars honked and racetrack winners whooped. It was, of course, not the defeat I feared it was. For in my eighteenth year, while earning $10 an hour as a Teamster parking cars at the state fair in a miserable dirt lot, I soon realized that I had, in fact, become a reader.

By senior year in college, finishing my last classes in cognitive psychology, I was fully under the spell of literature. Sitting at the seminar table with my fellow seniors, I placed my stack of James Joyce books, which included *Ulysses*, along side their psychology texts. And while they spoke of cognitive dissonance, I thought instead of Molly Bloom and plump Buck Mulligan, Stephen Dedalus, and the majestic beauty of the English language. Months later, I joined the Peace Corps, leaving soon thereafter for Tunisia where I spent my mornings helping create a school for special needs children and the rest of the day and every evening reading books I brought back each week from the American Cultural Center in Tunis. Over the course of those two years, I read everything: novels, all the major sacred texts, histories, biographies, poetry—you name it, I read it.

> **"**I WAS MAKING TREMENDOUS PROGRESS, FILLING UP MY WORD HOARD EVERY DAY. UNTIL ONE BOOK MADE ME FEEL COMPLETELY STUPID.**"**

After leaving Tunisia two years later, I traveled across Europe (reading *Anna Karenina*) to Japan, where I spent my days enjoying Kawabata, Oe, and Mishima, then returned home to earn my teaching credential (and read Rosenblatt, Moffett, and Atwell). Under the guidance of my professor Dorothy Petit, I was introduced to the world of young adult literature. At the insistence of Pat Hanlon, my master teacher, I joined NCTE and began reading professional journals. Two other professors, Rosemary Patton and Catherine Lucas, provided further direction, prescribing Joan Didion, Frank Conroy, Loren Eisely, and all the other essayists that would ultimately have a strong influence on me, as well as my reading and writing.

As I moved into this profession where I have found a home, I encountered a long line of wise, generous, and patient reading mentors. Sandy Briggs, who taught across the hall, turned me on to audio books, which I still listen to every day on the way to and from work. Paul Mariani, poet and professor: he walked me into the world of poetry one summer in Amherst where, during a National Endowment for the Humanities institute, we read Williams and Berryman

" . . . I RETURNED REGULARLY TO THOSE AUTHORS THAT HAD, BY THAT TIME, BECOME MY COMPANIONS ALONG THE WAY: HEANEY, WOOLF, MIKE ROSE, LOREN EISLEY, SENECA, AND MILOSZ. **"**

daily. And, most important of all, that day when, in my third year of teaching, I received a note from Carol Jago in response to one of the first articles I ever wrote for a journal, asking, "What are you reading?" It's a question she's continued to ask me ever since, first through notes, then letters, eventually by email, and now through tweets. She tells me what I have to read, wonders whether I have read this book or that poet, and did I see that latest *New Yorker* article by so-and-so about such-and-such, and what do I mean I don't read the *American Scholar*? And *of course, Carol! Yes* I will definitely read *The Emperor of All Maladies.* Carol, yes, I promise by NCTE, so we can discuss it!

Meanwhile, through my thirties I read to my children, all those books I had never read when growing up, discovering for the first time with my oldest son, Tolkien, Lewis, Le Guin, all those wonderful Harry Potters, *Where the Red Fern Grows*, and so many more until he was twelve. Then in my forties, having lost my father and gained three children who themselves were growing up, I returned regularly to those authors that had, by that time, become my companions along the way: Heaney, Woolf, Mike Rose, Loren Eisley, Seneca, and Milosz. Although by that time I was as likely to read these and all other books on my iPhone or iPad, listen to them in the car, or curl up with my prized first editions of Heaney actually on paper, between hardcovers.

Until it became my time, my place, my role to say, as so many had for me along the way, *You have to read this!* and to ask, *Have you read . . . do you know . . . ?* Or simply, as Carol so long ago first asked me: *What are you reading?* This is the *curriculum vitae*, the course of my reading life, my life course, the one that began there in Sacramento so many years back, where one day the boy I was sat under a tree and read that book that began the journey that would lead me to the man I have become.

PAUSE & REFLECT Write your own reading autobiography, identifying those books, moments, people, or experiences that played a key role in your development as a reader.

Reading: Past, Present, and Future

In the beginning, there was the word and it was spoken. Before we worried about reading characters scratched onto clay tablets, we read a man's character by looking in his eyes, listening to his voice, and assessing his actions. Men then thought what was written took flight when spoken aloud, and thereby entered the world of the living; whereas what was written lay dead on the page, lifeless until spoken—read aloud (Manguel 1996). Thus early "Typographic Man" (McLuhan 1994) came into existence only when the Talking Era, which lasted for 150,000 years, gave way to the "Manuscript Era," which went from roughly 3500 BC to 1450 AD (Poe 2011, 71). On our way to writing books, we marked up walls, carved symbols and figures into clay tablets, eventually scribbling first on papyri, then on animal skins (parchment). Around the mid-1400s, Gutenburg changed everything, thus ushering in the Print Era (111).

For centuries, reading was a skill available only to those in power: clergy, political leaders, wealthy merchants, and scholars. Gutenberg revolutionized all that in the time it took him to print his first little 42-line Bible in 1454 (Manguel 1996, 133). Of course, Gutenberg didn't change things for everyone, at least not immediately. Throughout the era of slavery, slaves were whipped, even hung, for learning to read. Teaching a slave to read was both "unlawful and unsafe," as Frederick Douglass wrote, for if you taught a slave to read "there [was] no keeping him" (2000, 44).

Whether control came from the slave owners or the government, the goal was the same: to control the mind and, in some ways, the spirit, for as Frederick Douglass wrote, "once you learn to read you will be forever free" (2011). How dangerous it must then have appeared to those in power to see a slave read aloud, to hear the fledgling voice speaking those words. So it was that reading began to move from the private reserves of individual and institutional power into the general public as books became increasingly available and people learned how to read them.

In Gutenberg's era, several hundred books were published each year, a figure that rapidly grew over time, with approximately 6000 published in 1900 (the number of books a Kindle can hold!) and an average of 225,000 published each year now (Poe 2011, 143). Instead of controlling *who* reads, as they did in the past, governments now control—or at least attempt to control—*what* people read, which now includes not only books but websites, text messages, and tweets. We saw this during many of the Arab uprisings in 2010 and 2011 when governments tried to shut down or otherwise prevent access to Internet providers and cell phone service companies.

The ideal of the contemplative reader has always been just that, though: an ideal. The Print Era entered into a prolonged battle for people's attention with the first radio broadcast, a battle that only intensified as film, and later television, ushered in the Audio-Visual Era (Poe 2011, 167). Whatever promise of wisdom these different media may have initially offered, it is clear that television, which so dominated the Audio-Visual Era (1850–1990), failed to deliver us to some better place, though there are, of course, exceptions. Instead, this Audio-Visual Era has, along with the Internet Era (222), brought us to a point in time when our "old linear thought process [which was calm, focused, undistracted] . . . is being pushed aside by a new kind of mind that wants and needs to take in and dole out information in short, disjointed, often overlapping bursts—the faster, the better" (Carr 2010, 10).

" FOR CENTURIES, READING WAS A SKILL AVAILABLE ONLY TO THOSE IN POWER: CLERGY, POLITICAL LEADERS, WEALTHY MERCHANTS, AND SCHOLARS. GUTENBERG REVOLUTIONIZED ALL THAT IN THE TIME IT TOOK HIM TO PRINT HIS FIRST LITTLE 42-LINE BIBLE IN 1454. "

Which brings us to the present era when 43 percent of the seniors taking the 2011 SAT read at a level appropriate for college; it is also worth noting that 1.65 million students took the SAT in 2011, making it the largest group ever to do so. Yet, it is also a time when many worry about the "slow erosion of our humanness and our humanity" (Carr 2010, 220), the loss of "narrative imagination" and empathy that come from reading and discussing the lives, ideas, and experiences of others similar to and different from ourselves (Nussbaum 2010, 95). If, as Miedema writes, "reading is the making of a deeper self" (2009, 65), we have fallen short and ended up in what Carr (2010) calls "the shallows"—a place where he fears we are unable to think about anything too deeply for too long. Poe, reflecting on the cumulative effect these different media have had on our collective and individual spirit over the last millennia, concludes that "the media, and particularly the modern media, have had a rather less positive impact on our spiritual well-being" (275).

Although not referring to it as "spiritual well-being," Wilhelm and Novak (2011), Miedema (2009), Newkirk (2012), and Edmundson (2004) share this same concern for the psychic and existential health of kids suffering *readicide*, which Gallagher defines as "the systematic killing of the love of reading, often exacerbated by the inane, mind-numbing practices found in schools" (2009, 2). Elsewhere, Gallagher (2011a) reiterates his argument for the importance of reading, including the classics: "they . . . offer wisdom . . . and 'imaginative rehearsals for the real world,'" an argument Jago emphatically seconds, saying such books serve as both "mirrors . . . [that allow kids] to reflect . . . and windows . . . that offer readers access to other worlds, other times, other cultures" (2004, 5). In a country so bent on improving reading scores on various tests, we have managed, largely as a result of our efforts to improve reading scores, to make kids *not* want to read. We have, as a society, done our part to help realize Huxley's vision of our future:

> What Orwell feared were those who would ban books. What Huxley feared was that there would be no reason to ban a book, for there would be no one who wanted to read one. Orwell feared those who would deprive us of information. Huxley feared those who would give us so much that we would be reduced to passivity and egoism. Orwell feared that the truth would be concealed from us. Huxley feared the truth would be drowned in a sea of irrelevance. Orwell feared we would become a captive culture. Huxley feared we would become a trivial culture, preoccupied with some equivalent of the feelies, the orgy porgy, and the centrifugal bumblepuppy. (Postman 1985, vii)

While we are not as far gone as Huxley feared, it is difficult to say we are too far from it when we look at certain trends in reading and the quality programming that fills so many hours of television broadcasting. Huxley here is talking, as Birkerts is elsewhere, about the inability to focus, to sustain one's attention in a "culture saturated with vivid competing stimuli [in which even] practiced readers [complain] that it is hard to maintain attentive focus" (Birkerts 2010, 39). One wonders whether we have lost, as a culture, the capacity not only to attend to but also to enjoy reading that asks us to do a little work in exchange for the subsequent rewards. Where, we wonder, is the notion of pleasure we, as teachers, associate with reading? When did it become a form of punishment to so many? In *The Lost Art of Reading*, David Ulin despairs that his 15-year-old son Noah hated reading *The Great Gatsby*. The assignment "involved annotation, which Noah detested; it kept pulling him out of the story to stop every few lines and make a note, mark a citation, to demonstrate that he'd been paying attention to what he read. . . . 'It would be so much easier if they'd let me just *read* it,'" Noah said (2010, 1).

> **" IN A COUNTRY SO BENT ON IMPROVING READING SCORES ON VARIOUS TESTS, WE HAVE MANAGED, LARGELY AS A RESULT OF OUR EFFORTS TO IMPROVE READING SCORES, TO MAKE KIDS *NOT* WANT TO READ. "**

Atwell (2007a) might claim that Noah feels he is being prevented from entering the "reading zone" because of all the "pedagogic strings attached" that ultimately prevent him from entering the "reading state . . . where all is clear and right . . . and [we] feel a connectedness that cannot be duplicated [even if it] becomes a blur to [us] as soon as [we] have finished it" (Birkerts 1994, 84). Miedema says that choice about *how* we read is just as important as the choice of *what* we read: "This freedom [to choose how as well as what one reads is what] brings back the pleasure of reading" (2009, 16).

What is our role as teachers in all this? As Gandhi said: We must be the change we wish to see in the world. We must be—or become—reading mentors, book whisperers, role models, text masters to our many apprentices. In addition to being guides and gurus ourselves, perhaps most important, *we must be and remain readers ourselves*, reading and discussing with our students and colleagues whatever we read not only for work as teachers but also for our lives as human beings. As Donalyn Miller, the "Book Whisperer" herself, writes:

> My credibility with students and the reason they trust me when I recommend books to them stems from the fact that I read every day of my life and that I talk about reading constantly. I am not mandating an activity for them that I do not engage in myself. I do not promote reading to my students because it is good for them or because it is required for school success. I advocate reading because it is enjoyable and enriching. When my students think about me in the future, I want them to remember me as a reader with a book in my hand and a recommendation on my lips. (2009, 106)

In my own classes, I take this role of mentoring young readers pretty seriously, passing on articles and recommendations to students constantly once I know their interests and talents.

PAUSE & REFLECT What would your students say about you as a reader based on the way you discuss your own reading in class?

As Tatum (2009) demonstrates through his work with African American boys, we teachers must share our own "textual lineage" with students, discussing with them those "texts (both literary and nonliterary) that are instrumental to [our own] human development," which caused us "to think differently about [our] life and [moved] us to read other texts" (xiv). If we do not discuss such a lineage, share with students the role reading has played and continues to play in our daily lives, we cannot expect them to follow us. As one of my students said once to Sam Intrator and Robert Kunzman (2009) regarding how I talked about books and reading in class, "It's really cool . . . Mr. Burke talks about books as if they really mattered."

In the future, reading may well return, ironically, to those earliest days when words were spoken or written, though not on the clay tablets of the past but those made of light, able to bring those written letters off the page not just in spirit but truth as we project them (as holographs) into space as our ancestors once thought we did by speaking them (see *Hamlet on the Holodeck: The Future of Narrative in Cyberspace* by Janet Murray, 1998, or the T. S. Eliot *Wasteland* iPad app). Thus will all the previous eras—talking, print, audiovisual, and Internet—join to create a new era in which reading words on a page will only be a preference. A conversation similar to the one we have already had about doing math in your head versus on a calculator will inevitably ensue with all the attending passions. In such a world, "reading" will be more akin to *thinking*.

Do I love listening to a Cormac McCarthy novel read by Matt Damon on my iPhone at 65 mph as I drive to work in the morning? Or the latest David McCullough history read by McCullough himself? Who wouldn't?! Am I *reading*? Sure I am. But I am not reading *actively*, as I

> **"**IN THE FUTURE, READING MAY WELL RETURN, IRONICALLY, TO THOSE EARLIEST DAYS WHEN WORDS WERE SPOKEN OR WRITTEN, THOUGH NOT ON THE CLAY TABLETS OF THE PAST BUT THOSE MADE OF LIGHT . . .**"**

do when I have a pencil in my hand; nor am I reading closely as I do when I can *re-*read passages for the pleasure or insight that second reading brings. I am not reading deeply as I do when I sit and read a professional journal or any other demanding text that requires time and attention. These issues of depth, of attention, and of the ability to read closely, critically—they are central to the Common Core. I can *enjoy* a good, even a challenging book while driving at 65 mph but I cannot understand the complexity of its ideas. To do that, I must be able to do what I teach my students to do: read, re-read, question, and challenge the text.

> **So in the future, which is already here, we will need to develop students' textual intelligence . . .**

So in the future, which is already here, we will need to develop students' textual intelligence (Burke 2001, 163), teaching them how to read different texts in different ways according to their purpose and the demands those texts make on readers' attention and knowledge. We will have to teach them, as Sir Francis Bacon observed long ago, that "some books are to be tasted, others to be swallowed and some few to be chewed and digested; that is, some books are to be read only in parts; others to be read, but not curiously; and some few to be read wholly, and with diligence and attention" (Jacobs 2011, 110). We will have to create opportunities and cultivate environments that support this type of reading instruction and, when necessary, teach students how to read these different texts in these different ways, even as we create other opportunities for reading as a pleasure. Love (2012) sums up this dilemma best: "How then to best love a book? If we love books [only] at a gallop, we are certain to forget much of the scenery we encounter. If we love at a trot, we will never feel the wind against our face. The only solution, it seems, is to love again and again, with different, deliberate speeds" (72).

PAUSE & REFLECT How do you talk about your own reading in class or with students on the side? What do you do, or how could you do more, to be a reading mentor to students?

What We Read: The Common Core State Standards and Beyond

For our purposes in the classroom, the quick answer to the question of what we have students read is: those types of texts spelled out in the Common Core Standards or whatever guidelines define our curriculum in the future. The balance between literary and informational texts will certainly shift as we work to better prepare our students for college and careers. One is inclined, as they might be at a restaurant, however, to inquire as to the source or consistency, the portions and ingredients of these recommended daily doses rich in intellectual and cultural fiber.

As the Common Core Standards document itself notes, regarding its own recommended readings:

> To become college and career ready, students must grapple with works of exceptional craft and thought whose range extends across genres, cultures, and centuries. Such works offer profound insights into the human condition and serve as models for students' own thinking and writing. Along with high-quality contemporary works, these texts should be chosen from among seminal U.S. documents, the classics of American

literature, and the timeless dramas of Shakespeare. Through wide and deep reading of literature and literary nonfiction of steadily increasing sophistication, students gain a reservoir of literary and cultural knowledge, references, and images; the ability to evaluate intricate arguments; and the capacity to surmount the challenges posed by complex texts. (National Governors Association 2010, 35)

These different types of texts serve many ends, some instructional, others more personal and existential. As with any balanced diet, one cannot be healthy if he or she consumes just one type of food.

This means creating opportunities for students to read not only fiction and nonfiction but also alternative interpretations and critical perspectives about those literary texts as well as artworks that explore related themes. It means inviting students to read informational texts from print publications in addition to examining other informational texts about the same topics that combine, for example, graphic and quantitative information (called infographics), and slide shows or videos found online that offer yet other perspectives on a given subject.

As for quantities of any one type of text, Jago (2011b) describes the National Assessment Governing Board's position on reading, saying that students "in order to be prepared for college and the workplace . . . need to read informational text as well as literature, [with] 70 percent of what students read over the course of a school day [reflecting] the kinds of texts that high school graduates will be assigned in college and for other postsecondary pursuits." In its position statement, the International Reading Association describes "excellent reading teachers" as those who "include a wide variety of fiction and nonfiction genres" such as novels, biographies, magazines, and poetry (2000, 197).

Gallagher, picking up on the food motif, uses a "50/50 approach," which he describes in *Readicide*: "I love strawberries, but if they were the only food I was allowed to eat, I wouldn't like them for long. . . . [To help my students] read for enjoyment . . . I have adopted a 50/50 approach in my classroom. . . . I want half their reading to be academic, and half . . . recreational . . . [so as] to mix up the reading diet of my students" (2009, 82). Middle school teacher Donalyn Miller requires her students to read 40 books each year in her class, dividing up her reading by genre, with students reading: poetry anthologies (5), traditional literature (5), realistic fiction (5), historical fiction (2), fantasy (4), science fiction (2), mystery (2), informational (4), auto/biography or memoir (2), and chapter book choices (9) (2009, 78).

Miller, Gallagher, Jago, and the others here emphasize the amount and type of reading students should do; less obvious, but just as important, is the difficulty or sophistication of the texts the students read. Such difficulty can be measured in terms of themes as well as language, style, or genre; yet difficulty is, ultimately, "a social construct, [one] endorsed by schools, rather than a simple objective property, [a concept] that lives in the eye of the beholder" (Purves 1991, 2). As the Common Core State Standards (CCSS) call for "complex texts" that exhibit "exceptional craft and thought" and demonstrate "steadily increasing sophistication," the idea of measuring the complexity of texts is now as important as it is elusive. Difficulty has traditionally been determined by length of words and sentences, as well as the familiarity of those words; new methods examine such concepts as "syntax, 'narrativity,' word abstraction, and 'cohesion,' [which refers to] how well the text makes connections for the reader [in order to] facilitate understanding" (Gewertz 2011, 12).

The CCSS document identifies three domains of difficulty for any text: *qualitative dimensions* (levels of meaning or purpose, structure, language conventionality and clarity, and knowledge demands); *quantitative dimensions* (word length or frequency, sentence length, and text cohesion—all of which can be easily measured by computers); and *reader and task considerations* (motivation, knowledge, experiences; purpose, complexity of the assigned task or questions) (National Governors Association, CCSS Appendix A, 2010, 4). Such notions of complexity differ in various ways from those used in recent years: *independent* (accessible, readable, comprehendible), *instructional* (less familiar in style, format, features, or content), and *frustration-level* (which is what I encountered when I tried to read *Finnegans Wake*: language that makes no sense to the reader and ideas that are completely unknown to the reader) (Kinsella and Feldman 2006, 10).

Focusing more specifically on the question of the "literary merit" of texts in Advanced Placement English courses, Gilmore (2010) claims that such complex and sophisticated literature:

1. Entertains the reader and is interesting to read.
2. Does not merely conform to the expectations of a single genre or formula.
3. Has been judged to have artistic quality by the literary community (teachers, students, librarians, critics, other writers, the reading public).
4. Has stood the test of time in some way, regardless of the date of publication.
5. Shows thematic depth: The themes merit revisiting and study because they are complex and nuanced.
6. Demonstrates innovation in style, voice, structure, characterization, plot, and/or description.
7. May have a social, political, or ideological impact on society during the lifetime of the author or afterward.
8. Does not fall into the traps of "pulp" fiction such as clichéd or derivative descriptions and plot devices, or sentimentality rather than "earned" emotion.
9. Is intended by the author to communicate in an artistic manner.
10. Is universal in its appeal (i.e., the themes and insights are not only accessible to one culture or time period). (7)

Stotsky (2010a) suggests that:

One source [of declining reading scores] may be what many American secondary students are currently reading and the difficulty level of what they read. According to a 2009 report by Renaissance Learning, the company that produces Accelerated Reader (a computerized database to keep track of what K–12 students read in participating schools across the country), the Harry Potter series and other contemporary young adult fantasy series (by Stephanie Meyer in particular) are among the most widely read books by secondary school students. . . . Ten of the top 16 most frequently read books by the 1500 students in the top 19 percent of reading achievement in grades 9–12 . . . were contemporary young adult fantasies. The database does not indicate whether the books students read were assigned or self-selected (e.g., for book reports), but it is easy to identify those likely assigned by English teachers—such titles as *To Kill a Mockingbird, Night, Of Mice and Men*, and *The Kite Runner*. [The data suggest] that high school students going on to college have had few common reading experiences aside from contemporary young adult fantasies. Moreover, almost all the books they read are relatively easy to read. (8)

PAUSE & REFLECT List the books you teach (include those you hope to teach in the future if you wish): How would you rate their complexity and the logic of their arrangement in terms of growing complexity?

With such a sustained assault on the quality of what high school students read, it is easy to see how many prominent critics and columnists blame young adult literature for the decline in reading ability, saying as Francine Prose does, that "the caged bird cannot read" because too many schools have "traded complexity for diversity" (1999, 76). Gurdon condemns young adult literature (YA lit) not for being too simple but too "rife with explicit abuse, violence, and depravity" (WSJ.com website, 2011), arguing it is not only intellectually inferior but "observably infectious," thereby *causing* the self-destructive behaviors and abuse (by making it seem normal), that the books examine. These condemnations of YA lit are dismissed, among others, by Atwell (2010) and Groenke and Scherff (2010). Lesesne offers the helpful metaphor of "reading ladders" as a way to frame the discussion of "meeting students where they are" and helping them where they need to be (2010, 3). She goes on to suggest that students be matched with books based on a new set of four Rs: rigor, relevance, relationships, and response (2).

> **Recommended Reading**
>
> We love a list, and so I include here some established sources for books we should read. Lists should be living, though, evolving over time to reflect our changing society and the zeitgeist; to that end, other resources listed change every year, some every month. When I asked Carol Jago for such a list, she said, "We need to stop looking for a definitive list and be constantly on the lookout for ideas for books."
>
> - National Council of Teachers of English
> - International Reading Association
> - American Library Association
> - Schoollibraryjournal.com
> - Modern Library 100
> - Poetry 180
> - Reading Rants
> - YALSA
> - Teen Reads
> - Prize-winning: Booker, Nobel, Pulitzer
> - Award-winning: National Book, Pictus, Newberry
> - Online: bookwhisperer.com, caroljago.com, GoodReads.com, professornana.livejournal.com, Shelfari.com

YA lit authors themselves passionately defend their work and the genre as a whole, citing the troubling statistics related to abuse, bullying, and the general feeling of alienation that so often define those confusing and painful years; these same YA authors also include in their defense the many letters they receive from readers who often say it was books such as theirs that kept them alive or helped them learn to accept themselves.

Teen blogger Emma responded to Gurdon's *Wall Street Journal* column via her *Booking Through 365* blog, saying that she had:

> seen YA books expose darkness, reveal depth, find flaws, give hope, change minds, break hearts and then repair them. Good literature rips open all the private parts of us— the parts people like you have deemed too dark, inappropriate, grotesque or abnormal for teens to be feeling—and then they stitch it all back together again before we even realize they're not talking about us. They're talking about their characters. (2011)

The point is that we read both to grow our minds and heal our hearts; that we need books that build our stamina and take us to places where we can meet people and do things we would

FIGURE 5.1 Keenan and Jack, two freshman, take time during our periodic personal reading time to enjoy their books.

never dare to do in real life; that we need them to understand the person we are, were, or hope to someday become. (See Figure 5.1.)

Kittle (2008) and Fletcher (2011) focus on the *uses* of reading to improve one's writing. They advocate the use of what they call "mentor texts," which Robb (2010) defines as "a text you use for teaching students about craft, technique, usage, and genre. These can be texts published by professional writers or student texts" (51). Such reading would fall into what many call "craft study," the focus of all such reading being to train the student to see, understand, and eventually emulate the writer's moves on the way to creating their own.

Tatum (2009) makes a compelling argument for the use of "enabling texts," which he defines as those texts that help students "broker positive relationships and improve [students'] lives" (55). The Declaration of Independence is, in Tatum's estimation, such a text as it "led African American males to act on their own lives" (56); other enabling texts help students understand themselves and those forces that affect them, while simultaneously providing students with a "*road map* and *a plan of action*" (57). These enabling texts are, in many respects, a much deeper form of the mentor texts discussed earlier; these texts, according to Tatum, help students "express their viewpoint and define who they are as informed by their many and varied contexts" (57) so long as these texts are "mediated by educators" committed to creating such relationships and improving the lives of their students.

Here's my point: You can find inner-city teachers who can get kids of all colors and cultures to read anything, even *Moby Dick* or *Henry V*, if you come at it the right way—framing it with questions students want to examine, using methods that ensure their success even as those same methods severely challenge them. And you can bring all the YA lit you want into a class but accomplish nothing if you impede its potential. What we need—and it is possible through both the CCSS or the Advanced Placement English courses—is a curriculum that invites students to answer the essential questions we all ask—a curriculum that is neither fun nor frustrating but, instead, is a transformative literacy experience, one that allows students to adopt all those different personae outlined in Chapter 1.

In such a class, what students read reflects Tatum's model of "multiple literacies" that include *academic literacy* (skills and strategies), *cultural literacy* (awareness of the historical and cultural influences that shape one's identity), *emotional literacy* (ability to manage emotions and beliefs), and *social literacy* (ability to work with and speak to a range of people in different contexts) (2005, 35). Yet the texts we choose must not be treated as standards-based delivery systems created to teach students the literary elements or the components of an argument; such reductionist approaches strip the life and deeper learning from whatever we have students read, turning the *Odyssey* into a workbook or Lincoln's speeches into test prep exercises. What we seek is "reading that pleases and profits, that together delights and instructs" (Dehaene 2009, 328). As Rosenblatt writes, "the value of the text seen as a source either of information or experience is lost through its primary use as a basis for teaching skills" (2005, xxx). It's like eating food only for the nutrients and not the pleasure of the meal or the company.

The texts we invite students to enter should serve as a "third space," which provides students a feeling of sanctuary, "a place where the needs, problems, questions, interests, discourses, and funds of knowledge of . . . students' home lives come into conversation," where they can think deeply about the text and the questions it raises (Wilhelm 2010, 56). Such texts, when they evoke these third spaces, capture the power Canada (1998) describes when he writes about the need for mentors in the lives of urban youth, or when Wilhelm and Novak write about books "being the change" we all hope to see reading achieve at its best, at its richest, its deepest. That was the space I entered that distant day, when I opened up *Bless the Beasts and the Children* and read away the afternoon. Something changed; I changed.

What of my own classes, then? What do *my* students read? The following snapshot covers a portion in the fall semester during which I happened to be writing this chapter but it is quite representative of my overall reading curriculum for the year.

Senior College Prep English

- *Independent Reading:* Each semester students read three autobiographies or biographies of people they admire and who lives in the world in a way students aspire to. We call it the Life Studies Project, the idea being that they will learn from studying the lives of others lessons and ideas that apply to their own. Colin, for example, who wants to study business, read the biographies of several different CEOs, beginning with the Steve Jobs' biography by Isaacson. Amber, who wants to be a cook, read books, such as Grant Achatz's *Life on the Line*, that detail how they became chefs and how they think about food.

- *Expert Project:* Weekly reading of content related to their Expert Project topic. Texts may be in any available media form or medium about important developments related to their yearlong inquiry (see assignment details in Figure 5.2). They must discuss and write about these key findings in a Critical Notes review of their latest reading selection (see sample in Figure 5.3). Spring semester they use all these notes and articles as the basis for a large research paper and formal presentation.

- *What Makes Us Who We Are:* Students read a wide range of informational texts, essays, fiction, and new media texts such as blogs, tweets, videos (TED talks, documentaries), and other text types—all exploring this big question of what makes us who we are. The eight-week unit examines food (Are We *Really* What We Eat?), clothing and media (Things Are Not Necessarily as They Appear to Be), and priorities (What Is Your Credo?), during which students read a range of literary and nonfiction texts that culminates in the writing of a credo paper they can use for their college applications. They read these closely and critically, taking notes, discussing them, often annotating the readings if given photocopies. Each subsection (e.g., Are You Really What You Eat?) of the larger unit (What Makes Us Who We Are?) culminates in a different type of essay that draws on the readings for ideas, evidence, or examples of what such a paper should be like. So, for example, all the readings about food lead to a descriptive essay in which students examine the intersection of food and culture.

Advanced Placement English Literature and Composition

- *Independent Reading:* As the list in Figure 5.4 shows, students choose three books or one author; they read one book from the list or by their chosen author each grading period (every six weeks). At the end of that grading period, they write an in-class essay that

The Expert Project: A Yearlong Inquiry into One Subject

Mr. Burke/English 7-8CP

Overview
Everything is interesting if you dig deep enough and spend enough time with it. And as we get older we begin to discover what interests us, often because we have greater abilities or they just fascinate us more for some reason we may not even understand. This project invites you to pick a topic and explore it in great depth over the course of the year, examining it through a wide range of media and from different perspectives. The important thing is to choose a subject about which you want to become a knowledgeable expert (well, perhaps a Level 1 Expert!).

Requirements
Over the course of the year each of you will do the following:

- ❑ Choose a topic that fascinates you and will merit a yearlong inquiry
- ❑ Submit a formal proposal about what you want to study, how, and why
- ❑ Read/watch/listen to: articles, tweets, blogs, podcasts, broadcasts, books
- ❑ Complete your Critical Notes on what you read/watch each week
- ❑ Write a major paper spring semester that includes words, images, infographics
- ❑ Present your findings to the class, adapting your paper into a slide presentation

Standards
The following come from the Common Core Standards for English:

1. Read closely to determine what the text says explicitly and to make logical inferences
2. Cite specific textual evidence when writing or speaking to support conclusions
3. Determine central ideas or themes of a text and analyze their development
4. Summarize the key supporting details and ideas
5. Analyze how and why individuals, events, and ideas develop and interact
6. Assess how point of view or purpose shapes the content and style of a text
7. Integrate and evaluate content presented in diverse formats and media, including visually and quantitatively, as well as in words
8. Delineate and evaluate the argument and specific claims in a text, including the validity of the reasoning as well as the relevance and sufficiency of the evidence
9. Analyze how two or more texts address similar themes or topics in order to build knowledge or to compare the approaches the authors take
10. Read and comprehend complex literary and informational texts independently

Fall Semester
Fall semester you will gather information, monitor your topic through the media, and develop your initial ideas about it, which you will then explore in greater depth spring semester through the paper you will write and the presentation you will give. Each week you will:

- ❑ *Learn more about your subject* by reading, viewing, or listening to one of the following media (all of which you should, by semester's end, have sampled): article, blog, Twitter feed, Facebook feed, or other social network sources by an established person in that field
- ❑ *Take Critical Notes* on whatever you read, view, or listen to, discussing not only the message but also the media and its meaning
- ❑ *Update your Works Cited* for the project, keeping track of all sources cited as you go
- ❑ *Discuss your subject and ideas* about it with others and/or the class when time allows

Topics

Environment	Finance/Economics	War/Military	Media	Religion/Faith
Technology/Science	Law/Crime	Transportation	Health/Medicine	Politics/Gov

FIGURE 5.2 An overview of The Expert Project for my seniors. It was intended to create a context for reading over the course of the semester a wide range of texts that were all related to one topic or question.

Critical Notes

Name: _____ Period: _____ Date: _____

Do all work on the back or a separate sheet of paper

1. *Identify the source and subject* of your inquiry this week:

I read/viewed/listened to	
. . . which was about	

2. *Collect Works Cited* information

Author:	Pages:
Title:	URL:
Type:	Issue:
Date Pub'd:	City Pub'd:
Date Accessed:	Publication:

3. *Before you read*, do the following on the backside or a separate sheet of paper:
   - ❏ Generate 2–3 questions about the text based on the title or some other element.
   - ❏ Identify what you understand to be the actual subject of the text.
   - ❏ Predict what you think the text will say about its subject.
   - ❏ Jot a couple sentences summing up what you know about this subject.
   - ❏ Create a Purpose Question (PQ) based on the title of the article or other text.

4. *As you read*, take notes here on key ideas, quotations, or details related to the subject of the article and your actual subject for the Expert Project.

5. *After you finish reading*, list the main idea and three supporting ideas from the article.

6. *Media critique:* Evaluate the media and how effective it was in achieving its original purpose. Use these questions to help you:

• Who created this message or text?
• Who is the intended audience? (**Note**: Just because it's *about* kids or parents doesn't mean the audience is kids or parents. The real audience might be companies who want to sell to kids or parents, or employers who want to understand the new generation of employees. Ask who benefits from this information.)
• What techniques do they use to get my attention?
• Who is *not* included or discussed in this message?
• Why are they creating or sending this message?
• Which values, lifestyles, or points of view does this message represent and/or leave out/ignore?

7. *Respond/react*: What are your own thoughts about this subject and article? Elaborate on your ideas as the purpose here is to add new ideas from here and other sources for your paper in the spring.

8. *Connect and reflect*: How does your work this week relate to previous weeks? What are the big ideas that are emerging as the weeks pass and you learn more about your subject?

Do all work on the back or a separate sheet of paper

FIGURE 5.3 Students had to use this Critical Notes sheet to help them read everything from tweets and Facebook posts to essays and videos more intentionally and critically as part of their Expert project.

AP Lit Independent Reading Requirement

Mr. Burke (2011–12)

Introduction You cannot succeed in this class or on the AP exam if you do not read voraciously during the course of the year. *What* you read matters as much as *how* you read; thus the list below includes many titles, all of which will challenge you. All the books listed meet the College Board's standards for "works of equal literary merit." Please do not read books not on this list or authors not approved; these will not be eligible and thus you will receive no credit. Short story collections, books read in previous classes, and plays are not acceptable for this assignment either, though I do love short stories and plays, and encourage you to read and enjoy them both on your own.

Readings Read *three* of the following books during the fall semester. **You must read one book and write the required paper at the end of each grading period.**

1. Achebe, Chinua — *Things Fall Apart*
2. Patchett, Ann — *State of Wonder* or *Bel Canto*
3. Alarcon, Daniel — *Lost City Radio*
4. Alvarez, Julia — *In the Time of the Butterflies*
5. Atwood, Margaret — *Oryx and Crake* or *The Blind Assassin*
6. Barry, Sebastian — *A Long Long Way*
7. Burgess, Anthony — *A Clockwork Orange*
8. Coetzee, J. M. — *Waiting for the Barbarians*
9. Crace, Jim — *The Pesthouse*
10. Danticat, Edwidge — *The Farming of Bones*
11. Eggers, Dave — *What Is the What?* or *Zeitoun*
12. Ellison, Ralph — *Invisible Man*
13. Flaubert, Gustave — *Madame Bovary* (Lydia Davis translation recommended)
14. Forrester, E. M. — *A Passage to India*
15. Franzen, Jonathan — *Freedom*
16. Gordimer, Nadine — *The Pick-Up*
17. Greene, Graham — *The Quiet American*
18. Heller, Joseph — *Catch-22*
19. Homer — *Iliad* (Fagles or Lombardo translation)
20. Jin, Ha — *Waiting*
21. Joyce, James — *The Portrait of the Artist as a Young Man*
22. Kafka, Franz — *The Trial*
23. Kesey, Ken — *One Flew over the Cuckoo's Next*
24. Khadra, Yasmina — *The Swallows of Kabul*
25. Kingsolver, Barbara — *The Lacuna* or *The Poisonwood Bible*
26. Marquez, Garbiel Garcia — *One Hundred Years of Solitude* or *Love in Time of Cholera*
27. McCarthy, Cormac — *Blood Meridian*
28. Murakami, Haruki — *After Dark*
29. Pessl, Marisha — *Special Topics in Calamity Physics*
30. Petterson, Per — *Out Stealing Horses*
31. Price, Richard — *Freedomland* or *Lush Life*
32. Robinson, Marilyn — *Gilead* and/or *Home*
33. Roth, Philip — *The Plot Against America* or *American Pastoral*
34. Roy, Arundhati — *The God of Small Things*
35. Smith, Zadie — *White Teeth* or *On Beauty*
36. Solzhenitsyn, Aleksandr — *One Day in the Life of Ivan Denisovich*
37. Tan, Amy — *The Bonesetter's Daughter*
38. Verghese, Abraham — *Cutting for Stone*
39. Virgil — *The Aeneid* (Fagles or Lombardo translation)
40. Wilde, Oscar — *The Picture of Dorian Gray*
41. Woolf, Virginia — *Mrs. Dalloway* or *To the Lighthouse*
42. Wroblewski, David — *The Story of Edgar Sawtelle*
43. Yehoshua, A. B. — *A Woman in Jerusalem*

FIGURE 5.4 Sample independent reading list for my AP class from the fall semester. It changes each year but retains this essential form. In this spring, they create their own reading list as part of a semester-long inquiry project, though the books must still be appropriate for the AP Lit exam.

emulates the AP test by way of integrated AP-exam practice. The prompts all come from released free-response items on past AP exams. I typically give them four to choose from on the day of the in-class exam.

- **Weekly Poem:** Each week students begin class by reading or rereading that week's chosen poem, which is rarely longer than 25 lines, worthy of close study, and connects to the larger ideas in whatever major work we are studying at that time (see Figure 5.5). We read, for example, Dickinson's "Much Madness Is Divinest Sense" when we get to the part of *Hamlet* that explores madness in Hamlet and Ophelia. Each day we read for a different reason, a different purpose meant to develop their close reading skills. On Friday, they use their notes to guide them in writing a 15- to 20-minute critical analysis of the poem in their notebooks.

- **Tragedy: The Great Encounter:** During this three-week unit, students read several Greek tragedies, as part of the larger study of tragedy and what Roche calls "The Great Encounter." Roche explains this encounter: "We need to be told that man is but a limited and contingent creature, subject to sudden disrupting forces. . . . Whatever our circumstances, we can achieve and endure through to essential greatness. It is not what fate has in store for us that matters but what we do with it when it comes" (1991, ix). As part of our study, we read not only the plays themselves but also critical essays and articles from various magazines and newspapers that use principles of Greek tragedy, for example, to make sense of certain CEOs who fail. *Brief* clips (5–10 minutes at most) from films, such as *Margin Call* or *The Smartest Guys in the Room*, carefully analyzed, become texts we study. Also included in the unit are readings from Aristotle on the nature of tragedy. The unit culminates in a substantial paper in which they must define tragedy, including ideas, examples, and evidence from a range of sources, including but not limited to those we read in class as part of this unit.

In both classes, I see the curriculum as a "conversation" that enables students to participate in and maintain the "living traditions of knowing and doing" English (Applebee 1996, 126). Thus I choose the various texts based on the conversations they invite us to have about craft and conscience, language and law, or other important concepts that integrate the teaching of skills and knowledge that form the core of the humanities. What students read is often shaped by how we ask them to read those texts, for it is through the transaction between my students and these texts that they are themselves changed as people but also as readers—or so I hope. As Virginia Woolf wrote in her own meditation of how we read, when we have "fed greedily and lavishly upon books of all sorts—poetry, fiction, history, biography—and [have] stopped reading and looked for long spaces upon the variety, the incongruity of the living world, we shall find that [our taste for reading] has changed . . . [that] it is not so greedy, [that] it is more reflective" (1986, 268). My own thoughts about what

FIGURE 5.5 Katie and Ally work together to read the weekly poem. Although most of the reading for these weekly poems is done individually, they sometimes join forces to read a particular passage or to compare their interpretations.

my students read, regardless of whether it is literary or informational, are captured best by Judith Langer, who treats

> literature as a way of thinking, rather than as a type of text—as one aspect of intelligent and literate thought that brings with it particular reasoning and problem-solving strategies. From this perspective, literary thinking has the potential to be useful in all of life's contexts, across the life span. Through literature, students learn to explore possibilities and consider options; they gain connectedness and seek vision. They become the type of literate, as well as creative, thinkers that we'll need to learn well at college, to do well at work, and to shape discussions and find solutions to tomorrow's problems. (2011a, 2)

In my own classes, this is what I see: students reading a range of texts, both literary and informational, moving back and forth along Rosenblatt's efferent-aesthetic continuum (2005, 13), which suggests that, more than the actual text type, it is the reader's "predominant stance" that determines the nature of the reading event. In other words, the informational text of the newspaper article or recipe can be read as a legitimate literary (or, in Rosenblatt's terms, *aesthetic*) text if the reader adopts such a predominantly aesthetic stance; just as the reader can, if adopting a predominantly efferent stance, read a poem only for the facts, or the main idea (Rosenblatt 2005, 104). Unfortunately, such a reading experience would not lead to the literate, creative thinkers Langer describes in the previous quote. Reading a short story by Jennifer Egan (2011) written in the form of a two-page to-do list, however, would.

How We Read: Teaching Reading as a Process

To speak of a "reading process" suggests there is some process we all use when reading; however, as Rosenblatt states in her transactional theory of reading: "There is no such thing as a generic reader or a generic literary work; there are in reality only the potential millions of individual readers of individual literary works.... The reading of any work of literature is, of necessity, an individual and unique occurrence involving the mind and emotions of some particular reader" (1995, 32). Experienced, effective readers, according to this theory, each have a process but it is idiosyncratic—specific to their own personal or cognitive needs. Such readers do not just belly flop into a text and start thrashing around: Whether consciously or not, experienced readers prepare themselves to read. Depending on their purpose, the type of text and its demands, the process may take more or less time. Each of us goes through a series of rituals designed to get us into that reading space (as athletes speak of "getting their head into the game" or "getting their game face on"), where we can relax; read; pay attention to; and, if possible, enjoy what we read. Such a process is, then, as much mental (even physical for some) as it is cognitive. Italian novelist Italo Calvino (1979) guides his reader through the process:

> Find the most comfortable position: seated, stretched out, curled up, or lying flat. Flat on your back, on your side, on your stomach. In an easy chair, on the sofa, in the rocker, the deck chair, on the hassock. . . . Stretch your legs, go ahead and put your feet on a cushion, on two cushions, on the arms of the sofa, on the wings of the chair, on the coffee

" EXPERIENCED . . . READERS DO NOT JUST BELLY FLOP INTO A TEXT AND START THRASHING AROUND . . . "

table, on the desk, on the piano, on the globe. Take your shoes off first. . . . Adjust the light
so you don't strain your eyes. Do it now, because once you're absorbed in reading there
will be no budging you. . . . Try to foresee anything that might interrupt your reading . . .
Anything else? Do you have to pee? All right, you know best. (4)

In his memoir, *My Dyslexia*, Philip Schultz, winner of the Pulitzer Prize for poetry, offers a
much more internal, complex, and less romanticized description of his own reading process,
which is all the more fascinating given that he is a prize-winning poet:

I love everything about books, except actually reading them. . . . The act of translating
what for me are the mysterious symbols of communication into actual comprehension
has always been a hardship for me. I often read a sentence two or three times before I
truly understand it; must restructure its syntax and sound out its syllables before I can
begin to absorb its meaning and move on to the next sentence. . . . For reasons I'll never
fully understand, or perhaps don't even want to, I dislike the peculiar, obstinate, slightly
out-of-control way in which my mind behaves when I'm reading. I can never just sit down
and begin reading, I must first trick myself into it by playing endless games of solitaire
on my computer, or reheating my tea or taking another walk with my dog. . . . And while
reading I must sell myself a bill of goods, convince myself that what I'm reading is fascinating and valuable, so compelling that it's worth the effort. . . . This argument, and it
is an argument, isn't always easy to buy into and sometimes I quit out of frustration and
exhaustion. (2011, 26)

Focusing specifically on the novel, Umberto Eco likens the reading process to a "walk in
the fictional woods" or a garden of seemingly endless forking paths (1994, 6). Readers are, he
points out, required to make "choices" at every turn while reading narrative texts, each decision leading the reader deeper into or out of the narrative woods. Through these choices as to
which path to take, we create the text with the author, thereby linking our reading process to the
author's composing process and becoming the "author's fellow-worker and accomplice." Or,
as Rosenblatt argues, the meaning of the text "comes into being during the transaction between
the reader and the text" (2005, 7).

Once we enter the woods of this text, Eco (1994) suggests we must then decide how we will
walk through them: choosing one path to get through as quickly as possible or walking around
the woods "so as to discover what the woods is like and find out why some paths are accessible
and others are not" (27). He adds that any such walk through a garden or forest depends on
us "lingering in the woods" (50) if we are to truly enjoy our time there. Such lingering might
include taking time to study different aspects of the text. This process further includes taking
time to consider other "possible woods" whether they be those imagined by other authors or
those the current work we are reading invites us to consider. Eco concludes his description of
the reading process by pointing out the obvious: We must, as readers, eventually leave these
woods, returning to the real world where we connect what we read in the book to what we encounter in our daily lives where we "look for a story of our origins, to tell us why we were born
and why we have lived" (139).

Eco offers a memorable way of describing the process, but its focus on narrative texts limits it as a complete model of all that goes on while we read. Wolf (2007) gives a more scientific

description of this complex process, emphasizing the extent to which, during the time spent reading, you:

> engaged an array of mental and cognitive processes: attention; memory; and visual, auditory, and linguistic processes [which further involved] your brain's attentional and executive systems [which] plan how to read. Next, your visual system raced into action, swooping quickly across the page, forwarding its gleanings about letter shapes, word forms, and common phrases to linguistic systems awaiting the information. These systems rapidly connected subtly differentiated visual symbols with essential information about the sounds contained in words. Without a single moment of conscious awareness, you applied highly automatic rules about the sounds of letters in the English writing system, and used a great many linguistic processes to do so. This is the essence of what is called the alphabetic principle, and it depends on your brain's uncanny ability to learn to connect and integrate at rapid-fire speeds what it sees and what it hears to what it knows. (8)

As if all these simultaneous processes were not complex enough, we must add all the subsequent and equally simultaneous processes through which we comprehend the literal and figurative meaning of the written text. This part of the reading process involves semantic systems that check each word read against all known uses and possible meanings of that word in the brain's memory, trying to determine which ones apply most to this word in this context. Thus, when students read the opening of *Lord of the Flies* and first encounter the word *fair* used to refer to the boy we will come to know as Ralph, they must test its use out against the roughly 10 different meanings of the word; as Golding uses it over and over, never referring to Ralph for the first few pages as anything but "the fair boy," the reader must check each time to see whether the word is being used in the same or some deeper way—one intended to include all the different connotative meanings of the word.

In addition to the semantic process, we must add the grammatical system, as well as the conceptual system that begins to use all this information to make inferences. To make these inferences about the meaning of the words, sentences, and text as a whole, the brain must then—remember, this is all taking place faster than we can even conceive if we are reading well—synthesize all this information, integrating our predictions about what it means with our current background knowledge to arrive at what we hope is the pleasure we call understanding (Wolf 2007, 10).

Ultimately, this scientific description, while elegant in detail, somehow falls short when applied to the 35 students who crowd into my classroom each period. With kids from so many different backgrounds in my classes, I find Rosenblatt's transactional theory more useful and apt: "We 'make sense' of new situations or make new meanings by applying, reorganizing, revising, or extending public and private elements selected from our personal linguistic-experiential reservoirs" (2005, 5). When a girl who grew up in Serbian bomb shelters but mastered English well enough in three years to thrive in my AP Lit class sits next to a Latino boy whose parents clean offices in Silicon Valley, and both discuss *Heart of Darkness* with a girl whose father is a CEO of a major Silicon Valley technology firm—well, let's just say they are not necessarily the same readers reading the same text, though my job is to guide them to a place where each is able to offer a responsible, defensible reading of that text. (See Figures 5.6 and 5.7.)

Students:	Teachers:
BEFORE	
• Access and/or gather background knowledge about the topic, text type, or text itself • Assemble any potentially necessary materials such as pencils, highlighters, sticky notes, reference works • Consider whether to print the text (if online) to be able to mark it up and increase the amount they will read • Decide how to read it: surface, deep; skim, slow; literal, figurative; critically, close—or just for fun! • Determine the purpose before reading • Find or create a quiet environment for reading • Generate questions, predictions, and associations related to the text itself and topic in general • Make a plan: Choose a strategy, technique, or tool appropriate to the text or purpose • Preview the text (for information related to its length, genre, subject, organization, style, features) to assess how to read it and how long it will take • Read (and listen for) any directions—on handouts, in textbooks, on whiteboard, from teacher or the text itself	• Anticipate students' emotional, cognitive, and cultural response to the text prior to assigning it • Assess students' skills, knowledge, and needs • Clarify how you and your students will use this text: To teach? To generate? For background information? • Create the appropriate environment for reading • Decide which strategies or techniques students will use • Prepare students with necessary skills and knowledge • Determine the objective in light of course goals, students' needs, and course standards • Establish how students will be assessed and on what • Evaluate the demands of the text and tasks as they relate to difficulty, time, readiness, and maturity • Explain why they are reading this—and reading it this way • Frontload key vocabulary, concepts, or knowledge • Model how to read, write about, or discuss the text • Provide or work with students to generate a Big Idea or Essential Question designed to challenge and engage
DURING	
• Connect what they read to their own experiences, other classes/texts, and the world at large • Evaluate the importance of details in relation to purpose • Keep objective or purpose question (PQ) in mind • Monitor their comprehension as they read • Pay attention to how the text is organized and the purpose this organization ultimately serves • Read actively, taking notes, annotating, asking questions, making inferences, drawing conclusions • Stop when confused to fix the problem or ask for help • Use all their senses—sight, sound, smell, touch, and taste—to visualize and bring the text to life • Use the assigned strategy or technique or choose one that will help them better understand and remember	• Adjust the level of demand—if required tasks are too challenging or not engaging enough—as needed based on your observations or results on assessments • Assess students' knowledge and comprehension throughout by most effective and least intrusive ways to evaluate their success and the methods used • Determine the level of intervention or instruction needed based on feedback or observations: explain, ask, verify; clarify, model; or have students generate ideas and questions, problems and possible solutions to them • Evaluate students' use of strategies or introduce new ones in light of struggles while reading or need to challenge and engage students at highest levels • Monitor students' levels of engagement, understanding, effort, making adjustments as needed • Check in with those students with special needs regularly to be sure they understand what to do and how to do it
AFTER	
• Assess that students completed the text, understood it, and can demonstrate that understanding through discussion, an exam, or some other way • Decide what matters most and how to remember it • Determine whether they can answer their initial PQ or have achieved their objective(s) • Discuss, represent, or write about the text and its connections to their own lives, other studies, and the world outside of school • Pause and reflect on their process: what they did, how it did/did not help them understand the text • Reread as needed to improve or extend their understanding beyond the surface or literal level • Retell, relate, or respond in their own words to the text	• Decide what evidence you are willing to accept that they read and understood the assigned text • Assess students' performance and readiness (for subsequent tasks, toward mastery) through testing, writing, discussions, or other measures • Evaluate what, if anything, you should re-teach based on assessment data and determine how best to re-teach it • Decide whether to have students re-read and if so, for what purpose, using which technique

FIGURE 5.6 The Process of Understanding and Thinking About What We Read

Reading Process Self-Evaluation

Name: _____ Period: _____ Date: _____

BEFORE	
1. I gather any materials (highlighter, notebook, sticky notes, etc.) I might need.	Always Usually Sometimes Rarely Never
2. I choose a place without distractions to do my reading.	Always Usually Sometimes Rarely Never
3. I make sure I have a dictionary within reach.	Always Usually Sometimes Rarely Never
4. I go over any directions for the assigned reading.	Always Usually Sometimes Rarely Never
5. I preview (skim) the assignment to determine what it's about, how long it will take me, and how difficult it is.	Always Usually Sometimes Rarely Never
6. I make a plan for how to take notes based on the assignment.	Always Usually Sometimes Rarely Never
7. I set a goal or establish a purpose (by asking a question).	Always Usually Sometimes Rarely Never
8. I make predictions about what I will read before beginning.	Always Usually Sometimes Rarely Never
9. I ask myself what I already know about this subject, this story, or this author.	Always Usually Sometimes Rarely Never
10. I decide which reading strategy/strategies will be most useful.	Always Usually Sometimes Rarely Never
DURING	
11. I revisit my objective or guiding question to focus my attention and help in evaluating information.	Always Usually Sometimes Rarely Never
12. I make connections to myself, the world, and other texts/studies.	Always Usually Sometimes Rarely Never
13. I identify the main idea and supporting details.	Always Usually Sometimes Rarely Never
14. I use previous experience and background knowledge to understand new information about the subject or story.	Always Usually Sometimes Rarely Never
15. I take notes, annotate the text, or highlight important details.	Always Usually Sometimes Rarely Never
16. I keep a list of questions about things I do not understand.	Always Usually Sometimes Rarely Never
17. I look up words I do not understand in the dictionary.	Always Usually Sometimes Rarely Never
18. I summarize what I read (in my head and/or in my notes) as I go.	Always Usually Sometimes Rarely Never
19. I make predictions about what will happen as I read.	Always Usually Sometimes Rarely Never
20. I monitor my understanding as I go and stop to use various "fix up" strategies when I get confused.	Always Usually Sometimes Rarely Never
21. I ask questions about what I read as I go.	Always Usually Sometimes Rarely Never
AFTER	
22. I stop and ask whether I know the answer to the Purpose Question I asked when I first began reading.	Always Usually Sometimes Rarely Never
23. I re-read all or part of the text to answer remaining questions, examine the author's style, or review for tests.	Always Usually Sometimes Rarely Never
24. I evaluate all that I read to determine what is most important to remember in the future (e.g., for tests, papers, discussions).	Always Usually Sometimes Rarely Never
25. I use one or more strategies to help remember these details.	Always Usually Sometimes Rarely Never

Reading Improvement Plan

Based on your evaluation above, make a plan for what you will do to improve your reading performance. In your plan, identify just those actions (3–5) that you can do immediately to get rapid results; then discuss how you accomplish your plan and why it will make a difference.

FIGURE 5.7 Students complete the Reading Process Self-Evaluation in the beginning of the year and at the end to reflect on their practices.

Thus, I close this section with Rosenblatt's transactional theory of the reading (and writing) process, its efferent-aesthetic texts aligning nicely with the Common Core and NAEP categories of informational and literary text.

> From the transactional point of view, *reading* always implies both a reader and a text in a reciprocal relationship. A *text* by itself is simply a set of marks or squiggles on a page. These become a sequence of *signs* as they meet the eyes of the reader. He [or] she engages in a dynamic, fluid, reciprocal to-and-from, back-and-forth process of choosing at each moment meanings that can be merged to make tentative sense of the text. A *reader* implies someone whose past experience enables him or her to make meaning in collaboration with a text. . . . *Meaning—whether scientific or aesthetic, whether a poem or a scientific report—happens during the interplay between particular signs and a particular reader at a particular time and place.* . . . Hence each reader's memory will have a unique accumulation of various encounters with [for example, the word *fair*] carrying different mixtures of ideas and feelings, denotations and connotations. (2005, x)

In an era when students too often want to base their "reader's response" on the assertion that "that's what I think," Rosenblatt's theory demands "responsible reading" (xxiv). Her theory requires that students—all readers—take into account the text, its words, their meaning, and, when creating meaning of those words, passages, or actions, find support in the text for the interpretation they offer. Through such a "complex, nonlinear, recursive, self-correcting transaction" (9), the reader synthesizes the different elements to arrive at "the meaning called novels, poems, or plays" (1) by discussing and writing about those texts.

What does all this look like in action? The following is one sample taken from a CP senior English class which was reading an article by Steven Greenhouse (2003) titled "Going for the Look but Risking Discrimination" in which the author examined evolving practices for hiring young people in Abercrombie & Fitch stores. For this 1500-word article, we read it in a variety of ways, which I will outline later, but first here is the opening so that you can get a sense of the article's subject and the issues involved:

"What does all this look like in action?"

> A funny thing happens when Elizabeth Nill, a sophomore at Northwestern University, goes shopping at Abercrombie & Fitch.
>
> At no fewer than three Abercrombie stores, she says, managers have approached her and offered her a job as a clerk.
>
> . . . Ms. Nill is 5-foot-6 and has long blond hair. She looks striking. She looks hip. She looks, in fact, as if she belongs in an Abercrombie & Fitch catalog.
>
> Is this a coincidence? A fluke? No, says Antonio Serrano, a former assistant Abercrombie store manager in Scranton, PA. It's policy.
>
> "If someone came in with a pretty face, we were told to approach them and ask them if they wanted a job," Mr. Serrano said. "They thought if we had the best-looking college kids working in our store, everyone will want to shop there."

We are reading this in order to examine arguments made by and about the media as part of a larger unit that will culminate in students writing an argument about some aspect of advertising. Here are the things I do relative to teaching this one article:

BEFORE

- Project an image of two Abercrombie & Fitch (A&F) models on the screen in class prior to giving them the article itself, asking them to generate questions that would help them "read" such ads. As we do this, I facilitate the discussion, asking them to elaborate on why they would ask a certain question or what they might expect to find in response to it.

- Generate words that describe the two models (go online and search for "Abercrombie & Fitch models" and you will get a quick sense of what we were looking at), asking them to sometimes refine their search terms or offer others specific to the clothing, the mood, the style. (See Figure 5.8.)

FIGURE 5.8 Andres reads images from various ad campaigns as part of our investigation of media in general and advertisements in particular.

- Take them to the library for a quick stint on the computers to conduct an image search for A&F and whatever other brands they may wear or wish they could. While they search (which, at times, causes me to worry I will lose my job if the principal comes in a sees what comes up!), they jot down nouns, verbs, and adjectives that describe what they see. I am trying to adjust their attention for the visual texts and the written arguments they will read once they begin reading the article.

- Back in class, they use their notes from the computer session to generate some thoughts about the models and ads, what they notice, any questions that arise. Someone asks why the ads for A&F (or others), which is selling clothing, so often feature models without any clothes on. I ask them to jot down their thoughts, their initial guesses.

- After we briefly discuss their ideas about the models and advertisements, I ask them to synthesize what they saw, said, and think in a paragraph using their list of nouns, verbs, and adjectives to help them write with greater precision and description.

- I give them the article, which I have formatted with extra-wide left margins for annotations and notes, line numbers in the margins for easy reference during discussion, and boxes at strategic places where they should stop and jot down ideas in response to questions (e.g., What does the store say its rationale is for this marketing strategy?). I ask them to look at the title ("Going for the Look, but Risking Discrimination") and generate a couple questions that occur to them. We then work together to shape a "Purpose Question" (PQ) they can write down on the front page and use to guide their reading. We arrive at: "What is 'the look' and how does going for it 'risk discrimination'?"

- We take several minutes to discuss the word **discrimination**—its meanings, connotations, and how it might apply to this article, this subject. We talk about the more sophisticated usage of "discriminating tastes" when it comes to fine foods and the more unfortunate notion of discriminating against people based on appearance, group affiliation, and so on.

- I introduce and discuss the homework, which is to read the article that night for the gist, underlining anything that seems related to the PQ we just developed. I tell them to read with a pencil, not a highlighter; pencils, I say, allow you to make notes in the margin to explain why you underlined something. Using my document camera, I model for them what to do in the time remaining, reading the opening aloud as I interrupt myself to comment on what I would write down and why and how it relates to the PQ.

DURING

- They read as directed that night, applying the strategy as we discussed.

- The next day, they come in with the article marked up, annotated, and ready to discuss before reading it more closely for its arguments, key ideas, and rhetorical strategies. They huddle into small groups of three to five to share what they found. I circulate to observe, assess, and make sure all did the work. A few students with reading difficulties were not entirely sure what to do but did read it as evidenced by their notes in the margins. (See Figure 5.9.)

- We discuss what they found in response to the PQ. While they share their ideas, I ask them to provide examples or otherwise elaborate on what they noticed that relates to the PQ, which remains our main focus so far.
- I open up the discussion for a few minutes to engage them further (and draw in more students) by connecting it to their own lives. I ask them to jot down what they think about the practices the article discusses, the idea that the models all represent the "classic American look," which I note only two of us in the class could be said to possess. Then they use their notes to help them participate in the discussion, thus allowing me to ask reluctant participants what they wrote down.

FIGURE 5.9 Back in class, students discuss their findings about the images and further discuss the article by Greenblatt that served to frame the whole unit.

AFTER

- After the discussion, we revisit our PQ to determine whether we can answer it or not. It is not necessary or appropriate at this point to have any other sort of assessment as the work in class proves they did read it and the coming work will require them to read it again for new reasons.
- With the time remaining in class, I tell them they are going to re-read the article now for the elements of argument as part of a larger unit on argument and the effect of advertising on people in general and kids in particular. I tell them to reread the article specifically to identify the arguments used by Abercrombie & Fitch, its lawyers, and all other interested parties to justify its hiring practices. They are only reading to find the arguments used to support the practice and the evidence that supports their assertions. Why? Because when doing close reading, especially with such a large, diverse class, I find students learn best when they process one aspect at a time so they can train their attention to read for that one element.

FIGURE 5.10 Monique and Julianne engage in collaborative reading of a challenging informational text, using this technique to slow down and help them read for the arguments the author makes about corporate ethics.

- After discussing the article the next day, during which we focus on the arguments *for* Abercrombie & Fitch's hiring practices, students work in small groups of two to three where they discuss the article (skimming and scanning at this point to find, and then re-read those arguments *against* the practice and the evidence cited). It is good to have them collaborate on the reading at this point as the slow patient work of close reading is not always engaging for all when they first learn to do it (see Figure 5.10); working with others, however, makes it more interactive and enables them to help each other find, evaluate, and analyze the counterarguments and evidence that supports their analysis. Also, this approach allows me to circulate and observe, assess and guide as needed.
- Finally, I ask them to write a summary of the article, its arguments, counterarguments, and their supporting evidence. To ensure they understand what I want them to do, I give my students a handout titled Summary Notes (see Figure 5.11). It includes the elements of an effective summary, sample verbs to use when writing one, and an example of a good summary. We talk about the article as I stand at the laptop, which projects a blank document on the screen, cursor blinking. Having set Microsoft Word to a 24-point font, I lead a brief discussion about the subject of the "Going for the Look" and what the writer says about it. I clarify that a summary takes no position on an issue and allows the use of the author's words. On the screen, guided by the sample they also have in hand, I type, "In

Summary Notes

Name: _____ Period: _____ Date: _____

Subject: _____

BEFORE
1. Determine your purpose.
2. Preview the document.
3. Prepare to take notes.

DURING
4. Take notes to help you answer these questions:
   - Who is involved?
   - Which events, ideas, or people does the author emphasize?
   - What are the causes?
   - What are the consequences or implications?
5. Establish criteria to determine what is important enough to include in the summary.
6. Evaluate information as you read to determine whether it meets your criteria for importance.

AFTER
7. Write your summary, which should:
   - Identify the title, author, and topic in the first sentence.
   - State the main idea in the second sentence.
   - Be shorter than the original article.
   - Begin with a sentence that states the topic (see sample).
   - Include a second sentence that states the author's main idea.
   - Include 3–5 sentences in which you explain—in your own words—the author's point of view.
   - Include one or two interesting quotations or details.
   - Maintain the author's meaning.
   - Organize the ideas in the order in which they appear in the article.
   - Use transitions, such as "according to," and the author's name to show that you are summarizing someone else's ideas.
   - Include enough information so that someone who has not read the article will understand the ideas.

Sample verbs: The author . . .
- argues
- asserts
- concludes
- considers
- discusses
- emphasizes
- examines
- explores
- focuses on
- implies
- mentions
- notes
- points out
- says
- states
- suggests

Sample summary written by a student

In "Surviving a Year of Sleepless Nights," Jenny Hung discusses *success and how it may not be so good.* Hung points out that having fun is better than *having success and glory.* Jenny Hung survived a painful year because of having too many honors classes, getting straight A's, and having a GPA of 4.43. Why would any of this be bad? It's because she wasn't happy. She describes working so hard for something she didn't really want. At one point she says, "There was even a month in winter when I was so self-conscious of my raccoon eyes that I wore sunglasses to school." She says she often stayed up late doing work and studying for tests for her classes. After what she had been through, she decided that it was not her life and chose her classes carefully once sophomore year came around.

_____

_____

_____

_____

_____

_____

_____

_____

_____

_____

_____

_____

_____

_____

_____

_____

_____

_____

_____

_____

FIGURE 5.11 Summary Notes is one of several structured note-taking approaches and reading strategies to use as we encounter increasingly more complex texts throughout a unit or semester.

'Going for the Look, but Risking Discrimination,' Steven Greenhouse . . ."—then stop and ask which verbs might work best there. We come up with a few words together, finally arriving at *examines*, then taking a minute to discuss why that word is better than *discusses* or *argues*, which we conclude he does not do as this is an article not an opinion piece. Armed with the beginning, with all their notes and the article read and reread, they go home to write their summary. (See Figure 5.12.)

- A week later, after reading other articles and watching some commercials and videos (from Dove Beauty Campaign and documentary *Still Killing Us Softly*), in the same critical ways, we return to the Greenhouse article and others, using their notes, summary, and annotations to write a paper in which they each construct an argument about advertising, culling evidence from the articles and elsewhere to support their claims. (See Figure 5.13 on the next page.) As we move from reading to writing about what we read, I often begin by facilitating a discussion which I then capture, in their words not mine, on the laptop to show them what they are saying and what the writing they are to do sounds like.

FIGURE 5.12 Dean uses the Summary Notes guidelines to help him read more closely but also to improve his ability to summarize what he reads.

Throughout this sequence, the point has not been to get the article read and move on to the next, but to read for depth, to develop students' ability to apply and extend previously acquired skills, and to create a context for learning new lessons about argument, rhetoric (visual and written), and language. Also, the point has been to engage in a sustained, substantial discussion about the article's ideas and the larger unit of inquiry about the forces that shape their identities and ways of thinking about and viewing the world. It has been a good few days of rich discourse about both craft and content, during which students analyzed advertisements, connected the learning to their own lives, and studied texts very closely as part of an emphasis on reading but also in preparation for an ambitious analytical writing assignment to follow. The reward was days of engaging discussions as a whole class and in small groups.

The example provided here examines informational texts intended to persuade and explain (advertisements and newspaper articles) as part of a unit that would go on to consider other media (commercials, documentaries, websites) and additional expository writings (essays, more newspaper articles). Although engaged here in what Rosenblatt called *efferent* reading (for information, the facts, the arguments), students would follow a similar process with aesthetic or literary texts—reading, annotating, and re-reading and discussing a poem such as Yeats' "Second Coming." It is a poem to which we return throughout the year in my AP class in various contexts and by way of measuring their progress as advanced analytical readers of literary texts.

What some might see as taking too long, I see as effective reading instruction at the high school level. Lincoln's Gettysburg Address is only 265-words long, yet Garry Wills wrote a 320-page book in 1992 about the speech, reminding us of the rewards of close reading of specific texts and the discipline such reading demands of both the reader and the teacher.

Argument Organizer

Name: _____

Subject
What is the subject of your argument?

Subject

Claim
What is the main point you will argue?

Claim

Reason
Why should readers accept your claim?

Reason

Evidence
- Facts
- Figures
- Statistics
- Observations
- Examples
- Quotations

Evidence	Evidence	Evidence

Acknowledge and Respond
to other perspectives on the subject

Acknowledge	Respond

FIGURE 5.13 The Argument Organizer works just as well to help students read for arguments as it does to help them construct their own (if used as a prewriting tool).

Principles and Practices: Effective Reading Instruction

Like so many other things, you know great reading instruction when you see it; however, as a useful standard or model for improving individual teachers' teaching, this statement leaves a bit too much to the imagination. Alvermann (2001) sums up effective adolescent literacy instruction by saying that:

> It must take into account a host of factors, including students' perceptions of their competencies as readers and writers, their level of motivation and background knowledge, and their interests. To be effective, such instruction must be embedded in the regular curriculum and make use of multiple forms of texts read for multiple purposes in a variety of learning situations. Because many adolescents of the Net Generation will find their own reasons for becoming literate—reasons that go beyond reading to acquire school knowledge or mastery of academic texts—it is important that teachers create sufficient opportunities for students to engage actively in meaningful subject matter projects that both extend and elaborate on the literacy practices they already own and value. (24)

The following traits of excellent reading instruction are supported by major reports focusing on middle and high schools. Each element is accompanied by several sources and examples to illustrate the practice at the secondary level:

1. **Teachers provide direct instruction throughout the reading process**, focusing on comprehension strategies (making inferences, drawing conclusions, synthesizing, visualizing, asking questions) that prepare students to read a variety of complex texts; in this context, they teach academic literacies such as taking notes, annotating texts, discussing and writing about those texts. Such direct instruction eventually gives way to modeling, then guided practice, and, finally, independent application of these skills and strategies (Torgesen et al. 2007; Biancarosa and Snow 2006; Langer 2002; Alvermann 2001; IRA 2000; Fielding and Pearson 1994).

   - Students learn specific question strategies such as Reporter's Questions (who, what, when, where, why, how?), and Question Answer Relationships (QAR), which involve two main categories: "in the book" questions and "in my head questions" (Rafael, Highfield, and Au 2006, 22).

   - Students are taught and required to use question strategies, such as SOAPSTONE, for specific genres such as poetry (What is the **s**ubject? **O**ccasion? **A**udience? Author's **p**urpose? Who is the **s**peaker? What is the **tone**?)

   - Students learn to use structured note-taking strategies or graphic organizers to improve comprehension, then use these notes when writing.

Essential Reading

The following reports on reading are important to become familiar with and are available online:

- *Reading Next*
- *Reading Between the Lines*
- *Academic Literacy Instruction for Adolescents*
- *Reading to Achieve: A Governor's Guide to Adolescent Literacy*
- *Lessons and Recommendations from the Alabama Reading Initiative*

- Students learn specific strategic sequences such as Reciprocal Teaching, which involves: summarizing, then generating questions, then clarifying, and finally predicting.

- Teachers model the use of strategies while reading out loud to the class about which questions to ask while reading, when to ask them, how to ask them, and why. (See Figure 5.14.)

2. **Teachers integrate instruction throughout the content of their courses**, teaching skills and knowledge within a meaningful context that allows students to connect what they learn to what they already know, to what they are currently learning, to their own lives, and to the world beyond school (Gallagher 2009; Biancarosa and Snow 2006; Tatum 2005; Smith and Wilhelm 2002; Alvermann 2001; IRA 2000; Guthrie and Wigfield 1997).

FIGURE 5.14 I read aloud frequently in all my classes, thinking aloud about what it means, what the author is doing—whatever is most relevant to our current focus in the class. Even advanced classes need this so they can hear what the text sounds like when read by a knowing reader.

- Students analyze the author's use of figurative language while reading literary texts (see Figure 5.15). In the process, the teacher explains what figurative language is, shows how writers use it, and discusses why they do; then the teacher directs students to use the strategies provided to identify, make sense of, and analyze the use of such language in the poem they study.

- Students work to master the elements of formal argument within the context of studying written, visual, and spoken arguments in different media; then, using a structured note-taking strategy, apply those elements to the articles they read and advertisements they analyze.

- Students reading essays, speeches, or poems examine rhetorical strategies such as repetition and the use of examples to emphasize certain aspects of a text or ideas. After the teacher directs their attention to examples and discusses how such devices affect the meaning of the text, students indicate examples of these various elements on their photocopy of the text, making a note in the margin about the effect of that usage. They then write a paragraph in which they analyze the use of repetition, citing and analyzing evidence from the text to show how they arrived at their choices.

- Students develop their ability to discuss all types of texts using appropriate academic language, using posters, handouts, or language from the whiteboard to guide them using a handout like the one shown in Figure 5.16.

FIGURE 5.15 Freshman discuss the text and use sticky notes to identify and analyze key moments in the stories we read.

Name: _____

Directions Fill in the "Read" section as you read; then, using those notes, summarize the text in the second section ("Retell"). Relate this text or topic to other texts you have recently read or ideas you have discussed, making whatever connections you can between them. Finally, jot down your own thoughts, making personal connections to the text or topic in the "Respond" section.

1. Read: Jot down the most important ideas using bullets.	**2. Retell:** Use your notes from #1 to summarize the text.

3. Relate: Connect the text to other topics or readings.	**4. Respond:** Express your thoughts about the text and topic.

FIGURE 5.16 Four R Notes works well for both fiction and informational texts.

3. **Students read interesting or real-world texts for authentic reasons** to increase engagement and motivation, thereby improving their overall reading capacity. To achieve such heightened, sustained engagement, the teacher must allow students to choose what they read, how they read, or what they focus on while they read (Schmoker 2011; Atwell 2009; Gallagher 2009; Smith and Wilhelm 2002, 2006; Guthrie and Wigfield 1997, 1997; Applebee 1996; Smith 1988).

- Students reading a typical whole-class novel, such as *To Kill a Mockingbird*, choose which character or theme they follow as they read so as to ensure that they are more attentive and engaged. Yes, of course, Atticus Finch is a moral exemplar worthy of studying; yet, every character in *Mockingbird* merits and will sustain the engaged reader's attention, yielding substantial rewards.

- Students read two books: a whole-class core novel, such as *Their Eyes Were Watching God*, and a second, self-selected novel, biography, or nonfiction work about a subject they choose to examine over the course of the semester.

- Students are organized into groups (called literature circles, inquiry circles, book clubs, or shared inquiry groups) and assigned either a whole-class novel or a high-interest book unique to each group that does not require significant instructional support to understand. In these groups, students generate the guiding questions and engage in the discussion independently, while the teacher circulates to observe, nudge, challenge students (see Figure 5.17).

FIGURE 5.17 Students discuss the books in different literature circles after I gave booktalks about each of them.

- The teacher provides a range of ways to read and respond to the book so as to invite greater motivation based on students' natural inclinations. So, for example, students could take notes and mark up the text in the traditional ways, chat with classmates online, or blog, tweet, or vlog (video blog).

- The teacher invites students to perform the text or portions of it live word for word or through modernized adaptations.

4. **Students engage in regular, authentic discussions** in class and online about a variety of texts, using conversation not only to comprehend but also to extend their thinking (Daniels and Harvey 2009; Torgeson et al. 2007; Biancarosa and Snow 2006; Alvermann 2001; Langer and Close 2001; Nystrand 1998, 2006; Beck et al. 1997; Fielding and Pearson 1994).

- Students participate in a seminar as a character from a book the class is reading or an expert on some aspect of that book, discussing the book from that perspective and providing evidence from the text to support their ideas. (See Figure 5.18.)

- Students jot down questions about a text the class is reading, pass these up to the teacher, who then asks a student to choose the questions the class will discuss, freeing up the teacher to monitor, guide, challenge, or simply listen to and observe the class during the discussion.

- The teacher invites an expert into the class to speak about a subject related to the book being read or the topic the class is examining through a variety of texts. This expert, such as the lawyer I invited to come to our class, guides us through the discussion about, in my own case, the idea of laws—where they come from, how they are used and interpreted—as part of our discussion of *Antigone*.

- Students reading a short piece of complex text, such as a poem or a passage from a Shakespeare play, underline passages of the text they *do not understand*, then turn to talk with a partner about only these portions, drawing on each others' knowledge to fill in the gaps and make useful inferences about the meaning.

- Students pair up to read a difficult informational text collaboratively after first generating a purpose question they should be able to answer when they finish. Student A reads the first paragraph, stops, and discusses with Student B what the most important piece of information from the paragraph that relates to the purpose question; then, after reaching agreement, Student B reads the second paragraph, stops, and the process repeats. The point is not always to finish the reading but to *use* the reading to foster rich discussion about the topic, the text, and the ideas it raises. Afterward, the whole class engages in a discussion to tie it all together before moving ahead. (See Figure 5.10.)

FIGURE 5.18 Students participating in a forum about power as it relates to several plays we read. Each student represents Macchiavelli (a different reading his *Prince*), a character in the plays, or one of the playwrights.

5. **The teacher provides targeted, strategic instruction** to the whole class, specific groups of students, or individuals as needed, paying attention not only to English learners, for example, but also to the advanced readers in the class—teaching all students through such instruction how to advance their skills (Fisher, Frey, and Lapp 2011; Echevarria, Vogt, and Short 2008; Biancarosa and Snow 2006; Langer 2002; Schoenbach et al. 1999).

- The teacher models for the whole class how to make an inference about a character. The teacher walks the class through predetermined passages, such as the scene in *Heart of Darkness* in which Conrad describes the immaculate European accountant in his bright white suit. After modeling which questions to ask and what to pay attention to, the teacher asks the students to make a similar inference about the Africans as depicted in the chapter.

- The teacher circulates around the room while groups discuss Robert Frost's poem "Out! Out!" as part of an inquiry into family relations. While moving from one group to the next, the teacher notices that the students as a class struggle with certain details that are all related to personification. Instead of doing the same focused lesson eight times for each group, she calls the class together briefly to clarify the meaning and purpose of personification—what it is, how it works. Then, she asks students to find examples in the poem and explains how they contribute to the poem's meaning. Having shown that they understand, the groups resume their discussions and the teacher continues to circulate to monitor their understanding and performance as she moves around.

- The teacher notices several English learners struggling to use a specific reading strategy or understand a text. The teacher calls the students together into a small group and models the strategy for them, thinking out loud while doing so, about what she is doing, how, and why. The teacher then has students practice the strategy while watching, adjusting or praising their performance as needed.

- The teacher sits down with a small group that is having a difficult time identifying the different elements of an argument in an essay; to help, the teacher draws a quick version of the Argument Organizer tool (refer to Figure 5.13) sometimes used in class, then walks them through the article quickly but patiently, using the organizer to help them identify the different elements and understand how they work in this essay.

6. **The teacher selects texts that grow progressively more complex** than those students previously read, or asks students to read in increasingly sophisticated ways beginning with texts similar to those they have already read (Stotsky 2010b; Perkins 2009; Stigler and Hiebert 2009; Biancarosa and Snow 2006; ACT 2004).

- The teacher begins the semester with a collection of short stories, all more or less equally difficult but still accessible enough so that students can focus on how to read them (i.e., using the methods the teacher is introducing) without having to struggle to understand them at this point. Having shown some initial mastery of the techniques, students then move on to read additional, more demanding short stories, which the strategies learned will help them read successfully. This might include reading the texts as "conversations" with each other to consider an idea common to all from multiple perspectives.

- Students read, for example, one of Shakespeare's sonnets, discussing what it means and why they think that; then to this one sonnet, the teacher adds one or more other sonnets of Shakespeare's (or another poet's) and asks students to read them as a set to examine the subject of love across texts, drawing evidence from the poems to support their interpretations.

- Students begin each class by reading the same poem chosen for its depth, merit, and complexity. Each day students read the poem for a different purpose, each day's focus demanding more of the reader than it did the day before. So Monday, students might read Yeat's "Second Coming" for any line that grabs them and write about it; by Wednesday, however, they might be reading for imagery and language that relates to Yeats's notion of recurring cycles. Come Friday, students might read the poem one last time to synthesize all the different aspects they have considered, then analyze the poem in a short in-class writing in which students examine how these different elements contribute to the poem's meaning.

- The teacher brings together a set of short, complex texts—both literary and informational, fiction and poetry, literary criticism and cultural commentary—to create a sequence of readings that build on each other but all relate to a larger anchor text such as a major literary work. These supplemental or secondary texts should grow more difficult (as well as the ideas themselves) as the unit progresses. Sophomores reading *Lord of the Flies*, for example, might begin by reading a short article about the traits of leaders; this would be followed by doing some research on specific tyrants from the twentieth century, then examining their motives and character traits. Students would then read *Lord of the Flies*, focusing on those qualities of the leaders they chose to study as reflected in its primary characters. During or after reading the novel, once students have established a solid foundation for their inquiry, they might then read a more advanced article by someone like psychol-

FIGURE 5.19 I meet with Antonella and Vincent to discuss their reading of *1984* as they work on their presentations about power.

ogist Howard Gardner (1995) in which he offers psychological profiles of the different types of leaders (see Figure 5.19). All of this would culminate in a paper or presentation in which students compare their appointed or chosen world leader to, say, Jack or Ralph from the novel.

- Students begin the year by reading personal narratives that all examine a common subject (e.g., first jobs). Then they move on to read more critically a second series of essays, this time being more analytical about the changing nature of work in the twenty-first century. To these might be added written passages or quantitative data from government labor reports about trends in the modern workplace. The unit might conclude with a chapter from a book that examines the place of work in our lives and society; such a book might draw on extensive research and include narrative, analytical, written, and quantitative content all in one multimodal text.

7. **Teachers have students write intensively and frequently about what they read**, using writing to help them understand and think more deeply about what they read. This writing should not privilege personal response over analysis of the texts but balance the two as one (personal) increases engagement and the other (analytical) prepares students for career and college-level writing, reading, and thinking (Applebee and Langer 2011; Graham and Hebert 2010; Biancarosa and Snow 2006; Alvermann 2001; IRA 2000).

- Students write to understand what they read; this means writing summaries and paraphrases, but also personal responses through which they begin to explicate the texts in order to better comprehend them.

- Students take notes or annotate a text for a specific reason or theme, then use those notes to guide their analysis of or response to the text they read.

FIGURE 5.20 Notebooks offer readers a wide range of tools to help them read more critically.

- All students keep a Reader's Notebook as a way of capturing ideas, jotting down notes about what they read, and rehearsing for the larger, more complex analytical writing assignments to come. (See Figure 5.20.)

- Teachers provide models and direct instruction to show students *how* to write about texts in the required ways; they may also offer students more analytical sentence frames (see Figure 4.4) to help students formulate interpretations and arguments.

- Students mimic either mentor texts or professional examples (of informational or literary texts) the teacher provides in order to understand the form and its features through emulation; for example by writing a sonnet or a counterargument students learn what one is and how it works.

8. **Assess students before, as, and after they read a text** using a variety of means—both formative and summative, formal and informal, integrating assessments—so as not to make the test seem like the reason they are reading the text. Also, use the information from the assessments to improve and inform instruction, especially for those whose performance suggests they still do not understand what they read (Biancarosa and Snow 2006; Echevarria, Vogt, and Short 2008; Langer 2002; IRA 2000).

- The teacher observes students as they discuss a text in groups, posing informal questions designed to test whether the students understand the reading and, if they do, how well.

- The teacher passes out index cards and asks students to write about what happened during the previous night's reading and why it matters to the story. So, for example, the teacher might ask students reading *Bless Me, Ultima* to say what happened to Ultima's owl in the chapter they read as homework. If they read the chapter, students will know the answer, the questions being such that any student should be able to answer them. These questions should only take a minute to answer; once collected, they provide the teacher with a way to begin the day's discussion about the text (see Figure 5.21).

Bless Me, Ultima Chap. 16-17

1. "The owl will scratch out your other eye—"
He crouched as if to pounce on me, but he remained motionless, thinking.... He straightened up and smiled, as if a thought had crossed his mind, and he said, "Ay cabroncito, your curse is that you know too much."

The Question: To whom is Tony speaking? What does this person want to do? What idea does Tony give to this person without realizing it?

2. The mystery of God is a major subject of chapter 17: What does Antonio have to say about it? What kind of questions does he keep asking himself and wondering about?

FIGURE 5.21 I project these quiz questions from my computer; students answer on index cards.

- Teachers create a formal multiple-choice exam about the text similar to the one students might take on the common assessment, released AP exam, or final. Such exams can be formatted so that students can defend their answers in the margin to further develop their test wisdom and overall critical reasoning.

- Students generate a list of words (or choose several from a list that the teacher gives them) that best describe some aspect of the text (tone, main character, diction, plot), then choose the *one* they think *best* describes that aspect. Then, the students explain why, providing evidence from the text to support and illustrate their assertions.

- Teachers provide a range of ways to show what students know but also develop their reading and writing skills. Students, for example, might be allowed to keep a reading notebook or blog, as if they were one of the characters, to show how well they understand the book. Or they might perform or visually represent some aspect of the text, explaining what they did and why and how it relates to the text.

9. **Provide time in class and outside to support extensive reading** of both assigned and self-selected texts to increase engagement; develop students' identity as readers; and improve stamina, speed, and fluency (Gambrell et al. 2011; Atwell 2007a; NCTE 2004; Smith and Wilhelm 2002; Pilgreen 2000; Schoenbach et al. 1999; Fielding and Pearson 1994).

- Students use the first 10 minutes of class to read from self-selected books while the teacher meets with individual students at her desk to discuss the self-selected book they are reading or their progress as readers.

- Students get the last 10 minutes to begin the assigned reading, during which time the teacher circulates to check with students to see that they are reading it as assigned and can understand the text.

- Teachers remember to tell students to take time that night to read their required or self-selected reading, keeping in mind that they cannot easily do it if they assigned too much other work.

- Teachers read with students during in-class silent reading time to model the practice of reading. (See Figure 5.22.)

FIGURE 5.22 I rarely provide time in class to read the novels; *The Kite Runner*, however, was so long and we had so little time that I made a point of allowing them the last ten minutes to get a jump on that night's homework.

10. **Use a variety of instructional strategies to** support and enhance reading instruction within a classroom that supports, even encourages, intellectual risk-taking from students at all ability levels and invites metacognitive conversations about students' reading processes (Echevarria, Vogt, and Short 2008; Torgesen et al. 2007; Bacevich and Salinger 2006; Langer 2002; Greenleaf, Schoenbach, Cziko, and Mueller 2001).

- Students use graphic strategies to help them visualize the action and better see the connections between ideas, characters, or texts. In my AP Literature class, for example, after students finish reading *Crime and Punishment*, I draw a circle with a dot outside it and tell them the whole novel can be summed up with that diagram, then ask them to try it out (Burke 2011, 155). Or I give students a painting, such as Casper

FIGURE 5.23 Students discuss a painting as they try not only to read the artwork itself but also consider how it might relate to Edna Pontellier in Chopin's *The Awakening*.

David Friedrich's *Wanderer Above a Sea of Fog* (1818), and ask them to explain how it relates to all the major works they have read that semester. (See Figure 5.23.)

- Students generate their own questions and use other devices to help them think well beyond the literal and into the interpretive and analytical domains about texts, their ideas, and their construction.

- Students reading a book that focuses on the future and/or technology such as *Brave New World* pick one strand of technology or a trend the book suggests will be part of the future society. They research this technology or trend (e.g., communication) back to its origins and 20 years into the future, examining the likely iterations of it and discuss the implications. In addition, they write about what the author of, for example, *Brave New World* would say about this and why they think that.

- Students exploring a subject through a collection of literary or informational texts adapt these texts into a high-quality collage, documentary, or other digital project that requires them to synthesize key ideas from the different works (see Figures 5.24a and b).

- Students take time whenever possible—before, throughout, and after—to reflect on their reading process, performance, and progress, using such metacognitive processes to deepen their understanding of their own ways of working.

FIGURE 5.24a The front of Dylan's "Sniper" cartoon offers a nice visual summary of the story's key moments; on the back, however, the same layout shows an analysis of the meaning and importance of each of these squares/screens.

Randy Bomer (2011) captures the complexity of the teacher's job when determining what role to play in a reader's experience and to what extent teachers should interject themselves:

> I kneel down beside Diedra, who has chosen for her independent reading a collection of short stories. At first, she is so into her reading that she does not even realize I am there. This is bad for me. . . . I am caught in a tension, one that exists in my mind because it exists in the field of literacy education. Should I speak to her or leave her alone? On one side of the tension in our field are people like Stephen Krashen and Nancie Atwell who might tell me to be quiet and let her read since it is the experience of sustained engagement with meaningful text that will lead her to all she needs to know about reading. . . . On the other side . . . are people like P. David Pearson, Carol Booth Olson, [and] Ruth Schoenbach . . . who [suggest] that it is important to provide students with external support for particular, valued habits of thinking in the midst of their reading. (56)

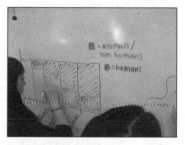

FIGURE 5.24b Kira and others draw out their ideas about *Frankenstein* and the boundary between human and nonhuman.

The list of ideas in Figure 5.25 seeks to honor both sides of Bomer's argument: students need both the freedom to graze and the guidance to grow as they move into more complex texts and the ideas in those texts. They also need us not only as guides but also as fellow travelers who are reading alongside them.

Overview of Reading Strategies and Essential Skills

Reading Strategies	Reading Skills
Establish a Purpose Readers establish a meaningful, appropriate purpose in light of the text and assigned task to help them better identify what is important and monitor their comprehension while reading.	**Skim the Text** Readers glance over an entire text, guided by a purpose or guiding question, and look at headers, titles, captions, introduction and conclusions, any graphics or sidebars.
Access and Acquire Background Knowledge Readers consider what they already know and get the knowledge they need to read and understand the text.	**Determine the Author's Purpose** Readers examine the author's purpose (to inform, persuade, explain, or describe) and the strategies used to achieve that purpose.
Make Predictions Readers predict what will happen or what the author will say about a subject based on previewing the text and their prior knowledge.	**Identify the Main Idea and Supporting Details** Readers discern the subject, main ideas, and supporting details of the text to determine what the author is saying about the subject and which details matter most in light of the subject.
Monitor Comprehension Readers constantly assess how well they understand what they read *as they read*; they revisit their purpose and stop to resolve any confusion *as they read*.	**Understand Text Structures/Patterns** Readers analyze how the text is organized (list, order of importance, cause-effect, compare and contrast, spatial, chronological order) and any other such patterns (repetition) they notice.
Make Inferences Readers make informed guesses about meaning based on what they know and learn about that subject while reading.	**Take Notes** Readers take structured, purposeful notes in the margins, on sticky notes, or in notebooks about insights, questions, ideas.
Draw Conclusions Readers determine the meaning based on information they gather as they read: because a, b, and c happen, the character must be . . .	**Ask Questions** Readers constantly ask questions about everything—the type of text, author's purpose, genre conventions, even what questions to ask. Foremost are: who, what, when, where, how, why, and "So what?"
Making Connections Readers connect what they read to their own lives, other texts, past/present studies, and current/historical events.	**Evaluate the Credibility and Quality of a Text** Readers evaluate the source, its credibility, purpose, and quality in light of genre conventions, and overall validity to determine whether it is reliable.
Summarize and Paraphrase Readers offer no analysis or synthesis; instead, they retell the important events or ideas in their own words; when paraphrasing, readers translate the text into their own words. A summary of a book can be a paragraph; paraphrases are as long as the text the reader seeks to understand.	**Troubleshooting the Text** Readers figure out the source of their confusion and use one or more of the strategies listed to the left to solve their comprehension problems. This may include talking to others about the text.
Visualize Readers bring the text to life through their senses, performing, drawing, or producing a multimedia representation of or response to the text.	**Write and Talk About the Text** Readers establish a meaningful, appropriate purpose in light of the text and assigned task to help them better identify what is important and monitor their comprehension while reading.
Re-read Readers reread words, passages they do not understand or wish to better understand as they read or after, returning to gain a deeper understanding and appreciation of the text or the author's craft.	**Chunk the Text** Readers break the text into smaller "chunks" to improve comprehension and better identify where comprehension breaks down.
Synthesize Readers determine the meaning based on ideas, information, and events as they read and after they finish, revising their understanding as needed.	**Reflect on Reading** Readers pay attention to and take time to think about what questions they asked and which strategies they used so they can know what to do in the future when reading similar texts.

FIGURE 5.25 Overview of Reading Strategies and Essential Skills for College-Ready Readers

Let's be honest: It has never been easier *not* to read: websites, study guides, audiobooks, and more—such sources abound, allowing students to get the gist of whatever we might be teaching. And if we teach these texts only for the facts, reducing reading to a series of endless multiple choice questions, we should not be surprised that students turn to such outlets for the answers to the *Hamlet* exam since that is all the adults seem to care about anyway (or so I imagine they would reason). The strategies and approaches outlined in Figure 5.25, those used by effective teachers, are of little use if the teacher does not read well, constantly, authentically. Nothing sells reading more than a passionate teacher, an engaged practitioner who walks the talk when it comes to reading. To this end, I talk to my classes and students on the side constantly about what I read, why I read it, how I find it to read, and how I read it.

> **NOTHING SELLS READING MORE THAN A PASSIONATE TEACHER, AN ENGAGED PRACTITIONER WHO WALKS THE TALK WHEN IT COMES TO READING.**

Reading for your own reasons will always find its way into the classroom, into your teaching, and, if we are lucky, into students' minds where, like a seed, it plants itself and grows over time in the rich soil of their own imagination. When I finish a magazine, such as the *New Yorker*, I ask myself which of my students would find something in it most interesting. Today, for example, I finished the latest edition and immediately knew I had to give it to Wren, a brilliant girl in my class of seniors whose brain ranges across many disciplines in an effort to feed itself. In this way, I not only model my own divergent reading and enhance my credibility in students' eyes, but I also serve as a mentor of minds through the words I pass along in this way. Later, at home, sometimes a blog, article, or other digital content demands I share it with some student, as I did today with James Han, a National Merit Finalist whose mind never seems to satiate itself.

Questions Readers Should Always Ask of Any Type of Text

- Which type of text is this (story, poem, essay, mixed media, etc.)?
- Why did the author/creator choose this form over another?
- What is the subject of this text?
- What is the author saying about this subject?
- What is the author's purpose in writing/creating this text?
- Which techniques does the author use to achieve this purpose?
- What do I need to know to be able to read this critically?
- How is this text organized/designed?
- How does that organizational approach support the author's purpose?
- To what extent can I trust the author, creator, or narrator of this text?

Type: Fictional Story

Common Core Standards Domain: Literature

Description:	Before
Fictional story includes short stories and novels, as opposed to *creative nonfiction* or other forms of nonfiction that use novelistic techniques to tell stories about actual events or people. Fiction falls under what the Common Core calls "imaginative fiction."	• Preview the text, taking time to think about the title, any images, pull quotes, and pre- or post-questions. • Predict what the story will be about. • Activate background knowledge about the era, genre, subject, etc. • Formulate a "Purpose Question" (PQ) . • Determine how to read the text in light of the PQ and any task that would be done after reading the text (e.g., writing an essay).

Sources of Difficulty

- Ambiguity
- Background Knowledge
- Empathy
- Irony
- Language
- Narrator Reliability
- Structure
- Style
- Subject
- Text Length
- Vocabulary

Key Features/Literary Terms

- Ambiguity
- Antagonist
- Character
- Conflict
- Conventions
- Diction
- Exposition
- Falling Action
- Flashback
- Foreshadow
- Genre
- Imagery
- *In media res*
- Irony
- Mood
- Plot
- Point of View
- Protagonist
- Resolution
- Rising Action
- Setting
- Structure
- Suspense
- Symbols
- Theme
- Tone

Sentence Frames

- The author uses *x* to create *y* in order to emphasize *a* and its affect on *b*.
- By using *x*, the author creates *y*, thus emphasizing how *a* affects *b*.
- In order to emphasize how *a* affects *b*, the author uses *x*, which creates *y*.

Readings and Resources

- *Fresh Takes on Literary Elements* (Smith and Wilhelm 2010)
- *The Making of a Story* (LaPlante 2007)

During

- Read with your PQ in mind.
- Ask questions as you read: who, what, when, where, how, why, so?
- Determine who is telling the story, why are they telling it—and if the person is reliable.
- Identify the source or nature of the conflict in the story, and how this conflict shapes the story through people's response to it.
- Which words would you use to describe the tone of the story as you read?
- Look for those crucial moments when something—the tone, characters, relationships, the mood, or focus—changes: what changed, how, and why?
- What do the main characters want more than anything? Why? What are they willing to do to get it? What does this tell us about them?
- How is the story organized? Why does the author arrange it this way?
- What stands out as you read about the author's style?
- How do these stylistic elements contribute to the meaning of the story?

After

- Answer, if you can, your PQ, now that you have finished the story.
- Reflect on the shape of the story: where and when did it begin—and end?
- How did the main character change over the course of the story?
- What *caused* these changes to the main character?
- Identify the key moments in the story and how they relate to the story's themes, character development, and plot structure.
- Return to the title: What new insights come to mind after reading the story?
- What did the author say about the main subject or idea of the story?
- What was the author's attitude toward this subject or idea?
- What connections can you make between this story and your own life, other readings, or the world at large?
- Re-read the story or portions of it to clarify any lasting confusion or examine other aspects of the story, such as style, now that you know the basic story.

FIGURE 5.26a Overview: Reading Fiction

Type: Informational Texts: Essay

Common Core Standards Domain: Informational

Description

Informational texts include essays, articles, websites, and any other documents used to inform, explain, or persuade. The form, function, and features of the informational text depend on the author's purpose and subject. They can be functional or highly stylized, carefully crafted documents. Increasingly, they may contain diagrams, photographs, or video if written for or read on tablets or computers.

Sources of Difficulty

- Author's stance or perspective
- Background knowledge
- Diagrams/Graphics
- Document design or layout
- Language
- Structure
- Style
- Subject
- Textual features
- Vocabulary

Key Features/Literary Terms

- Allusion
- Analogy
- Anecdote
- Appeals
- Argument
- Assertion
- Audience
- Bias
- Connotation
- Context
- Conventions
- Counterargument
- Credible
- Diction
- Evidence
- Figure of speech
- Graphics
- Jargon
- Perspective
- Purpose
- Rhetoric
- Source
- Structure
- Transition
- Tone

Sentence Frames

- The author adopts a _____ tone throughout in order to suggest _____.
- Broken into three distinct parts, the essay illustrates how ____ is created.
- The author shows not only how _____ is created but why it matters.

Readings and Resources

- *Strategies that Work* (Harvey and Goudvis 2007)
- *The Reader's Handbook* (Burke 2002)

Before

- Scan the entire text, noting the title, any images, subheadings, its length, and general degree of difficulty, source, author, any information before or after the text that would provide further context or support.
- Use all available clues—the title, context, images—to determine the subject.
- Predict what the text will say about this subject.
- Activate background knowledge about the era, genre, subject, etc.
- Formulate a "Purpose Question" (PQ).
- Determine how to read the text in light of the PQ and any task that would be done after reading the text (e.g., writing an essay)

During

- Read with your PQ in mind.
- Ask questions as you read: who, what, when, where, how, why, so?
- How is this text organized—and to what end?
- Evaluate the quality of the sources for any evidence or details offered.
- What strategies does this author use to achieve his or her purpose?
- Does the author consider other perspectives, particularly those that challenge the author's main idea?
- If the author uses any other features—links, images, video, graphics—what purpose do these serve?
- Did you feel you could trust this author as you are reading?

After

- Answer, if you can, your PQ, now that you have finished the story.
- What do you think about this subject now compared to before you read this article?
- What do you still not understand?
- What new questions or understandings does this text raise?
- What might you re-read in the text to discover or better understand?

FIGURE 5.26b Overview: Informational Texts

Struggling Readers: Help Them to Help Themselves

All our students should be struggling readers most of the time: School is, after all, where we go to learn what we do not know or cannot yet do. This tension between knowing and not-knowing, being able and unable, brings into relief the cognitive and emotional aspects of reading (Beers 2003, 13) as well as the social and cultural dimensions (Tatum 2005; Schoenbach et al. 1999) that drive or undermine the learning process. I see these various factors of anxiety and avoidance play out as often in my Advanced Placement English Literature classes as I do my College Prep or reading classes: Most people, especially if they feel vulnerable, seek to avoid what threatens their dignity, their sense of themselves as competent, or even gifted. Give most AP Lit kids a poem by Emily Dickinson and watch them wrestle with its many allusions, ambiguities, and abstractions; the strugglers in such advanced classes just stay quiet about it and pretend they get the poem's meaning. If you ask students, as I often do, to underline the parts of the poem they do *not* understand, you'll often be lucky to see more than a couple lines marked; yet ask them what some difficult line that is unmarked means, and they will frown and say they have no idea.

What is the source of these reading difficulties? What explains the boy who can read, understand, and analyze the most complex baseball statistics or a best-selling book, such as Michael Lewis' *Moneyball*, but cannot grasp a demanding literary or informational text about something unfamiliar? Some (Hirsch 2007; Marzano 2004) argue the problem is a lack of background knowledge. Thus, to return to the baseball example: Hirsch cites a study that found a very low-level reader (as measured by reading tests) who knew everything about baseball could perform at advanced levels on a serious assessment of complex texts if they were about baseball, whereas the high-level readers who knew nothing about baseball performed far-below grade level on the same exam (69).

Of course, background knowledge is hardly the only cause of reading difficulties. A more complete list follows, based on an adaptation of my Four Cs of Academic Success model (Burke 2004):

- *Commitment:* Students are not engaged; refuse to read or avoid reading because they believe they will fail; do not feel challenged; have no identity of themselves as someone who can or does read the assigned text; dismiss the text or associated tasks as unimportant; do not give themselves permission to try or you to teach.

- *Content:* Students lack the necessary knowledge about the text, topic, genre, conventions, language, or discipline they must know to read the text or complete the tasks based on the reading.

- *Competencies:* Students do not possess or have not yet mastered the skills needed to read the assigned text, use the required tools or strategies, or complete the associated tasks such as writing about or discussing the text in a particular way.

- *Capacities:* Students struggle for reasons related to speed, stamina, confidence, or attention; others have serious problems that stem from processing speed, mental stamina, limited attention, or confidence—any one of which can derail an otherwise adept reader. Students taking tests of one sort or another can be particularly troubled by these issues, or more emotional aspects such as anxiety.

Many of these points are illustrated in Philip Schultz's description of his own reading process as someone with dyslexia (2011, 202). Devlin (2000), though writing about math, captures the sense of disorientation students often feel when learning a new academic discipline, comparing the experience to entering a new house:

> When we enter a house for the first time, we of course find it unfamiliar. By walking around for a while, however, looking into various rooms and peering into cupboards, we quickly get to know it. But what if we cannot enter the house, and our own knowledge of it comes from the instructions and plans that were used to build it? Moreover, what if those instructions and plans are written in a highly technical language that we find intimidating and incomprehensible? What if, try as we may, we cannot form any mental picture of the house? Then we are not going to get much of a sense of what it is like to live there. We are not going to be able to enter the house even in our imagination. (2000, 128)

The student whose work is shown in Figure 5.27 was in a transitional class for English learners, and gives us important insights about the experience of becoming a reader at the same time one is learning the language.

Sources of Trouble

The following can cause students trouble when reading:

- **Attention:** problems with hyperactivity, distraction, impulsivity, prioritizing, stamina
- **Language:** difficulty processing words, grammar, characters, abstract concepts; lack of or confusion related to vocabulary
- **Cognition**: issues related to organizing, analyzing, evaluating importance or meaning of words, quantitative information, visual displays
- **Perception:** challenges in discriminating between auditory or visual stimuli, including lectures, films, and other forms of auditory/visual presentation
- **Expression:** obstacles to writing, speaking, or graphically representing ideas; extends to include spelling, handwriting, speed of output, or stamina related to writing
- **Speed:** difficulties associated with speed of reading or writing about reading
- **Socialization:** complications associated with working in groups on tasks related to texts or discussing those texts due to social anxieties
- **Memory:** limits or other problems connected with remembering what they read or should keep in mind while reading
- **Emotions:** responses to content student read about or ideas that arise during discussion of readings; can include fear, depression, even trauma associated with topics students may have experienced personally, especially those related to war, abuse, or death

Even the most distinguished writers grapple with some texts, those that make unprecedented demands by using forms or introducing features previously unknown to them. What then, can we do to help all our struggling readers gain the confidence, motivation, and skills they need if they are to meet the demands of our class now and the world after they graduate? The most honest answer is: all those strategies and techniques already discussed, but more intensively, frequently, and with greater intention (Torgesen et al. 2007; Allington 2006; Beers 2003; Ruetzel, Camperell, and Smith 2002; Schoenbach et al. 1999).

From their survey of the research, Johannessen and McCann (2009) identify the following instructional approaches as having a reliable effect on reading achievement: connecting to students' interests outside school; guiding students through the process of learning how to read challenging texts in different genres; using a range of interactive exercises such as quickwrites, anticipation guides, role-plays or other such drama-based activities (70). Modeling and frequent, high level student-led discussion also produce effective results. Finally, the authors

Reading Reflection (page 1)

Name: Marcos   Period: 3°

ELD 3-4 Reading Reflection- Spring 2   5 Final

You have spent a lot of time working on various reading strategies this past year. Please think about each question and answer it as clearly and thoughtfully as possible, paying attention to punctuation, spelling and grammar. If you need more room to write, you may use a sheet of binder paper. (Worth 30 points)

1. Think about reading in your native language compared to reading in English. What are some of the challenges you have faced in learning to read English?

it's hard Because in Brasil is totaly different from here and I din't even Learn every thing there so it's going to Be hard when I go Back to Brasil, cuz Like I'm going t have to Learn all over again.

2. What do you most enjoy about reading?

Here honestly I hate reading But sometimes I Line to read magasige and only Book that I Like.

3. What do you NOT enjoy about reading?

I do not enjoy reading Because the Books are Lond and Boring and some Book that I Like in the end they don't have a good Endo

4. Do you prefer reading silently or aloud? Why?

I prefer reading silently Because I'm only reading to my sel and I don't get nervosf, But when I read Lould when I miss a word or pronoced wrong everyone start Laphing @ me.

5. Think about your DEAR reading in this class. Write about your DEAR reading experience, comparing the first time you did it to the end of the year. What have you noticed about your independent reading?

I have notice that I get Better at reading and I not Missing that much word Line @ the Begining of the year. I think that I improve more and I still want to improve more and more.

6. What are some things that distract you or make you lose your concentration when you are trying to read silently?

what make me Lose my concentration when I trying to read silently is Noisy and when peopll are doing an activite Like talhing or singing.

FIGURE 5.27 Marcos' completed reading reflection sheet

Reading Reflection (page 2)

7. What is your ideal environment for silent reading? Describe the scene.

for silent reading you shold seperete every one and tell them to read the Book that ways was going to Be easier.

8. What are at least three things to think about when reading orally in front of an audience?

- I get really nervose
- I'm aftaid when I miss the student start Laphi
- and it's hard to malle eyes contact.

9. Describe yourself as an oral reader.

- at the Begining I was shy Like almost every one in c But Latter I din't carp any more. I don't think I'm hella reading But yeah I think I read in a normal Level.

10. The first time you did an oral reading in front of the class this year, how did you feel?

I felt really nervose Because I think that was my First time in this school year that I did a oral reading

11. Compare that feeling to the last time you read orally. How were the feelings the same? Different?

I felt different now I don't carl coz I did a Lot of time already. Now I not scare Like the Last time now I know all my class mates so it did cha a Lot not only that and my reading too.

12. You participated in two Literature Circles this semester. What was your favorite thing about Literature Circles?

My favorite thing about Literature Circle is that we can decide ahos in our group and you coild talk to them about other stuff not on the Literature Books.

FIGURE 5.27 Continued

Reading Reflection (page 3)

13. What was your least favorite thing about Literature Circles?

My Least farcrith thing aBout Littlave circles is th we Learn How to have a discusion on the Book as a group

14. Now that you have read novels, plays and short stories this year, have you become more interested in reading? Less interested? What do you think the reason is for your answer? I think Less interested Because I never Lined to read Book and I think I nevel will. I Knew up read short stories, plays, novels and ect: But some of the stories plays .. was Boring. that's why I don't Like reading i; . think that is Boring.

15. Describe how you feel about your reading progress this year.

I think that I improve a Lot Because Last year I cot too much so I din't study at all But m I do. so that's why I think I improve my readi· and my writing too.

16. What are at least two things you need to work on to continue to become a better reader?

• I know that I hate reading But for me te contin to Learn I'm going to read Book.

• Study more so I can Improve my reading an my writing .·.

FIGURE 5.27 *Continued*

stress the centrality of embedding skills within the context of meaningful inquiries that make connections to students' lives and experiences outside of school, pausing throughout such sequences to reflect on the process of their own learning so that students can identify and internalize those "questions that good readers ask when they read literature" (71).

Ruetzel, Camperell, and Smith (2002) single out three "validated comprehension strategies appropriately taught in the context of real discussions (that is, grand conversations, book clubs, and literature circles) that fit the general specifications associated with transactional strategies instruction" (337):

- *Elaborative interrogation:* Students use *why* questions to process informational texts, activating their prior knowledge and experiences, which they use to weave the facts from the texts into a larger tapestry of understanding that also facilitates the recall of the salient details.

- *Text organization instruction:* Students learn about different ways of organizing texts and the features common to those types, while also learning various comprehension strategies, including activating background knowledge.

- *Social and self-regulatory process instruction:* Students develop self-regulating behaviors and a sense of self-efficacy (i.e., they believe they can learn and use strategies that will improve reading skills). A thumbnail sketch of such instruction shows the teacher first explicitly teaching comprehension strategies; then modeling how to use these strategies on a task that is challenging but achievable; then setting goals for their performance in the reading of the text and use of the techniques; and, finally, evaluating their effort and the results, reflecting on what worked and why so they know what to do again in the future. (345)

It is not always easy to spot the struggling readers. Students can pretend to understand anything from C. S. Lewis to T. S. Eliot, using those resources available online and in the school halls (aka their friends) to tell them "what the story really means." When writing, they cannot hide: they have to show their cards, though of course students can just not do the assignment, dismissing it as "stupid" and saying "I could read and get it if I wanted but it's so *boring* I can't be bothered." Reading, however, is different: You can fake it; get the facts, the summaries, even the analyses of many smart people on the Internet.

Beers notes:

> There is no single template for the struggling reader. . . . We cannot make the struggling reader fit one mold or expect one pattern to suffice for all students. Not all struggling readers sit at the back of the room, head down, sweatshirt hood pulled low, notebook crammed with papers that are filled will half-completed assignments, a bored expression. . . . Now think for a moment about that girl who sits three seats back, usually over toward the side of the room [who is] quiet, neat, and offers quick smiles . . . or the boy who always keeps that class laughing. He's cute, well-dressed, well-liked, and willing to run any errand for you. If you call on him, he sometimes knows the answer, but most often he says something witty that gets the class laughing and, for a second, even you forget that he hasn't answered the question. . . . Or picture that new girl from Vietnam or Cambodia or Russia or Mexico who barely speaks English . . .and then think about that student who is your gifted reader . . . bound for AP English, if not already there . . . who can stumble over ideas, worry over words, get lost in a sequence of events, become confused over who is the narrator. Another struggling reader. (2003, 15)

Teri Lesesne (2009) offers five characteristics that reluctant readers consider when choosing a book to read: "title, cover, author, opening that hooks, and ability to recommend to friends" (2).

We gain our greatest understanding, however, not from scholars of literacy but the students themselves, in their own words. Zaniesha entered high school as a student in my ACCESS program (Burke 2005) as a wonderful young woman who struggled to meet the demands of school as a freshman. By year's end she had become a voracious and confident reader and went on to attend a good university after graduating. Here she reflects on her progress over the course of her freshman year:

> When we started school in August, I wasn't really interested in reading. I would rather have just asked someone else what the book was about instead of reading it to myself. Being in the [ACCESS] class made me strive harder than I did last year because I wanted to prove myself to my teachers, parents, and peers. Being in the ACCESS class helped me progress in my reading. By the end of September, I was reading eight pages in fifteen minutes compared to five pages in fifteen minutes when school began.
>
> By January, I was reading 12–13 pages in fifteen minutes. Reading started to become more interesting to me and when the 15 minutes were up, I saw myself wanting more time to read. Then I started challenging myself to read harder and longer books. In the beginning of the year, I never saw myself wanting to read every day, let alone a 350-page book.
>
> Now in May I have learned and changed so much as a reader and a student. I am able to read a 600-page book and over 20 pages in 15 minutes. There are still some things that I need to improve on like sticking with a book when I start it and focusing a little more on short-term goals as opposed to trying to see the big picture in the beginning. As a student, there is only one thing that I want and that is to have a 4.0 GPA sometime next year. As a reader, I want to keep striving to be the best reader I can be.

One last point warrants discussion: your ability as the teacher to empathize with students' struggles as readers, as learners. Some teachers, those elite readers who seem to have spent their first months reclining in the crib reading their first Jane Austen novel, often cannot conceive of what is so difficult about a given text; nor does the teacher of many years always remember, after having read *Lord of the Flies* dozens of times, how complex the language or concepts really are. *Isn't it obvious that Piggy's "specs" represent civilization and, when they are shattered, the demise of that civilization?* One easy and often revelatory thing you can do to better grasp the demands of your assignments is to ask students to jot down on a card or their homework the next day just how long it took them to read (and do any accompanying assignments) the chapter you told them would "only take about twenty minutes." There is, within those who have always struggled to make sense of what they read, a culture to which we must respond with consideration and respect, even as we strive to push them. Such culturally responsive teaching uses the cultural knowledge and prior experiences of students to help them grow more confident and comfortable by teaching to and through their strengths (Gay 2010).

PAUSE & REFLECT After thinking about who struggles in your class—and why—find a text you are sure will initially defeat you when you read it. You might try reading some of Chaucer's *Canterbury Tales*—in the original Middle English. Or better yet, try a novel or poem in some language you studied in high school but never quite mastered. Of course, there's always *Finnegans Wake*. Reflect on the experience and how you responded cognitively and emotionally to it.

Advanced Reading: Turning Them into "Crafty Readers"

It is easy to think only of the strugglers: They are the houses on fire, the ones you need to tend to *now*, whom you rush to help *asap*. And, of course, there are the other kids taking up the great middle of your class, who mostly come, mostly do their work, mostly at the good-enough or sometimes even great level. But what about the voracious minds that devour a book or three a week *in addition to all that school assigns them*?

In the absence of any spotlight on these students, any reports about their performance, these advanced readers are often overlooked, receiving no "curricular differentiation that meets or challenges their abilities . . . [because] there are so many other students [reading] below grade level that it is hard to justify not working with them" (Fisher 2008). Of the 36 states that submitted reports on gifted students, 10 provide *no* money for gifted education and 4 spent less than $1 million (National Association for Gifted Children 2011, 2). A 14-year study of high school valedictorians found "that the great majority of former high school valedictorians do not appear headed for the top of adult achievement arenas" (Arnold 1995, 287), the conclusion being that such students learned to "do school" (Pope 2003) better than their peers:

> Working hard, trying your best, conforming to the system, excelling at academic tasks, focusing your efforts, avoiding distractions, enjoying learning: these items form the short list of how one becomes a high school valedictorian. . . . [They] were "good kids" whose laurels resulted from conforming to the system of schooling. (Arnold 1995, 41)

One gets the feeling, however, reading Arnold's *Lives of Promise*, that these valedictorians, whose greatest ambition seems to have been to complete and comply, were challenged more often by the volume than the complexity of the work they did. Thus many teachers of advanced classes (though many advanced readers are in the regular or College Prep courses) will ask students to read as many as 25 to 30 pages a night in *The Odyssey* or *Beloved*, often requiring them to take notes or answer questions that are largely designed to prove students did the reading. While such assignments develop the reader's stamina (and, perhaps, patience!), they necessarily do not build intellectual muscle. Advanced reading is about not only *what* students read but *how* they read it (King-Shaver and Hunter 2003, 35). Fifth graders can easily read Hemingway's *Old Man and the Sea*; to them, however, it would amount to little more than a story of a man, a boy, and a big fish. Read in high school, however, Hemingway's "simple, straightforward" novel merits close study for its style and themes. Just as one can read such accessible texts in rigorous ways, so, too, can complex texts be reduced to their facts, as Rosenblatt recounts the teacher who asked the class, "What facts does this poem teach you?" (2005, 102).

Some imagine that a class, such as AP Lit, ensures students will be reading as they would in college, for indeed such is the mission and nature of the program; yet a study of AP programs found that "the AP experience is not uniform . . . the quality of AP courses differ[ing] tremendously by high school and even by teacher" (Sadler, Sonnert, Tai, and Klopfenstein 2010, 265). Thus, some teachers ask their students to read *Heart of Darkness* as if it were a study guide for the upcoming AP Lit exam; others treat it as a case study of power, a work of literary art, or an allegory for modern corporate greed, supplementing the reading of the novel itself with a range of critical theory and other such readings. Or they read *Heart of Darkness* and *Siddhartha*, focusing on the use of archetypes in both as they compare the similarities and differences between the two novels.

What I am suggesting is reading that uses comprehension as the first rung on a much greater ladder that resembles Figure 3.14. If, as Postman and Weingartner wrote, "students enter school as question marks and leave as periods" (1969, 60), I want such advanced reading to greet them like a rap on the forehead from a Zen master as they enter the class. I am, ironically, challenging us to cultivate the type of reading that Thomas and Brown (2011) capture in their analysis and description of elite gamers who learn "much more than facts, figures, and data. They shared their interests, developed their passions, and engaged in a play of imagination. They learned to participate and experiment. In that sense, something larger was always being addressed, built, created, and cultivated" (31). In other words, to develop students' skills and disposition to "look and look again is best taught by practice in paying attention to texts—in close reading" (Berthoff 1999, 671).

Yes, yes, you are thinking, It's all very nice. But what does it look like? The following examples represent a wide range of possibilities, none of which are specifically or necessarily for advanced classes; rather, they involve students engaging in "close readings and close observations [that] sharpen hard, dull wits (and bright, confident wits) because they offer occasions to enjoy a pleasure in the exercise of the mind [and to] practice Practical Criticism by rehabilitating looking and looking again and reading slowly—and a gain—would thus be to reclaim the Imagination, the agency of the active mind" (Berthoff 1999, 680). Here, then, are some ideas and assignments to consider for advanced reading:

- Have students first read one or more nonfiction texts (anything from *The Declaration of Independence* to Ted Kaczynski's Unabomber manifesto, an op-ed from the latest newspaper to an essay such as Thoreau's "Civil Disobedience") to create a critical or conceptual frame for the subsequent texts, which may include fiction, informational texts, media, or art. Use the initial framing text(s) to create a lens through which you examine the primary texts. For example, students would read Camus' essay "The Myth of Sisyphus" prior to or during the study of Kafka's *Metamorphosis* in order to examine the idea of work and its effect on Gregor and his family, or historian Tony Judt's brilliant essay "Night" (2010), in which he seeks to understand his illness by comparing himself to Gregor as ALS consumes his body.

- Provide students with a model or metaphor of some sort that they can apply to the text to help them dig deeper into its structure and meaning. This might entail, for example, giving students the ODONO Model (see Figure 5.28), or one of many different variations of the Journey Cycle, then asking them to apply it to a demanding literary text as they

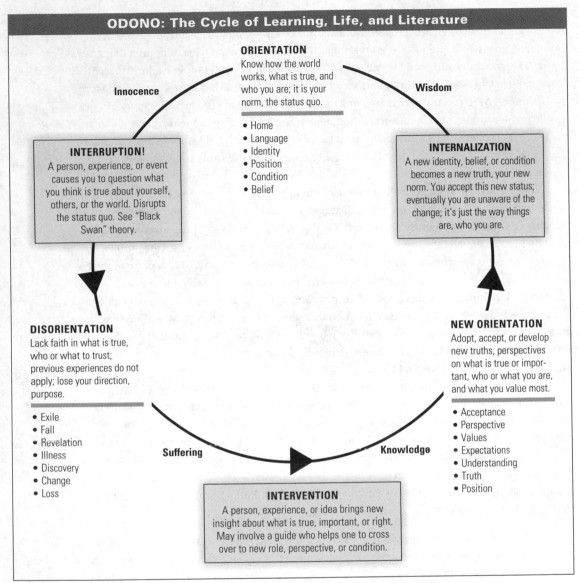

ODONO: The Cycle of Learning, Life, and Literature

ORIENTATION
Know how the world works, what is true, and who you are; it is your norm, the status quo.

- Home
- Language
- Identity
- Position
- Condition
- Belief

Innocence

INTERRUPTION!
A person, experience, or event causes you to question what you think is true about yourself, others, or the world. Disrupts the status quo. See "Black Swan" theory.

Wisdom

INTERNALIZATION
A new identity, belief, or condition becomes a new truth, your new norm. You accept this new status; eventually you are unaware of the change; it's just the way things are, who you are.

DISORIENTATION
Lack faith in what is true, who or what to trust; previous experiences do not apply; lose your direction, purpose.

- Exile
- Fall
- Revelation
- Illness
- Discovery
- Change
- Loss

Suffering

INTERVENTION
A person, experience, or idea brings new insight about what is true, important, or right. May involve a guide who helps one to cross over to new role, perspective, or condition.

Knowledge

NEW ORIENTATION
Adopt, accept, or develop new truths, perspectives on what is true or important, who or what you are, and what you value most.

- Acceptance
- Perspective
- Values
- Expectations
- Understanding
- Truth
- Position

FIGURE 5.28 The ODONO Cycle works at all levels and offers students a powerful way to read at more advanced levels given the simplicity of its format. It is not the same as the Journey Cycle, though they complement each other.

read; they should gather examples and make notes about how these examples relate to the different stages of the model.

- Offer students a theme or invite them to come up with their own that they then use to read the assigned (or chosen) text(s) closely, drawing details and making inferences from it as they read. For summer reading, as one example, we asked our AP Literature students to find two books of appropriate AP literary merit that explored the idea of separate worlds in whatever way that idea might apply to the texts.

- Assign students roles that require them to research that person's theories, principles, and ideas; then, apply those to the primary text, reading the book *as if they are* the assigned role. Just think how much more demanding (and interesting!) it is to read *Lord of the Flies* as if you were Anne Frank, Sigmund Freud, Hannah Arendt, or Friedrich Nietzsche. Students can follow up this reading by participating in a full-class forum *in character* and, if time allows, writing an analytical response as that character. (See Figure 5.18.)

- Provide students with readings, criteria, or other resources related to a philosophical or critical theory, which students then apply to the literary text as they read. The teacher can introduce postcolonial theory to *all* her students prior to having them read, for example, *Heart of Darkness*, which they then read through the requisite postcolonial lens. Or the teacher can provide a short reading that summarizes the key themes of existentialism, which students then apply to existential novels they read in literature circles. A final example would allow the teacher to ask students to choose any of the different critical theories (see Figure 5.29) to use when reading a given literary work. Another handout, shown in Figure 5.30, reflects a more specific theory, often called Archetypal or Mythological theory, which students at all grade levels can use with reasonable dexterity due to the familiarity of the ideas

- Teach students the more advanced elements of argument, rhetoric, or style and ask them to read for those specific elements, examining how the author uses this in a written or visual document. Instead of just reading Shakespeare's sonnets as *sonnets*, read them as arguments that make powerful use of many different rhetorical devices.

- Ask students to research a period in history with a rich literary treatment and create a list of proposed readings through which they will explore that era, making inferences about what it was like, why it was the way it was, and why it is worth studying. Students could, for example, read a collection of books that explore the 1920s, including obvious masters such as Fitzgerald and Eliot, but also less familiar authors such as Ford and Beckett.

- Assign students different perspectives from which to read a text or some portion of it. These perspectives should be, if not in opposition to each other, at least divergent to generate creative tensions, productive dissonance that inspires great conversation. In his Genesis Seminar, for example, Burton Visotzky, a rabbi and Midrash scholar, holds an ongoing conversation about what the *Book of Genesis* means and how we might apply it to our lives in modern times (1996). In these sessions, he brings together financiers, lawyers, psychologists, and others to generate insights and new meanings based on their expertise. A variation on this idea would be to not only have students emulate this but to invite to your class local lawyers, psychologists, architects to help generate new and productive readings.

- Have students use graphs or other such tools to represent the more complex dynamics in the novel or play they are reading. When reading *Frankenstein*, for example, students can draw a plot graph to represent the degree to which Victor Frankenstein and his wretched creation exhibit human traits (what you notice is that for much of the story, Dr. Frankenstein becomes more of a monster as the monster becomes more human, acquiring language, sophisticated ideas, and a wide range of emotions).

- Use the Brady-Johnson Program in Grand Strategy Seminar from Yale, which asks students to study literary, philosophical, and primary source documents in order to solve problems of statesmanship (through Grand Strategy). Visit the Yale University website

The Basics: Critical Theory

Critical Theory	Features	Questions/Strategies
Deconstruction Criticism Emphasizes unity and coherence. Examines the incongruities and flaws in meaning by analyzing the ways we assign value to one thing—a group, category, idea—over another based on our assumptions and biases about such "constructs" as race and gender. Stems from a desire to resist the authority of someone/something that has power over you. Language cannot express an absolute truth.	• Ignores details about the author, era, or reader. • Emphasizes the meaning, purpose, and effect of elements to the whole. • Analyzes why we think, feel, or believe as we do. • Requires that we challenge our own assumptions, biases, and expectations. • Rejects the notion of a "correct" reading, arguing that all are "misreadings."	• What idea, character, or relationship is essential to the text; which are outcast, rejected, or not validated? • What contradiction do you find within the text—e.g., opposing viewpoints on a topic—and how do they undermine your reading? • Who or what enjoys a privileged status within the text, on what basis, and to what end? • Is there another way to read this scene, passage, or text? On what basis? • How is the author using language to convey ideas about what is true?
Feminist (Gender) Criticism Grows out of a belief that historical bias against women, nonwhite, and marginalized authors, characters, and people in general contributes to the meaning in the text. Focuses on systems or rules and the roles that govern or affect men and women, including language. Looks as much as what is said, done, depicted, or included at what is left out, ignored, or omitted.	• Examines the way gender or identity affects meaning. • Focuses on bias, perspective, status, but also who and what gets published in the first place. • Believes that women read, write, think, and live differently; that these differences are meaningful, valid points of interest worth studying.	• How does gender or identity contribute to the meaning of the text? • How are women depicted, treated, or discussed in this text? • How would a woman read or respond to this text? What are the implications? • How is this text a response to the era in which the author wrote it? • How does the author use language (including imagery, and figurative speech) to describe men and women in this story?
Historical Focuses on the extent to which the author's personal experiences, historical era, and events contribute to the meaning of the text.	• Emphasizes the role the author's personal experience plays in shaping meaning. • Examines effect of historical era and events on meaning of the text.	• When was the author writing this text? • Where is the author from? • What personal experiences or values of the author shaped this text? • How does history affect meaning here?
Marxist Criticism Such critics use a set of social, economic, and political principles to understand and change society, especially the relationship between classes based on power, position, and money. Behaviors, thoughts and values are determined by economic factors, based on the idea that art and literature are fundamentally elitist and able to be understood and enjoyed only by the rich and powerful.	• Stresses the conflicts within society, especially economic differences between the classes. • Considers social, economic, historical, and political elements. • Concentrates on who has power, how they got it, what they do with it. • Evaluates literature and art in terms of impact on class struggle. • Examines the ideology that informed its creation and the time in which it was created or set.	• What underlying assumptions govern a society, its institutions, and people? • Who has power? What is the source of that power? How do they use it? • What is the author's ideology? • What is the author's purpose as it relates to the lives of those who read and/or are represented by this story? • What is the author's attitude toward the members of the different classes?
Mythological Criticism Seeks to understand why certain stories, symbols, and characters elicit universal human reactions. Recurring motifs and patterns like the heroic journey represent this. Includes also archetypes, fables, myths, and rituals such as sacrifice, exile, Cinderella, or Icarus. Emphasizes images common to all across cultures and eras.	• Shares some ideas with Psychological Criticism, but draws also on religion and philosophy, art, and anthropology. • Focuses on motifs, patterns, symbols, images, and archetypes. • Examines purpose, meaning, and effect of these stories like return of the Prodigal Son or hero's journey, among others.	• What recurring or universal motifs, imagery, or symbols does the author use—and to what effect? • What myths, legends, or folktales does the author use—and how? • What archetypes does the author incorporate, either directly or through allusion, and how do these archetypes contribute to the meaning of the text?
New Criticism (Formalism) Prevailing school of literary criticism since 1920s; this traditional approach emphasizes close reading and each element's contribution to the meaning as opposed to the author's biographical or psychological details or the historical period in which it was written.	• Ignores details about the author, era, or reader. • Emphasizes the meaning, purpose, and effect of each element on the whole; dismisses the reader's response as a valid reading or interpretation. • Stresses the importance of stylistic elements (e.g., ambiguity, irony, diction) and their effect on the meaning of the text.	• How does x contribute to the meaning of the text? • When, how, why does the author use and create tension, irony, and ambiguity? • What opposes what and how does this opposition contribute to the text's meaning? • Which strategies or devices does the author use and how do these contribute to the text's meaning?

FIGURE 5.29 The Basics. Critical Theory. Not all critical theories are appropriate for most classes; the idea is to choose those that will deepen the reading of the text at hand without distracting from the text itself.

© 2013 by Jim Burke from *The English Teacher's Companion*, Fourth Edition. Portsmouth, NH: Heinemann.

Critical Theory	Features	Questions/Strategies
Philosophical (Existential) Some argue that literature should teach morality and examine philosophical ideas. Others suggest that literature is a means for considering the fundamental "philosophical problems," which remain constant across the ages. Some, such as Sartre, write literature *as philosophy*, using the story to explore a concept.	• Predicated on certain concepts or principles such as "free will." • Concerned with the moral conduct of characters. • Interested in the extent to which the characters accept responsibility for their actions. • Examines literature through the four philosophical problems of knowledge, conduct, governance, and purpose.	• What moral principles govern characters' actions? • How do these principles affect the meaning of the text? • Is there a specific philosophical concept that the author is trying to illustrate? • Who or what is the character trying to become and by what process? • What would the character say to the questions, "Who am I?" "Whose am I?" "What am I?" and "Why am I here?"
Postcolonial Criticism A powerful lens through which to view how the colonial powers treated and, through literature, depicted their subjects; moreover, to view how those subjects responded to their colonizers. Involves a complex mix of politics, psychology, and anthropology.	• Examines relationship between colonial powers and their subjects. • Focuses on the role race, power, and identity play in the treatment and depiction of characters and situations through the stories. • Looks at how the colonized are "othered," a process that dehumanizes or marginalizes subjects.	• Examine the text for references to or depictions of colonizers or the colonized to see whether they are treated as an "other" or a brother. • Ask whose values inform or are reflected in the language and imagery of the story. • How do the concepts of race, identity, and power play out in the story? • How are women treated by men from the colonial power and their own country?
Postmodern Criticism Grew out of World War II as a response to the terror and destruction of the war. A continual effort to break away from tradition and conventional forms and styles. Embraces the anxiety (and exhilaration) that comes with a world dominated by simultaneous, often contradictory images, ideas, language, cultures, truths.	• Blends genres and styles, themes, and conventions to expose absurdity of modern world. • Often playful and critical, making reader aware of conventions.	• What techniques does the author use to create awareness of the rules that govern the story—which he then violates? • Does the author join seemingly unrelated elements or genres—to what effect?
Psychological Criticism Strongly influenced but not limited to Freud and psychoanalysis, this school also considers theories, such as Maslow's "hierarchy of human needs" and other established models of human development.	• Focuses on the interior life of the author and characters, especially needs and motives. • Analyzes patterns of behavior (e.g., Oedipus Complex). • Connects to psychological events or experiences in life of characters or author, as well as *zeitgeist* of era.	• What does the character want more than anything else—and why? • What unconscious factors most influence the character's development or actions? • What developmental model or theory applies to and gives insight about this literary text? • How does the character think about, feel about, or react to key events or characters?
Reader's Response Criticism Meaning exists in the reader not the text; there is no authoritative reading. Emphasizes subjective or ideal response to the text, thus allowing for multiple readings of the same text. Readers *cannot* say the text means whatever they think it does; must offer responsible reading.	• Offers an "ideal reading" based on what the reader thinks the text implies. • Focuses on the process by which the *reader* creates meaning instead of interprets the author's intentions. • Invites readers to respond to what they notice or affect of text and elements on them as they read.	• What expectations do I have about what this text means? • How do these expectations influence my reading? • What do I think this text means? Why? • What connections can I make between this text and my own experience? • Which elements—words, images, or devices—affect me most as I read? How?
Structuralist Criticism Codes, signs, and systems govern social and cultural practices, especially communication through language, symbols, or patterns. All means by which we communicate involve signs, which are assigned meaning by the culture. Focuses on language as a way to understand and represent the world.	• Focuses on how a text creates meaning not what it means. • Identifies and analyzes the codes and logic within these systems, how they're used, and why. • Examines how patterns, signs, and other linguistic structures motivate readers to respond.	• How does the text's form or structure contribute to the meaning? • What goes with or against what—why? • What sign systems—sports, music, art, manners—govern this text? • What system(s), pattern(s), or element(s)—words, stanzas, chapters, characters, or narrators control the text or express its ideas?

Useful Critical Theory Links:

1. http://en.wikipedia.org/wiki/Literary_theory
2. www.iep.utm.edu/l/literary.htm
3. www.kristisiegel.com/theory.htm#marx
4. www.cla.purdue.edu/academic/engl/theory/index.html
5. http://bcs.bedfordstmartins.com/virtualit/poetry/critical.html
6. http://theory.eserver.org/

FIGURE 5.29 *Continued*

Roles, Rites, and Responsibilities: A Gallery of Archetypes

Archetype	Description	Examples
Roles and Figures		
The Hero	• Born (sometimes) into the role; at other times, chosen; has a specific purpose • Discovers identity, strengths, or self through trials • Embodies the values of the culture he represents and that claims him or her	Oedipus, King Arthur. Beowulf, Odysseus, Hamlet, Victor Frankenstein, Antigone
The Scapegoat	• Blamed for the community's crisis • Killed, punished, or exiled as a way of restoring the community to its former condition	"The Lottery," Muggles (*Harry Potter*)
The Outcast	• Banished from a group/society for a crime against others or being different • Destined to become a wanderer	Cain, Gregor Samsa, Bartleby
The Devil	• Represents evil incarnate or "the Dark Side" • Offers wealth, fame, or knowledge in exchange for possession of hero's soul	Lucifer, *Dorian Gray*, Mephistopheles, Faust
The Mentor	• Represented by wise elder, the teacher, intellectual or spiritual guide • Trains, prepares, and guides those under his or her care	Tireseias, Obi Wan Kenobi, Atticus Finch
The Magician	• Includes witches, good and bad; power to transform others and themselves • Represents the ability to control nature, people, situations for good or ill purposes	Circe, Gandalf, Merlin
The Innocent	• Includes the maiden but also the uninitiated boy; vulnerable • Possesses faith in goodness of themselves and others, the world at large	Ophelia, Holden C, Sonya in *Crime & Punishment*
The Trickster	• Represents chaos and disorder to show absurdity of others' rules and ideas • Teaches others lessons by undermining existing rules and limits	McMurphy (*Cuckoo's Nest*), Yosarian (*Catch-22*)
Star-Crossed Lovers	• Requires two lovers from opposing groups, cultures, or families • Opposed by families; conducted in secret often; destined to end tragically	Romeo and Juliet, *Thousand Splendid Suns*
The Shadow	• Represents the force(s) that oppose the hero's goal; equated with "dark side" • Motivated by some previous injustice, offense; seeks retribution	Iago, Kurtz (in *Heart of Darkness*)
The Martyr	• Characterized by charismatic leadership of the dispossessed, lost • Sacrifices him- or herself for good of others that they may live or live free	Jesus, McMurphy in *Cuckoo's Nest*
The Ally	• Known for his or her loyalty, devotion to the hero and his or her task, quest • Exists to help the hero; may come to the role reluctantly at first; others born to it	Sam Ganges in *LOTR*, Virgil to Dante in *Inferno*
The Guardian	• Represents the forces that prevent the hero from beginning the quest • Manifests itself as a person, a group, a condition, or a concept embodied in law	The Law (Kafka parable); suitors in *Odyssey*
The Temptress	• Characterized by sensuous beauty, intellect, or power • Appeals to hero and ultimately brings about his downfall	The Sirens, Cleopatra, Circe
The Platonic Ideal	• This woman is a source of inspiration and a spiritual ideal, for whom the protagonist or author has an intellectual rather than a physical attraction	Dante's Beatrice, Petrarch's Laura
Scenarios		
The Quest	• Searches for an object, solution that will solve a problem or save a community • Includes many trials along the way	*Frankenstein*, Stephen Dedalus in *Portrait of the Artist*
The Task (Trials)	• Saves, recovers, destroys, or otherwise completes a task • Saves society, self, and/or others by completing the task	Hercules' 7 trials; Frodo and his ring
The Initiation	• Requires undergoing a series of experiences that transform the individual • Enters into larger community through the process	Child to adult, novice to master
The Fall	• Comes as a consequence of overreaching or hubris • Requires having achieved position and respect in eyes of others	Oedipus, *Satan*, Brutus
Symbols		
Light-Dark	• Light signifies hope, purity, innocence, enlightenment, honesty • Dark in its various forms (shadow, night, etc.) implies ignorance, despair, evil	*Heart of Darkness*
Water-Desert	• Water represents purity, birth or rebirth, passage of time • Deserts bring to mind wandering, loss, sterility, absence, state of being lost	Odysseus, Siddhartha, Huck Finn, Moses
Heaven-Hell	• Heaven suggests the Promised Land, the place of the gods and The Good people • Hell is the damned, evil/darkness, those punished by the gods, those who fell	*Inferno*, Greek myths, *Paradise Lost*, *The Road*
Death-Rebirth	• Death manifests itself in actual death but also figurative loss of self, identity • Rebirth comes about by return from journey, resurrection, new identity	Jesus motif, Odysseus

FIGURE 5.30 Roles, Rites, and Responsibilities: A Gallery of Archetypes

© 2013 by Jim Burke from *The English Teacher's Companion*, Fourth Edition. Portsmouth, NH: Heinemann.

for more information about the program, samples of recent syllabi, and articles describing the program in detail.

- Read widely about a significant subject of importance to the students and society at large over the course of a semester or even, if possible, a year. This idea of "learning in depth" (Egan 2010) over an extended period of time cultivates more advanced reading as student immerse themselves deeper into the subject and increasingly demanding texts, which their rapidly improving background knowledge allows them to read with little or no support. (A sample of this assignment is discussed on page 148.)

- Identify a subject worthy of sustained, deep inquiry as a class and, after reading the primary text, research what others have said about this subject, gathering notes from your supplemental readings; also, have students interview people of different groups (age, gender, and so on) for their perspectives on this topic, applying those new insights to a re-reading of the text to help them see what they could not before. The best example of this idea is Simon Wiesenthal's *The Sunflower: On the Possibilities and Limits of Forgiveness* (1998) in which, after detailing his own experience in the concentration camps that led to the question about forgiveness, Wiesenthal interviews world and spiritual leaders who have grappled with this question of forgiveness in countries such as Germany, South Africa, and Ireland.

- Consult books, such as *Reading Like a Writer* (Prose 2006), *How to Read Literature Like a Professor* (Foster 2003), *The Literature Workshop* (Blau 2003), and *Protocols of Reading* (Scholes 1991), all of which explain and illustrate advanced reading, demystifying the act by identifying the questions and habits of such readers. You can also study critical editions of books you teach, focusing your attention on the notes and supplemental essays. Longman Cultural Editions of books, such as *Heart of Darkness,* typically include not only extensive notes but also critical essays and a second complete text (e.g., *The Man Who Would Be King* in the case of Conrad's novel) to examine. Other critical editions are available from W. W. Norton, Bedford-St. Martin's, and The Modern Library. A third type of critical edition, similar to the others just mentioned but different in a powerful way, are books such as *The Annotated Alice* (Carroll 1999), *The Annotated Pride and Prejudice* (Austen 2010), *A Jane Austen Education* (Deresiewicz 2011). In addition, such books as *Lectures on Literature* (Nabokov 1980) and *The Art of Shakespeare's Sonnets* (Vendler 1997) in which these professional readers model for you how they read these different texts. Only by committing to advanced reading yourself can you expose and guide students through it with any success.

A final thought about advanced reading. In his book *The Crafty Reader*, Scholes (2001) concludes his argument for such reading by emphasizing, as I will here through his words, that

for those of us with middling gifts in the way of pure intelligence, serious attention to craft of reading can take us quite far. We may acquire what is thought of as "intelligence" simply by using our minds as well as we can and giving them the equipment they need, which is to be found in the books and other texts around us. Reading is the route to intelligence, not the goal of it. It is proper attention to the craft of reading that will make the reader crafty. (243).

Crafty. I like that. It's much more evocative than *advanced*. To be "crafty," one must be smart like a fox, which is pretty much how I want my students to be when it comes to reading, for it is just such a curious, adept mind that our world demands of those who will contribute to our collective success and security in the new world we are creating.

PAUSE & REFLECT Return to the Teaching by Design page (Figure 3.14) and evaluate what your students read and how they read it according to that scale. Does "difficult" or "advanced" reading in your class mean more pages or more complexity?

PAUSE & REFLECT Before reading the following section on assessment, write about what you assess, when, how, and why you assess it. Discuss also how you use the data from tests to refine your teaching or curriculum.

Using Assessment to Improve Reading—and Teaching

Reading assessment threatens to overshadow so much of our work, so we worry that the on-slaught of testing will render our curriculum meaningless and reduce our jobs to merely pre-paring students to take exams. Despite its flaws, assessment, which is not necessarily the same as testing, remains a crucial element of our work; it is one we must use to hold not only our students but also ourselves accountable as we work to improve their performance—and our own. Moreover, assessments will make no lasting difference if students do not learn to evaluate themselves, if they do not study their own performance, using whatever feedback is available to facilitate improvement. Tests themselves present one other challenge we will briefly discuss here: Tests are *texts* themselves, each governed by its own conventions making its own cogni-tive demands just as informational or literary texts do. In other words, tests are a genre we must actively teach students how to read just as we teach them to read poems, websites, or advertise-ments (Calkins, Montgomery, and Santman 1998; Schoenbach et al. 1999; Afflerbach 2004).

Reading assessment these days raises a hornet's nest of complicated questions, only a few of which we will discuss in this chapter; the others will be examined in more detail in the assessment chapter:

- What do we want students to know, be able to do, or remember before, during, or after reading a text that is so important we should take time to assess their knowledge, ability, or retention in that domain?

- How can we best determine the extent to which students learn, remember, and can use what they read?

- Does a particular exam assess students' performance and progress in such a way that it yields data we can also use to measure how effective our instruction was and guide our subsequent teaching of this material in the future?

- To what degree do our assessments align with relevant standards and provide useful information regarding students' performance on and progress toward meeting those standards?

- How (and when) can we best teach students to *read* tests (as their own legitimate read-ing genre) without overshadowing or displacing the more meaningful content of our curriculum?

- How might we better embed preparation for assessments—our own or those required by the state or the College Board—into our curriculum so classes do not seem like test-preparation courses but offer, instead, a rich experience that examines important questions while simultaneously teaching, in context, the skills and knowledge students need to do well on such exams?

Afflerbach (2007) argues that, when assessing reading performance, we must also apply a more demanding conceptual framework of reading that represents its complexity and invites more sophisticated assessments than the narrow, standardized tests often reflect. To this end, he offers the definition provided by the Program for International Assessment (PISA) in its most recent report: "Reading literacy is understanding, using, reflecting on and engaging with written texts in order to achieve one's goals, to develop one's knowledge and potential, and to participate in society" (OECD 2010, 24).

Afflerbach advocates adopting this notion of "reading literacy," instead of simply "reading," which

> is often understood as simply decoding, or even reading aloud, whereas the intention of [the PISA] survey is to measure something broader and deeper. Reading literacy includes a wide range of cognitive competencies, from basic decoding, to knowledge of words, grammar and larger linguistic and textual structures and features, to knowledge about the world. It also includes metacognitive competencies: the awareness of and ability to use a variety of appropriate strategies when processing texts. Metacognitive competencies are activated when readers think about, monitor and adjust their reading activity for a particular goal. (OECD 2010, 24)

Reading assessments in particular have a variety of audiences: students, of course, but also teachers, parents, administrators, politicians, and taxpayers (Afflerbach 2007, 6). Such assessments also serve a range of purposes. State or national standardized tests hold teachers and students accountable, providing one window on what students have learned as evidenced by what they can do on such exams.

In addition to the audiences, assessments come in a variety of forms and serve diverse purposes. Teacher observations and more informal assessments such as comments in discussions and written responses, offer daily feedback to the teacher about what students are able to do or may need to learn in the context of the current unit. Quizzes or major tests give the teacher a larger picture of how much and how well the students learned what he or she taught; whether the teacher takes time to reteach certain skills or content based on these results depends on different constraints such as time and the importance of those skills or that knowledge for subsequent units. If, for example, test results clearly show students do not understand the current chapter from *The Odyssey*, there is little reason to move to the next one, especially if we are asking them to read independently.

Additional assessments include projects based on texts read, interpretive performances, visual or graphic renderings of texts (e.g., as graphs, diagrams, or even cartoons). In short, the point of the assessments is to determine where the students are, what they learned, and how effective one's own teaching was on a given occasion or over the course of a unit. As Figure 5.31 shows, however, each type of assessment has both advantages and disadvantages

Summary of Reading Assessments

Assessments	Advantages/Disadvantages
Multiple Choice Represented by quizzes and big tests designed to cover a wide range of content that can be quickly processed by machine. Found in class or on high-stakes or AP exams.	**Advantages**: Efficient, consistent, quickly graded for timely feedback. **Disadvantages**: Possible interference from test anxiety and test-taking; emphasizes identification and recall over critical thinking and insight.
Short Answer Requires a 1–2 sentence response to a question or a specific prompt.	**Advantages**: Requires more than identification depending on how questions framed; quickly graded for prompt feedback. **Disadvantages:** Wording of the answer; possible inconsistency in evaluating.
Cloze Statements Demands that readers complete a statement designed to show their comprehension of the text. Response can be as short as one word or a phrase that completes a sentence.	**Advantages**: Must know and remember to show understanding; requires some thinking. **Disadvantages:** Emphasizes memory; structure may prove difficult for students with language or cognitive difficulties.
Constructed Response Asks students to respond to a question with a brief explanation of some passage or idea from the text. Response reveals whether student read and how well they understood the assigned text. Students *can* generate their own questions.	**Advantages**: Offers students opportunity to explain, think, generate ideas and connections. **Disadvantages:** Prompt language may make it difficult for some; others may struggle to achieve brevity.
Teacher Conference Involves sitting down 1:1 or as a small group to discuss the text with the teacher, who will ask questions, evaluate quality of responses, degree of participation (if group). In more intensive situations, the teacher can ask students to read a passage aloud to assess them for accuracy, speed, word recognition, and other aspects of miscue analysis.	**Advantages**: Individualized; supportive, responsive; teacher can ask students to clarify or elaborate. **Disadvantages:** Takes time; not all teachers able to manage time, conversations, and rest of class during conferences.
Essay (Timed) Gives students most or all of a period to write an actual essay about the text(s) they read. Text may be one they chose for personal reading, one the teacher assigned, or one they have not seen before the exam.	**Advantages**: Reveals depth and complexity of understanding of the text being written about. **Disadvantages:** Possible interference from writing task and pressure of time undermines ability to convey understanding of the text and its finer ideas.
Discussion (Group) Puts the teacher on the periphery of discussions (informal or more structured, such as lit circles) where they observe, occasionally ask questions to clarify or test the thinking of; best if teacher takes notes or otherwise captures the quality and pattern of responses.	**Advantages**: Smaller setting allows greater comfort and provides glimpse into depth and authenticity of understanding of the text; also more engaging. **Disadvantages:** Some struggle to find way into the discussion or do not know conventions of academic discussion.
Discussion (Class) Requires the teacher to facilitate a full-class discussion of a text; also, asks the teacher to monitor participation and quality of response throughout the discussion, often by making notes and marks on a seating chart.	**Advantages**: Give-and-take of discussion shows fluency of understanding; engaging for some. **Disadvantages:** Social anxiety or lack of familiarity with conventions of academic discussion interferes with students' ability to show what they know.
Performance Invites students to demonstrate understanding through dramatic interpretation (with possible written or spoken discussion of what their performances reveals about their understanding of the text).	**Advantages**: Engaging, motivating; accesses other talents, interests. **Disadvantages:** *Not* an area of strength for all; potential inequities in skill raise question of fairness in grading. Insight about understanding not always evident; often no time to ask follow-up questions.

FIGURE 5.31 A Summary of Reading Assessments

Summary of Reading Assessments

Assessments	Advantages/Disadvantages
Teacher Observation Includes level of engagement, independence, insight reflected in comments, writing, or other contexts, including tests.	**Advantages**: Situated; see student in action; get a sense of fluency and depth of knowledge; can measure speed, comprehension, accuracy, and more in private. **Disadvantages:** Possible bias; cannot observe all students in larger class.
Essay (Process) Allows students to discuss, get feedback on, and revise their essay over several days.	**Advantages**: Controls for the interference from the *timed* essay and shares all the similar advantages listed above. **Disadvantages:** Takes time; variability in grading due to possible bias; writing may be weakness that still interferes.
Portfolio Includes a wide range of possibilities, including dialectic journals, reader responses, graphic or visual explanations designed to show understanding and support close reading. Could possibly include more artistic responses such as drawings, cartoons, or collage, which students should be asked to explain in relation to the text, but also practice essays or other written responses that serve to assess.	**Advantages**: Flexibility; allows for wide range of responses that give insights about performance, understanding. Evidence of processes and understanding is more authentic as it is a record over time, not an isolated day. **Disadvantages:** Difficult to provide timely response or view students' efforts on regular basis in the portfolio or notebook.

FIGURE 5.31 *Continued*

worth considering when choosing how to assess students' reading abilities or understanding of a particular text.

As I write this chapter, the end of the fall semester is coming to a close, teachers are trying to finish strong even as they prepare for the upcoming holidays. During these last weeks of the semester, one gets a good overview of the range of approaches and attitudes toward assessment. First, there is the Intensive English class, taught by Ms. Morgan; it is a double-period class into which freshman are placed based on their reading scores on the state exam in eighth grade and uses the same curriculum as the regular or College Prep (CP) and Advanced Standing (AS) freshman classes. In this class, students take the district's common assessment exam for the first half of the two-hour final period; in the second hour, they write an in-class essay about *The Kite Runner*—the last novel they read though they took longer and approached it differently than the other freshman who also read it.

Ms. Morgan, who also teaches AS freshman English, spends the week prior to the final preparing her students to write, going back through *The Kite Runner* with them to teach them how to gather details and organize them with advanced knowledge of the prompt as a guide. On the day of the final itself, these struggling readers can use their notes, bring their book, and request extra time if they need it. Ms. Morgan gives them, along with the writing directions (they get a slimmed down version prior to the final), a template for the essay, which they can use or not. Ms. Morgan simply wants to focus on assessing their reading and sees the template as one way to minimize the interference that their anxieties about testing and writing might otherwise cause.

Later that day, in her AS ninth-grade class, Ms. Morgan gives her AS students the same standards-aligned common assessment—as required of all freshman teachers regardless of level—for the first hour, after which her students also write an in-class essay about the last novel of the year, *The Kite Runner*. The prompt is the same for her AS and Intensive English classes, but the standards for the AS students are higher and they were not given the extensive support leading up to the final, Ms. Morgan used that time instead to explore the bigger ideas in the book as she focused on more advanced reading skills.

Meanwhile, the CP freshman English teachers, who teach all the other students not in Intensive English or AS English, begin with the same common assessment exam that focuses primarily on reading comprehension of informational texts similar to those they will encounter on the state exam in the spring. Following that, students write an in-class essay about their independent reading books from the semester. Students are able to bring one sheet of notes on their different self-selected books, though they did not know the prompt—there were several to choose from actually—they would write about on the final.

A tour of the other English classes during finals week reveals a range of assessments and expectations. Some administer large multiple-choice exams meant to hold students accountable for the books they read and the grammar they studied; such tests also allow teachers—several of whom have small children and are already straining under the demands of the fast-approaching holiday season—to scan and grade them quickly so they can use the winter break to recover, spend time with family, and, of course, shop. Others in the department have students deliver presentations or performances based on texts they read; one teacher arranges a culminating forum on *One Flew Over the Cuckoo's Nest* in which students participate as different characters from the book or experts called in to offer their opinions about aspects of the novel. Some teachers, not all, collect Reader's Notebooks that they have used as an ongoing and supplemental assessment of students reading over the course of the semester. One of the AP language teachers divides the two-hour final between a practice AP exam and an in-class letter to the school board (written in the computer lab). The exam requires students to show their understanding of not only *Huck Finn* but the elements of rhetoric they studied that semester as they craft their argument to the school board, either defending the teaching of the novel or arguing that it should not be taught due to its language.

What about my own classes? My CP senior class, which meets first period, shows up in varying states of disarray. The first hour they write an in-class essay, which asks them to discuss all three books they read for their Life Study independent reading requirement. In short, they have to write one essay in which they discuss common themes or lessons learned from all three (e.g., books by or about CEOs, coaches, historical figures). Even though they did not receive the actual prompt ahead of time, we discussed its gist; this gave them enough information to prepare themselves, which in this case meant they could bring in notes and their books. Several students showed up with laptops and asked if they could write their essay on them (see Figure 5.32). Although they had not inquired prior to the final, I consented, aware of the concerns doing so raised. Computers proved especially helpful for students with learning difficulties. The model shown in Figure 5.33 offers my students a useful model for their own lives and a framework within which to examine those lives they study through biographies and memoirs.

FIGURE 5.32 Sam, Joey, and Dasha use their computers to write in-class essays at the semester's end.

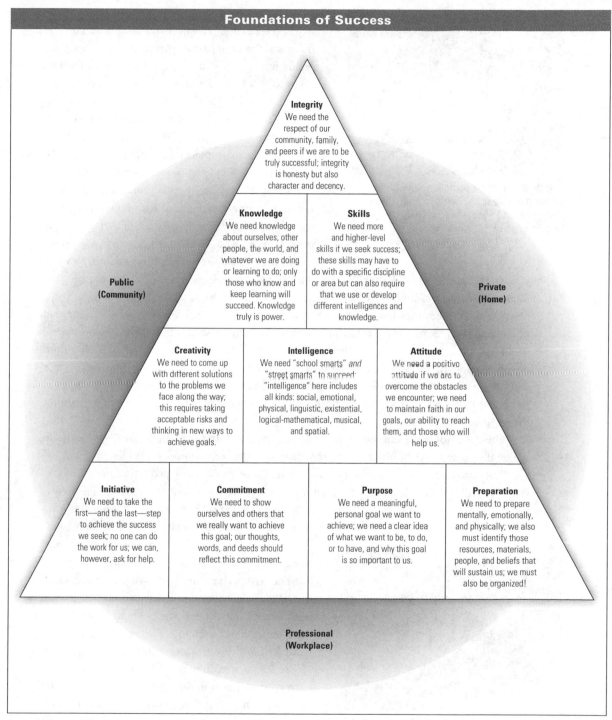

Foundations of Success

Integrity
We need the respect of our community, family, and peers if we are to be truly successful; integrity is honesty but also character and decency.

Knowledge
We need knowledge about ourselves, other people, the world, and whatever we are doing or learning to do; only those who know and keep learning will succeed. Knowledge truly is power.

Skills
We need more and higher-level skills if we seek success; these skills may have to do with a specific discipline or area but can also require that we use or develop different intelligences and knowledge.

Public (Community)

Private (Home)

Creativity
We need to come up with different solutions to the problems we face along the way; this requires taking acceptable risks and thinking in new ways to achieve goals.

Intelligence
We need "school smarts" and "street smarts" to succeed; "intelligence" here includes all kinds: social, emotional, physical, linguistic, existential, logical-mathematical, musical, and spatial.

Attitude
We need a positive attitude if we are to overcome the obstacles we encounter; we need to maintain faith in our goals, our ability to reach them, and those who will help us.

Initiative
We need to take the first—and the last—step to achieve the success we seek; no one can do the work for us; we can, however, ask for help.

Commitment
We need to show ourselves and others that we really want to achieve this goal; our thoughts, words, and deeds should reflect this commitment.

Purpose
We need a meaningful, personal goal we want to achieve; we need a clear idea of what we want to be, to do, or to have, and why this goal is so important to us.

Preparation
We need to prepare mentally, emotionally, and physically; we also must identify those resources, materials, people, and beliefs that will sustain us; we must also be organized!

Professional (Workplace)

FIGURE 5.33 The Foundations of Success model

FIGURE 5.34 Lourde, obviously with Christmas on her mind, uses her notes to write the final in-class essay about her Life Study book before heading off for winter break.

The second hour required these students to write an essay about *Siddhartha* using their copious notes and the draft paragraphs we typically wrote together in class most days. The actual prompt asked them to write an essay about how *Siddhartha* corresponds with the ODONO Model (see Figure 5.28). When they finished, students turned in their *Siddhartha* final attached to all their reading notes that provide a more complete assessment of my students' reading performance and progress (see Figure 5.34).

In my AP class, they spent the first hour writing about their last independent reading book, a novel chosen from a list I provide for the fall semester. The prompt? Four past AP Lit exam prompts, any one of which they can choose and write about by way of showing their critical reading skills (and progress toward taking the AP exam in the spring). As Figure 5.35 shows, students could bring in an index card with character names on them and a few notes, although they had no idea what the prompt would be and so could not prepare in any specific way. Some students had taken the opportunity to study one author over the course of the semester for their independent reading; thus Savannah, who read three Phillip Roth novels, could write about her third book but also connect it to the others as part of her discussion of Roth's work as a whole. It's a nice option that makes no added demands on them or me, but provides students a more cohesive experience and the opportunity to study an author they appreciate.

The AP students spent the second half of the class submitting their five-page essays in which they discussed *Siddhartha, Frankenstein,* and *Metamorphosis* using elements of archetypal theory, which we had studied while reading these books. They also returned their books (which I will have to scan in and reshelf myself since we have no more textbook clerks due

FIGURE 5.35 Seniors in my AP Literature class are allowed only an index card for names to help them on their in-class essays about independent reading books as part of their semester final.

to budget cuts) and I collected their Reader's Notebooks, which provide a rich record of their reading—of novels, critical essays, poems, plays, and more—over the course of the semester. I only collect and assess the notebooks twice each semester, though I check them informally throughout the semester while they write in them. Finally, I took home the seating chart I used to keep track of their participation in class discussions of the books we read (see Figure 5.36). Instead of receiving three grades (one each grading period), they get one large grade (the equivalent of a major paper). They can improve on each grade in subsequent grading periods, using their performance data from the seating chart and my comments in conferences about their discussion of literature in the class.

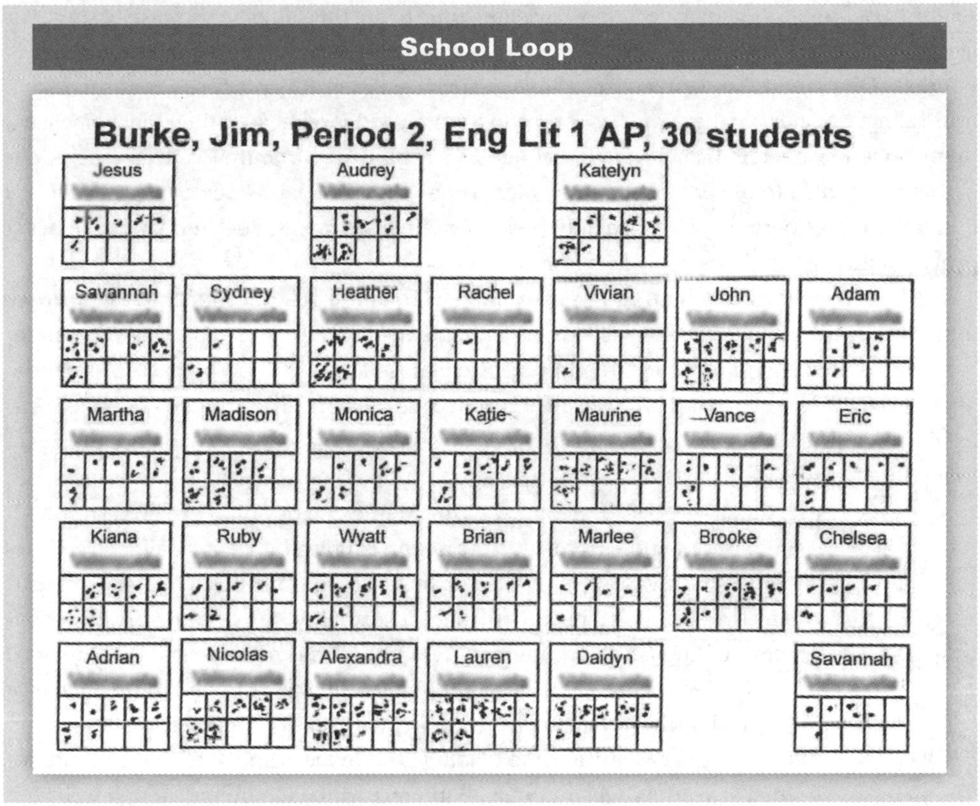

FIGURE 5.36 Our school uses a student management system called *School Loop*, which allows me to print up seating charts. Each box below the name represents a week, each dot a question asked, comment made, or contribution to class discussion.

These assessments and the others throughout the semester complement my teaching and support students' learning instead of disrupting it. It's not a single number on a single day; rather, assessment is embedded throughout the course—there to help them read and me teach better. It is, in short, *balanced* and useful. We will take up these issues and more, all in greater depth, in the next chapter on assessment.

Final Thoughts Re: Reading

Of the discussing of books—and reading—there is no end as Ecclesiastes (sort of) tells us. Nor is it a discussion likely to come to any neat resolution soon. As I have said elsewhere in this chapter, certain changes are already upon us such as the option to listen to instead of read a book by pressing a button (text-to-speech). Tablet computing will inevitably accelerate these changes in ways we will both love and loathe, I expect. We even have such helpful books as *How to Talk About Books You Haven't Read*, which one can, of course, download as an audio book if one does not even want to read a book about not reading books (Bayard 2009). In short, real reading seems to be something many feel they have little time to do; this often, in the case of students, leads teachers to "talk through" texts (or show the video) that some assume students can or will not read. Often many students come to "regard such compensatory practices as normal," and thus safely assume that they don't *need* to read the assigned text because their teacher will tell them what they need to know about it (Schoenbach et al. 1999, 8). Or they can, as generations before them, turn to the original or some digital equivalent of SparkNotes, though I confess I find these tools liberating: They give me cause to create assignments such guides would never prove useful on if students tried to use them.

When we consider the writing side of the literacy equation, few question it: We write more than ever now in both our personal and professional lives. Reading seems to be different for reasons the aforementioned PISA report suggested: the changing nature of text. As Eisner defines it, literacy involves "the ability to encode or decode meaning in any of the symbolic forms used in a culture" (2004, 8). *In any of the symbolic forms used in a culture.* We have tended to treat literature as an end, a cultural inheritance we must pass on. As Scholes writes, however, "literary works . . . are a means to, not the end of, studies in English" (2011, xv). Here, Scholes returns to the notion of English that, as a field, he believes must shift away "from privileging literature to studying a wide range of texts in a wide range of media—so that . . . 'textuality' can become the main concern of English departments" (xv). A quick survey of magazines, political campaign media strategies, and online and social media trends makes it difficult to deny the force and urgency of Scholes's argument.

> **"**FACEBOOK OFFERS INTERESTING POSSIBILITIES FOR THOSE WHO CAN USE IT TO DISCUSS BOOKS OUTSIDE OF CLASS.**"**

The very nature of the reading experience is and will become more social as readers seek not only to interact with each other through websites, such as goodreads.com, but also respond to each other *as they read* through what the *Huffington Post* calls "augmented reading." This approach to reading asks readers to use any one—or all!—of several social media sites (e.g., Twitter, Facebook, Flickr, Instagram) to provide more of a "guided experience that includes sharing pictures of where you are reading, what you are reading, what you are thinking *as you read it*, and arranging a large meet-up at a café with other readers of the same book" (Ellis 2011). As I discussed in Chapter 2 (Who We Teach), such interactivity is the *norm* for the current generation of youth, and will only become more so in the future as tools and texts evolve to support such reading.

Facebook offers interesting possibilities for those who can use it to discuss books outside of class. One group offers surprising depth if used in a way to achieve that insight, including adopting the names of the characters when posting to discuss *Rosencrantz and Guildenstern Are Dead*. Obviuosly, for permissions reasons, we can't show these pictures or exchanges, but these type of online groups are increasing.

Even though it is not a practical answer to the many questions this chapter raises, I will close with several analogies I often think about when it comes to reading these days. First, there is the question of authenticity: Are we and our students reading "real" texts that examine in all their complexity real ideas, the big questions that simultaneously develop students' skills? Here I will let Tom Newkirk respond: "Those who argue for a cultural, or in Michael Pollan's terms, an ecological, approach to reading—one in which literacy is a meaningful, invested activity—are seen as hopeless romantics. But who's being impractical here? Real food, real reading. Something to consider" (2009b, 29).

The second idea about what real reading might look like today in such an interactive digiverse comes, ironically, from the past: the religious tradition of exegesis or Midrash—a term that "derives from *darash,* meaning "to study," "to search," "to investigate," "to inquire"; it means "to go in pursuit of" (Bruns 1987, 628). Clerics developed this approach to reading the sacred texts as a way to bring to life "a canon . . . that is closed," in which all meanings appear to have been established, making the reader's experience too passive and treating the reader as a vessel to be filled with what others have decided the text truly means. Midrash focuses on the reader's personal struggle to comprehend, to interpret, and to apply the text in a way that renders it a vital document, one which, as with our Constitution, keeps it relevant and *alive* through ongoing, serious arguments about what it means and how it applies to our lives and to our society today.

My final thought is that texts and the reading of them—whether literary or informational, print or auditory, paper or plastic (screen)—are much like a labyrinth. On the one hand, the labyrinth of one's life. People wander through it, guided this way and that by the signs we must learn to read and by those texts that give us ideas about how to proceed, which lead us to the center where, as with all good reading, we discover sides of ourselves or come to better understand ourselves as we are. But the texts themselves are also labyrinths, some of which (*Hamlet, Huck Finn,* even the more "modern" *Catcher in the Rye*) are old and established, but others are new and still shifting about (blogs, tweets, mixed-media productions) even as we learn to make our way into or through them. To accompany and guide us through these texts, we need the stories, the ideas, the truths, and the techniques that have emerged over the years and that reading allows us to consider either in the company of others (in class or online) or in the "dark cathedral of [our] skull" (Lux 1997, 77).

> **"** ARE WE AND OUR STUDENTS READING 'REAL' TEXTS THAT EXAMINE IN ALL THEIR COMPLEXITY REAL IDEAS, THE BIG QUESTIONS THAT SIMULTANEOUSLY DEVELOP STUDENTS' SKILLS? **"**

It was in this privacy of his own mind that poet Jimmy Santiago Baca, after stealing a book from the receiving clerk at the jail, found himself alone in his cell later, looking at a page (of what turned out to be a poem by Wordsworth) he could not understand other than the word *pond*; somehow though he realizes a man is walking around in the poem (2001, 99). This one word, which he claims that night as *his* word—"I kept spelling the word: p-o-n-d, keeping it as mine" (100)—awoke in him "memories of Mother at the pond, in the sun, the breeze blowing over her, and all of us lying in the grass and napping as dragonflies skimmed the surface and fishes popped the silver surface, rippling rings" (100). Thus, at the center of his labyrinth, there in prison, Baca (2010, 2001) found—as did Malcolm X—not only himself but the light by which he would lead himself back out of that concrete labyrinth and into a life he devoted to creating not just literature but lives for "adolescents on the edge," such as he once was, through his work as a passionate advocate for literacy.

Recommended **Resources**

BOOKS

- *With Rigor for All*, Carol Jago (Heinemann 2011).
- *Readicide: How Schools Are Killing Reading and What You Can Do About It*, Kelly Gallagher (Stenhouse 2009).
- *"You Gotta BE the Book": Teaching Engaged and Reflective Reading with Adolescents*, Jeff Wilhelm (Teachers College/NCTE 2008).
- *Reading for Their Life: (Re) Building the Textual Lineages of African American Adolescent Males,* Alfred Tatum (Heinemann 2009).

ONLINE

- Readwritethink.org
- International Reading Association (www.reading.org)

CHAPTER SIX

Speaking and Listening

Speech is the mirror of the soul: as a man speaks, so is he.
—Publilius Syrus, from *Sentences* (circa 43 A.D.)

Introduction: Can We Talk?

As I walked toward my English class senior year, I began preparing for the presentation I was to give that day. My topic was syllabication, something we needed to know about in the era of the typewriter. I had not prepared at all; nor did I really have a good understanding of the subject, but I had the basic idea. How difficult could it be? Ken Kitchener (he insisted we call him by his first name) called me up to the chalkboard from his chair in the corner. Our room had no desks, only couches, beanbag chairs, and rugs on which we sprawled our lazy adolescent bodies. I sauntered up, quickly trying to think of a word I could easily divide.

"Let's say you had a very basic word you needed to break up," I began casually, the chalk confidently poised in my fingers as I moved to write the word. "Take, for example . . . the word . . . *participation*," I said, then went to divide it, at which point everything went horribly wrong: did you break it after the *r* and before the *t*? or was it after the *t*? And so it went: I lost all confidence and began improvising. Why did I get a B– for my utter failure? Because I made everyone laugh so hard. I embraced the mess of it all and turned it into a performance. This is my first memory of public speaking.

Something else happened that senior year, though—something unexpected: I was placed, without my consent and against my clearly stated (but perhaps ineffectively expressed!) wishes, into a Reader's Theater class in the drama department. If you do not know Reader's Theater, I will say only that the emphasis is almost entirely on reading, performing with your voice, hands, and face; you sit at a music stand with the script before you, focusing not on what to say but on how to say it. My first line, which I waited until the end of the play to speak, was: "I think he went that a-way, Sheriff!" It was one line; and in the next play, I had a few more. By year's end, I was selected to emcee the senior talent show. Nothing in all my time in high school caused me to feel such confidence in myself as these early efforts to speak before people.

PAUSE & REFLECT Recall your own experiences in school with speaking in class. How did you feel about speaking—in groups or before the class—when you were a student?

Effective speaking these days depends as much on what you say as on what you use to say it: video, images, software applications, audio, infographics, and stories. Of course some (Duarte 2010; Guber 2011; Atkinson 2005) would say that everything is a story, the only difference being which of these different media we use to tell it. For what runs through all these efforts to communicate, even when it seems not to apply, is the importance of and our ability to tell a story well enough to please or to persuade (see Figure 6.1). It is through stories that we create and reinforce our sense of community, as Brooks (2011a) notes in his book *The Social Animal: The Hidden Sources of Love, Character, and Achievement*:

> Even during small talk, we talk warmly about those who live up to our moral intuitions and coldly about those who do not. We gossip about one another and lay down a million little markers about what behavior is to be sought and what behavior is to be avoided. We tell stories about those who violate the rules of our group, both to reinforce our connections with one another and to remind ourselves of the standards that bind us together. (288)

Through conversation, we not only create communities but also engage in the more intimate social intercourse of establishing relationships with and courting one another. Again Brooks, illustrating the role communication plays in our development and success, writes:

> Words are the fuel of courtship. Other species win their mates through a series of escalating dances, but humans use conversation. . . . [If] a couple speaks for two hours a day, and utters on average three words a second . . . the couple will have exchanged about 1 million words before conceiving a child. That's a lot of words, and plenty of opportunities for people to offend, bore, or know each other. It's ample opportunity to fight, make up, explore, and reform. If a couple is still together after all that chatter, there's a decent chance they'll stay together long enough to raise a child. (13)

If and when we *do* have children, we raise and shape them through the words we use, the range of and frequency with which we use these words when we speak to our children, and the tone we use when speaking to them. Citing recent research in child development, Brooks observes that "children raised in poor families have heard 32 million fewer words than children raised in professional families. On an hourly basis, professional children heard about 487 'utterances.' Children growing up in welfare homes [heard] about 178" (106). One could argue,

Communication in Varying Classroom Settings

FIGURE 6.1a We must be able to speak comfortably and effectively with our students individually.

FIGURE 6.1b We must also be able to confer with groups of students about the work but also about whatever else might get in the way of their success. This is the mentoring part of our work.

FIGURE 6.1c We must be comfortable speaking to groups, not something that comes naturally to all of us, certainly not to me.

Photograph © Marc Fiorito

as Brooks does, that the individual and social consequences of not developing children's verbal abilities are profound: "Students from the poorest quarter of the population have an 8.6% chance of getting a college degree [, while] students in the top quarter have a 75% chance of earning a college degree" (107).

Finally, if those same devoted, verbally engaged parents are to provide for that child, they must communicate not only with each other and their children but also those with whom they work. They need to speak as effectively with customers as they do with those colleagues with whom they collaborate. Again, we return to the importance of story: The same skills we use to tell stories to our children at night are those we must bring to work in the morning if we are to communicate effectively the merits of our products, our company, and even ourselves.

As Daniel Pink observes, "the whole new mind in this new era demands . . . not just argument but STORY. When our lives are brimming with information and data, it's not enough to marshal an effective argument. . . . The essence of persuasion, communication, and self-understanding has become to ability to fashion a compelling narrative" (2006, 66). Guber (2011) adds that "stories put all the key facts into an emotional context. . . . And the building blocks of all compelling stories whether they're told in person, in the pages of a book, or via actors on the screen or monitor, are *challenge*, *struggle*, and *resolution*" (20).

FIGURE 6.2 Trevor combines his graphic skills with his speaking skills to share what he learned about Africa over the course of the semester. His map consists of images of Africans he chose and arranged.

FIGURE 6.3 Fiona and Fietonga, discuss a novel to better understand it.

PAUSE & REFLECT   What role does (or will) speaking and listening play in your classroom? Provide examples and discuss them in relation to their effect on student learning.

Speaking: Past, Present, and Future

Margaret Wheatley, author and mentor of many leaders, reminds us that "before there were classrooms, meetings, or group facilitators, there were people sitting around talking" (2002, 56). Prior to such discussions, people had only gestures and sounds to convey danger and desire. When our ancestors first spoke, they used those capacities they inherently possessed but had not previously discovered or developed to communicate with those around them. Then they created images, conveying to others through shapes and figures how they lived, how they hunted. These were the original PowerPoint presentations: Our most distant relatives combining words with images to explain where they went, what they found, what they did, and how they did it.

Today we have come nearly full circle. We see people on television standing in front of wall-sized lighted screens where they point to and sometimes manipulate colorful icons representing, among other things, animals and the geography of a certain region being discussed. The fire of the ancient past now burns inside the screen of the present, but those who will persuade us best today will use what they did in the past: stories. Sure, the stories about the animals now include statistics and streaming video; still, these are just today's tools used to bring alive what the storytellers of the ancient past did with echoes inside the cave and hands shaping the light to look like the animals outside the cave.

My own approach to speaking changed the day I saw astronaut Sally Ride when she spoke at a state reading conference. She just showed us images of space and the crew moving through it, of our receding planet filling a window of their shuttle. No bullets. No animations. Just stories. Images. Her voice. I left that day and bought a projector and a digital camera, committed to bringing teachers into the space of my classroom through my own images,

Students will be expected to use these tools, techniques, and technologies (and those we have yet to imagine) to promote their work, their business, their ideas, and their name. Future college graduates will still craft the traditional resume but will invest the full measure of their talent and time into producing a more dynamic resume for YouTube, Tumblr, and LinkedIn. Now we write but do so more and more as words to be read aloud (performed) for videos, podcasts, and new formats that will emerge and evolve. We will each become our own individual media outlet, managing our own personal channel—a trend we already see to some extent through Facebook, SlideShare, YouTube, and Twitter.

PAUSE & REFLECT What are your thoughts about this idea that we must each be our own "media outlet"? Do you agree? Disagree? What are the implications for your class, department, or school?

Speaking and Listening: What the Common Core State Standards Say

What then to actually teach? Curiously, despite all the discussion so far about the role of story and all the ways winning people use it, we do not see it in the documents that guide our teaching; all the more ironic given that our nation's leaders use stories about our national fate, or the Sputnik era, to persuade us that we need these standards. While useful and unobjectionable, the standards seem hardly to capture the range and complexity of skills the world demands of students once they graduate and begin trying to make both a living and a life. See the Standards on the inside front and back covers.

In a report titled *Are They Really Ready to Work?*, the Conference Board and other organizations committed to preparing students for the modern workforce, found that oral communication and related skills—collaboration, professionalism, and teamwork—ranked significantly higher than reading or writing when employers were asked which skills they valued most. What's more, the higher the education level, the greater value placed on oral communication: employers of high school graduates ranked oral communication third (behind professionalism/ work ethic and teamwork/collaboration), 70.3 percent saying it was "very important" (Casner-Lotto 2006). Those hiring people with two-year or technical school diplomas ranked these same oral skills even higher (82 percent rating them as "very important"). It is the last category, however, those with a four-year college diploma, that really stands out the most: Oral communication leaps to number one, with 95.4 percent of employers saying such skills are "very important" (9).

Why are these oral skills so important, worth so much more, especially as we move up into the higher-level jobs? Because it is through these public and personal interactions that we form, in our own mind and others', the impressions that help us keep or eventually cost us our jobs, customers, and, ultimately, our business. It is during such oral exchanges between people that we demonstrate what Aristotle called our

FIGURE 6.4 Carmen and Gina discuss *Of Mice and Men*, a good example of students working to help each other overcome gaps in experience, knowledge, or ability.

ethos, which he identified as one of the three modes of persuasion in his *Rhetoric*: "Persuasion is achieved by the speaker's personal character when the speech is so spoken as to make us think him credible. We believe good men more readily than others; this is true generally whatever the question is, and absolutely true where exact certain[ty] is impossible and opinions are divided" (1984, 24). What makes us think someone credible? Of what does *ethos* consist? Certain words consistently appear when discussing this subject, all of which form a separate set of standards students must learn and internalize if they are to be effective speakers: credibility, character, intelligence, and virtue.

Osborn and Osborn (1997) identify four qualities that are vital to making the right impression when speaking: competence, integrity, likability, and forcefulness (32). They describe these in more depth, but sum up the essence when they write, "competent speakers seem informed, intelligent, and well prepared . . . [as well as] ethical, honest, and dependable. [In addition, good speakers] rate high on [likability because they] radiate goodness and goodwill, which inspire audience affection in return . . . [since] audiences are more willing to accept ideas and suggestions from speakers they like . . ." and find force-

> See Peter Connor's Ground Rules for Online Discussion (http://teaching.colostate.edu/tips/tip.cfm?tipid=128) for a solid set of netiquette standards. Discussion now takes place in a wide variety of contexts, through a range of media and means.

ful (33). We know what forceful is when we see and hear it, but in short it is what a speaker conveys when he or she is passionate, decisive, committed, and enthusiastic. (See Figure 6.4.)

Summing up the importance of speaking and listening, especially as it relates to English learners (ELs), Short and Fitzsimmons (2007) conclude:

> [O]ral language development is . . . important because it facilitates English literacy development . . . [and] to be academically literate, students must be able to engage in the oral discourse of the classroom as well as the reading and writing activities in the lessons. Therefore, teachers should integrate all four language skills in their lessons, and oral language practice should not be sacrificed for more time on reading and writing. (34)

These speaking and listening skills become even more vital for those students who enter postsecondary institutions, where 95 percent of the University of California professors identified listening as essential to success in college. Such a skill is, according to the report, a prerequisite since "full participation in intellectual discussions and debates depends upon clear speech and use of the vocabulary of the discipline" (Intersegmental Committee 2002, 27).

But enough talk! Let's get down to the business of what it looks like to do and, more important, to teach these standards to students.

PAUSE & REFLECT Of all these different standards, which do you think are the most important? What is missing? Or, in your opinion, not quite correct?

Principles and Practices: What to Teach and How to Teach It

We will focus on the four types of speaking most common to the classroom, the workplace, and our adult lives: interviews, discussions, speeches (or presentations), and performances. I address listening within the context of each of these, showing how and why to integrate it into the context each of these provides. I organize them in this sequence—from interviewing to performing—based on the rationale that interviewing is most often more intimate, personal, or otherwise comfortable for those uncomfortable with speaking in public; performance is the most risky or potentially embarrassing form of speaking, taking place as it does before the full class or an even larger audience (see Figure 6.5). This rationale suffers, of course, from several flaws, most notably that what I suggest is safe (e.g., interviewing) can often be anything but comfortable. Still, the idea is to arrange speech acts as a progression from least to most difficult, stressful, or complex.

PROVIDING THE NECESSARY CONDITIONS IN THE CLASSROOM

Before looking at interviewing, or any of the other types of speaking we will discuss, we must identify the necessary conditions that will ensure that both you and your students succeed. Brown and Isaacs (2005) offer the following design principles for hosting conversations that matter:

- Set the context
- Create hospitable space
- Explore questions that matter
- Encourage everyone's contribution
- Cross-pollinate and connect diverse perspectives
- Listen together for patterns, insights, and deeper questions
- Harvest and share collective discoveries (40)

A safe, supportive environment is essential. Why? Because, as Jerry Seinfeld says, most people would rather be in the coffin than delivering the eulogy (2008, 120). Fear of presenting to an audience remains the number one phobia of people in the United States (DeNoon 2006). Although presentations may inspire a particularly intense feeling of dread or anxiety in most, speaking to others in any social situation has become a greater source of anxiety in recent years for one reason: shyness. The Shyness Institute at Stanford reports that the percentage of

	Interviewing	Discussing	Speaking/Presenting	Performing

Examples of Each Type	• Panel interview
	• 1:1 Interview
	• Exit interviews
	• Surveys
	• Conducting interviews
		• Book chats with teacher
		• Writing conferences
		• Literature circles
		• Full-class discussions
		• Conversation pairs
		• Shared inquiry
		• Harkness discussion
		• Socratic Seminar
		• Fred Friendly Seminar
		• Inquiry Circles
			• Presentation
			• Speech
			  • persuasive
			  • informational
			  • procedural
			• Lecture
			• Debate
			• Booktalks
				• Oral interpretation
				• Read-aloud
				• Reader's theater
				• Dramatic performance
				• Spoken word
				• Word for word

Digital Versions	• Phone interviews • Email interviews • Video interviews (Skype)	• Online discussions (e.g. Facebook, Twitter, Skype, chat, other) • Phone (text message, Twitter, voice, video chat)	• Multimedia presentation • Online presentation (Skype, YouTube, Prezi) • Podcast • Digital storytelling	• Movie • Podcast
Qualities of Effectiveness	• Ask clear, appropriate questions • Come prepared to ask and respond to others' questions • Pose follow-up questions to get more information and show you are listening • Capture information from subject in notes, recording device (without distracting)	• Responsive audience • Interactive participant • Challenge assumptions, assertions, positions • Ask up-take questions to solicit more details • Allow the discussion to open up, unfold • Authentic, open-ended	• Compelling subject and details about it • Surprising perspective on the subject • Fluent speech and thought • Eye contact • Forceful voice, presence • Interactive, includes audience	• Prepared/well-rehearsed • *In* character • Staged • Engaged • Compelling
Listening Skills	• SLANT (**S**it up, **L**ean forward, **A**ctively listen, **N**od, and **T**rack the speaker) all the time • Make eye contact with the speaker the whole time • Respect others' opinions by listening and thinking about what they said (appear engaged) • Do not laugh, have side conversations, handle cell phone, or do other work • Restate questions or ideas to show you are listening	• Use appropriate academic language to refer to and discuss ideas and texts • Refer and respond to others' comments by way of introducing your own ideas • Use up-take language when referring to or elaborating on others' ideas and observations • Ask questions of speaker that show you listened to them • Restate or paraphrase comments or key ideas	• Identify key ideas when listening to speeches and presentations • Take detailed notes during talk • Pose thoughtful questions when appropriate about content from the talk • Make connections between the ideas in talk and your own ideas, recent studies, and other texts	• Show interest in the performance by laughing or otherwise responding appropriately • Respond and behave in ways that do not distract the performers • Listen for intonation and other cues that contribute to character development and meaning • Do not have side conversations, use cell phones, or otherwise distract the performers
When to Use/Teach?	• To gather information for research project • To generate ideas and information for paper, project, speech • To get background information on era, event, experience prior to reading book on subject	• To increase student engagement • To improve comprehension • To help students digest information and ideas they read, study, write about, view • To mix up instructional modes and include kids throughout the period	• As alternative to a paper or project • To add energy to the class • To challenge students to overcome fears • To create opportunities to which they must rise—and thereby feel achievement	• To allow alternative way into a subject, text, or assignment • To tap into students' strengths prior to focusing on their weaknesses • To allow students to understand character, language, craft, author

FIGURE 6.5 Overview of Speaking and Listening

adults who are chronically shy rose from 40 percent in the 1970s to nearly 50 percent in the last decade, making chronic shyness the third most prevalent psychiatric disorder in the United States (Henderson 2008). Instead of treating so common a problem as a disorder, Henderson and her colleagues at the Shyness Institute have placed shyness within the more useful category of "social fitness," which considers "capabilities in demanding social situations as analogous to capabilities in demanding physical situations: one needs to get and remain fit if one expects to function. Social fitness is achieved through practice" (Henderson 2008).

PAUSE & REFLECT What are the big issues you see in your own students? Shyness? Struggles with learning English? Emotional or developmental difficulties? Cultural differences?

As one can imagine, these anxieties—or outright phobias—about speaking to others are only intensified if students have difficulties related to speaking that make humiliation seem inevitable. Another source of such anxiety is, of course, being an English learner; speaking in public is difficult enough without having to do it in a language you are still busy learning. We have a whole other set of students for whom speaking is inherently difficult though no less important to master: The number of students with autism spectrum disorders includes as many as 1 in 38 children (Wallis 2011, A4). Regardless of whether they have this specific disorder, Vygotsky argued that as teachers we should do anything we can do to "minimize or eliminate any environmental factors that could amplify the effects of the original point of concern" (Smagorinsky 2011, 6) that might undermine students' ability to participate in or benefit from our class.

What, then, can we do to ensure students succeed when speaking in groups or to an audience? In short, establish norms for a safe environment and enforce them clearly and consistently. Such standards, depending on the occasion, include:

- Establish clear objectives and criteria early on to help students prepare
- Ensure that everyone gets respect, attention, and applause
- Provide models (live, YouTube, videos of past students)
- Demystify the performance by telling students what they need to do
- Clarify expectations regarding appropriate behavior and attire
- Give students ample time to prepare and rehearse
- Assign a productive role or appropriate task to those students who must listen
- Ask students to double-check any technology—applications, hardware, media—they will use beforehand
- Teach students the strategies, skills, and knowledge that allow speakers to be calm, confident, clear, and compelling
- Do not do *anything* yourself that students, while speaking, would interpret as ignoring them: be visibly present to them

PAUSE & REFLECT Before reading the next section, make a list of your own job interview experiences. What stands out as you list the different jobs and remember the experience of interviewing for them? What do you wish your teachers had told or taught that you could tell your students?

Interviews: Asking and Answering Questions

If students cannot get past the interview they won't get the job, the scholarship, the spot at that college they want to attend—you know, that elite one that sends alumni out to grill prospective students about why the school should accept them. Interviewing is about *asking* the questions, too—a skill no less important for its practical applications while we are in school or later when we are out in the workplace gathering information, interviewing prospective employees, or evaluating contractors when remodeling our house. Asking questions offers alternatives to reading when it comes to gathering information about an era or event; such conversations also provide powerful opportunities for cross-generational or otherwise personal conversations with parents, grandparents, siblings, neighbors, and others.

Over the years, my students have interviewed—both in person and online—their parents; local and state politicians; civic and business leaders; and, one year, dozens of centenarians. Thus, oral history also falls into the category of interviewing, something many Holocaust, genocide, or Civil Rights centers involve students in since the survivors, witnesses, and participants are quickly passing away—one hopes with their story recorded for posterity. Those interested in interviewing or watching interviews with Holocaust survivors can find local resources and recommendations through the United States Holocaust Memorial Museum online. Participants in National Writing Project workshops in Birmingham, Alabama work with students, teaching them how to interview and write the stories of those who witnessed or participated in the Civil Rights movement. The stories then join others in the Civil Rights Museum there in Birmingham as part of the record of that time.

Interviews come in several forms, each one serving a different purpose—all of which are appropriate for the English class. My students:

- participate in mock job interviews
- conduct interviews of classmates
- pose interview-like questions to guest speakers
- gather information for research through interviews and surveys
- collect background knowledge through interviews about subjects we study
- interrogate (students acting as) authors or characters from books we read
- interview veterans, centenarians, survivors, participants, or witnesses of important historical events and eras

When having them prepare to interview someone, I provide students a handout that looks something like Figure 6.6 and take time to help them prepare their questions, plus teach them how to conduct or participate in the interview.

Examples of assignments or activities from my classes that incorporate interviews include:

- ***Icebreaker:*** Freshmen in the first week are eager to get to know each other and not yet ready to settle into the routine of serious academic work. I ask students to put together their academic notebook by Friday, complete with all the paper and extras; it's the outside, however, that we talk about on Friday. They must decorate the outside with images, art, photos, words—whatever—that reflect what matters most to them and shows who they are. We end the first week with kids interviewing each other about the binders, using information from their interviews to then introduce each other to the class.

Conducting Interviews: An Overview

Overview This assignment asks you to interview one or more people about a topic that we will be discussing in class in the weeks ahead. For your interview to be successful, you must prepare for it. When you finish, you will write a short synthesis paper about what you learned from your interview and research.

Goals This assignment will teach you how to:

- Generate and ask effective interview questions
- Arrange the questions in the best order
- Pose follow-up questions for more detailed answers
- Take notes while others respond to your questions
- Synthesize your notes and respond to the details in a short paper

Step 1 Generate a list of possible people to interview for this subject. Choose the people who will give the best information and be easiest to interview.

Step 2 Make a list of questions to ask these people. The questions should all be related to the topic you are investigating and should yield *interesting* and *relevant* information. (*Hint:* The "Reporter's Questions" are a good place to start.)

Step 3 Decide which questions to ask; you should ask no more than six or seven.

Step 4 Arrange your questions in the order in which you will ask them.

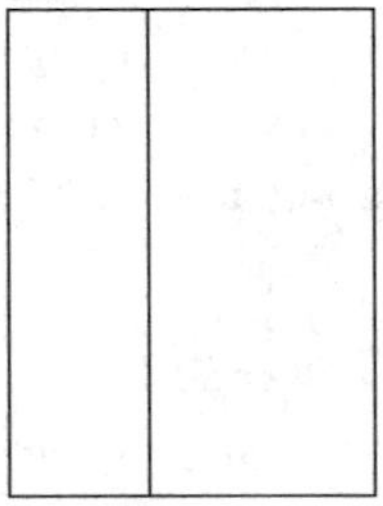

Step 5 Format your note-taking page: Write your questions in the left margin (see the example), leaving room between them for answers. If you have difficulty listening and writing at the same time, use a device, such as your phone, to record the interview; this will allow you to listen and then take your notes later from the recording.

Step 6 Conduct your interview. If interviewing more than one person, consider interviewing each separately so one person's answers do not influence the other person's. As you conduct the interview, take notes in short phrases, jotting down both key ideas and memorable phrases. Also, ask follow-up questions when the interviewee says something interesting or is not forthcoming. For example, if your interviewee says, "My family was not in favor of me marrying your mother," ask a follow-up question like, "What did that feel like?" or "How did you respond to that?" or "Why did they feel that way?" After you finish, go back over your notes and add any details you didn't have time to write down or you remembered after you finished.

Remember to thank the people you interview for taking time to answer your questions!

Step 7 Write a 1–2 page response to the interviews in which you synthesize (make connections between) the different details and discuss what they mean, why they are important. Include in your synthesis paper your own thoughts about what you learned from these people. What surprised you? What interested you most? Why? How do their comments correspond with what you thought *before* you interviewed them?

FIGURE 6.6 Conducting Interviews: An Overview

- **Guest Speakers:** I am always looking to invite people into our classroom. We ask lawyers to discuss the law when we read *Antigone*, psychologists to help us diagnose Raskolnikov when we read *Crime and Punishment*, or local experts—scholars, survivors, witnesses—to talk about genocide when we read books such as *Heart of Darkness* or *Night*. In these cases, the students serve as a panel, interviewing the speakers during or after their presentation. Figure 6.7 shows the handout designed to help students *prepare* for the discussion that we had in class with Helen Farkas about her experiences in Auschwitz. They were to prepare only questions. Figure 6.8 shows an article about her visit.

- **Mock Job Interviews:** As my seniors worked on their resumes, it occurred to me that the assignment would be much more powerful if they could put these documents to use. Our school career outreach counselor contacted the local Rotary Club about arranging mock interviews with real employers. More Rotarians responded than we could possibly use, reminding me once again that everyone wants to help the schools. Working with Mike Heffernan, the head of the Burlingame Rotary Club at that time, I let him lead us through the process. We developed likely interview questions for a standard office job, collaborating in the evenings via email to shape these questions and design the experience of the actual interviews.

    In class, I spent time preparing students for the big day, talking about what they should wear, how they should behave, what they should expect. I used the handout in Figure 6.6 to facilitate a discussion about the interviews before and after, using their answers here as the basis for a subsequent reflection on the whole experience. This was a first period senior English class and the holiday season was fast approaching. Could I expect anything of them, really? The trickiest demand was that they dress appropriately for the day—a request I feared they would dismiss. As the images in Figure 6.9 show, the students arrived and did a great job.

We interviewed all 35 seniors in one 50-minute period, each of them getting about a 10-minute interview, which most of the students felt was plenty of time and very authentic (and suitably stressful). That evening, Mike Heffernan, the Rotarian who had helped to arrange it all, sent me several pages of feedback from the entrepreneurs who gave up their time that morning to come in and do the interviews. Here are few representative examples:

"Generally, the students were prepared, except for two who did not know the job responsibilities. While those two did a good job for the rest of the interview but they lost out in terms of **'first impression'**—*and it's rare that you can ever totally recover."*

"I wish they had **used my name** *at least once. I tried to use their name several times, hoping that would encourage them to use my name. Using the interviewer's name is important—you paid attention; it's respectful."*

"All 5 interviewees **thanked me** *at the end. Good!"*

" **Maintain eye contact** *with the interviewer—even while you are formulating a response and then speaking. Especially make sure NOT to look upward when thinking about answers—it's OK to say 'I'm thinking . . .' but maintain eye contact, for sure."*

" **HAVE a GOOD TIME!**—*interviewers have to do this all day long, for multiple applicants; enthusiasm is contagious and they will remember you for it, and be grateful!"*

QuickSearch: Holocaust

Name: ______________________________ **Period:** ______ **Date:** __________

Use the following sites to guide your inquiry into the subject:

- www.ushmm.org/museum/exhibit/online/
- www.ushmm.org (then click on "Holocaust Introduction" under "History" heading)

Subject	Question (About Subject)	Prediction About/Reason for Question
Culture	How could such "cultured" men, who listened to classical music, had been educated at the best universities, and read the great authors (and called themselves Christians) commit these atrocities?	I predict that... This is an important question because . . .

Reflection/Response: After today's investigation, what thoughts do you have about the subject? What have you learned or thought about that you did not know or that seems especially important to you?

FIGURE 6.7 QuickSearch: Holocaust

ᴛʜᴇ DAILY JOURNAL
San Mateo County's homepage

Remembering the Holocaust
October 01, 2007, 12:00 AM By Heather Murtagh

At 23 years old, Helen Farkas found herself unable to sleep the night before she was to board a train ultimately taking her to Auschwitz — the now infamous concentration camp.

She passed the time by writing to her fiance who was taken into the military two years earlier. Farkas never was able to mail the letter to Joe. Farkas, an 86-year-old Burlingame resident and Holocaust survivor, told her story to Burlingame High School students Wednesday. The real-life history lesson helped explore the class' theme of survival — the theme of English teacher Jim Burke's lesson.

Farkas collected her thoughts about her experiences during World War II in a book, "Remember the Holocaust," which was published in 1995. Since the '70s, she has told her story to American students.

Heather Murtagh Helen Farkas speaks to a class at Burlingame High School last week to recount her experience during the Holocaust.

"It's hard. It's not a subject you enjoy telling, especially now as we're dying out — those of us who survived," she told the 26 freshmen. "It's an important lesson for you to know, not to learn — God forbid."

Farkas was born in Satu-Mare, Romania in 1920. She was the seventh of nine children and the youngest girl. Leading up to the war, she met her fiance Joe — a local soccer star. When the war began and news of killing people because of religion was released, Farkas' family didn't believe the news. At one point, the family's radio was confiscated.

"Can you believe men, women and children are being murdered for their religion? We could not. So, we lived in denial," she explained.

In 1944, Farkas and her family were forced into ghettos. A house that once held one family held four to five. Many possessions were left behind for the move. There were posters describing the evils of Jews. Those who weren't Jews avoided contact for helping a Jew could mean facing the same fate.

"We were doomed and we didn't even know it," Farkas explained. "We couldn't do anything about it. There was no hope for us."

After a couple of weeks the family was told it would be leaving to work by train in the morning. Farkas couldn't sleep all night. She wrote to Joe who had been forced into the labor camps shortly before Farkas was moved into the ghetto. That was the letter she never sent.

Farkas was loaded along with her sister into a cattle car on the train with about 80 or 90 people. There was no place to sit; not enough room to lie down; a pot for a bathroom; and no food or water. The trip to Auschwitz could take eight or 12 hours by train but instead took three days, allowing more important cargo to pass.

Arrival was like a cattle call. Farkas and the others were loaded off without steps. Children and elderly fell. An officer had the responsibility of separating those who had just arrived.

"With a flick of a thumb, he decided you life," she said.

Some people went to the left, others to the right. Farkas' mother and her sister's three children were sent to the left. Farkas' sister couldn't leave the children, so she followed.

The image of her mother walking away is etched into Farkas' mind. The family didn't know it at the time but those who went to the left were sent to the gas chamber and the crematorium.

"She was murdered at the same time as her children," Frakas said.

Farkas and her sister Ethel were chosen to work. The women had their head's shaved and were stripped naked. At first glance of each other the girls laughed. Laughter soon gave way to fear and tears began streaming. The girls were given rags to wear that were full of lice.

In October, the women were chosen to work in Purskau. They were to dig ditches designed as traps to slow the American and Russian tanks.

Sometimes, the women would hear shots in the distance while working.

"We'd think, 'Please God. Send down a few bombs for us.' We would rather die by bombs than through the gas chamber," Farkas said.

Farkas described lining up to move as the death march. People died of starvation or frost, even malnutrition. Those people were just left unburied. Only those who had worn shoes when taken to Auschwitz had shoes. Others wore wooden clogs, which often caused foot infections from the rubbing.

FIGURE 6.8 Article about Helen Farkas and her talk to our class about survival

FIGURE 6.9a Chris shakes hands with local Rotary Club member Suzanne Juptner as part of his interview.

FIGURE 6.9b After Chris presents his resume to the Rotary Club interviewer, he begins the actual interview.

FIGURE 6.9c Local Rotary Club president Mike Heffernan speaking to the class the day after the interviews to share observations and provide feedback from the interviewers.

As these comments remind us, speaking and listening are at least as much about *non-*verbal as verbal communication. These and other important details were further reinforced the next day when the Rotary president came into the class to take questions and offer more detailed feedback. Students themselves found the experience powerful and very practical as many of them had already experienced interviews or realized they would soon enough. As Rose shows throughout his book, *The Mind at Work* (2004), the ability to talk—with co-workers, bosses, and customers—is fundamental to both getting and keeping any decent job.

PAUSE & REFLECT What questions, concerns, or comments come to mind when you read and look at the images of the Rotary Club job interview sequence?

- **Exit Interviews**: In the weeks prior to the end of school, I ask students to reflect on their performance this year and to consider their current performance in light of their future goals for both school and career. These interviews prove especially useful and relevant in my senior classes when those final weeks can be so fragmented, especially in AP classes. Students complete these forms, then sit with me—usually in the hall, so we can have a quality private five-minute chat—as I go over their self-evaluation, affirming what I agree with and challenging them on what I do not (see Figure 6.10). This is like the conversation your doctor has with you after the checkup or the mechanic after the tune-up. It also gives us a space to bring some closure to the year and address any lingering issues or concerns—or simply thank them for a great year and wish them well as they launch out into the world. I am often surprised by how much these exit interviews mean to the students.

Again, technology offers abundant alternatives to the examples provided here. Interviews can now be conducted by email, Skype, or FaceTime. Such technologies allow a freshman like Lindsay Rosenthal to interview an astrophysicist at Harvard for her project or classes to ask questions of people who live halfway around the world in the country students are studying.

Text messaging and Twitter offer other useful, different possibilities for interviewing, all of which are valid and increasingly common (Robb 2010). Obviously, it is possible, thanks to these same applications and media, to bring experts and authors *into your classroom* to speak about their work or other ideas such as my students do when we bring people into our class.

FIGURE 6.10 Daniel and I discuss his work as he prepares for the final presentation of the year.

> **PAUSE & REFLECT** Before reading the next section, estimate the amount of time your students spend in discussion; identify the contexts and purposes of those discussions; and describe the structure of the discussions, paying specific attention to what they talk about and who decides which subjects they discuss.

Discussion: Thinking Out Loud and in Public

Let us begin by asking what actually *counts* as discussion and considering why discussion *should* count in the classroom. Discussion, conversation, dialogue, talking, and debate: These are not all the same. Many distinguish between "talk" and dialogue or conversation when studying the place and purpose of discussion in the classroom (Bakhtin 1986; Barnes 1992; Stock 1995; Applebee 1996; Nystrand 2006; Applebee, Langer, Nystrand, and Gamoran 2003; McCann et al. 2006). Based on their research, these scholars argue that dialogue is a process—a way of learning that "makes one say what one has never said before" (Zeldin 2000, 93).

Barnes arrived at the same conclusion based on his observation of classrooms where, "during exploratory talk, students built on each others' ideas, actually creating thoughts that no one in the group had previously conceived, [a process called] *working on understanding*" (Gilles 2010, 10). To put it more bluntly: Talk does not change people; conversation does (Zeldin 2000, 3), allowing us to see things anew from different perspectives. Thus, dialogue is generative: It creates new connections and concepts through "direct, face-to-face encounters" (Bohm 1996, xx), thereby confirming, as several books suggest, that we are smarter together than we are on our own (Surowiecki 2004; Shirky 2008; Fisher 2009). Cain (2012), however, offers strong evidence that real creativity more often begins in the individual's mind, as they work alone *before* coming to the group for comments. (See Figure 6.11.)

Researchers further distinguish between "recitational" talk and "presentational" talk (Barnes 2008, 2). Exploratory talk is "hesitant, rough draft conversation [during which] the speaker tries out new ideas"—something akin to what Smagorinsky says also happens as students begin to learn academic writing (2006). Such exploratory talk differs from presentational talk, which is "more polished . . . [and allows] students to report their findings" (Gilles 2010, 10) but not to reflect on, revise, or refine them. During presentational speaking, students merely repeat what they learned (or heard the teacher say) instead of constructing meaning through collaboration (Chinn, Anderson, and Waggoner 2001, 381) or what might be better described as authentic conversations (Langer and Close 2001; McCann 2006; Showkeir and Showkeir

Classroom Conversations

FIGURE 6.11a Elizabeth and Jessica use a graph to trace the tension as it rises and falls within the novel they are reading.

FIGURE 6.11b Freshman boys present the results of their group discussion about our different human needs and how they relate to the stories of survival we read.

FIGURE 6.11c Freshman participate in a fishbowl discussion of *Of Mice and Men*.

FIGURE 6.11d AP students conduct a symposium based on *The Awakening* in which students participate as characters from the story.

2008). Which mode dominates the class and informs the instruction depends in large part on the "instructional frame" the teacher adopts (Chinn et al. 2001, 381).

So, what type of "frame" *does* dominate instruction? According to McCann et al., "recitation, rather than authentic discussion, is the common mode of most classrooms" (2006, 10); or, as Goodlad (2004) describes it, the dominant mode of teaching is "frontal," which describes a style in which teachers lecture and lead large-group discussions. Nystrand (2006) makes a useful distinction between *authentic discussion*, which is dialogic, and *recitation*, which is "monologic" and thus leads to predetermined answers. Langer found that "in the most effective English classes, students engage in *dialogue* with their teachers and with each other as they build ever deeper and broader *understandings* . . . [through] conversations [which] are critical to student learning" (Angelis 2002, 3). Such "envisionments," as Langer (2011a) calls them, are only possible when the conversations are rich and recursive; then such "conversations [become] meetings on the borderline of what [we] understand and what [we] don't with people who are different from [ourselves]" (Zeldin 2000, 88). I intentionally use *we* here for if we ourselves do not engage with the ideas and the people in the room, our students surely will not.

What then are the elements of the "dialogic classroom" and the effective conversations that take place within it? Discussions come in an array of formats: from more structured discussion strategies like "shared inquiry" (Great Books 1999) and reciprocal teaching (Palinscar and Brown 1984), to relatively natural, organic approaches like Socratic seminars (Strong 1997; Copeland 2005), and literature circles (Daniels and Harvey 2009; Daniels 2002). Whatever their format, configuration, or purpose, certain elements are common to all major studies of classroom discussion. During such class discussions students and teachers:

- Ask authentic questions that require interpretation, analysis, and evaluation as students struggle to make sense of texts, topics, and information—as well as their own or classmates' questions, all of which are linked or contingent so as to develop a sustained line of inquiry and deeper understanding (Hillocks 1999, 27).
- "Explain, elaborate, or defend [their] position [interpretations, conclusions, or evaluations] to others, as well as to themselves . . . [in order] to integrate and elaborate knowledge in new ways" (Vygotsky 1978, 158).

- Pose follow-up questions or respond with "up-take" comments and queries (Nystrand 1998) designed to urge students to make connections to other classes, texts, or events in the world outside the classroom—as well as revisit ideas and interpretations—treating discussions as a recursive process of discovery not destinations to reach as quickly as possible.

- Generate and make room for multiple, even contradictory, perspectives by not only including others but enriching the discussion and using that tension between ideas to lead to new, previously unimagined ideas.

- Discuss topics that are meaningful and worth talking about, which allow both students and teachers to not only understand the text being studied but also the world at large, as well as themselves.

- Learn the skills, conventions, and background knowledge needed to participate in and contribute to the class or small-group discussions.

- Listen and respond to each other with respect and attention, even when students and teachers do not agree.

- Provide adequate time to develop ideas through the discussion; use discussion as a "medium of instruction" not a tightly scripted delivery system designed to arrive at a predetermined point or truth (Nystand 2006, 393).

- Use a variety of discussion formats (think-pair-share, reciprocal teaching, Socratic Seminar) and strategies (questions, passages, graphic organizers, sentence stems) to ensure that discussion deepens over time, is purposeful, and, in general, improves students' understanding of the text or subject being discussed.

If done right, discussions pay great dividends for teacher and student alike, transforming what might be a predictable lesson about *To Kill a Mockingbird* into a lively conversation about the moral dilemmas that make the book worth reading in the first place (Simon 2001; Intrator 2003; Wilhelm and Novak 2011). A discussion like this inevitably yields other substantial benefits. Comprehension improves. Engagement increases. Critical thinking advances. Writing, thanks to the opportunity such discussions provide to rehearse and refine thinking, shows substantial gains. And, key ideas and narrative details, because they were part of a rich exchange, are more likely to be remembered and able to be recalled long after that class ends. (See Figure 6.12.)

A certain mental agility or intellectual fluency emerges also, as with the musician who jams with others, conversation becoming like a jazz the student learns to play with increasing confidence and comfort as he or she learns the moves, gains a feel for the openings, and learns how to jump in and play with others. This is the sort of class experience that leads to envisionment-building, which Langer (2011a) describes as:

> . . . a function of one's personal and cultural experiences, one's relationship to the current experience, what one knows, how one feels, and what one is after. Envisionments are dynamic sets of related ideas, images, questions, disagreements, anticipations, arguments, and hunches that fill the mind during every reading, writing, speaking, or other experience [in] which one gains, expresses, and shares thoughts and understandings. Each envisionment includes what the individual does and does not understand, any momentary suppositions about how the world will unfold, and any reactions to it. An envisionment is always either in a state of change or available for and open to change. (10)

How Do Dialogue and Debate Differ from Each Other?

Dialogue:

- Is collaborative.
- Asks multiple sides to work toward shared understanding.
- Listens to understand, to make meaning, and to find common ground.
- Enlarges and possibly changes a participant's point of view.
- Creates an open-minded attitude: an openness to being wrong and an openness to change.
- Submits one's best thinking, expecting that other people's reflections will help improve it rather than threaten it.
- Calls for temporarily suspending one's beliefs.
- Searches for strengths in all positions.
- Respects all the other participants and seeks not to alienate or offend.
- Assumes that many people have pieces of answers and that cooperation can lead to a greater understanding.
- Remains open-ended.

Debate:

- Is oppositional.
- Requires two opposing sides try to prove each other wrong.
- Listens to find flaws, to spot differences, and to counter arguments.
- Defends assumptions as truth.
- Creates a close-minded attitude, a determination to be right.
- Asks people to submit their best thinking and defend it against challenges to show that it is right.
- Calls for investing wholeheartedly in one's beliefs.
- Searches for weaknesses in the other position.
- Rebuts contrary positions and may belittle or depreciate other participants.
- Assumes a single right answer that somebody already has.
- Demands a conclusion.

Source: Jeannie Murphy. "Professional Development: Socratic Seminars." Regions 8 and 11 Professional Development Consortia, Los Angeles County Office of Education, 6 Dec. 2000, www.lacoe.edu/pdc/professional/socratic.html.

FIGURE 6.12 Dialogue versus debate

As English teachers, we all value and recognize the joy and importance of good discussions; according to Nystrand (2006), "95% of English language arts teachers value peer discussion in literature instruction" (395). Such conversations are what brought most of us into teaching English, right? Those late nights in college spent passionately discussing the meaning of this book or that poem, arguing about which translation of Neruda or Rilke, which of all the poems was the best—The One. After studying 150 years of research on classroom discussion and conducting his own research in eighth- and ninth-grade language arts classrooms, Nystrand found that "discussion-based instruction, in the context of high academic demands, significantly enhanced literature achievement and reading comprehension" (400), a finding Langer and Close (2001) also emphasized in their study of discussion and its effect on literary understanding. Yet despite the repeated confirmation of Nystand's important 2006 conclusion, he also found that in the typical English language arts classroom today:

- Discussion practices vary widely in terms of format, function, and duration
- Teachers asked most of the questions (92 percent in eighth grade; 91 percent in ninth grade)
- Open-ended, whole-class discussion averaged less than one minute a day; 61.1 percent of classes observed had no discussion at all; only 5.6 percent had more than one minute a day; only one class out of the 54 studied averaged more than two minutes of discussion a day

- Only 11.1 percent of observed group work was autonomous or displayed significant student interaction in producing the outcomes; most work was collaborative seatwork with predetermined or correct answers
- Authentic, open-ended teacher questions and up-take (follow-up questions) significantly improved engagement and quality of discussion, but student-generated questions had the strongest effect
- Teachers undermine the purpose and potential of such class discussion when they "determine prior to class the sequence of questions they will ask and what answers they will accept or when they respond to correct student answers with a mere nod before moving on to the next question, often changing the topic of discourse" (400)
- What counts or is valued as knowledge in the classroom is determined by the questions the teachers ask, how they respond to their students, and how they structure groups and activities

One can easily see the press of time (and state tests) interfering here, causing teachers to feel they do not have time to properly prepare for and run such rich discussions. Other constraints are easy to imagine: large class sizes; so many kids with such diverse needs, all with such limited background knowledge; and the belief, held by some teachers, that discussion is really only appropriate and useful for the kids in honors or AP classes who can handle it. Indeed, several researchers (Tatum 2005; Delpit 2006) found that despite all the intellectual nutrients good discussion promises, students in lower-level classes, or schools that are in some form of program improvement, rarely have the opportunity to participate in authentic discussions—their curriculum being almost entirely limited to skills and knowledge needed to pass the state test or exit exam.

Delpit (2006) calls for such enriched instruction to be given to all, noting that "seldom are students encouraged to tackle deep moral issues they must tussle with . . . nor are they led to think about themselves as responsible agents for the larger world" (xvi). She elaborates on her concern for these students who are too often poor or nonwhite—or both: "We have given up the rich meaningful education of our children in favor of narrow, decontextualized, meaningless procedures that leave unopened hearts, unformed character, and unchallenged minds" (xiv).

PAUSE & REFLECT Revisit the reflection before reading this section of the chapter. In light of what you have read so far, how would you assess your own use of, and the quality of, discussion in your class?

Of the many constraints that impede use of discussion, those that interest me most are the ones about which I can do something. We all have plenty of students who are not fluent in academic discussions. Many of these students simply do not know how to jump in or what to say once they do enter the discussion. They lack the language or what Kinsella and Feldman, based on their work with ELs, call "participation structures" (2006, 1). They go on to identify the following qualities of effective classroom participation structures:

- high structure
- more student talk than teacher talk
- individual accountability
- tangible, visible "evidence checks" of student engagement

- individual reflection and writing ("prepared participation")
- relevant vocabulary and communicative language strategy development
- active listening accountability and development
- task-based social interaction between diverse peers
- rehearsal of information with peers prior to the unified class discussion
- unified class debriefing and synthesis of ideas
- a vivid connection/transition to the focal lesson content (3)

To address these obstacles to students' success, I do several things. First, I provide models: how to respond, enter into a discussion, frame a question, reiterate another's question, use a student's question as a springboard for your own comment, and so on. I also work with them to develop the language—the conversational and cognitive "moves"—needed to participate. The sentence frames, similar to those for writing, offer them a foothold to help them up and into the discussion; after a time, as they become more comfortable and confident in their abilities and what they have to say, they can leave these structures behind and join in on the jazz of the discussion as it unfolds. Expressed in a vaguely algebraic format, here is one sample of such moves, which I will usually sketch out on the board:

When X says y, he means z.

X believes, for example, that. . . .

This is obvious since early on X says . . .

We have spent some time already focusing on what happens during and the importance of good discussions; it seems worthwhile to clarify what those discussions should be *about*. Sure, conversations can help kids as readers, writers, and thinkers. But what are the *subjects* of these important conversations, what topics merit our precious instructional time? Briefly, discussions involve not just what the students read and write, but how they do so, which strategies they use during those activities. Moreover, these conversations might also invite students to connect the present to previous units or lessons, not to mention world events that students are currently studying. For example, when we were reading *Julius Caesar* as our country invaded Iraq to remove Saddam Hussein, we drew daily from newspaper articles and online sources that were almost eerie in their similarity to the opening act of Shakespeare's play. Finally, students will—or should—want to discuss those enduring questions that have always been at the heart of the humanities (Nussbaum 2010; Burke 2010; Parks 2000; Adler 1984); they should, however, also have to examine their own assumptions that inform their responses to these questions in the first place. As Parks (2000) says, "commitment to truth requires a questioning curiosity and ongoing and rigorous examination of one's most elemental assumptions" (18).

Let us examine all the preceding ideas by looking at what happens before, during, and after such a rich discussion as we have described so far.

PAUSE & REFLECT Reflecting on the past semester or year, what have been the subjects of your students' discussions? Which discussions and subjects did they enjoy the most? Why do you think that was?

Before: How to Prepare for and Launch a Successful Discussion

One could do worse than to begin any discussion by asking students to identify their assumptions about a given idea or subject; still, we are better off to begin by setting the table properly before we serve up the main course of the conversation itself (see Figure 6.13). What does this mean? In short, it means, thinking a bit like a dinner host who must decide how to arrange the room, whom to invite (to play the different roles any good dinner party demands!), what to serve, and, in the event one serves anything too exotic, how to conduct themselves during the meal. In other words, the teacher must make decisions about:

- The format or configuration (literature circles or reciprocal teaching? Small group or whole class? In class or online—or both?)
- The roles a given discussion format require (facilitator, respondent, timekeeper)
- The skills or knowledge students need or how you might otherwise prepare them (for discussing a particular subject, genre, or process)
- The rationale as to why they are having a discussion about this topic in this format (why they are being put into ongoing literature circle groups that will discuss *Crime and Punishment* in class and online for the next month)
- What they will actually discuss during these conversations (the author's craft, major themes in the work, big questions such as whether we are inherently evil)

Figure 6.14 offers a useful summary of the different discussion formats or activities. Yet discussion should not always be so highly structured: Much of the time I just tell students to "turn and talk" to a neighbor for a few minutes about an idea or specific question after having them first do some brief thinking on paper (a written conversation with themselves about what they think at this point). Regardless of which discussion method or activity you choose, the basic configurations are: solo, pairs, small groups (3–5), large groups (6–8), and full-class. The think-pair-share method follows a three-step process: first, discuss the topic or text with yourself (typically in writing); then, pair up with another, comparing your different ideas with each other for the allotted time; finally, share your initial ideas with a larger group before reporting out and extending the discussion with the whole class. If we are only having a quick conversation during which students compare interpretations of or responses to a text, I tend to go with the turn-and-talk approach, since our instructional time is so precious. However, if we are settling in for an extended discussion about an essential question or text, I will organize them into groups.

PAUSE & REFLECT What are your biggest questions and concerns when it comes to setting up and working with groups in your classroom? How do or would you address those?

Once I have decided which configuration or approach to take, I consider whether it calls for specific roles. Roles in literature circles have, in recent years, been deemphasized, largely in response to people getting too structured. Literature circles have evolved into "small, peer-led reading discussion groups [as opposed to] their original form [in which students] were reading

Joining the Conversation:
Questions and Comments to Help You Participate in Academic Discussions

Purpose	Comment Stems	Question Stems
Clarify Comments or questions intended to achieve greater clarity through evidence, examples, or summary.	• Your main idea appears to be that . . . • You seem to suggest that . . . • The author is saying that . . . • I'm saying that x means (or is) y . . . • My point is that . . .	• Can you explain why . . . ? • Why do you think that . . . ? • Are you saying that . . . ? • Is that the same as . . . ? • Can you give an example of that?
Elaborate Comments or questions designed to elicit more information, other perspectives, or related ideas.	• I would add that . . . • Another thing to consider is . . . • Other explanations exist, such as . . . • X, however, would disagree, saying . . . • Your comment raises the question . . .	• What other explanations are there? • Are there other interpretations? • Could you explain how you arrived at that idea (or interpretation)? • How is your idea different from X's? • Why do you think that?
Agree Comments or questions that establish your *shared* position in relation to others' through sympathy, agreement, or concession.	• Most would agree that . . . • I share your belief that . . . • I also think that . . . • You seem to believe, as X does, that . . . • Your position is the same as X's . . .	• Isn't that the same as . . . ? • So what you are saying is that you agree with X that . . . ? • I'm not sure I understand: How is your position different from X's? • Aren't you saying the same thing as X?
Disagree Comments or questions that establish your *opposing* position by challenging, questioning, or actively (but *respectfully*!) rejecting an idea or perspective.	• I'm not sure I agree that . . . since . . . • X thinks____, but I disagree . . . • While X suggests____, I think . . . • You seem to disagree with X since . . . • I have to disagree because . . .	• Isn't that different from what X just said? • X thinks . . . but you disagree, don't you? • Don't you disagree, though, since you said . . . ? • How can you say x when you think y?
Agree *and* Disagree Comments or questions that agree with or concede *part* of an idea but also challenge or otherwise reject another part of a stated position.	• I agree that . . . but can't accept that . . . • We both agree that . . . but I think differently about the idea that . . . • While I agree with you that . . . I reject the idea that . . . based on . . . • Yes, I share the author's view that . . . but think differently about . . . • You clearly agree that . . . but seem to disagree with the idea that . . .	• What part of the argument (or idea) do you agree with? • You don't disagree with everything X said, though, do you? • Even though you think . . . don't you agree with the idea that . . . ? • I see why you think _____, but you seem to also agree (or disagree) that . . . , don't you?
Respond Comments or questions that make connections between your own ideas and experiences, others' remarks, texts you've studied, other courses, or the world both past and present.	• X reminded me of . . . • This is similar to (or different from) . . . • The author's argument reminds me of . . . • I thought it was interesting that . . . • X really made me wonder why (how) . . .	• How is x similar to/different from y? • Isn't that related to what X said in . . . ? • Why do you think that's so important? • But isn't it possible that . . . ? • How does that compare/relate to . . . ?
Report Comments and questions that provide insights and an overview of results, investigations, or discussions to the larger group in a class discussion.	• We found that . . . • During our discussion we realized . . . • Our main points were . . . • We concluded that . . . • Our most important discovery was . . .	• What did you discover? • What surprised you most? Why? • How did you arrive at that result? • What did you realize this time that you had not before? What did you do differently this time?

When participating in an academic or formal discussion remember to:

• Acknowledge others' comments before making your own (e.g., "Picking up on what Juan said . . .")
• Listen and process what others are saying (instead of merely looking for your chance to jump in)
• Show you are listening by responding to and acknowledging key ideas in others' comments (e.g., "Maria makes a good point when she says . . . I would add that . . .")
• Avoid slang or otherwise informal language more appropriate to discussions with friends
• Provide examples, details, or evidence when appropriate and possible to support or illustrate your ideas

FIGURE 6.13 Joining the academic conversation

Text-Focused Discussion Methods	
Literature Circles	These techniques all focus on the close reading and interpretation of texts, though most could be adapted to accommodate other uses. While each differs in some way, they all direct students to inquire into and provide reasons for their interpretations of written, visual, or other types of text. Some, such as reciprocal teaching, require that people play specific roles. In the case of peer response, students are reading and responding critically to each others' writing.
Inquiry Circles	
Shared Inquiry	
Midrash	
Reciprocal Teaching	
Collaborative Reading	
Peer Response	
Book Group	
Symposium-Style Discussion Methods	
World Café	These techniques are not specific to texts; rather, they can be used to deepen understanding of both texts and concepts. Some, such as the Friendly Seminar (named after Fred Friendly), require participants to play specific roles or adopt personae (e.g., Freud) whose ideas you represent (in character) during the discussion. Can work with full-class or smaller groups.
Socratic Seminar	
Friendly Seminar	
Harkness Table	
Discussion Cards	
Jigsaw	
Media-Based or Written Discussion Methods	
Written Discussion	These and other similar techniques not listed here tap into the power of social media and its use in discussing ideas outside the classroom. Written discussions can be used to prepare for in-class conversations with others; they can also serve as an end in themselves. Threaded discussions and social media-based conversations, depending on how they are conducted, might use Twitter, Facebook, or GoogleDocs. Others, depending on their technology setup, might use video conferencing, live chat, or other interactive technologies to enhance discussions. These techniques can be used to discuss texts but are also powerful tools for talking about other subjects or processes.
Threaded Discussion	
Text Message Discussion	
Social Media Discussion	
Video Conferencing	
Moodle	
Passing Notes	
Journal Swapping	
Blogging	
Discussion Activities and Methods	
Think-Pair-Share	With the exception of "hot groups," these methods are all reasonably familiar and thus able to be adapted to many different uses. Hot groups are formed amidst crisis and given problems to solve. They are perfect for generating ideas and solutions. Speed dating allows for two-minute conversations about a given open-ended topic or question, after which people get up and seek new conversational partners for another round. These all tend to be high-energy, often collaborative, methods that kids enjoy.
Turn-and-Talk	
Speed Dating	
Fishbowl	
Hot Group	
Debate	
Tools to Jump Start or Deepen Discussions	
Survey/Questionnaire	Just as a BBQ needs something to get the fire going, so, too, do discussions. These tools, which can be used in most of the previously mentioned discussion methods, help frame or begin the discussion; they also help the conversation go deeper through questions or texts, for example, designed to challenge assumptions and get kids to elaborate on their ideas or make new connections. Several of these tools require someone, usually the teacher, to assemble a collection of scenarios, quotations, or survey questions on a given subject; students' responses to these conversation starters provide the way into the larger dialogue about the subject or text. These tools invite spirited collaboration, which is then followed by full-class discussion of responses.
Question(s)	
Quotation(s)	
Text/Excerpt	
Case Study/Scenario	
Opinionnaire	
Image/Art	
Film/Video	
Metaphor/Analogy	
Graphic Organizer	
Visual/Graphic Representation	
Sticky Notes	
Connections	

FIGURE 6.14 Overview of Discussion Techniques

chapter books or novels . . . [that they divided] into three or four sections [they would then] meet every few days to discuss as [the reading] unfolded" (Daniels and Harvey 2009, 198).

Still, it can be useful to ensure people have a specific role to play as they learn how to behave in and contribute to such groups. An alternative strategy, one with fewer roles, would be reciprocal teaching (Palinscar and Brown 1984), which involves four distinct activities—summarizing, questioning, clarifying, and predicting. These can be divided up among the members as roles and responsibilities instead of a collective activity done by all. As with literature circles, these four roles can be rotated so that each student learns how to summarize, question, clarify, and predict under such circumstances.

Brookfield and Preskill (2005, 113) and Isaacs (1999, 201) suggest alternative roles that cannot be assigned but are simply roles we must all learn to play as the dialogue demands in any given context. Their roles focus on challenging assumptions, keeping a record of the discussion, identifying emerging ideas or themes, and those questions that are not being asked—but should be if the discussion is to get down into the good stuff (see Figure 6.15). Isaacs, borrowing ideas from group systems theory, identifies four "players" essential to "thinking together": opposers, movers, followers, and bystanders (202). These, or other such roles, can be discussed and defined with the class as part of the preparation for a particular discussion.

It is easy to think that because conversation is natural, it comes easy to us. Some students seem to have been born in the midst of conversations they just jumped into and kept alive with the force and fire of their own intelligence. But such academic discussions are *not* natural. Those few kids in our classes who make it all look so easy? They are often the children of lawyers, politicians, leaders, or others who make a living talking and have raised their children at a dinner table rich in conversations. In my open enrollment AP classes, in which anyone who wants to can enroll, many students are silent, looking away when the searchlight scans the room and falls on them. When I talk with these students after class, they say things like: *I didn't know what to say! I had no idea how to get into the discussion! Everything I wanted to say had already been said! I was afraid I would sound stupid!* When I ask students in struggling reading classes or CP English classes why they said nothing during the larger class discussion, even though I usually already know (from having read or heard their ideas while I circulated) that they had good ideas to offer, they give the same answers.

FIGURE 6.15 Sometimes it helps to design discussions to ensure urgency and engagement through arguments. Make them reach consensus as in this case where they must arrive at the one word they think best describes a character in a novel.

Whatever the format of the discussion, or the subject, students need to know how the game is played. This means we need to take time, *before the conversation* begins, to introduce the language appropriate to their role or this topic. Teaching them the terms for sonnets, however, or rhetoric, does not prepare them to make "the moves" academic discussion (and writing) demand of students. To "enter the conversation about ideas . . . [we must] demystify academic [discussion for students] by isolating its basic moves, explaining them clearly, and representing them" as forms students can learn, first through mimicry, and later through practice, and the free jazz of performance (Graff and Birkenstein 2010, ix).

To that end, we must not only give students the language moves but also explain and model how to use them in action. Such moves include not only what to say but how to respond with what Nystrand (1998) calls "up-take," which he defines as a way of following up or responding to students' comments. All of these different aspects of dialogue apply equally if these discussions are to take place online, where a whole new set of skills or knowledge may be required if students are to participate as intended and learn as expected. Again, school is a country, a place with its own language, customs, and conventions; we must teach students how to learn—and live—while they reside there (Burke 2004).

In addition to language and conventions of academic discussion, this is the point—before the actual discussion begins—to get them warmed up, stretched out, and ready to roll. Langer and Close (2001) suggest such scaffolding as notetaking from readings, sticky notes on which students record their initial ideas about a topic or text, or quick writes to help them gather their rough-draft thinking prior to the discussion (9). Adler and Rougle (2005), drawing on their own research in the area of class discussions, refer to such prediscussion activities as "seeding the conversation" (37)—an initial investment that yields greater "buy-in" (42) and, ultimately, success. (See Figures 6.16a and b.) One might make the obvious comparison, to extend the seeding metaphor, to preparing the soil before putting in the plant: When properly placed in well-prepared soil, plants thrive (as do the students and the discussions we hope to help them have).

One final element merits further time and attention before entering the conversation itself: assessment. Students need to know what counts and how to achieve success. If using the appropriate up-take or other academic language matters, make it count; if evidence that students listened is important, make it count. This is most easily done by providing students with a rubric or generating with them the criteria by which they will be assessed. One way I monitor and assess participation in discussion is by putting a dot next to each student's name on my seating chart (see Figure 5.36), with each box representing a week in the grading period. Each dot equals a student posing or responding to a question or otherwise contributing to a discussion. In addition, I use the rubric in Figure 6.17 to assess their general participation in full-class

FIGURE 6.16a Give students other texts, in this case a set of paintings chosen to invite a discussion about stories, to start the discussion.

FIGURE 6.16b Claire and Cassie look closely at the text to find evidence to illustrate the different stages of the journey diagram they have drawn to explain *Siddhartha*.

Class Discussion Rubric

Name: _____ Period: _____ Date: _____

Six-Week PR   12-Week PR   Semester

	Preparation and Participation	Knowledge and Ideas	Listening and Responding
Exceeds the Standard	• Show *exceptional* preparation, having read the required (even additional) material, and make insightful or significant connections • Collaborate with peers to create a stimulating, insightful conversation that welcomes all students and perspectives (in-class or online) • Initiate and participate actively in full-class and small-group discussions in ways that improve the class measurably	• Elaborate on your own or others' ideas by making insightful or compelling observations about other texts, topics, or events • Extend your own or others' ideas by providing unexpected evidence or connections to support and/or illustrate your idea • Generate compelling questions or connections that advance the discussion and challenge existing interpretations	• Respond to others' ideas by posing imaginative, compelling questions, summarizing key ideas, or challenging assumptions • Show respect for others' ideas by acknowledging, referring to, or complementing others when agreeing or disagreeing • Respond to specific ideas others mention, using those conventions and vocabulary appropriate for academic discussions
Meets the Standard	• Come prepared, having read the required material, and make insightful or significant connections • Work with peers to create and sustain a substantial conversation that welcomes all students and perspectives (in-class or online) • Initiate and participate in full-class and small-group discussions in ways that sometimes improve the class	• Elaborate on your own or others' ideas by making appropriate and useful connections to other texts, topics, or events • Build on your own or others' ideas with appropriate examples or quotations from the text • Generate relevant questions or connections that advance the discussion or challenge existing interpretations	• Respond to others' ideas by posing useful, perceptive questions, summarizing main ideas, or challenging basic assumptions • Show respect for others' ideas by acknowledging and referring to them when agreeing or disagreeing • Respond to the ideas others mention, using those conventions and vocabulary appropriate for academic discussions
Approaches the Standard	• Come moderately prepared, having read the required material, and make connections that show understanding and possible insight • Work with peers as directed to complete tasks; may show more strength in one area (in-class or online, full class or small group) more than another • Initiate few discussions; participation focused on task completion more than exchange of ideas or authentic discussion	• Elaborate on your own or others' ideas by attempting to make connections to other texts, topics, or events • Attempt to build on your own or others' ideas with examples or quotations from the text (which may not be relevant) • Generate plausible questions or connections that attempt to advance the discussion or challenge existing interpretations	• Respond to others' ideas with relevant but obvious questions; summarize basic ideas; may attempt to challenge assumptions • Show some respect for others' ideas by referring to them when agreeing or disagreeing • Respond to some ideas others mention, attempting to use those conventions and vocabulary appropriate for academic discussions
Misses the Standard	• Show no apparent preparation; may not have read or have thought enough about material to make insightful or significant connections • Resist or avoid working with peers under most circumstances (in-class or online, full class or small group) • Refuse or do not contribute to full-class and small-group discussions; chronic absences also apply here: must be present to participate	• Make unrelated or no connections to other texts, topics, or events • Miss opportunities to build on your own or others' ideas with examples or quotations from text • Ask unrelated or no questions or make connections that advance the discussion or challenge existing interpretations	• Respond to others' ideas with unrelated questions or none; do not summarize or challenge ideas or assumptions • Show little or no respect for others' ideas when responding, agreeing or disagreeing • Respond to others' ideas or use those conventions and vocabulary appropriate for academic discussions rarely or never

Well Done	Work On

FIGURE 6.17 Class Discussion Rubric

© 2013 by Jim Burke from *The English Teacher's Companion*, Fourth Edition. Portsmouth, NH: Heinemann.

discussions over the grading period. On other occasions, I simply tell them I am evaluating the quality of their contributions; to that end, I will move around and make notes on cards or the seating chart based on my observations over the course of several days during which such sustained conversations are happening.

Gilles (2010) offers an excellent vignette of a middle school language arts teacher who takes time to "help her students learn the ground rules of conversation":

> Stephanie [the teacher] begins by finding some articles that sixth graders will find relevant and also a bit controversial, such as an article on sagging pants . . . or child labor. She tells students that we can all learn from one another because our lives are so different. She asks students to read the article and "mark it up"—in other words, ask questions and make comments directly on the article. She then partners students and places one partner from each pair in the center ring, while the other partner is in the "peanut gallery" outside the ring. The peanut gallery partner is responsible for keeping track of what the person inside the circle is doing. . . . After about 10 minutes, the whole class debriefs the conversation . . . , getting them to discuss not only what they said about the topic but how they performed in the discussion (12).

DURING: HOW TO START, SUSTAIN, AND EXTEND THE CONVERSATION

Gilles places such discussions as I just mentioned in the *before* section, treating them as warm up for the main event. I use many of the same techniques, but consider them part of the discussion, perhaps a transition from *before* to *during* the conversation. It doesn't matter whether we disagree on the terms; what matters most is that we both agree that the following can be used to either jump start the conversation about a text or idea, or can serve as tools to *create* and sustain the discussion itself throughout the allotted time. (See Figure 6.18.) A good discussion, after all, is a bit like one of those circus acts with all the plates spinning on the end of poles balanced on the performers' noses. It's not enough to get it started; you have to keep adding new plates (or ideas) to the act to achieve the necessary sense of challenge and engagement, to create the feeling that something is going on here with which they want to be involved. Figures 6.19 through 6.21 show discussion starters and handouts and Figure 6.22 shows Roberto and Travis talking through their model of the stages of life before presenting it to the class.

What are *we* as the teacher doing during these conversations that are catching fire in our classrooms? Mostly helping to keep it burning and growing the way firefighters ignite a "controlled burn." We are monitoring the flow and degree of participation; we are evaluating the quality of the content and posing questions to improve that quality (see Figure 6.23). In their report *Improving Literary Understanding Through Classroom Conversations*, Langer and Close (2001) list the following roles the teacher plays during such rich and emerging discussions: tapping understanding, seeking clarification, inviting participation, orchestrating discussion; focusing ideas, shaping arguments, linking concerns, [and] upping the ante," by which they mean providing "new and less obvious ways to think about their ideas and concerns, such as asking "How is the view of the characters in this play different from our modern view?" (15).

Starting and Sustaining the Discussion

Technique	Examples
Students and/or teachers	**Students or teachers**
Write to gather their thoughts, a technique that has the added benefit of helping both the student and you assess the students' knowledge and position as the conversation begins	• Jot ideas in notebook in response to question, prompt, or text • Exchange ideas by writing online via blogs, threaded discussions, social networks, survey sites, or other means
Generate or use criteria or categories that students then apply to the character or text in the subsequent discussion	• Identify stages of life, types of characters, criteria for evil, or core principles in philosophy (e.g., existential themes)—then apply to character or story • Use model such as Maslow's "Needs" hierarchy, Kohlberg's levels of moral reasoning, or diagnostic criteria (e.g., psychopath) and apply to character
Develop questions and connections based on their own experiences, prior knowledge, or reading	• Ask students to jot questions down on index cards, which an elected student (or panel of students) then draws from to lead discussion • Provide a handout with specific types of questions (e.g., factual, inferential, applied) each student must pose, then use as part of a Socratic Seminar in class
Provide a range of subjects to choose so that students can read the book and participate in discussions about topics that are important to them	• Identify all major themes or subjects in a book; let students choose ones they like and participate in an ongoing discussion about that subject as it relates to the book, themselves, and the world • List a related set of topics—economics, politics, justice, philosophy—common throughout a book; allow students to choose one, focus on that throughout book, and come ready to discuss in class each day or as assigned
Host a symposium on the text or topic that deepens and extends thinking	• Pose and respond to others' questions about the text or topic as a whole; can also focus on specific aspect or idea • Participate in a symposium as a character from book, history, or recent news; anchor all comments in that persona, using their voice
Use graphic organizers or other visual explanation to foster collaborative discussion about the text or topic as it relates to the tool	• Huddle around a graphic organizer (e.g., the decision tree or journey cycle), using its structure to facilitate conversation about text or topic • Create a map of region, neighborhood, or house, discussing how these elements factor into the story or relate to the theme
Create or use a metaphor or analogy, then apply to the text or topic to advance students' thinking in new, more analytical directions	• Tell students reading about a subject like war to create their own metaphor or analogy for war; then apply to the story they are reading for the class • Put a metaphor or analogy on the board and ask students to have a discussion about how it applies to the story or idea
Examine a set of quotations or statements, choosing one and using it to start or extend the discussion	• Gather provocative statements from any popular quotations website; enter a given subject (e.g., forgiveness, evil, law) and choose the ones that relate most to your topic or text; ask students to choose and respond to one, then discuss with others and connect it to the text being studied
Offer students a scenario (or series of) that they must discuss and use to help them think about the central questions in the text or topic under discussion	• Create a series of scenarios that vary by degree or type and ask students to agree or disagree, then extrapolate underlying principles, which they then apply to text or topic in discussion. *Examples:* 1. Scientists who created atomic bomb are evil. 2. Man who dropped the atomic bomb is evil. 3. President who ordered creation and dropping of the bomb is evil. And so on…
Read supplemental texts to generate new ideas and insights into the primary text or topic; these texts can be from different genres so long as they spark new thinking	• Give whole class a newspaper article about subject related to the primary text or topic; ask them to respond and relate it to the primary text • Divide the class into smaller groups, giving each a different article to read and relate to the text or topic in a subsequent class discussion
Ask students to examine a graphic or image in order to foster and further their thinking about the text or topic; graphic can be a chart, a visual explanation, or any other form intended to convey ideas	• Draw a figure on the board (e.g., a circle with a dot outside of it) and ask students to have a generative discussion in which they come up with as many connections or interpretations as possible between the diagram and the primary text or topic • Display an image—photograph, sculpture, painting—to the class (or give different groups different images) and ask them to examine it in light of the primary text or topic and be prepared to contribute to full-class discussion
Generate three more possible interpretations of a text, character, or event; provide viable support for each, selecting the best one and developing it in detail	• Come up with a word that *best* describes a character, setting, or event; then ask students to come up with three more that are at least as good with evidence to support • Challenge students to come up with three more viable interpretations of a particular text and explain how they are different and why each is a valid interpretation
Interrupt the discussion to provide provocative questions, observations, or statements by way of helping them blast through to the next level	• Interrupt their group discussions, which you have determined are stuck at a certain level, and give them a question, a supplemental text, or whatever else you think will help them move to the next level. This might be a short text or paragraph that seems to challenge everything they have said. It might also be something of a riddle, such as "How is Character X like an egg?" • Interrupt the group discussion and direct them to return to writing and, by way of this written conversation, come up with the next generation of ideas

FIGURE 6.18 Starting and Sustaining the Discussion

AP English Literature

Overview There is no *one* way to read a text; rather, there are many—each one is informed by different principles and criteria, some historical, some mental, and others more political. This assignment asks you to choose one of the critical theories listed below and do all the activities listed.

Standards The AP Literature Course Outcomes state that the student:

- Uses knowledge of relevant social/cultural/historical contexts to interpret texts
- Analyzes the use of textual features, devices, and organizational patterns, and how they connect multiple levels of ideas, themes, and meanings in texts
- Uses knowledge of relevant critical perspectives to clarify and elaborate the meaning of texts
- Develops an appropriate topic, research question, interpretation, thesis, or assertion
- Integrates evidence from a variety of primary and secondary sources into an original composition

Requirements Each of you must do the following:

1. Choose your theory from this list, which the attached handout describes in greater detail:

   - Marxist/Economic
   - Psychological/Analytical
   - Postmodernism
   - Philosophical/Existential
   - Mythological/Archetypal
   - Deconstruction
   - New Criticism (Formalism)
   - Feminist/Cultural Studies
   - Structuralism

2. Research your topic (see links below for useful sites), guided by these questions:

   - What are the key elements of this theory?
   - What are the origins of this theory or these ideas?
   - What are the limits or constraints of this theory?
   - What other theories is it similar to or different from?
   - How does this theory explain or otherwise apply to *Hamlet*?
   - How can your theory (a.k.a. your critical lens) be applied to history or world events?

3. Respond to the text through the lens of your critical theory in one or more of the following:

   - Google Group (or some other platform with similar interfaces—Facebook, Schoolloop)
   - Blog (a group blog to which you all contributed and responded separately from other one)

4. Facilitate a class discussion about a given scene or act, synthesizing your research and reading of the text. This presentation should:

   - Define the theory, outlining the key elements of it
   - Apply the theory, showing how these elements apply to *Hamlet*
   - Demonstrate your ability to effectively organize information on *not more than five slides* for the purpose of defining and persuading (use to accept your reading of *Hamlet*)

5. Use your notes and annotations to write a formal critical essay of *Hamlet* in which you examine the play through the lens of your chosen theory. The paper should:

   - Be 4–5 double-spaced typed pages
   - Cite at least five critical sources in addition to *Hamlet* and Meyer. These may not include any quote sites, or student support sites, but must be from actual documents you research, read, and use
   - Include a properly formatted (MLA) Works Cited page, including all sources used

Recommended links for more information on critical theory

1. http://en.wikipedia.org/wiki/Literary_theory
2. www.iep.utm.edu/l/literary.htm
3. www.kristisiegel.com/theory.htm#marx
4. www.cla.purdue.edu/academic/engl/theory/index.html
5. http://bcs.bedfordstmartins.com/virtualit/poetry/critical.html
6. http://theory.eserver.org/
7. www.phillwebb.net/Default.htm

FIGURE 6.19 This assignment for my AP Literature class asks students to examine *Hamlet* through the lens of critical theories.

A while ago Mr. Burke gave me some documents about essays others have written on *Hamlet* from deconstructionist viewpoints. Two of my favorite ideas that those authors brought up were:

- the idea that Hamlet, by being confusing and uninterpretable, is trying to destroy the "very idea of a text itself"
- the idea that the phrase "good night" changes throughout the text. The essay traced the phrased throughout Hamlet, showing how the meaning of the phrase changed at different points in the play.

Anyway it was pretty interesting. If I were less tired right now I would write more than two ideas. I'll probably revisit this post tomorrow.

—cschubiner

Comment [15]: relates to grace's paragraph at the topic "Act 2 Scene 2 line 210 "Words. Words, Words" I felt this was an Interesting quote to support deconstructionism because Hamlet is reading a book obviously not just for words but for an idea.

—OOBanteil

Food for thought: Besides the ease with which the hierarchy between poetry and prose can be overturned, there is one other significant concept that necessitates our attention: the fact that such a dichotomy is inescapably self-referential. Similar to the concept yin and yang, 'prose' would bear absolutely no meaning if it was not juxtaposed with 'poetry'

—JACK

Comment [16]: oh really? how so? i really would like some evidence here. without evidence, your articulate ramblings are just that—ramblings.

—cechubiner

The idea of opposite is consistent with all things, the would be no joy with out pain. no sun with out rain, it is only by having the collective juxtaposition that we get the individual ideas. This should clear up any confusion that may have existed, or maybe I'm still rambling . . .

—PD

I've been thinking for a while. In my essay, I'm most likely going to deconstruct Hamlet himself. Is he mad? Or is he sane? Or is he sometimes mad, sometimes sane, and sometimes feigning madness? That's probably what I'll focus most on, although i could branch off to question whether he actually loves Ophelia and whatnot. Anyway, when reading I've found that I could interpret Hamlet in multiple ways. It seems like just when I've found his true character, he says or implies something that makes my earlier interpretation incorrect. In my essay, I'll attempt to mention many of these interpretations, concluding that each interpretation has adequate support it the text to be considered valid. However, since many Interpretations are valid, they're all invalid, as there's only one correct interpretation. Thus, the only true things we know of Hamlet are on the surface, and any attempts at analyzing his character further are futile, and any conclusions drawn are disprovable.

—cschubiner

JACK's ramblings about opposites are what I was talking about when I said "opposite binary oppositions", Clay. The fact that there are various underlying meanings in Hamlet that if read correctly read (even though there is no correct reading of a text when deconstructing it) can completely obscure meaning. Anyway, for my essay I'll be focusing on Hamlet's sanity, too. I'll attempt to justify that he is both insane and not insane arid that he feigns insanity at some times to continue the play that goes on within the play. I figure that since I initially wanted psychology I could involve mental issues into a paper on deconstructionism, meh.

—cschubiner

Comment [17]: ARE YOU SAYING YOU DONT LIKE THIS TOPIC?!?!?!?!? !!?!?!?!?!?!?!?!!'??!!?!?!?!?!?!?!

—1gmphillips

It's called sarcasm love...

—PD

Roll, Grace. Oh look, I've Involved colloquial language in this discussion now. Nerd points? nerd points to karen!

By the way, this "small" discussion Is 9 pages long. WIN.

—Karen

FIGURE 6.20 Here a group of students uses GoogleDocs to have a conversation about possible topics for the *Hamlet* paper in Figure 6.19.

SENTENCE STARTERS

Prior Knowledge

- I already know that . . .
- This relates to . . .
- This reminds me of . . .

Asking Questions

- I wonder why . . .
- What if . . .
- Why is it . . .

Making Connections

- That's like in the book when . . .
- That reminds me of what we studied in history . . .
- This is similar to when . . .
- I can relate to that because . . .

Summarizing

- The main idea is . . .
- Everyone seems to think . . .
- The most important points are . . .

Comparing

- _____ is like _____ because . . .
- Steinbeck and Obama are saying the same thing . . .
- Steinbeck and Obama agree that . . . but I think _____ would not agree about . . . because . . .

Clarifying/Revising

- What I mean is . . .
- Another way of saying this is . . .
- I didn't mean to imply . . . but. . . .
- At first I thought . . . but then I realized x and now think . . .

Reflecting and Relating

- In the end, I believe . . .
- I first thought . . . but now think . . . because . . .
- While I realize . . . I think . . . because . . .
- This is relevant to my life because . . .
- My conclusion at this point is that . . .

Overview

We have finished reading *Of Mice and Men* and will use this week to bring the inquiry (and the semester!) to a close. Instead of writing a paper or giving presentations, which we don't have time to do well, I thought we would combine writing and discussion by having a Socratic Seminar online. In short, a Socratic Seminar asks students to consider a subject from different perspectives, asking questions that help them and their classmates clarify and extend their thinking about the subject they are studying.

Objectives

My intention is to use the discussion to:

- Learn how to post written responses to an online blog
- Consider a question from several different perspectives
- Pose questions to other students, the text, and the author that lead to new and deeper thinking about the subject
- Elaborate on your thinking through written discussion
- Make connections to the text, yourself, other texts, and the world
- Provide support for your ideas from the text or other reliable sources

Grading

- Your grade on this assignment will be based on the quality of your participation in class and online, as well as the quality of your work as spelled out in the Objectives section above. This is equivalent to a major assignment, so do your very best.

Step One

- Log on to the blog: http://mrburkesfreshmen.blogspot.com
- Read the directions, including Barak Obama's remarks
- Post a response to Obama's ideas and the question, "Am I my brother's keeper?" As part of your response, you need to connect these ideas to *Of Mice and Men* somehow, using examples from the text to develop and support your ideas. This should be a thoughtful, well-developed response, not just a couple sentences dashed off.

Step Two

- Read most of the other responses from your classmates on the blog
- Post *two questions* in response to other people's posts. These questions should invite people to clarify or defend their ideas. For example, you might ask, "What about if everyone did what you suggest? What would be the effect of that?" or you might ask, "How would you relate that to George's relationship with Lennie?"

Step Three

- *Respond* to at least *two* questions or postings
- Your responses should be well developed. Use some of the sentence starters in the margin to help you get started if you are stuck

Step Four

- Read through most of the responses, jotting down notes about big and common ideas that appear throughout the different comments.
- Write a final commentary that ties together your own thoughts and those of others, but also adds one last idea, perhaps your final thought about this subject of "my brother's keeper"
- Include in this last comment new ideas or opinions you have about this subject and what led you to these new thoughts

FIGURE 6.21 *Mice and Men* Online Socratic Seminar handout

FIGURE 6.22 Eventually, students use the stages model as the basis for a writing assignment that requires evidence from the text to support it.

Depending on how the discussion, regardless of the format, is going, you may have other roles to play that vary by group or student. Those still learning how to participate in academic discussions may be struggling to jump in; in such a situation, they need guidance and language—examples of how to make this intellectual and social move without causing offense. Others may be forgetting the purpose of the discussion; thus, you need to reiterate it, perhaps recalibrating or redefining it as needed. If students' ideas or responses seem stuck at a particular level, guide them by asking prompting questions to get to the better ideas. Focus on the language, the questions, and how these work to get at the better ideas. Obviously, some may be drifting off topic; the reason for this, however, may not be as simple as it seems—they may have no idea how to proceed or not understand the text or the task. Thus, you may need to pause the conversation to check for understanding and, as needed, teach or reteach relevant skills or knowledge they need to proceed.

PAUSE **&** REFLECT Describe your role in a typical class discussion. If you are brave enough, have a student, colleague, or student teacher record the number of times you speak and code them (e.g., a column for Ask Question, Respond with Answer, etc.). Reflect on what the results tell you about your teaching style.

Engaging Minds Through Discussion

FIGURE 6.23a The class faces off for a discussion of whether Tookie Williams should be put to death after reading three different perspectives arguing one action or another.

FIGURE 6.23b Speed dating conversation about the question "What does this book have to say about how we should live our lives?" Each chat is two minutes, then up and move, until time at end, when we debrief and discuss as a class. It was one of the first days of spring and they needed a change.

One of the most important skills and types of knowledge—both for teacher and student—is what is known as "up-take"—a range of responses during a discussion that validate what a speaker says while getting them to delve still deeper into that subject. To some extent, the sentence frames in Figure 4.4 offer a wide range of responses that can be used for uptake. Such exchanges take on the more natural give-and-take of authentic conversations, a student or the teacher acting a bit like those workout partners you see in the gym sometimes goading their mate to the next level, though in the English class it generally involves less barking and sweat. Up-take questions and responses are vital for, as Nystrand found in his study of classroom discourse, "the vast proportion of teacher questions (a) are test questions, (b) get a response, (c) do not involve uptake, and (d) elicit a report of what is already known (1998, 37).

Up-take is not a generic response of "tell me more!" Rather, it includes a variety of forms and levels. In some situations, the person responding is pushing the speaker to elaborate on what he or she just said, asking for evidence or explanation. Under other circumstances, uptake may involve the teacher or another student reiterating what one student just said or linking several students' comments in order to model how to better use academic vocabulary. Respondents, whether teachers or students, often use uptake to make those connections some students are not yet able to see due to a lack of background knowledge or skills as a reader. Connecting all these forms of uptake is the importance of nudging the students from wherever they are to where they need to be by way of guiding, modeling, and directly instructing them as needed (Vygotsky 1978).

After: How to Extend the Benefits of the Discussion

Discussion is rarely the end point; it is, instead, a means—the way to get students *into* and help them move *through* the text or the topic (see Figure 6.24). But what about the great *beyond* after the discussion concludes? While the discussion was by no means a mere side dish (to return to our earlier analogy of a conversation being like a meal), it is best treated as a means of developing a wide range of communication and social skills and preparing students for some culminating action such as writing an essay (or taking an exam). The primary options when students finish the discussion include:

- Collect all notes and other evidence of preparation for or participation in the discussion to check for understanding and effort

- Use all notes and ideas from the discussion as the basis for a paper, presentation, or other culminating project that synthesizes all these previous conversations and investigations

- Reflect on their performance and the process, identifying those areas of strength and those they need to improve

- Debrief on the discussion to identify, whether it was for one period or much longer, key ideas and insights about both the subject and the experience of discussion, including which strategies, questions, or stems worked best

Photograph © Marc Fiorito

FIGURE 6.24 During discussions or preparation for them, my role is to circulate around the room and clarify, challenge, evaluate, and assess their performance and needs.

These last few points about reflection and debriefing are especially important if you are using techniques that are new to you or your students. The obvious example of such new directions would be online discussion in its many variants, though you may be making new efforts to include any type of discussion in your class. A significant and constantly growing chorus of voices from the research and classroom communities are making online discussions a part of their classes (Albright, Purohit, and Walsh 2002; Robb 2010).

While such discussions are often the primary means for the conversation taking place, others use these technologies in more responsive ways (Kahn 2007; Jewell 2005)—setting up blogs and discussion boards, or turning to Twitter and similar platforms to supplement longer, more traditional discussions taking place in class. Others, including myself, integrate the online and the class discussions from the beginning, making them complements to each other to provide for a wider range of ways into the discussion (Bowers-Campbell 2011). Such integration has the added benefit of using discussions in class or online to prepare for or extend these discussions when students go home or return the next day to continue them.

> **"** THE WORLD FOR WHICH WE ARE PREPARING THE KIDS REQUIRES AN AGILITY ACROSS PLATFORMS AND PROGRAMS THAT MAKES THIS A VALID APPROACH . . . **"**

I used to structure these discussions in an attempt to keep them within the confines of the school software. Now, however, I tend to make a list of the available options, including Facebook, Google Groups, and even Twitter. I tell students they need to send me the information that allows me to monitor and respond as needed (digital up-take, essentially). I realize this freedom may not exist at all schools, but the world for which we are preparing the kids requires an agility across platforms and programs that makes this a valid approach so long as I know they are safe (and working well!).

As this section has discussed at length, successful discussions—online or in class—require serious planning and preparation, much of which may not be visible to students. Ironically, to the extent that these discussions do not rely on us or appear to be led by the students themselves, such discussions require all the more effort on our part. It is hard work to exclude oneself from the discussion or at least the primary responsibility for running it. My students' comments, which follow, suggest that both in-class and online discussions are useful and engaging; no doubt discussion, especially online, will be a significant part of work in and outside of schools in the future.

Jeff Wilhelm (2010), one of our most thoughtful practitioners, offers perhaps the best conclusion to this section on discussion; these words appeared at the end of an article he wrote about the "power and pleasures of dialogue":

> Finally, I just have to add that real learning [which comes from such meaningful dialogue] is fun. In contrast, being told what to think is not empowering or interesting or fun. Nobody I know, student or adult, likes being told what to think or do. I've just read two recent books: *The Art of Conversation* (Blyth 2009) and *How to Have a Beautiful Mind* (de Bono 2004); both emphasize not only the fun of true dialogue, but how to engage in it. The many suggestions in these books show how conversational and dialogic "moves" can be taught to people if they are interested in . . . wisdom. . . . Both books make the point that dialogue is in the service of understanding and of growing wisdom; monologue cannot be. (58)

PAUSE & REFLECT After reading this section on class discussions, what is most important for you to remember? Why is this so important for you?

PAUSE & REFLECT Describe your greatest success or failure as a speaker. What happened? How did the audience respond? How did *you* respond?

Stand and Deliver: Speaking and Presenting

Speaking and presenting are so important that the Boy Scouts of America even offers a Public Speaking merit badge! As one might expect, it's not enough to just give a speech and get the badge: After a brief introductory speech, the scout must then prepare a longer (3–5 minutes) talk on a chosen topic, followed by a two-minute impromptu talk his counselor assigns—all of which culminates in a formal presentation that uses images or other media to convey the information and ideas to the community (meritbadge.com 2011). Leave it to the Boy Scouts to so helpfully sum up the history of speaking and its evolution in the last century: the five-minute icebreaker or personal introduction one might have given (and still does, actually) at the first Rotary Club meeting they attended has now become the one-minute elevator pitch with full media included. What's that? No time to hear it? That's okay: I'll tweet you the link to my personal YouTube or SlideShare channel for you to access from home, work, or your smartphone while you take the elevator to your office.

The public speaking merit badge was created, I should add, in 1932; obviously, much has changed since then. Today, colleges have begun to invite students to submit "video essays," which students then post on YouTube, sending the university the hot link (Quillen 2010, 50) as an alternative to the more traditional written essay. In the business world, the same has happened with "video resumes." Not to be outdone, publishers have begun producing "vooks." What is a *vook*? Even though the form is still evolving, it is a "digital mashup of video and books, with a dash of popular social networks . . . thrown in for seasoning" (Evangelista 2010, D1). What do these all have in common? They are all various forms of public speaking (see Figure 6.25), the only differences between them being the purpose, audience; occasion; and, in many cases, the means by which they are viewed or delivered (e.g., YouTube versus a device like the iPad). My friend Mark, a chef for a popular chain of restaurants, creates new recipes all the time; he then describes them through presentations for cooks around the country who view these demonstrations online in a password-protected online digital classroom.

Whereas the previous section about discussion focused on an activity that is both a skill and an instructional strategy, this section looks at a distinct skill, one that is elusive to master but can—and must—be effectively taught if teachers take the time it requires. And time *is* a factor when it comes to public speaking.

Discussions and interviews can be used in a variety of contexts, some of which are more efficient than others in terms of the time they take. Speeches? Presentations? They take time. Time to compose. Time to rehearse. Time to set up, deliver, take down all posters, slide sets on the projector, visuals taped to the board. Time (for all 35 of my students) to give. Time to teach students the skills and knowledge (i.e., design, format, argument, story, speaking, and much more) they need to learn if they are to do these well and make it worth the time it takes you to teach and each student to give them.

Types of Public Speaking

Speech	Debate	Presentation	Performance
• Types	• Types	• Types	• Types
• Prepared	• Lincoln-Douglas	• Ballroom	• Scripted
• Extemporaneous	• Oxford	• Conference room	• Impromptu
• Live or recorded	• Policy	• Café table	• Live or recorded
• Purposes	• Formal	• Elevator pitch	• Purposes
• Inform	• Informal	• Live or recorded	• Persuade
• Persuade	• Live	• Purposes	• Demonstrate
• Explain	• Purpose	• Inform	• Entertain
• Demonstrate	• Persuade	• Persuade	• Inspire
• Entertain	• Occasions	• Explain	• Occasions
• Inspire	• Community event	• Demonstrate	• Personal event
• Occasions	• School assignment	• Occasions	• Community event
• Personal event	• Media: Not permitted?	• Community event	• School event
• Community event	• Length: Specified	• Professional event	• School assignment
• Professional event	• Attire: More formal	• School assignment	• Media: Optional
• School event	• Digital alternatives	• Media: Audio, video, print	• Length: Situational
• School assignment	• None	(handouts), artifact display	• Attire: Situational
• Media: Optional		• Length: Situational	• Digital alternatives
• Length: Situational		• Attire: Situational	• Podcasts
• Attire: Situational		• Digital alternatives	• Skype (or similar)
• Digital alternatives		• Podcasts	• Video (via YouTube)
• Podcasts		• Skype (or similar)	
• Skype (or similar)		• Video (via YouTube)	
• Video (via YouTube)			
Sample Assignments	**Sample Assignments**	**Sample Assignments**	**Sample Assignments**
• How to do _____	• Should we (be allowed to) _____?	• Elevator pitch based on a story or idea	• Reader's Theater
• Personal introduction	• _____ was wrong to do X: Agree/Disagree	• Book trailer (on video)	• Read aloud
• Booktalk	• X is _____: Agree/Disagree	• Formal presentation on topic, theory, or text (e.g., What is Marxist literary theory and how does it apply to *Hamlet*? Or: Power in general and in *1984* in particular)	• Perform scenes
• The importance of X	• Debate (one group vs. another) whether X is guilty, evil, legal, etc.	• Newscast	• Produce movie
• The best _____ of all time			• Hot Seat: Author
• Tell a story			• Hot Seat: Character
• Book trailer (on video)			• Word for word (perform story as a play)
• The history of _____			• Digital storytelling
			• Dramatic interpretation
			• Spoken word
Questions to Ask	**Questions to Ask**	**Questions to Ask**	**Questions to Ask**
• What's the subject?	• What's the subject?	• What's the subject?	• What's the occasion?
• Who's the audience?	• What's my position?	• Who's the audience?	• What is the proper tone?
• Why should they care?	• What is the opposing side's position?	• Why should they care?	• What do I want them to leave knowing, feeling, or believing about this subject, character, book, or author?
• Why is this important?	• What is the weakest part of their argument?	• Why is this important?	• What's my purpose?
• How should I organize it?	• What must I achieve immediately?	• How should I organize it?	• Which techniques, media, or information can help me achieve my purpose?
• What's the occasion?	• How can I achieve that?	• What's the occasion?	
• What is the proper tone?	• What evidence do I have?	• What is the proper tone?	
• What do I want them to leave knowing, feeling, or believing?	• How should I organize it?	• What do I want them to leave knowing, feeling, or believing?	
• What's my purpose?	• Which techniques, media, or information can help me achieve my purpose?	• What's my purpose?	
• Which techniques, media, or information can help me achieve my purpose?		• Which techniques, media, or information can help me achieve my purpose?	

Note: Keep in mind the connection between speaking and writing outlined in Figure 4.3 which covers the four primary types of writing: informational, persuasive, expressive, imaginative.

FIGURE 6.25 Types of Public Speaking

But it is time we must take, for as with so many other aspects of our discipline, speaking increasingly merges with writing; yesterday's speech is today's talk is tomorrow's instructional video delivered to colleagues or customers via the Internet, the smartphone, or some other digital device designed to teach, inform, or persuade. And no more of these *long* speeches! The world is on the run! This is the era of the "elevator pitch," which Scott Brown sums up as not "a sound bite [but] an idea in miniature: a full three-master [ship] built to scale in a bottle. It's got to be complete, logical, and watertight, stem to stern" (2010, 98). The term and concept have evolved only slightly from the original one that asked you to imagine you stepped into an elevator with someone like Bill Gates and you had exactly one minute, during which Mr. Gates could not get away, to present your big idea. Go! As I have said throughout the book: ours is an economy of attention. (See Figure 6.26.) Just as writers must know how to construct messages to get and keep that attention, so, too, must speakers, whether they are speaking live, online, or on a smartphone while standing in line at the market.

Two important ideas at the heart of this section—rhetoric and the composing process— are treated in such detail in the writing chapter it seems unnecessary to address them here in any detail. Before we look at samples of these different types of speaking in the class, let us briefly review, by way of discussing the role of assessment up front, what effective speakers do, especially in presentations; the rubric shown in Figure 6.27 focuses on this.

SPEECHES

If I am asking students to speak for the first time that year, I will survey the class about their feelings, asking them to tell me how they feel. This has the effect of showing I care and am committed to a successful experience; it has the added benefit of giving me a sense of where the student stands. Look how much information I get from Ruby Ruiz, a freshman in my reading class, by asking her to reflect on her experience with and ability as a speaker:

> I am an average speaker. The reason I consider myself an average speaker is because I feel comfortable talking to other people but I sometimes don't feel comfortable talking in front of a big crowd. Another reason that I consider myself an average speaker is because sometimes I have trouble telling others my views and ideas. The reason I have trouble telling others my views and ideas is because sometimes I am scared of what they will think. I always listen to what people have to say because I know that if I want people to listen to me then I have to pay attention to them, too.

The basic, easy speeches you can do are the introductory ones, sometimes called "icebreakers" because they are generally given at the beginning of a class to help everyone get to know each other. You can do these very quickly and informally by asking two people to interview each other and then briefly introduce each other while standing in front of the class or by their seats (see Figure 6.28). In the right class, in the right circumstances, it accomplishes a lot by way of creating community even as it challenges them to do what is difficult within constraints that generally feel safe (see Figure 6.29).

A more formal introductory speech, such as the one my colleague Diane McClain requires of her students, might be given early in the year. This speech requires students to prepare

Name: _____ Period: _____ Date: _____

Overview

The following ideas are designed to help you speak to either one person (e.g., a coach, a teacher, a prospective employer in an interview) or a large group in a formal setting. Speaking in front of people is considered, by many Americans, the most stressful experience imaginable. These strategies can help ease some of that stress by getting you prepared.

Preparation

First, clarify your topic. Try the business card test: you have only the side of a business card to state your main idea. Aside from that, the following points are essential, even if they do seem obvious.

- Preparation: know your material "cold" so that you can worry not about what to say but about how to say it.
- Rehearsal: this might mean walking around your bedroom all afternoon repeating your lines over and over; it might also mean practicing in front of friends, parents, mirrors, even video cameras or tape recorders.
- Audience: how you speak, what you include, and how you act will be determined by the answers to a few simple questions: To whom am I speaking? Why am I speaking to them? What do they know—and what must I explain? How much time do I have?
- Tools and aids: what, if any, visual or other aids (props, handouts, transparencies, poster, computer presentation, video) should I use to convey this information to my audience most effectively?

Visual Aids

When your purpose is to convey complex or abundant information to your audience, use visual aids to help them keep track of your main ideas. These aids also let the audience know what to expect. For instance, based on the example provided in the box below, the audience can relax, knowing the speaker will take questions after the presentation. Consider using one of the following:

- Posterboard
- Overhead transparencies (made with colored pens or copied)
- Presentation software such as PowerPoint, Keynotes, or Prezi
- Handout with the same information as displayed on your visual aids so listeners don't have to take notes but can pay closer attention or supplement your notes with their own

Characteristics of Effective Speeches or Presentations

- **Visual aids:**
  - Are clearly visible and readable to all members of the audience
  - Use large basic fonts, such as Helvetica, for clarity and neatness
  - Include minimal text for emphasis and readability
  - Use concrete, precise words that will not confuse the audience
  - Do not include graphics or images that compete with the information

> - **Overview of presentation**
>   - Background
>   - Current status
>   - Proposed changes
>   - Implications
>   - Summary and questions

- **Effective, engaging speakers:**
  - Pace their speech so that each word gets the proper enunciation and emphasis.
  - Look at their audience as much as possible.
  - Project and inflect their voices in order to engage the audience and emphasize those ideas they feel are particularly important.
  - Use humor or other such devices to engage and maintain their audience's attention.

- **Effective presentations:**
  - Provide an overview of the presentation at the beginning.
  - Provide a summary of the important points in the presentation at the end.
  - Provide strong supporting data or examples to clarify the ideas for the audience.
  - Follow a logical, coherent progression from idea to idea.
  - Avoid any theatrics or other acts that will undermine the speaker's ability to effectively convey the information to the audience.
  - Anticipate the audience's questions and answer them.
  - Restate questions from the audience to clarify (and provide time to compose a thoughtful response to the question).
  - Use transitions to clearly mark where one idea ends and the next begins; these transitions also make for a more fluid, coherent speech.

- **Presentation Strategies:**
  - **Note cards:** these can contain either cue words or main ideas across the top of the card, followed by ideas or scripts as needed.
  - **Outline:** helpful, abbreviated script that supports but allows you to speak instead of read. Also helpful as a checklist of what you've discussed.
  - **Memorize:** if you have time, memorize what you will say, especially if you are presenting your information dramatically. Actors reading off 3 x 5 cards doesn't work too well.
  - **Write your outline or script in larger type and triple-space it** so you don't have to search through the document to find your place.
  - **Have style:** whether this is the handouts, your way of speaking, your humor, or the guiding metaphors and analogies you use to help listeners understand, make sure your speech engages their attention and their heart if at all possible. Give them something to remember.
  - **Avoid words you can easily trip over** during the course of your speech. This is particularly important for speeches that cause the speaker stress.
  - **Monitor your audience:** if you see that you are losing them, adjust your speech, improvise, project yourself more forcefully.
  - **Cue words:** on note cards or outlines, such words, if the speaker is well prepared, allow the one to recall all he or she wants to say about a topic. Example: *Implications* signals the memory to recall the list of five different implications for the expanded use of technology in every aspect of our lives.

FIGURE 6.26 Elements of an Effective Speech or Presentation

Rubric: Multimedia Presentation

Name(s): _____ Topic: _____ Grade: _____

FOCUS and DEVELOPMENT
Examines the extent to which each slide establishes a focus and develops that focus through examples, details, data, or images.

5. Provides compelling focus with rich details.
- ☐ Presentation offers insight about important ideas
- ☐ Individual slides each have a clear, compelling focus
- ☐ Slides include specific examples, details, evidence
- ☐ Slides relate to and develop main idea of presentation
- ☐ Images or data add insight/meaning to ideas

3. Creates general focus with related details.
- ☐ Presentation shows understanding of important ideas
- ☐ Individual slides have an identifiable main idea/focus
- ☐ Slides include basic/few examples, details, evidence
- ☐ Slides connect to main idea of presentation
- ☐ Images or data add limited insight/meaning to ideas

1. Lacks focus and relevant details.
- ☐ Presentation lacks insight; ignores important ideas
- ☐ Individual slides lack a clear, compelling focus
- ☐ Slides include no examples, details, or evidence
- ☐ Slides show no connection to idea of presentation
- ☐ No images or data; if there are, add no substance

ORGANIZATION
Applies to order of slides, ideas on slides, and transitions from one idea to the next.

5. Establishes effective organization that adds value.
- ☐ Intro/conclusion slides sum up key ideas concisely
- ☐ Slides have organizing header at top in large font
- ☐ Ideas arranged in clear, concise bullets
- ☐ Slides follow logical progression to achieve objective.

3. Creates practical organization that adds order.
- ☐ Intro/conclusion slides include key ideas
- ☐ Slides have an ineffective header or lack header
- ☐ Ideas arranged in bullets in way that distracts/confuses
- ☐ Slides follow a logical progression; partially effective

1. Offers no or flawed organization; confuses.
- ☐ Intro/conclusion slides missing or do not organize information
- ☐ Slides have confusing header or no evident header
- ☐ Ideas not arranged in bullets; blocks of text
- ☐ Slides lack logical progression; confuse audience

LANGUAGE
Considers both the speaker's written and spoken language; focuses on diction as well as factors such as concision, parallel structure, clarity.

5. Uses language that is precise and powerful.
- ☐ Words are precise, effective, clear
- ☐ Sentences are concise, in appropriate style
- ☐ Sentences and other content has parallel structure
- ☐ Syntax and grammar clarify and emphasize

3. Uses language that is general and predictable.
- ☐ Words are familiar, generic, predictable
- ☐ Sentences are sometimes concise, in appropriate style
- ☐ Sentences and other content may lack parallel structure
- ☐ Syntax and grammar do not always clarify and emphasize

1. Uses language that is flawed, vague, inappropriate.
- ☐ Words are vague, incorrect, unfamiliar
- ☐ Sentences lack conciseness; may be inappropriate style
- ☐ Sentences and other content lacks parallel structure
- ☐ Syntax and grammar confuse and undermine purpose

DELIVERY
Refers to speaker's presence, gestures, voice, interactions with/use of technology in presentation, and overall ethos.

5. Offers energetic, dynamic presentation of information.
- ☐ Preparation is evident in everything speaker does
- ☐ Presence is commanding, rehearsed, confident
- ☐ Voice projects, emphasizes through intonation
- ☐ Presentation conveys knowledge, insight, energy
- ☐ Technology and delivery complement each other

3. Offers useful, pedestrian presentation of information.
- ☐ Preparation is evident but could be more thorough
- ☐ Presence has some energy; not rehearsed, confident
- ☐ Voice sometimes projects; some emphasis in tone
- ☐ Presentation shows some knowledge, insight, energy
- ☐ Technology and delivery complementary at times

1. Offers lackluster, confusing presentation of information.
- ☐ Preparation not evident; seems rushed; winging it
- ☐ Presence is underwhelming; no energy, confidence
- ☐ Voice does not project; monotone, without emphasis
- ☐ Presentation conveys little knowledge, insight, energy
- ☐ Technology and delivery not in sync; a distraction

DESIGN
Refers to layout, appearance, and configuration of slides, including fonts, style, color, images, and other features.

5. Unifies and complements elements and purpose.
- ☐ Background of slides complements content
- ☐ Elements work together to enhance message
- ☐ Fonts are appropriate size, style, color
- ☐ Images placed and formatted to add meaning; relevant
- ☐ Elements are consistent, related throughout slides

3. Serves and signals elements and purpose.
- ☐ Background of slides neither complements nor distracts
- ☐ Elements work together at times to enhance message
- ☐ Fonts are mostly appropriate size, style, color
- ☐ Images placed and formatted; complement and distract
- ☐ Elements are consistent, related throughout slides

1. Undermines elements and purpose.
- ☐ Background of slides distracts from content
- ☐ Elements undermine or distract from message
- ☐ Fonts are not appropriate size, style, color
- ☐ Images confuse; show no evidence of intent; random
- ☐ Elements not consistent, unrelated throughout slides

CONVENTIONS
Includes punctuation, spelling, grammar, and usage.

5. Uses conventions to add to meaning and purpose.
- ☐ Sentence style and pattern is rhetorically effective
- ☐ Punctuation adds clarity, meaning to content
- ☐ No errors in punctuation, spelling, grammar, or usage

3. Observes general conventions.
- ☐ Sentence style and pattern sometimes rhetorically effective
- ☐ Punctuation adds some clarity, meaning to content
- ☐ Some errors in punctuation, spelling, grammar, or usage

1. Undermines message through errors and flaws.
- ☐ Sentence style and pattern is rhetorically effective
- ☐ Punctuation adds clarity, meaning to content
- ☐ Many errors in punctuation, spelling, grammar, or usage

FIGURE 6.27 Multimedia Presentation rubric

FIGURE 6.28 Students introduce each other as part of their Toastmasters Introduction speech.

FIGURE 6.29 Ronai and Jesus read through the assigned speeches in the textbook to get ideas for their own speeches.

carefully and listen to their classmates as they evaluate their performance using the criteria shown in Figure 6.30. Which criteria you use will depend on the occasion and purpose.

Another quick but useful type of speech you can have kids give—an informal talk, really—is a booktalk. These come in a variety of forms and lengths, including the more ambitious "book trailer"—modeled after the trailer for an upcoming film. My preferred style, however, is to ask kids, especially in my reading classes, to give the briefest of one-minute talks right after a period of silent reading in class. Still, as with even the most seemingly simple task, students need to know what the performance looks like, so I provide one like the following. I did this one day while reading with the kids in class early in the year:

> I am reading *A Perfect Peace* by Amos Oz. This book makes me think about marriage and what it should be like. Yonathan, the main character, does not love his wife. He shows her no respect, often humiliating her in front of others.
>
> I think marriage should be something you are proud of. You cannot hide from who you really are in a marriage. Marriage is, or can be, a difficult experience. It teaches you to be a better person if that is a lesson you are willing to learn.

Instead of just turning them loose each day to remember my example—this was, remember, a class for struggling readers—when it is their turn to give such a talk, I created the following template to guide them:

> My name is . . .
> I'm reading _____ by _____ .
> One thing this book makes me think about is
> The author thinks . . .
> But I think . . . because . . .

Life Lesson Speech: Checklist and Evaluation

❏ **Topic Target**: All sections filled in with details, topics, domains.

❏ **Speech Prep Notes**: Completed organizer about a specific topic from target.

❏ **Speech Draft**: Complete written text of speech (rough draft) that would take at least two minutes to deliver (about the length of what I provided in the example). It must have the bold subheadings as part of the organization of the speech.

❏ **Speech Outline**: Organized into outline form, using bold headings from draft to organize. Follows basic format of my example.

❏ **Index Cards**: Adapt the outline to index cards following example provided in *Writer's Inc* (page 427). Due Friday.

❏ **Deliver Speech**: Each person should come well prepared and ready to give their speeches starting on Tuesday of next week.

❏ **Self-Assessment and Reflection:** Complete the self-assessment assignment and reflect on your performance and thoughts about this speech in particular, the process, and public speaking in general.

Speech Evaluation

Name: _____ Period: _____ Date: _____

CATEGORY	SCORE	COMMENTS
Subject		
Focus (5) • Your speech has *one* subject • You establish your focus (main idea) clearly and effectively • Each part of your speech (introduction, body, and conclusion) has a specific focus		
Organization (5) Your speech: • Uses one or more organizational patterns • Maintains organization throughout • Has an introduction, body, and conclusion		
Development (5) You develop the ideas in your speech by using: • Supporting details • Examples • Stories • Explanations		
Ethos (5) • Likability: You had a friendly, positive attitude when speaking; you won over the audience • Integrity: You were honest, credible, and conscientious • Forcefulness: You were confident, enthusiastic, and in control of yourself • Competence: You were prepared, and you knew your topic well		
Completion (5) You satisfied all requirements regarding: • Time • Subject • Type of speech		
TOTAL SCORE (OUT OF 25)		

FIGURE 6.30 Life lesson speech checklist

Having received a model and such a structured guideline, students are more willing and proceed to do work that feels successful to them as readers, writers, and speakers of course.

What follows is a complete instructional sequence (in the form of the steps and accompanying handouts) for a CP freshman class. This was a class with almost twice as many boys as girls. Lots of kids with special needs or from EL backgrounds, kids still in Transitional English—all of them "energetic" and pathologically social. I loved them. All 32 of them. But they needed structure, models, guidance, and time.

We had been reading speeches and essays about the lessons people had learned from their lives or others'. In fact, the Big Question around which the whole unit was organized was, "What can I learn from the lives of others that can help me with my own?" The goal was to take them through the entire composing process, until they arrived at the podium to give their speeches and needed no cards to read but could speak confidently and comfortably while looking at us and projecting their voices. Each of the following handouts describes what we did and how we did it. I should say that the speeches were and kids not only had fun but worked very hard, and learned much along the way. I should add that while they worked on their own speeches, they read, watched videos, and critiqued the figurative language and speaking styles of Martin Luther King, Jr., Nelson Mandela, Caesar Chavez, Susan B. Anthony, and President Obama.

> **" I should add that while they worked on their own speeches, they read, watched videos, and critiqued the figurative language and speaking styles of Martin Luther King, Jr., Nelson Mandela, Caesar Chavez, Susan B. Anthony, and President Obama. "**

As this was a unit and a complex set of skills that were new to these excitable ninth graders, I needed to provide clear, useful examples for them to follow at every stage. Also, providing these models and precise directions allowed me to better understand what I was after and what they needed to do or learn. Thus, I did much of the assignment with them as we went, at each step taking time to model, debrief, and help them, ultimately, prepare for and give the speeches that made them so proud in the end. Figure 6.31 shows the assignment sheet all students received and Figure 6.32 is a notetaking tool sample.

Few experiences give students the feeling of achievement that having to "stand and deliver" do. Also, the ability to speak well and in public determines what is possible for many of our students in many fields. (See Figures 6.33 and 6.34.) Edwin Tufte (1997) goes so far as to suggest that scientists' inability to speak with clarity, economy, and persuasiveness resulted in the *Challenger* shuttle disaster as they were unable to quickly convey their message in time to delay the launch. It is only by doing what they cannot or did not think they could that students build the confidence they need to become who or what they will be as adults.

PAUSE & REFLECT As you finish the speech section, what comments, questions, or concerns arise, especially as you apply the ideas here to your own class?

PRESENTATIONS

The previous section focused on speeches, none of which require visual or other aids. Presentations differ from speeches, however. We associate presentations primarily with the workplace

Life Lessons: A Speech

Overview

This assignment culminates in a 2- to 3-minute speech about an important lesson you or someone else learned from experience. Sometimes lessons are deeply personal, even humiliating. Other lessons seem small and obvious but can have large effects on us over time—that is, the obvious realization that "hard work does pay off," though it may take time!. For this assignment, choose a lesson you or someone else learned, one that is appropriate, interesting, and important.

Standards

This assignment addresses the following standards:

- Deliver focused and coherent oral presentations that convey distinct perspectives and solid reasoning
- Use gestures, tone, and vocabulary appropriate to audience and purpose
- Choose logical patterns of organization to inform and persuade (LS 1.3)
- Choose appropriate techniques for developing the introduction and conclusion (LS 1.4)
- Deliver narrative presentations that communicate significance of events in a sequence; locate those events in specific places; use sensory details; and reflect appropriate pacing (LS 2.1)

Requirements

This assignment requires that you:

- Complete the Topic Target or Mind Map for brainstorming ideas
- Develop an outline for your speech using the Speech Prep Notes
- Write up the actual speech according to the directions that follow—be sure to do *all* steps
- Rehearse to prepare: can use cards to prompt but cannot read your speech text!
- Reflect on performance and content
- Assess others according to rubric/criteria provided

Directions

Everyone has experiences from which they learn lessons that shape their values, lead to important realizations, and affect the decisions they make or the way they live. Choose *one* lesson you or someone else learned and give a 2- to 3-minute speech in which you:

- Identify the lesson
- Describe the context in which you or someone else learned this lesson
- Explain how you or someone else learned this lesson
- Discuss the effect this lesson had on you or someone else then and over time
- Assess and convey the meaning and importance of that lesson as it relates to the person who learned it and your audience

Assessment

Your speech and the preceding steps will be evaluated according to the criteria outlined on the attached rubric

FIGURE 6.31: Freshman students give this Life Lessons speech.

or community meetings, and on occasion, products people (in person, online, or on television—try to sell us. As the notion of text and composition evolves to include a wider range of forms, functions, and features and to be viewed/read/consumed on an ever-expanding range of devices, all educational, political, commercial, or functional (how-to) texts will come to resemble presentations.

Even though speaking will always mean standing in front of a group however large and talking about some subject to them, presenting now includes forms that do not require the "presenter" to speak or to be present, if the presentation is created for online delivery, for the presentation. This is what Weissman (2009) calls a "virtual presentation," which he describes as a presentation that "combines the Internet and related electronic technologies to enable [a

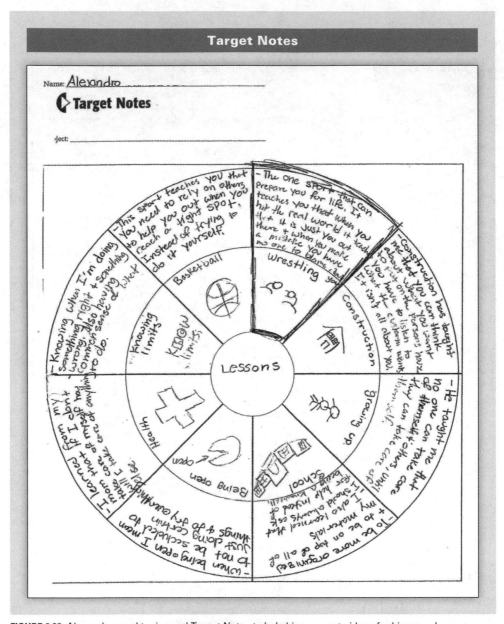

FIGURE 6.32 Alesandro used topics and Target Notes to help him generate ideas for his speech.

person] to present *and exchange* information and ideas with distant audiences without your physical presence" via software platforms such as Adobe® Connect™, or WebEx™ (215). In such cases, which we see all the time online, on television, or via our smartphones, the presentation can be viewed simultaneously by one or a million as the movie like presentation, with that smooth, familiar voice-over, plays for us in the private theater of our office computer, smart phone, or car.

Jerry Weissman, who has written several of the most influential books about presenting, observes that most presentation slides remain, even today, little more than electronic versions of the flipcharts of the past. This style of presentation suffers from what he calls the "presentation as document syndrome" (2009, xx) for we too often mistake the tool (presentation software) for the tale (story), which is where the power lies. As Weissman says, "*you* are the storyteller, not your slides" (2009, x).

One of the reasons I like the concept of FODP (Focus, Organization, Development, and Purpose) is that it applies equally to essays and paragraphs as much as it does to websites, presentations, and blogs (see page Figure 4.6 for more detailed description of FODP). What are the most common flaws, or complaints, about presentations? That they:

FIGURE 6.33 Two boys read and respond to each others' speeches to refine them prior to rehearsing and delivering them.

FIGURE 6.34 Jesus delivers his speech to the class.

- Undermine clarity by being too abstract; they are not *about* anything in particular and thus are not useful; they do not tell a coherent or meaningful story

- Lack concrete examples or specific evidence that can help people see and understand what you are saying

- Need (but rarely ever have) a compelling lead that establishes the speaker's own credibility and engages the audience

- Organize information without a specific end in mind using the best organizational patterns by which to achieve that end (see Figure 4.18 for an overview of these different organizational patterns)

- Overwhelm the audience by trying to say too much; it would be better to spend more time focusing on fewer ideas and examining these in depth

To avoid these common problems, Atkinson (2005) suggests we use the different views—Slide View, Notes View, and Normal View—of the presentation software itself to analyze the effectiveness of our presentation.

Abela (2008, 2010) does not dismiss the value or use of what he calls "Ballroom Style" presentations emphasized and popularized by Reynolds (2008, 2011) and Duarte (2008, 2010); however, he does make a compelling, research-based argument for an alternative, a style more appropriate for many situations when the presenter's goal is to inform and persuade, instead of to inspire and motivate, as with the Ballroom Style. He calls this the "Conference Room" approach. All these presentation masters are right; their books, however, do not fully capture the way presenting has evolved even in the few years since they wrote them. To address these gaps and give you a more detailed sense of the difference between the types of presentations, I created Figure 6.35.

Four Types of Presentations

Convention Hall	Conference Room	Café Table	Computer
Present in large room, to large audience, with full media complement and no handouts; there to inspire, instruct, and inform. Presenter must be compelling and charismatic. Similar to Steve Jobs when he addressed Apple users.	Present in small room to limited audience, with handout but no/few slides; there to facilitate, persuade, explain, help people act, decide. Presenter must be logical, credible, practical. Similar to sales meeting or board meeting.	Present in intimate setting, at small table, using tablet, laptop, and/or handouts; there to explain, persuade about product, service, or self. Presenter must be comfortable, confident. Similar to conversation or interview.	Present through video delivered online, on digital display (such as iPad or laptop), email attachment, or smartphone. All speaking done as voice-over delivered in conjunction with high-quality video production. Similar to informercial.
Meaningful	Useful	Useful	Useful/Meaningful
50–1000s	5–25	1–4	1 (or millions if online)
20–60 minutes	As long as necessary	20–120 minutes	5–15 minutes
Purpose is to inspire, challenge, motivate, unify, and instruct.	Purpose is to guide, persuade, explain; to help others act or decide.	Purpose is to explain, establish credibility, relationship; to persuade and inform.	Purpose is to inform, seduce, inspire, sell, or persuade; to get audience to call, contact.
Print materials are optional; if used, given after for review; do **not** print and distribute the slides; Handouts to complement slides.	Print materials are vital; used to stimulate discussion, direct discussion; any slides are to complement the printed documents.	Printed materials are optional but appropriate as presentation is more of a conversation. Slides may distract; use handouts to stimulate, or direct discussion.	Printed materials are only available as a download or link to a subsequent webpage to request more information about person, product, or service.
Uses story, words, images, and media (some data?) to appeal to emotions.	Uses story, evidence, charts, words (some media?) to appeal to logic.	Uses story, evidence, images, charts, words, and media to appeal to logic.	Uses story, evidence, images, charts, words, media to appeal to emotion and/or logic.
Interactive: it allows audience chance for Q and A (or electronic devices to respond to presenter).	Interactive via questions, interruptions, pauses for comments; more of a discussion.	Very interactive via questions, interruptions, pauses for comments; a conversation.	Not interactive (since has no live presenter); interactivity can come through buttons, links, other user features.
Use approximately 1 slide per minute of speaking.	Use as few slides as possible: 0–10 maximum.	Use as few slides as possible: 0–10 maximum.	Use approximately 1 slide per minute; it may appear more like a movie than series of slides.
Look is bold, colorful, visually WOW! but simple, minimalist.	Look is functional, no color, visually complex but clear; dense with data or details.	Look uses features of convention and conference style as appropriate.	Look is bold, colorful, visually WOW! but simple, minimalist; like a movie.
Uses 0–8 words, in large, stylish fonts that may complement an image.	Uses as many words as needed on handout in small, basic font with no image to add power or punch.	Uses as many words as needed on handout in small, basic font; may also include elements of convention style for some slides.	Uses 0–8 words, in large, stylish fonts that may complement an image; would be accompanied by an appropriate voice-over.
Representative applications include: PowerPoint, Keynote, or Prezi.	Representative applications include: PowerPoint, Google Presentation (or possibly Keynote).	Representative applications include: PowerPoint (or possibly Keynote).	Representative applications include: PowerPoint, Keynote, Prezi, Quicktime, or other video platforms
Organized as a story, nonlinear, with multiple themes.	Organized as a story, linear, one theme; may use chronological, hierarchical, and comparative structures.	Organized as a story, linear, one theme; may use chronological, hierarchical, and comparative structures.	Organized as a story, one or more themes; may use chronological, hierarchical, and comparative structures.
Tone is humorous, inspirational, passionate; spoken as a leader.	Tone is serious, objective, businesslike; spoken as problem solver.	Tone is serious but warm, objective but committed; spoken as problem solver.	Tone is seductive, practical, or humorous—whatever is right for audience, subject, or occasion.

To see model presentations, visit the following sites:

- www.slideshare.net/contest/worlds-best-presentation-contest-2009
- www.prezi.com/explore
- www.thersa.org
- www.garrreynolds.com/presentation
- www.duarte.com/work/
- www.poworltd.oom/_blog/Blogs

FIGURE 6.35 Four Types of Presentations

© 2013 by Jim Burke from *The English Teacher's Companion*, Fourth Edition. Portsmouth, NH: Heinemann.

Most presentations incorporate or otherwise depend on computers and presentation software. What is your experience with designing and giving presentations? Which programs do you know and use? Is this an area of strength or weakness for you? Explain.

The different presentations types sound a bit as though we were training students all to speak at conventions around the country. What do these different types of presentations look like in the classroom? The Convention Hall works well when students have a large, abstract idea to present such as the topic of power shown in Figure 6.40. Other possibilities might include presenting about subjects, such as evil or love, or a larger question: What does it take to be a survivor? I realize the Figure 6.35 says a Convention Hall presentation is for 50 to thousands of people; it is, ultimately—a style, a way of approaching a presentation that is most commonly used in that context. Students do their planning on notebooks as shown in Figure 6.36.

The Conference Room style of presentation would be more appropriate for discrete information that requires greater structure, more details and evidence, and more of an argument or explanation. One example of such a presentation would be to assign different critical theories to

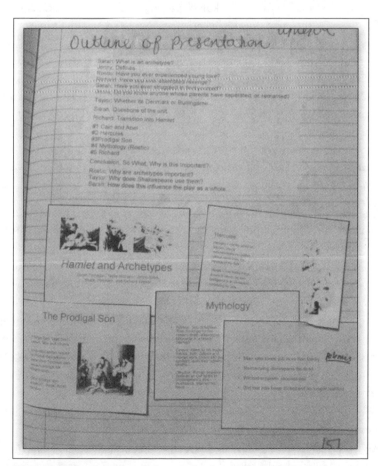

FIGURE 6.36 Sample outline of presentation from a notebook which shows a student preparing a presentation on a critical theory as it applies to *Hamlet*.

" THESE
PRESENTATION
FORMATS ARE ALSO
USEFUL AS A STEPPING-
STONE TOWARD THE
LARGER AUDIENCE
OF THE FULL CLASS,
A TRANSITION MANY
STUDENTS, ESPECIALLY
ENGLISH LEARNERS OR
THOSE WHO STRUGGLE
WITH PUBLIC
SPEAKING, NEED OUR
HELP TO MAKE. **"**

each group, making them responsible for a detailed presentation about their assigned theory that draws examples from the assigned text (e.g., *Hamlet*) as evidence.

The Café Table and Computer style presentations each have their place also. The Power Project mentioned later in this section was supposed to be delivered as a Convention Hall presentation; due to time constraints, we changed to a Café Table and Computer style presentation mode, which ended up working well. These presentation formats are also useful as a stepping-stone toward the larger audience of the full class, a transition many students, especially English learners or those who struggle with public speaking, need our help to make.

These examples raise the question of possible configurations for presentations. Speeches must be delivered by one person; presentations, however, are ideally suited for groups of up to six, depending on the situation and instructional goals. Certainly pairs are easy, often ideal, very efficient, and consistent with the collaborative nature of today's modern workplace. Another possibility would allow students the option to present in lieu of a paper or some other project. This freedom allows kids to play to their strengths when it suits your instructional goals. Of course, if you are teaching students how to give a certain type of presentation or to write a specific type of paper, all need to do that; however, if you are looking for ways to assess students' understanding of a novel, why *not* allow them to write a paper, make a presentation, produce a movie, or give an interpretive performance designed to show their understanding of a character or a theme?

Few activities have more ways they can go wrong than a presentation and the time these crises take is time we cannot afford to lose. When students give presentations, they *must* do the following *before* the period and day they are presenting:

- Make sure the version of the presentation software they used outside of class on another computer is compatible with the equivalent software on the computer you will use in the classroom

- Check that the file of their presentation is downloaded (unless they are copying it over via a flash drive) onto the class computer and opens to avoid relying on the Internet; also, ensure the program loads and works well

- Double-check all fonts and other features of their slides if they are presenting on a different computer than the one on which they created the slide set; also, be sure all video, audio and image links embedded into the slides are loaded and ready to work!

- Bring a backup of the presentation file on a separate hard drive or flash drive in case their computer fails

- Ensure that they have the power adaptor and LCD projector adaptor for their specific computer; *do not rely on the teacher* to have the same version

- Give the projector itself a trial run; if possible, check the number of lamp hours remaining on the bulb to avoid a crisis

- Copy your handouts, if you have any, at least a day in advance, but do not, however, distribute them until it is necessary; otherwise, students will look at them and ignore the presenter
- Evaluate presentations again for appropriate content
- Time it out! We have no time for the five-minute presentation that takes 25 minutes to give!

I would like to tell you I learned these things from books and studies done far from my class; sadly, no. I know them all from having made these mistakes myself or having students do the same, often when there was no time left! Of course, no matter how many times one checks the adaptor or the software, one cannot anticipate or prevent such disasters. On the first day of senior final presentations one year, for example, a girl passed out after the first slide of a presentation about crime that was not graphic but was too much for the girl. Within minutes, five kids had called 911, the desks were all pushed back, and the boy who asked for an extension on his presentation as I entered the classroom earlier was quietly giving thanks for such divine intervention as the principal ushered everyone out so the paramedics could tend to the fallen girl.

The sample shown in Figure 6.40 was done in a senior class as the culminating project for *1984*, which we read as a case study in power. Instead of jumping right into the computer lab to start designing slides on the screen, students generated ideas and took notes as they read, reminded periodically that these would serve as the basis for their final project. All books on presentations, when discussing the composing process, emphasize the importance of sitting down first with pencil and paper (some suggest sticky notes as a useful alternative) instead of turning on the computer or focusing on design. Figure 6.37 displays the assignment sheet for the storyboard template that turns into a presentation outline as shown in Figure 6.36. Also see Figure 6.38 for a blank storyboard template.

> **"I WOULD LIKE TO TELL YOU I LEARNED THESE THINGS FROM BOOKS AND STUDIES DONE FAR FROM MY CLASS; SADLY, NO. I KNOW THEM ALL FROM HAVING MADE THESE MISTAKES MYSELF OR HAVING STUDENTS DO THE SAME . . ."**

PAUSE & REFLECT Reflect on this section about presentations, some of which may be new to you. What new questions and ideas does it raise for you? What are the implications of those ideas to your classroom?

PERFORMANCES

All public speaking involves performance. Given the place of English within the arts, however, it is only appropriate to look for opportunities for performance in class when reading drama, poetry, literature, or great speeches. Such opportunities, while making the class more engaging for most students, offer more than just good intelligent fun: performance, if done well, increases comprehension and, in some, retention. Often it does the same for students' confidence, as my own experiences described at the beginning of this chapter show (see Figures 6.39 and 6.40).

Presentation: On Power for English 8CP

Mr. Burke

Overview: As we have read *1984* over the last few weeks, we have focused on the subject of power. It is, we all realize by now, a more complex subject—and a more personal one—than we perhaps understood at first. Another aspect of power we have not studied is speaking or, in this case, presenting. People with power use language and charisma to persuade us to do, think, believe, or feel certain things.

Objectives: This project has several objectives that amount to teaching you to:

- Generate clear and compelling ideas
- Convey the ideas using images and words
- Organize the ideas into slides
- Use the slides to complement your presentation
- Present the ideas in a clear and compelling way

Requirements: Each *team* must do the following, all of which will be submitted:

- Brainstorm ideas for topic, designs, content, visuals
- Create a storyboard (see Figure 6.38) using the model provided, sticky notes, or any other form you prefer but works in the same way
- Design a slideset of approximately 7 to 10 slides in PowerPoint, Keynote, Prezi (see prezi.com), or Google Presentation (in GoogleDocs) that follow the elements of effective presentations (see Peformances section)
- Write up notes, specific to each slide, that you *do not read* when you present
- Create a handout that sums up your key ideas; this is the audience "take away"
- Deliver the presentation on the appointed day using the slides
- Evaluate your own and others' presentations using the guidelines provided

Elements: Your presentation/slides should include the following:

- **Focus**: Subject + main idea (your point or opinion about the subject)
- **Organization**: Slides and content arranged to achieve an effect and purpose
- **Development**: Visuals and words, but *no more than seven words on a slide*
- **Purpose**: Your presentation should have a specific purpose; each slide should have one, and also one that is related to the primary purpose of the presentation
- **Design**: Slides are visually appealing and rhetorically effective: *no bells or whistles*

In addition, your presentation/slides should include:

- **Memorable Language**: When speaking, you should come up with phrases so smart, so witty, so insightful that people will want to tweet them to others
- **Figurative Speech**: Include a metaphor, simile, or analogy to make your subject more clear and compelling, but also more memorable
- **1984 Content:** Include examples and quotations from the novel
- **Other Content:** Present examples and quotations from other sources, including the world, your own experience, history, or your other classes

Recommended Resources: The following sites offer excellent examples of effective presentations/slides:

- www.microsoft.com/office/powerpoint-slidefest/do-and-dont.aspx
- www.slideshare.net/contest/worlds-best-presentation-contest-2009
- www.thersa.org/
- www.garrreynolds.com/Presentation/index.html

FIGURE 6.37 Presentation outline/assignment sheet

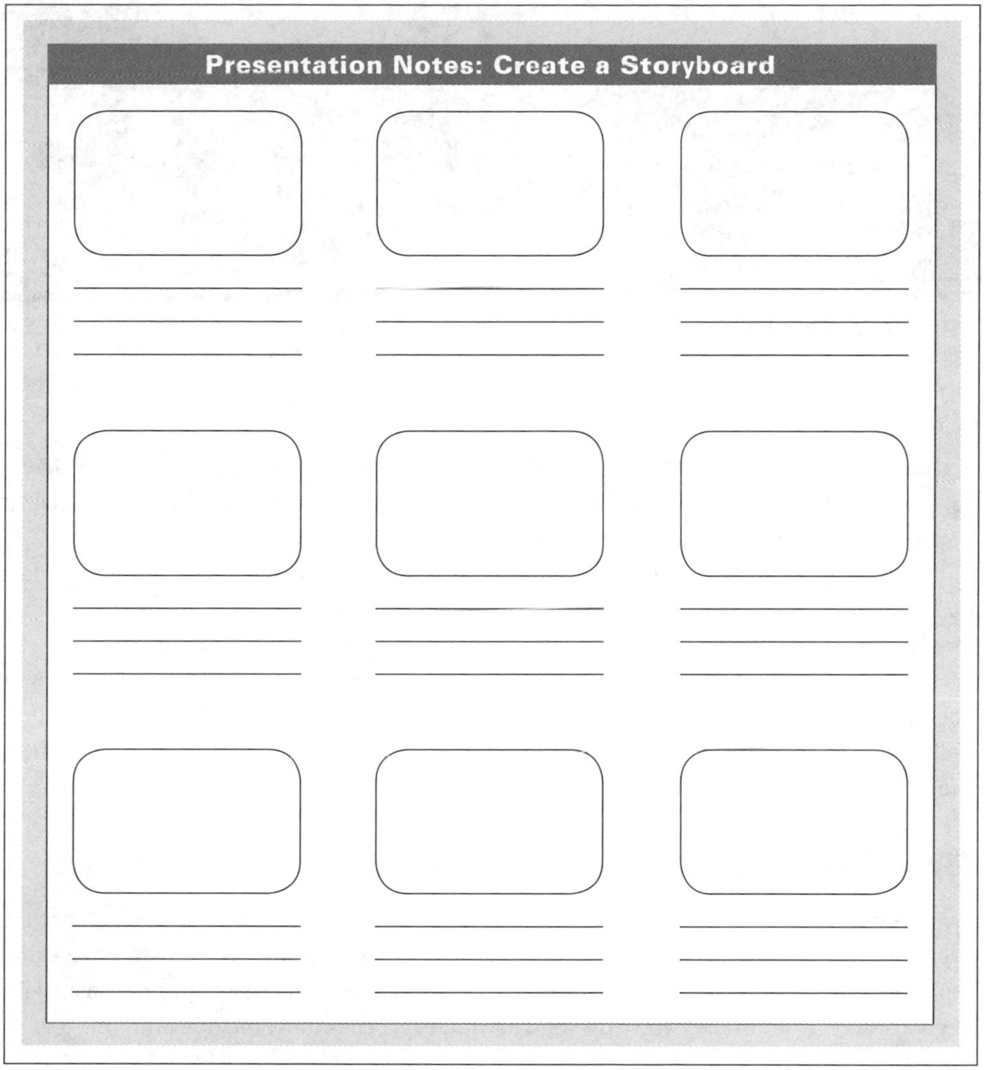

Presentation Notes: Create a Storyboard

FIGURE 6.38 Storyboard template (students must use this to begin the design process)

FIGURE 6.39 Kayvon and Patrick brainstorm and discuss their ideas for their presentation on power in *1984*.

FIGURE 6.40 Colin and Vincent fine-tune their great presentation before the Big Show begins.

FIGURE 6.41 Students presenting to peers during gallery

FIGURE 6.42 A group rehearses for performance of *Romeo and Juliet* on the steps outside my class.

It is not the responsibility of the English class to work to improve on performance outside of speaking or presenting; we have little time for that. Besides, that is what drama and speech classes are for: to *really* learn to perform and speak.

What we can do in our English classes, however, is to make room for the small performances that fit into our days, whether these are poems or passages, short stories or scenes from plays—all of which help bring students in and bring the texts alive if we can create the sort of atmosphere that allows such risks and rewards as performance invites (see Figures 6.41 and 6.42). A list of the different types of performance might include monologues, read alouds, impromptu enactments, and reader's theater. Some of these take less than a minute and others a full period or more depending on your goals and time available.

Final Thoughts: Telling the Story of Our Lives

If students are to succeed in their personal and professional and their public and their private lives, we must help them learn to speak not only before a class but also with others, often—and especially—those different from themselves. We must develop in them not just the basic skills of giving a speech but the knowledge of what such speeches must include and how people listen to and respond to them.

If we want students to write great life stories with their days, we must help them find their voices and the courage it sometimes requires to use the voices to tell their stories or the story of someone else. There is a moment in the movie *The King's Speech*, which tells the story of King George VI's struggles to overcome his stuttering, when he wants to give up and retreat into the false security of his silence; however, in that moment, he sees a newsreel of Hitler using his voice, his ability to inspire millions of people with speech, and realizes that he must learn to speak not for himself but for his country—perhaps even the world. He realizes that if he cannot communicate with people, including those within his own family, he will lose his country.

The stakes for us and our students may not be as dire as that, but the stakes are high, for our classes are filled with thousands, hundreds of thousands of students who have yet to discover or develop their voices. Ours is the enterprise of working with students to help them rise in the world, a process that depends on proper and powerful speech.

The goal, of course, is not to rid any of our students of the speech natural to their culture or personality, but rather to add to their languages the capacity and knowledge to speak in any circumstance to anyone about any subject for any personal or professional purpose. As Bailey (2007) stresses, all teachers now have to be "language teachers" (205) who teach the gateway academic language needed to succeed in school, during discussions or meetings, in interviews or presentations. Without that language and the ability to use it well, students are effectively barred from the larger culture of power they seek to claim as their own, while seeking still to maintain their own identities in the process (Delpit 2006, 24).

Recommended **Resources**

Print

- *Academic Conversations: Classroom Conversations: Classroom Talk That Fosters Critical Thinking and Content Understandings*, Jeff Zwiers and Marie Crawford (Stenhouse 2011).
- *Comprehension and Collaboration: Inquiry Circles in Action*, Stephanie Harvey and Harvey Daniels (Heinemann 2009).
- *Speaking Volumes: How to Get Students Discussing Books—And Much More*, Barry Gilmore (Heinemann 2006).
- *slide:ology: The Art and Science of Creating Great Presentations*, Nancy Duarte (O'Reilly 2008).

Online

- Toastmasters (www.toastmasters.org/)
- American Rhetoric (www.americanrhetoric.com/)
- TED Talks (www.ted.com/)
- Slideshare: (www.slideshare.net/)
- Prezi (http://prezi.com/)

CHAPTER SEVEN

Language Study

Vocabulary, Grammar, and Style

> You cannot enter any world for which you do not have the language.
> —Wittgenstein

Introduction: The Language of Learning, Literature, and Life

Although this whole book and, to a great extent, our work is made up of words, it seems best to begin by acknowledging that we are worried about language and declaring that *it matters* to us that people honor Coleridge's call to "use the best words in the best order," to achieve their intended effect. Moreover, when they read, we want our students to recognize that the writer chose that word, crafted that sentence, put those words in that order for a specific purpose. We can often feel, when talking to students about language, as though we are offering them a quivering bright green Jello mold filled with chunks of everything they loathe.

Spelling is not an obsession with me; it's the phrase "it doesn't matter" that troubles me— and those at the universities who warn incoming freshman; according to Conley (2003) that

> Grammar is the basis for good writing. Good writing demands that writers consistently use proper sentence structure . . . and understand [how] words . . . function within a sentence. It is also important to understand the specific ways correct grammar makes writing clearer and helps [students] communicate more effectively.(18)

Thus, the subject of this chapter is not mere "vocabulary" or "grammar" but the meaning and importance of these words, for "sentence craft and sentence appreciation are not trivial pursuits. They engage us in the stringent and salutary exploration of the linguistic resources out of which our lives and our very selves are made" (Fish 2011, 159).

In case this sounds too grandiose, consider that the Common Core Standards emphasize "'close reading' [which] confines initial study to the text itself, [asking] students to make sense of it by probing its words and structures for information and evidence" of the deeper meaning of the text and author's purpose in writing it (Gewertz 2011, 6). In this same analysis of close reading in the Common Core, Gewertz describes a teacher who developed sample lessons around the standards. These lessons asked students to examine the text for its meaning and structure, looking for the answers in the text itself, guided by questions such as "Wh[ich] words did [the author] use to characterize what happened next?" (6).

This is the sort of attention Francine Prose finds lacking in even the students who take her MFA writing seminars, those who traded close reading for political reading, guided by their own opinions with little regard for the words and what they actually mean. Prose responds to these deficits by challenging her students (and us) to read like writers by "lingering over every word, every phrase, every image, considering how it enhanced and contributed to the story as a whole" (2006, 11). Balancing his respect for the traditions of the past and those we are creating in the present, Christopher Johnson (2011) offers the following at the end of his introduction to the new emphasis on what he calls "microstyle":

> When I'm reading and writing, I'm hyperaware of the words and phrases I encounter and use—not in an "is it correct?" way, but in a "how does it work?" way. When I consider the fragments that make up normal verbal life, I see specimens of the diverse flora and fauna of our new verbal ecosystem. (31)

Johnson and Prose both capture the combined role that language plays in both reading and writing, which is often neglected in discussions of vocabulary, though a study by Fearn, Farnan, and Rodenberg demonstrated that vocabulary instruction during the writing process related to their writing task was effective (2003, 26). Let us then begin our inquiry into which elements of this "verbal ecosystem" we should teach and how we can do it best so that students have at their disposal all that our language offers those who master it.

> **"LET US THEN BEGIN OUR INQUIRY INTO WHICH ELEMENTS OF THIS 'VERBAL ECOSYSTEM' WE SHOULD TEACH AND HOW WE CAN DO IT BEST ..."**

What we are talking about—at the word, sentence, or whole-text level—is craft. Each word, each sentence is a thread in some larger text (from *texere*, meaning to weave) our students or an author is creating. Everything about craft challenges the way many are being asked to work. In his meditation on craft, Sennett (2008) writes:

> Pride in one's work lies at the heart of craftsmanship as the reward for skill and commitment. Craftsmen take pride most in skills that mature. This is why simple imitation is not a sustaining satisfaction; the skill has to evolve. The slowness of craft time serves as a source of satisfaction. . . . [Slow] craft time also enables the work of reflection and imagination—which the push for quick results cannot [do]. (294)

In addition to time, craft also demands a conscience—a sense that it matters how well things are done, made, written, or spoken. Some people dismiss such granular details about language as meaningless, perhaps because they do not know the rules or elements, and thus wish to avoid confronting their own knowledge gaps. No doubt years of reliance on spell-checkers, grammar checkers, and autocorrection functions within various applications or on cell phones have undermined those habits of mind that (we hope!) students developed in their earlier years under the guidance of their teachers.

What then is the aim of this chapter? To explore those elements of language—vocabulary, grammar, usage, and style—that students must master as readers, writers and speakers to develop in them not just a consciousness of these elements but a conscience about their correct and effective use.

What Students **Need to Know About and Be Able to Do** with Language

It is both discouraging and revealing that the entire first page of the Writing section of *Understanding University Success* (Conley 2003) focuses exclusively on correctness. Conley lays out here the standards for university-level work as described by the institutions and professors he interviewed for his study of what students must know in all disciplines to succeed in college. In the Reading section, vocabulary earns special attention as a crucial standard for comprehension: Successful students

> understand vocabulary and content, including subject-area terminology; connotative and denotative meanings; and idiomatic meanings, [and] exercise a variety of strategies to understand the origins and meanings of new words, including recognition of cognates and contextual clues. (22)

The remainder of this chapter focuses on language study in English language arts classes—that is, looking closely at vocabulary, grammar, and style, which includes rhetoric. These three domains are well represented in the Common Core Standards for language.

As a corollary to these standards, the questions asked on common assessments in various districts and states offer a relevant, if somewhat narrow, perspective on what the standards mean in the world as tested by districts and the state. Here are some representative question stems I collected along the way after looking at different district and state exams (although, admittedly, not yet aligned with the Common Core Standards):

- Which sentence in the first paragraph (from a passage students had to read first) is NOT consistent with the overall tone of this essay?
- Which words could BEST be added to the beginning of this sentence to make a smoother transition from the previous sentence?
- Which sentence in the story "Eleven" is a fragment?
- Which of the following words would be the best replacement for the word *have*?
- Which of the following words would be the best replacement for those words underlined in this passage?
- The author's use of the word *moved* in line 15 establishes a tone of . . .
- Which of the following answers best explains why the author used alliteration in line 13?
- The poet uses irony in the last stanza of the poem in order to . . .
- Why does the speaker repeat the phrase "we will not forget" throughout his speech?
- Which of the following does the speaker contrast in his speech?
- How does the writer's repeated use of the passive voice complement her purpose in this piece of writing?

Vocabulary: Teaching Words, Words, Words

When I first came to Burlingame High School, we had a professional development day to discuss the place of writing and portfolios in our English curriculum. As the day neared its end, the department chair, a nice woman who had taught at the school for many years, grew visibly disturbed when we seemed to have reached a consensus that we would begin having the kids keep writing portfolios. When someone asked her why she was so upset, she finally confessed that she spent so much time in her classes on vocabulary instruction that her students would have nothing to put in the portfolios.

With 51 minutes each day, I struggle as you must to fit it all in. As Don Graves used to say to me, "Teachers' classes are like five-pound bags into which everyone is always trying to stuff ten pounds of grain!" Various studies repeatedly show that vocabulary gets short shrift in the English classroom, where between reading, writing and assessing students' progress in those areas, vocabulary consistently loses out despite its central role in both reading and writing (National Governors Association 2010, 32; Beck, McKeown, and Kucan 2002; Feldman and Kinsella 2005).

Recognizing teachers' struggles, Graves begins his 2006 book, *The Vocabulary Book,* by stating that there are "three crucial facts about vocabulary . . . to keep in mind . . . when planning vocabulary instruction":

1. *The vocabulary learning task is enormous!* Estimates of vocabulary size vary greatly, but a reasonable estimate . . . [is that] books and other reading materials used by school children include [more than] 180,000 different words.

2. That there are far more words to be learned than we can possibly teach is not an argument that we should not teach any of them.

3. *There is increasing evidence that many children of poverty enter school with vocabularies much smaller than those of their middle class counterparts.* (3)

Despite these challenges, robust vocabulary instruction is paramount for our students since a strong vocabulary is a prerequisite for reading the complex texts described in the Common Core Standards and those texts students will read in college (Blachowicz, Fisher, Ogle, and Watts-Taffe 2006, 526).

❝With 51 minutes each day, I struggle as you must to fit it all in.❞

As many have noted, however, not all words are so important as to require that we teach them (Beck, McKeown, and Kucan 2002; Baumann and Kame'enui 2004; Graves 2006). In recent years, words have been sorted into several categories based on their frequency, "academic vocabulary" often (see Figure 7.1) being singled out as a priority for all, but especially English learners (Zwiers 2008; Fisher and Frey 2008; Bailey 2007; Marzano 2004). This trend has been accompanied by a tendency to generate its own vocabulary problems: Everyone seems to want to come up with their own terms for what Baumann and Graves conclude should be called "academic vocabulary" (2010, 9).

Adding to the discussion about these different types of words is the question of which words are so important that the teacher should take the necessary time to teach and assess students' knowledge of them. Beck, McKeown, and Kucan (2002, 2008) offer a three-tier model, which the Common Core frameworks use as the basis for their vocabulary standards:

- **Tier One words** are the words of everyday speech usually learned in the early grades, albeit not at the same rate by all children. They are not considered a challenge to the average native speaker, though English-language learners of any age will have to attend carefully to them. While Tier One words are important, they are not the focus [of instruction or the Common Core Standards].

Academic Vocabulary

These words come from commonly assigned textbooks, state exams, class assignments, and state standards documents.

1. abbreviate	61. concise	121. elements	181. integrate	241. plausible	301. series
2. abstract	62. conclude	122. emphasize	182. intent	242. plot	302. set
3. according	63. conclusion	123. employ	183. intention	243. point	303. setting
4. acronym	64. concrete	124. equal	184. interact	244. point of view	304. show
5. address	65. conditions	125. equivalent	185. intermittent	245. portray	305. signal
6. affect	66. conduct	126. essay	186. interpret	246. possible	306. significance
7. alter	67. confirm	127. essential	187. introduce	247. preclude	307. simile
8. always	68. consequence	128. establish	188. introduction	248. predict	308. skim
9. analogy	69. consider	129. estimate	189. invariably	249. prefix	309. solve
10. analysis	70. consist	130. evaluate	190. investigate	250. prepare	310. source
11. analyze	71. consistent	131. event	191. involve	251. presume	311. spatial
12. annotate	72. consistently	132. evidence	192. irony	252. preview	312. specific
13. anticipate	73. constant	133. exaggerate	193. irrelevant	253. previous	313. speculate
14. application	74. constitutes	134. examine	194. isolate	254. primary	314. stance
15. apply	75. consult	135. example	195. italics	255. prior	315. standard
16. approach	76. contend	136. excerpt	196. judge	256. probable	316. state
17. appropriate	77. context	137. exclude	197. key	257. procedure	317. statement
18. approximate	78. continuum	138. exercise	198. label	258. process	318. strategy
19. argue	79. contradict	139. exhibit	199. likely	259. produce	319. structure
20. argument	80. control	140. explain	200. list	260. profile	320. study
21. arrange	81. convert	141. explore	201. literal	261. project	321. style
22. articulate	82. convey	142. expository	202. locate	262. prompt	322. subject
23. aspects	83. copy	143. extract	203. logical	263. proofread	323. subjective
24. assemble	84. correlate	144. fact	204. main	264. property	324. subsequent
25. assert	85. correspond	145. factor	205. margin	265. propose	325. substitute
26. assess	86. credible	146. feature	206. mean	266. prose	326. succinct
27. associate	87. credit	147. figurative	207. measure	267. prove	327. suggest
28. assume	88. criteria	148. figure	208. metaphor	268. purpose	328. sum
29. assumption	89. critique	149. focus	209. method	269. quotation	329. summarize
30. audience	90. crucial	150. footer	210. model	270. quote	330. summary
31. authentic	91. cumulative	151. foreshadow	211. modify	271. rank	331. support
32. background	92. debate	152. form	212. monitor	272. rare	332. survey
33. body	93. deduce	153. format	213. motivation	273. rarely	333. symbolize
34. brainstorm	94. defend	154. former	214. narrative	274. reaction	334. synonym
35. brief	95. define	155. formulate	215. narrator	275. recall	335. synthesize
36. calculate	96. demand	156. fragment	216. never	276. reduce	336. table
37. caption	97. demonstrate	157. frame	217. notation	277. refer	337. technique
38. category	98. depict	158. frequently	218. note	278. reflect	338. term
39. cause	99. derive	159. general	219. notice	279. regular	339. test
40. character	100. describe	160. genre	220. objective	280. relate	340. theme
41. characteristic	101. detail	161. graph	221. observe	281. relationship	341. thesis
42. characterize	102. detect	162. graphic	222. occur	282. relevant	342. timeline
43. chart	103. determine	163. header	223. opinion	283. rephrase	343. tone
44. chronology	104. develop	164. heading	224. oppose	284. report	344. topic
45. citation	105. devise	165. highlight	225. optional	285. represent	345. trace
46. cite	106. diction	166. hypothesize	226. order	286. request	346. trait
47. claim	107. differentiate	167. identify	227. organize	287. require	347. transition
48. clarify	108. dimension	168. illustrate	228. origins	288. requisite	348. translate
49. class	109. diminish	169. imitate	229. outline	289. respond	349. typically
50. clue	110. direct	170. imply	230. pace	290. responsible	350. unique
51. code	111. discipline	171. inclined	231. paraphrase	291. restate	351. utilize
52. coherent	112. discover	172. include	232. participation	292. results	352. valid
53. common	113. discriminate	173. incorporate	233. passage	293. reveal	353. variation
54. compare	114. discuss	174. indicate	234. pattern	294. review	354. vary
55. compile	115. distinguish	175. indirect	235. perform	295. revise	355. verify
56. complement	116. domain	176. infer	236. perspective	296. root	356. viewpoint
57. complete	117. draft	177. influence	237. persuade	297. rule	357. voice
58. compose	118. draw	178. inform	238. place	298. scan	
59. composition	119. edit	179. inquire	239. plagiarism	299. score	
60. conceive	120. effect	180. instructions	240. plan	300. sequence	

FIGURE 7.1 Academic vocabulary word list

- **Tier Two words** (what the Standards refer to as *general academic words*) are far more likely to appear in written texts than in speech. They appear in all sorts of texts: informational texts (words such as *relative, vary, formulate, specificity,* and *accumulate*), technical texts (*calibrate, itemize, periphery*), and literary texts (*misfortune, dignified, faltered, unabashedly*). Tier Two words represent subtle or precise ways to say relatively simple things—*saunter* instead of *walk*, for example. Because Tier Two words are found across many types of texts, they are highly generalizable.

- **Tier Three words** (what the Standards refer to as *domain-specific* words) are specific to a domain or field of study (*lava, carbretor, legislator, circumference, aorta*) and key to understanding a new concept within a text. Because of their specificity and close ties to content knowledge, Tier Three words are far more common in informational texts than in literature. Recognized as new and "hard" words for most readers (particularly student readers), they are often explicitly defined by the author of a text, repeatedly used, and otherwise heavily scaffolded (e.g., made part of a glossary). (Common Core State Standards, Appendix A 2010, 33)

Feldman and Kinsella (2005), who focus on the needs of English learners, offer a useful alternative to the three-tier model for choosing which words to teach:

- Choose "big idea" words that name or relate to the central concepts addressed in the passage (e.g., *democracy, independence, fossil fuels, ecology*).

- Choose high-use, widely applicable "academic tool kit" words that students are likely to encounter in diverse materials across subject areas and grade levels (e.g., *aspect, compare, similar, subsequently*).

- Choose high-use "disciplinary tool kit" words that are relevant to your subject area and that you consider vital for students to master at this age and proficiency level (e.g., *metaphor, policy, economic, application, species*).

- Choose "polysemous" (multiple meaning) words that have a new academic meaning in reading in addition to a more general, familiar meaning (e.g., *wave* as in "wave of immigrants" vs. a greeting or ocean wave).

- Especially when dealing with narrative texts, identify additional academic words (not included in the reading selection) that students will need to know in order to engage in academic discourse about the central characters, issues, and themes. (10)

Once you have chosen the "target words" (Coyne, Simmons, and Kame'enui 2004, 41), it is often helpful to know how familiar students are with these words. Several methods for evaluating students' word knowledge prior to studying the words have been developed over time. Some suggest levels of understanding; typically, Level One on such a model would be "have not seen or heard this word" and Level Four would be something akin to "Know it and can use it correctly." Beck, McKeown, and Kucan suggest word knowledge be evaluated on a continuum from "no knowledge" of a given word to a "rich contextualized knowledge of the word's meaning, its relationship to other words, and its extension to metaphorical uses, such as understanding what someone is doing when they are *devouring* a book" (2002, 10).

While their continuum offers more insight than mine, I need something I can give kids on the fly; get a quick read on where they are; and, using that information to adjust my plans, move into the unit—get to the teaching. To this end, I use a scale that can be adjusted for quick use in class by a show of hands:

0 = Never heard or seen it; I have no idea what it means.

1 = Have seen or heard it, but have no sense of what it means.

2 = Know it but cannot explain or use it.

3 = Know it and understand it when I see it; not sure how to use it in writing.

4 = Know it and can use it with confidence.

Principles and Practices for Effective Vocabulary Instruction

Graves (2006) identifies four components of an effective vocabulary program, which others (Baumann and Kame'enui 2004) have adopted or endorsed based on their own studies:

1. Provide rich and varied language experiences
2. Teach individual words
3. Teach word-learning strategies
4. Foster word consciousness (6)

The remainder of this section will examine each of these components in some detail, offering samples of what each of these elements looks like in the classroom. The goal of vocabulary instruction should be a systematic, comprehensive, and integrated program of words chosen and taught within the context of a unit or a text that students are motivated to read. Under such circumstances, they then are more likely to view vocabulary as a means to a desired end. With that in mind, let us look more closely at what it is we can *do* as teachers to improve our game in this area of the English curriculum.

1. PROVIDE RICH AND VARIED LANGUAGE EXPERIENCES

What does it mean to provide such experiences to improve students' vocabulary and their performance in school? In short, it means having students read a whole bunch of books and other texts (Tier Two titles) that students can manage, with some effort, to read. It means the room is saturated with language, reading, words read silently *and* aloud, seen and heard, in some rare cases even tasted or smelled! Representative activities as part of such a rich environment include:

- Explore a word or related set of words that apply to readings for the period, week, or course of a unit. For example, the word *border*, which is the subject of a collection of poems in our anthology, allows for a rich discussion of language through consideration of synonyms (from visualthesaurus.com) and images of different borders, as well as the many different definitions and connotations that come up when discussing this word.
- Provide students with one or more texts that explore a word or set of words related to a particular subject of interest to the class. When reading *Crime and Punishment*, for example, my students read three op-eds examining the notion of redemption in the case of Tookie Williams, one of the founders of the Crips gang. Two of the articles are written by

the same reporter at the *San Francisco Chronicle* who argues that he is a saint (for what he has done since) in one, and that he is a monster (for what he did before) in the other. Williams himself wrote the third article in response to the reporter's. All three articles, in conjunction with the part of *Crime and Punishment* we are reading, offer a rich exploration of the idea of redemption and the language associated with it.

- Tell students in literature circles that each night someone must look for key or interesting words in the assigned reading, then bring these words up the next day to discuss, having looked into the word's meaning(s) and history prior to class.

- Ask students to go through a paper they are writing and find all the *to be* verbs (*is, was, were, am, are, be, been, being*) and then replace them with more active, precise, or nuanced verbs.

- Read aloud to your students—poetry, fiction, great primary source documents, speeches—no matter what class you teach. My AP Literature students often note that they understand the poems better when they hear how I pronounce and speak the word, showing through my intonation where emphasis and meaning lies.

- Bring in words (advertisements, headlines, campaign materials, magazine covers, products, parking tickets, job applications—anything with meaningful language!) to show students how they are used or how you use them in certain circumstances. I often bring in examples of letters I write to officials, agencies, businesses or applications and ads I see.

- Ask students to engage in close reading of complex texts. When Claudius, for example, gives his inaugural speech after marrying Gertrude and "though [the memory of] his dear brother's death . . . be green" (1.2.2–3), I ask students to read through the speech for any word(s) that are associated with two (e.g., *pair, both, we, our*, and many more), then examine the implications of the use of such words in this context.

- Keep a dictionary handy: I have one I pass to a student during discussions, asking them to look up some word that is central to our discussion. I also have a good dictionary on my class computer, which is right there to consult for etymologies, synonyms, and antonyms. Note, however, as Marzano (2004) and Feldman and Kinsella (2005) point out, that many dictionaries are at best vague and for those still learning English downright confusing.

2. TEACH INDIVIDUAL WORDS

Graves (2006) lists several benefits for teaching specific words to students. For one, it lightens the load of the estimated 50,000 words that students need to be able to read by the end of high school. By teaching students individual words, teachers also expand the vocabulary students have on hand to read, write, or talk about the subjects they study. To this end, readers also gain a boost in reading comprehension through the growth in their word bank. One other benefit, which matters more than it might appear, is the extent to which our own knowledge of and enthusiasm for language enhances our own credibility when we say that words matter (59). Here are some ways to reach these ends:

- Introduce, review, and require students to use key terms over time as part of a unit or the general study of your class. These words might be domain-specific academic vocabulary such as literary terms students learn, study, and use when reading, writing and talking about literature. The word *hubris*, for example, seems to return regularly throughout the course of my senior English class, so I spend time developing their understanding of that when we look at Sophocles' plays early in the year so they have a foundation to build on as we use the word.

- Examine individual words in the context of an array of words with similar but different meanings. When trying to teach students the meaning of a given word (*credible*), place it on a continuum with other words to either side that express the more complete range of that idea, discussing with students where one term (*trustworthy*) ends and another (*feasible*) begins.

- Identify prerequisite words you must teach prior to having students read or write about a topic. Prior to having students write an analytical paragraph about data from online surveys they conducted, for example, we spent time defining, discussing, and using *reliability/reliable*, *credible/credibility*, and *valid/validity*.

- Provide robust direct instruction of essential words. Feldman and Kinsella (2005) offer the following steps in such a process, which is especially effective for English learners:

  1. *Pronounce the word:* After you pronounce it correctly for the class so they can hear it spoken, have students say it as a class several times, even breaking it down to emphasize syllables if it is a longer, more unusual word.

  2. Explain what the word means in language that is familiar to the students, providing when possible synonyms or familiar phrases to link this new word to their prior knowledge.

  3. Provide several examples of the new term to show how it is used in a sentence in different contexts so they grasp the wider application of the word. It is a good idea to offer sentence frames [that] require the students to use the target word to complete the sentence (e.g., if teaching the word *austere*, the teacher might say to the class, "Like a monk, the father in the poem lived an _____ life or a life of _____.").

  4. Elaborate on the words and their meaning by having students generate their own additional examples and visual representations of the words.

  5. Assess their understanding throughout the instructional process, using informal means to check for understanding as evidenced through correct use of the words taught. Feldman and Kinsella encourage teachers to "go beyond simple memorization or matching tasks and require students to demonstrate some deeper level of thinking and understanding (6).

- Provide deliberate, sustained vocabulary instruction as a *process* by following these steps, which Marzano (2009) says show a strong effect on learning and remembering the words or terms:

  1. Provide a description, explanation, or example of the new term.

  2. Ask students to restate the description, explanation, or example in their own words.

  3. Ask students to construct a picture, pictograph, or symbolic representation of the term.

  4. Engage students periodically [throughout the process] in activities that help them add to their knowledge of the terms in their vocabulary notebooks.

  5. Periodically ask students to discuss the terms with one another.

  6. Involve students periodically in games that enable them to play with terms. (84)

- Use intensive vocabulary instruction to engage students with the greatest needs and their peers at the other levels within your classes. Morgan Hallabrin, who teaches open-enrollment AP Literature and "Intensive English" classes for incoming freshman reading more than three grade levels below ninth grade, developed the following process for teaching what she calls "major concept words" in her classes:

  1. Introduce the word in the context of the unit, assignment, or text you are about to teach. Her example to me was *hubris* as an overarching idea for a mythology unit in her Intensive English class as part of a larger background knowledge sequence leading up to reading the version of *The Odyssey* in the freshman textbook.

  2. Provide sample sentences for students to see, read, hear, and speak as a group.

  3. Define the word collaboratively, using the dictionary together to make sense of the word, its meaning(s), its history.

  4. Discuss how the word changes through tense and use (as a noun, verb, adjective—if more than one of these apply).

  5. Analyze the word's characteristics, breaking it down and coming up with some visual way to represent the word or concept.

  6. Offer examples and nonexamples of the word's correct use in different contexts and in relation to the unit on mythology.

  7. Ask students to then generate three sentences of their own using the word in different ways and contexts.

  8. Write sentences using sentence starters to help students use the words in more complex, sophisticated ways as part of their study.

As with all intensive vocabulary instruction, Morgan's approach takes time, roughly 30 to 40 minutes for such a sequence for a major concept word. Yet it reflects the characteristics of effective direct vocabulary instruction described by Marzano (2004, 30), as Morgan's regular use of silent reading also embodies other elements of effective vocabulary instruction (Marzano 2004, 42). Both Morgan, in her classroom, and Marzano, through his research into "classrooms that work," recognize the often absurd constraints of time that teachers face given all that they must teach. Marzano and teachers like Morgan show, however, that such vocabulary instruction is possible and that it works.

3. Teach word-learning strategies

As students wade deeper into the waters of our language, they inevitably encounter words they do not know but must learn to make sense of if they are to understand what they read and use those words when they speak and/or write. They must become strategic readers, able to crack the code of the language that resists their attempts to understand it. To do this, they must acquire the ability to use a range of tools and techniques, which I discuss next. These strategies are not, however, universally applicable or always effective. Beck, McKeown,

> **"** As students wade deeper into the waters of our language, they inevitably encounter words they do not know but must learn to make sense of if they are to understand what they read and use those words when they speak and/or write. **"**

and Kucan (2002) identify, for example, four distinct types of context, only two of which offer help; the other two consistently lead to misreadings or at least confusion.

One of these problematic contexts, which they call "misdirective," tends to suggest almost the opposite of what the context might appear to imply a given words means. Consider this sentence as an example: "Will, who always obeyed his parents and made every effort to show them respect, appeared *indifferent* to all that his mother said." The word *indifferent*, preceded as it is by the words *obeyed* and *respect*, would make it difficult for the reader who does not know *indifferent* to conclude that it certainly was not a form of obedience or respect.

The other type of context that trips readers up, according to Beck, McKeown, and Kucan, is "nondirective," which simply offers no help, as in this example: "The first thing one noticed about Frances was her *inscrutability*." Here, the reader finds no hooks to hang a prediction on, nothing to give them a foot up into the meaning of the italicized word. Finally, two other contexts—general and directive—offer the attentive, strategic reader assistance, the first by offering some minimal information, the second by directing the reader to the word's meaning through evident, useful clues (2002, 4). These authors suggest using the strategies in the following subsections.

Model for Students

Use models to show how to identify and use context clues. I like Janet Allen's description (1999) of how she learned to approach this strategy as a teacher:

> Talking through the process (thinking aloud) gives students the opportunity to hold the teacher's thought processes up as a mirror for their own thinking. . . . When I talked with students about context, the only reference point I ever used was the surrounding text of the sentence. As I have worked through my understanding of context, I now see it in a much larger sense. Contextual clues come in two varieties: semantic/syntactic and typographic. Semantic and syntactic clues (knowledge of words and knowledge of structure) help readers predict words in several ways. Knowing that a larger piece of text is discussing cause and effect helps readers anticipate cue words like motivation, impetus, or consequence. If an essay is designed to show sequence, we might anticipate words like chronologically. . . . Teachers have the opportunity to show students not only how semantic and syntactic cues help readers, but also how typographic cues such as pictures, graphs, charts, glossaries, and footnotes aid readers in understanding new words. (25)

Use Images

Images will *show* them what the words mean. So many words refer to objects, places, or other subjects that are foreign to students, especially those who have not had the experience of traveling beyond their local environment. Image search functions, such as Google Images, provide us access to a visual database I could not imagine when I began teaching in the 1980s. So when I am teaching a novel like *Bless Me, Ultima*, I go into Google and search for terms—"dust devil," "adobe houses," "golden carp"—to show my students. Looking these up in a dictionary would not help students because these are visual terms meant to evoke imagery in the reader's mind. I then project these on the screen and we discuss them. One warning, however: Do *not* search for such terms in real time in front of your students. You would be shocked to see what comes up when searching for innocent words like *golden carp* or *trestle bridge*! This visual strategy seems particularly helpful when it comes to references to places, objects, or people from a region or era with which students are unfamiliar. No doubt, it would also help English learners who often have the concept but not the image or the words for it.

Teach Students How to Use Word Parts

This is a way for them to understand unknown words. "Word parts" include prefixes and suffixes, word roots and etymologies. Even though research raises questions as to the effectiveness of this as a dominant element of any vocabulary program, Graves emphasizes spending more time on fewer parts for deeper instruction to increase retention and understanding (2006, 103). Roots and etymologies differ from prefixes; these can be taught in groups or "families" to give students more systematic approach to attacking unfamiliar words (Blachowicz and Fisher 2002, 196).

Create Semantic or Concept Maps

These will help students see and build connections between words and ideas. Blachowicz and Fisher (2002) distinguish between "brainstorming maps," which get students to think about the extent of a new important concept. Preparing to read an article about World War I, for example, the teacher would write "WWI" in the center and then help the students generate subcategories—participants, causes, weaponry, and so on. Some go so far as to fill a whole wall with such maps, having students add to them as the class reads the assigned texts. "Semantic maps" resemble brainstorms but instead of categories, these maps focus on the relationships between words. Blachowicz and Fisher (2002) explain:

> [T]he difference between a semantic map and a brainstorming map, for us, is that in the former the teacher determines the major vocabulary terms and concepts that will appear, while the students generate examples. . . . While a semantic map addresses the relationships between words, it allows students to generate new information based on their reading and learning. In this way, it expands their understanding of central concepts. (98).

They suggest the following steps when developing a semantic map (see Figure 7.2):

1. The teacher selects a keyword and target words.
2. The keyword is written at the center of the map; the target words are listed at the side.
3. Students generate words related to the keyword and target words.

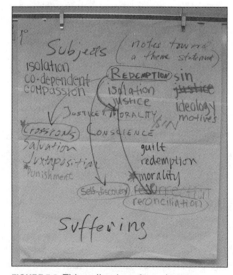

FIGURE 7.2 This collection of words are part of an exploration of the notion of redemption. Note how words are clustered to highlight the connections between them.

4. Relationships between the keyword, target words, and student words are discussed.

5. The map is constructed (or copies of an incomplete map are handed out for completion).

6. The students add to the map or maps as they read or work on the topic. (Blachowicz and Fisher 2002, 98)

Use the Vocabulary Self-Collection Strategy (VSS)

Require students to use the VSS. This strategy (Marzano 2004; Blachowicz and Fisher 2002; Ruddell and Shearer 2002), which asks students to collect their own vocabulary words as they find them, "provides high personal motivation . . . by emphasizing children's selection of personal important words from text" (Ruddell and Unrau 2004, 1493). The premise is that students "learn new words not by hearing them explained with other new words, but rather from ongoing and extended transactions with the words, their peers, and their teacher within the context of life and classroom experience" (354)—a premise borne out in the study these authors conducted with at-risk middle school students. Ruddell and Shearer outlined the Vocabulary Self-Collection Strategy used in their study:

1. Each student selected one word each week on Mondays from any source so long as they thought it was worth studying.

2. They nominated their words for the class list, during the process of which the students explained where they found their word, what they thought it meant, and why they thought it should be added to the list. The teacher nominated a word, too, following the same steps.

3. The class decided on the final words for that week, then defined them, refining the definitions through class discussion and consulting additional reference sources as needed.

4. Students recorded the words and the finalized definitions in their vocabulary journals.

5. Students studied the words throughout the week, discussing them, creating semantic maps, doing semantic feature analysis, and other interactive activities.

6. They took a test at the end of the week that assessed their ability to spell, explain, and write meaningfully about each word.

7. The class reviewed the words every three weeks, after which students were tested on five words randomly selected from the list. (355)

> **❝** SUCH AWARENESS COMES FROM PLAY AND PRACTICE, USE AND INCLUSION OF WORDS, PHRASES, AND LANGUAGE THAT EXPANDS STUDENTS' GENERAL SENSITIVITY TO SUCH WORDS. **❞**

4. FOSTER WORD CONSCIOUSNESS

As Scott and Nagy define it, word consciousness "refers to the knowledge and dispositions necessary for students to learn, appreciate, and effectively use words. Word consciousness involves several types of metalinguistic awareness, including sensitivity to word parts and word order" (Scott and Nagy 2004, 201). Such awareness comes from play and practice, use and inclusion of words, phrases, and language that expands students' general sensitivity to such words. Johnson, Johnson, and Schlichting (2004) list eight distinct categories of logology (word play):

1. *Onomastics:* nicknames, place names, business names, and more specialized types such as nicknames and pseudonyms.

2. *Expressions:* idiomatic expressions, proverbs, slang, catch phrases, clichés, and slogans.

3. *Figures of speech:* similes, metaphors, hyperbole, euphemisms, and oxymorons.

4. *Word associations:* synonyms, antonyms, collocations, coordinates, superordinates-subordinates.

5. *Word formations:* affixes, compounds, acronyms, initialisms, portmanteaus, neologisms.

6. *Word manipulations:* anagrams, palindromes, rebuses.

7. *Word games:* alphabetic, alliterations, rhymes, riddles, puns, tongue twisters.

8. *Ambiguities:* ambiguous words, phrases, and sentences. (181)

To these categories I would add one other approach that I have found effective in engaging and improving students' word consciousness. *Translations* offer compelling opportunities to examine the shades of meaning for words and phrases (Larochelle 2011, 61). To do this create a parallel version of several different translations of a specific passage from works we commonly teach—*The Odyssey, The Stranger, Crime and Punishment,* or the plays of Sophocles—and look at the words used to evoke the character's actions, tone, or persona. A variation on this would be to display a list of words (or provide a handout) that might be used in a specified place in a sentence and have students try them out, choosing the one they think is most effective and explaining why. (See Figure 7.1.) A more sophisticated alternative would be to have students themselves generate the words and then analyze the effectiveness of the different words. Also see the figurative language tool in Figure 7.3.

What this fourth category comes down to is to celebrate and have great fun with language in your class as often as possible. When you see bloopers on signs or funny signs (e.g., Slow Village Ahead. . . . When Flashing Stop A Head . . . Wolf Crossing Slow), bring them into your class and laugh together. Make room for puns and double entendres, as well as for your own awe for the beauty of a line or a word. But also bring into your class the language of politics, language that often shows us, for good or ill, how words can be used to affect the way people think, feel—and act. Frank Luntz, one of the most influential masters of words for political purposes, crafted phrases such as "Contract with America" and the "death tax" (2007, 149). Luntz illustrates the power of words to illicit a response when he describes his "dial sessions," which use dials as

the research equivalent of the EKG that measures a combination of emotional and intellectual responses and gets inside each [focus group] participant's psyche, isolating his or her emotional reaction to every word, phrase, and visual. Participants hold small wireless devices in their hands . . . [and turn] a computerized numerical display that range from 0 to 100 . . . on a second-by-second basis on their immediate, visceral, personal reactions [to words they see or hear people using]. (78)

Name: _____

Directions   Speakers often use figurative language to add both style and power to their words. As you read the assigned speech, jot down *five* different lines of powerful figurative speech (see example below). Underline the actual figurative speech in the quotation. Following my example, explain what the speaker **means** and offer some evidence as to why you think that is what he means. When you finish, use your notes to **write a paragraph** about the speech, focusing on how and why he uses figurative language.

Literal: What He Says	Figurative: What He Means	Rationale: Why You Think This
Ex: "[The Emancipation Proclamation] <u>came as a joyous daybreak to end the long night of their captivity.</u>"	Ex: He means that the Emancipation Proclamation was like the light at the end of the tunnel. The slaves suffered with no hope it seemed of ever being free. It is like the door opening and bringing in light to someone in solitary confinement.	Because the Emancipation Proclamation freed all the slaves. This news saved the slaves by bringing joy and hope into their lives the way light comes into the darkness and helps us find our way. When we see the "light at the end of the tunnel" we know we will make it. Until that news came they were captive, slaves, property. The E.P. set them free, restored their humanity.
1.		
2.		
3.		
4.		
5.		

Please use these notes to help you write a paragraph on the back (or a separate sheet of paper).

FIGURE 7.3 Figurative Language close reading handout. Use such tools to direct their attention; add an example and discuss or model it to be sure they develop confidence that they can do this.

Let me sum up this section on vocabulary instruction with Marzano's succinct list of the "characteristics of effective direct vocabulary instruction":

1. Effective vocabulary instruction does not rely on definitions.
2. Students must represent their knowledge of words in linguistic and nonlinguistic ways.
3. Effective vocabulary instruction involves the gradual shaping of word meanings through multiple exposures.
4. Teaching word parts enhances students' understanding of terms.
5. Different types of words require different types of instruction.
6. Students should discuss the terms they are learning.
7. Students should play with words. (2004, 70)

Grammar, Style, **and** Rhetoric

People *judge* us by how we use language when we speak and write. We need only slip up once— all it takes is a wrong preposition, a misplaced apostrophe—around a "grammar ranter," and the verdict is in: They assume we are ignorant and immoral as they simultaneously validate their own belief that they are superior in these areas (Dunn and Lindbloom 2011). As Shaughnessy (1979) observes, "when a writer breaks the rules of word order that govern the English sentence, he usually disturbs the reader at a deep level, forcing him to re-cast mentally the deviant sentence before he can proceed to the next one" (90). She goes on to add that "even slight departures from the code [of correct writing] cost the writer something. . . . [since] a person who does not control the dominant code of literacy in a society that generates more writing than any society in history is likely to be pitched against more obstacles than are apparent to those who have already mastered that code" (13). Lindemann dismisses those who show such "linguistic intolerance," who see the offenders as "corrupting the English language" as "ethnocentric" (2001, 69), a charge Delpit (2006) and Gilyard (1991) echo in their observations about language and "codes of power."

It is these students Shaughnessy (1979) speaks of when describing the "true outsiders," who attended the same schools as their peers but

> were nonetheless strangers in academia, unacquainted with the rules and rituals of [academic] life, unprepared for the sorts of tasks their teachers were about to assign them. Most of [these students] had grown up in one of New York's ethnic or racial enclaves [where they spoke] languages or dialects at home and never successfully reconciled the worlds of home and school, a fact which by now had worked its way deep into their feelings about school and about themselves as students. (3)

Here we see what our discussion of grammar will emphasize throughout: grammar and our language use are inextricably connected—through writing, reading, and speaking—to our own sense of competency and our general identity. Lacking the language structures needed to express sufficiently complex ideas or do so correctly, students withhold themselves from the academic enterprise, keeping to the margins or not showing up at all to avoid being humiliated. The importance and implication of this reluctance to engage, to join the conversation become all the more urgent given the call to enroll and encourage more underrepresented students in advanced classes.

If, on the other hand, we teach students *how* to "enter the conversation" (Graff, Birkenstein, and Durst 2010, 141), as writers, speakers, or readers, they will feel able to engage in the exchange of ideas taking place in class, online, on the page, and in their heads as they attempt to "read for the conversation [which] is more rigorous and demanding than reading for what one author says" (147). Still not sure how this relates to the study of grammar? Consider these comments from Graff, Birkenstein, and Durst in which they reflect on their own emerging understanding of what close reading and academic discussion demands in a college freshman composition class:

- "[E]ntering the class discussion] requires the same sorts of disciplined moves and practices used in many writing situations, particularly that of identifying to what and to whom you are responding" (141).

- "[Students] need to make it clear to listeners that they [are changing the direction of the conversation]" by using "metacommentary to highlight [a] key point so that listeners can readily grasp it" (144) and follow them as they shift the discussion's focus.

- "We eventually realized that the move from reading for the author's argument in isolation to reading for how the author's argument is in conversation with the arguments of others [in a given field] helps readers become active, critical readers rather than passive recipients of knowledge. On some level, reading for the conversation is more rigorous and demanding than reading for what one author says" (147).

Graff, Birkenstein, and Durst (2010) provide several examples of such close reading. Here is one that is a useful example of how close attention to the language makes it important to include reading and speaking in the discussion of grammar, style, and rhetoric, and vocabulary:

> If you read the passage this way, however, you would be mistaken. Draut [the author] is not questioning whether a college degree has become "the ticket to middle-class security," but whether most Americans can obtain that ticket, whether college is within the financial reach of most Americans. You may have been thrown off by the "but" following the statement that college has become a prerequisite for middle-class security. However, unlike the "though" in Zinczenko's opening, this "but" does not signal that Draut will be disagreeing with the view she has just summarized, a view that in face she takes as a given. (150)

PAUSE & REFLECT What are your thoughts about and experience with such social judgments based on one's language as they speak or write it? Visit the blogs Unnecessary Quotations, Apostrophe Abuse, or Grammar Vandal to test your own tolerance for such errors—or just for the fun the sites offer.

If we are to make room for such close study of language in our curriculum, the question then is how this study of grammar can improve students' ability not only to write but to speak and read with greater skill and confidence. Studies going as far back as the 1950s concluded grammar instruction showed no effect on thinking or writing (Lindemann 2001; Hillocks 2008;

Smith, Cheville, and Hillocks 2006; Smith and Wilhelm 2007); these studies, however, most often looked at grammar taught in isolation, which Graham and Perin (2007) discuss in their report *Writing Next*:

> Grammar instruction in the studies reviewed involved the explicit and systematic teaching of the parts of speech and structure of sentences. The meta-analysis found an effect for this type of instruction for students across the full range of ability, but surprisingly, this effect was negative. This negative effect was small, but it was statistically significant, indicating that traditional grammar instruction is unlikely to help improve the quality of students' writing. Studies specifically examining the impact of grammar instruction with low-achieving writers also yielded negative results (Anderson, 1997; Saddler and Graham, 2005). Such findings raise serious questions about some educators' enthusiasm for traditional grammar instruction as a focus of writing instruction for adolescents. (20)

Studied in context, however, grammar can improve performance (Graham and Perin 2007; Weaver 2008; Fearn and Farnan 2005). As Graham and Perin subsequently note:

> However, other instructional methods, such as sentence combining, provide an effective alternative to traditional grammar instruction, as this approach improves students' writing quality while at the same time enhancing syntactic skills. In addition, a recent study (Fearn and Farnan, 2005) found that teaching students to focus on the function and practical application of grammar within the context of writing (versus teaching grammar as an independent activity) produced strong and positive effects on students' writing. Overall, the findings on grammar instruction suggest that, although teaching grammar is important, alternative procedures, such as sentence combining, are more effective than traditional approaches for improving the quality of students' writing. (21)

Therefore, we will focus here on grammar studied in the context of reading, writing, and speaking, bypassing the traditional emphasis on error, which is often evidence of *growth* as writers struggle to master new and more complex forms (see the Top 20 Most Common Writing Errors listed in the sidebar here). In addition, we will consider grammar as it relates to all aspects of communication. Close reading, as mentioned before, is central to the Common Core State Standards (CCSS), which places "a high priority on the close, sustained reading of complex text . . . Such reading focuses on what lies within the four corners of the text. It often requires . . . that students . . . read and

---

The Top 20 Most Common Writing Errors

This list shows the most common errors in college freshman writing according to Lunsford and Lunsford (2008). It has evolved since first appearing in 1986, the most recent version reflecting the effects (both good and bad) technology has had on writing. Conducted by Lunsford and Lunsford through the 2008 Stanford Study of Writing, they found these to be the most common errors:

1. Wrong word
2. Missing comma after an introductory element
3. Incomplete or missing documentation
4. Vague pronoun reference
5. Spelling (including homonyms)
6. Mechanical error with a quotation
7. Unnecessary comma
8. Unnecessary and missing capitalization
9. Missing word
10. Faulty sentence structure
11. Missing comma with a nonrestrictive element
12. Unnecessary shift in verb tense
13. Missing comma in a compound sentence
14. Unnecessary or missing apostrophe (including its/it's)
15. Fused (run-on) sentence
16. Comma splice
17. Lack of pronoun–antecedent agreement
18. Poorly integrated quotation
19. Unnecessary or missing hyphen
20. Sentence fragment (795)

re-read deliberately and solely to probe and ponder the meanings of individual words, the order in which sentences unfold, and the development of ideas over the course of the text" (Coleman and Pimentel 2011, 4).

Such targeted instruction also benefits English learners who, understandably, find such close study of texts difficult when they are still busy learning the language. Studies of English learners who received direct instruction in the use of various close reading techniques for informational and primary source documents showed significant gains over those who did not receive such instruction in how to "deconstruct the meaning" of these passages (Gebhard and Martin 2011, 303). During such instruction, students were taught "how texts were structured and made coherent through the use of temporal markers and other cohesive devices; unpacking meaning clause by clause to see how participants were omitted or verbal processes transformed into nouns or became nominalized; and identifying participants, processes, and circumstances in key passages to become aware of [the choices writers make]" (303).

Gebhard and Martin (2011) close by saying that "students are more likely to be prepared to engage in this kind of strategic semiotic work if they have been in classrooms with teachers who have a critical awareness of language and how to apprentice students [for] playing high-stakes language games" (304). A useful approach (referred to as the RSVP model) for close reading appears in *Reading Between the Lines* (ACT 2006), which focuses on the demands of college-level reading:

Relationships (interactions among ideas or characters)

Richness (amount and sophistication of information conveyed through data or literary devices)

Structure (how the text is organized and how it progresses)

Style (author's tone and use of language)

Vocabulary (author's word choice)

Purpose (author's intent in writing the text) (15)

The ACT report includes a table that offers a continuum of complexity to further clarify the idea of complexity as it relates to language (see Figure 7.4). If considered from the perspective of not only writing but also of reading, this table makes it very clear—to me, at least—how central the study of language is in general, and of the sentence in particular when it comes to close reading. Describing her early, undergraduate encounters with such careful attention to language, Francine Prose (2006) recalls developing the "ability to look at a sentence and see what's superfluous, what can be altered, revised, expanded, and, especially, cut . . . [until one sees] that sentence shrink, snap into place, and ultimately emerge in a more polished form: clear, economical, sharp" (2). Although she is emphasizing her efforts as a writer in this context, her remark emphasizes all the more the work the reader must do when reading the piece to determine why these words were kept, used, arranged in this order, and have the effect they do on the story and its reader.

To illustrate what she means by "close reading," Prose recounts her high school teacher who required them to read through *Oedipus Rex* and *King Lear* and "circle every reference to eyes, light, darkness, and vision, then draw some conclusion on which [they] would base

Degree of Text Complexity			
Aspect of Text	**Uncomplicated**	**More Challenging**	**Complex**
Relationships	Basic, straightforward	Sometimes implicit	Subtle, involved, deeply embedded
Richness	Minimal/limited	Moderate/more detailed	Sizable/highly sophisticated
Structure	Simple, conventional	More involved	Elaborate, sometimes unconventional
Style	Plain, accessible	Richer, less plain	Often intricate
Vocabulary	Familiar	Some difficult, context-dependent words	Demanding, highly context dependent
Purpose	Clear	Conveyed with some subtlety	Implicit, sometimes ambiguous

FIGURE 7.4 This table, which displays the Degree of Text Complexity, comes from ACT's *Reading Between the Lines* report exploring college readiness.

[their] final essay" (4). To a certain degree this example is about word choice not grammar; however, once you begin to have students trace the sentence patterns, for example, to see how they reflect the internal condition of the protagonist, you are engaging in the same sort of close reading as Prose describes. When my students read *Crime and Punishment*, for example, they find throughout, if directed, grammatical patterns that reflect Raskolnikov's divided mind and conflicted nature (his name translates to mean *schism*).

The following is one such example from early on in the novel; note, as you read, how he swings back and forth, the sentences written (despite my few ellipses) in halting starts and stops, punctuated with anxiety, self-doubt, inner conflict; it plagues him throughout the rest of the novel.

> [Raskolnikov] was over his head in debt to the landlady and was afraid of meeting her.
>
> It was not that he was so cowardly and downtrodden, even quite the contrary. . . . He was crushed by poverty; but even his strained circumstances had lately ceased to burden him. . . . As a matter of fact, he was not afraid of any landlady, whatever she might be plotting against him. . . . This time, however, as he walked out to the street, even he was struck by his fear of meeting his creditor. (Dostoevsky, 1992, 3)

Now that we have established that language study is as much about reading as it is about writing, let's lift up the hood on this part of the curriculum and see what it involves and discuss how we can best teach it.

What Students (and Teachers) **Need to Know**

This area of the curriculum—the study of grammar—has "proven to be particularly nettlesome" for beginning teachers, many of whom feel they lack the necessary content knowledge and fluency within this domain but also feel torn between competing priorities: Am I teaching grammar to improve writing or to prepare for the state test? This should rarely seem to join together into one coherent set of expectations (Smagorinsky, Wilson, and Moore 2011).

In an attempt to bring some clarity and sense to this situation, Smith and Wilhelm (2007) propose two simple criteria for determining what to teach regarding grammar:

1. The term is so commonly used that teachers, texts, and tests presume that students know it.

2. The term is essential to being able to explain an important issue of style or correctness. (13)

Using these criteria, Smith and Wilhelm identify only 16 terms their research says are worth taking the time to teach:

- Adjective
- Adverb
- Agreement
- Antecedent
- Compound
- Conjunction
- Interjection
- Noun
- Participle
- Passive and active
- Phrase, clause, and sentence
- Preposition
- Pronoun
- Singular and plural
- Subject and predicate
- Verb (15)

To this reasonable list we must, of course, add the more detailed language standards described in the Common Core Standards.

Figure 7.5, a two-page reference, provides teachers who may not have thought so much about the finer points of the sentence an overview. Many of us know or have known the anxiety of one teacher who felt she had little or no "formal preparation in the principles of writing practice . . . [and therefore] had few pedagogical tools to carry out writing instruction [that would allow her] to anticipate how her students would respond, and so had little procedural knowledge of how to prepare her students for the processes needed to complete the tasks she assigned" (Smagorinsky, Wilson, and Moore 2011, 289).

What is my ultimate objective, what am I trying to teach my students when it comes to grammar, usage, style, and rhetoric? How to write clearly, correctly, and cogently about a range of topics and texts; but also how to speak about the way grammar and usage function within the texts they read closely and write about throughout the year (see Figure 7.6). In addition to

Forms an Functions: The Sentences

Name and Description	Examples Used in Academic Writing
FUNCTION	
Declare (Declarative) Makes a statement; tells us something about a person, place, thing, or idea	Upon entering the woods, the speaker in Frost's poem encounters "two roads [that] diverged in a yellow wood."
Question (Interrogative) Poses a question; expresses interest, consternation, wonder, curiosity, challenge	Why does Frost, after initially saying the paths were different, say they are "really about the same"?
Exclaim (Exclamatory) Indicates strong emotion, surprise, power, passion	The narrator in Frost's poem is himself divided into two "I's," two selves!
Command (Imperative) Demands action; tells what to do; includes an implied subject (*You!*); suggests authority, confidence	**Write** an essay in which you examine the attitude of Frost's speaker toward the road. **Include** in your response examples from the text. **Avoid** summary.
Wonder (Conditional) Such "If . . . then . . " sentences speculate about what something would be like under certain conditions	If, however, Frost wrote it in the third person instead, the tone of the poem and our relationship with the speaker would fundamentally change, as would the meaning of the poem.
STRUCTURE	
Simple One independent clause, no dependent clauses; can have single or compound subject; single or compound predicate; capable of complexity, nuance	a. Literary critics provide perspective. b. Literary critics and other scholars provide perspective. c. Literary critics provide perspective and challenge our assumptions.
Compound Two or more independent clauses joined by a semicolon, or by a comma and a coordinating conjunction	a. Literary critics provide perspective, but some are more insightful than others. b. Literary critics provide perspective; some are more insightful than others.
Complex One independent clause and 1+ dependent clauses	a. Although some question the validity of such critical interpretations, literary critics do provide a useful perspective. b. Literary critics provide a useful perspective, though some interpretations, such as those provided by Marxists, seem more political than literary.
Compound-Complex 2+ independent clauses and 1+ dependent clauses	a. Literary critics provide perspective, but because they too often mix their interpretations with political motives, they lack credibility in the eyes of many readers.
RHETORIC	
Periodic AKA: left-branching sentence that puts the subject at the end. Creates tension, suspense, emphasis; causes confusion if left branch is too long	In contrast to other writers of his time, who still embraced the more ornate language of the previous era, **Hemingway created a new style.**
Cumulative AKA right-branching or loose sentence; begins with main idea (independent clause), then adds details (phrases! clauses). Establishes main idea immediately for emphasis; each addition builds on the others for a cumulative effect	**Hemingway created a new style**, one that stood in contrast to other writers of his time, who still embraced the more ornate language of the previous era.
Interrupted AKA: midbranching sentence. Interrupted by phrases/clauses that are parenthetical, creating a pause or disrupting the flow. Creates tension, distraction; allows for emphasis, suspense, elaboration; set off by dashes or parentheses though enclosing	**Hemingway**, rejecting the more ornate language of the previous era, **created a new style.**

FIGURE 7.5 Forms and Functions: The Sentences

(continues)

Forms an Functions: The Sentences

Name and Description	Examples Used in Academic Writing
RHETORIC (*continued*)	
Centered Begin with phrases or clauses, followed by the base clause, which is modified by one or more additional phrases or clauses	Rejecting the more ornate language of the previous era, **Hemingway created a new style**, one that stood in stark contrast to other writers of his time, who were paid by the word, unlike Hemingway, who, as a journalist, sent his stories by telegraph.
Balanced The phrases or clauses are equivalent and parallel in struc-ture, meaning, or length; suggests relationship between *x*, *y*, and *z* due to parallel structure; emphasizes differences especially well	**Hemingway created** a new style, one that stood in stark contrast to the past; however, **Fitzgerald made** from the familiar something new that was honored even as it re-jected that same past.
Inverted The predicate precedes the subject, thus inverting the natu-ral order of the subject followed by the action	**A new style it was**, one that Hemingway shaped with his own two hands; **an enduring voice it would remain**, one mocked and mimicked, but always his own.
Antithetical Structure used to convey the contrary or opposing elements in a sentence	Hemingway created a style that was **new but old**, shaped as it was by the Bible; that was **simple yet complex**, saying as much through omission as by inclusion; that was **American yet European**, influenced as he was by the writers, such as Joyce, who had migrated to Paris.
Chiasmus *Chi* is Greek for *X*; think of it as criss-cross or a reversal of grammatical structures in successive clauses or phrases; it can help reinforce antithesis or otherwise express relation-ships between elements	Hemingway **created a new style; this style in turn cre-ated** Hemingway, for **it became his signature—a style immediately as recognizable** as "Papa" himself was.
Passive Consists of the verb to be and a past participle (e.g., *was + taken*); the subject is often implied or serves as the object If used judiciously, it can improve cohesion and allow the writer to emphasize something other than the normative subject	Such a style, **used** by authors to capture the sense of alien-ation **felt** by those who lived abroad, **was mistaken** as simple, even childish by less sophisticated readers.

FIGURE 7.5 *Continued*

direct instruction and periodic review of these concepts, I bring in anything I see in the news that relates to language as we are studying it. In part this is to reinforce my argument about the importance of such knowledge. Here are samples of what I have brought in lately:

1. The *Idea Transplant* blog titled "Every Sentence Should Matter" by Jan Schultink offers advice about giving effective corporate presentations, in which he notes that "every sentence should matter." Schultink (2011) argues, after returning to read fiction after a "25-year [hiatus] to overcome the bad memories of high school teachers forcing me to read this genre against my will," that it adds substance and power when the presenter believes "every sentence actually matters" and recognizes that "beautiful sentences are also more memorable and hence more persuasive."

2. A blog by critic Stanley Fish about President Obama's prose style in which Fish performs a close reading of Obama's 2009 inaugural address. In the blog, Fish notes that Obama's style is "incantatory rather than progressive"; the cadences ask for assent to each proposition ("That we are in the midst of a crisis is now well understood")

Language of Composition: Rhetorical Terms and Devices to Know and Teach

- Declarative
- Interrogatory
- Periodic sentence
- Cumulative sentence
- Loose sentence
- Ad hominem
- Ad populum
- Aesthetic
- Agency
- Aim
- Allegory
- Alliteration
- Allusion
- Ambiguity
- Amplify
- Analogy
- Anaphora
- Anecdote
- Annotation
- Antagonist
- Antecedent
- Antimetabole
- Antithesis
- Aphorism
- Apologia
- Apologist
- Apostrophe
- Appeal
- Apposition
- Archaic diction
- Argument
- Arrangement
- Assertion
- Assonance
- Attitude
- Audience
- Authority
- Bandwagon
- Begging the question
- Bias
- Bildungsroman
- Canon(ical)
- Catharsis
- Causality
- Chiasm(us)
- Cite
- Claim

- Climax
- Coherence
- Cohesion
- Colloquial
- Common ground
- Concession
- Conclusion
- Connotation
- Consonance
- Context
- Contradiction
- Coordination
- Counterargument
- Credible
- Declaim
- Declare
- Deduction
- Deliberative
- Denotation
- Device
- Diction
- Discursive
- Document(ation)
- Doppelganger
- Elegiac
- Ellipsis
- Enumeration
- Epigram
- Epiphany
- Epistolary
- Epithet
- Eponym
- Equivocation
- Ethos
- Euphemism
- Euphony
- Evidence
- Exemplum
- Explication
- Extended analogy
- Fable
- Fact
- Fallacy
- Figurative
- Figure of speech
- Foil
- Generalization

- Genre
- Heuristic
- Hortatory
- Hyperbole
- Hypophora
- Idiom
- Imagery
- Implied metaphor
- In medias res
- Induction
- Inference
- Inversion
- Irony
- Isocolon
- Jargon
- Judicial
- Juxtaposition
- Litotes
- Logos
- Maxim
- Metaphor
- Metonymy
- Mode
- Modifier
- Mood
- Narrative
- Narrative intrusion
- Negate
- Nominalization
- Nostalgia
- Objective
- Occasion
- Omission
- Onomatopoeia
- Opinion
- Oxymoron
- Panegyric
- Parable
- Paradox
- Parallelism
- Parataxis
- Parenthesis
- Parody
- Partition
- Pathos
- Periprasis
- Persona

- Personification
- Perspective
- Polemic
- Precedent
- Prejudice
- Premise
- Propaganda
- Propose
- Prose
- Pun
- Realism
- Recursive
- Red herring
- Refutation
- Repetition
- Reversal
- Rhetoric
- Rhetorical question
- Sarcasm
- Satire
- Scheme
- Simile
- Slang
- Soliloquy
- Source
- Stance
- Straw man
- Subject
- Subjective
- Subordinate
- Syllogism
- Synecdoche
- Syntax
- Synthesis
- Tautology
- Testimony
- Thesis
- Tone
- Topic
- Transition
- Trope
- Understatement
- Unity
- Voice

FIGURE 7.6 Language of Composition: Rhetorical Terms and Devices to Know and Teach

rather than to a developing argument. The power is in discrete moments rather than in a thesis proved by the marshalling of evidence. (Fisher 2009; NYT blog)

3. A column by David Brooks titled "Poetry for Everyday Life" in which he discusses the way metaphors, which he notes—citing research by James Geary—we use every 10 to 25 words, shape our thinking. "Most important," Brooks notes, is that "being aware of metaphors reminds you of the central role that poetic skills play in our thoughts. If much of our thinking is shaped and driven by metaphor, then the skilled thinker will be able to recognize patterns, blend patterns, apprehend the relationship and pursue unexpected likenesses." (2011b; NYT online)

How to Teach Grammar, Language, and Style

What then does the research, to which I will add examples from my classes, tell us about effective instruction in grammar? It identifies the following techniques as reliable and effective in improving students' use of language in all areas, even though the emphasis is on writing, with consequential benefits to reading as well. Before proceeding, we should acknowledge that many teachers do not feel free to pursue their own approaches to teaching grammar because their content in this area comes only from the textbook the district may have purchased; this is in spite of the fact that more of the textbooks now feature work by such people as Jeff Anderson, whose ideas about language study are both engaging and effective. Nonetheless, for those who *are* able to make decisions about how to approach grammar, the following sections describe approaches I have found effective and that are, in general, supported by research.

Sentence Combining

This is considered one of the most effective instructional approaches available, one which works well with a wide range of students. The basic idea is to combine two or more kernel or base sentences into more syntactically complex sentences (Smith, Cheville, and Hillocks 2006, 268). Research on sentence combining emphasizes the increased syntactic maturity as measured by the number of words in clauses and the number of clauses in each sentence (268). Strong suggests that sentence combining leads to improved reading also by teaching students to "pay attention to words so that their patterning [is] better understood" (1986, 2).

You can use sentence combining in various ways: have students work independently on a handout or sentence combining problem displayed to the class; ask students to work together to solve the problem of transforming three sentences into one; work with them from your station at the computer, document camera, whiteboard, or overhead projector to solve it together; by thinking out loud as you do so, students can hear your thinking process (Saddler 2007; Strong 1986, 2001).

There are books you can buy with sentences you can adapt to your class; I prefer, instead, to create my own so I can link them to whatever we are reading, thereby increasing the connection between the different aspects of the English curriculum. Often, though not always, I will draw on sentence combining as part of our brief but focused writing response to the weekly poem. Thus, each day we might read that week's poem, then they solve that day's sentence-combining exercise on their own before we discuss it as a class. As you can see in Figures 7.7 through 7.9, each day's task is more challenging and invites a discussion of their writing after words.

Sentence-Combining Slides

1. Barack Obama lived in Springfield, Illinois.
2. He is the 44th President of the United States.
3. Springfield is the hometown of Abraham Lincoln.

1. **Barack Obama** lived in *Springfield, Illinois.*
2. **He** is the 44th President of the United States.
3. *Springfield* is the hometown of Abraham Lincoln.

1. **Barack Obama** lived in *Springfield, Illinois.*
2. **He** is the 44th President of the United States.
3. *Springfield* is the hometown of Abraham Lincoln.

Barack Obama, the 44th President of the United States, previously lived in Springfield, Illinois, the hometown of Abraham Lincoln.

FIGURE 7.7 Sample sentence-combining slides that show the sequence and method for teaching combining. This would be the equivalent of Langer's "separate" instruction. What is missing is the color I typically use to further highlight the different patterns.

Sentence-Combining Slides

1. Siddhartha's father refused to allow him to leave home.
2. As a Brahmin, his father believed Siddhartha should stay at home and take over the family after he died.

1. **Siddhartha's father** refused to allow him to leave home.
2. As **a Brahmin**, his **father** believed Siddhartha should stay at **home** and take over the **family** after he died.

Siddhartha's father, **a Brahmin**, refused to allow Siddhartha to leave home, believing, instead, that **he** should stay at **home** and take over the **family** after he died.

Siddhartha's father, **a Brahmin**, refused to allow Siddhartha, **his only son**, to leave home, believing, that Siddhartha should instead stay at home and take over the family after his father died, **an honor any son should want to accept**.

FIGURE 7.8 As the sequences unfold, the sentences or other such work grow more complex. This would be mostly consistent with Langer's notion of text as simulated, followed by integrated when students apply these ideas to their own papers.

Sentence-Combining Slides

1. Frost uses understatement.
2. Frost emphasizes the emotional distance between the family members.
3. Frost refers to all of the family members in the third person.

Frost uses understatement to emphasize the emotional distance between the family members, all of whom he refers to in the third person.

1. The saw represents the menace.
2. Menace lurks just below the surface of the otherwise "calm day" in the poem and our lives.
3. Frost ascribes an almost predatory hunger to the saw.

1. **The saw** represents the **menace**.
2. **Menace** lurks just below the surface of the otherwise "calm day" in the poem and our lives.
3. Frost ascribes an almost predatory hunger to **the saw**.

The saw, to which Frost ascribes an almost predatory hunger, represents the **menace** that lurks just below the surface of the otherwise "calm day" in the poem and our lives.

FIGURE 7.9 Note the use of academic sentences instead of descriptive or narrative. This is the sort of sentence students need to master in our classes.

Sentence Composing

A variation on sentence combining, this robust approach developed by Killgallon (1998) combines four techniques to create a strong model with the following steps:

- *Sentence unscrambling*, which "provides a close look at how professional writers structure their sentences" (7)

- *Sentence imitating*, which asks students to "to use sentences by professional writers as models for sentences . . . in which [students maintain or emulate] the structure of the model but not its content" (9)

- *Sentence combining*, which requires students to "impose a structure on a given amount of content—presented as a list of sentences—experiment with possible combinations, then compare their results with the original sentence" and the specified structure the lesson was teaching (12)

- *Sentence expanding* presents to the student "a shortened version of a professional sentence [to which] students must provide their own additions . . . in a way that will result in a smooth blend with the rest of the professional writer's sentence" (15).

Killgallon organizes his approach around real sentences from real writers. Here is a sample sequence in which he teaches the appositive phrase.

- *Unscrambling*
    1a. struggled as usual
    b. she
    c. to maintain her calm, friendly bearing
    d. a sort of mask she wore all over her body
        —from "The Blind Man" by D. H. Lawrence

- *Imitating*
    A tall, rawhide man in an unbuttoned, sagging vest, he was visibly embarrassed by any furnishings that suggested refinement.
        —from "Early Marriage" by Conrad Richter

- *Combining*
    - *Model:* In her wallet she still carried a picture of her husband, a clean-shaven boy in his twenties, the hair parted on one side.
        —Jhumpa Lahiri, *Unaccustomed Earth*
    a. a constant reminder of his marriage
    b. he always stored a suit of white linen
    c. in his closet
    d. a dried flower pinned to one lapel

- *Expanding*
    My bed was an army cot, /. (add appositive phrases at the slash mark)
        —from "The Night the Bed Fell" by James Thurber

PAUSE & REFLECT You solved them all, right? What do you think of Killgallon's method and the sentence combining approach? How do they compare with what you do?

If I have one reservation about Killgallon's (and many others') approach, it is not with the method itself but the nature of the samples. Because they are all wonderful sentences from fiction, they do a remarkable job of helping students to write more sophisticated narrative sentences; my students, however, need to learn to write such sentences *about* literature and informational texts in the context of analytical writing. To that end, my sentence combining and composing activities, as Figure 7.10 shows, emphasize analytical prose.

I generally use other, more algebraic frames, often on the fly in class, to nudge students' thinking in these more analytical directions. Such work is typically done in their notebooks; later, on the subsequent paper, I have them identify and focus on their use of whatever grammatical constructions I am using. This emphasis on analytical writing (instead of learning to write sentences like D. H. Lawrence) has one other important benefit: it makes them write from the perspective of a close reader who is trying to articulate what Frost means, how he creates some effect, why he chose this image or that word; thus, the writing enhances and improves the reading.

Sentence Composing

Verbal Phrases

Describing in precise detail a "dimpled spider" and "white heal-all," Frost questions the origins and intent of such a "design of darkness."

Verbal Phrases

1. **Describing in precise detail a "dimpled spider" and "white heal-all,"** Frost questions the origins and intent of such a "design of darkness."

Verbal Phrases

1. Describing in precise detail a "dimpled spider" and "white heal-all," Frost questions the origins and intent of such a "design of darkness."

2. Frost, **describing in precise detail a "dimpled spider" and "white heal-all,"** questions the origins and intent of such a "design of darkness."

FIGURE 7.10 These are my variations on Killgallon's lessons; the key difference is that his are from great fiction writers and my examples are from academic writers.

Sentence Templates

Graff, Birkenstein, and Durst offer the most developed, clear, and effective approach to such templates for academic writing, which they argue go all the way back to ancient Greece and Rome where the use of "rhetorical *topoi* . . . model passages and formulas that represented the different strategies available to public speakers" (2010, xxii). You can find examples of these templates in the writing chapter (see Figure 4.4), but here are a few examples from Graff, Birkenstein, and Durst to illustrate what they look like and how these templates differ when it comes to "the moves that make academic writing," as Graff, Birkenstein, and Durst (2010) call them:

- ***Introducing what "They Say"***
  - A number of _____ have recently suggested that _____.
  - In their recent work, *Y* and *Z* have offered harsh critiques of _____ for
    _____.

- ***Introducing "Standard Views"***
  - Many people assume that_____.
  - Conventional wisdom has it that _____.

- ***Introducing an Ongoing Debate***
  - In discussions of *X*, one controversial issue has been _____. On the one hand, _____ argues _____. On the other hand, _____ contends _____. Others even maintain _____. My own view is_____ (222).

The algebraic nature of these templates (alternately called "stems," "kernels," "frames," and "structures" by many) often appeals to kids, offering a more practical view of what we are trying to teach; this is an approach that is unhindered by what type of sentence or grammatical construction it is and thereby makes more clear what the writing should *do*. I also like such templates because we can use them to capture good thinking, tossing up on the board a template like Figure 7.11, to help us see what made a student's example, just offered in our discussion of a text, so effective. In other words, these templates can be specific to a rhetorical or grammatical structure you want to teach, or they can be more informal, generated in the context of the discussion of a text or topic and not specific to any one grammatical structure.

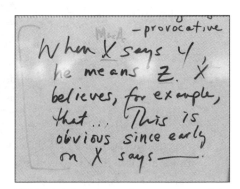

FIGURE 7.11 Sample template structure or "algebraic" structure, the sort I often dash on the board to guide our thinking—give it a shape.

Structured Notes

A variation on the algebraic structure of the template approach, structured notes (formatted on paper or digital display) work to teach both analytical writing and reading, those two aims so central to our work but difficult to integrate seamlessly. As Figure 7.12 shows, I put up what looks like a spreadsheet on the board, using a form of reporter's questions (Five Ws and an H, as some call them) to give structure to our discussion, then capture the details of that discussion; again, the

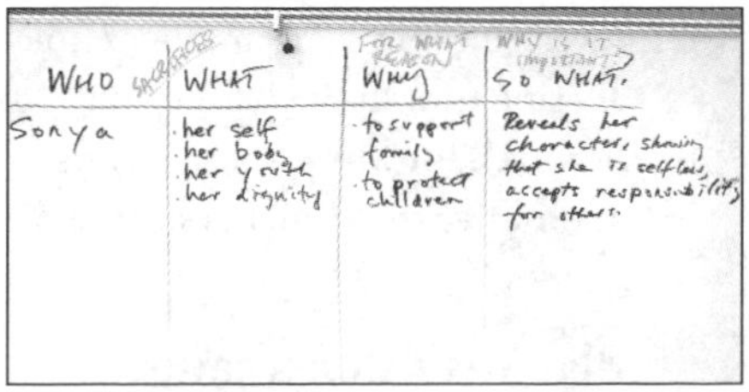

FIGURE 7.12 This example comes from our work on *Crime and Punishment*, but the method words well for any class, on any level, with any book.

emphasis is on analytical writing about literary or informational texts in structured notes to show them how it works. Then they gather more through group discussions meant to further focus their attention on the text we are analyzing. Eventually, we use the spreadsheet notes to craft analytical sentences.

A more technology-based approach is to give groups a highly structured section of an informational text and, asking students to work in groups, have them break down the short passage into some variation on the previously mentioned spreadsheet format. My seniors, for example, as part of a larger unit about success, read excerpts from a very challenging article by Philip Zimbardo on his "time perspective theory" after first watching a wonderful six-minute "TED Talk" in which Zimbardo explains the theory. After modeling for them how I want them to take notes, they jot their ideas down. As I watched them work in their groups, I realized we could increase the demands of the assignment and create opportunities to talk about parallel structure, verbs, and sentences in general if we used even more structure on the assignment.

"WHETHER WRITING THEIR OWN PAPERS OR STUDYING OTHERS', STUDENTS CAN IMPROVE THEIR UNDERSTANDING OF PUNCTUATION BY PLAYING PURPOSEFULLY WITH IT . . ."

So, we took their notes to the computer lab the next day and, working in teams, they typed up their notes into one slide per team in PowerPoint. This had the added benefit of creating an authentic context to teach them how to insert tables and format cells. Figure 7.13a through 7.13d show the sequence, which culminated in a class forum where students discussed Zimbardo's ideas prior to writing a summary and analysis of his model— a demanding writing task that the structured notes had ideally prepared them to do.

Let me conclude with a few more succinct examples of activities you can fit in and use to guide your teaching of language when working on reading or writing:

Author's Choices

Direct students' attention to the choices writers made, asking them to examine the effect the choice of some rhetorical device or grammatical structure makes on the meaning. What, for example, is the purpose of repeating that same simple sentence structure five times when the writer clearly knows how to write other types of sentences?

Consider Alternatives

After examining the author's choices, students can generate alternative sentence patterns, discussing how their changes affect the meaning. They might end this discussion by providing a rationale for why the writer chose the one he or she did (and why it was more effective than the alternative the students suggested).

Play with Punctuation

Whether writing their own papers or studying others', students can improve their understanding of punctuation by playing purposefully with it to see how a period affects the meaning

FIGURE 7.13a Students break down the language of the article they are reading to create a parallel structure.

FIGURE 7.13b After getting their ideas down on the butcher paper, the groups, which for various reasons were large that day, then transcribed their words into one Power-Point slide.

Future-Oriented People

Verbs	What	Reasons/Implications
Resist	Temptations	To gain more in the long run
Plan	To succeed	For fulfillment
Sacrifice	Personal time	To get ahead
Challenge	Themselves	To improve in the future
Accept	Delays	To achieve better goals in the long run
Anticipate	Courses of action	So future consequences can be avoided
Analyze	Situations	For a clear path forward
Increase	Efficiency	To get more done in less time
Pay attention	To responsibilities	To optimize outcomes

FIGURE 7.13c This is what their finished product looked like after sending it to me.

Future-Oriented People

Resist	temptations	to gain more in the long run
Plan	to succeed	for fulfillment
Sacrifice	personal time	to get ahead
Challenge	themselves	to improve in the future
Accept	delays	to achieve better goals in the long run
Anticipate	course of action	to avoid future consequences
Analyze	situations	to determine the clear path forward
Increase	efficiency	to get more done in less time
Meet	obligations	to optimize outcomes

FIGURE 7.13d I took their slide and, in order to squeeze in a bit more attention to design, created a duplicate to show them other options and to create a discussion.

differently than a semicolon, or a comma over a dash—or colon, if that seems an available option. In her book *Rhetorical Grammar*, Martha Kolln (2003) offers a concise example of the difference punctuation can make on the meaning of the sentence by illustrating the effect of different choices on what seems like the same sentence:

1. I loved the book, but I hated the movie.
2. I loved the book; but I hated the movie.
3. I loved the book; I hated the movie.
4. I loved the book; however, I hated the movie.
5. I loved the book: I hated the movie.

To reinforce the idea that grammar is not just about writing but is very much a necessary part of the discussion about reading, I include Kolln's explanation of the difference between these five sentences:

The first one we might think of as the basic compound-sentence rule, the comma-plus-conjunction, which puts fairly equal emphasis on the two clauses. The next three, with the greater pause the semicolon will give the reader, put more emphasis on the second clause. But there are differences among them, too. Seeing the bare semicolon of (3), the reader will sense a kind of tight finality—no argument, no concessions; the addition of *however* in (4) adds a note of deliberation, a degree of thoughtfulness in coming to a decision about the movie. The colon in (5) commands special attention: The reader will pause and give even more attention to the word of contrast, *hated*, than in the other four versions. (2003, 278)

Move the Pieces Around

Students often lack a sense of the elasticity of sentences, the way syntax allows a writer to swap one part of the sentence for another, or move a phrase from the place before the subject to after it. Such moves often, though not always, change the meaning or the sound and shape of the sentence. Have students try writing the same sentence in different arrangements, changing as little as possible aside from the portion they move. Here is a sample I displayed on the document camera for them to see what I mean. Again, note the emphasis on academic as opposed to narrative writing:

1. In order to show *X*, Updike uses *Y*, suggesting . . .
2. Updike uses Y to show *X*, suggesting . . .
3. Suggesting . . . , Updike uses *Y* to show *X*.

Here are three possible sentences I provided to show them what I mean. They are not award-winning sentences, but even the discrepancies between them allow for intelligent discussion of the quality of one over another.

1. In order to show *the dog's character*, Updike uses *personification*, suggesting that this dog has become a member of the family.
2. Updike uses *personification*, suggesting that this dog has become a member of the family, in order to show *the dog's character*.
3. Suggesting that this dog has become a member of the family, Updike uses *personification* to show *the dog's character*.

Writing about sentences, which depends on students reading for grammar, rhetoric, syntax, and style, is challenging to many students. It requires a level of critical distance from and insight about the sentence the student is analyzing. As I mentioned in Figure 7.2, students often lack immediate access to the language needed to think analytically or express their ideas once they have examined the sentence or subject in depth. For those students, who include but are not limited to English learners, the list in Figure 7.14 offers the words they need.

Language of Literature: Style Analysis: Sentences

Directions Use the following word lists to improve your sentence fluency through precise, active words specifically related to writing about and analyzing the author's style at the sentence level.

Example Dostoevsky reveals the conflicted nature of Raskolnikov's mind through his use of punctuation; each ellipsis, semicolon, dash or comma is meant to mimic the halting and unbridled nature of Raskolnikov's mind. As his name, which translates to mean schism suggests, it is divided—at war with itself.

Nouns		Verbs		Adjectives	
Action	Interruption	Adapt	Hint	Abstract	Interrupted
Adjective	Inversion	Add	Illustrate Imitate	Active	Introductory
Adverb	Jargon	Adopt	Imply	Adjectival	Jargon-filled
Agent	Language	Affect	Infer	Allusive	Journalistic
Agreement	Length	Aim	Influence	Ambiguous	Lackluster
Allusion	Logic	Alienate	Inform	Analogous	Linguistic
Analogy	Metaphor	Appear	Inspire	Anemic	Long
Antecedent	Model	Argue	Intend	Antithetical	Low
Antithesis	Modifier	Arrange	Interrupt	Appositional	Lyrical
Argument	Move	Borrow	Introduce	Balanced	Masterful
Arrangement	Movement	Break	Invert	Beautiful	Modern
Balance	Narrator	Build	Join	Biblical	Modified
Brevity	Noun	Cause	Lead	Bloated	Monotonous
Character	Object	Challenge	List	Blunt	Musical
Characteristic	Paragraph	Characterize	Mark	Brief	Nuanced
Chiasmus	Parallelism	Choose	Mention	Classical	Objective
Choice	Passivity	Cohere	Model	Clear	Organized
Clarity	Pattern	Combine	Move	Clichéd	Parallel
Clause	Period	Compare	Narrate	Coercive	Passive
Cohesion	Personification	Complain	Notice	Coherent	Pedantic
Colon	Phrase	Complement	Orchestrate	Cohesive	Periodic
Comparison	Prodicato	Compose	Paint	Colloquial	Persuasive
Conoioion	Proposition	Compress	Pose	Common	Prepositional
Conjunction	Pronoun	Conclude	Praise	Complex	Quirky
Constraint	Punctuation	Connect	Punctuate	Compound	Rambling
Contradiction	Purpose	Consider	Question	Concrete	Rapid
Contrast	Question	Construct	Quote	Conditional	Recursive
Convention	Reference	Contain	Recall	Connotative	Redundant
Coordination	Repetition	Contradict	Refer	Conventional	Repetitive
Craft	Rhetoric	Contrast	Reiterate	Coordinated	Rhetorical
Dash	Rhythm	Contribute	Report	Crafty	Rhythmic
Design	Semicolon	Coordinate	Resist	Cryptic	Seamless
Device	Series	Craft	Restate	Cumulative	Short
Dialogue	Simile	Create	Reveal	Dangling	Simple
Diction	Slang	Deconstruct	Shape	Declarative	Spare
Discourse	Stress	Derive	Show	Denotative	Structural
Economy	Structure	Describe	State	Dependent	Stylistic
Effect	Style	Diminish	Struggle	Derivative	Subordinated
Element	Subject	Disrupt	Subordinate	Direct	Subtle
Ellipses	Subordination	Distract	Suggest	Discursive	Syntactical
Emphasis	Suggestion	Economize	Summarize	Economical	Traditional
Exclamation	Summary	Elaborate	Trace	Elegant	Transcendent
Exposition	Surface	Emphasize	Transform	Elevated	Transitional
Feature	Syntax	Employ	Transition	Elliptical	Unconventional
Figure of speech	Technique	Enhance	Undermine	Elusive	Vague
Focus	Tense	Equate	Unify	Emphatic	Verbal
Focus	Tension	Evoke	Violate	Exclamatory	Well-made
Form	Text	Exclaim	Weave	Fragmented	
Fragment	Theme	Explain		Grammatical	
Function	Tone	Explicate		High	
Genre	Topic	Explore		Humorous	
Grammar	Transition	Focus		Idiosyncratic	
Image	Type	Follow		Imperative	
Imagery	Unity	Force		Independent	
Imitation	Variety	Forge		Indicative	
Influence	Voice	Form		Indirect	
Intention	Words	Fragment		Intentional	
				Interrogatory	

FIGURE 7.14 Language of literature—style analysis: sentences

Closing Thoughts

Many teachers love grammar; others avoid it. Some simply dismiss it, as if it were a chore they simply did not have time to do—and probably never will. Yet it is the DNA of our language, of our *thought*. Perhaps a more apt analogy would be to compare it to the wood from which so much in our lives is made, for what we are really discussing in this chapter is not only craft—the tools and techniques—but also the materials we use to make things, in this case, words, sentences—and meaning.

As with all professional communities, ours has its divisions. In the case of language usage, Garner identifies two: descriptivists and prescriptivists (2009, location 1315). Garner, who diplomatically characterizes himself as a "descriptive prescriber" (1400), explains the difference between the two types: "Prescribers seek to guide users of a language—including native speakers—on how to handle words as effectively as possible. Describers seek to discover the facts of how native speakers actually use their language" (1328). This distinction, alive and well, returns us to the beginning of this section, to the "grammar ranters" Dunn and Lindbloom (2011) described, to the idea—and *ideal*—of perfection, correctness, conscience.

As one would expect given their devotion to the study of writing, Lunsford and Lunsford offer a balanced, judicious way of thinking about these issues in their article titled "'Mistakes Are a Fact of Life': A National Comparative Study," which opens by discussing the dream of correctness and the much messier reality of errors:

> Perhaps it is the seemingly endless string of what have come to be called "Bushisms" ("We shouldn't fear a world that is more interacted") and the complex response to them from both right and left. Perhaps it is the hype over Instant Messaging lingo cropping up in formal writing and the debate among teachers over how to respond. . . . Perhaps it is the long series of attempts to loosen the grip of "standard" English on the public imagination. . . . Or perhaps it is the number of recent reports, many of them commissioned by the government, that have bemoaned the state of student literacy and focused attention on what they deem significant failures at the college level . . .
>
> Whatever the reasons, and they are surely complex, multilayered forms of language use have been much in the news, with charges of what student writers can and cannot (or should and should not) do all around us. (2008, 782)

We want our students to write cogent prose that is as correct as it is capable of achieving whatever outcome the writer seeks. We also want students to read the whole range of texts as they were meant to be read: not only for their content but their character, for their beauty *and* their force, for their arguments and their agreements, for the way they sound and the way they mean. Here we see the personae from Chapter 1 alive in the classroom where we want students to be able to read, write, speak, and think from many angles.

Recently, I asked my students to "read like a lawyer" ("who is doing this assignment as pro bono work," I added) a passage from *Crime and Punishment*. We talked briefly about what this meant, how one would do it, and why it was an important mind-set to be able to adopt. This allowed us to look at the choices Dostoevsky made, choices which would allow both the defense and the prosecuting attorneys to find evidence of Raskolnikov's guilt and innocence (by reason of insanity). "Reading like a lawyer," however, also anticipated the arguments they would have to make as writers soon; thus they had to think about the language and rhetorical moves needed to frame their case and the evidence that would support their arguments. It meant looking at Dostoevsky's word choices, sentence structure, narrative design, and other moves he made that allowed us—by some linguistic sleight-of-hand—to be simultaneously disgusted by and feel symphathy for an ax-murdering intellectual with megalomaniacal dreams of being the next Napoleon.

In this same senior class sat a wonderful young woman named Julia who is the very embodiment of Hermione Granger. All this talk of perfection and error reminds me of when Julia was in my freshman honors class. Their end-of-the-year project, which they had much of the second semester to work on, asked them to study a subject in depth through books, research, and interviews. Julia chose perfectionism, something she said she had struggled with all her life (and, at least in my class, seemed to have won the battle—did she ever even lose a point?).

> **"** . . . WHAT WE ARE REALLY DISCUSSING IN THIS CHAPTER IS NOT ONLY CRAFT—THE TOOLS AND TECHNIQUES—BUT ALSO THE MATERIALS WE USE TO MAKE THINGS, IN THIS CASE, WORDS, SENTENCES—AND MEANING. **"**

On the day of her final presentation, on which they had to submit their written paper and give a serious presentation, more of a mini-dissertation defense than a school presentation, really, she began by saying, without any awareness of the mistake, "It is not easy being perfect and is something I have struggled with my whole life." To the class' credit, no one laughed. After her otherwise excellent presentation, class ended and they all went off to take other finals. I took a few minutes to sit down and skim through her hefty report on the trials of being perfect. By the end of the first page, I had, alas, found about five of the Lunsfords' errors. I smiled, put the paper, along with the others, in my bag to read that night, as one school year ended and the dream of perfection for the next school year was already forming itself in my exhausted June brain.

Recommended **Resources**

Print

- *Mechanically Inclined: Building Grammar, Usage, and Style into Writer's Workshop*, Jeff Anderson (Stenhouse 2005).
- *Image Grammar: Teaching Grammar as Part of the Writing Process*, Harry R. Noden (Heinemann 2011).
- *Critical Passages: Teaching the Transition to College Composition*, Kristin Dombek and Scott Herndon (Teachers College Press 2004).
- *Analyzing Prose*, Richard A. Lanham (Continuum 2003) and *Style and Statement*, Edward P. J. Corbett and Robert J. Connors (Oxford 1999) are both so rich it is impossible to recommend one over the other.
- *Style: The Basics of Clarity and Grace*, Joseph M. Williams (Pearson Longman 2006).

- *They Say/I Say: The Moves that Matter in Academic Writing*, Gerald Graff and Cathy Birkenstein (Norton 2010).
- *The St. Martin's Handbook*, Andrea A. Lunsford (Bedford/St. Martin's 2011).
- *Bringing Words to Life: Robust Vocabulary Instruction*, Isabel L. Beck, Margaret G.McKeown, and Linda Kucan (Guilford 2002).

ONLINE

- The University of Chicago Writing Program Grammar Resources Page (http://writing-program.uchicago.edu/resources/grammar.htm)
- Purdue OWL (Online Writing Lab) (http://owl.english.purdue.edu/)
- Texas A & M Online Writing Center (http://writingcenter.tamu.edu/)

CHAPTER EIGHT

Assessing and Grading Student Learning and Work

In the name of excellence, we test and measure them—as individuals, as a group—and we rejoice or despair over the results. The sad thing is that though we strain to see, we miss so much. All students cringe under the scrutiny, but those most harshly affected, least successful in the competition, possess some of our greatest unperceived riches.

—Mike Rose, from *Lives on the Boundary*

Introduction: Assessing the Assessment Situation

In conducting research for his book, *The Energy to Teach* (2001), Don Graves asked me to keep track of everything I did for a week, jotting down what I did and quickly assigning it a value of TE (takes energy), GE (gives energy), or N (neutral). It was the energy equivalent of those personal finance exercises that require you to keep track of every penny then total it up at week's end to see where your money goes. Of the many pages of moments that made up my week, the Monday and Tuesday pages included these entries:

Monday—3:00-3:30: Met with student to discuss paper. GE

Tuesday—3:00-3:30: Met with student to discuss paper. TE

At the end of the week, I sent my data off to Don, who eagerly began his analysis of it for the study. He called the next week to ask about a few things. "So you met with students from the same class, at the same time, two days in a row, to do the same thing (talk about a paper). But on Monday, it gave you energy and on Tuesday it took energy: What was the difference?" "That's easy, Don," I explained, "the kid on Monday wanted to talk about how to be a better writer, so it was a satisfying conversation I didn't mind staying after school to have. The other kid, the one on Tuesday, just wanted a better grade, so instead of a good discussion about writing he just kept saying, in one way or another, 'So if I did that would it be an A?' over and over. So it took a lot of energy to smile and say, 'Well, let's just focus on improving your writing and the grades will follow.'"

Assessment and grading challenge us all, threatening to turn what should be mentoring into a minefield of potential trauma, if we do not approach these opportunities to guide our students with the right mind-set and intentions. Here's a story to illustrate what I mean:

A colleague of mine, relatively new to the profession, had a student in her AP Literature class who had not taken any advanced classes until senior year. This lack of experience at the advanced level, combined with a general lack of skill, made it difficult for him to do well; as the semester went on, his grade went down and he grew increasingly discouraged. The very committed teacher told him she would help him revise two essays so he could catch up with his classmates, most of whom had been in advanced classes for three years. By semester's end, his grade was a respectable 79 percent.

He felt she should show consideration for all his progress and hard work by bumping the grade up to a B–. She felt otherwise, explaining that she had given him extensive feedback that allowed him to improve his performance and his grade but that he was not working to a different standard than the others. By way of consideration, however, she encouraged him to write her a letter explaining why he should receive the higher grade. His letter, which came the next day, was a vicious rant—filled with expletives in which he vented his anger at her, his peers, and the class which, despite his progress, he felt was fixed, making it impossible for him to earn a higher grade. Thus, his next conference and opportunity for feedback about his performance came not from his devoted teacher but the school safety officer and dean, who suspended him for four days for threatening a teacher.

PAUSE & REFLECT Take time to respond to these opening stories. What issues or concerns do they raise for you? How would you respond? Why would you respond that way?

I begin with these stories not to scare readers (though they no doubt will) but to acknowledge the challenges we face when we discuss assessment and grading, two aspects of our work that have taken on much greater weight during the era of standards and increased competition to get into good colleges. They also consume a disproportionate amount of our energy, taking time that could be better spent improving our teaching to defend our assessments, or the grades themselves. Consider the stress of the following example, which illustrates my point all too well: One day I saw a staff member standing in the doorway of an English teacher's classroom. She was clearly angry. Suddenly this usually happy colleague, who helped us with so much, screamed from the threshold of her son's teacher's classroom, to which she had come to challenge her son's final grade—"a B+ is *useless*!" Then she stormed off down the otherwise quiet halls of the empty school.

As these anecdotes show, assessment and grading are complicated. Here are a few examples:

- When teachers say *assessment*, most students, parents, and administrators think: *testing, grades, consequences.*

- What is the relationship between the standards, assessments, curriculum, and grades for my course?

- What are assessments and grades used for and based on in my school and the colleges to which students apply?

- How do students feel about the different assessments? Are some assessments, for example, more considerate of their strengths and progress than others? And, how do their emotions affect students' performance on these exams?

- What role—if any—should effort, improvement, and natural ability play in determining grades?

- Can assessments ever be valid and equitable given the "confounding variables" of language, knowledge, and culture, which make success on such tests often seem beyond the reach for "racially and linguistically diverse students"? (Murphy 2007, 231)

- Who is—or should be—responsible for the content of assessments, the criteria used to evaluate them, and the process by which these measurements are used to improve performance and determine students' grades?

All of which is to say that assessment matters. At its best, assessment provides students and teachers with reliable, useful data about what students know and learn, while also providing feedback so that they can perform even better in the future. At its best, assessment celebrates and validates the hard work of students and teachers, both of whom see in the results a confirmation of their own potential.

At its best, assessment motivates students to learn in ways that increase their comprehension and improve their memory of the material at the same time (Belluck 2011). At its best, assessment does for us all what it did for one teacher who reflected on her experience with assessment after her administrator asked, "How do you know the kids are really getting it?" She wrote:

> I discovered holes in my curriculum. I once dismissed standardized testing for its narrow focus on a discrete set of skills, but I learned that my self-made assessments were more problematic. It turned out they were skewed in my favor. I was better at teaching literary analysis than grammar and punctuation. When I started giving ongoing standardized assessments, I noticed that my students showed steady growth in literary analysis, but less growth in grammar and punctuation. I was teaching to my strengths instead of strengthening my weaknesses. (Nyamekye 2011, 24)

" AT ITS BEST, ASSESSMENT CELEBRATES AND VALIDATES THE HARD WORK OF STUDENTS AND TEACHERS, BOTH OF WHOM SEE IN THE RESULTS A CONFIRMATION OF THEIR OWN POTENTIAL. "

At its worst, however, assessment, which has the power to "set the standards for what counts as good writing" (Hillocks 2003, 64), instead strips writing of all meaning, resulting in "70 percent of Illinois teachers interviewed [saying they] were hammering away at the five-paragraph theme" until it was all the children of Illinois knew of writing. The consequence, after nearly 10 years of incessant "hammering away," was that students "came to see the five paragraph theme and the shoddy thinking that goes with it as the solution to any writing problem, thus leading a whole generation of incoming college freshman in Illinois to require remediation so they could meet the demands of college-level writing and thinking (Hillocks 2003, 70).

At its worst, assessment causes such anxiety and fear that it undermines the very progress it hopes to measure. Such is the case with many students when it comes to writing, "Internet plagiarism [having become] so common that [many teachers] replaced written assignments with tests and in-class writing" (Gabriel 2010). These multiple choice tests many will use to "assess" writing wind up reducing a complex, elegant craft to answers that can neatly fit a standardized format, as in this example from an actual high school exam:

A standard essay body paragraph usually has:

    a. No quotes

    b. 1 to 2 quotes

    c. 3 to 4 quotes

    d. 4 to 5 quotes

The remainder of this chapter will look at the finer points of creating and using various assessments to help kids learn and remember so that they can apply their knowledge to a variety of situations. Since I considered assessment in each major curriculum chapter, this one focuses more on the guiding principles, important types, and best practices of assessment, in general, which you can adopt or adapt to meet the needs of your students.

PAUSE & REFLECT Before reading any further, describe in some detail your assessment policies, practices, or philosophies. What are the sources of these ideas? If you are not yet a teacher, what will your policies be, and what is the rationale behind such policies?

Assessments: An Overview of Different Types

As Douglas Reeves observed, "The nation *is* overtested, but . . . underassessed, [a] distinction [that] is essential, as many schools continue to engage in summative testing—educational autopsies that seek to explain how the patient died but offer no insight into how to help the patient improve" (2006, location 124). Reeves' diagnosis offers an apt and compelling comparison of American schools regarding the two main forms of assessment: formative and summative. (See Figure 8.1 for an overview of the different elements of these assessments.)

The larger question is whether formative writing assessment actually *improves* student writing if taught with great focus while assessing it at the same time. After their extensive meta-analysis of formative writing assessments at the middle and high school levels, Graham, Harris, and Hebert (2011) put forth the following recommendations:

1. **Use Formative Writing Assessment to Enhance Students' Writing**

- *Provide feedback.* Writing improves when teachers and peers provide students with feedback about the effectiveness of their writing.

- *Teach students how to assess their own writing.* Writing improves when students are taught to evaluate the effectiveness of their own writing.

- *Monitor students' writing progress.* Writing improves when teachers monitor students' progress on an ongoing basis.

Types of Assessments: An Overview

	Classroom Formative Assessments	Common Formative Assessments	Summative Assessments
Definition	"Formative assessment is a planned process in which assessment-elicited evidence of students' status is used by teachers to adjust their ongoing instructional procedures or by students to adjust their current learning tactics" (Popham 2008, 6)	"Specially designed [assessments] by participating teachers of . . . secondary course/department teams who all teach the same content standards to their students. They provide educators with many benefits, including a sharper focus for instruction around a common core curriculum and those particular curricular areas needing attention. . . . They are used as pre-assessments to inform participating teachers, individually and collectively, the degree to which the students already know or have yet to learn the particular [standards] they are about to teach" (Ainsworth and Viegut 2006, 23)	"Takes place when educators collect test-based evidence to inform decisions about already-completed instructional activities such as when statewide accountability tests are administered each spring to determine the instructional effectiveness of a state's schools during the soon-to-be-completed school year . . .[or] the final exam a teacher administers . . .to [determine] an appropriate grade" (Popham 2011, 271)
Qualities	• Assessment <u>for</u> learning • Informal assessment • A <u>process</u> not necessarily a test • Can be open-ended to allow for multiple responses; can also be closed, in which case there is one correct answer	• Assessment <u>for</u> learning • Also known as benchmark exams • Pre- and posttests • Generally not open-ended except for possible writing prompt; otherwise, similar to summative assessments in design and spirit	• Assessment <u>of</u> learning • A <u>test</u> not a process • No pre- and posttest • No open-ended questions except for essay prompts that may appear

Source	• Assessment created or chosen by:
	  • Individual teacher
	  • Informal team of teachers
	  • Authorized resource (textbook)
		• Assessment created or chosen by:
		  • Department grade-level team
		  • District grade-level team
		  • School site instructional leaders
			• Assessment created by:
			  • Government
			  • District
			  • College Board
			  • Teacher
			  • Department/district

Focus	• Individual student performance • Individual teacher performance • Comparable to a photo album of the student's work over time	• Performance of student and teacher • Performance of school, district • Comparable to a few photos of a student at different times throughout the year	• Performance of student and teacher at the end of a course or semester • Performance of department, school, district, specific subgroups • Comparable to a single photograph of a student on that day at that time
Audience	• Individual teacher • Students • Parents	• District • Department • Grade-level team • Teacher • Student • Parent	• Government • School board • District • Administration • Community • Department • Teachers • Students • Parents
Locus	• Internal: These assessments come from within the school and classroom where they are taken and are typically administered by teachers in their own classrooms during regular school hours	• Internal: These assessments come from the school or district the student attends and are typically administered by teachers in their own classrooms during regular school hours	• Internal/External: These assessments come from the teacher (final exams) or outside sources (district, state, or national exams or end-of-course exams such as AP tests)
Purpose	• Generate data <u>now</u> to help individuals • Yield information <u>now</u> to guide choices about what to teach, how best to teach it • Measure current performance and progress in light of ultimate goal • Serve to aid and improve instruction and understanding	• Generate data <u>now</u> to help individuals • Get information <u>now</u> about effectiveness of teacher, methods, or curriculum • Measure understanding and progress <u>now</u> to predict performance on summative assessments <u>later</u> • Serve to aid and improve instruction and understanding but also hold both teachers and students accountable • Help teachers meet unit goals	• Generate data about how all students at each grade level are doing relative to standards or other objectives • Measure degree of mastery of a course of study in a given class • Determine effectiveness of schools and programs with different students • Serve to hold schools, departments, and teachers accountable
Assessed	• Constantly • Daily • Weekly • In regular class by students' own teachers as part of curriculum	• Every 4–8 weeks • In regular class (usually) by students' own teachers (usually) as part of curriculum	• 1–2 times a year • In a novel setting often (classroom of other teacher, library, or other large room) by proctors who may not be familiar to students; or in class by regular teachers

FIGURE 8.1 An overview of the assessments most commonly used in schools

(*continues*)

Types of Assessments: An Overview

	Classroom Formative Assessments	Common Formative Assessments	Summative Assessments
Analysis	• Assessments scored, evaluated, and otherwise analyzed by individual teacher who created or chose the assessment and will use the data to better instruct his or her students	• Assessments scored, evaluated, and otherwise analyzed by grade-level teams at school or district who will use the data to improve performance of students, teacher, and schools	• Assessments scored and analyzed by state agencies, or College Board readers who will use the data to evaluate school programs; or scored by teachers on final course exams

Response	• Assessment data allows:
	  • Teacher to change approach
	  • Teacher to alter curriculum
	  • Student to alter or revise
	  • Teacher can respond immediately by changing content or approach
		• Assessment data allows
		  • Grade-level team to respond
		  • Teachers to adjust instruction
		  • Students to change performance
		• Teacher can respond quickly by changing content or approach
			• Assessment data allows:
			  • Teacher to determine final standing
			  • Teacher to make changes in future
			  • Student no chance to improve
			• Little or no feedback to individual students

Impact	• Assessment can:
	• Disrupt curriculum/instruction
	• Complement curriculum/instruction
	• Supplement (if created by students)
		• Assessment can:
		  • Disrupt curriculum/instruction
		  • Complement curriculum/instruction
			• Assessment will:
			  • Disrupt instruction up to a week
			  • Determine future course or college opportunities for some students

Needs	• Students with special needs can:
	  • Get extended time
	  • Demonstrate understanding by alternative means
	  • Use permissible aids
	• Teachers control assessment, so able to adjust task, text, topic, or test
	• Teacher can adjust assessment criteria for special needs students
		• Students with special needs can:
		  • Get extended time
		  • Use permissible aids
		  • Teachers do not control assessment, so unable to adjust task, text, topic, or test
		• Teacher cannot adjust assessment criteria for special needs students
			• Students with special needs can:
			  • Get extended time (if on IEP)
			  • Use permissible aids (if on IEP)
			  • Teachers do not control assessment, so unable to adjust task, text, topic, or test
			• Teacher cannot adjust assessment criteria for special needs students on external exams (e.g., state) but can do so on internal exams (e.g., final exam)

	You can intervene here using data from classroom formative assessments	You can intervene here using data from common formative assessments	

Sample Assessments	• Selected Response/Short Answer
	  • Multiple-choice questions
	  • Short-answer questions
	  • Fill-in questions
	  • Matching items
	  • True/false items
	• Written Response
	  • Timed essay
	  • Process essay
	  • Document-based question (DBQ)
	  • Extended written response
	  • Blog, wiki, or other social media
	  • Original story, poem, or other
	  • Online written discussion of text
	  • Notebook/notes
	• Performance/Presentation
	  • Slide presentation
	  • Speech
	  • Oral reading
	  • Socratic Seminar/forum
	  • Class or small-group discussion
	  • Multimedia production
	• Personal Communication
	  • Student-teacher conference
	  • Online response/discussion
	  • 1:1 discussion with peer
		• Selected Response/Short Answer
		  • Multiple-choice questions
		  • Short-answer questions
		  • Fill-in questions
		  • Matching items
		  • True/false items
		• Written Response
		  • Timed essay
		  • Document-based question (DBQ)
		  • Extended written response
			• Selected Response/Short Answer
			  • Multiple-choice questions
			  • Short-answer questions
			  • Fill-in questions
			  • Matching items
			  • True/false items
			• Written Response
			  • Timed essay
			  • Document-based question (DBQ)
			  • Extended written response
			  • Final paper or major report
			• Performance/Presentation
			  • Speech
			  • Presentation
			  • Performance
			  • Teacher interview

Considerations Common to All

- Academic vocabulary of prompts, directions, question stems
- Genre conventions of tests and each type of test in particular (e.g., multiple-choice, short-answer, document-based essay)
- Genre conventions of each type of text read (e.g., poem, image, infographic, and so on)
- Tasks common to tests
- Alignment with standards for state, national, and Advanced Placement exams

FIGURE 8.1 *Continued*

2. **Apply Best Practices for Assessing Writing in the Classroom**

* *Allow students to use the mode of writing in which they are most proficient when completing a writing assessment.* Writing improves when students are assessed in the format with which they are most experienced—pencil and paper, or word processing.

* *Minimize the extent to which presentation forms, such as handwriting legibility or computer printing, bias judgments of writing quality.* Writing assessment improves when teachers judge the quality of student writing and do not allow factors such as handwriting or computer printing, to bias their judgment.

* *Mask the writer's identity when scoring papers.* Writing assessment improves when teachers do not allow their knowledge of who wrote a paper to influence their judgment.

* *Randomly order students' papers before scoring them.* Writing assessment improves when teachers score papers randomly rather than allow a previous paper's score to influence their judgment.

* *Collect multiple samples of students' writing.* Writing assessment improves when teachers assess students' writing in a variety of genres. This finding supports the decision by the authors of the Common Core Standards to emphasize students' mastery of many different types of writing, since writing is not a single generic skill.

* *Ensure that classroom writing assessments are reliably scored.* Writing assessment improves when teachers use procedures for ensuring that particular aspects of writing, such as quality and its basic attributes, are measured reliably. (16)

As many observe, formative assessments show a strong effect on student learning and improved instruction (Graham, Harris, and Hebert 2011; Marzano 2010; Popham 2011; Reeves 2007). Which ones you use, or your school requires, depends on the school's culture and conditions. Certainly English, with all its different modes—speaking, discussing, writing, reading, learning language, creating projects, and so much more—places a more complex burden on the teacher when it comes to choosing the right assessment for the job given the other constraints of time and curriculum we face. Some teachers are free to create their own rubrics or other scoring criteria when assessing writing; others must use measures or methods adopted by their departments, schools, or districts.

Instead of going into the minutia of assessment, we will skip to the practical and see what these ideas look like in the classroom. A brief review of several key aspects will serve us well; however, we are so undone by all the testing much of the time that we forget effective assessment is essential to our own and students' progress. First, we must remember that assessment serves a variety of purposes by allowing us to:

* determine students' readiness to learn and current level of knowledge or ability in a given area before we teach them

* monitor students' progress over the course of our instruction

* evaluate the effectiveness of our own instruction at key junctures

* measure their progress so we can assign them a final grade

These are the main reasons *why* we assess; but what about *what* we assess—or should? Popham (2011) suggests two key "assessment targets" that are most related to English: cognitive assessments (those that deal with intellectual processes) and affective assessments (those that measure students' attitudes and interests). In addition to these two targets, there remains the issue of assessing students' progress toward the standards, which, presumably, have been aligned with the curriculum and formative assessments in the first place.

Whether your school adopts "Power Standards" (Ainsworth and Viegut 2006) or simply aligns its curriculum with state or national standards, its ability to match standards with instructional goals will depend on your ability to develop a plan for how students will reach those goals and turning them into language students can understand (Zmuda and Tomaino 2001; M. Conley 2005; Stiggins and Chappuis 2012). This last idea—that students should be able not just to understand but to *use*, even develop assessments as part of learning to assess their own and their peers' work—garners strong support from several studies (Stiggins and Chappuis 2012; Graham, Harris, and Hebert 2011; Davies 2007).

Integrating Assessment into the Course

Langer (2002) found that successful middle and high school teachers integrated assessment (and preparation for high-stakes tests) into the curriculum, using the assessments to deepen and support the learning, even as it allowed teachers to prepare students for upcoming state exams. Part of this process means, for example, treating tests as texts that students must be taught to read; therefore, when they read other texts, they will have a more keen eye that can spot questions they will encounter on tests later. In her study, Langer observed that more than 80 percent of effective teachers integrated skills and knowledge that would eventually be tested into their ongoing curriculum (see Figure 8.2). Specifically, she noted that:

> In effective schools, test preparation does not mean more practice of test-related items. Rather, the focus is on the underlying knowledge and skills needed to do well in course-work and in life, as well as on the tests, and these become part of the ongoing English language arts learning goals and the students' ongoing received curriculum. (2002, 17)

In addition to such curricular integration, effective schools foster a culture of improvement through regular conversations about the content and conventions of the exams themselves. Many teachers in such schools actually took the tests themselves to better understand their demands, something I have regularly done and find very instructive. As the report concludes, schools with a strong learning culture focused on students' learning, measuring the effectiveness of the instruction through the tests; whereas the more traditional or common approach emphasized preparing for the tests themselves, the goal being to improve test scores instead of student learning (Langer 2002, 23).

What follows are techniques I have found effective and efficient (i.e., when integrated they do not, as a rule, disrupt my curriculum but complement it) with classes at all grade and ability levels:

- *Weekly Poem:* In my Advanced Placement class, I pick one poem (or, in the spring, a pair with a common theme) from our anthology to read each day that week at the beginning of class. We read it the first day for the gist, perhaps taking time for a more personal connection and some quick jottings about the poem's subject (see Figure 8.3). Each day, for the first 10 to 15 minutes, we re-read, each day more closely, with more intent, taking

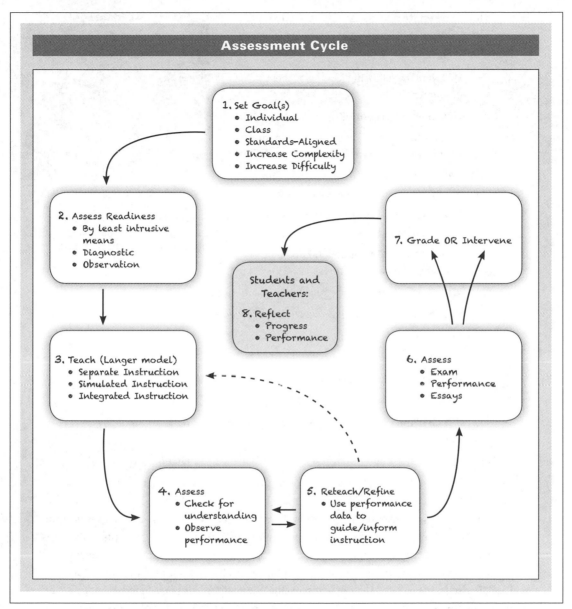

Assessment Cycle

1. Set Goal(s)
   • Individual
   • Class
   • Standards-Aligned
   • Increase Complexity
   • Increase Difficulty

2. Assess Readiness
   • By least intrusive means
   • Diagnostic
   • Observation

3. Teach (Langer model)
   • Separate Instruction
   • Simulated Instruction
   • Integrated Instruction

Students and Teachers:
8. Reflect
   • Progress
   • Performance

7. Grade OR Intervene

6. Assess
   • Exam
   • Performance
   • Essays

4. Assess
   • Check for understanding
   • Observe performance

5. Reteach/Refine
   • Use performance data to guide/inform instruction

FIGURE 8.2 As this model illustrates, the assessment cycle is ongoing throughout the instructional process.

notes as we go to prepare for Friday when we will write (for about 15 minutes) a practice in-class essay in which students tie it all together. Throughout the week, we discuss the poem, working on our analytical reading by focusing, for example, on the poet's use of imagery; it never feels like test preparation. The poems are also chosen for their ability to connect to the major work of literature we are reading at that time (see Figure 8.4).

• ***Incorporate Test Question Stems:*** While we teachers cannot copy state or other major exams we administer, we can often take time while we are sitting there to study them. I went through a variety of exams one year and jotted down representative question stems to use when we discuss or write about literary or informational texts. Here are samples from my list; you can gather your own:

FIGURE 8.3 Students benefit from time spent engaging in close reading. Such sustained reading of a single text creates a context for teaching essential skills as well as discussing the ideas and craft of the text.

- Which of the following _____ best characterizes the . . .
- How does *X* feel about *Y*?
- What is the meaning of the line *xyz* in the context of passage #3?
- What is the meaning of the word *x* as it is used in the following sentence?
- Which statement best summarizes *X*'s attitude toward *Y*?
- Which of the following statements best describes the way *X* perceives *Y*?
- What does *x* imply in the context of this sentence . . . ?
- Which statement best characterizes *X* as presented in the two passages?
- Which phrases from *x* and *y* best summarize *z*?
- *X* is an example of which of the following . . . ?
- Which of the following statements best describes the author's purpose?
- Which of the following does *not* belong?
- Which of the following *x*, *y*, and *z*s would you include to make your essay more _____?
- Which word would best replace *x* in the following sentence?
- Which of the following is the best way to combine sentences *x*, *y*, and *z*?

In addition to using released tests or those I have created to mimic state or AP exams, it can be very useful to have students create their own test questions or writing prompts. This trains them to look for the type of content one would include on such exams; moreover, it acclimates them to the language of tests as they use that language to frame their own questions (see Figure 8.5). It also has the added benefit of increasing engagement and buy-in to what is going on in class. Stiggins and Chappuis (2012), discussing the value and benefits of student-generated exam questions, say:

> Students who participate in the thoughtful analysis of quality work to identify its critical elements or to internalize valued achievement targets become better performers. When students learn to apply these standards so thoroughly that they can effectively evaluate their own and each other's work, they are well on the road to becoming better performers in their own right. (12).

The following examples offer some sense of what it looks like when we invite our students to take over and create the test—or evaluate it.

Poem Analysis

"The Convergence of Twain" and the "Titanic" April 9, 2008

During a disaster, social ranks are not apparent. When the Titanic sank, "crowds of people" including "servants" and the "well fed" were at Mother Nature's mercy (Titanic, 5/6). In the poem "The Convergence of Twain," Thomas Hardy glorifies the Titanic as being a strong creation, but also uses diction to convey the ship's vulnerability when it is hit by the iceberg which symbolizes the clash of social classes. To contrast Hardy's point of view, Slavitt's poem "Titanic" is more direct with the horror of the sinking masterpiece and the abolishment of the hierarchy structure. For example, Slavitt's use of exclamation points indicates that what the people on the ship are experiencing is complete horror. On the other hand, Hardy structures his poem into parts, which slows down the pace of the poem. Hardy's combination of the iceberg "with the intimate welding" of the ships bow symbolize the separation of the rich and the poor and their immediate alliance once there was a threat of danger (the Convergence of Twain, 23). Slavitt conveys the same concept except it is more direct: "To go down... we all go down" illustrates the fall of all social classes when the Titanic was sinking (Titanic, 4). Both authors, whether they allude or directly state it, construct their poem around social class.

FIGURE 8.4 Victoria's analysis of two poems, while short, shows us that such daily work on poems (or any other text read in a similar way) creates opportunities for integrating analytical writing.

It is not enough, however, to just have them create sample test questions in response to required or self-selected readings for class. Students need to know the conventions of the tests themselves as well as the elements from which they are made (see Figure 8.6). Here are some suggestions for what to teach students in this area.

Teach students to read the language of tests. Not only must the reader make sense of the way words are used—denotative versus connotative meanings that bring the tricky ambiguities into the test—but they must also note the type of words used. Consider how the following types of words function within a test to clarify or confuse the reader:

- ***Directive words:*** These words are especially important on an essay exam because they provide specific directions. The rubric for a particular test might say, for example, "Extent to which the writer accurately *defines* the problem." If you *evaluated* the problem, you might be off-topic and thus get penalized. Directive words include: *define, compare, contrast, explain, describe, evaluate, list, identify, summarize, interpret, differentiate, review, outline, prove, analyze.*

Name: _____ Date: _____ Period: _____

Test Title:	
Vocabulary Question	
• is a word you *probably* don't know • can *usually* figure out the meaning from context clues • be aware of connotative and denotative meanings	
Factual Question	
• find the answer *in the text* • skim to find the passage with the answer • question usually includes key words to help locate passage	
Critical Thinking Question	
• find the answer *between the lines* • asks you to make an inference based on clues in the text • might be about style, main idea, author's purpose, tone, etc.	
Essay Question	
• asks you to write a specific amount • incorporates several tasks: analyze, compare, summarize, persuade, define, evaluate, discuss • asks for a statement about a subject you have studied • expects supporting details or examples	
Discussion Question	
• interests you and the rest of the class • makes students think as they talk • allows more than one answer, response, or possible perspective	

FIGURE 8.5: The Testmaker Tool helps students better understand the language and structure of tests by asking them to develop their own test questions. They can use this tool with either personal choice books or required texts.

© 2013 by Jim Burke from *The English Teacher's Companion*, Fourth Edition. Portsmouth, NH: Heinemann.

Name: _____   **Period:** _____   **Date:** _____

Question Type	Example	Notes
Vocabulary	Which of the following best defines *resolute* in the sentence, "The President was *resolute* in his efforts to . . ."	• Word • Defined • Explained
Factual	How long did the Wright brothers' first plane stay in the air?	Find the answer *in* the text, *on* the page
Analytical	How——and why—does the character change by the end of the story?	Find the answer *between the lines*; make an inference
Essay	Agree or disagree: Choose one invention from the Industrial Revolution that continues to benefit us today. Discuss three ways in which this invention has made life easier or better for people. Be sure to provide examples.	Draw from source to illustrate and support what you are saying about the subject

Question Type	Factual
Question	Why did George and Lenny leave their last jobs?
Answer	Because Lenny was accused of raping a woman so they had to get out of town.
Evaluate (1–10)	10
Explain	This is a *very* important question because it gives us essential information about both men and foreshadows later events in the story.
Question Type	
Question	
Answer	
Evaluate (1–10)	
Explain	

FIGURE 8.6 The Test Creator works in a similar way to the Testmaker Tool but asks students to focus more on evaluating the quality of their questions and answers.

© 2013 by Jim Burke from *The English Teacher's Companion*, Fourth Edition. Portsmouth, NH: Heinemann.

- ***Quantitative words:*** Examples include *always, most, never, equal, sometimes, usually, almost, often, all, none.* In *How to Study in College,* Walter Pauk (1997) organizes these qualifiers into what he calls "families" that form a continuum Pauk argues is useful for true/false and multiple-choice questions:

  - All-most-some-none [no]
  - Always-usually-sometimes-never
  - Great-much-little-no
  - More-equal-less
  - Good-bad
  - Is-is not

- ***Technical words:*** These are specific subject-matter words that students must know to read the test successfully. Such words include *adjective* or *onomatopoeia, irony* or *imagery.* (See Figure 7.14.)

- ***Procedural words:*** These words might appear in the directions or the teacher's discussion of the test. They include words like *rubric, standard, DBQ,* or *procedure.* (See extensive list of academic vocabulary words in Figure 7.1.)

Many of the strategies outlined next are already a part of your curriculum. We have students read for meaning, find supporting details, annotate texts, and summarize what they read all the time. The following list of types of questions, while overlapping in places, provides a set of cognitive abilities students need to have if they are to be effective readers of tests:

- Analytical (*Explain the causes of Holden Caulfield's troubles as a result of his brother's death.*)
- Synthesis (*After reading this story what would be the best title and why?*)
- Identification (*Identify all of the verbs in the following passage.*)
- Definition (*Which of the following best defines the word* antiquated?)
- Authorial intention (*What was Miller trying to say about the McCarthy Era in* The Crucible?)
- Cause and effect (*Identify the main causes of aggression according to the article.*)
- Perspective (*How does the writer feel about this subject?*)
- Categorical questions (*Which of the following genres best describe this passage?*)
- Inferential (*Based on his actions, what does this character fear?*)
- Evaluative (*Which of the two passages offer the most cogent argument?*)
- Speculative (*If you read on, which of the following outcomes would you expect?*)
- Connotative (*What does the word* essence *mean based on the author's use of it in the previous sentence?*)
- Sequential/logical (*How does the argument of _____ contribute to the larger treatment of . . . and . . . ?*)
- Comparative (X *and* Y *are similar in that they both . . .*)
- Purpose (*Device* X *is most commonly used to . . .*)

Finally, after considering all these items, one faces the more basic, but still important, task of teaching students—especially those who lack the necessary background—how to actually read tests as a genre in their own right. Whatever you do in terms of assessment, you need to be sure students have clear directions for the tasks involved. I suggest creating a standard set of directions by way of helping them develop routines when it comes time to take or practice for standardized tests. Here then are the techniques I teach students who must take major standardized exams for which the school—and, in some cases, they—can experience serious consequences:

Test-Taking Strategy Directions

- ***Set a purpose:*** Turn the title (e.g., "Matter") into a PQ: What is matter?

- ***Skim and scan:*** Depending on how much time students have for the test, they should flip through to get a sense of the terrain: number and type of questions, what's easy, what's difficult, how much time it should take. This will orient students and allow them to prioritize their time and attention. Skim the heading, first lines of paragraphs, and questions (but not the answers).

- ***Do the easy ones first:*** As with pick-up-sticks, students get just as much credit for the easy ones as the difficult ones. After skimming through the test, they should knock out the ones they know so they have the time they need to read the others more closely. This will also activate students' background knowledge, thus making it more likely they can figure out the more difficult questions.

- ***Try to answer the question before looking at the answers:*** Paired with the previous strategy, this method gets students primed to know the answer when they see it; if they have already determined the answer in their heads, they know what to look for when they check the list of possible answers.

- ***Paraphrase the question in their own words:*** This should help them better understand what they are being asked.

- ***Read all the possible answers first before answering:*** Test makers depend on inattentive readers to make mistakes that conscientious readers will not. Even if students see the answer they know is right, they must learn to read through them all to make sure there is no surprise hiding under answer E (e.g., "All of the above").

- ***Make a plan:*** Use these strategies:
  - Underline keywords in each question
  - Put a dot (•) next to any possible answers
  - Use P.O.E.: Process of elimination to rule out answers that cannot be right
  - Draw a line from the correct answer to the words in the text that provide evidence for your answer

- ***Watch out for traps:*** Some tests use the word *not* to trip students up; teach students to stop and ask themselves what the question is really asking. Avoid answering questions that include information from the passage, especially on standardized test, because these are often designed to distract from the actual answer. Instead, look for answers that respond to the question.

- ***Read recursively:*** Good readers habitually circle back around to check what they are reading and thinking against what they have already read to see that they agree. This habit also keeps them attentive to what they are supposed to be doing. On an essay test, for example, after reading and underlining the key words in the directions, students should pause periodically to re-read the prompt and any accompanying scoring guides. This will help them measure the extent to which they are answering the question; it might also provide useful information to spark new ideas for their essay.

- **Read the answer sheet:** Students need to understand how it works. A group of students once neglected to do this on a district reading test, resulting in a score for many of −2.6. We calculated this to mean they were reading at the level of a fetus nearing its third month.

- **Answer questions in the order that works best:** Students should work through the test in the order that makes the most sense to them and will help them read it best. If reading the multiple-choice and fill-ins will help remind them of all they should address in their essay, so be it. One important point, however: They must use some sort of system to indicate which questions they have to still answer and be sure to erase any such marks before turning in the test.

- **Trade and Grade:** If you're doing a sample test in class for practice, this is a good idea, especially if you allow time for students to discuss the exam with each other and the class.

- **Pause and Reflect:**

  - How did you do?
  - What went wrong?
  - What went well?
  - How to do better next time?

Questions to Ask When Reading a Test

- Why is that the best answer?
- What is the question for which this is the answer?
- Why did I not choose that answer?
- How did I arrive at this answer?
- Is this answer based on my experience and opinion or on information found in the text on which I'm being tested?
- Where else can I look for this information (e.g., another section of the test)?
- What does that word mean in this context?
- What does the rubric or other scoring guide suggest I need to understand or look for in this question?
- What are they actually trying to test?
- Is it better to guess or leave it blank?

PAUSE & REFLECT After reading the previous section about teaching students to read and take tests, pause to reflect on your experiences with giving and taking tests. Have tests been easy for you or have they been part of your own academic struggle?

This is all, as I have discussed here and elsewhere, pretty personal stuff for me (Burke 2004, 2005). I knew nothing about taking tests when I graduated from high school. But I learned, slowly improving, patiently acquiring the necessary strategies for taking tests, as had my father before me. After dropping out of high school, he took the lowest-paying job with the state printing plant where, after learning how to study and take tests, he advanced by examination. By the time he retired 38 years later, the only position above his was filled by an appointment from the governor.

Writing **on Demand**

We are quick to resist and even dismiss the writing-on-demand genre as a distraction, an intrusion, a discordant note in the otherwise elegant music we want our curriculum to make. We often regard this genre as inauthentic, useless, even meaningless. And yet, our students encounter this genre everywhere: on final exams, formative assessments, district and state assessments; not to mention college placement exams and those tests, such as the SAT, ACT, and Advanced Placement, that are central to the college-bound student's future success. Even after they graduate, depending on their career path, students find themselves facing still more timed writing tests as they attempt to enter graduate school, upper management, or positions in civil service; this is the case for those applying to be firefighters in the town where I teach. As Janet Angelillo (2005) writes, "Writing to prompts is a way of life; it is the reality of much real-world writing, so we teach it from a sense of duty. . . . Let's teach it because we know it is a skill they need" (155).

In other words, timed writing is a legitimate genre of writing, one that requires a specific set of skills and type of knowledge if students are to succeed not only in school but also in their adult lives. Gere, Christenbury, and Sassi (2005) go so far as to say that *"most writing is writing on demand"* (5), then go on to outline their "crucial assumptions" about such writing, arguing that good writing and writing on demand are not contradictory; that assessment is an integral part of effective writing instruction; that writing prompts can be approached rhetorically (5).

Timed writing—also referred to as writing on demand—is a genre of particular concern to most teachers given national trends in K–12 education that suggest students are writing less and, when they *do* write, are more likely to be writing or preparing for a writing exam provided by a department, district, state, or organization such as the College Board (Graham, Harris, and Hebert 2011; Applebee and Langer 2009, 2011; Gere, Christenbury, and Sassi 2005; Hillocks 2002). Calfee and Miller (2007) distinguish between two types of such writing prompts: "stand-alone" and "text-based" prompts (278). The authors refer to the first of these prompts as a "cold-turkey scenario" in which there is no preparation, no text to read or respond to; the second situation, however, includes some passage or a complete text the student must read either for background or as the basis of a critical analysis (see Figure 8.7).

Calfee and Miller concluded that text-based prompts resulted in the best performance by students in general as they offer students of all levels "a resource for the writing task . . . [which] lessens the

FIGURE 8.7 Students must learn how to perform on a variety of assessments. Freshmen students here write in-class essays about their independent reading books at the end of the grading period.

demands on memory and ensures all students have a common starting point for the task" (2007, 276). Such support is particularly helpful and important to English learners and students who need additional support on such timed and often high-pressure writing assessments. This last observation from Calfee and Miller—about helping students by giving them a foot up—addresses one final issue about writing assessment that repeatedly surfaces in discussions about formative writing assessment; for example, Graham, Harris, and Hebert (2011) note:

> Concerns have further been raised about the fairness of such assessments, as analyses of state writing tests reveal that what is assessed, how it is assessed, and how it is scored vary from state to state [and, I would add, from teacher to teacher, even, arguably, assignment to assignment with the same teacher] . . . and such differences have direct consequences for how many students [pass or fail]. (12)

Even at its best, assessment evokes images of students standing at the doorway to the next grade level, a program students need the grades to enter, or college itself. Some students are weighed out and asked to trust that the scales are balanced, accurate, and fair despite a long history that suggests fairness is an elusive ideal, especially when it comes to the inherently subjective assessment of writing. Even though multiple measures are implemented to achieve greater validity and consistency, Wilson (2006) challenges the reliability of such assessments, concluding along with others she cites, that writing assessment as typically practiced is "extremely unreliable" (20) and should be used as a guide not a gate.

Although the following suggestions would benefit all students, at least take time to consult this checklist for your English learners:

- Know who *all* your English learners are
- Allow them additional time
- Permit them to bring notes or use index cards
- Tell them they can use their books
- Define any unknown words in the prompt, directions, or text
- Direct them to use the BOSS or ABCD strategy (see Gallagher 2006)

The primary purpose of such formative assessments, according to Calfee and Miller (2007), "is to establish the degree to which the student is making progress—and, if he or she is not, to find out how to help the student move ahead" (274). But even here, within the constraints of assessing their performance and progress, and preparing for summative measures to which we must all answer, we can reach for meaning. I attempt this, for example, during our time each day reading, discussing, and writing about the weekly poem, all of which culminates in a 15-minute in-class practice essay on Fridays. We work daily on writing but do so within the context of a larger question about, for example, borders (a theme that both poems share). This is so that the poems, our discussion of them, and the experience of writing about them have some greater meaning than merely practicing for the AP exam so many months away.

Checklist: Writing on Demand

- Create a *text*-based prompt.

- Give students time, paper, and the message they should prepare *before* they write.

- Discuss successful and unsuccessful samples of writing before beginning.

- Tell students to use the writing process model.

- Remind students to use strategies when writing.

- Display useful academic language and strategies on classroom walls.

- Provide the criteria by which they will be assessed.

- Establish and maintain a quiet, focused environment while they write.

- Require students to reflect on their performance when they finish.

When it comes to such writing, we are always serving at least two masters: assessing what students know and using the occasion to actively teach them how to write essays. While our inclination with timed writing is to get it over with and get back to business, we must realize that such instruction *is* our business. To this end, we must use the occasion of on-demand writing not only to prepare for this one but to teach students how to do well on *all* such exams. This means making room for both instruction on and reflection about their performance.

Some years ago I was preparing a group of sophomores for the upcoming state exam. To do this, I downloaded sample essay prompts from the state education department website and copied them for the students, along with the rubric that would be used by the state to assess them. I should note that this was a class of underachieving students, all of whom read several grades below the tenth-grade level.

Before they wrote, I had them jot down things they knew they needed to remember to do on the exam; in addition, I asked them to list those areas they personally needed to watch for and check on throughout the writing process. Finally, I told them to go through and underline what they needed to *do* and to *include* in their essays according to the prompt. I then followed up by reading each line in the prompt and asking them, "What, if anything, did you underline in that sentence?" We would then discuss what they underlined, whether they should have, or why they did not underline those things they should have. The prompt was fairly common, though these are not its exact words: *Write an essay about someone who has played an important role in your life. Discuss what they taught you and how it has shaped your life*. I then directed them to write the essay, having left them the time they needed to write.

> **"**WHILE OUR INCLINATION WITH TIMED WRITING IS TO GET IT OVER WITH AND GET BACK TO BUSINESS, WE MUST REALIZE THAT SUCH INSTRUCTION *IS* OUR BUSINESS.**"**

During the writing of their essays, I looked for an appropriate "pause point" (Gawande 2009, 126) to have them reflect on their performance so far. After about 10 minutes, I noticed that most of the kids were writing away, filling the page; a few others, however, had one

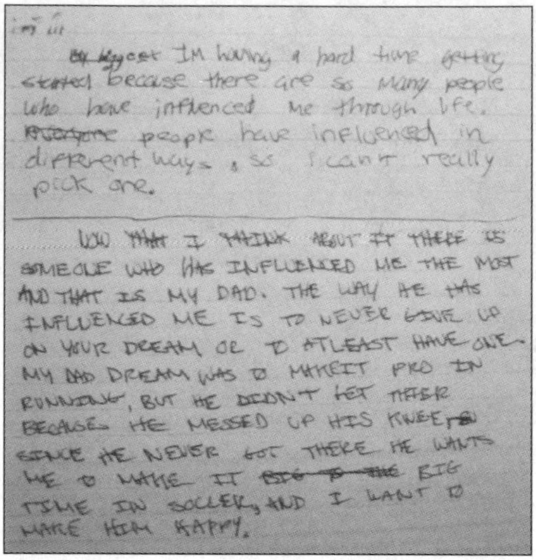

FIGURE 8.8 Eduardo's reflections, followed by the beginning of the practice essay he wrote in class as part of our preparation for the state exit exam.

sentence, or a page of notes but no writing. I told everyone to finish the sentence they were writing and draw a line across the page. Underneath this line, I asked them to reflect on what they had done so far to write what they had. "If you asked questions such as 'Who has taught me the most important lesson?' or 'Why was *that* the most important lesson?' then jot those down. If, however, you have a blank page, write down what is going on, why you have no writing so far." They all kept writing now, even the kids who had not been writing. After a few minutes, I told them to draw a line across the page and resume writing their essay. I didn't want to ask them to discuss what they wrote because I didn't want to take them out of the stream of writing for too long. I noticed those, most notably Natalie and Eduardo, who had *not* been writing were now galloping across the plains of the page. (See Figure 8.8.)

After they finished writing, students assessed themselves using the state rubric, then jotted down a few quick insights about what they did that helped and what was difficult—and *why*; these were subjects to which we would return in the coming days as we debriefed and prepared for the state exit exam. Then, finally, they turned in their essays and left. I quickly thumbed through to find Natalie's and Eduardo's to see what they wrote during and after the reflection. In short, Natalie, who had a very difficult life outside of school and serious self-esteem issues, wrote that every time she was about to put down a word, she would hear her mother's voice saying *Oh yes, that's a brillllliant idea!* in her sarcastic voice, so Natalie would not write it down. Once she could name the enemy (her mother) and explain the effect on her (to herself), she wrote the solid essay I knew she could.

Eduardo, whose Latino culture placed family first, said that his problem was that he had so many people who had influenced him profoundly, among them his father, his mother, and his uncle, who had taught him soccer. Eduardo explained after that he feared disrespecting the other two if he wrote about one. After honoring and recognizing the importance of all these people, Eduardo wrote about his father, getting off to a usable beginning of what he could no doubt turn into a better essay given more time. Eduardo was, it seemed to me, suffering from a form of cultural interference here, which when removed (through reflection), freed him up to write what he really felt.

> **" After honoring and recognizing the importance of all these people, Eduardo wrote about his father . . . "**

It is this sort of responsive teaching that Tatum (2005) refers to and calls for in his expanded notion of literacy when he writes: "Literacy instruction must be planned in ways to advance multiple literacies which should [include]: academic, cultural, emotional, and social literacy. . . . [And such] instruction must take place in responsive environments" (35).

Teaching Timed Writing: What It Looks Like

As we near the end of the semester in my AP Lit class, it is time to wrap things up, give them a chance to show me what they know and have learned about *Siddhartha* as well as writing in general and literature in particular. On-demand writing is of particular importance as a skill for those students who must not only master this genre if they are to survive the AP exam in May but also thrive in college when they arrive in the fall; there they will take placement exams and those dreaded essay exams in those cute little blue books. Concern has grown in recent years about students' writing performance in college (National Commission on Writing 2003; American Diploma Project 2004; Perin 2007; Applebee and Langer 2009) both in terms of quality and quantity as students are "not . . . given assignments requiring writing of any significant length or complexity" (Applebee and Langer 2009, 21). These reports raise important questions about writing in the secondary classroom, for if most of the writing done is timed, in-class writing (as opposed to more fully developed process writing), the likelihood of feedback and critical discussions is diminished considerably.

> **"**ONE REASON I DEVOTE TIME TO DIRECTLY TEACHING TIMED WRITING IN MY AP CLASSES IS THAT I HAVE A WIDE RANGE OF ABILITIES IN THE CLASS.**"**

What then, does it look like to *teach* students how to write on demand for summative assessments? While the following sequence comes from my AP Lit class, it offers an instructional sequence that can be adapted to a wide range of classes and assignments. One reason I devote time to directly teaching timed writing in my AP classes is that I have a wide range of abilities in the class. Our district's open enrollment policy allows anyone who chooses to enroll in AP Literature to do so, which means I have a lot of kids who need deliberate instruction to reach their potential. The following sequence describes what I did in the days leading up to the AP exam; one could easily adapt it to any other such summative assessment for which students might be preparing.

1. Give all the students "The Basics: Writing a Timed Essay" handout (see Figure 8.9) two days before the final, making this the last minilesson of the semester and on an area of urgent importance to many for whom this remains a difficult genre. It also engages them, as they must know how to write such essays in other classes and for college. On the back of their handout is the rubric I will use to assess their performance (see Figure 8.10); I encourage them to dedicate more time to examining what the rubric *really* says, for though we have used it all year long, they still have not internalized all its elements.

2. Ask them to skim it and indicate those areas they need to work on or which are unfamiliar to them; then jot down a few thoughts about those items and this genre in general in their notebook, after which I direct them to turn and talk to a neighbor for a minute to hear what others have to say on this topic (see Figure 8.11).

3. Provide students with copies of the unannotated sample timed essay like the one they will be writing; this is, however, not a topic they would see nor a book about which any of them could write on the upcoming test, so I am not giving away the keys to the kingdom here. We take time to break down the prompt, going through line by line, guided by the question, "Is there anything there you should underline because

The Basics: Writing a Timed Essay

Writing a brilliant essay about a topic and a text you may never have seen before is difficult! You have to think and act fast if you are going to write something you can turn in with pride at the end of the allotted time. After reading these strategies for writing a timed essay, consult the annotated sample prompt, rubric, and paper. Note that most readers realize you are writing under difficult circumstances for readers who are trained to "reward you for what you do well, not punish you for what you do wrong" as they say when scoring the AP Literature and Composition essays.

BEFORE
Preview, Pick, and Prepare

1. Preview all prompts (if you have choices) and pick the topic about which you can write the best essay (which may be different from the one about which you would *most* like to write).
2. Analyze the prompt, paying close attention to what you must *do* and *include*; this means identify and underline the required nouns and verbs (e.g., *compare* and *contrast*, *textual evidence* and *literary devices*).
3. Read and take useful notes—in the margins or on a separate piece of paper—related to your chosen prompt if you are writing about a text included in the test; if there is no text, proceed to the planning stage.

Plan

4. Generate compelling, specific ideas that are clearly related to the prompt.
5. Gather examples, quotations, evidence, or details from appropriate sources or the text you are analyzing.
6. Revisit the prompt to confirm that your ideas, examples, and evidence are appropriate to the prompt.
7. Sketch out a brief writing plan, outline, or mind map *if time allows*; indicate the key connections and ideas.
8. Develop a thesis that is narrow and compelling, but also supportable and related to the prompt.
9. **Avoid** a formulaic thesis or restatement of the prompt itself if at all possible (to make a strong first impression).
10. Write Legibly: What the reader can't read, they skip, resulting in a lower grade.

DURING
Write

11. Establish your purpose and point quickly and in a compelling voice to make a strong first impression.
12. Use an organizational strategy appropriate to the prompt and your thesis, making sure it prevents writing a summary or mere description. Choosing a journey pattern, for example, gives the writer an analytical focus.
13. **Avoid** long introductions; instead, create a narrow, compelling argument you can then defend in the essay.
14. Organize each body paragraph around a specific topic sentence that makes an assertion related to your thesis (instead of beginning with description or narration, which takes time and does not advance your argument).
15. Integrate specific examples, evidence, and details—*and comment on these*, explaining what the quotations or examples mean, why they are important, how they relate to your thesis or topic sentence.
16. **Avoid** summary; if you find yourself summarizing, keep asking yourself, "So what?" and "Who cares?" and "How is that related to my claim or the point I was trying to make?"
17. Revisit the prompt, checking that you are doing or including *everything* it requires.
18. Monitor the time: You must write a *complete* essay with a beginning, middle, and end. Every second counts!
19. Take time to write well: You have no time to revise, so pay attention along the way to make sure that you:
    - ❏ Pay as much attention to *what* you write as you to *how* you write: voice and style matter!
    - ❏ Use strong verbs, precise nouns, and a variety of sentence types appropriate to your purpose.
    - ❏ Provide effective transitions to clarify and emphasize your ideas and the connections between them.
    - ❏ Organize your ideas in paragraphs that are visibly indented, fully developed, and purposefully arranged.
    - ❏ **Avoid** any grandstanding, editorializing, ranting, seeking pity, asking for mercy, or making excuses.
20. Conclude the essay, tying up all your ideas, connecting them to the thesis; however, do more than just restate what you have already said. Reach for the great closing line that delivers to the reader a final WOW!

AFTER
Revisit and Refine

21. Revisit the prompt and, if available, the rubric to make sure you have done *everything* the prompt asks.
22. Edit and proofread as needed depending on the number, type, and severity of your errors.
23. Follow any other minor directions for which you might be penalized: indicating which prompt you wrote about, attaching the prompts, scoring rubric, or notes you may have made to prepare to write.

Troubleshooting

- What if you do not understand the topic or the text you must write about?
- What if reading and writing are difficult for you and so you need more time to complete this assignment?
- What if you write better on the computer than on paper?

FIGURE 8.9 This one page summary discusses what successful writers do on timed writing assessments. We return to it throughout the year as part of our study of timed writing exams.

Student: _____ **Paper:** _____ **Score:** _____

Score	In your essay, you
9–8 **A+/A**	❏ exceed or satisfy all requirements outlined in the directions and/or prompt ❏ respond to the prompt clearly, directly, and fully ❏ approach the text analytically ❏ craft an appropriate and cogent argument ❏ incorporate abundant, effective evidence from the text to support and illustrate your argument ❏ achieve a degree of subtlety and insight through the combination of your ideas and writing ❏ have few/no GUM (grammar, usage, mechanics) errors and use GUM to improve meaning/effect ❏ make readers constantly think, "Great move!" "Insightful!" "Such a way with words . . ." "Wow!"
7–6 **A–/B+**	❏ exceed some and satisfy all requirements outlined in the directions and/or prompt ❏ respond to the prompt but not as clearly, directly, or fully as an 8–9 paper ❏ approach the text analytically, but do not develop your ideas to that higher standard ❏ craft an appropriate and plausible argument ❏ incorporate evidence from the text to support and illustrate your argument ❏ achieve moments of subtlety and insight through the combination of your ideas and writing ❏ have a few minor GUM (grammar, usage, mechanics) errors; use GUM to improve meaning/effect ❏ make readers often think, "Great move!" "Insightful!" "Such a way with words . . ." "Yes!"
5 **B**	❏ satisfy most requirements outlined in the directions and/or prompt ❏ respond to the prompt but lack full understanding of the topic, text, or task ❏ attempt to approach the text analytically but tend to summarize more than analyze ❏ craft a usable argument that shows understanding but limited insight ❏ use some/basic evidence from the text to support and illustrate your argument ❏ show some subtlety and insight through the combination of your ideas and writing ❏ have some intrusive GUM (grammar, usage, mechanics) errors; use GUM to little effect ❏ make readers occasionally think, "Nice move," "Thoughtful!" "Nice wording, shows potential"
4–3 **B–/C**	❏ satisfy most/some requirements outlined in the directions and/or prompt ❏ respond to the prompt incompletely, indirectly, or incorrectly in one or more ways ❏ show minimal analysis or no attempt to analyze; summarize with few insights about text ❏ craft an argument that is indefensible or otherwise flawed; may not *have* an argument ❏ use no substantial or relevant evidence from the text to support and illustrate your argument ❏ show no subtlety or insight through the combination of your ideas and writing ❏ have many possible GUM (grammar, usage, mechanics) errors; GUM not used to any effect ❏ make readers think, "Good idea there," "Wish writer had developed that," "I see potential here!"

2–1
 	
D/F
	❏ satisfy few or no requirements outlined in the directions and/or prompt
	❏ combine two or more serious problems in the following areas:
	  ❏ may not satisfy any of the requirements outlined in the directions and/or prompt
	  ❏ may not address the actual prompt
	  ❏ may indicate a serious misreading of the text (or suggest the student simply did *not* read it)
	  ❏ may offer little or no textual evidence
	  ❏ may use textual evidence in a way that suggests a failure to understand the text
	  ❏ may be unclear, badly written, or unacceptably brief
	  ❏ may have so many errors as to be difficult to read or understand
	  ❏ may have written an essay with great style but say nothing about the subject
	  ❏ make readers think, "You should have asked for help."

Grade	**What works:** / **What to work on:**

FIGURE 8.10 This is the rubric I use for the timed essays my AP students take, all of which use previously released AP free-response topics. It allows us to anchor our assessment in the AP course objectives without making the course seem like just a test-prep class.

FIGURE 8.11a Will first reads through the clean copy of the sample essay, jotting down what he thinks the writer did well.

FIGURE 8.11b Will and Richard then compare their comments, focusing on the differences between their analyses before looking at the annotated sample I created that identifies all the subtle details of the sample essay.

you must *do* or *include* it in your essay?" As we move through the prompt, I respond routinely with questions like:

- "Why do you think that?"
- "What would you include and why would that be important?"
- "Well, what is the question the prompt is asking you to answer?"

4. Direct them to now read and annotate the clean copy of the sample paper *on their own* (which I remind them was written in class and thus merits more forgiveness of those errors or flaws they may find). I tell them to make notes in the margin that identify what this writer does that makes it so successful, emphasizing that there is something to say in nearly every sentence, certainly every paragraph. As they do this, I circulate, goad, advise, direct their attention, ask questions, and clarify. I remind them to consult the rubric and The Basics: Writing a Timed Essay handout we previously discussed.

5. Tell them to now huddle up in pairs or threes to compare what they said, what they thought, focusing on things one person noticed or said that escaped the others.

6. Facilitate classwide discussion about what they noticed, going through the essay nearly line by line (since it is so brief), asking questions, directing their attention, using their observations and annotations to guide the discussion. In addition, since my goal is to teach them how to write such essays, I keep redirecting them back to the appropriate item in The Basics handout so we can revisit and discuss how that applies to the sample essay.

7. Distribute the annotated version (see Figure 8.12) and have them compare what I noticed with their observations. I ask them to use my annotated edition to guide their small-group discussion and generate questions and observations we can then use for our discussion.

Verbs are **bold**; nouns are *italic*.	**Prompt** In great literature, no scene of violence exists for its own sake. **Choose** a work of *literary merit* that **confronts** the reader or audience with a *scene or scenes of violence*. In a well-organized essay, **explain** how the scene or scenes **contribute** to the *meaning of the complete work*. **Avoid** *plot summary*.

Alexander T.

Per. 2/Burke

> Note the title: Adds insight, creates a frame.

We Are the Good Guys

> Opens with compelling imagery related to prompt.

The Road, by Cormac McCarthy begins with a human head on a stake in the middle of the road. It later follows with the boy staring at a bloody mattress with a woman on it, screaming because both of her legs have been sawed off. These examples of extremely graphic violence show the most animalistic side of human behavior, which McCarthy uses to demonstrate humanity's constant struggle with the inner beast.

> Provides narrow claim that addresses prompt without repeating it.

> Establishes critical frame and subject by third sentence.

We, as a species, are always torn between emotion and reason. ~~father about the surrounding~~ Oftentimes the struggle is greatest when we are put in the most dire circumstances. This is evident in *The Road*, where nuclear holocaust tests our humanity and then tests our basic will to survive, which are two very different things. The struggle between these things is emphasized by scenes of grotesque violence, which accentuate our animalistic flaws, and an innocent boy, who is present at these scenes of violence and who represents our future and our capacity to love.

> Begins second ¶ with focused statement related to previous ¶ and thesis.

> Introduces new point that builds on topic sentence; then examines use and meaning of violence.

> Situates and elaborates on previous idea, then illustrates with example.

> Contrasts two ideas with great style and rhetorical effect.

The boy often questions his father about the ~~father about the surrounding~~ surrounding violence, presenting an individual struggle between right and wrong that is representative of the entire species' struggle. ~~father about the surrounding~~ The questioning often involves the boy repeatedly asking whether they are the good guys or not, and why the bad guys want to eat them. McCarthy uses this loss of innocence throughout the novel to make the reader aware of not only the desperation the nuclear winter has caused but what we have done in times of great suffering. A boy and his father, scarred by the apocalypse of humankind, struggle to maintain their compassion and their essential humanity because it is their only valuable possession.

> Begins with narrative then shifts to analysis, reestablishing connection to thesis but introducing new ideas.

> Sustains focus on author's purpose and how he achieves it.

> Offers summary, then analysis of effect, followed by explanation of importance.

The combination of compassion and great violence illustrates the duality of our race. The scenes of violence in *The Road* question our worth, while the boy confirms it; he proves that even though a majority of us will commit atrocities and turn on one another in order to survive, there are a small few who justify our existence by maintaining grace in the worst of times.

> Expands idea and thesis of duality of our nature.

> Drills down to examine meaning, import of previous lines, link to larger themes.

The Road's dual image of carnage and compassion ~~father about the~~ shows us that it is not enough to simply survive, because to live without the things that make us so vulnerable is pointless. It tells us that it is not enough to simply survive, but we must prove that we are worthy of surviving.

> Uses repetition (shows, tells) to emphasize the final point in last line.

> Delivers Wow! last line, which transforms this in-class essay into a work of compelling ideas and fine writing.

FIGURE 8.12 This is the sample annotated essay discussed here. I use Microsoft Word's annotation tools to create the notes. The blocked-out portions represent those parts the student crossed out. I want students to see them so they learn they can do the same when writing their essays.

8. Project the same annotated edition of the essay on the large screen so I can go through and do a think-aloud in great detail, pointing out and elaborating on my annotations, asking them questions, redirecting them again to The Basics sheet that offers a summary of the skills and knowledge they need.

9. Tell them that they may, on the day of the exam, bring an index card with information on it to help them write the best essay they can. I tell them that if they use it to merely jot down facts—names of people and places—they will get little use of it; if, however, they jot down analytical frames (e.g., *X* changes as a result of *Y*, which suggests *Z*; this is important because . . .) that will be of use for most any prompt they might receive on that day (see Figure 8.13). I do not tell them the prompts, but I do give them the broadest outlines for the *Siddhar-tha* essay, telling them only this: "Focus on the key themes we have discussed. And no, you may not bring your book or use any other notes beyond what is on the index card."

FIGURE 8.13 Students need to learn to write the in-class essays under those conditions similar to the ones they will encounter on the test for which they are preparing. Jenna and others get to bring one index card with key information on it; over time, however, they do not get this help and must come in ready to write.

10. Direct them to write the essays—one on *Siddhartha*, one on their most recent independent reading book—in the two hours we have for final exams. I permit them to keep the index card out on their desks and, if they choose, the Basics: Writing a Timed Essay handout (see Figure 8.9) to use as a guide, a checklist throughout their process.

11. Score their essays using the AP rubric, noting which features of their performance stand out as I go and making samples to discuss when we return. It is winter break, the semester is over, and I have (for just my AP Lit class) 140 essays; thus, I offer few if any comments on any papers but gather examples and notes to discuss (see Figure 8.14).

12. Return and discuss essays on the first day back from winter break, making general observations, doing a think-aloud on the overhead with a sample essay that captures what we discussed, and focusing in particular on the one thing they can do next time to improve. In this case, the "one thing" is my observation, overwhelmingly apparent on this essay, that the strong writers use many more analytical verbs and substantial subjects in contrast with the less successful writers; their sentences begin with generic nouns and verbs that tend to narrate or summarize and thus not show any insight or construct any arguments that merit defending. To make this point, I take two papers—a high (8 out of possible 9) and a medium (5) and type up, in a two-column handout (it doesn't take that long!), the first 7–8 words from each sentence in the entire essay in the order in which they were written, then use this to guide our discussion. I then ask them to code each sentence beginning to indicate the source of the idea:

- If the sentence indicates an argument or observation the student (S) has come up with, they label it with an (S).
- If the sentence summarizes what the author (A) says or describes, they label it with an (A)

After they work though this—solo or in pairs, it doesn't matter to me—I have students return to and analyze their own essays using the same method.

Siddhartha Post-Final Analysis

Both of these are written in response to the same prompt:

The Cycle of Life and Learning: Throughout the *Siddhartha* unit, we have referred to the ODONO (Orientation-Disorientation-New Orientation) model, applying it to our own lives and the characters in the stories we have read. In this essay, you will use the ODONO model to explain Siddhartha's journey and to analyze what each person and experience along the way taught him and how that lesson led to his final enlightenment. Do not use the ODONO model to summarize. You may also want to incorporate into this essay ideas from the chapter on the hero's journey from Campbell, which we also read.

Note: The shaded portions indicate the paragraphs of each paper; the numbers correspond with each sentence in the essays. Thus, the paper that received an 8 had 18 sentences; the 5 paper had 34 sentences. As you read through each paper, code the sentence as follows: If the sentence offers an argument or observation the student created (i.e., that shows analysis, insight) put an *S* next to it; if, instead, the sentence describes what happens or what the author does (i.e., that summarizes the events or ideas), put an *A* next to it. If you are not sure, put a question mark.

8-Score Paper	5-Score Paper
1. Enlightenment, nirvana: these words imply a realization . . .	1. In *Siddhartha*, by Herman Hesse, the main character, Siddhartha realizes . . .
2. Also implied in these words, however, is a journey . . .	2. As he sets out on his journey, Siddhartha is confronted . . .
3. In Hesse's *Siddhartha*, the eponymous protagonist experiences . . .	3. Due to Siddhartha's need to search for enlightenment, he must put . . .
4. Through Siddhartha, Hesse suggests . . .	4. When Siddhartha leaves home, he goes . . .
5. Each time that Siddhartha loses orientation is clearly marked by . . .	5. At first, Siddhartha feels . . .
6. But each time he becomes disoriented, he does not . . .	6. The Samana's teaching was not . . .
7. Rather, Siddhartha's losses of orientation are better described as . . .	7. The Samanas helped Siddhartha realize . . .
8. His departure from the Samanas, for example, is explicitly depicted as . . .	8. Siddhartha also realizes that . . .
9. But this fact is less important than . . .	9. Govinda and Siddhartha then went . . .
10. Through this example, Hesse asserts that . . .	10. Siddhartha followed the teachings . . .
11. The enlightening effect of disorientation is best observed in . . .	11. Again, Siddhartha felt that he'd rather . . .
12. With young Siddhartha's departure, the protagonist makes . . .	12. Through Gotama, though, he finally realizes . . .
13. This disorientation teaches the greatest lesson . . .	13. Siddhartha wanted to be like Gotama . . .
14. In this way, Hesse shows us that . . .	14. Before Siddhartha leaves Gotama, he knows . . .
15. Essentially, to become disoriented is to move . . .	15. Govinda doesn't want Siddhartha to leave . . .
16. Disorientation refines our knowledge, bringing us closer . . .	16. Though Govinda taught Siddhartha always oriented themselves . . .
17. Like rough sandpaper smoothing a soft wood into a sphere, it serves . . .	17. While on his own, Siddhartha becomes confused . . .

FIGURE 8.14 The side-by-side samples help to illustrate very clearly the difference between those sentences that analyze and those that summarize. After going over these examples together, students evaluate their own essays (after they have been scored), coding them to determine the amount of summary and analysis.

(continues)

8-Score Paper	5-Score Paper
18. When the sandpaper stops grinding, we are left with something very concise, perhaps a single grain of truth, perhaps nothing at all.	18. As he travels alone, Siddhartha meets new people . . .
	19. At first, he meets a woman named . . .
	20. Siddhartha and Kamala become . . .
	21. Kamala teaches Siddhartha . . .
	22. She is a rich, beautiful woman and he is . . .
	23. However, after he finds enlightenment, there is . . .
	24. After being with Kamala, Siddhartha spends time . . .
	25. Siddhartha was new to his teachings . . .
	26. Vasudeva was able to help Siddhartha . . .
	27. At one point Siddhartha contemplated killing . . .
	28. And through these teachings by the river, Siddhartha finally found . . .
	29. On his quest for enlightenment, Siddhartha encounters . . .
	30. However, Siddhartha has an ability to adapt and accept . . .
	31. As he follows these ideas and teachings, though . . .
	32. Siddhartha went through the cycle of . . .
	33. Each person he encountered gave him insight and helped him. . . .
	34. These cycles continued throughout Siddhartha's life until he finally found enlightenment.

FIGURE 8.14 *Continued*

13. Reflect in their notebook about performance, process, and progress, identifying those lessons learned and what they need to do on such writing in the future to improve and achieve the better result they seek.

14. Make myself available to meet with students outside of class who want to further discuss their essays so they can continue to improve.

Alternative Approaches to Teaching Writing on Demand

The subsections that follow describe **some alternative on-demand writing** approaches that I have found useful.

Computer Lab

If you have access to a full-class lab, consider taking the class there for the period so students all have access to computers, which, at this point, most students find more comfortable for writing. Graham, Harris, and Hebert (2011) include this alternative approach as one of their final recommendations, though many schools forbid the practice of writing on computers because students do not take state tests on computers.

Administrators fear using computers will undermine students' performance on state exams when they are required to write by hand (Applebee and Langer 2011). There are potential problems, however, which you should take care to avoid given the often high-stakes nature of such exams: paper, ink, time, working machines, enough machines, and availability of the room. Other variations on this option include using a laptop cart if your school provides them, or, if you are in a 1:1 laptop school, giving students the option to write on their computers in class. (See Figure 8.15.)

FIGURE 8.15 Allowing students with different learning needs to use laptops to write in-class essays is one way to provide additional support. Joey was able to write with much greater speed and confidence on such occasions.

ABCD STRATEGY

Gallagher (2006) suggests a useful, succinct strategy you can teach students for writing timed essays which he calls the ABCD Method and sums up this way:

- **A**ttack the prompt:
  - Cross out any extraneous words in order to "prune the prompt."
  - Circle any word that asks you do something.
  - Draw an arrow from each circled word to what it asks you to do.
  - Transform the prompt into a checklist of the circled words and a list of what they ask students to do.
- **B**rainstorm possible answers:
  - Generate ideas using a brainstorm, cluster, or list.
- **C**hoose the order of your response:
  - Create some sort of a "map" that helps them "chart their course."
  - Develop some order as to what goes first, second, third, and so on.
- **D**etect errors before turning the draft in. (41)

Gallagher spends several pages going into greater detail about this strategy, which he uses with kids in his classes to get the results that make him such a great teacher.

SOAPSTONE STRATEGY

This approach offers a quick, useful device for analytical reading and writing under the pressure of time when you often forget what you should consider when preparing to write. Morse (2012) outlines the method (in bold italic), to which I have added additional comments:

- ***Who is the Speaker?*** The voice that is telling the story or describing the subject of the poem.
- ***What is the Occasion?*** What is the context or situation that the speaker or poet is describing or responding to?

- *Who is the <u>Audience?</u>* These are the people—or person—to whom the poet addresses this poem.
- *What is the <u>Purpose?</u>* What effect is the poet attempting to achieve?
- *What is the <u>Subject?</u>* The subject of the poem plus what the speaker or poet is saying about it expressed in a few words or phrases.
- *What is the <u>Tone?</u>* The attitude the author revealed through the speaker's voice.

STRUCTURED RESPONSE

Lomax (2009) offered a highly structured response to The Basics: Writing a Timed Essay handout shown in Figure 8.9, which I originally posted on my blog. As a teacher of ELs, he wrote, "I have to teach low-level Arabic learners who need a much more simplified formula, which generally goes like this:

- *Introduction 50 words:* Introduce the essay topic in general. Say what the essay question says in your own words.
- *Paragraph 1 (50 words):* To begin with, To start with, Firstly, First of all + rest of topic sentence (The topic sentence will introduce what this paragraph is about.) Advantage 1 Advantage 2 Advantage 3.
- *Paragraph 2 (50 words):* Now I will turn to, Now I will discuss, Turning to + rest of topic sentence (The topic sentence will introduce what this paragraph is about.) Disadvantage 1 Disadvantage 2 Disadvantage 3.
- *Conclusion (50 words):* In conclusion, To conclude, To sum up + general summary of essay ideas Your opinion / Any recommendations." (134)

Adding his own thoughts about using such a highly structured approach, Lomax, who teaches Arabic-speaking students who are studying English, says, "From this, I would be lucky if they get expressions like 'on the other hand' right, as their copying skills are also limited. As much as I hate this creativity crushing structure, it prepares them for what they will be marked on in the exam."

I understand and even share the concerns expressed by so many (Hillocks 2002; Wilson 2006) about the emphasis on timed writing. Yet, on-demand writing remains fundamental to the academic enterprise of which I am a part as a classroom teacher. Thus, I agree with those who argue for the inclusion and direct teaching of on-demand writing (Gallagher 2006; Angelillo 2005; Gere, Christenbury, and Sassi 2005; Burke 2004), believing as Gallagher says, that "writing on demand has become a gate-keeping issue. Students taught to write well have the key to unlock gates to better opportunities. Students who do not write well on demand risk being locked out" (2006, 41). This is what Delpit (2006) refers to as "the culture of power" into which she argues good teaching initiates all students (24). She goes on to define good teaching as "instruction that is constant, rigorous, integrated across disciplines, connected to students' lived cultures, connected to their intellectual legacies, engaging, and designed for critical thinking and problem solving that is useful beyond the classroom" (18).

PAUSE & REFLECT What questions remain or arise for you about assessment in general, or writing assessment in particular, after reading this chapter so far?

Grading Progress, Performance, and Process—**Not People**

A friend of mine had a student who submitted a major paper that turnitin.com found to be 90 percent unoriginal, showing nearly all the paper in bright red letters that indicate plagiarism. How to handle? Easy: copy the essay, print out the turnitin.com report, pass it on to the dean as required by school policies, and move on. Except it didn't stop there. Instead, the father, a very successful lawyer, challenged the teacher and the ruling, never once addressing or otherwise acknowledging that his son had in fact plagiarized his paper. This challenge went first from the dean to the assistant principal who asked the teacher what he wanted to do—*I'm not changing anything: the kid cheated*, he said. And so it went up the chain of command, eventually landing on the desk of the principal who provided unqualified support for the teacher's decision.

After *seven months*, during which the question of whether the student had, in fact, plagiarized the paper never became the issue, the teacher was summoned to the district superintendent's office where he was told that the father was now threatening to take his case before the school board if the teacher did not change the grade—to what?! The rightful grade the boy had "earned." The superintendent said the teacher had two choices: He could change the grade or stand his ground, either of which the district would support, but he should realize that it would take a lot of time and cost a lot of money to defend him and the district against this parent. The teacher said, "Well, I've stood my ground this long, I don't see why I should change now." The superintendent nodded, then shook his head, grinned, and suggested the teacher reconsider the other choice (changing the grade). This was not, it became immediately apparent, a suggestion nor had it ever been a real option.

PAUSE & REFLECT Jot down your response to these four "key philosophical questions" regarding your grading system:

- Why do you grade students?
- What composes a grade?
- Are grading standards flexible, absolute, or relative?
- How can good scores be skewed through faulty grading? (Brown and Isaacs 2004, 30)

We face so many different expectations—from students, parents, universities, as well as departments, administrators, and school boards—regarding grading. Here, I will offer an overview of possible practices and principles to consider, then share what I do and, why I do it that way. Then you can get busy grading this chapter in terms of how much it helped you understand or redefine your role and relationship when it comes to assessing, teaching, and grading your students and their work.

In her study of writing assessment in *Rethinking Rubrics*, Maja Wilson (2006) frames the subject of grading in a thoughtful way by looking at the grading policies of Linda Christensen. It's worth noting that Linda Christensen has written books about her teaching (see *Writing, Reading, and Rising Up: Teaching About Social Justice and the Power of the Written Word*, Rethinking Schools Press 2000), served as director of the Oregon State Writing Project, and worked as a language arts coordinator for Portland Public Schools in Oregon. It gets your attention, then, when Wilson declares Christensen's "dirty little secret: She hasn't graded a student paper in twenty-eight years" (80).

What?! Christensen (2000), as many of us have, struggled with the element of judgment inherent in grading and sought to come up with grading policies that were, she felt, more likely to allow students to "take risks—to engage in the formative exchange between thought and language . . . to recognize [and show that we value the writing process] by grading it" (81). This emphasis on the learning and writing process "leaves teachers free to encourage, praise, and support risks that [might] turn out badly" (81). Christensen's grading policy still arrives at a letter grade and uses points, but it places the value on the hard work students do—see the "three Ps" later in chapter—at each stage of their writing process instead of waiting until it's over and putting one definitive grade on it at the end.

How then should we think about grading? By what stars (or standards) should we chart our course through these rough waters? First, let's be clear what we are talking about here. Grading is separate from assessment, although they are certainly related. O'Connor defines grading as "the practice of reporting a number of letters as a summary of student performance" (2007, 126). Grading typically takes us away from assessment *for* learning and gets kids thinking about assessment for *grades*. Grades are the money in the market of our classes. What's more, several recent studies (Godfrey 2011; Goodwin 2011) suggest the currency of these grades increasingly suffers from inflation that threatens to undermine the integrity of the whole system.

Although teachers' attitudes toward and beliefs about grades no doubt run the gamut, we can all come to some reasonable agreement about a few things regarding grades and the process of arriving at them. O'Connor offers three "beliefs": grades are not necessary for teaching and learning to occur; grading is complicated; grading is subjective (2007, 128). In addition, the grades should make sense by some criteria established and communicated to the students; these grades should be fair. Finally, they should mean something to both student and teacher so that any grade earned has the substance of real achievement.

Yet there are many competing terms for and philosophies about grading floating around out there, some of them anchored in a past that will never return, others associated with a future that has not yet arrived but seems always about to if we read the latest journals. Most notably, we hear about "standards-referenced" grading practices (Marzano 2010, 119) and "standards-based" grading approaches (Marzano 2010; Guskey 2001), and "omnibus (letter) grades" (Marzano 2010). Despite the many benefits of such grading approaches, though, they have many shortcomings that prevent them from being effectively implemented in large classes such as mine. In addition, they take too long, demand a lot of work, result in report cards that are often too complicated for most parents, and fail to convey to parents any sense of their child's progress. Thus what promises insight and progress tends, at this point, to cause confusion and problems for all involved (Guskey 2001, 26).

Let me offer an example to help us think about grading. Two students, the same class, the same assignment—choose a book from a preapproved list of novels to read by the end of each six-week grading period. All of this culminates in the same task: write an in-class essay about any one of four prompts for that book from which they may choose on the day of the essay exam. Alejandro read *A Day in the Life of Ivan Ilich* (about 150 pages but on the list!); Savannah read *Cutting for Stone* (about 500 pages and on the list!) in the same six-week grading period.

Alejandro writes a brilliant essay that earns him an A based on criteria I provided ahead of time; Savannah, however, writes an essay, which, according to the same criteria, earns her a B. Is that fair? Savannah is, in this example, one of the best writers in the class, which explains why she is also the editor of the school newspaper. She always gets one of the top grades on her essays; in this instance, however, she got bogged down in the longer book and was tripped up by a prompt she struggled to get a good handle on in the allotted time of the test. Alejandro, who has never done so well on such papers, chose this book so he could really study it and focus on how to write about it.

Their grades make sense and are valid for several reasons. First, they were free to choose what they read and which prompt they wrote about. Also, the standards by which their writing was scored came from the College Board and are, in this case, the criteria by which their work will be evaluated when they write about similar books in response to the same sort of prompts in May when they take the AP exam. Finally, both were given examples (see preceding sequence for preparing students to write on demand) and strategies; both had equal opportunity to meet with me to discuss previous timed writing performances and get additional instruction to help them do well on this exam.

From this example, certain guiding principles emerge, which can be applied to and adapted to any class:

- Grades should be linked to specific learning goals, which, in turn, should be the focus of the instruction that leads up to the exam, paper, or performance.
- Grades should be aligned with those standards that apply to your course and the assignment itself.
- Grading criteria for assignments should be clearly established and communicated, whenever possible, prior to performance so that students may use the criteria as a guide and feel like the grading process was transparent and consistent.
- The grades are based on criterion-referenced performance standards (e.g., Exceeds the Standard, Meets the Standard, Approaches the Standard, and Misses the Standard), each level of which is described so as to make them clear to students before, during, and after what they did or should have done on the assignment.
- The grades apply only to the performance(s) being measured and cannot be supplemented through extra credit, which has nothing to do with learning and can, in some cases, penalize those who lack the resources to do the extra credit work. The exception, when it comes to writing, would be revision; this is as long as revision is an option available to all, and everyone can get the teacher's guidance to improve performance—then it is fair.
- The grading process for a class or assignment removes as much subjectivity as is possible. This includes, whenever possible, including checklists that would lead students to a more successful performance (Reeves 2011, 6; Gawande 2009) and the teachers to more consistent, reliable scores.
- Grades for assignments are not based on any personal characteristics of the students such as personality, attitude, appearance, handwriting, or behavior.
- Grades for the same assignment, in the same class, done in different teachers' classes should be consistent and evaluated using the same criteria, which are adopted or

otherwise created by the teachers of those classes. This is a surprisingly idealistic proposition despite the seemingly obvious logic of it. Absent any such grading standards and the structure to support it within a school or department—or at least between colleagues teaching the same subject—grading then falls to teacher biases based on individual tastes and priorities. In such a situation, we get: *Well I just think correctness is more important than ideas and style; after all, if it is not correct, no one will pay attention to their ideas in the first place!*

- The grades should recognize the value of the process, performance, and progress of each student on a given assignment. In the event, however, that the student shows tremendous growth the second half of the semester, it is fair and humane, so long as one is judicious and could explain the process whereby the grade was arrived at, to give such a student the B– if the grade total was 79 percent at semester's end. We all need to feel like our efforts will reap some reward, "else what's a Heaven for?"

  A different but related debate that has emerged in recent years, which we will not examine here, is the policy in a growing number of districts of allowing no zeros, even if the student did not turn in anything; typically, the rationale is that they were there and must have learned *something*. This last case is different from the ABCI strategy discussed next, which emphasizes learning and improving and rewards effort not absence.

Reeves sums up the discussion of grading by identifying four essential elements: accuracy, fairness, specificity, and timeliness (2011, 1). He concludes his study of grading, however, by saying "the acid test for any grading system . . . is the degree to which it is working. By 'working,' I mean whether students, teachers, and parents can use the feedback from the grading system to improve [their] performance" (123). Reeves's comment is telling, for we are all aware—from our own and our children's experiences in school—that teachers can use grades to punish, reward, threaten, prevent, celebrate, show favor, and provide feedback, as Reeves says.

Guskey (2000) offers several additional ideas, all guided by the principle of grades as feedback and opportunities to learn and improve. He offers the following guidelines:

- Grades work in reference to specific learning criteria, rather than "on the curve," to ensure consistent grade distribution from one teacher to the next and avoid creating a highly competitive and unhealthy environment.

- Identify what you want students to learn, what you will accept as evidence of their learning, and the criteria you will use to judge that evidence.

- Avoid using grades to punish since such actions diminish effort and engagement, often causing students to withdraw and dismiss low grades as meaningless; instead, consider using an A, B, C, or I (Incomplete) approach, and not assigning zeros but instead giving students an "I," thus suggesting that she or he can still learn from you and your class.

What do we grade, though? The finer details of categories and weighting, curves and other variations, are not our focus here. What to grade, however, is an important and useful question. To adapt a line we have all heard about testing: What gets graded is what gets done. In this scenario, however, points become the instructional equivalent of the little biscuits I hold over my dog's head to make her jump. (Sophie doesn't jump; she has trained *me* to give up and give it to her anyway, and will then reward me with her adorable enthusiasm and abiding love.) To treat students this way is to play to the strengths of the hungry elite kids and penalize those kids who find the prospect of doing meaningless things for an extra five points degrading. (*So, my paper is not an A because I did not do the cover page you said we would get five more points for if we did it*, the student thinks but does not say.)

Guskey and Jung advocate for grades based on three types of learning criteria and their related standards: product, process, and progress. These elements, they suggest, correct for what often seems to be an arbitrary "hodgepodge" (2009, 56) of factors that work against students working hard to learn and improve in the face of obstacles such as language acquisition, learning difficulties, and lack of academic literacies those at the top came into the class already possessing. Guskey and Jung (2009) explain each of the three Ps as follows:

- *Product:* Criteria focus on what students know and are able to do at a particular point in time, relating to the final evidence of their learning on, for example, their final exams, reports, projects, exhibits, and portfolios.

- *Process:* Criteria here apply to what students did in order to reach their current level of achievement. This would include, for example, effort, behavior, and work or study habits, but also evidence from their daily work, quizzes, and other smaller assignments over time.

- *Progress:* The criteria here consider how much students gained from their work and learning experiences in your class over time. The focus here is on how far they have come from where they were when they entered your class instead of merely focusing on the end result. (55)

What do I grade in my classes? My assignments fall into three buckets—big (think: projects, finals, major papers), medium (2-3-page papers, speeches), and little (those assignments we do in class or for homework that are not part of a larger assignment to which they might be attached).

- *Writing*

  Steps throughout the writing process (sometimes individually, other times as a whole sequence) are graded.

  - *Papers:* The final paper itself; revisions as measured by the extent to which students followed my suggestions, fixed those errors I indicated, and generally improved the paper. Timed writings are also included but graded by different criteria or standards depending on the performance.

  - *Short or Daily Writing:* Examples would include notes taken and used to write a paragraph about a text they read (thus I would collect both and count notes as first step, the paragraph as the second and include both in the grade); would also include written explanations of a completed graphic organizer or some graphic work they did such as a mind map or drawing of a metaphor related to a story we were reading (see Figure 8.16).

  - *Other Writing:* This might include surveys, blogs, wikis, and posts to online literature circle discussions on Facebook; or it might include more creative writing such as poems and stories.

- *Notebooks:* Several times a semester I evaluate students' notebooks, along with their the posts to the class blog, evaluating them using the scoring guide shown in Figure 4.47. Whatever the grade on the notebook the first time, it serves as a marker of where they are in terms of their thinking and use of the notebook. Instead of penalizing them, and to prevent those kids who would bloat out their notebooks with pages and pages of nothing, I give them very pointed feedback about their work and show them contrasting examples from classmates to help them see what I expect and what my standards look like. This first notebook grade is essentially a draft grade—it is version 1.0. Now that they know how they are doing, what they need to work on, they can improve their use of the notebooks. The next grade, then, replaces the previous one, giving them an incentive to do much better.

FIGURE 8.16 Jessica and other ninth graders show their initial understanding by drawing the poem; they then write an explanation of their drawing, after which they present them to the class as part of a full-class discussion.

- *Reading*
  - Miscellaneous small assessments such as index cards, reflective reading assessments
  - Annotations and other such note-taking work when I am teaching it or otherwise demanding it as preparation for a subsequent writing assignment
  - Large writing assignments or presentations that all the daily work prepared them to do (see Figure 8.17)
  - Tests or practice tests if related to the time of state testing

- *Speaking*
  - Formal speeches or presentations
  - Structured occasions such as a fishbowl, Socratic Seminar, literature circles, or forums, such as the one discussed earlier, where they participate as Machiavelli or a literary character in a forum on power in *Oedipus, Antigone*, and *Hamlet*
  - Class discussion (both in groups and as a class): One large grade, the equivalent of a major paper, which gets revised twice each semester. That is, I keep track on my seating chart of each time a student contributes a comment or question, and keep a mental note about the evolving quality of those contributions (so as to root out or otherwise diminish the value of the student who thinks all that matters is to keep tossing out questions and comments regardless of their value).

    For the first six-week grading period, they get a grade, which for many is a horrifying D or F because they may have said nothing, despite my entreaties, my coaching, my calling on them with the easiest of questions. Now they can work on this area of their performance, with a clear incentive to do so as the second six-week grading period will allow them to replace that initial grade if they improve. So it goes with the third grading period; thus, the student who gets an F for the first grading period can, if she really works on it, improve—just as she might with her writing—and earn an A by semester's end.

Of Mice and Men

Please answer all questions on a separate page

Introduction While reading *Of Mice and Men* we will pause to make some observations. These observations are intended to improve your ability to see and interpret key ideas and events in the story. Write your response to these questions on a separate sheet of paper *as you read*. It's fine to type your responses if you prefer. Responses to each question should be thorough, not just a few words or a single sentence.

1. **Exposition**: List five *key details* that provide background to the characters and the plot up to this point. Explain why each detail is so important to the story.

2. **Rising Action**: List and describe the events in Chapter 3 that increase the tension in the story and will lead to the climax? In a short paragraph, identify the events and explain *how* they affect the plot.

3. **Connect/Characterize**: Everyone respects Slim, especially Candy (p. 45) for whom "Slim's opinions were law." Write down a few reasons why people respect someone. Who is someone *you* respect, someone whose opinions are law? Explain *why* everyone respects Slim and how Slim is similar to or different from this person you respect so much.

4. **Infer**: Steinbeck includes a lot of animals in the story, including mice, rabbits, and dogs. Think about these animals and their relationship to the humans. What do you think Steinbeck is trying to say by using these animals? Why do you think that? Provide evidence to support your argument.

5. **Mood**: On pages 48–49, Steinbeck refers to "silence" repeatedly. What is the cause and meaning of the silence? Note that he personifies silence. Find some examples in which he personifies silence and explain how this technique affects the mood.

6. Develop two test questions based on the second chapter:

    a. **Right There (Literal) Question**: This is a factual question that you can answer by pointing "right there" on the page to find the answer. An example from *The Odyssey* would be, "What test did Odysseus pass that the suitors could not?" (Answer: Stringing his bow and shooting the arrow through a row of ax handles.) Answer the question and explain its importance.

    b. **Between the Lines (Inferential) Question**: This question is more complex. The answer cannot be pointed to on the page but must be *inferred* from other details in the story. An example from *The Odyssey* would be, "How would you characterize the relationship between Odysseus and his men?" Answer the question and explain its importance.

FIGURE 8.17 This is a good representation of what my freshman students do for homework over the course of reading a chapter from a novel.

- *Intangibles*

    - *Effort:* We have so many inclusion students and others with special needs of one sort or another. We all know the difference between Lourdes who, despite her learning difficulties that are compounded by her second language interference, worked harder than anyone in the class to do what, by one standard, would be a D or even an F; and then there is Jack who did the very minimum but also ends up with a D or an F. This is the gray area that often involves our compassion and humanity as much as our commitment to higher standards and professional integrity. Ultimately, on some level, a final grade needs to make sense to both teacher and student.

    - *Improvement:* There is no reason to make this seem more objective than it is; I will simply say our whole enterprise is predicated on improvement. We are in the improvement business. But people only work to improve to the extent they believe they can and will be rewarded in some way for doing so. Take for example Heather, who struggled much of the first half of the semester on her formal essays, but kept meeting with me and getting incrementally better grades on each paper, showing real and substantial growth. But those early grades may undermine her final grade—she ends up with a 78 percent or 89 percent. It's important for me to at least take that improvement into consideration on the report card.

Needless to say, it is an area requiring integrity and should not have anything to do with my feelings about her and her progress. If I show her some consideration that I do not show the surly, often withdrawn boy in the back corner who has nevertheless made similar gains, well, then I need to check myself and recalibrate my grading standards.

One other aspect of grading, one new to most of us, involves student information systems such as School Loop, Blackboard, or Schoology (among others); these allow teachers to post homework and other content (lesson plans, handouts, reference links, and so on), while also permitting us to keep our gradebook online for students and parents, counselors and colleagues to check at any time of the day or night. At my school, it is not a choice: You use School Loop or you will get sent to the principal's office. The administration does not, nor does my department, tell me whether I have to use categories (quizzes, tests, homework, and so on); nor do they tell me, if I do use categories (I do not), how much each category should count toward the final grade. But the categories are there to use; and the system is built as it is, to be used as it dictates, all of this leads over time to what Jaron Lanier, in his wonderful book *You Are Not a Gadget* (2010) calls "lock in," which amounts to a mind-set that eventually lets the preset or established categories and other functions determine what we do, how we do it, and how much it is worth to us.

It remains to be seen what grading, along with report cards and parent communications, will look like in the future as the Common Core Standards become our map for the territory ahead. Standards do not necessarily mean standardization, though in areas such as grades, it is easy to imagine a standardized, standards-based report card; the dream is to have a more objective system of grading, as people long ago did of a standardization of spelling, currency, and weights and measurements. I can't imagine such a system of standardization at the moment, but suspect we must anticipate and work to resist it in some form.

Final Thoughts

The road from Ds and Fs to As and Bs was, for me, a long but very satisfying one. We hate the grades unless we get them, doing the hard work that earns that elusive grade we never dreamt possible. Then the achievement of that success is a tremendous tonic to our spirit, giving us confidence that the way forward is possible. But these same grades can inflict a lasting harm, as this passage from Mary Pipher, an author whose books have sold millions of copies, reminds us:

> When I was in fifth grade, I wrote my first poem, a sonnet, comparing life to the seasons. My teacher gave me a big red C and scrawled "Trite" across the top of my poem. I gave up on my career as a writer. Between my dad's warning and the fact that I couldn't do better than a C in creative writing in Beaver City, Nebraska, I despaired. I thought writers were born geniuses and that I was a pedestrian person who worked hard but had no real gifts. (2009, 89)

One more story by way of a laugh and a lesson. A friend's daughter grew up loving *To Kill a Mockingbird*, reading it over and over several times a year. When she arrived at high school, the teacher said they would read *Mockingbird*, which thrilled the girl. When they finished, they were asked to write an in-class exam to assess their understanding of the book. The prompt was fairly straightforward: "Please choose the character you think is the most important and explain why, providing examples from the text to support and illustrate your ideas." And so the girl launched into it, writing a remarkable essay about why Scout was by far the most important character. When she got her paper back with a big *C* on it, she was confused. She asked the teacher, who said apologetically, "Oh, well that was because you got it wrong, dear!" The correct answer was Atticus, of course. Here we see what kids fear: Tests as traps and missed opportunities to show what they know and can really do.

All we need to know about these two words—*assess* and *grade*—is apparent in their etymology. *Assess* comes from *assesser*, based on Latin *assidere*, meaning "sit by." Thus to assess is, in spirit, to sit by and watch, listen, learn, and teach with patience how to do or know something. However, *grade*, originally from the French, or Latin *gradus*, meaning "step," was used to refer to a unit of measurement and later came to refer to degrees of merit or quality. There we have the difference, that judgment of "merit or quality," which leads to the belief that we are our grades. In the end, however, our students' grades are ultimately our own: Our success can only be measured by theirs.

Recommended **Readings and Resources**

Readings

- Afflerbach, Peter. *Understanding and Using Reading Assessment, K–12* (International Reading Association 2007).

- Ainsworth, Larry, and Donald Viegut. *Common Formative Assessments: How to Connect Standards-Based Instruction and Assessment* (Corwin 2006).

- Marzano, Robert J. *Formative Assessment and Standards-Based Grading* (Marzano Research Laboratory 2010).

- Popham, W. James. *Classroom Assessment: What Teachers Need to Know*, sixth ed. (Pearson 2011).

- Reeves, Douglas. *Elements of Grading: A Guide to Effective Practice* (Solution Tree 2011).

- Stiggins, Rick, and Jan Chappuis. *An Introduction to Student-Involved Assessment for Learning* (Pearson 2012).

- Wilson, Maja. *Rethinking Rubrics in Writing Assessment* (Heinemann 2006).

Resources

- WestEd Education Labs (www.wested.org)

- Released exams for instructional use available from your state department of education, College Board, and AP Central

- Common Core State Standards Assessment Consortia: Smarter Balanced Education Consortium or The Partnership for Assessment of Readiness for College and Careers (PARCC)

Abela, Andrew V. 2008. *Advanced Presentations by Design: Creating Communication That Drives Action.* San Francisco: Pfeiffer.

———. 2010. *The Presentation: A Story About Communicating Successfully with Very Few Slides.* Great Falls: Soproveitto.

Academy of Achievement. 2012. "The Voice of Triumph." Academy of Achievement. Website accessed 4/3/12.

ACT. 2004. "On Course for Success: A Close Look at Selected High School Courses That Prepare All Students for College," 48. Iowa City: ACT.

ACT. 2006. "Reading between the Lines: What the Act Reveals About College Readiness in Reading." Iowa City: ACT.

Adams, Caralee. 2011. "NAEP Study Finds Jump in Students Taking Tough Courses." *Education Week*, April 13, 2011, p. 6.

Adler, Mary, and Eija Rougle. 2005. *Building Literacy Through Classroom Discussion: Research-Based Strategies for Developing Critical Readers and Thoughtful Writers in Middle School.* New York: Scholastic.

Adler, Mortimer J. 1984. *The Paideia Program: An Educational Syllabus.* New York: Collier.

Afflerbach, Peter. 2004."Assessing Adolescent Reading." In *Adolescent Literacy Research and Practice*, edited by Tamara L. Jetton, and Dole, Janice A., 369–91. New York: Guilford.

———. 2007. *Understanding and Using Reading Assessment, K–12.* Newark: International Reading Association.

Ainsworth, Larry, and Donald Viegut. 2006. *Common Formative Assessments: How to Connect Standards-Based Instruction and Assessment.* Thousand Oaks, CA: Corwin.

Albright, J., K. Purohit, and C. Walsh. 2002."Louise Rosenblatt Seeks Qtaznboi@aol.com for Ltr: Using Chat Rooms in Interdisciplinary Middle School Classrooms." *Journal of Adolescent and Adult Literacy* 45: 692–705.

Allen, Janet. 1999. *Words, Words, Words: Teaching Vocabulary in Grades 4–12.* Portland: Stenhouse.

Alliance for Excellent Education. 2007. "High School Teaching for the Twenty-First Century: Preparing Students for College." In *Issue Brief.* Washington, D.C.: Alliance for Excellent Education.

Allington, Richard L. 2006. *What Really Matters for Struggling Readers: Designing Research-Based Programs.* Boston: Pearson.

———. 2011 "Reading Intervention in the Middle Grades." *Voices from the Middle* 19, no. 2: 10–16.

Alvarez, Julia. 2007. *Once Upon a Quinceanera: Coming of Age in the USA* New York: Viking.

Alvermann, Donna. 2001. "Effective Literacy Instruction for Adolescents." Chicago: National Reading Conference.

American Association of University Women. 1998. "Gender Gaps: Where School Fail Our Children." Washington, D.C.: American Association of University Women.

American Diploma Project. 2004. "Ready or Not: Creating a High School Diploma That Counts." In *American Diploma Project.* Washington, D.C.: ADP.

Anderson, A. A. 1997. "The Effects of Sociocognitive Writing Strategy Instruction on the Writing Achievement and Writing Self-Efficacy of Students with Disabilities and Typical Achievement in an Urban Elementary School." Unpublished doctoral dissertation. University of Houston, Houston,TX.

Anderson, Janna Quitney, and Lee Rainie. 2012."Millennials Will Benefit and Suffer Due to Their Hyperconnected Lives." Washington D.C.: Pew Research Center's Internet & American Life Project.

Angelillo, Janet. 2005. *Writing to the Prompt: When Students Don't Have a Choice*. Portsmouth: Heinemann.

Angelis, Janet. 2002."The Critical Role of Conversation in Learning." *English Update Newsletter*. Fall.

Applebee, Arthur N. 1981. *Writing in the Secondary School: English and the Content Areas*. Urbana: National Council of Teachers of English.

———. 1986."Musings . . . Principled Practice." *Research in the Teaching of English* 20, no. 2: 5–7.

———. 1993. "Literature in the Secondary School: Studies of Curriculum and Instruction in the United States." In *NCTE Research Report Number 25*. Urbana: National Council of Teachers of English.

———. 1994. "Toward Thoughtful Curriculum: Fostering Discipline-Based Conversation." *English Journal* 83, no. 4: 45–52.

———. 1996. *Curriculum as Conversation: Transforming Traditions of Teaching and Learning*. Chicago: University of Chicago Press.

Applebee, Arthur N. and Judith A. Langer. 2009."What's Happening in the Teaching of Writing?" *English Journal* 98, no. 5: 18–28.

———. 2011. "A Snapshot of Writing Instruction in Middle Schools and High Schools." *English Journal* 100, no. 6: 14–27.

Applebee, Arthur N., Judith A. Langer, Martin Nystrand, and Adam Gamoran. 2003. "Discussion-Based Approaches to Developing Understanding: Classroom Instruction and Student Performance in Middle and High School English." *American Educational Research Journal* 40, no. 3: 685–730.

Aristotle. 1984. *The Rhetoric and Poetics of Aristotle*. Translated by W. Rhys Roberts. New York: Modern Library.

Arnold, Karen D. 1995. *Lives of Promise: What Becomes of High School Valedictorians (a 14-Year Study of Achievement and Life Choices)*. San Francisco: Jossey-Bass.

Arum, Richard, Josipa Roksa, and Esther Cho. 2010. "Improving Undergraduate Learning: Findings and Policy Recommendations from the SSRC-ELA Longitudinal Project." Washington, D.C.: Social Science Research Council.

Atkinson, Cliff. 2005. *Beyond Bullet Points: Microsoft PowerPoint to Create Presentations That Inform, Motivate, and Inspire*. Redmond: Microsoft.

Atwell, Nancie. 1998. *In the Middle: New Understandings About Writing, Reading, and Learning*. Portsmouth: Heinemann.

———. 2002. *Lessons That Change Writers*. Portsmouth: Heinemann/firsthand.

———. 2007a. *The Reading Zone: How to Help Kids Become Skilled, Passionate, Habitual, Critical Readers*. New York: Scholastic.

———. 2007b. "The Pleasure Principle." *Instructor* 116, no. 5: 44–46.

———. 2009. "Myths of Independent Reading." *Teachers College Record*.

———. 2010. "The Case for Literature." *Education Week*. February 8, 2010. Available at: http://www.edweek.org/ew/articles/2010/02/10/21atwell_ep.h29.html.

Austen, Jane. 2010. *Pride and Prejudice: An Annotated Edition*. Edited by Patricia Meyer Spacks. Cambridge: Belknap.

Baca, Jimmy Santiago. 2001. *A Place to Stand*. New York: Grove.

———. 2010. *Stories from the Edge*. Portsmouth: Heinemann.

Bacevich, Amy, and Terry Salinger. 2006. "Lessons and Recommendations from the Alabama Reading Initiative: Sustaining Focus on Secondary Reading." Washington, D.C.: American Institutes for Research.

Bailey, Alison L. 2007. *The Language Demands of School: Putting Academic English to the Test*. New Haven: Yale University Press.

Bakhtin, M. M. 1981. *The Dialogic Imagination*.Translated by Caryl Emerson and Michael Holquist. Edited by Michael Holquist. Austin: University of Texas Press.

———. 1986. *Speech Genres and Other Late Essays*. Translated by Vern W. McGee. Edited by Caryl and Michael Holquist Emerson. Austin: University of Texas.

Barnes, Douglas. 1992. *From Communication to Curriculum*, second ed. Portsmouth: Heinemann.

Barnes, Douglas. 2008. "Exploratory Talk for Learning." In *Exploring Talk in School*, edited by Neil Mercer and Steve Hodgkinson eds. Los Angeles: SAGE.

Bateman, Walter L. 1990. *Open to Question: The Art of Teaching and Learning by Inquiry*. San Francisco: Jossey-Bass.

Bauerlein, Mark. 2008. *The Dumbest Generation: How the Digital Age Stupefies Young Americans and Jeopardizes Our Future (or, Don't Trust Anyone under 30)*. New York: Penguin.

———. 2011. "Too Dumb for Complex Texts?" *Educational Leadership* 68, no. 5: 28–33.

Baumann, James F., and Michael F. Graves. 2010. "What Is Academic Vocabulary?" *Journal of Adolescent and Adult Literacy* 54, no. 1: 4–12.

Baumann, James F., and Edward J. Kame'enui. 2004. *Vocabulary Instruction: Research to Practice*. New York: Guilford.

Bayard, Pierre. 2009. *How to Talk About Books You Haven't Read*. New York: Bloomsbury USA.

Bazerman, Charles, ed. 2008. *Handbook of Research on Writing: History, Society, School, Individual, Text*. New York: Lawrence Erlbaum.

Bazerman, Charles and Andrea Lunsford. 2005. "Taking the Long View: Observations from the Stanford Study of Writing in Its 4th Year." Conference on College Composition and Communication, San Francisco, CA.

Beck, Isabel L., Margaret G. McKeown, Rebecca L. Hamilton, and Linda Kucan. 1997. *Questioning the Author: An Approach for Enhancing Student Engagement with Text*. Newark: International Reading Association.

Beck, Isabel L., Margaret G. McKeown, and Linda Kucan. 2002. *Bringing Words to Life: Robust Vocabulary Instruction*. New York: Guilford.

———. 2008. *Creating Robust Vocabulary: Frequently Asked Questions and Extended Examples*. New York: Guilford.

Beckett, Samuel. 2006. "Worstward Ho." In *Samuel Beckett: The Grove Centenary Edition Volume Poems, Short Fiction, Criticism*, edited by Paul Auster, 471. New York: Grove.

Beers, Kylene. 2003. *When Kids Can't Read: What Teachers Can Do*. Portsmouth: Heinemann.

———. 2009. "The Genteel Unteaching of America's Poor." Urbana: National Council of Teachers of English.

Belluck, Pam. 2011. "To Really Learn, Quit Studying and Take a Test." *New York Times*, January 20, 2011.

Bernabei, Gretchen. 2005. *Reviving the Essay: How to Teach Structure without Formula*. Shoreham: Discover Writing Press.

———. 2010. Personal correspondence.

Bernabei, Gretchen, Jayne Hover, and Cynthia Candler. 2009. *Crunchtime: Lessons to Help Students Blow the Roof Off Writing Tests—and Become Better Writers in the Process*. Portsmouth: Heinemann.

Berthoff, Ann E. 1999. "Symposium: Reclaiming the Active Mind." *College English* 61, no. 6: 671–80.

Biancarosa, Gina, and Catherine E. Snow. 2006. "Reading Next: A Vision for Action and Research in Middle and High School Literacy: A Report to Carnegie Corporation of New York." Washington, D.C.: Alliance for Excellent Education.

Birkerts, Sven. 1994. *The Gutenberg Elegies: The Fate of Reading in an Electronic Age*. New York: Fawcett Columbine.

———. 2010. "Reading in a Digital Age." *The American Scholar*, 32–44.

Blachowicz, Camille, and Peter J. Fisher. 2002. *Teaching Vocabulary in All Classrooms*, second ed. Upper Saddle River: Merrill/Prentice Hall.

Blachowicz, Camille, Peter J. Fisher, Donna Ogle, and Susan Watts-Taffe. 2006. "Vocabulary: Questions from the Classroom." *Reading Research Quarterly* 41, no. 4: 524–39.

Blau, Sheridan. 2003. *The Literature Workshop: Teaching Texts and Their Readers.* Portsmouth: Heinemann.

Bloom, Harold. 1995. *The Western Canon: The Books and School of the Ages.* New York: Riverhead.

———. 2000. *How to Read and Why.* New York: Touchstone.

Blyth, Catherine. 2009. *The Art of Conversation: A Guided Tour of a Neglected Pleasure.* New York: Gotham.

de Bono, Edward. 2004. *How to Have a Beautiful Mind.* London: Ebury.

Bohm, David. 1996. *On Dialogue,* edited by Lee Nichol. New York: Routledge.

Bomer, Randy. 2011. "What Makes a Teaching Moment: Spheres of Influence in Professional Activity." *English Journal* 101, no. 1.

Boscolo, Pietro, and Carmen Gelati. 2008. "Best Practices in Promoting Motivation for Writing." In *Best Practices in Writing Instruction,* edited by Steve Graham, Charles A. MacArthur, and Jill Fitzgerald. New York: Guilford.

Bowers-Campbell, Joy. 2011. "Take It out of Class: Exploring Virtual Literature Circles." *Journal of Adolescent and Adult Literacy* 54, no. 8: 557–67.

Brandt, Deborah. 2001. *Literacy in American Lives.* New York: Cambridge University Press.

Brannon, Lil, Sally Griffin, Karen Haag, Tony Iannone, Cynthia Urbanski, and Shana Woodward. 2008. *Thinking Out Loud on Paper: The Student Daybook as a Tool to Foster Learning.* Portsmouth: Heinemann.

Bransford, John D., Ann L. Brown, and Rodney R. Cocking. 2000. *How People Learn: Brain, Mind, Experience, and School.* Washington, D.C.: National Academy Press.

Bridgeland, John M., John J. Dilulio, Jr., and Karen Burke Morison. 2006. "The Silent Epidemic: Perspectives of High School Dropouts." Washington, D.C.: Civic Enterprises.

Brizendine, Louann. 2006. *The Female Brain.* New York: Broadway.

———. 2010. *The Male Brain.* New York: Broadway.

Brogan, Chris. 2010. "Virtually There." *Entrepreneur,* December 21, 2010, p. 43.

Bromberger, Lee. 2009. "Comment on 'How to Write a Timed Essay' Blog." In *Jim Burke: The English Teacher's Companion,* edited by Jim Burke. San Francisco.

Bronson, Po. "The Creativity Crisis." *Newsweek,* July 10, 2010.

Brookfield, Stephen D., and Stephen Preskill. 2005. *Discussion as a Way of Teaching: Tools and Techniques for Democratic Classrooms,* second ed. San Francisco: Jossey-Bass.

Brooks, David. 2011. *The Social Animal: The Hidden Sources of Love, Character, and Achievement.* 2011: Random House.

———. 2011b. "Poetry for Everyday Life." *New York Times,* April 12, 2011.

Brown, Juanita, with David Isaacs. 2005. *The World Café: Shaping Our Futures through Conversations That Matter.* San Francisco: Berrett-Koehler.

Brown, Scott. 2010. "Scott Brown on the Art of the Elevator Pitch." *WIRED,* November 29, 2010.

Bruce, Bertram C. 2007. "Diversity and Critical Social Engagement: How Changing Technologies Enable New Modes of Literacy in Changing Circumstances." In *Adolescents and Literacies in a Digital World,* edited by Donna E. Alvermann. New York: Peter Lang.

Bruns, Gerald L. 1987. "Midrash and Allegory: The Beginnings of Scriptural Interpretation." In *The Literary Guide to the Bible,* edited by Robert Alter and Frank Kermode, 625–45. Cambridge: Belknap.

Buckner, Aimee. 2005. *Notebook Know-How: Strategies for the Writer's Notebook.* Portland: Stenhouse.

Buehl, Doug. 2009. *Classroom Strategies for Interactive Learning,* third ed. Newark: International Reading Association.

Burke, Jim. 1999. *I Hear America Reading: Why We Read What We Read*. Portsmouth: Heinemann.

———. 2001. *Illuminating Texts: How to Teach Students to Read the World*. Portsmouth: Heinemann.

———. 2002. *Tools for Thought: Graphic Organizers for Your Classroom*. Portsmouth: Heinemann.

———. 2004. *School Smarts: The Four Cs of Academic Success*. Portsmouth: Heinemann.

———. 2005. *Accessing School: Teaching Struggling Readers to Achieve Academic and Personal Success*. Portsmouth: Heinemann.

———. 2006. *Letters to a New Teacher: A Month-by-Month Guide to the Year Ahead*. Portsmouth: Heinemann.

———. 2007a. *50 Essential Lessons: Tools and Techniques for Teaching English Language Arts, Grades 9–12*. Portsmouth: Heinemann.

———. 2007b. "Teaching the English Language Arts in a "Flat" World." In *Adolescent Literacy: Turning Promise into Practice*, edited by Robert E. Probst, Kylene Beers, and Linda Rief, 149–65. Portsmouth: Heinemann.

———. 2009. *Content Area Writing*. New York: Scholastic.

———. 2010. *What's the Big Idea? Question-Driven Units to Motivate Reading, Writing, and Thinking*. Portsmouth: Heinemann.

———. 2011. "The Shape of Ideas." *Journal of Adolescent and Adult Literacy* 55, no. 2: 155.

———. 2012. "Connecting the Classroom, Community, and Curriculum." *English Journal* 101, no. 4: 17–28.

Buzan, Tony. 2010. *The Mind Map Book*. London: BBC.

Byrne, David. 2003. "Learning to Love PowerPoint." *WIRED*, September 11, 2003.

Cain, Susan. 2012. *Quiet: The Power of Introverts in a World That Can't Stop Talking*. New York: Crown.

Calagione, Sam. 2009. "The Way I Work: Dogfish Head's Sam Calagione." *Inc.* July

Calfee, Robert C., and Rozanne Greitz Miller. 2007. "Best Practices in Writing Assessment." In *Best Practices in Writing Instruction*, edited by Steve Graham, Charles A. MacArthur, and Jill Fitzgerald, 265–85. New York: Guilford.

Calkins, Lucy, Kate Montgomery, and Donna Santman. 1998. *A Teacher's Guide to Standardized Reading Tests*. Portsmouth: Heinemann.

Calvino, Italo. 1979. *If on a Winter's Night a Traveler*. Translated by William Weaver. San Diego: Harcourt Brace.

Canada, Geoffrey. 1998. *Reaching up for Manhood: Transforming the Lives of Boys in America*. Boston: Beacon Press.

Carr, Nicholas. 2010. *The Shallows: What the Internet Is Doing to Our Brains* New York: W. W. Norton.

Carroll, Lewis. 1999. *The Annotated Alice: The Definitive Edition*, edited by Martin Gardner. New York: W. W. Norton.

Carter, Marcia, Anita Hernandez, and Jeannine Richison. 2009. *Interactive Notebooks and English Language Learners*. Portsmouth: Heinemann.

Annie E. Casey Foundation. 2011. "America's Children, America's Challenge: Promoting Opportunity for the Next Generation." In *2011 Kids Count Data Book: State Profiles of Child Well-Being*. Baltimore: Annie E. Casey Foundation.

Casner-Lotto, Jill, and Mary Wright Benner. 2006."Are They Really Ready to Work?: Employers' Perspectives on the Basic Knowledge and Applied Skills of New Entrants to the 21st Century U.S. Workforce." New York: The Conference Board.

Cazden, Courtney B. 2001. *The Language of Teaching and Learning*. Portsmouth: Heinemann.

Chinn, Clark. A., Richard. C. Anderson, and Martha A. Waggoner, 2001. "Patterns of Discourse in Two Kinds of Literature Discussion." *Reading Research Quarterly* 36: 378–411.

Christensen, Linda. 2000. *Writing, Reading, and Rising Up: Teaching About Social Justice and the Power of the Written Word*, Milwaukee: Rethinking Schools Press.

Cohen-Solal, Annie. 2007. "Introduction." In *Existentialism Is a Humanism*. New Haven: Yale University Press.

Coiro, Julie, Michele Knobel, Colin Lankshear, and Donald J. Leu. 2008. *The Handbook of Research on New Literacies*. Mahwah: Lawrence Erlbaum Associates.

Coleman, David, and Susan Pimentel. 2011. "Publishers' Criteria for the Common Core State Standards in English Language Arts and Literacy, Grades K–2." Washington, D.C.: Common Core State Standards.

College Board. 2010. "Teachers Are the Center of Education: Writing, Learning and Leading in the Digital Age." New York: College Board, the National Writing Project and Phi Delta Kappa International.

———. 2011. "42 Percent of 2011 College-Bound Seniors Met Sat College and Career Readiness Benchmark." *College Board's Press Room* .

College Board Advocacy and Policy Center. 2010a. "Sixth Annual AP Report to the Nation." New York: College Board.

College Board Advocacy and Policy Center. 2010b. "The Educational Crisis Facing Young Men of Color: Reflections on Four Days of Dialogue on the Educational Challenges of Minority Males." New York: College Board Advocacy and Policy Center.

Collier, Lorna. 2009. "Everyday Writing: Words Matter More Than Ever in 21st Century Workplace." *The Council Chronicle*: March 6–10.

Conley, David T. 2003. "Understanding University Success." In *A Report from Standards for Success*. Eugene: Association of American Universities.

———. 2005. *College Knowledge: What It Really Takes for Students to Succeed and What We Can Do to Get Them Ready*. San Francisco: Jossey-Bass.

Conley, Mark W. 2005. *Connecting Standards and Assessment through Literacy*. Boston: Pearson.

Connor, Peter. 2012. "Netiquette: Ground Rules for Online Discussions." Colorado State University.

Connors, Robert, and Cheryl Glenn. 1999. *The New St. Martin's Guide to Teaching Writing*. Boston: Bedford/St. Martin's.

Conroy, Pat. October 24, 2007. Personal communication.

Cooper, Susan, and Mary Lyn Bourque Loomis (eds.). 2001. "National Assessment of Educational Progress Achievement Levels 1992–98 for Reading." Washington, D.C.: National Assessment Governing Board.

Copeland, Matt. 2005. *Socratic Circles: Fostering Critical and Creative Thinking in Middle and High School*. Portland: Stenhouse.

Corbett, Christianne, Catherine Hill, and Andresse St. Rose. 2008. "Where the Girls Are: The Facts About Gender Equity in Education." Washington, D.C.: American Association of University Women Educational Foundation.

Corbett, Edward P. J., and Robert J. Connors. 1999. *Classical Rhetoric for the Modern Student*, fourth ed. New York: Oxford University Press.

Cortese, Antonia, and Diane Ravitch. 2008. "Still at Risk: What Students Don't Know, Even Now." In *A Report from Common Core*, edited by Frederick M. Hess, 3. Washington, D.C.: Common Core.

Council of Chief State School Officers and the National Governors Association for Best Practices. 2010. "Common Core State Standards for English Language Arts." Washington, D.C.: Council of Chief State School Officers and the National Governors Association Center for Best Practices.

Cox, Rebecca D. 2009. *The College Fear Factor: How Students and Professors Misunderstand One Another*. Cambridge: Harvard University Press.

Coyne, Michael D., Deborah C. Simmons, and Edward J. Kame'enui. 2004. "Vocabulary Instruction for Young Children at Risk of Experiencing Reading Difficulties," edited by James F. Baumann and Edward J. Kame'enui. New York: Guilford.

Crawford, Matthew. 2009. *Shop Class as Soulcraft: An Inquiry into the Value of Work*. New York: Penguin.

Csikszentmihalyi, Mihaly. 1990. *Flow, or the Psychology of Optimal Experience.* New York: Harper.

Csíkszentmihályi, Mihály, and Barbara Schneider. 2000. *Becoming Adult: How Teenagers Prepare for the World of Work.* New York: Basic.

———. 2008. *Flow: The Psychology of Optimal Experience.* New York: Harpers Perennial.

Culham, Ruth. 2010. *Traits of Writing: The Complete Guide to Middle School.* New York: Scholastic.

Cullen, Dave. 2010. *Columbine.* Lebanon: Twelve.

Cushman, Kathleen. 2010. *Fires in the Mind: What Kids Can Tell Us About Motivation and Mastery.* San Francisco: Jossey-Bass.

Cziko, Christine. 1998. "Reading Happens in Your Mind, Not in Your Mouth: Teaching & Learning 'Academic Literacy' in an Urban High School." *California English* 3, no. 4: 23–25.

D'Angelo, Frank J. 1985. *Process and Thought in Composition.* New York: Little, Brown.

Damon, William. 2008. *The Path to Purpose: Helping Our Children Find Their Calling in Life.* New York: Free Press.

Daniels, Harvey. 2002. *Literature Circles: Voice and Choice in Book Clubs and Reading Groups*, second ed. Portland: Stenhouse.

Daniels, Harvey, and Marilyn Bizar. 2004. *Teaching the Best Practice Way: Methods That Matter, K–12.* Portland: Stenhouse.

Daniels, Harvey, and Stephanie Harvey. 2009. *Comprehension and Collaboration: Inquiry Circles in Action.* Portsmouth: Heinemann.

Darling-Hammond, Linda. 2009. "Recognizing and Enhancing Teacher Effectiveness." *The International Journal of Educational and Psychological Assessment* 3: 1–22.

———. 2010. *The Flat World and Education: How America's Commitment to Equity Will Determine Our Future.* New York: Teachers College Press.

Darling-Hammond, Linda, and John Bransford, ed. 2005. *Preparing Teachers for a Changing World: What Teachers Should Learn and Be Able to Do.* San Francisco: Jossey-Bass.

Davenport, Thomas H., and John C. Beck. 2002. *The Attention Economy: Understanding the New Currency of Business.* Cambridge: Harvard University Press.

Davidson, Cathy N. 2011. *Now You See It: How the Brain Science of Attention Will Transform the Way We Live, Work, and Learn.* New York: Viking.

Davies, Anne. 2007. "Involving Students in the Classroom Assessment Process." In *Ahead of the Curve: The Power of Assessment to Transform Teaching and Learning,* edited by Douglas Reeves, 31–57. Bloomington: Solution Tree.

Dehaene, Stanislaus. 2009. *Reading in the Brain: The Science and Evolution of a Human Invention.* New York: Viking.

Delpit, Lisa D. 2006. *Other People's Children: Cultural Conflict in the Classroom.* New York: New Press.

Denby, David. 1996. *Great Books: My Adventures with Homer, Rousseau, Woolf, and Other Indestructible Writers of the Western World.* New York: Simon and Schuster.

DeNoon, Daniel J. 2006. "The Truth About Phobias." Accessed March 12, 2011, WebMD.com.

DeParle, Jason. 2009. "Struggling to Rise in Suburbs Where Failing Means Fitting In." *New York Times,* April 18, 2009, p. A1.

Deresiewicz, William. 2011. *A Jane Austen Education: How Six Novels Taught Me About Love, Friendship, and the Things That Really Matter.* New York: Penguin.

Devlin, Keith. 2000. *The Math Gene: How Mathematical Thinking Evolved and Why Numbers Are Like Gossip.* New York: Basic Books.

Dombek, Kristin, and Scott Herndon. 2004. *Critical Passages: Teaching the Transition to College Composition,* Language and Literacy Series. New York: Teachers College.

Dorning, Mike. 2011. "Portion of U.S. Working Men Falling Along with Their Wages." *San Francisco Chronicle,* August 28, 2011.

Dostoevsky, Fyodor. 1992. *Crime and Punishment*. Translated by Richard Pevear and Larissa Volokhonsky. New York: Everyman's.

Douglas, Levin, and Sousan Arafeh. 2002. "The Digital Disconnect: The Widening Gap Between Internet-Savvy Students and Their Schools." In *Pew Internet and American Life Project*. Washington, D.C.: Pew Research Center.

Douglass, Frederick. 2000. *Narrative of the Life of Frederick Douglass, an American Slave*. New York: Modern Library.

———. 2011. Frederick Douglass Organization.

Duarte, Nancy. 2008. *slide:ology: The Art and Science of Creating Great Presentations*. Sebastopol: O'Reilly.

———. 2010. *Resonate: Present Visual Stories That Transform Audiences*. Hoboken: John Wiley and Sons.

Dunn, Patricia A., and Ken Lindbloom. 2011. *Grammar Rants: How a Backstage Tour of Writing Complaints Can Help Students Make Informed, Savvy Choices About Their Writing*. Portsmouth: Heinemann.

Dyson, Freeman. 1999. "This Side Idolatry." In *The Pleasure of Finding Things Out: The Best Short Works of Richard P. Feynman*, edited by Jeffrey Robbins, ix. Cambridge: Perseus.

Echevarria, Jana, MaryEllen Vogt, and Deborah J. Short. 2008. *Making Content Comprehensible for English Learners*. Boston: Pearson.

Eco, Umberto. 1994. *Six Walks in the Fictional Woods*. Cambridge: Harvard.

Edmundson, Mark. 2004. *Why Read?* New York: Bloomsbury.

Egan, Jennifer. 2010. *A Visit from the Goon Squad*. New York: Anchor.

———. 2011. "To Do." *Guardian*.

Egan, Kieran. 2010. *Learning in Depth: A Simple Innovation That Can Transform Schooling*. Chicago: University of Chicago Press.

Eisner, Elliot W. 2004. "Preparing for Today and Tomorrow." *Educational Leadership* 61, no. 4: 6–10.

Elbow, Peter. 1990. *What Is English?* New York: Modern Language Association of America.

Ellis, Justin. 2011. "Huffpo Launches a Book Club around Augmented Reading." *Huffington Post*.

Emma. 2011. "There Are Whole Lives in These Bookshelves." In *Booking Through 365*.

Erickson, Tamara J. 2009. "Gen Y in the Workforce." *Harvard Business Review*, February: 25–30.

Evangelista, Benny. 2010. "How a "Vook" May Change E-Reading Experience." *San Francisco Chronicle*, January 23, 2010.

Fearn, Leif, and Nancy Farnan. 2005. "Writing on Demand: The Influence of Time." *California English* 11, no. 1.

Fearn, Leif, Nancy Farnan, and J. Kris Rodenberg. 2003."Vocabulary for Writing." *California English*: 26–30.

Feldman, Kevin, and Kate Kinsella. 2005."Narrowing the Language Gap: The Case for Explicit Vocabulary Instruction." In *ReadAbout*. San Francisco: Scholastic Corporation.

Feynman, Richard. 1999. *The Pleasure of Finding Things Out: The Best Short Works of Richard P. Feynman*, edited by Jeffrey Robbins. Cambridge: Perseus.

Fielding, Linda G., and P. David Pearson. 1994. "Synthesis of Research: Reading Comprehension: What Works." *Educational Leadership* 51, no. 5.

Fine, Sarah. 2010. "Moving Forward with the Common Core." *Education Week*, October 20, 2010, 18–19.

Fish, Stanley. 2011. *How to Write a Sentence (and How to Read One)*. New York: Harper.

Fisher, Anne. 2009. "When Gen X Runs the Show." *Time*, May 14, p. 35–38.

Fisher, Douglas, Nancy Frey, and Diane Lapp. 2011."What the Research Says About Intentional Instruction." In *What Research Has to Say About Reading Instruction*, edited by S. J. Samuels and Alan E. Farstrup, 359–79. Newark: International Reading Association.

Fisher, Douglas, and Nancy Frey. 2008. *Word Wise and Content Rich: Five Essential Steps to Teaching Academic Vocabulary*. Portsmouth: Heinemann.

Fisher, Lef. 2009. *The Perfect Swarm: The Science of Complexity in Everyday Life*. New York: Basic.

Fisher, Tamara. 2008. "Advanced Readers." In *Unwrapping the Gifted*. Bethesda: *Education Week*.

Fletcher, Ralph. 1996. *Breathing in, Breathing Out*. Portsmouth: Heinemann.

———. 2011. *Mentor Author, Mentor Texts: Short Texts, Craft Notes, and Practical Classroom Uses*. Portsmouth: Heinemann.

Fletcher, Ralph, and Joann Portalupi. 1998. *Craft Lessons: Teaching Writing K-8*. Portland: Stenhouse.

Fliehman, Sara. "Heretical Thoughts: Is English as a Subject Too Fiction-Centric." Available at: http://englishcompanion.ning.com/forum/topics/heretical-thoughts-is-english.

Flower, Linda. 1997. *Problem Solving Strategies*. Boston: Wadsworth.

Foster, Harold M., and Megan C. Nosol. 2008. *America's Unseen Kids: Teaching English/Language Arts in Today's Forgotten High Schools*. Portsmouth: Heinemann.

Foster, Thomas C. 2003. *How to Read Literature Like a Professor*. New York: Harper Perennial.

Francis, David R. 2001. "Why Do Women Outnumber Men in College?" National Bureau of Economic Research.

Frankenberg, Erica. 2006. "The Segregation of American Teachers." In *The Civil Rights Project*. Cambridge: Harvard University Press.

———. 2008. "Are Teachers Prepared for Racially Changing Schools?" Los Angeles: The Civil Rights Project.

Freeman, David, and Yvonne Freeman. 2007. *English Language Learners: The Essential Guide*. New York: Scholastic.

Friedman, Thomas L. 2007. *The World Is Flat: A Brief History of the Twenty-First Century*. New York: Farrar, Straus and Giroux.

Friedman, Thomas L., and Michael Mandelbaum. 2011. *That Used to Be Use*. New York: Farrar, Straus and Giroux.

Fry, Richard. 2009. "The Rapid Growth and Changing Complexion of Suburban Public Schools." Washington, D.C.: Pew Hispanic Center.

Fry, Richard, and Felisa Gonzales. 2008. "One-in-Five and Growing Fast: A Profile of Hispanic Public School Students." Washington, D.C.: Pew Hispanic Center.

Fry, Richard, and Passel, Jeffrey. 2009. "Latino Children: A Majority Are U.S.-Born Offspring of Immigrants." Washington, D.C.: Pew Hispanic Center.

Gabriel, Trip. 2010. "To Stop Cheats, Colleges Learn Their Trickery." *New York Times*. July 5, 2010.

Gaddis, John Lewis. 2002. *The Landscape of History: How Historians Map the Past*. New York: Oxford University Press.

Gallagher, Kelly. 2006. *Teaching Adolescent Writers*. Portland: Stenhouse.

———. 2009. *Readicide: How Schools Are Killing Reading and What You Can Do About It*. Portland: Stenhouse.

———. 2011a. "Can Reading Be Saved?" *Education Week* 4, no. 2: 22.

———. 2011b. *Write Like This: Teaching Real-World Writing Through Modeling and Mentor Texts*. Portland: Stenhouse.

Gallagher, Winifred. 2009. *Rapt: Attention and the Focused Life*. New York: Penguin.

Gambrell, Linda B. 2007. "Promoting Pleasure Reading: The Role of Models, Mentors, and Motivators." *Reading Today*, 16.

Gambrell, Linda B., Barbara A. Marinak, Heather R. Brooker, and Heather J. McCrea-Andrews. 2011. "The Importance of Independent Reading." edited by S. Jay Samuels and Alan E. Farstrup. Newark: International Reading Association.

Gardner, Howard. 1995. *Leading Minds: An Anatomy of Leadership*. New York: Basic.

———. 2006. *Multiple Intelligences: New Horizons in Theory and Practice*. New York: Basic Books.

Garner, Bryan. 2009. *Garner's Modern American Usage*. New York: Oxford University Press.

Gawande, Atul. 2009. *The Checklist Manifesto: How to Get Things Right.* New York: Metropolitan Books.

Gay, Geneva. 2010. *Culturally Responsive Teaching: Theory, Research, and Practice,* Multicultural Education Series. New York: Teachers College Press.

Gebhard, Meg, and J. R. Martin. 2011. "Grammar and Literacy Learning." In *Handbook of Research on Teaching the English Language Arts,* edited by Diane Lapp and Douglas Fisher. New York: Routledge.

Gee, James Paul. 2007. *What Video Games Have to Teach Us About Learning and Literacy. Second Edition: Revised and Updated Edition.* New York: Palgrave Macmillan.

Gere, Anne Ruggles, Leila Christenbury, and Kelly Sassi. 2005. *Writing on Demand: Best Practices and Strategies for Success.* Portsmouth: Heinemann.

Gewertz, Catherine. 2011. "Teachers Tackle Text Complexity." *Education Week,* March 14, 2011.

Gilles, Carol. 2010. "Making the Most of Talk." *Voices from the Middle* 18, no. 2: 9–15.

Gilligan, Carol. 1993. *In a Different Voice: Psychological Theory and Women's Development.* Cambridge: Harvard University Press.

Gilmore, Barry. 2010. "Standing on Merit: The Role of Quality and Choice in Student Reading." In *Engaging Students with Literature: A Curriculum Module for AP® English Literature and Composition,* 5–13. New York: College Board.

Gilyard, Keith. 1991. *Voices of the Self: A Study of Language Competence.* Detroit: Wayne State.

Gladwell, Malcolm. 2010. "Small Change: The Revolution Will Not Be Tweeted." *New Yorker,* October 4, 2010, p. 38–47.

Graff, Gerald, and Cathy Birkenstein. 2007. *They Say/I Say: The Moves That Matter in Academic Writing.* New York: W. W. Norton.

Glenn, Cheryl, and Melissa A. Goldthwaite. 2008. *The St. Martin's Guide to Teaching Writing,* sixth ed. Boston: Bedford/St. Martin's.

Godfrey, Kelly E. 2011. "Investigating Grade Inflation and Non-Equivalence." New York: College Board.

Godin, Seth. 2007. *The Dip: The Little Book That Teaches You When to Quit (and When to Stick).* New York: Portfolio.

———. 2010. *Linchpin: Are You Indispensable? : How to Drive Your Career and Create a Remarkable Future.* New York: Portfolio.

Goleman, Daniel. 2006. *Emotional Intelligence: Why It Can Matter More Than IQ.* New York: Bantam.

———. 2007. *Social Intelligence: The New Science of Human Relationships.* New York: Bantam.

Good, Thomas L. 2010. "Forty Years of Research on Teaching 1968–2008: What Do We Know Now That We Didn't Know Then?" In *On Excellence in Teaching,* edited by Robert Marzano. Bloomington: Solution Tree.

Goodlad, John. 2004. *A Place Called School.* New York: McGraw-Hill.

Goodwin, Bryan. 2011."Grade Inflation: Killin with Kindness?" *Educational Leadership* 69, no. 3: 80–81.

Goodyear, Dana. 2008."I (Heart) Novels." *New Yorker,* 62–68.

Gourevitch, Philip, ed. 2006. *The Paris Review Interviews, Vol. 1.* New York: Picador.

Graff, Gerald, Cathy Birkenstein, and Russel Durst. 2010. *They Say/I Say: The Moves That Matter in Academic Writing,* second ed. New York: W. W. Norton.

Graham, Steve, and Michael Hebert. 2010."Writing to Read: Evidence for How Writing Can Improve Reading." Washington, D.C.: Alliance for Excellent Education.

Graham, Steve, Charles A. MacArthur, and Jill Fitzgerald. 2007. *Best Practices in Writing Instruction (Solving Problems in the Teaching of Literacy).* New York: Guilford.

Graham, Steve, Karen Harris, and Michael Hebert. 2011. "Informing Writing: The Benefits of Formative Assessment." In *A Carnegie Corporation Time to Act Report.* Washington, DC: Alliance for Excellent Education.

Graham, Steve, and Dolores Perin. 2007. "Writing Next: Effective Strategies to Improve Writing of Adolescents in Middle and High Schools—a Report to Carnegie Corporation of New York." Washington, D.C.: Alliance for Excellent Education.

Graves, Donald H. 2001. *The Energy to Teach*. Portsmouth: Heinemann.

Graves, Michael F. 2006. *The Vocabulary Book: Learning & Instruction*. New York: Teachers College.

Gray, James, and Robert Benson. 1982. *Sentence and Paragraph Modeling*. Vol. 17, Curriculum Publications. Berkeley: Bay Area Writing Project.

Great Books Foundation. 1999. *An Introduction to Shared Inquiry*, fourth ed. Chicago: Great Books Foundation.

Greenhouse, Steven. 2003. "Going for the Look, but Risking Discrimination." *New York Times*.

Greenleaf, Cynthia, Ruth Schoenbach, Christine Cziko, and Faye Mueller. 2001."Apprenticing Adolescent Readers to Academic Literacy." *Harvard Education Review*, no. 1: 79–129.

Gregory, Marshall. 1997. "The Many-Headed Hydra of Theory Vs. The Unifying Mission of Teaching." *College English* 59, no. 1: 41-58.

Groenke, Susan L., and Lisa Scherff. 2010. *Teaching YA Lit Through Differentiated Instruction*. Urbana: National Council of Teachers of English.

Guber, Peter. 2011. *Tell to Win: Connect, Persuade, and Triumph with the Hidden Power of Story*. New York: Crown.

Gurdon, Meghan Cox. 2011. "Darkness Too Visible." *Wall Street Journal*.

Gurian, Michael, Kathy Stevens, and Kelley King. 2008. *Strategies for Teaching Boys and Girls: Secondary Level*. San Francisco: Jossey Bass.

Guskey, Thomas R. 2000. "Grading Policies That Work Against Standards . . . And How to Fix Them." *National Association of Secondary School Principals* 84, no. 620: 20–29.

———. 2001. "Helping Standards Make the Grade." *Educational Leadership* 59, no. 1: 20–27.

Guskey, Thomas R., and Lee Ann Jung. 2009."Grading and Reporting in a Standards-Based Environment: Implications for Students with Special Needs." *Theory into Practice* 48: 53–62.

Guthrie, John T., and Allan Wigfield, ed. 1997. *Reading Engagement: Motivating Readers Through Integrated Instruction*. Newark: International Reading Association.

Guzzetti, Barbara, and Margaret Gamboa. 2005. "Online Journaling: The Informal Writings of Two Adolescent Girls." *Research in the Teaching of English* 40, no. 2: 168–205.

Harrington, Mary Kay. 2002."English Placement Test." In *Focus on English*. Long Beach: California State University.

Harrison, Robert Pogue. 2012. "The Book from Which All Our Literature Springs." *The New York Review of Books*. February.

Harvey, Stephanie, and Anne Goudvis. 2007. *Strategies That Work: Teaching Comprehension for Understanding and Engagement*, second ed. Portland: Stenhouse.

Haven, Cynthia. 2009. "The New Literacy: Stanford Study Finds Richness and Complexity in Students' Writing." *Stanford University News*.

Hayes, Tom. 2008. *Jump Point: How Network Culture Is Revolutionizing Business*. New York: McGraw-Hill.

Hemphill, F. Cadelle, Alan Vanneman, and Taslima Rahman. 2011. *Achievement Gaps: How Hispanic and White Students in Public Schools Perform Mathematics and Reading on the National Assessment of Educational Progress*. Washington, DC: National Center for Education Statistics.

Henderson, Lynne. 2008. "The Social Fitness Model." In *The Shyness Blog*. Palo Alto: The Shyness Institute.

Hephzibah, Roskelly, and David A. Jolliffe. 2005. *Everyday Use: Rhetoric at Work in Reading and Writing*. New York: Pearson Longman.

Herrington, Anne, Kevin Hodgson, and Charles Moran, ed. 2009. *Teaching the New Writing: Technology, Change, and Assessment in the 21st Century Classroom*. New York: Teachers College.

Hicks, Troy. 2009. *The Digital Writing Workshop*. Portsmouth: Heinemann.

Hillocks, George Jr. 1999. *Ways of Thinking, Ways of Teaching*. New York: Teachers College.

———. 2002. *The Testing Trap: How State Writing Assessments Control Learning*. New York: Teachers College Press.

———. 2003. "Fighting Back: Assessing the Assessments." *English Journal* 92, no. 4: 63–70.

———. 2008. "Writing in Secondary Schools." In *Handbook of Research on Writing: History, Society, School, Individual, Text*, edited by Charles Bazerman, 311–30. New York: Lawrence Erlbaum.

———. 2009a "Needed: A Revolution in the Teaching of Literacy." *English Leadership Quarterly* 32, no. 1: 8–10.

———. 2009b. "A Response to Peter Smagorinsky: Some Practices and Approaches Are Clearly Better Than Others and We Had Better Not Ignore the Difference." *English Journal* 98, no. 6: 23≠29.

Hirsch, E. D. 1988. *Cultural Literacy: What Every American Needs to Know*. New York: Vintage.

———. 2007. *The Knowledge Deficit: Closing the Shocking Education Gap for American Children*. Boston: Houghton Mifflin Harcourt.

———. 2009. *The Making of Americans: Democracy and Our Schools*. New Haven: Yale University Press.

Hotz, Robert Lee. 2009. "A Wandering Mind Heads Straight Toward Insight." *Wall Street Journal*, 2009, p. A11.

Humes, Karen R., Nicholas A. Jones, and Roberto R. Ramirez. 2011. "Overview of Race and Hispanic Origin: 2010." Edited by U.S. Census Bureau. Washington, D.C.: U.S. Department of Commerce.

Hyerle, David. 2009. *Visual Tools for Transforming Information into Knowledge*. Thousand Oaks: Corwin.

International Reading Association. 2000. "Excellent Reading Teachers: A Position Statement of the International Reading Association." *Journal of Adolescent and Adult Literacy* 44, no. 2: 193–99.

Intersegmental Committee of the Academic Senates of the California Community Colleges et al. 2002. "Academic Literacy: A Statement of Competencies Expected of Students Entering California's Public Colleges and Universities." Sacramento, CA.

Intrator, Sam M. 2003. *Tuned in and Fired Up: How Teaching Can Inspire Real Learning in the Classroom*. New Haven: Yale University Press.

Intrator, Sam M., and Robert Kunzman. 2009. "Who Are Adolescents Today: Youth Voices and What They Tell Us?" In *Handbook of Adolescent Literacy Research*, edited by Randy Bomer Leila Christenbury, and Peter Smagorinsky. New York: Guilford.

Isaacs, William. 1999. *Dialogue and the Art of Thinking Together: A Pioneering Approach to Communicating in Business and in Life*. New York: Currency.

Ito, Mizuko, Heather Horst, Matteo Bittanti, danah boyd, Becky Herr-Stephenson, Patricia G. Lange, C. J. Pascoe, and Laura Robinson. 2008. "Living and Learning with New Media: Summary of Findings from the Digital Youth Project." Chicago: The John D. and Catherine T. MacArthur Foundation Reports on Digital Media and Learning.

Jackson, Maggie. 2009. *Distracted: The Erosion of Attention and the Coming Dark Age*. New York: Prometheus.

Jacobs, Alan. 2011. *The Pleasures of Reading in an Age of Distraction*. New York: Oxford University Press.

Jago, Carol. 2002. *Cohesive Writing: Why Concept Is Not Enough*. Portsmouth: Heinemann.

———. 2004. *Classics in the Classroom: Designing Accessible Literature Lessons*. Portsmouth: Heinemann.

———. 2009. "Crash! The Currency Crisis in American Culture." In *President Perspective*, 1–6. Urbana: National Council of Teachers of English.

———. 2011a. *With Rigor for All: Meeting Common Core Standards for Reading Literature*, second ed. Portsmouth: Heinemann.

———. 2011b. "The Common Core/Uncommon Sense." In *High School Bits*: Bedford/St. Martin's.

Jensen, Eric. 2005. *Teaching with the Brain in Mind*, revised second ed. Alexandria: Association of Supervision and Curriculum Development.

Jewell, Vivian. 2005. "Continuing the Classroom Community: Using Online Discussion Boards." *English Journal* 94, no. 4: 83–87.

Johannessen, Larry R., and Thomas M. McCann. 2009. "Adolescents Who Struggle with Literacy." In *Handbook of Adolescent Literacy*, edited by Randy Bomer Leila Christenbury, and Peter Smagorinsky, 65–79. New York: Guilford.

Johnson, Christopher. 2011. *Microstyle: The Art of Writing Little*. New York: W. W. Norton.

Johnson, Dale D., Bonnie Von Hoff Johnson, and Kathleen Schlichting. 2004. "Logology: Word and Language Play." In *Vocabulary Instruction: Research to Practice*, edited by James F. Baumann and Edward J. Kame'enui. New York: Guilford.

Judt, Tony. 2010. "Night." *New York Review of Books*, January 14, p. 23.

Kafka, Franz. 1987. *Letters to Friends, Family, and Editors*. New York: Schocken.

Kahn, Elizabeth. 2007. "Building Fires: Raising Achievement through Class Discussion." *English Journal* 96, no. 7: 16–18.

Karp, Josh. 2010. "Does Digital Media Make Us Bad Writers." Available at: http://spotlight.macfound.org/featured-stories/entry/does-digital-media-make-us-bad-writers.

Keniston, Kenneth. 1965. *The Uncommitted: Alienated Youth in American Society*. New York: Harcourt, Brace, and World.

Killgallon, Don. 1998. *Sentence Composing: The Theory Booklet*. Portsmouth: Heinemann.

King, Stephen. 2010. *On Writing: A Memoir of the Craft*. New York: Scribner.

King-Shaver, Barbara and Alyce Hunter. 2003. *Differentiated Instruction in the English Classroom: Content, Process, Product, and Assessment*. Portsmouth: Heinemann.

Kinneavey, James L. 1971. *A Theory of Discourse: The Aims of Discourse*. Englewood Cliffs: Prentice-Hall.

Kinsella, Kate, and Kevin Feldman. 2006. "Essential Features of Structured, Inclusive Academic Discussions." In *San Mateo County English Language Learner Conference*. San Mateo: San Mateo County Office of Education.

Kirby, Dawn Latta, and Dan Kirby. 2007. *New Directions in Teaching Memoir: A Studio Workshop Approach*. Portsmouth: Heinemann.

Kirkpatrick, David. 2010. *The Facebook Effect: The Inside Story of the Company That Is Connecting the World*. New York: Simon and Schuster.

Kittle, Penny. 2008. *Write Beside Them: Risk, Voice, and Clarity in High School Writing*. Portsmouth: Heinemann.

———. 2011. Personal correspondence.

Kolln, Martha. 2003. *Rhetorical Grammar: Grammatical Choices, Rhetorical Effects*. New York: Longman.

Kopetz, Patricia B., Anthony J. Lease, and Bonnie A. Warren-Kring. 2006. *Comprehensive Urban Education*. New York: Pearson.

Kopytoff, Verne G. 2011. "Blogs Wane as the Young Drift to Sites Like Twitter." *New York Times*, February 21, p. B1.

Kress, Gunther. 2007. *Literacy in the New Media Age*. London: Routledge.

Kress, Gunther, and Theo Van Leeuwen. 2001. *Multimodal Discourse: The Modes and Media of Contemporary Communication*. London: Arnold.

Lampert, Magdelene. 2001. *Teaching Problems and the Problems of Teaching*. New Haven: Yale University Press.

Langer, Ellen. 1997. *The Power of Mindful Learning*. New York: Perseus.

Langer, Judith A.1995. *Envisioning Literature: Literary Understanding and Literature Instruction*. New York: Teachers College/International Reading Association.

———. 2002. *Effective Literacy Instruction: Building Successful Reading and Writing Programs*. Urbana: National Council of Teachers of English.

———. 2004a. "Developing the Literate Mind." In *International Reading Association Annual Convention*. Orlando, FL. International Reading Association.

———. 2004b. *Getting to Excellent: How to Create Better Schools*. New York: Teachers College Press.

———. Email, July 16, 2010.

———. 2011a. *Envisioning Literature: Literary Understanding and Literature Instruction*. New York: Teachers College.

———. 2011b. "The National Study of Writing." Paper presented at the National Council of Teachers of English, Chicago, November.

Langer, Judith A., and Elizabeth Close. 2001. *Improving Literary Understanding Through Classroom Conversation*. Albany: Center on English Learning and Achievement.

Lanham, Richard A. 1993. *The Electronic Word: Democracy, Technology, and the Arts*. Chicago: University of Chicago Press.

———. 2006. *The Economics of Attention: Style and Substance in the Age of Information*. Chicago: University of Chicago.

Lanier, Jaron. 2010. *You Are Not a Gadget: A Manifesto*. New York: Knopf.

Lankshear, Colin, and Michele Knobel. 2006. *New Literacies: Everyday Practices and Classroom Learning*. New York: Open University Press.

Larkin, Ralph W. 1979. *Suburban Youth in Cultural Crisis*. New York: Oxford University Press.

Larochelle, Paul. 2011. "Found in Translations: Using Multiple Versions of Translated Text for Close Analysis of Language." *English Journal* 100, no. 4: 61–65.

Lave, Jean, and Etienne Wenger. 1991. *Situated Learning: Legitimate Peripheral Participation*. New York: Cambridge University Press.

Lee, Jr., Michael John, Franes Contreras, Keon M. McGuire, Adriana Flores-Ragade, Anita Rawls, Kelcey Edwards, and Roxana Menson. 2011. "The College Completion Agenda: The Latino Edition." In *Latino Edition*: College Board.

Lemov, Doug. 2010. *Teach Like a Champion*. San Francisco: Jossey-Bass.

Lenhart, Amanda, Sousan Arafeh, Aaron Smith, and Alexandra Macgill. 2008. "Writing, Technology, and Teens." Washington, D.C.: Pew Internet and American Life Project.

Lent, ReLeah Cossett and Jimmy Santiago Baca. 2010. *Adolescents on the Edge: Stories and Lessons to Transform Learning*. Portsmouth: Heinemann.

Lesesne, Teri S. 2009. "Reaching Reluctant Readers: Suggestions for Igniting the Spark." *English Leadership Quarterly* 31, no. 3: 2–3.

———. 2010. *Reading Ladders: Leading Students from Where They Are to Where We'd Like Them to Be*. Portsmouth: Heinemann.

Lewin, Tamar. 2006. "At Colleges, Women Are Leaving Men in the Dust." *New York Times*, July 9, 2006, p. 17–19.

Lickona, Tom, Eric Schaps, and Catherine Lewis. 2003. "Character Education Partnership's Eleven Principles of Effective Character Education." Washington, D.C.: Character Education Partnership.

Lipstein, Rebecca and Ann K. Renninger. 2007. "Interest for Writing: How Teachers Can Make a Difference." *English Journal* 96, no. 4: 79–85.

Lindemann, Erika. 2001. *A Rhetoric for Writing Teachers*, fourth ed. New York: Oxford University Press.

Lomax, Nathan. 2009. "Comment on 'How to Write a Timed Essay' Blog." In *Jim Burke: The English Teacher's Companion*, edited by Jim Burke. San Francisco.

Lopez, Shane J. 2009. *Gallup Student Poll National Report*. Washington, D.C.: Gallup.

———. 2009. "Engagement, Performance on Standardized Tests, and The Gallup Student Poll."

Love, Jessica. 2012. "Reading, Fast and Slow." *The American Scholar*, 72.

Lunsford, Andrea. 2008. "Stanford Study of Writing." Stanford: Stanford University Press.

Lunsford, Andrea, and Karen J. Lunsford. 2008. "'Mistakes Are a Fact of Life': A National Comparative Study." *College Composition and Communication* 59, no. 4: 781–806.

Luntz, Frank. 2007. *Words That Work: It's Not What You Say, It's What People Hear*. New York: Hyperion.

Lux, Thomas. 1997. "The Voice You Hear When You Read Silently." *New Yorker*, July 14, 1997, p. 77.

MacArthur, Charles A. 2007. "Best Practices in Teaching Evaluation and Revision." In *Best Practices in Writing Instruction*, edited by Steve Graham, Charles A. MacArthur, and Jill Fitzgerald. New York: Guilford.

MacArthur, Charles A., Steve Graham, and Jill Fitzgerald. 2006. *Handbook of Writing Research*. New York: Guilford Press.

Magazine Publishers of America. 2004. "Teen Market Profile." New York: Magazine Publishers of America.

Mahiri, Jabari. 2004. *What They Don't Learn in School: Literacy in the Lives of Urban Youth*. New York: Peter Lang.

Manguel, Alberto. 1996. *A History of Reading*. New York: Penguin.

Maran, Meredith. 2010. "'Goon Squad': Jennifer Egan's Time-Travel Tour De Force." In *Fiction*: Salon.com.

Marzano, Robert J. 2004. *Building Background Knowledge for Academic Achievement: Research on What Works in Schools*. Alexandria: Association for Supervision and Curriculum Development.

———. 2007. *The Art and Science of Teaching: A Comprehensive Framework for Effective Instruction*. Alexandria: Association for Supervision and Curriculum Development.

———. 2009. "Six Steps to Better Vocabulary Instruction." *Educational Leadership* 67, no. 1: 83-84.

———. 2010. *Formative Assessment and Standards-Based Grading*. Bloomington: Marzano Research Laboratory.

Marzano , Robert J., and John S. Kendall. 2007. *The New Taxonomy of Educational Objectives*, second ed. Thousand Oaks: Corwin.

Marzano , Robert J., and Deborah J. Pickering. 2005. *Building Academic Vocabulary*. Alexandria: Association for Supervision and Curriculum Development.

Marzano, Robert J., Deborah J. Pickering, and Jane E. Pollock. 2004. *Classroom Instruction That Works: Research-Based Strategies for Increasing Student Achievement*. Alexandria: Association for Supervision and Curriculum Development.

Mathews, Jay. 1988. *Escalante: The Best Teacher in America*. New York: Henry Holt.

———. 2010. "Help Pick Non-Fiction Books for Schools." *Washington Post*, February 21, 2010.

McCann, Thomas M., Larry R. Johannessen, Elizabeth Kahn, and Joseph M. Flanagan. 2006. *Talking in Class: Using Discussion to Enhance Teaching and Learning*. Urbana: National Council of Teachers of English.

McLuhan, Marshall. 1994. *Understanding the Media: The Extensions of Man*. Cambridge: MIT Press.

Mead, Sara. 2006. "The Evidence Suggests Otherwise: The Truth About Boys and Girls." Washington, D.C.: The Education Sector.

Meritbadge.com. 2011.

Miedema, John. 2009. *Slow Reading*. Duluth: Litwin.

Miller, Donalyn. 2009. *The Book Whisperer: Awakening the Inner Reader in Every Child*. San Francisco: Jossey-Bass.

Morse, Ogden. 2012. "Soapstone: A Strategy for Reading and Writing." College Board website.

Murphy, Leo Ruth, and Sandra. *Designing Writing Tasks for the Assessment of Writing*. Norwood: Ablex, 1988.

Murphy, Sandra. 2007. "Culture and Consequences: The Canaries in the Coal Mine." *Research in the Teaching of English* 42, no. 2: 228–43.

Murray, Donald M. 2001. *The Craft of Revision*, fourth ed. Fort Worth: Harcourt College.

———. 2004. *A Writer Teaches Writing*. Boston: Thomson.

Murray, Janet. 1998. *Hamlet on the Holodeck: The Future of Narrative in Cyberspace*. Cambridge: MIT Press.

Nabokov, Vladimir. 1980. *Lectures on Literature*. San Diego: Harvest.

Nagin, Carl and the National Writing Project. 2006. *Because Writing Matters: Improving Student Writing in Our Schools*, revised and updated edition. San Francisco: Jossey-Bass.

National Adolescent Literacy Coalition. 2007. "Foundational and Emergent Questions: Smart People Talk About Adolescent Literacy." In *A Report by the Steering Committee of the National Adolescent Literacy Coalition*. Washington, D.C.: National Adolescent Literacy Coalition.

National Association for Gifted Children. 2011. "2010-2011 State of the Nation in Gifted Education: A Lack of Commitment to Talent Development." Washington, D.C.

National Center for Education Statistics. 2009. "The Condition of Education 2009." Washington, D.C.: National Center for Education Statistics.

The National Commission on Writing in America's Schools and Colleges. 2003. "The Neglected "R": The Need for a Writing Revolution." 2003. New York: The National Commission on Writing in America's Schools and Colleges.

National Center on Education and the Economy. 2007. "Tough Choices or Tough Times: The Report of the New Commission of the Skills of the American Workforce." San Francisco, CA.

NCTE. 2004. "A Call to Action: What We Know About Adolescent Literacy and Ways to Support Teachers in Meeting Students' Needs." Urbana, IL: National Council of Teachers of English.

NCTE. 2008. "The NCTE Definition of 21st Century Literacies." National Council of Teachers of English. Available at: www.ncte.org/positions/statements/21stcentdefinition.

National Endowment of the Arts. 2005. "2004 Annual Report." Washington, D.C.: National Endowment of the Arts.

National Endowment for the Arts. 2008. "2007 Annual Report." Washington, D.C.: National Endowment for the Arts.

National Endowment for the Arts. 2009. "Reading on the Rise." Washington, D.C.: National Endowment for the Arts.

National Governors Association. 2010. *Common Core State Standards for English Language Arts and Literacy in History/Social Studies, Science, and Technical Subjects*. Washington, D.C.: NGA Center and CCSSO.

Newkirk, Thomas. 1997. *The Performance of Self in Student Writing*. Portsmouth: Heinemann.

———. 2005. *The School Essay Manifesto: Reclaiming the Essay for Students and Teachers*. Shoreum: Discovery.

———. 2009a. *Holding on to Good Ideas in a Time of Bad Ones: Six Literacy Principles Worth Fighting For*. Portsmouth: Heinemann.

———. 2009b. "Reading, Science, and Reductionism." *Education Week*, March 4. 2009.

———. 2010. "The Case for Slow Reading." *Educational Leadership* 67, no. 6: 6–11.

———. 2011. "Literacy and Loneliness." *University of New Hampshire Magazine*, Durham: NH. .

———. 2012. *The Art of Slow Reading: Six Time-Honored Practices for Engagement*. Portsmouth: Heinemann.

Newkirk , Thomas and Richard Kent, ed. 2007. *Teaching the Neglected "R": Rethinking Writing Instruction in Secondary Classrooms*. Portsmouth: Heinemann.

Nielsen, Jakob. 2008. "How Little Do Users Read?" In *Jakob Niesen's Alertbox*.

———. 2010. "iPad and Kindle Reading Speeds." In *Jakob Nielsen's Alertbox*.

Nussbaum, Martha C. 1995. *Poetic Justice: The Literary Imagination and Public Life*. Boston: Beacon Press.

———. 2010. *Not for Profit: Why Democracy Needs the Humanities*. Princeton: Princeton.

Nyamekye, Ama. 2011. "Putting Myself to the Test: A Teacher Finds Positives in Testing." *Education Week*, August 31, 2011.

Nystrand, Martin. 1998. "English: Not Just for English (Class) Anymore." *English Update*.

———. 2006. "Research on the Role of Classroom Discourse as It Affects Reading Comprehension." *Research in the Teaching of English* 40, no. 4: 392–412.

Nystrand, Martin, with Adam Gamoran, Robert Kachur, and Catherine Prendergast. 1997. *Opening Dialogue: Understanding the Dynamics of Language and Learning in the English Classroom.* New York: Teachers College.

O'Connor, Ken. 2007. "The Last Frontier: Tackling the Grading Dilemma." In *Ahead of the Curve: The Power of Assessment to Transform Teaching and Learning*, edited by Douglas Reeves. Bloomington: Solution Tree.

Obama, Barack. 2007. *Dreams from My Father: A Story of Race and Inheritance.* New York: Crown.

OECD. 2010. "Pisa 2009 Results: What Students Know and Can Do: Student Performance in Reading, Mathematics and Science (Volume I)." Organization for Economic Cooperation and Development. Washington, D.C.

Olsen, Laurie, and Ann Jaramillo. 1999. *Turning the Tides of Exclusion: A Guide for Educators and Advocates for Immigrant Students*, The California Tomorrow Equity-Centered School Reform Series. Oakland: California Tomorrow.

Olson, Carol Booth, and Robert Land. 2007. "A Cognitive Strategies Approach to Reading and Writing Instruction for English Language Learners in Secondary School." *Research in the Teaching of English* 41, no. 3: 269–303.

Osborn, Michael, and Suzanne Osborn. 1997. *Public Speaking*, third ed. Boston: Houghton Mifflin.

Palinscar, Annmarie Sullivan, and Ann L. Brown. 1984. "Reciprocal Teaching of Comprehension-Fostering and Comprehension-Monitoring Activities." *Cognition and Instruction* 1, no. 2: 117–75.

Parks, Sharon Daloz. 2000. *Big Questions: Mentoring Young Adults in Their Search for Meaning, Purpose, and Faith.* San Francisco: Jossey-Bass.

Pauk, Walter. 1997. *How to Study in College*, sixth ed. New York: Houghton-Mifflin.

Payne, Lucile Vaughn.1969. *The Lively Art of Writing.* New York: Signet.

Pearson, David P., and Margaret C. Gallagher. 1983. "The Instruction of Reading Comprehension." *Contemporary Educational Psychology* 8: 317–44.

Pérez, Angel B. 2012. "Want to Get into College? Learn to Fail." *Education Week.*

Perin, Dolores. 2007. "Best Practices in Teaching Writing to Adolescents." In *Best Practices in Writing Instruction*, edited by Charles A. MacArthur Steve Graham, and Jill Fitzgerald. New York: Guilford.

Perkins, David. 2009. *Making Learning Whole: How Seven Principles of Teaching Can Transform Education.* San Francisco: Jossey-Bass.

Pew Internet. 2009. "Generational Differences in Online Activities." Washington, D.C.: Pew Internet.

Pew Research. 2010. "The Rise of Intermarriage." Washington, D.C.: Pew Research.

Phillips, Anna M. 2012. "High School Admissions Letters Go Out to Students." In *School Book.* New York: *New York Times.*

Piercy, Marge. 1982. "The Seven of Pentacles." In *Circles on the Water.* New York: Knopf.

Pilgreen, Janice L. 2000. *The SSR Handbook: How to Organize and Manage a Sustained Silent Reading Program.* Portsmouth: Heinemann.

Pink, Daniel. 2006. *A Whole New Mind: Why Right-Brainers Will Rule the Future.* New York: Riverhead.

Pipher, Mary. 2005. *Reviving Ophelia: Saving the Selves of Adolescent Girls.* New York: Riverhead Books.

———. 2009. *Seeking Peace: Chronicles of the Worst Buddhist in the World.* New York: Riverhead.

Plato. 1997. "Phaedrus." In *Plato: Complete Works*, edited by John M. Cooper, 506–56. New York: Hackett.

Poo, Marshall T. 2011. *A History of Communications: Media and Society from the Evolution of Speech to the Internet.* Cambridge: Cambridge University Press.

Pope, Denise Clark. 2003. *Doing School: How We Are Creating a Generation of Stressed-out, Materialistic, and Miseducated Students*. New Haven: Yale University Press.

Popham, W. James. 2008. *Transformative Assessment*. Alexandria: Association for Supervision and Curriculum Development.

———. 2011. *Classroom Assessment: What Teachers Need to Know*, sixth ed. Boston: Pearson.

Postman, Neil. 1985. *Amusing Ourselves to Death: Public Discourse in the Age of Show Business*. New York: Penguin.

Postman, Neil, and Charles Weingartner. 1969. *Teaching as a Subversive Activity*. New York: Delacorte.

Prose, Francine. 1999. "I Know Why the Caged Bird Cannot Read: How American High School Students Learn to Loathe Literature." *Harper's*, September, 76–84.

———. 2006. *Reading Like a Writer*. New York: Harper Collins.

Purves, Alan C. 1990. *The Scribal Society: An Essay on Literacy and Schooling in the Information Age*. New York: Longman.

———, ed. 1991. *The Idea of Difficulty in Literature*. Albany: State University of New York.

Quate, Stevie, and John McDermott. 2009. *Clock Watchers: Six Steps to Motivating and Engaging Disengaged Students across Content Areas*. Portsmouth: Heinemann.

Quillen, Ian. 2010. "Video Essays Play as Auditions for College." *Education Week*, April 7, 2010, 50.

Rafael, Taffy E., Kathy Highfield, and Kathryn H. Au. 2006. *QAR Now: A Powerful and Practical Framework That Develops Comprehension and Higher-Level Thinking in All Students*. New York: Scholastic.

Rampey, B. D., G. S. Dion, and P. L. Donahue. 2009. "Neap 2008 Trends in Academic Progress," edited by Institute of Education Sciences National Center for Education Statistics. Washington, D.C.: U.S. Department of Education.

Ravitch, Diane. 2001. *Left Back: A Century of Battles over School Reform*. New York: Simon and Schuster.

———. 2010. *The Death and Life of the Great American School System: How Testing and Choice Are Undermining Education*. New York: Basic Books.

Reeves, Douglas. 2006. "Foreword." In *Common Formative Assessments: How to Connect Standards-Based Instruction and Assessment*. Thousand Oaks: Corwin.

———. 2007. "From the Bell Curve to the Mountain: A New Vision for Achievement, Assessment, and Equity." In *Ahead of the Curve: The Power of Assessment to Transform Teaching and Learning*, edited by Douglas Reeves. Bloomington: Solution Tree.

———. 2011. *Elements of Grading: A Guide to Effective Practice*. Bloomington: Solution Tree.

Reynolds, Garr. 2008. *Presentation Zen: Simple Ideas on Presentation Design and Delivery*. Berkeley: New Riders.

———. 2011. *The Naked Presenter: Delivering Powerful Presentations with or without Slides*. Berkeley: New Riders.

Richardson, Will. 2010. *Blogs, Wikis, Podcasts and Other Powerful Web Tools for Classrooms*. Thousand Oaks: Corwin.

Rico, Gabriele. 2000. *Writing the Natural Way*. New York: Tarcher/Putnam.

Rideout, Victoria J., Ulla G. Foehr, and Donald F. Roberts. 2010. "Generation M2: Media in the Lives of 8- to 18-Year-Olds." Menlo Park: Kaiser Family Foundation.

Rief, Linda. 2007. *Reader's-Writer's Notebook*. Portsmouth: Heinemann.

Ritchtel, Matt. 2011. "In Classrooms of Future, Stagnant Scores." *New York Times*.

Robb, Laura. 2010. *Teaching Middle School Writers: What Every English Teacher Needs to Know*. Portsmouth: Heinemann.

Robelen, Erik W. 2010. "Education Attainment Rises for Americans across Race, Ethnicity." *Education Week*, May 19, 2010, p. 6.

Roberge, Mark M. 2003. "Generation 1.5 Immigrant Students: What Special Experiences, Characteristics and Educational Needs to They Bring to Our English Classes?" In *37th Annual TESOL Convention*. Baltimore.

Robinson, Ken. 2009a. "Creativity in the Classroom, Innovation in the Workplace." (whitepaper) Available at: principalvoices.com.

———. 2009b. *The Element: How Finding Your Passion Changes Everything*. New York: Penguin.

———. 2011. *Out of Our Minds: Learning to Be Creative*. London: Capstone.

Roche, Paul. 1991. "The Great Encounter." In *The Oedipus Plays of Sophocles*. New York: Meridian.

Rodriguez, Richard. 2002. *Brown: The Last Discovery of America*. New York: Viking.

Romano, Tom. 2009. "Defining Fun and Seeking Flow in English Language Arts." *English Journal* 98, no. 6: 30–37.

Rooney, Patrick, William Hussar, and Michael Planty. 2006."The Condition of Education 2006." In *The Condition of Education*. Washington, D.C.: United States Government.

Rose, Mike. 2004. *The Mind at Work: Valuing the Intelligence of the American Worker*. New York: Viking.

———. 2005. *Lives on the Boundary: A Moving Account of the Struggles and Achievements of America's Educationally Underprepared*. New York: Penguin.

———. 2009a. *Why School? Reclaiming Education for All of Us*. New York: New Press.

———. 2009b. Observing Classrooms: What Journalists and Teachers Might Have in Common." *English Leadership Quarterly* 32, no. 1: 4–5.

———. 2010a."A Lesson for Teachers." *Los Angeles Times*, June 4.

———. 2010b. "When the Light Goes On." *The American Scholar*, Spring: 72–76.

———. 2011. "Making Sparks Fly." *American Scholar*.

Rosenblatt, Louise M. 1995. *Literature as Exploration*. New York: Modern Language Association.

———. 1999. "Theory and Practice: An Interview with Louise M. Rosenblatt." *Language Arts* 77, no. 2: 158–70.

———. 2005. *Making Meaning with Texts: Selected Essays*. Portsmouth: Heinemann.

Rosin, Hanna. 2010. "The End of Men." *Atlantic Monthly*, July/August: 56-70.

Ruddell, Martha Rapp, and Brenda A. Shearer. 2002. ""Extraordinary," "Tremendous," "Exhilarating," and "Magnificent": Middle School at-Risk Students Become Avid Word Learners with Vocabulary Self-Collection Strategy (VSS)." *Journal of Adolescent and Adult Literacy* 45, no. 5: 352–63.

Ruddell, Robert B., and Norman J. Unrau. 2004. "Reading as a Meaning-Making Construction Process: The Reader, the Text, and the Teacher." In *Theoretical Models and Processes of Reading*. Newark: International Reading Association.

Ruetzel, Ray D., Kay Camperell, and John A. Smith. 2002. "Hitting the Wall: Helping Struggling Readers Comprehend." In *Improving Comprehension Instruction: Rethinking Research, Theory, and Classroom Practice*, edited by Linda Gambrell Cathy Collins Block, and Michael Pressley, 321–53. San Francisco: Jossey-Bass.

Russell, Michael, and Lisa Abrams. 2004. "Instructional Use of Computers for Writing: The Effect of State Testing Programs." *Teachers College Record* 106, no. 6: 1332–57.

Saddler, Bruce. 2007. "Improving Sentence Construction Skills through Sentence-Combining Practice." In *Best Practices in Writing Instruction*, edited by Steve Graham, Charles MacArthur, and Jill Fitzgerald, 163–178. New York: Guilford.

Saddler, Bruce, and S. Graham. 2005. "The Effects of Peer-Assisted Sentence-Combining Instruction on the Writing Performance of More and Less Skilled Young Writers." *Journal of Educational Psychology*, 97: 43–54.

Sadler, Philip M., Gerhard Sonnert, Robert H. Tai, and Kristin Klopfenstein. 2010. *AP: A Critical Examination of The Advanced Placement Program*. Cambridge: Harvard Education Press.

Sadowski, Michael. 2008. *Adolescents at School (Second Edition): Perspectives on Youth, Identity, and Education.* Cambridge: Harvard University Press.

Said, Edward W. 1994. *Orientalism.* New York: Vintage.

Salahu-Din, Hillary Persky, and Jessica Miller. 2008. "The Nation's Report Card: Writing 2007." Washington D.C.: U.S. Department of Education.

Santos, Fernanda. 2012. "A System Divided: To Be Black at Stuyvesant High." *New York Times.*

Schmoker, Mike. 2011. *Focus: Evaluating the Essentials to Radically Improve Student Learning.* Alexandria: Association of Supervision and Curriculum Development.

Schmoker, Mike, and Gerald Graff. 2011."More Arguments, Fewer Standards." *Education Week.*

Schoenbach, Ruth, Cynthia Greenleaf, and Christine Cziko. 1999. *Reading for Understanding: A Guide to Improving Reading in Middle and High School Classrooms.* San Francisco: Jossey-Bass.

Scholes, Robert. 1991. *The Protocols of Reading.* New Haven: Yale.

———. 1998. *The Rise and Fall of English: Reconstructing English as a Discipline.* New Haven: Yale University Press.

———. 2001. *The Crafty Reader.* New Haven: Yale University Press.

———. 2011. *English After the Fall: From Literature to Textuality.* Iowa City: University of Iowa.

Schuessle, Jennifer. 2009. "Get a Life, Holden Caulfield." *New York Times*, 2009, p. WK5.

Schultink, Jan. 2011."Every Sentence Should Matter." In *Idea Transplant*, edited by Jan Schultink.

Schultz, Philip. 2011. *My Dyslexia.* New York: W. W. Norton.

Scott, Judith A., and William E. Nagy. 2004. "Developing Word Consciousness." In *Vocabulary Instruction*, edited by James R. Baumann and Edward J. Kame'enui. New York: Guilford.

Seinfeld, Jerry. 2008. *Seinlanguage.* New York: Bantam.

Selsberg, Andy. 2011. "Teaching to the Text Message." *New York Times*, March 20, 2011.

Sennett, Richard. 2008. *The Craftsman.* New Haven: Yale.

Shaughnessy, Mina. 1979. *Errors and Expectations: A Guide for the Teacher of Basic Writing.* New York: Oxford University.

Shaw, George Bernard. 1916. "Pygmalion." Available at: Bartleby.com.

Shepard, Lorrie A. 2000. "The Role of Assessment in a Learning Culture." *Educational Researcher* 29, no. 7: 4–14.

Shirky, Clay. 2008. *Here Comes Everybody: The Power of Organizing without Organizations.* New York: Penguin.

Short, Deborah J., and Shannon Fitzsimmons. 2007. "Double the Work: Challenges and Solutions to Acquiring Language and Academic Literacy for Adolescent English Language Learners—a Report to Carnegie Corporation of New York." Washington, D.C.: Alliance for Excellent Education.

Showkeir, Jamie, and Maren Showkeir. 2008. *Authentic Conversations: Moving from Manipulation to Truth and Commitment.* San Francisco: Berrett-Koehler.

Shulman, Lee. 1999. "Foreword." In *Ways of Thinking, Ways of Teaching*, edited by George Hillocks. New York: Teachers College.

Sieff, Kevin. 2011. "Asian Americans Outpacing Peers." *Washington Post*, p. B.5.

Simon, Katherine G. 2001. *Moral Questions in the Classroom: How to Get Kids to Think Deeply About Real Life and Their Schoolwork.* New Haven: Yale.

Sion, Ronald T. 2004. "Three Pragmatic Tools of Character Education." *English Leadership Quarterly* 26, no. 4: 2–3.

Smagorinsky, Peter. 2006. *Research on Composition: Multiple Perspectives on Two Decades of Change.* New York: Teachers College Press.

———. 2009. "Is It Time to Abandon the Idea of 'Best Practices' in the Teaching of English?" *English Journal* 98, no. 6: 15–22.

———. 2011. "Confessions of a Mad Professor: An Autoethnographic Consideration of Neuroatypicality, Extranormativity, and Education." *Teachers College Record* 113, no. 8.

Smagorinsky, Peter, Elizabeth Anne Daigle, Cindy O'Donnell-Allen, and Susan Bynum. 2010. "Bullshit in Academic Writing: A Protocol Analysis of a High School Senior's Process of Interpreting Much Ado About Nothing (Fix Title to Italics)." *Research in the Teaching of English* 44, no. 4: 368–405.

Smagorinsky, Peter, Amy Alexandra Wilson, and Cynthia Moore. 2011. "Teaching Grammar and Writing: A Beginning Teacher's Dilemma." *English Education* 43, no. 3: 262–92.

Smith, Frank. 1988. *Joining the Literacy Club: Further Essays into Education.* Portsmouth: Heinemann.

———. 1998. *The Book of Learning and Forgetting.* New York: Teachers College.

Smith, Mary Ann (ed.). 2011. "Writing Assignment Framework and Overview." 1998 Berkeley: National Writing Project, 2011.

Smith, Michael W., Julie Cheville, and George Hillocks, Jr. 2006. ""I Guess I'd Better Watch My English": Grammars and the Teaching of the English Language Arts." In *The Handbook of Writing Research,* edited by Charles A. MacArthur, Steve Graham, and Jill Fitzgerald, 263–75. New York: Guilford.

Smith, Michael W., and Jeffrey D. Wilhelm. 2002. *"Reading Don't Fix No Chevys": Literacy in the Lives of Young Men.* Portsmouth: Heinemann.

———. 2006. *Going with the Flow: How to Engage Boys (and Girls) in Their Literacy Learning.* Portsmouth: Heinemann.

———. 2007. *Getting It Right: Fresh Approaches to Teaching Grammar, Usage, and Correctness.* New York: Scholastic.

Sommers, Nancy. 2009. "Revision Strategies of Student Writers and Experienced Adult Writers." In *The Norton Book of Composition Studies,* edited by Susan Miller. New York: Norton.

———. 2010. "Responding to Student Writers." In *Creating Community in the Classroom.*

Spandel, Vicki. 2009. *Creating Writers: Through 6-Trait Writing Assessment and Instruction,* fifth ed. Boston: Allyn & Bacon.

Stanovich, Keith E. 1986. "Matthew Effects in Reading: Some Consequences of Individual Differences in the Acquisition of Literacy." *Reading Research Quarterly* 21: 360–406.

Sternberg, Robert J., Linda Jarvin, Elena L. Grigorenko. 2009. *Teaching for Wisdom, Intelligence, Creativity, and Success.* Thousand Oaks: Corwin.

Stiggins, Rick, and Jan Chappuis. 2012. *An Introduction to Student-Involved Assessment for Learning.* Boston: Pearson.

Stigler, James W., and James Hiebert. 2009. *The Teaching Gap: Best Ideas from the World's Teachers for Improving Education in the Classroom.* New York: Free Press.

Stock, Patricia Lambert. 1995. *The Dialogic Curriculum: Teaching and Learning in a Multicultural Society.* Portsmouth: Heinemann.

Stotsky, Sandra. 2010a."Let's Spread the Blame for Reading Underachievement." *Education Week,* December 8: 24.

———. 2010b. "Literary Study in Grades 9, 10, and 11: A National Survey." In *Forum: A Publication of the Association of Literary Scholars, Critics, and Writers,* edited by Kate Oser. Boston: Association of Literary Scholars, Critics, and Writers.

Straight, Susan. 2009. "Reading by the Numbers." *New York Times.*

Strong, Michael. 1997. *The Habit of Thought: From Socratic Seminars to Socratic Practice.* Chapel Hill: New View.

Strong, William. 1986. *Creating Approaches to Sentence Combining,* Theory and Research into Practice. Urbana: National Council of Teachers of English.

———. 2001.*Coaching Writing: The Power of Guided Practice.* Portsmouth: Heinemann.

Surowiecki, James. 2004.*The Wisdom of Crowds: Why the Many Are Smarter Than the Few and How Collective Wisdom Shapes Business, Economies, Societies and Nations.* New York: Doubleday.

Swanson, Christopher B. 2010. "Progress Postponed: Graduation Rate Continues Decline." In *Diplomas Count,* 22–28. Bethesda: *Education Week.*

Tapscott, Don. 2008. *Grown up Digital: How the Net Generation Is Changing Your World.* New York: McGraw-Hill.

———. 2009. *Grown up Digital: How the Net Generation Is Changing Your World.* New York: McGraw-Hill.

Tatum, Alfred W. 2005. *Teaching Reading to Black Adolescent Males: Closing the Achievement Gap.* Portland: Stenhouse.

———. 2009. *Reading for Their Life: (Re)Building the Textual Lineages of African American Adolescent Males.* Portsmouth: Heinemann.

Tavernise, Sabrina. 2012. "Poor Dropping Further Behind Rich in School." *New York Times*, February 10.

Taylor, Paul, and Scott Keeter. 2010. "Millennials: A Portrait of Generation Next." In *Milliennials*, edited by Rich Morin. New York: Pew Research Center.

Thomas, Douglas, and John Seely Brown. 2011. *A New Culture of Learning: Cultivating the Imagination for a World of Constant Change.* Palo Alto: Thomas and Brown (Self-Published).

Thompson, Clive. 2009. "The Future of Reading in a Digital World." *WIRED.*

———. 2011. "Secret Messages in the Digital Age." *WIRED*, February 18.

Toffler, Alvin, and Heidi Toffler. 1999. "Foreword." In *Rethinking the Future: Rethinking Business, Principles, Competition, Control, Leadership, Markets and the World,* edited by Rowan Gibson. London: Brealey.

Tomlinson, Carol Ann. 1993. "Progression: Toward Independent Learning over Time." *Middle School Journal* 25: 55–59.

Torgeson, Joseph Debra Houston, Lila Rissman, Susan Decker, Greg Roberts, Sharon Vaughn, Jade Wexler, David Francis, and Mebel Rivera. 2007. "Academic Literacy Instruction for Adolescents." Portsmouth: RMC Research Corporation, Center on Instruction.

Trubek, Anne. 2012. "Use Your Words." *WIRED*, February: 19.

Tufte, Edwin. 1997. *Visual Explanations: Images and Quantities, Evidence and Narrative.* Cheshire: Graphics Press.

Turner, Mark. 1996. *The Literary Mind: The Origins of Thought and Language.* New York: Oxford University Press.

Turner, Robin. 2008. *Greater Expectations: Teaching Academic Literacy to Underrepresented Students.* Portland: Stenhouse.

Ulin, David L. 2010. "The Lost Art of Reading: Why Books Matter in a Distracted Time."

Vendler, Helen. 1997. *The Art of Shakespeare's Sonnets.* Cambridge: Belknap.

Visotzky, Burton L. 1996. *The Genesis of Ethics: How the Tormented Family of Genesis Leads Us to Moral Development.* New York: Three Rivers.

———. 1962. *Thought and Language.* Cambridge: MIT Press.

Vygotsky, Lev S. 1978. *Mind in Society: The Development of Higher Psychological Processes.* Cambridge: Harvard University Press.

———. 1986. *Thought and Language.* Translated by Kozulin. Cambridge: MIT Press.

Wagner, Tony. 2006. "Rigor on Trial." *Education Week*, 26–30.

———. 2008. *The Global Achievement Gap: Why Even Our Best Schools Don't Teach the New Survival Skills Our Children Need—and What We Can Do About It.* New York: Basic Books.

Wallis, Claudia. 2011. "Study in Korea Puts Autism's Prevalence at 2.6%, Surprising Experts." *New York Times*, June 9, 2011, p. A4.

Weaver, Constance. 2008. *Grammar to Enrich and Enhance Writing.* Portsmouth: Heinemann.

Weber, Chris. 2002. *Publish with Students: A Comprehensive Guide.* Portsmouth: Heinemann.

Weisenthal, Simon. 1998. *The Sunflower: On the Possibilities and Limits of Forgiveness.* New York: Schocken.

Weissman, Jerry. 2009. *Presenting to Win: The Art of Telling Your Story.* Upper Saddle River: Financial Times.

West, Cornell. *Race Matters*. 2001. Boston: Beacon.

Wheatley, Margaret. 2002."Some Friends and I Started Talking . . ." *Utne Reader*, 56.

Whitaker, Sonya. 2010. *The Culturally Responsive Teacher: How Understanding Culture Positively Impacts Instruction and Student Achievement (DVD)*. Portsmouth: Heinemann.

White, Dennis. 2010. "Foreword." In *Fires in the Mind: What Kids Can Tell Us About Motivation and Mastery*. San Francisco: Jossey-Bass.

Whiting, Sam. 2003."The New Generation Gap: English Is Hard Enough Even When It's Your First Language." *San Francisco Chronicle*, December 14, p. B-1.

Whitmire, Richard. 2010. *Why Boys Fail: Saving Our Sons from an Educational System That's Leaving Them Behind*. New York: Amacom.

Wiebe, Todd J. 2006."College Students, Plagiarism, and the Internet: The Role of Academic Librarians in Delivering Education and Awareness." Available at: wwwmlaforum.org.

Wiggins, Grant. 2010. "What's My Job: Defining the Role of the Classroom Teacher." In *On Excellence in Teaching*, edited by Robert Marzano, 7–30. Bloomington: Solution Tree.

Wilcox, Bonita L. 2004."Character Education in the Language Arts Curriculum." *English Leadership Quarterly* 26, no. 4: 1–2.

Wilhelm, Jeffrey D. 2007. *Engaging Readers and Writers with Inquiry: Promoting Deep Understandings in Language Arts and the Content Areas with Guiding Questions*. New York: Scholastic.

———. 2008."*You Gotta Be the Book: Teaching Engaged and Reflective Reading with Adolescents*. New York: Teachers College.

———. 2010. "Creating 'Third Spaces': Promoting Learning Through Dialogue." *Voices from the Middle* 18, no. 2: 55–58.

Wilhelm, Jeffrey D., and Bruce Novak. 2011. *Teaching Literacy for Love and Wisdom: Being the Book and Being the Change*. New York: Teachers College.

Williams, James D. 2003. *Preparing to Teach Writing: Research, Theory, and Practice*. Mahwah: Lawrence Erlbaum.

Williams, Joseph M. 2006. *Style: Lessons in Clarity and Grace*. New York: Pearson.

Willis, Judy. 2006. *Research-Based Strategies to Ignite Student Learning: Insights from a Neurologist and Classroom Teacher*. Alexandria: Association for Supervision and Curriculum Development.

Wills, Garry. 1992. *Lincoln at Gettysburg: The Words That Remade America*. New York: Touchstone.

Wilson, Douglas L. 2006. *Lincoln's Sword: The Presidency and the Power of Words*. New York: Vintage.

Wilson, E. O. 1998. *Consilience: The Unity of Knowledge*. New York: Knopf.

Wilson, Maja. 2006. *Rethinking Rubrics in Writing Assessment*. Portsmouth: Heinemann.

Wolf, Maryanne. 2007. *Proust and the Squid: The Story and Science of the Reading Brain*. New York: Harper.

Wolf, Mikyung, Amy C. Crosson, and Lauren B. Resnick. 2006. "Accountable Talk in Comprehension Instruction." Pittsburgh: Learning and Research Development Center.

Woolf, Virginia. 1953. *The Common Reader*. San Diego: Harcourt.

———.1986. "How Should One Read a Book?" In *The Second Common Reader*, edited by Andrew McNeillie, 258–70. San Diego: Harcourt.

Yancey, Kathleen Blake. 2008. "2008 NCTE Presidential Address: The Impulse to Compose." Paper presented at the NCTE Annual Convention, San Antonio, Texas, November 23, 2008.

Yavorcik, Carin. 2009. "National Children's Health Survey Report Finds Autism Prevalence Now 1 in 91." Autism Society.

Yazzie-Mintz, Ethan. 2010."Charting the Path from Engagement to Achievement: A Report on the 2009 High School Survey of Student Engagement." Bloomington: Center for Evaluation and Education Policy.

Zakaria, Fareed. 2008. *The Post American World*. New York: W. W. Norton.

Zeldin, Theodore. 2000. *Conversation: How Talk Can Change Our Lives*. Vol. 2. Mahwah: HiddenSpring.

Zemelman, Steven, Harvey Daniels, and Arthur Hyde. 2005. *Best Practice, Today's Standards for Teaching and Learning in America's Schools*. Portsmouth: Heinemann.

Zinsser, William. 1998. *On Writing Well: The Classic Guide to Writing Nonfiction*. New York: Harpers.

Zmuda, Allison, and Mary Tomaino. 2001. *The Competent Classroom: Aligning High School Curriculum, Standards and Assessment—a Creative Teaching Guide*. New York: Teachers College Press.

Zull, James. E. 2002. *The Art of Changing the Brain: Enriching the Practice of Teaching by Exploring the Biology of Learning*. Sterling: Stylus.

Zwiers, Jeff. 2008. *Building Academic Language: Essential Practices for Content Classrooms, Grades 5–12*. San Francisco: Jossey-Bass.

Essential resources for teaching English/ language arts

from Jim Burke